FOUR STARS
★ ★ ★ ★

FOUR STARS

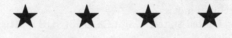

★ ★ ★ ★

MARK PERRY

Houghton Mifflin Company

BOSTON · 1989

For information about permission to reproduce selections
from this book, write to Permissions, Houghton Mifflin
Company, 2 Park Street, Boston, Massachusetts 02108.

Library of Congress Cataloging-in-Publication Data

Perry, Mark, date.
  Four stars.
    Bibliography: p.
    Includes index.
      1. United States.   Joint Chiefs of Staff — History.
  I. Title.
UA23.7.P47 1989   355.3'3042'0973   88-32073
ISBN 0-395-42923-4

Printed in the United States of America

P 10 9 8 7 6 5 4 3 2 1

To Nina

ACKNOWLEDGMENTS

I would first like to thank Nina Perry for her unfailing confidence, patience, and advice during the three years that it took to write *Four Stars*. She often sacrificed her own work to help me see this book to completion. Special thanks are due to my son, Cal, and my daughter, Madeleine. Gratitude is also owed to our respective families: my sisters, Anne and Lois, Jack Brown, and Laurel, Peter, and Litsa Mikhalevsky. This book would not have been possible without the support of two close and special friends, Terry Balderson and Captain N. S. Mikhalevsky.

The idea for a book on the American high command was first broached by me to my resourceful agent, Gail Ross, who voiced her constant encouragement in the face of clear obstacles. Great gratitude is owed to John Sterling, my editor at Houghton Mifflin, for his unyielding persistence, editorial vision, amazing prescience, and impeccable good grace. My manuscript editor, Luise Erdmann, will always have my thanks. During the course of this work, a number of close professional associates graciously gave me time to complete this book. My thanks go to the staff and leaders of Vietnam Veterans of America, most especially to Mary Stout, Bobby Muller, John Terzano, Jim Pechin, and the editorial staff at *The Veteran:* Mokie Pratt Porter, Alexa Davis, Gayle Garmise, Lori Kenepp, Michael Keating, and Deborah Needleman. I am particularly indebted to Washington reporter John Prados, for reading and commenting at length on the manuscript, and to William Triplett, who helped identify and document specific episodes in JCS history during the Vietnam era.

The story of the JCS could not have been told without the cooperation of scores of military officers. In particular, I owe gratitude to General Bruce Palmer, who set me on this course and, at important moments in my research, pointed the way to new information. I am indebted to former members of the JCS for their cooperation. They showed unfailing trust and confidence, invited me into their homes for long discussions, and endured hours of return phone calls to confirm reported incidents in JCS history. My thanks go most especially to Generals Andrew Goodpaster, Hamilton Howze, David Jones, Harry Kinnard, Edward Lansdale, Lyman Lemnitzer, Edward C. Meyer, John W. Vessey, and William Westmoreland, and Admirals Eugene Carroll, James Holloway III, Gene LaRocque, Thomas Moorer, and Elmo Zumwalt, Jr. Colonels William Corson, Alexander McColl, George McGarigle, Rob Paschall, Harry Summers, and Major Steve Trueblood provided critically important insights. My appreciation to Clark Clifford, for spending an afternoon talking about the JCS's role in the Vietnam conflict, and to Sam Adams, Tony Cappaccio, Tom Gervasi, George McT. Kahin, Noel Koch, Lawrence Korb, David Morrison, Philip Odeen, Dina Rasor, and Frank Snepp for providing background material and personal insights on the Department of Defense and on critical incidents in JCS history.

The Joint Chiefs of Staff Historical Division provided essential material on the early years. Historians serving with the JCS and dozens of officers currently on duty at the Pentagon were patient and cooperated with my incessant requests for information. In particular, I wish to thank Willard Webb of the JCS Historical Division, Bernard Nalty and the historians at the Office of Air Force History, military historian Richard K. Sommers of the Senior Officer Oral History Program at the Army War College, and a score of officers of the Naval Historical Center and the Marine Corps Historical Center for giving me access to important interview transcripts of officers who served at the Pentagon. The staffs of the Library of Congress and the National Archives and Records Service took time to find specific documents. I am indebted to the public affairs staff of the Department of Defense: Frank Falatco, Lieutenant Commander William Hamilton, Major Clay Magee, Carolyn Piper, and Betty Sprigg are just a few of those who took the time to help. At the State Department, I am indebted to Chip Beck (USN, ret.). Obviously, many of the anecdotes related here have been reported to me by a number of high-ranking civilian officials who could not be quoted by name. I am particularly grateful for the cooperation of four such sources who currently serve or have served with the JCS. In one other case, I am grateful for the work of an official who provided enormous amounts of raw data on the workings of the JCS, often at risk to his own position.

Public testimonies of defense and military officials are critical to understanding the issues discussed here. The cooperation of the House and Senate Armed Services committees in providing information and in spending untold hours in hunting for important legislative background material is much appreciated. Arch Barrett of the House Armed Services Committee — probably the foremost authority on military reform, the issues that surround it, and the personalities involved — spent hours speaking with me in the midst of the fight over the Goldwater-Nichols bill. His long conversations and his constant attention to the details of the debate when he could hardly afford to spend the time are very much appreciated.

Two important aides to the Senate Armed Services Committee spent several days during the same period outlining the issues involved and provided me with essential materials. Their often blunt comments on individual commanders and their detailed description of the behind-the-scenes political maneuvering mean that their names must remain anonymous. I am indebted to them for the detailed chronology of the reform debate that is presented in the last part of the book.

Quite naturally, many of the lesser-known incidents involving the JCS in the immediate past included the use of Special Forces and military intelligence assets. The sensitive nature of some of these operations — including closely guarded JCS activities — made them particularly difficult to document. Thankfully, a number of experts on covert operations were willing to share their reminiscences of past operations and current troubles in the Special Forces program. Although the handful of officers involved do not wish to be identified, they have my thanks for their cooperation.

Richard Billings helped me formulate much of my thinking on this sensitive subject. Thanks are also due to Scott Malone, who provided his own notes and personal knowledge in a career of talking with this nation's twilight warriors, as well as Michael Pilgrim, whose firsthand knowledge of the defense and covert operations bureaucracy helped clear up some early misconceptions. Colonel William Corson provided an extremely valuable, if brief, commentary on the military debate surrounding the use of the Special Forces, as did a number of other former Special Forces officers, many of whom are now retired and value their privacy.

It is impossible to write about military affairs without referring to those who first led the way. I am grateful to Andrew Cockburn, James Fallows, Roger Franklin, Joseph Goulden, Seymour Hersh, Fred Kaplan, Stanley Karnow, Nick Kotz, Edward Luttwak, Neil Sheehan, Richard Stubbing, Strobe Talbott, Patrick Tyler, George Wilson, and countless others whose initial research on the American military in the 1980s has been particularly helpful. Innumerable colleagues in Washington, Chicago, and New York have shown great loyalty, confidence, and support for this project over the last several years: Scott Armstrong, Asa Baber, Leslie Bates, Lisa Berger, George Black, Howard Bray, Isolde Chapin, David Corn, Ken Cummins, Jeff Danziger, Joseph Foote, Jeff Goldberg, Ron Goldfarb, Jim Hougan, Marc Leepson, Dan Moldea, Victor Navasky, Tom O'Neill, Kate Patterson, Peter Ross Range, Ira Rosen, Philip Stern, Bill Thomas, Tom Von Stein, Doug Valentine, Danny Wexler, Tim Wells, and many others have been of great help. I also want to thank Washington Independent Writers, the National Security Archives, and the Center for Military Procurement for their continued interest.

Finally, my abiding gratitude to the scores of Army, Navy, Air Force, and Marine officers for talking with me about their experiences with the JCS. Information on JCS officers from public records, testimonies, and personal reminiscences is essential in any work of this type, but it is not an adequate substitute for personal memories. There is almost universal admiration for the JCS members who led this nation during the 1950s, '60s, and '70s but who were not alive to give a personal account of their service. Even the best known of these officers have faded from history. But the legacy of their service, I found, has not faded from the memories of those with whom they served and who continue to speak of them with deep admiration and respect.

Arlington, Virginia
OCTOBER 1988

CONTENTS

INTRODUCTION

Civil-military relations in the United States, especially at the highest levels where political and strategic issues become entwined, have not always been close and harmonious. In fact, the history of those relations contains several stormy chapters.

General Bruce Palmer, Jr.

EVERY MILITARY OFFICER should look like Kirk Douglas: the square jaw, the steady eyes, the chest that seems made for a crisp uniform and a bright display of medals. The mythology about our military might also require that every officer live up to the standard set by Marine Colonel "Jiggs" Casey, the character Douglas played in the 1964 thriller *Seven Days in May*. Colonel Casey is the movie's hero — he single-handedly foils a plot of the Joint Chiefs of Staff to overthrow the U.S. government. His commitment to civilian rule is far more important than whatever political views he might have, and at a crucial point in the movie he offers a laconic, but powerful, assertion of his faith in the Constitution: "It seems to have worked so far. I sure wouldn't want to be the one to change it."

The movie tells a spellbinding story, but it perpetuates a myth about the American high command and its relationship to elected leaders that continues to have an almost universal appeal. It leads us to believe that most members of the military are a little like Jiggs Casey: they may have strong political commitments, but they remain unswervingly loyal to their commander in chief. The Joint Chiefs of Staff (JCS), the nation's most visible symbol of the military, is the embodiment of that myth. Even now, it is often perceived as an institution that is directed by political eunuchs whose programs and policies are above partisan concerns. As this book tries to show, nothing could be further from the truth.

xiii

But if Jiggs Casey perpetuates a myth about the military, the movie's villain poses an important question. Played by Burt Lancaster, General James Mattoon Scott believes that the United States is courting disaster by agreeing to a disarmament pact with the Soviet Union, and the pact provokes him to stage a coup. As the movie opens, Scott is called to testify before Congress, where he is confronted by a wily southern senator. The senator listens as Scott condemns the disarmament pact and then responds acidly: "From the chairman of the Joint Chiefs of Staff I would welcome and respect any judgments having to do specifically with military considerations, but in so far as his political attitudes are concerned, these, I'm sure, we could dispense with." But Scott is not easily intimidated. It is at this point that he poses the critical question: "Senator, we're talking about the survival of the United States. Is my uniform a disqualification in that area?"

The forty-year history of the JCS is a story of its tremendous growth and influence on U.S. foreign policy. What began as a committee of military advisers in 1947 slowly became the most powerful group of military officers in America. Given its enormous power, it's surprising that so little is known of its activities. The JCS's penchant for secrecy is justifiable: few would argue that sensitive military information should not be publicly available. But information about the JCS's operations, programs, and ideology is another matter, and it provides the foundation for much of the reporting in this book. Equally important are the officers themselves, and only by focusing on individual leaders — as distinguished from the system that produced them — can the role and impact of the JCS be fully understood.

Not surprisingly, a shroud of secrecy surrounds the deliberations of the JCS. It holds regular meetings, but its discussions are rarely attended by civilian officials. It also holds "special sessions" — secret assemblies with only JCS members in attendance. No notes are taken. The need for secrecy is obvious: the JCS has complete knowledge of American troop dispositions, deployment force capacities, airlift capabilities, and nuclear warfighting strategies. Less technical discussions, however, are also hidden from public view, meetings that reflect its opinions of presidents, Secretaries of Defense, members of Congress, and new weapons systems, deliberations that determine political strategies to increase military influence.

Although the JCS is careful to protect information about its operations, the institution — its structure and mandate — is described in the National Security Act of 1947 and the Goldwater-Nichols Defense Reorganization Act of 1986. The JCS comprises the four-star leaders of the nation's combat services — the Army, Navy, Air Force, and Marines — and a chairman and vice chairman, who meet three times weekly in a large, windowless room in the Pentagon called the tank.

Though the six men do not command combat troops, their decisions determine the nation's military policies. During an international crisis, they are responsible for the lives of millions of Americans. Despite this power, the role of the JCS has been largely ignored throughout its tenure.

The members of the JCS are the planners and coordinators of the most powerful military establishment in the world. They are responsible for overseeing the activities of the world's fourth largest Army, its most powerful Air Force, and a 600-ship Navy that maintains a presence in every major ocean.

The Army has close to 800,000 soldiers organized in eighteen divisions; another 850,000 soldiers serve in ten reserve or National Guard divisions. Four Army divisions are stationed in Europe, one in South Korea.

The Navy has 590,000 sailors deployed in four fleets: one in the Atlantic, one in the Pacific, one designated for action in the western Pacific and Indian oceans, and one in the Mediterranean and eastern Atlantic. The fleets total 16 aircraft carriers, 38 ballistic missile submarines, 100 nuclear-powered attack submarines, over 1,000 aircraft, and 200 cruisers and destroyers. Deployed with the Navy are 190,000 U.S. Marines in three divisions. Another division of 50,000 Marines stands in reserve. Marine aviation units deploy some 400 aircraft. The Navy is the most diverse of the three services: it not only deploys fleets in the world's major oceans, it maintains its own air and land forces.

The U.S. Air Force organizes its approximately 600,000 servicemen and women into three separate commands. The Strategic Air Command (SAC) controls 325 bombers and over 1,000 intercontinental ballistic missiles (ICBMs). It is responsible for maintaining the nation's strategic nuclear defense system. Because of the critical nature of its mission, the head of SAC reports directly to the JCS. The Aerospace Defense Command is responsible for the air defense of the United States, Canada, and Mexico, with command of some 1,800 interceptor fighters. The Military Airlift Command (MAC) is responsible for airlifting American military personnel in 350 long-range and 200 medium-range transports.

The services work together in a highly complex arrangement of "unified" operational commands composed of forces from two or more services that have regional responsibilities. There are seven in all: Readiness Command, Central Command, Space Command, Southern Command, and commands for the Atlantic, Pacific, and Europe.*

---

* CINCs (or "sinks") are four-star commanders of each of the world's military regions. CINCPAC, for example, is the commander in chief of the Pacific Command (or PACOM), a unified command that includes subcommands for forces in the Far East, Korea, Japan, and the U.S. Pacific Fleet.

Each regional command unifies a variety of Army, Navy, and Air Force units for regional defenses and is controlled through a CINC, or commander in chief. The Army is responsible for the defense of western Europe, with a four-star commander in chief in charge of American forces (CINCEUR) and an American four-star officer serving as head of all NATO forces (a SACEUR: Supreme Allied Commander, Europe). The Navy is in charge of the Pacific, including those combined U.S./Republic of Korea forces stationed in South Korea. The two jobs are considered the best command assignments of their respective services. The Air Force considers control of SAC its top command position. The three Air Force commands operate independently and are called "specified" commands.*

Thirty-five percent of all military personnel serve outside the United States, on American bases in Europe, the Philippines, South Korea, aboard Navy ships patrolling the Indian, Mediterranean, Atlantic, and Pacific oceans, in B-52s on constant patrol over northern Canada, and in military assistance programs in dozens of countries around the world. At no other time in its peacetime history has the United States deployed so many of its forces outside its borders. Behind this is a highly organized chain of command. The president issues orders to the nation's unified and specified commands through the Secretary of Defense.

Command authority bypasses the JCS, though in actual practice all orders for unified and specified commanders are routed through it; military decisions made by the president, or by the Secretary of Defense acting on his behalf, are made "with the advice" of the JCS. There is little doubt, as one defense expert notes, that "the JCS is far more than an advisory body; it is firmly established as an integral part of the chain of command." Each of the nation's top military officers has a civilian counterpart. The secretaries of the Army, Navy, and Air Force are responsible for maintaining their services' readiness by assessing their needs and by waging budget battles in Congress to meet those needs. Thus, each service's military chief has two responsibilities: he is responsible for making interservice decisions affecting the entire military (under the leadership of a JCS chairman) and decisions affecting only his own service (reporting to a civilian secretary).

While civilian secretaries maintain forces, the JCS employs them. The JCS is responsible for planning America's future wars and for making certain that combat units have the personnel and material necessary to carry out the nation's security goals. The JCS establishes the nation's combat doctrine, mandates weapons development priorities,

---

* In 1987, Congress established a Special Operations Command, unifying the forces of each service's special operations units.

writes the military budget, determines military force composition, and monitors defense readiness. All joint programs (those affecting units from two or more services) are the responsibility of the JCS.

Four Stars is an account of the JCS's forty-year battle to gain a larger role in making decisions on American foreign policy. The JCS can be best understood when its relationship to civilian leadership is examined and illuminated. More precisely, *Four Stars* examines what General Andrew Jackson Goodpaster once called "the inescapably weak points in the structure," the places where, as he said, "the military and the civilian come together."

In its early years, the JCS was more preoccupied with internal matters than with foreign policy. In fact, in its first two decades, its officers were known more for their arguments with each other than for their disagreements with civilian officials; it is a story of vicious intramural contests over allocation of resources, service missions, and operational roles.

From the moment it was established, the new high command struggled to expand its domination, first over the military services and then over individual combat officers. In the mid-1950s, these service disagreements escalated, evidenced by a clear break between the JCS leadership and the president. Later, a triumvirate of Air Force and Army generals engaged in a vicious competition that was only resolved by the controversial promotion of a legendary military officer as JCS chairman. His appointment and the adoption of his strategic views led to America's most destructive postwar military crisis.

The most significant incident in the JCS's existence occurred in August 1967, when the entire U.S. high command threatened to resign over the civilian handling of the Vietnam conflict. The events of 1967 reinforced its commitment to winning a major role in determining just when and where the American government would use military power. That crisis allows for a novel interpretation of American postwar national security policy: everything that occurred in the twenty years before 1967 made the crisis inevitable; everything that occurred afterward made military reorganization, the end of this forty-year history, essential.

In the 1970s, reform efforts sparked by a visionary group of JCS officers were derailed by domestic crisis and economic dislocation. Nor were its efforts made easier by the 1980 election of a conservative president intent on rebuilding American military might. The 1983 bombing of the Marine barracks in Beirut was public evidence that the JCS had failed to attain its most important goal: to hold civilian leadership accountable for the use of American troops in faraway conflicts.

The inability of the American high command to win a clear military victory in the years since 1947 is a subject much commented on in almost all the recent books on the nation's defense establishment. The examples constitute a well-known litany of failure, stark reminders that all is not well with the American military: the unsatisfactory conclusion of the Korean War, the failure at the Bay of Pigs, the shattering defeat in Vietnam, the embarrassing incompetence of the Iranian rescue mission, the criminally unjustified death of 241 Marines in Beirut, and the almost comic chaos of the Grenada invasion. All of these incidents spurred public doubts about the military's ability to promote American ideals and interests as well as to defend the homeland.

These tragedies eventually sparked a broad examination of American military leadership, an intergovernmental conflict pitting a broad-based coalition of reform advocates against a stubborn but successful Secretary of Defense. After four years of acrimonious discussion — during which a powerful JCS chairman conducted a highly political and personal battle against an entrenched opposition — Congress passed the Goldwater-Nichols Reorganization Act of 1986, giving the JCS new and more significant powers. It gave the JCS a major role in the determination of American foreign policy. The debate will continue: should the chairman's position be strengthened even further? Do the services retain too much influence? Should America's unified commanders be given greater responsibilities?

The most important but unstated question is whether the American people will demand that their military leaders do more than just obey orders, an issue that cannot be decided by an act of Congress. Just as no law can guarantee military victory, no single piece of legislation can ensure loyalty, dictate foresight, or codify reasoned dissent. The passage of military reform legislation is only a partial answer to the fundamental question that lies at the heart of this work and at the center of the JCS's continuing struggle with civilian leaders. Only the American people can decide whether they want a silent, unquestioning military or one that plays a formative role in the democratic process.

FOUR STARS

★ ★ ★ ★

1

AN ADMIRAL
AND A GENERAL

★   ★   ★   ★

All members of the JCS have expressed from time to time
their firm belief that the military must always be controlled by civil authorities.

General Omar Bradley

AT THE END OF 1939, it was clear to most of the military that the
United States would soon be involved in a worldwide conflict. They
believed that Japan's brutal invasion of Manchuria in the early part of
the decade and Germany's conquest of Poland, back in September,
made the coming struggle inevitable. These concerns, however, were
more than offset by the military's supreme confidence in its ability to
lead men in battle. The only thing it lacked was a unified command
structure that could manage the conflict. It was a critical handicap: on
the eve of World War II, the nation's top officers were engaged in a bitter debate over which service's strategic plan for victory should be
endorsed by the president. The resolution of this debate, the nation's
need to hear a single military voice, led directly to the establishment
of the Joint Chiefs of Staff (JCS).

The JCS is one of those handful of official government bodies that
was actually established *before* Congress could give it official sanc-
tion. In the 1920s, the nation's two services communicated through a
Joint Army-Navy Committee, a group that was no more than a pro
forma bow to a coordinated command. Even so, by the beginning of
1940 this titular committee was beginning to argue over just which
service would have the primary responsibility for fighting what most
officers believed would be a two-front war. The Army and Navy
squared off publicly in January 1941, eleven months before the attack
on Pearl Harbor, when they became embroiled in a debate over the

degree to which the United States should support British war aims in Europe. The services weren't splitting hairs; at stake were resources, personnel, and glory.

The Navy led the charge, claiming that the future war should be its concern. On the horizon loomed Japan, which, the Navy believed, should be dealt with first. Its position was actually aligned closely with isolationist policies and was rife with unashamedly anti-British sentiments: naval leaders doubted that Britain's interests could ever coincide with America's, and they reminded their civilian superiors of Great Britain's traditional opposition to American maritime interests. The American people, the Navy said, weren't interested in helping Great Britain retain its influence in Europe or in shedding blood for the British colonial empire. The Navy had a powerful and well-placed advocate in the person of Fleet Admiral William D. Leahy. While not nearly as strongly anti-British as some of his colleagues, Leahy nevertheless advocated naval dominance in military policy. He was joined by Admiral Ernest J. King, a hard-drinking tactical genius who had been shunted aside by the "old boys" during the 1930s. King just didn't seem to fit the Navy's "dress white" peacetime tradition of officers who were known more for their sophistication than for their battle-wagon prowess. As a result, he was unceremoniously exiled to the North Atlantic at a time when few thought that that theater would matter.

This Army-Navy quarrel was exacerbated after America entered World War II, when it became clear that the services would be forced to coordinate their operations. Recognizing this necessity, in early February 1942, President Franklin D. Roosevelt directed both services to establish a "joint coordinating body," with greater responsibilities than the pro forma (and now clearly outdated) Joint Board of the Army and Navy. Roosevelt knew he would need such a command staff if the American military was to work successfully with the sophisticated and highly organized British Chiefs of Staff Committee in designing an overall strategy to win the war. According to the official JCS history, the body was directed to advise the president on "war plans and strategy, military relations with allies, the munitions, shipping and manpower requirements of U.S. forces, and matters of joint Army-Navy policy." This body, the U.S. Joint Chiefs of Staff, met officially for the first time on February 9, 1942.

The establishment of the JCS did not resolve the growing feud over which service would take the lead in designing U.S. war strategy. Ernest King — just returned from the North Atlantic — argued for the adoption of what became known as the Pacific First approach, which held that the United States should defeat Japan before dealing with Germany. In addition to showing a traditional mistrust of the

British, the strategy had a logic of its own: Japan had launched a direct attack on the United States (that is, the U.S. Navy); it considered America its primary enemy, sought hegemony in the Pacific (the "American lake"), and had conquered the Philippines, an American colony. There was more than a service principle at stake: the Navy believed that the war against Japan was a war between two fleets as well as two nations. Naval officers argued further that the British seemed to be doing quite well against the Germans and could probably hold them off indefinitely, or at least until Japan had been defeated.

The Navy wasn't alone in its parochial concerns. Just after Roosevelt established the JCS, General Dwight D. Eisenhower drew up a memo detailing his own (and the Army's) view of American military strategy. He argued for an immediate buildup of American forces in Great Britain, a move that implied an early landing of Allied forces on the European continent. For he and other Army leaders believed that the Japanese offensive in the Pacific had, by early 1942, run its course. The United States could turn its attention to Europe, thereby keeping Great Britain in the war. Eisenhower's memo viewed the conflict as a war between two of the world's most powerful armies, a position that would fully commit the United States to the concept of "total war," without which, Army leaders believed, a total victory could not be won. They told their Navy colleagues that the defeat of Germany would give the United States a greater voice in postwar European affairs and thereby undercut England's position on the Continent. They argued further that Russia's entrance into the war didn't reinforce the Navy's position after all, but was a compelling reason that the United States needed to put its primary focus on the Continent or be cut out of a postwar European settlement that was certain, especially after 1942, to include the Soviet Union.

Eisenhower's memo reflected an earlier Army position known as Operation Victory, an ambitious mobilization plan that called for the deployment of a 210-division force backed by tiers of bombers and ships. The plan horrified naval officers, who believed the American people would never agree to such large-scale mobilization. In addition, it would undermine America's real value as an arsenal and breadbasket. For Roosevelt, there was never really any debate; his intention all along was to fight in Europe first, though clearly not because of pro-Army prejudice (Roosevelt had, after all, been Assistant Secretary of the Navy). But what Roosevelt gave with his right hand he took back with his left: having accepted a Europe First strategy, he vetoed any thought of mobilizing 210 divisions.

Basically, Roosevelt believed that Germany was the greatest threat America faced and worried about the slim but very real possibility that the Soviets might defeat Germany *without* an allied invasion of

France. This was something, as Winston Churchill continually reminded him, that neither the United States nor Great Britain could tolerate. Roosevelt agreed. When Army Chief of Staff George Marshall attempted to use the Pacific First strategy as a bludgeon against British war plans, Roosevelt told him to drop the argument because it antagonized the British.

The interservice debate didn't end with Roosevelt's decision. While Roosevelt foreclosed the Army-Navy rivalry, thereby soothing the British, he kept the debate alive within the American military as a means of spurring what he considered a useful argument over military strategy. In other words, while Roosevelt silenced Marshall's use of the Pacific First plan for political purposes, he allowed Ernie King to pose the question continually in administration circles, thereby unintentionally institutionalizing service rivalry.

Ever since, military commanders have continually noted that not only did the United States win the war despite service rivalry, it might well have won *because* of it. Public opinion and congressional sentiment were clearly on the Navy's side. Throughout the first two years of the war there were even, as Eisenhower sarcastically noted in his wartime diary, "insinuations" that the War Department, an Army fiefdom, had "conspired" to "expose the Navy to defeat at Pearl Harbor for the sake of maneuvering America into war in Europe." So it was that in the midst of the most horrifying world conflagration in human history, service rivalries were translated into a classic Washington battle of bureaucracies, with the Navy Department in a showdown against the War Department.

For those who believe the American military rejected narrow service concerns the moment of the Pearl Harbor attack, the Army-Navy feud is a sobering reminder of just how deep, and pervasive, service rivalries have always been. On a more practical level, while Roosevelt refused to use this competition as a stick against British designs in the Balkans and the Mediterranean, he failed to intervene when it dictated clearer strategic visions, more stringent uses of military resources, and narrower military timetables. In effect, the Navy's Pacific First strategy served as a handy brake on the Army's penchant for more men, more resources, and more firepower. It is a ploy the Navy has used, with some success, to this day.

The residue of the Army-Navy competition in defeating the Axis is still apparent, and it amuses historians and writers who cover military affairs. Navy officers continue to argue that "we won that war," scoffing at Army pretensions that "if you haven't fought the Germans, you haven't fought a war at all." The Air Force, a relative latecomer to the debate, had its own claim — that the strategic bombing of German and Japanese cities tipped the balance in favor of the Allies — which the Army and Navy consider "preposterous." In 1942, a number of officers realized that the service competition was counterproductive, even self-defeating. Eisenhower, for one, came to despise it and wanted to resolve it. The feud became so bitter, and so public, that in Congress the competition between the War and Navy departments raised political questions about the nation's ability to wage a united war. But it took a number of significant wartime incidents, and their public revelation, to provide the initial impetus for reform of the American high command.

The first such incident occurred just after America entered the war. In February 1942, word began to trickle back to Congress that, at the Anglo-American Arcadia conference in Washington, the American military planning staff had performed poorly in comparison with the "large and smoothly functioning British staff." It became apparent that the American military command was dangerously disorganized, unfocused, and all but inept, which not only led to a broad questioning of American military planning skills, but embarrassed top military leaders and their commander in chief.

The shortcomings of the JCS were most apparent, however, during the Casablanca Conference of 1943, which hoped to work out arrangements for the final invasion of Europe. The British Chiefs of Staff Committee had done its homework, knew it, and even lorded it over the Americans. What could the Americans provide, how soon, and in what quantity? the British Combined Chiefs of Staff Committee asked. No one seemed to have an answer. What was the grand strategy of the United States? The answer came down to, well, we haven't decided yet. What training mechanisms would the Americans initiate in preparation for the European conflict? Sorry, the JCS answered; that hasn't been determined. The British officers were amused, Leahy, King, and Marshall were humiliated, Congress was puzzled, and, worst of all, Roosevelt was embarrassed.

At George Marshall's instigation, the JCS took the lead in reforming the American command system after Casablanca. In early 1943, it ordered a "comprehensive reappraisal and reorganization of the supporting structure of the Joint Chiefs of Staff," which included a detailed study of how the British system operated. This led to the establishment of a number of logistics and planning committees within the JCS, as well as to the appointment of Joint Deputy Chiefs of Staff, to handle "the burden of detailed and routine matters" coming before the JCS. As the war progressed, the system evolved to include a number of joint committees — on intelligence, civil affairs, postwar policy, and industrial production — each of them mirror images of the British structure.

The closer the new JCS came to replicating the well-oiled British system, the better it worked — though it never worked as well as it should or could have. Even now, when retired military leaders *harrumph* about the welter of officers, directorates, planning staffs, and committees making up the burdensome JCS system and proudly proclaim that "we did a better job in World War II with half the staff," they're speaking from personal perspectives colored by victory. The American war was, at best, a triumph of industrialization, not military planning; of more, not better. And while American soldiers and sailors were rarely short of courage, they never had to rely on it to win. There were always plenty of bullets, ships, planes, and tanks to go around, and in the end materials, not finesse, proved to be the difference.

So the victory celebration at war's end was dampened by an assessment of American military capabilities, which resulted in moves to reform the high command. One effort was initiated within the military itself, in early 1944, when top Army and Navy commanders testified before Congress on the necessity of a new, "unified" military command system. That fall, the JCS conducted a survey of the nation's top military commanders on the same subject and appointed a special committee to plan the necessary reforms. With the end of the war in sight, the JCS Special Committee on Reorganization of National Defense was hard at work on a postwar military command establishment. The committee eventually recommended the creation of a single defense agency presided over by a Secretary of the Armed Forces, the creation of an Air Force, and the appointment of an overall "commander of the Armed Forces supported by an Armed Forces General Staff." Not surprisingly, the senior Navy officer on the committee disagreed with the report's conclusions.

A number of other independent reports were submitted in this period, though few agreed with the Special Committee's report. The most important one was written by a committee headed by investment banker Ferdinand Eberstadt, a protégé of Secretary of the Navy James Forrestal. Eberstadt concluded that "under present conditions," service unification — by which he meant the establishment of one service of all arms — would not improve the nation's security, but that a coordinated military system of three services and three service secretaries, united under a single command, would.

In the end, this report gained the most widespread backing, and Congress began writing legislation based on its conclusions. The Navy, fearing an overhaul of its traditional role, began writing a plan reflecting its own prejudices: independent commands under independent services, with coordination in the hands of a strong executive. Clearly, the Navy report was a result of its wartime experiences, when it had been allowed to act in almost total isolation during the campaign against the Japanese in the central Pacific. The Army, which supported Eberstadt, answered with a plan of its own, written by Lieutenant General J. Lawton Collins, based on the recommendations of a board of senior officers. The board endorsed the Eberstadt report, calling for a single cabinet-level officer to represent military concerns. The Army also advocated the creation of a separate Air Force, with all three services placed under the jurisdiction of the Joint Chiefs, which would be given full responsibility for the military budget.

The Navy wouldn't have any of it. During hearings on the Eberstadt plan, Navy witnesses argued that a new national security apparatus would strip the Navy of its air and Marine amphibious units. To resolve the problem (it was important that all parties "sign on"), Secretary of War Robert Patterson and Secretary of the Navy Forrestal appointed two officers to work out a compromise. In the end, the final bill was the product of General Lauris Norstad and Admiral Forrest Sherman, who hammered out the postwar military structure of the nation for four months. They then presented it to President Harry S. Truman, who, in February 1947, passed it on to Congress without major revision. It had been almost five years since the first official meeting of the JCS.

The Norstad-Sherman plan was the genesis of the National Security Act of 1947, a bill that had been created through compromise and controversy but whose legislative success was assured after two years of almost constant debate: it was signed into law by Truman on July 26, 1947. The bill, Public Law 253, is still considered one of the most important pieces of postwar legislation. Not only did it officially name the JCS as the highest military body in the nation, it created the United States Air Force, established a unified Department of Defense, established the Central Intelligence Agency, designated a National Security Council to coordinate policy for the president, and mandated the appointment of civilian secretaries to lead the military services.

PL 253 was, in reality, a grand compromise between the Army and the Navy. The Army won a unified military cabinet agency in the form of a Department of Defense and succeeded in making the Air Force a separate service. In exchange, the Navy's maintenance of its own air and marine wing remained inviolate. The bill seemed certain to satisfy both services; in 1947, there was little reason to believe that the mammoth changes engendered in the act would continually be debated and redebated. Nor was there reason to believe that the new JCS would soon be involved in a bitter debate over the role of the American high command in determining military and foreign policy.

Proponents of the bill point out that the National Security Act simply made into law what was already fact. The establishment of the National Security Council, for instance, was simply a redesignation of the State-War-Navy Coordinating Committee that had served Roosevelt during the war. The CIA was actually a postwar version of the Office of Strategic Services. The Department of Defense united the Navy and War departments, albeit with a larger staff, more money, and an enlarged mission. The creation of a separate Air Force, the bill's defenders noted, was a foregone conclusion; by the end of the war, the Army Air Corps was operating as a separate command. Even the Joint Chiefs of Staff was simply a continuation of the arrangement that had been in existence since 1942. In fact, the two different staffs (the old JCS, and the new, 1947 JCS) were so closely linked that, in some cases, the wartime structure was merely "painted over." For instance, World War II's Joint Staff Planners became the Joint Strategic Plans Committee, and the Joint Intelligence Staff became the Joint Intelligence Group.

The National Security Act did, however, add another layer to the "national command authority," interposing a powerful Secretary of Defense between the president and his primary military advisers. It wasn't too long before the cabinet position was the subject of military barbs. A number of officers began to describe the secretary as the Deputy Commander-in-Chief or the Deputy President, who, they even now pointedly remind military detractors, "isn't elected by anyone." While the JCS was established as a military adviser to the president, it actually met more often with the Secretary of Defense. The act was precise: the JCS not only had no operational authority, it didn't even have the right to "sign off" on the military budget, a provision that would cause enormous problems. But there were other problems as well.

The act made no provision for a JCS chairman, and, until an amendment to the act was passed in 1949, the JCS was simply a committee of three contentious service leaders. With postwar budget constraints and the nation's insistence on demobilization, the new system was sure to be tried. The first test of the actual power of the JCS came in 1949 and is known in the military as the Revolt of the Admirals.

While the military command structure might not have been the well-oiled machine that everyone supposed, particularly in the wake of the American victory, there was little doubt that the country had the command talent to wage war. During the war, the United States had developed what is still considered the most talented military leadership in its history. In the Pacific, Admirals William "Bull" Halsey and Chester Nimitz and General Douglas MacArthur led American forces in the conquest of Japan. In Europe, Generals Eisenhower, Patton, and Bradley fashioned America's conquest of Germany.

Other, younger men also emerged at the top of the military ladder during the war who would lead the nation for the next two decades. In the Navy, Admirals Arleigh Burke, Arthur Radford, Robert Carney, and Louis Denfeld were recognized as future leaders. In the Army, Generals James Gavin, Matthew Ridgway, and Maxwell Taylor were given key postwar assignments to acknowledge their wartime contributions. The new service, the blue-suited Air Force, began to build a formidable strategic attack force led by four-star officers: Curtis LeMay, Nathan Twining, Carl Spaatz, Hoyt Vandenberg, and Thomas White.

Each one of these officers would eventually be called on to provide military leadership, and inevitably each of them would be forced to grapple with a problem that none of them could have imagined before the war. The problem was so knotty, yet so fundamental, that its solution is still elusive: Who should control the country's nuclear arsenal, and under what circumstances should it be used? The first commander to grapple with this problem was Admiral Louis E. Denfeld. It was to prove his undoing.

Retired naval officers don't like to talk about the former Chief of Naval Operations. Denfeld, a Naval Academy graduate, was a highly decorated battleship commander in World War II. Soft-spoken, almost deferential, he served as Deputy Chief of Naval Operations for personnel under war hero Chester Nimitz after the end of the war and became CNO in 1947. Just two years later he was forced to resign because of an internal JCS spat that spilled over into the Navy and that still symbolizes the worst aspects of service rivalry. In essence, Denfeld was the victim of a feud that pitted the Navy against the Air Force.

Denfeld's predecessor, Nimitz, was as plodding and patient as Denfeld was deferential. Nimitz was made for war, not peace, a stubborn Dutchman from Texas whose stock-in-trade was telling vaguely off-color jokes. He didn't take long to tell people that he not only had a difficult time accepting the new command arrangements of 1947, he also disagreed with the clear implication that the Air Force, not the Navy, should be responsible for the nation's nuclear forces.

In his final report as CNO, Nimitz made the Navy's position clear. He began with the obvious: The U.S. Navy had a monopoly on the seas. The British Navy had been virtually destroyed during the war, and the Soviet Navy was nonexistent. Moreover, the Navy's emphasis on the deployment of aircraft carrier task forces meant that the United States "could establish offshore, anywhere in the world, air fields" that were "virtually as complete as any air base ever established." For this reason, Nimitz said, the Navy should be granted the lion's share of the nation's available military resources.

Nimitz said his argument was not intended to denigrate the roles of the Army or Air Force, nor was it pro-Navy. He was a patriot, he said, and was talking about national security. But what he was actually talking about was control of the nation's nuclear arsenal, a point that became clear when Denfeld subsequently told Congress that the Navy needed funding for a large aircraft carrier that could deploy new, high-performance jets armed with nuclear weapons. Just after Nimitz filed his report, the Air Force, led by Chief of Staff Carl Spaatz, protested the building of the Navy's "supercarrier," saying that it undermined the intent of the 1947 act. Secretary of Defense Forrestal told the services to resolve the problem themselves and, in true JCS fashion, suggested the appointment of a committee to fashion a compromise.

Denfeld, quick to follow in Nimitz's shoes, disagreed. The press had already publicized the Navy–Air Force feud, he said, and it was clear that the American people wanted the problem handled quickly. Then, too, Forrestal's proposed committee would include three officers, one from each service. Denfeld believed their deliberations could not be left to chance: not only would the Air Force officer resolve the problem in the Air Force's favor, the same would be true of the Army representative, General Albert Wedemeyer. As it turned out, Denfeld didn't have to worry about Wedemeyer, who had his own problems with the Air Force. Wedemeyer, and the Army, suspected that the Air Force was trying to gain control of the continental air defense system, an Army fiefdom.

For Denfeld, the aircraft carrier represented more than just a new weapons system for the Navy; it was to be his stamp on the service, a legacy he would leave to his colleagues, especially Nimitz, in whose shadow he had served all his life. It's difficult to find an officer who played a more active role in the Navy during the first four decades of the twentieth century. It's also difficult to find an officer whose career made less of an impact.

Denfeld was "from the boats," the battleships that formed the main fighting force of the Navy before, during, and just after World War I. They were the ships of the future, when (or so almost everyone thought) they would be the ultimate terror — bigger, faster, more powerful than any weapon on land or sea. But on the morning of December 7, 1941, it took the Japanese just thirty minutes to send their gray hulks below the surface of Pearl Harbor, and with them went dozens of careers. By the end of the war, battleship commanders were as obsolete as their ships; the war was being won by aircraft carriers and by the aviators who commanded them. The battleship commanders bitterly resented the death of the "real" Navy; for them, the ships represented the service as it was intended. They also felt that the battleships had actually won the war, were even uselessly sacrificed to protect the carriers in the Battle of the Solomons, when dozens of ships went below the waves of Ironbottom Sound. The aviators were not impressed and irreverently called the battleships "targets."

This realization made Denfeld the primary defender of the Navy's aircraft carrier. He had spent most of his career as an organized and hardworking administrator — he had only seen action in the Pacific during the war's last six months — and he was, or so his colleagues soon thought, desperate to prove his leadership in the new aviator-dominated service. A man who prided himself on his political acumen (not for nothing did he serve as an aide to the explosive King for three years), Denfeld moved quickly to force a confrontation with his colleagues on the JCS. Therefore, when the Secretary of Defense suggested that the Navy and Air Force resolve their differences and write a roles and missions statement endangering neither, Denfeld refused.

The military was split; in early 1948, the service chiefs told the Secretary of Defense that they could not agree on a common position. It was the no-nonsense Air Force general, Carl Spaatz, who had been one of the few American "aces" in World War I, who got to the heart of the issue. The real question, he told his colleagues, was whether there should be "three Services, specialists in their normal fields, operating as a team of the National Military Establishment or whether the Services shall be free to duplicate, within each one of them, forces and equipment for which another Service has primary responsibility."

Precisely. But for the Navy the issue went even deeper; not only was its aircraft carrier and high-performance jets armed with nuclear bombs vulnerable to Air Force claims that it, and not the Navy, should be the premier strategic service, control of the bomb itself was at stake. In essence, the Navy believed that if the construction of its supercarrier was stopped by the Air Force, it would be successful in pressing its claim as the nation's one service with control over nuclear weapons. If the Air Force won that control, it would become the most important service, winning the most promotions, attention, and money. It was the Navy versus the Air Force, with the Army holding an important position as an onlooker.

Omar Bradley, appointed the Army's chief of staff in February 1948, had initially entered the fray to protect what he considered the Army's traditional role: the responsibility for the tactical air defense of the continental United States. But in March 1948, Bradley actually sided with the Air Force by arguing that the Navy should *not* be allowed to deploy Marine units larger than divisions. So there were really three disagreements: over which service should control nuclear weapons, over whether the Navy should be allowed to build a supercarrier, and over the size of the Marines.

At the beginning of the month, Secretary of Defense James Forrestal called the Joint Chiefs of Staff to a meeting at the Key West Naval Base to sort through these increasingly complex problems. The four-day meeting resulted in what has come to be known as the Key West Agreement, which laid out major policy guidelines, some of them still in force. At Key West, Louis Denfeld made a major and (as it turned out) career-ending concession: he agreed that the Air Force would have responsibility for strategic bombing. The Navy never had any intention of intruding on Air Force responsibilities, Denfeld protested, but only wanted to protect the role of naval aviation, a commitment he had made to Nimitz and his fellow officers. Carl Spaatz nodded his approval. The Air Force didn't oppose the Navy's carrier, he assured Denfeld, but just wanted to make sure that its role in the new national security structure was protected. In the spirit of conciliation, Omar Bradley conceded that the Navy should be allowed to deploy Marine units, he just wanted to protect the Army's premier tactical role. The Navy agreed to deploy no more than four Marine divisions "or have a field unit headquarters higher than a corps." What had begun as a shouting match ended with a series of compromises that Denfeld was convinced gave approval for the construction of the Navy's supercarrier. The Key West Agreement was officially adopted in an executive order issued March 26, 1948.

But there was a serious problem. For all its attempts at clarification, the agreement actually failed to concur on the major issue dividing the chiefs: it never even touched on which service should control the nation's nuclear arsenal. Within days, Spaatz was back on the stump, arguing that the agreement had granted the Air Force direct supervision of the JCS's Armed Forces Special Weapons Project, which meant "exclusive control" of nuclear weapons. He went on to say that divided control of nuclear weapons would result in "uncoordinated, and even conflicting requests and instructions," on strategic use of the weapons. Bradley agreed with Spaatz's characterization; Denfeld didn't.

Convinced that not only was the construction of the supercarrier in danger but also that his job as CNO was on the line, Denfeld reiterated the Navy's position: the Key West Agreement did not say that the Navy should be denied use of nuclear devices. Spaatz had agreed to the construction of a Navy carrier, Denfeld said, and therefore clearly agreed that the Navy should have a nuclear role. Moreover, he argued, the Air Force proposal could actually harm national security by denying naval use of the weapons during combat operations. Once again, Forrestal was forced to intercede; he called another meeting of the chiefs, this time at Newport Naval Base on August 20, 1948. The two-day meeting ended with a compromise, as before. The director of the Armed Forces Special Weapons Project, designated as the arm of the military developing nuclear weaponry, would report to the Air Force chief of staff. But the office itself would be available to all the services. In addition, the Newport Agreement made clear that each service was responsible for "programming and planning" its own role and mission, a statement that allowed the Navy some leeway in deploying nuclear weapons.

But the debate wasn't over. Spaatz's convenient loss of memory about the Key West Agreement had embarrassed Denfeld, who was smarting from what he viewed as a plot on the part of the Air Force to stop the Navy's supercarrier. In December, Denfeld got his revenge. For an officer who prided himself on conciliation, who had always maintained that successful leadership consisted of being able to suggest and not order — a distinct difference in philosophy from the Navy's pantheon of tyrants — the next move was well out of character. Clearly, Denfeld was feeling pressure from the newly empowered heroes of the Japanese war, the Navy's aviators, who were beginning to doubt that a battleship commander could adequately defend, let alone understand, their point of view.

In December, General Hoyt Vandenberg, who had taken Spaatz's place as the Air Force chief of staff, told the JCS that Air Force studies indicated that Soviet air capabilities were modest, that the United States could carry out a nearly unimpeded strategic air offensive if necessary. Denfeld said he wasn't entirely convinced by Vandenberg's figures and asked that they be reviewed by the JCS's Joint Intelligence Committee. Vandenberg was enraged. It looked like a typical Navy ploy to him, another attempt to rewrite the Key West Agreement. He knew that if the Air Force study could be compromised, the Navy could claim a larger role in the deployment of nuclear forces, including the deployment of its planned supercarrier, the U.S.S. *United States.* Denfeld pleaded innocent; he wasn't trying to win approval of a new carrier, he said (a claim that would haunt him in days just ahead), because the Air Force had already agreed to such a carrier. Vandenberg lapsed into silence.

Denfeld's ploy worked initially: a preliminary report of the Joint Intelligence Committee said that Denfeld was right, Vandenberg had "oversimplified" Soviet air capabilities and had ignored some pertinent data. The JCS directed the JIC to investigate further. Had Vandenberg's rosy picture substantially underestimated Soviet capabilities? At the end of August 1949, nine months after Vandenberg's initial assessment, the JIC reported that he had underestimated, by some 400, the number of bombers available to the Soviet Union — a startling conclusion, considering that the Soviet Union actually had no strategic bombers at the time. Denfeld had won the first round in his continuing fight to build the supercarrier.

On March 28, 1949, Harry Truman appointed Louis Johnson as the new Secretary of Defense with a mandate to cut the defense budget.

Johnson, a plain-spoken man, couldn't understand all the controversy but vowed to get to the bottom of it and launched an immediate investigation of the Navy's aircraft carrier proposal. However, he had already made up his mind about the carrier — and about quite a few other things. Reviewing the Navy–Air Force feud and the debate on strategic arms, and mindful of Truman's desire to cut military expenditures, Johnson decided to cancel the supercarrier. The news came on April 23, barely a month after he had taken office. Denfeld, his standing among his colleagues clearly endangered, fought back. He told a Senate Armed Services subcommittee a month later that the full JCS had approved the carrier, that it was necessary in order to accommodate newer aircraft, and that it was essential for national security. Even the Air Force, he said, citing the Key West Agreement, had approved its construction.

Remembering Denfeld's criticism of Vandenberg's views, the Air Force struck back. One week after Denfeld's Senate testimony, Carl Spaatz told a gathering at the National Press Club that the Air Force had *never* agreed to allow the Navy to build a carrier. Spaatz's claim did its damage. In the office of the CNO, naval officers grilled a defensive Denfeld on the details of the Key West Agreement. Had the Air Force approved the supercarrier or not? And if so, what had he agreed to in return? His answers were a major embarrassment and a damaging admission. Yes, Denfeld said, the Air Force had approved a new carrier, no matter what Spaatz said. Truman himself, he added, had approved its construction. And yes, he had agreed to the Air Force's premier role in strategic bombing, but, he argued, it had been a good exchange.

Unbeknownst to Denfeld, however, Truman had decided to back Johnson's decision despite his earlier promise; the battle between the Navy and Air Force was becoming unseemly and politically embarrassing for the president; he wanted it to end. Denfeld, who was perhaps the first but almost certainly not the last person to underestimate Truman, pointed out that the budget already contained funds for the carrier. It had to be built. With that, Vandenberg finally got his revenge. He didn't care what the budget said; he had never approved it anyway. "The 1949 budget," he told his colleagues, "was prepared and submitted on a unilateral basis. It was not coordinated or examined in detail by the Joint Chiefs of Staff. Hence, I cannot at this time approve or disapprove one particular part of the budget of one Service without the thorough consideration of the programs and budget requirements of all three services."

The public sniping was almost more than Truman could stand, and, meeting with the JCS in March and April 1949, he expressed his anger. He told the military officers assigned to the White House that he had recently "called in those fellows [the Joint Chiefs] on this business of presenting a united front to these questions" and he expected "that that would be done." Denfeld loyally retreated into silence, but only for the time being. The battle over the supercarrier had been costly and embarrassing, and Denfeld belatedly realized that his reputation as a Navy partisan was at stake. Not the least of his worries was the resignation of Secretary of the Navy John L. Sullivan, who quit over Johnson's decision to cancel the carrier. Denfeld decided to stay on, but he knew his Navy colleagues were questioning his decision. In fact, not only did they believe that Denfeld should have resigned in protest with Sullivan, by late April they believed that Denfeld had become a decided handicap in their battle for the carrier. The admirals were in revolt.

In the eyes of the Navy's newest and strongest branch, the admirals of naval aviation, Denfeld had made a key mistake: he had cut a deal with the Air Force, thereby agreeing not only to the concept of strategic bombing but also to the funding of a new fleet of strategic bombers — *Air Force bombers.* In return, the Navy had won a paltry and, without the control of nuclear weapons, useless compromise, the building of the U.S.S. *United States.* Now, even that had been canceled. In mid-1949, top Navy officers met in a round of high-level meetings to try to find a way out of the dilemma.

In the first and one of the most bitter JCS battles, Denfeld was caught in a classic squeeze play that was to plague a number of his successors. It was, after all, a new environment. Before 1947, the JCS was an equal — no, more — in the nation's foreign policy apparatus. Then the services had direct access to the president, while the Secretary of War and the Secretary of the Navy were shunted aside to less "operational" roles; the "action" had been in the field, not in the Gold Room. There were different tests then, of heroism, decisiveness, of actual command.

But times had changed. After the war, military commanders were expected to fight different battles in different environments. While Louis Denfeld might lead by example as Ernie King's aide or on the bridge of the U.S.S. *Wisconsin* off Okinawa, the spare atmosphere of the tank called for different talents, talents that were, in many ways, more brutal than even those required during the heat of combat. In the end, Denfeld just wasn't prepared and so became the new system's first victim. Still, in the middle of 1949, Denfeld hoped he could not only retrieve the situation and his position as JCS chairman but also that he could win the increasingly bitter fight between the Air Force and the Navy.

Unfortunately, Denfeld's defense of his role as CNO occurred in the middle of congressional efforts to reform the National Security Act in the early summer of 1949. The changes had been suggested by a commission headed by former president Herbert Hoover and were designed to do two things. First, Congress decided to institutionalize "the right [of the military] to speak out against administration policy before the Congress" (the better to criticize Truman's austere military budgets) and, second, to unite the JCS by appointing a nonvoting chairman to serve as spokesman for the military high command (the better to head off just the kind of service fighting characterized by the aircraft carrier debate).

If Denfeld's deal with the Air Force had been a hard pill for the Navy to swallow, the decision of Congress to appoint a JCS chairman was even worse. The top naval officers had consistently opposed the appointment of such a high-level official and had won the first round of the debate back in 1947, when the National Security Act was drafted. Now, the Navy was not only stuck with a JCS chairman, it was in danger of losing its vaunted supercarrier. What was worse, the Air Force would undoubtedly be rewarded for its efforts by winning funding for its newest bomber, the B-36, which it claimed would be the first line of defense for the United States in the atomic age.

There was only one thing to do: the admirals decided to strike back at the Air Force, but this time without Denfeld. Arleigh Burke and Arthur Radford, both high-ranking naval line officers and war heroes, were picked for the duty. Their job was not just to defend the Navy but to make certain that the Air Force was denied funds for the B-36. Denfeld was in no position to object. Thinking that the U.S.S. *United States* would go forward and with the Key West Agreement in his pocket, Denfeld had approved Joint Emergency War Plans that included strategic nuclear bombing of the Soviet Union during the first day of a future war. Everyone knew, including Denfeld, that his position endorsed the deployment of the Air Force's new plane.

The opening shot of the B-36 debate was fired by Cedric Worth, a civilian analyst to the Undersecretary of the Navy who prepared an anonymous and, as it turned out, totally false document charging that the Air Force's new plane was a "billion dollar blunder." Worth's paper was a political bombshell: the only reason the construction of the B-36 had continued despite its "mediocre capabilities," Worth claimed, was because the Secretary of Defense and the Secretary of the Air Force had a financial interest in it and owed political favors to Consolidated-Vultee Aircraft, its manufacturer. These claims made national headlines and spurred congressional hearings. Under the leadership of Congressman James Van Zandt, whom the official JCS history called "a champion of Navy interests," the House Armed Services Committee launched an immediate investigation. But it did not merely investigate Worth's claims of impropriety; at the prodding of Navy officers, it decided to air the entire issue of strategic nuclear war publicly. Included in the armed services' mandate was an investigation of whether the cancellation of the U.S.S. *United States* "was sound."

In the course of its preparations for the hearings, the JCS was asked specifically whether it favored a national military strategy that relied on strategic bombing. The question went to the heart of the issue. Ever the team player and now clearly boxed in by his Key West handshake, Louis Denfeld decided he had no choice: he had to keep his part of the agreement or lose face with the JCS. He therefore agreed with the JCS on the importance of strategic bombing and, by extension, with the Air Force on the need for strategic bombers.

Denfeld's honesty cost him the support of Burke and Radford, who told him that they felt no obligation to support the Key West accords; the Navy's interests came first. They would testify, they said, that the Navy disagreed with the Air Force strategic bombing concept, regardless of their commanding officer's opinions. The central point of the Navy's position was presented by master strategist Arthur Radford, who was best known for his uncanny ability to tell just what the enemy was planning. Part of the Navy's "carrier gang," he focused on the B-36. True to form, Radford said, the Navy rejected the Air Force's conception of strategic warfare. The operations envisioned by the Air Force, he argued, simply wouldn't work; they could not be carried out with currently available aircraft, and the results (in any event) would not be in the long-term national security interests of the United States. He argued further that the American people had actually been misled by the Air Force, tricked into believing that any future war would be "cheap and easy." At issue, he said pointedly, was "the atomic blitz."

"Can the B-36 be intercepted and destroyed in unacceptable numbers," Radford asked rhetorically. "Yes," he answered. Denfeld knew that Radford's argument was groundless: the Air Force had never claimed that the B-36 would be the sole strategic bomber; it planned to use B-29s and B-50s, not the B-36, as primary carriers for nuclear warheads. Denfeld also knew that Radford had based his claim of B-36 vulnerability on American interceptor technology, which was unavailable to the Soviet Union. Based on current reports, Radford had said, the B-36 was vulnerable not only at 25,000 feet but also at 40,000 feet and at night. What he failed to mention, as Denfeld well knew, was that the Soviet Union didn't have antiaircraft capabilities that could intercept bombers at that altitude. Not only was the B-36 not vulnerable to the Soviets, it's difficult to determine just what American aircraft might have been.

Radford summed up his presentation, and the Navy's position, by

arguing for a different American strategy, one keyed to tactical support of American defenses in Europe, the likely point of a Soviet
attack. The focus of an American counterstroke should be against
those forces by tactical fighters, he claimed, not questionable strategic
attacks on Soviet territory. Therefore, control of the seas was essential, and only the Navy could provide it. Implicit in Radford's testimony was the Navy's clear position that the United States could
continue to control the seas only if Congress overruled the Secretary
of Defense and the president and approved the supercarrier.

By then it was clear that Denfeld's job was in jeopardy. To save it,
Denfeld moderated his position; he tried to agree with Radford (and
his fellow admirals) by attempting to support the JCS position in favor
of strategic bombing at the same time that he supported the Navy's
parochial position: "I fully support the broad conclusions presented to
this committee by the naval and marine officers who preceded me,"
Denfeld said. He went on to argue that the Air Force must pay far
greater attention to "precision and selectivity." It was a delicate
dance, and it failed. Denfeld simply could not transform strategic
bombing into tactical bombing.

The Air Force's defense of the B-36 was keyed to the acceptance of
strategic bombing as a decisive means of waging war. During the final
days of hearings on the B-36, Air Force Chief Vandenberg rejected the
Navy's contentions that the Air Force was attempting to find a "cheap
and easy" means of waging war. "A prime objective of this country
must be to find a counter-balance to the potential enemy's masses of
ground troops other than equal masses of American and Allied ground
troops," he argued. "No such balancing factor exists other than strategic bombing." This argument was seconded by the Army. The Navy's
primary mission was not to "attack land targets," JCS Chairman Bradley said, but to face down "the Russian fleet" and the "menace of the
submarine."

The testimony of Vandenberg and Bradley tipped the balance
against the Navy, even though it had produced its top officers, including some of the most widely respected combat admirals in American
history. Although Radford and Burke led the Navy charge, their position was seconded by four officers who had reached the peak of their
careers in the naval war against Japan: Chester Nimitz, Ernest King,
William Halsey, and Raymond Spruance. Despite this heady combina-
tion of brass and stripe, the Navy eventually lost the battle. The B-36
was funded, strategic bombing was vindicated, the U.S.S. *United
States* was dismantled, and the position of chairman of the Joint
Chiefs of Staff was created.

For one of the few times in history, the Navy had been routed. Its
defeat can be easily attributed to its misleading descriptions of the

capabilities of the B-36 as well as to the result of an investigation that Worth had made unfounded claims of conflict of interest against the Secretary of the Air Force. More important, as the hearings went on, it became apparent to the congressional committee that the controversy actually had little to do with either the B-36 or the supercarrier and that the strategic debate was actually peripheral to the Navy's concerns. In fact, Denfeld's testimony and actions as CNO showed that the Navy didn't really disagree with the Air Force on nuclear weapons. What was at issue, the committee found, was the concept of unification under the JCS system.

In only one area did Congress agree with the admirals. They had testified that each service should be left to "design and develop its own weapons" and that "the views of a particular service are entitled to predominant weight in the determination of the forces needed by that service to fulfill its mission." Congress agreed. The JCS system did not "insure at all times adequate consideration for the views of all services," its final report said. Yet even this was a minor victory. To ensure the "adequate consideration" the Navy deemed necessary, Congress instituted the office of JCS chairman, a position strongly opposed by the Navy.

The year 1949 had not been good for the Navy, and now, with the B-36 scandal over, there seemed only one thing left to do. In October, the naval officers who had opposed Denfeld's Key West handshake unceremoniously demanded his resignation: "The authority of the Joint Chiefs of Staff, the Secretary of Defense and the President had been challenged" by the high command of the nation's Navy, and someone had to be sacrificed. Denfeld's only fault was his inability to control his subordinate commanders and silence his former bosses. Secretary of the Navy Francis P. Mathews requested his relief, and on October 27, President Truman approved his transfer to "other duties."

Mathews detailed Denfeld's sins: "Integrity of command is indispensable at all times. There can be no twilight zone in the measure of loyalty to superiors and respect for authority existing between various official ranks." The words are pointed: Denfeld was the odd man out in the Navy hierarchy. For "integrity of command," read "failure to agree with Navy policy"; for "authority existing between various official ranks," read "failure to toe the Navy line." The reassignment of Denfeld, interpreted ever after as the first firing of a member of the JCS, rippled through the military establishment during the late fall of 1949. For a time, the JCS was stunned into paralysis. The Navy had been vanquished, the Air Force vindicated, and the Army seemed clearly in charge of the American high command. During its first two years, the JCS had been caught up in service debates; it wasn't until 1950 that it could settle down enough to begin grappling with the growing military power of the Soviet Union, a threat that had to be met with an austere $13 billion military budget. The JCS knew it was impossible.

To oppose the Soviets, the JCS believed the United States needed a massive military buildup in all areas, a commitment to support and rearm America's allies, and a redirection of national financial resources — all of which, as the JCS well knew, Truman was unwilling to do. There were hard choices ahead, including the withdrawal of American forces from nations that would then have to be responsible for their own defense. The choices were difficult but necessary.

As the JCS looked at the situation maps of the world in early 1950, it saw some key "hot spots." Europe, especially Berlin, was obviously coveted by the Soviets. Taiwan was under pressure from the Chinese mainland, and in Indochina, the French were involved in a major war against Vietnamese nationalists supported by the Soviets and Chinese. If the United States was to make good its policy of containment, these three areas would be the first to receive aid. The bulk of the commitment would be made to Europe, which posed the greatest threat to American interests. And although the situation was bleak in some regions, there were areas in which local forces could be counted on to oppose communist inroads: the Middle East seemed calm; the British and Americans had made remarkable progress in ending the Greek civil war; South America seemed safe for the moment; and Taiwan would be aided covertly and defended with the help of the U.S. Navy. Even in South Korea, which the JCS believed was outside the American defense perimeter, the Army of the Republic of Korea was making great strides, a judgment that was soon proven decidedly overconfident.

The U.S. military mission — the Korean Military Advisory Group (KMAG) — found that Korea's army was improving, that it was fast becoming the "border security" force necessary to fend off a North Korean attack in the rugged hills along the 38th Parallel. The head of KMAG was "enthusiastic" about South Korea's ability to defend itself, even to the point of recommending that the Koreans not be sent tanks for their defense; if South Korea was attacked, tanks would be virtually useless in the mountains along its northern border.

It was a good thing: the JCS had already approved a Joint Outline Emergency War Plan, which reflected the official U.S. military policy in the Far East. The JCS plans included the defense of the Philippines, Japan, and Okinawa. Taiwan would be defended if possible, but the JCS didn't think the undermanned and denuded American occupation army stationed in Japan could really stop a full-scale communist offensive on the Asian mainland. As the official JCS history noted: "In the face of an expected Soviet/satellite thrust westward, the United States would seek to hold a bridgehead on the continent or to return as soon as possible." That left Korea out.

The JCS's initial frustration over Truman's austere defense budget was alleviated somewhat when the president decided to reconsider his position on a military buildup as a result of Soviet moves. In addition, in the midst of the B-36 controversy and the relief of Denfeld, the Soviets had exploded their first nuclear bomb, several years ahead of U.S. expectations. Soon afterward, Truman asked his key advisers to reexamine U.S. strategic objectives. The result was NSC-68, one of the first and certainly one of the bleakest policy papers ever issued by the new National Security Council (NSC). The NSC was fast becoming a competitor of the JCS: that the NSC would be assigned a leading role in writing what was then considered a purely military assessment was a clear signal that the opinion of the JCS was not as valued in 1950 as it had been in 1940.

NSC-68 portrayed the American struggle against the Soviet Union as a "basic conflict" of "freedom versus slavery." It stated that should the Soviet Union attack, its offensive would include a military "overrun" of Western Europe, "air attacks" against Great Britain, and "atomic attacks" against North American targets. Four courses of action were proposed to meet this threat: a continuation of current policies, a withdrawal of military forces to the American mainland, a full-scale war, and "a rapid build-up of political, economic and military strength in the free world." As with so many other NSC studies to come, the NSC's recommendation was telegraphed as part of the paper's assessment. Three of the possibilities were straw dogs: almost everyone believed the United States would fall behind under "current policies," no one seriously considered isolationism an option, and no one wanted war. That left the buildup of the free world's political, economic, and military strength, which NSC-68 recommended as "the only means short of war which may eventually force the Kremlin . . . to negotiate acceptable agreements on issues of major importance."

Truman wasn't totally convinced. Not wanting to bust the treasury, he circulated NSC-68 to the Bureau of the Budget, which sent back its assessment. It claimed that NSC-68 "oversimplified issues and grossly overemphasized military considerations. . . . The neat dichotomy between 'slavery' and 'freedom' is not a realistic description either of the situation today or of the alternatives as they appear to present themselves to large areas of the world. . . . The gravest error of NSC-68 is that it underplays the role of economic and social change as a factor in 'the underlying conflict.' " This response convinced the president that the military situation was not as grave as his top advisers thought, and he directed the Secretary of Defense and the JCS to establish their military priorities with the budget assessment, not NSC-68, in mind. Uncertain just where the danger lay, and perhaps chastened by the swift departure of Denfeld, the chiefs' proposed buildup was modest. The American military would defend Europe, recommend an increase in defense appropriations "for exposed Alaskan airfields" and "modernization of Army equipment," and draw a security line in Asia just west of Japan and the Philippines. There would be no American presence on the Asian mainland.

The 1951 budget had been decided and the battle for the 1952 budget was about to begin. It would include another reassessment and an expansion of military strength to ward off Soviet designs in Europe. NSC-68 notwithstanding, the president and his Secretary of Defense remained committed to "lower spending levels" in 1952. In the wake of what naval officers were now calling the Denfeld "execution" — the CNO had departed to swift, but certain, obscurity — the chiefs decided to go along with the president. Even Omar Bradley was satisfied with the president's proposals. The military would "make do"; the United States could not defend everything, everywhere, all at once. On the morning of June 25, 1950, all of that changed when North Korean troops invaded the South.

The invasion of South Korea was not unexpected, though its timing was something of a surprise. Despite their public pronouncements, KMAG believed that sooner or later the North Koreans would strike south, that the war would be bloody, but that in the end South Korea would be able to hold off the attack. The only officer who disagreed was Douglas MacArthur, the one hero of World War II who rivaled Eisenhower, who outshone Marshall, and who was most often named as a candidate for president. MacArthur initially disagreed with the proposed withdrawal of American troops, which had been stationed in South Korea since the Japanese surrender, and was only convinced of the necessity of the move because of "political considerations." In a cable to the Department of the Army in early 1949, MacArthur had said that the establishment of a South Korean defense force equal to a fight with the North Koreans was "not within the capabilities of the U.S."

Reaction to the communist attack on South Korea was glacial. JCS members, with the probable exception of Bradley, were not immediately informed, and there was little sense of panic in Washington, one of the few places that remained unconcerned with the new, faraway war. When KMAG reported that the North Korean attack had "achieved tactical surprise" — a report issued just twenty-four hours after the invasion — Secretary of State Dean Acheson's special assistant, John Foster Dulles, cabled Washington that to "sit by while

Korea is overrun by unprovoked armed attack would start a world war." Bradley, and the other members of the JCS, seemed unconcerned. The general, one of the most well liked officers in American history, told his colleagues that Korean forces were expected to hold off the communists "unless the Russians actively participate." He believed that South Korea's fall, while unlikely, was clearly possible: "If Korea falls, we may want to recommend even stronger action in the case of Formosa," he said. There was no statement, no hint, that American troops should or even needed to intervene.

Sunday, June 25, was a critical day in Washington. While the American military establishment continued to be optimistic about South Korea's chances, the State Department and the president himself remained unsure. Dean Acheson's position on American intervention was critical, and he eventually succeeded in reinforcing Truman's own thinking. "To back away from this challenge, in view of our capacity for meeting it, would be highly destructive of the power and prestige of the United States," Acheson later reflected.

His doubts about South Korea's ability to fight alone spurred Truman to call a meeting of eleven of his top advisers at Blair House on Sunday evening. Present were Secretary of State Acheson and Secretary of Defense Johnson; the secretaries of the Army (Frank Pace), Navy (Francis Mathews), and Air Force (Thomas Finletter); the chiefs of staff of the Army (J. Lawton Collins), Navy (Forrest Sherman), and Air Force (Hoyt Vandenberg), and the new chairman of the JCS (Omar Bradley). In addition, Acheson brought along three able assistants, Undersecretary James Webb, Assistant Secretary Dean Rusk, and Recording Secretary Philip Jessup.

The meeting began with a discussion of the situation in Formosa, an approach that historians would consider peculiar in light of the Korean crisis. But the Formosa discussion, led by Johnson and Bradley, was well in line with American strategic thinking at the time. Neither man believed that Korea could be defended with the troops at hand, whereas Formosa could be adequately protected by the U.S. Seventh Fleet. Furthermore, when Johnson and Bradley had returned from a trip to Formosa just hours earlier, they had been greeted by a policy memo from MacArthur, who argued for a "complete defense" of the island in the wake of the North Korean invasion. Neither Acheson nor Truman was impressed with MacArthur's argument and, after a short dinner, the discussion turned to Korea. As expected, Acheson made the case for intervention, outlining four distinct steps that would sharply escalate American involvement. They included assessing Korea's military needs, dispatching supplies to defend Seoul, naval and air support for the possible evacuation of American dependents, and deploying the Seventh Fleet to Korean waters.

The official JCS history states that Acheson's recommendations were "endorsed, tacitly or explicitly, by all those present." This characterization is inexact. The chiefs were puzzled by Acheson's program; neither Bradley nor Collins believed that the United States should send ground troops to defend South Korea, saying that the American troops in Japan were not prepared to enter the conflict. Both generals felt that the United States could not defend its interests in other parts of the world while fighting a war in Korea. It couldn't be done, Bradley said, at least not without full mobilization. But Hoyt Vandenberg and Forrest Sherman disagreed, at least partly. Vandenberg believed the Air Force could have a decisive impact on the outcome of the battle and confidently told the president that if the South Koreans couldn't stop the invasion, he could. On the other hand, Sherman emphasized the protection of the Korean coastline, a predictable comment considering that was all the Navy could do. Nevertheless, he believed that such protection could turn the tide of battle.

Bradley and Collins reiterated the Army's position: if the United States intervened, a massive number of troops would be needed in order to win the war. The Air Force and Navy could not win the battle alone, no matter what Vandenberg or Sherman said. Truman made a quick decision, accepting Acheson's recommendations while directing the JCS to study the Korean situation. The JCS was to draw up plans for intervention that included bombing Soviet airfields in the Far East.

When this gathering reconvened almost twenty-four hours later, it was clear that the situation in Korea had gotten much worse. Once again, Collins and Bradley advised Truman to ignore Air Force arguments that it alone could win the war, and again Acheson pleaded for a stronger stand. MacArthur's cables were particularly troubling: the Far East commander predicted that Seoul would fall and noted that the Korean army was in full retreat. The situation was going from bad to worse — either that or, as a number of chiefs would later intimate, MacArthur was "hitting the panic button." Bradley noted MacArthur's tone, but he still recommended that the president move slowly in taking further steps that would escalate the conflict. There was still no reason to believe, he said, that the United States needed to intervene. Within five days, Bradley and the rest of the JCS changed their thinking.

It was an odd turnaround: both Vandenberg and Sherman had begun their presentations to Truman on June 26 by arguing that Air Force and Navy intervention would be decisive, but by June 30 they were saying that the deployment of ground troops was in the nation's interest. Yet Bradley and Collins, who had argued against intervention, now believed there might be no other way to save South Korea. The JCS position on the war was beginning to solidify. Bradley and Collins realized that the news from South Korea was bound to get worse and that in the face of South Korea's imminent military collapse, arguments against intervention were starting to sound hollow. But their task, as they saw it, was to give sound military advice to the civilian leadership; in their estimation, American intervention should only be a last desperate measure.

On the night of June 29, Douglas MacArthur returned to Japan after a firsthand assessment of the situation in Korea. In a detailed summary, he made his position clear: "The Korean army is entirely incapable of counter action and there is grave danger of a further break-through. . . . The only assurance for the holding of the present line, and the ability to regain later the lost ground, is through the introduction of U.S. ground combat forces into the Korean battle area." This report was the last straw.

At 5:00 A.M. on June 30, 1950, President Truman gave permission for the commitment of American ground troops in the fight to save South Korea. Collins, the first JCS member informed of the decision, called his colleagues. Sherman, who had been so confident of the Navy's ability to stop North Korea, put his thoughts on the action in a memo to the JCS. His words are a fitting description of its position on intervention. "The decision had been taken on the recommendation of General MacArthur, who was on the spot," Sherman wrote. "I had some apprehensions about it, and in the following days I felt that the decision was a sound one. It was unavoidable, but I was fully aware of the hazards involved in fighting asiatics on the Asiatic mainland, which is something that, as a naval officer, I have grown up to believe should be avoided if possible." Bradley's opinion, on the other hand, was an outspoken indictment of the American commitment, which he knew was likely to degenerate into a no-win slugging match with the dedicated and disciplined North Koreans. "Korea is the wrong war, at the wrong time, in the wrong place," he said.

Doubts permeated the entire military establishment, but the assessments were still far from defeatist. There were two worries. The first was a military paradox: that the war could be won if, and only if, it could be contained, that is, if the Chinese did not become involved or if the United States did not take steps to extend the war to the Chinese mainland. The second stemmed from the first: the military officer most likely to extend the war was MacArthur, and he was the American commander in Korea.

The deputy Army chief of staff for operations and plans, General Matthew Ridgway, outlined these worries to Bradley, the JCS chairman, soon after Truman's announcement. Ridgway, an awe-inspiring general whose forceful personality was making itself felt throughout the Army, said that he doubted MacArthur would stop at a nominal commitment of American troops and warned that he would be hard, perhaps impossible, to control. Given the opportunity, Ridgway said, MacArthur would interpret his orders liberally, not literally. His tendency, Ridgway believed, would be to widen the war. The otherwise reticent, almost painfully modest Bradley agreed, but he reminded Ridgway that MacArthur was on the scene. In the end, he said, it was MacArthur or no one; the JCS had to support its commander on the ground.

Douglas MacArthur is the subject of more biographies than any other military officer in American history. His life has been catalogued, examined, criticized, esteemed, and vilified in equal parts since his death, in 1964. Through the work of hundreds of historians and archivists, his achievements, shortcomings, battles, and ambitions have served as a convenient, if somewhat misleading, snapshot of the American military in the first half of the twentieth century. His papers rival the collections of past presidents; his diaries and reminiscences are culled for important military information; his speeches are memorized and quoted. For millions of Americans he remains the quintessential general — a hero, a conqueror, and, finally, a legend. Yet we know little of the real MacArthur, the flash of his military genius forever obscuring his obvious insecurities. He was a momma's boy and a hero, a man of petty cruelty who became a beneficent conqueror, a general whose power over a conquered Japan could have transformed him into a tyrant but didn't, but whose chafing under the slightest guidance made him a near-hysteric.

MacArthur was undoubtedly the most complex military figure of this time, even more puzzling than the war-loving George Patton, certainly more mysterious than the beloved Bradley. If he had left the military in 1949, before Korea, he might well be considered the greatest general in American history. It was Korea, and MacArthur's bitter but inevitably futile conflict with the JCS, that proved his undoing.

It is now clear that from the moment of America's intervention in Korea, the JCS took steps to restrain MacArthur's plan to widen the war. It is also now plain that MacArthur understood this and took steps to circumvent its orders. In the end, the JCS was caught in the middle: between its loyalty to a fellow commander and its oath to obey civilian leadership. Still, its position on MacArthur remains unclouded by either personal opinion or service rivalry: when MacArthur initiated policies that essentially circumvented higher military authority (especially *after* the Chinese intervention), the JCS moved swiftly and decisively to have him removed.

Its problems with MacArthur began just two months after the North Korean attack. After hesitantly agreeing to American intervention,

Forrest Sherman and Lawton Collins visited MacArthur in Tokyo on August 20, 1950, ostensibly to assess the situation in the Far East. In fact, their mission was an attempt to dissuade the general from his reported scheme to flank North Korea's forces on the peninsula. MacArthur had initially communicated his new strategic view to the JCS on July 7, saying that the Korean War would be won by an amphibious assault on Korea's west coast, a suggestion that stunned the chiefs. The war had barely started; the few American forces available had retreated to a small perimeter around Pusan, at the end of the peninsula; and the buildup of troops and material had barely begun. A counteroffensive now, at the very onset of American intervention, wouldn't and couldn't succeed.

It was a harebrained scheme. MacArthur wanted to put American troops ashore at the port of Inchon, just 150 miles north of Pusan on the Yellow Sea. Storming Inchon would be like trying to storm Big Sur: Inchon didn't have beaches, "only piers and seawalls," and the currents and tides were murderous. MacArthur thought it would work even if everyone else didn't or, given the force of his personality and his consummate self-confidence, maybe because they didn't.

When Sherman visited the Far East commander's headquarters, he heard harsh words. Pipe in hand, dress blouse casually open at the neck (MacArthur's personal dress code influenced a generation of generals to affect the same informality, even the same sunglasses), MacArthur rudely lectured the World War II hero on naval tactics. "My confidence in the Navy is complete," he said arrogantly, "and in fact I seem to have more confidence in the Navy than the Navy has in itself." It was the closest he came to an insult during the meeting, implying that the assault was not a question of good tactics but of manhood. This fact was not lost on the CNO, who, under the circumstances, could hardly back down. "I wouldn't hesitate to take a ship in there," Sherman said confidently, looking at the map of Inchon Harbor. "Spoken like a true Farragut," MacArthur snapped back. With his eyes lifted to the heavens, he concluded his argument: "I can almost hear the ticking of the second hand of destiny. We will act now or we will die." Collins had his own view of MacArthur's comment. "Ask not for whom the second hand of destiny ticks," he reportedly told Sherman just after this meeting. "It ticks for thee."

The Inchon landing went forward, but the JCS could barely contain its fears. Even Sherman had second thoughts. Within twenty-four hours of his Tokyo briefing, he confided to Collins: "I wish I had that man's optimism." Collins concurred but went even further, calling the landing a "5000 to 1 shot." Even so, the JCS approved the plan, and on September 17, American troops braved the high walls of Inchon and struck east toward Seoul. Within days they routed the North Koreans.

Within two weeks they retook the capital of South Korea. It was a brilliant tactical maneuver: MacArthur's landing at Inchon saved the war for the Americans and vindicated the hero of the Philippines. The chiefs fell silent.

Yet, even in the midst of victory, intimations of MacArthur's downfall could be felt. One of America's premier combat officers and a future member of the military's renowned "Never Again Club" ("We should *never again* fight another war like Korea"), James Gavin, toured the battlefield and reported sighting "an elaborate arrangement of hard stands and revetments" at North Korean airfields. Gavin, a kind of "Mr. Wizard" of the Army (and described as "a dead ringer for Frank Sinatra" by a fellow officer), had been sent east to cull such intelligence as a member of the Pentagon's Weapons Systems Evaluation Group; what he saw were preparations far in excess of any North Korean expertise. He reported his findings and his personal conclusions to the JCS: the Chinese were prepared to intervene in Korea. MacArthur's aides dismissed Gavin's findings, arguing that if the Chinese planned any involvement, they would almost certainly know about it. The JCS history of the Korean conflict disagrees with this staff assessment, however; it notes that at the same time that MacArthur's staff was refuting Gavin's observations, the Far Eastern Command's military intelligence section was reporting a significant buildup of Chinese troops in Manchuria, just across the North Korean border.

Having pried the North Koreans from their siege of the Pusan perimeter, MacArthur's troops struck north across the 38th Parallel. Despite the pace of events, MacArthur's decision to invade North Korea was not made lightly or unilaterally. For one of the few times in his career, MacArthur waited for clear instructions. On September 11 (only two months since the war began), he received high-level approval to "conduct the necessary military operations either to force the North Koreans behind the 38th parallel or to destroy their forces." There was an important caveat, however: MacArthur was to conduct his operations *unless* there was a threat of intervention by China or the Soviet Union; as JCS Chairman Bradley described it, "We all agree that if the Chinese Communists come into Korea, we get out."

MacArthur's job was to win the war in such a way as to make certain that the Chinese did *not* intervene. The JCS thought the task was possible: by stopping short of the Chinese border, by refusing to bomb Chinese hydroelectric plants on the Yalu River, and by deploying South Korean troops in defensive positions in the final march past the North Korean capital, MacArthur could signal American intentions, limit the war to the Korean peninsula, and short-circuit any Chinese plans. But that's not what happened.

At the very least, MacArthur stretched Washington's limits on his military operations; at most, he disobeyed his orders. The evidence seems incontrovertible: on October 17, MacArthur drew a "halt" line across North Korea 30 miles beyond the limit set by the JCS just two weeks earlier, a wispy disregard for order that, according to the official JCS history, "unilaterally introduced changes into a plan that had received the formal approval of his superiors." Oddly, the JCS made no response. On October 20, MacArthur issued another circular to his subordinate commanders: they were to prepare to move rapidly to the North Korean border. The JCS now broke its silence. In a cable, the JCS reminded MacArthur of its September prohibition; he glibly responded by saying that his moves were "a matter of military necessity." This answer outraged Collins, who told Bradley that MacArthur's behavior constituted a flagrant disregard of orders. Bradley agreed: MacArthur was stretching the limits of his responsibility; he was playing with politics and taking actions designed to bring China into the war.

Still, the Joint Chiefs refused to countermand his order. Although MacArthur had stretched his orders, had flaunted his stars, had even manipulated the chiefs, he was a winner, a victorious combat commander.* In effect, the JCS found it hard to criticize him for success — he had retrieved a seemingly irretrievable situation. In any case, by the time the JCS could issue a new directive, the moment had passed. Victory was at hand: by late October, the North Koreans had been defeated and mopping-up operations had begun. The JCS was even planning to redeploy the American troops from Korea to Europe. Its earlier fear, that China would intervene and change the course of the war, seemed out of the question. Even the CIA was optimistic, reporting that it was unlikely the Chinese would enter the war.

Nevertheless, on October 26, 1950, eighteen Chinese divisions totaling 180,000 men moved into North Korea, and within two weeks U.N. troops were being pushed back by the Chinese Army. The JCS was "baffled"; if the Chinese wanted to intervene, why do it with only 180,000 men, why not with a million? MacArthur was also confused, though in a November 4 cable to the chiefs he confidently reported that he doubted the Chinese would intervene *in force* and urged the JCS not to make any "hasty decisions." One day later, he changed his mind and took the step that finally led to his dismissal: he ordered the bombing of the bridges linking North Korea to China. In view of his earlier cable, the November 5 order came as a surprise. The chiefs, at the instigation of civilian leaders, asked MacArthur for an explana-

---

*For a time, the five-star MacArthur outranked his military superior on the JCS, Chairman Omar Bradley, who won his fifth star just after the Inchon landings.

tion. His tone stunned them. In just twenty-four hours, he had swung from mild optimism to near hysteria. "Men and material in large force are pouring across all bridges over the Yalu from Manchuria," he said. "The only way to stop this reinforcement of the enemy is the destruction of these bridges. . . . Every hour that this is postponed will be paid for dearly in American and other United Nations blood. . . . I cannot overemphasize the disastrous effect, both physical and psychological, that will result from the restriction which you are imposing. I trust that the matter be immediately brought to the attention of the President as I believe your instructions may well result in a calamity of major proportions for which I cannot accept the responsibility without his personal and direct understanding of the situation."

In one breathless message, MacArthur had changed his view of the war, demanded a major escalation, questioned the integrity of the JCS, predicted a calamity, put the onus for defeat on the military leaders in Washington, and made a direct and unprecedented appeal to the president. The cable was stunningly out of character. MacArthur prided himself on his coolness under fire, and, while he didn't flout death (like Patton), his studious detachment — often accompanied by a well-rehearsed and appropriately eloquent speech — was hardly a charade. Fearful of the consequences and obviously unhinged by his tirade, Truman gave in.

That MacArthur was on the edge of panic was now universally accepted by the U.S. high command. On November 6, General George Marshall, the architect of America's victory in World War II, the conscience of the American military, and perhaps the most highly respected officer in uniform, decided he needed to calm MacArthur personally. He cabled MacArthur from Washington, opening his message with reassuring words: "This is a very personal and informal message to you from me." The former Army chief of staff, a Quaker who refused to work more than eight hours in any one day, assured MacArthur that "we all realize your difficulty in fighting a desperate battle in a mountainous region under winter conditions" and admitted that political considerations were adding to his pressure. Trying to convey hope, even empathy, Marshall reassured MacArthur that these were only "necessarily limiting conditions" in the conflict and that they were "unavoidable."

It is clear now that Marshall's message was not only meant to calm MacArthur, it was designed to make sure that there was no "stampede" in Korea, a clear possibility given the general's state of mind. The cable seemed to serve its purpose: the flighty MacArthur steadied; the U.N. troops stiffened and then held. Calmer now, perhaps embarrassed by his earlier panic, MacArthur switched gears: the U.N. command would launch an offensive in mid-November, he announced with a flourish. It would be the last thing the Chinese expected. The planning had already begun, he explained to the JCS. It would, once again, turn the war around.

In Washington, the JCS was near despair, its last remnant of respect for the aging warrior washed away by the Custer-like gallantry of calling for a final charge while surrounded by Indians. The JCS needn't have worried; the deadline for the offensive came and went, came again and was again postponed. MacArthur positioned his troops and ignored the warnings of his subordinate commanders. Finally, on November 24, he launched his assault against the remnants of the staggering North Korean Army. Four days later, the Chinese came to its aid, this time in force. The JCS soon realized that MacArthur's offensive was a disaster and that his time had run out. As Collins told a colleague, "He has to go. It's past time." At 1:00 A.M. on November 28, MacArthur cabled his assessment of the Chinese intervention to the JCS: "We face an entirely new war." Meanwhile, the JCS was making plans to appoint an entirely new commander.

In the years after MacArthur's dismissal, political commentators and historians have emphasized his disagreement with President Truman. The final blowup, they contend, was a political contest centered on MacArthur's inability, or unwillingness, to follow a direct order from his commander in chief. The implication, notwithstanding strong contradictory evidence, is that MacArthur's battle with Truman and his subsequent firing is a classic example of the ongoing civilian-military tussle for national supremacy. The evidence from JCS files and from histories of the period suggests otherwise. Far from being a civilian-military contest, the MacArthur incident reflects a military struggle revolving around the place of the JCS in the nation's high command. The battle was truly joined when the JCS received MacArthur's November 5, 1950, cable. From that day forward, the JCS moved to convince civilian leaders that the American Army in Korea needed a new commander. The JCS gave MacArthur every chance, including the opportunity to retrieve the situation after the failure of his offensive in late November.

When MacArthur proposed an amphibious landing at Inchon, the chiefs had allowed him to go forward despite strong reservations. But they hadn't panicked or overruled their ground commander. In November, when the Chinese intervened, the action had stunned MacArthur. His cables to the JCS were shrill. It was a bad performance. In the month that followed, he pleaded with the JCS for a withdrawal from the Korean peninsula. The continued battering of the U.N. forces seemed to support the view. While the State Department continued to look for a negotiated settlement, the JCS made plans for the withdrawal. In that time of panic, however, the members of the JCS took on a new role, one usually left to a field commander. Despite MacArthur's plea for a withdrawal, the JCS decided to plead optimism in the face of defeat, to imbue MacArthur with a confidence they themselves did not have. And they continued to search for a new commander.

When General Walton Walker, the commander of the U.S. Eighth Army in Korea, was killed on December 22, the JCS sent Matthew Ridgway to take his place. Ridgway had been cautioning the chiefs on MacArthur's handling of the war since the very beginning. Before his assignment to Korea, he had uncharacteristically upbraided Vandenberg for failing to tell MacArthur what to do. When the Air Force chief of staff protested that it wouldn't do any good, Ridgway angrily suggested that MacArthur be fired. Vandenberg was surprised by Ridgway's outburst, though he knew that Collins held the same views.

Despite Vandenberg's surprise, Ridgway's statement obviously had an impact. Ridgway was one of "Marshall's generals," a student of war with a clear sense of what soldiers could and could not do. For him, command was basic to morale, and morale to victory. MacArthur, he thought, was beaten, but the Americans weren't. In the months that followed, it became clear that Ridgway was right. Soon after he took command of the Eighth Army (making him second in command to MacArthur), the JCS began to ignore MacArthur's warnings of impending doom and placed a greater reliance on Ridgway's ability to save the situation.

For the combat commanders of the Eighth Army, Ridgway's arrival was a pivotal event. Colleagues looking back on the period marvel at how the future Army chief of staff "changed the situation enormously — he was just a breath of air. We knew we could win with him." Lieutenant Colonel Harold K. Johnson, a commander in the battered American 1st Cavalry Division and "no admirer of MacArthur's," remembers Ridgway's arrival as Eighth Army commander: "General Ridgway promptly began to hold conferences with division commanders and their principal subordinates and to visit subordinate units. . . . General Ridgway talked forcefully, and encouragingly. The sheer force of his personality turned the situation in Korea." We can do it, Ridgway said; *you* can do it.

Ridgway's performance was initially considered nothing less than remarkable, but as the Eighth Army continued to hold against massed Chinese attacks, it reinforced the JCS view that MacArthur had panicked while Ridgway hadn't. This outlook was reflected in a January 1951 cable to MacArthur in which the JCS spelled out its requirements: he would inflict "maximum damage" on the enemy and only evacuate Korea when he considered it "essential." MacArthur protested the directive in a return message. It was impossible to hold both Korea and Japan, he said. Washington must choose between the two. The tone rivaled his November 5 hysteria: "As I have pointed out, under the extraordinary limitations and conditions imposed upon the command in Korea its military position is untenable, but it can hold for any length of time up to its complete destruction if overriding political considerations so dictate."

Secretary of State Dean Acheson was disgusted. "Here is a posterity paper if ever there was one," he said, "with the purpose not only of clearing MacArthur of blame if things went wrong but also of putting the maximum pressure on Washington to reverse itself and adopt his proposals for widening the war." Acheson, never one to mince words, told Truman that MacArthur was "basically disloyal." For George Marshall and the JCS, the cable was evidence that MacArthur had lost his grip. "When the general complains of the morale of his troops, the time has come to look into his own," Bradley remarked.

While the JCS and State Department searched for a negotiated settlement of the conflict and Ridgway moved his revitalized Eighth Army back north toward the 38th Parallel, MacArthur again argued for permission to bomb military installations in China. In light of JCS cables on the war, MacArthur's request was extraordinary. From the moment of the North Korean invasion, the JCS had made the administration's position clear: the United States did not want a fight with China. But MacArthur had another surprise in store. In March, he commented publicly that the reunification of Korea was America's goal, a statement that led directly to a confrontation with the president. Korea's reunification had not been an administration goal for quite some time, at least from the time of the Chinese intervention. Furthermore, MacArthur began making public his own concern that Washington wasn't fighting the right war, telling a number of foreign diplomats that his strategy included fighting China. He also reiterated his belief that Nationalist Chinese troops should be used in Korea, an option ruled out by the administration in August 1950, soon after the war began. MacArthur's statements and his meeting with the diplomats openly defied Truman's policy and his instructions from the JCS. The White House was so disturbed that the JCS was directed to issue a warning to the general. It cabled MacArthur on March 24, cautioning him against making public statements and issuing specific instructions on clearing any future statements with the administration. The cable was a direct order. He disobeyed it.

In a letter to Congressman Joseph Martin, MacArthur openly criticized administration policy as well as Truman's refusal to deploy the Nationalist Chinese troops. Finally, on Friday, April 6, the American high command began a full review of MacArthur's actions in Korea during a special session. Bradley favored MacArthur's dismissal, but he suggested that the president make the final determination on the basis of a written recommendation from the JCS. In the political battle that was sure to result, the opinion of professional officers would be invaluable. Everyone agreed: the JCS would recommend MacArthur's dismissal and pass its decision on to the president. George Marshall was called in and told of the decision by Bradley. After reviewing Mac-Arthur's communications with the JCS, Marshall endorsed the recommendation. Not only should MacArthur be fired, he said, he "should have been fired two years ago." Marshall wondered why the JCS had put up with him for so long. The JCS took just two hours to decide: MacArthur had not simply questioned American policy, he had openly challenged it. Military officers used another term: insubordination.

Today, the role of the JCS in the dismissal of MacArthur is often overlooked, dampened by all the events that followed. We now take for granted that combat officers are responsible to a four-star staff that is part of an accepted chain of command. In 1951, however, the concept of an essentially intermediary command structure, one that stood between elected civilian officials and combat commanders, was not only new, it was unprecedented — as revolutionary a concept as any in the history of the republic. In one sense, the three years before 1951 were a distinct failure for the JCS: the new staff had failed to short-circuit service prerogatives, which resulted in the dismissal of Louis Denfeld.

In 1951, the question was far different. The issue was not simply whether the JCS would reassert civilian control of the military (which was, after all, never very much in doubt), but whether it would assert its own control of the military. On that question hinged the future importance of the command staff. Despite the 1947 National Security Act, the importance of the JCS very much depended on its perception by the combat leaders, the men in the field who actually fought the nation's wars. Without the appearance of command, without the ability to make the most difficult decisions (and the dismissal of MacArthur was one of the most difficult the JCS ever had to make), the Joint Chiefs would become a powerless committee, no more important to the nation's conduct of foreign policy than the old joint service structure of the 1920s and 1930s.

In this sense, then, the meeting on April 6, 1951, was a turning point in JCS history, as pivotal and far-reaching as any that has ever taken place. That the JCS was actually making history was not lost on the participants: each member was mindful that he was not only deciding the future of the national command establishment, he was doing so under the clear threat that his action would ignite a public controversy, would embolden the defenders of perhaps the greatest military hero ever produced by the nation. If there is any irony here, it consists solely in this: if the JCS had dismissed a lowly platoon commander, the impact of its decision would have been lost to history. It needed MacArthur to establish its primacy, which made the members even more cautious in their deliberations. Nor was the group unmindful of the impact of its decision on the course of its staff; once done, the action would be irretrievable, the course of the JCS would itself be set. For the foreseeable future, no military commander could claim that the four officers of the JCS were commanders in name only; they would hold actual power.

The JCS session was intended to be an assessment of MacArthur's military capabilities. In fact, that discussion was over after fifteen minutes, when the chiefs agreed that MacArthur's conduct of military operations was questionable: he had lost the confidence of his troops, his command was causing continuing morale problems, and he was attempting to undercut Ridgway's standing with the Eighth Army. The talk turned to political considerations. Collins and Vandenberg argued that MacArthur's dismissal would cause a storm of protest, sow doubts about American war aims, and cast aspersions on the military. Still, Collins finally said, it was clear that the general was no longer capable of carrying out American policies. Ridgway had been right all along: given any latitude, MacArthur would interpret his orders liberally, picking and choosing those he would obey. This policy might have worked in World War II but was impossible in an age of nuclear weaponry. The JCS put its views on the record: MacArthur would be relieved and Ridgway named as his successor. The decision, it noted, was made on purely "military grounds." Within hours, President Truman seconded this judgment.

On April 11, 1951, MacArthur was informed of the decision in a cable from JCS Chairman Bradley: "I have been directed to relay the following message to you from President Truman: 'I deeply regret that it becomes my duty as President and Commander in Chief of the United States military forces to replace you as Supreme Commander, Allied Powers; Commander in Chief, United Nations Command; Commander in Chief, Far East; and Commanding General, U.S. Army Far East.' "

2

FLIMSY, BUFF,
AND GREEN

★　　★　　★　　★

These laborious processes exist because each military
department feels obliged to judge independently each
work product of the Joint Staff. Had I allowed my interservice and inter-allied staff to be similarly organized . . .
during World War II, the delays and resulting indecisive-
ness would have been unacceptable to my superiors.

Dwight D. Eisenhower

DURING ITS FIRST TWO YEARS, which ended with the reassignment
of Admiral Louis Denfeld in November 1949, the JCS regularized its
means of dealing with civilian leadership, developed a national military strategy, designed a method of planning military budgets, and
structured the new chain of command. With few exceptions, these
procedures and operations are still in force today. But from the very
beginning, the structure of the Office of the Joint Chiefs of Staff has
been the focus of widespread controversy. Critics say it is too bureaucratic, confusing, and redundant. JCS staff members respond that the
interlocking and confusing organization is designed to untrack the
kind of infighting that destroyed Denfeld's career in 1949 and led to
MacArthur's dismissal in 1951.

The chairman of the JCS, as the highest-ranking officer in the American military, is responsible for overseeing the business of the Army,
Navy, Air Force, and Marines in the "joint arena" (military matters
that affect two or more of the armed services). The chairman and a
vice chairman control the work of the JCS through an independent
staff led by a three-star director, appointed by the chairman to serve
for three years. By tradition, this position is rotated among the three

services.* Under the chairman's guidance, the director and his eight to ten assistants control the work of six military directorates: manpower and personnel (referred to as J-1), operations (J-3), logistics (J-4), strategic plans and policies (J-5), command, control, and communications (J-6), and force structure and resources (J-8). In addition, five separate JCS offices report to the director on joint activities in specialized areas: the Joint Analysis Directorate coordinates military studies, the Joint Secretariat is the historical and management division, the Joint Special Operations Agency coordinates interservice paramilitary and intelligence operations, the Directorate for Information and Resource Management is the technical analysis arm, and the Office of the Inspector General is the internal legal watchdog.

The director of the JCS also receives reports from the military's own intelligence office, the Defense Intelligence Agency, and from five other offices that represent the American military internationally (for example, the U.S.-Mexican Defense Commission). In all, the director receives reports from sixteen different directorates and offices under his control. In addition, five of eleven Department of Defense agencies report to the JCS: the Defense Logistics Agency, the Defense Communications Agency, the Defense Intelligence Agency, the Defense Mapping Agency, and the Defense Nuclear Agency.

Despite this complex organization, all final decisions in joint matters are left in the hands of the JCS itself — the chiefs of staff of the Army and Air Force, the Chief of Naval Operations, and, since 1969, the commandant of the Marines. These four chiefs are assisted by operations deputies (called OPDEPS, or sometime DCSOPS, or "desk ops" in Pentagonese). These officers perform the same kind of functions for the four individual service chiefs as the director of the JCS performs for the chairman; they are powerful three-star officers responsible for conducting the day-to-day business of the services on the JCS.

But the JCS staff, and the services' OPDEPS, are responsible only for the business of the American military that affects all the services. In this sense, the members of the JCS are "dual hatted": they represent their services on joint matters and determine service policies that involve only single-service interests. In fact, each of the four service chiefs has a staff of his own that is a mirror image of the JCS staff; it is solely concerned with Army (or Air Force, or Navy, or Marine) matters

---

* There are three military departments: the Army, Navy, and Air Force. The commandant of the Marines is part of the JCS, though his "service" is part of the Department of the Navy and therefore reports to the Secretary of the Navy. That the Navy has its own army is a constant source of friction for the JCS staff.

and has no influence on policies that affect all the services. For example, the Air Force chief makes decisions in the joint arena by relying on the assessment of his operations deputy, who receives reports on such matters from the director of the JCS. On the other hand, the Air Force chief makes decisions in his own service by relying on the assessment of his vice chief, who receives reports from the military staff of the Department of the Air Force. In addition, the four chiefs are "dual hatted" in one other significant sense: each reports to a presidentially appointed civilian head of the service. The Air Force chief of staff, for instance, is responsible to the Secretary of Defense as well as to the Secretary of the Air Force.

Given this almost incredible complexity, it's no wonder that the JCS has established a set of procedures that are designed to dampen the inevitable friction that results from competing interests among the services. Unfortunately, the procedures adopted by the JCS on October 6, 1947, are as confusing as its organizational chart; they can only be sorted out by referring to what the JCS staff calls a MOP 39. JCS Memorandum of Policy 39 is a highly significant, partly secret, and indispensable command guide developed by the first staff to regularize procedures; it's a road map of just how the JCS operates, resolves service disputes, and determines military policy. Since it was first issued, it has undergone seventeen revisions, but its core remains the same, a testament to the JCS's desire to wring a consensus on military policies from a divided service structure despite a number of important congressionally mandated JCS reorganizations.

According to the MOP 39, any policy decision made by the chiefs is the result of a paper trail that begins with the issuance of a directive or memorandum outlining an issue raised by the president, Secretary of Defense, Congress, DoD agency, or military field commander. Thousands of such directives are sent to the JCS each year; close to 25,000 were issued in 1986 alone. The directive (or memorandum) activates what JCS officers call the "flimsy, buff, green" or "flimsy, buff, green, red-striped" procedure. The first step is taken by the secretary of the JCS (a one-star officer in the Joint Secretariat), who assigns the directive to one of the JCS's sixteen offices. It is summarized on "flimsy" paper and acted on within the designated office or passed on to a special committee of "action officers" from each of the services appointed by the director of the JCS. If a decision cannot be reached by the action officers, the paper is recirculated to the appropriate JCS office, with appended dissents and comments, on "buff" paper, and then finally sent back to the director.

Most issues are decided in the "buff" stage and become military policy. But if differences remain or one of the services has a strong disagreement with the proposed action, the director decides the issue himself and returns the paper to the service action officers. If the action officers agree with the director, the decision becomes policy. Usually this "buff" decision ends the process, and the final military policy is printed on green paper. But in a very few cases there are still unresolved issues that must be decided in a meeting of "service planners," a committee of service operations deputies. At this point dissent, while unusual, is a clear sign that the issues are of overriding policy concern. Some 10 percent of all military issues pass this OPDEPS or "green" stage and are forwarded for a final decision to the members of the JCS, who resolve the issue by consensus or compromise.*

The OPDEPS are central to this process, filling the same role for the head of the service that a top White House assistant fills for the president. These operations deputies — or Little Chiefs, as they are sometimes called — have their hand on the pulsebeat of all military issues. In effect, while the Little Chiefs don't decide the most important JCS issues, they determine what the most important issues are — a job as important as any in the military. These "gatekeepers" — yet another phrase used by civilian defense officials to describe the role of the OPDEPS — decide an issue in the joint arena by unanimous vote, thereby removing the item from the official JCS agenda.

A failure to reach a compromise at the deputy level means that the green paper is forwarded to the JCS for its consideration. This occurs most often when the issue involves a policy that would have a direct impact on force structures or weapons systems. After the JCS decides the issue, the decision is printed on red-striped paper and passed on to the Secretary of Defense. The process usually takes about three weeks and involves nearly half of the JCS staff.

In select cases, the JCS insists on the issuance of "flimsy, buff, and green" procedures in order to assess different arguments, though it knows it will have to make the final decision. In the early years, when Omar Bradley was the JCS chairman, this occurred most frequently when the JCS regularized the nation's new command structure and needed to gather a variety of opinions from each service. In some cases, especially when the JCS is attempting to reach an all-service position on a key foreign policy issue, the director of the JCS will initiate the "flimsy, buff, and green" procedure three or four different

---

* At each stage of this complex process, dissenting opinions are added to the original memo so that officers further up the line can study the positions of their own services. In addition, some flimsy, buff, green studies are passed on to officers in one of the eleven DoD agencies for comment.

times, the result being a green document the size of a metropolitan telephone directory.*

The JCS meets every Monday, Wednesday, and Friday, usually within hours of a meeting of the operations deputies, who set the JCS agenda. This tradition, established in August 1949 by Omar Bradley, sometimes changes due to the outside commitments (tours, speaking engagements, crises, and testimonies) of JCS members. While major issues, policies, and plans that affect all the services come under full JCS scrutiny, not all military decisions are made by the chiefs, but are delegated to assistants, deputy chiefs, heads of agencies, or unified commanders.

Nevertheless, there are five decision-making areas the chiefs always consider without their operations deputies and without issuing a directive to the JCS secretary: selected combat operations, nominations for the Medal of Honor, military reorganization plans, three-star and four-star promotions (from lists in a "stud book"), and decisions on major weapons systems.

Few JCS officers deny that the system's drawbacks are significant, that the procedures often undermine individual command initiative, and all too often substitute consensus for foresighted and original military policies. These complex procedures provide a far different routine than that enjoyed by officers in field commands. Put simply, assignment to the JCS means that an officer has not only lost a chance to gain valuable command experience, he has entered a world of directorates, bureaus, and agencies resembling a Rube Goldberg contraption which operates by procedures so predictable that they are almost rituals. It's little wonder that assignment to the JCS is considered a dead end by many military professionals.

"It's the kiss of death," one lieutenant colonel said. "When I got my orders I thought, Well, I might make it to colonel, but that's about it." For others, a JCS assignment "is like entering Disneyland." While an Army or Air Force colonel or Navy captain commands power and respect in field assignments (and generals are rarely seen), the Pentagon provides a mirror image of the experience; colonels, majors, captains, even rear admirals and brigadier generals, are common sights. Among top officers, where command is prized above prestige, few if any JCS jobs, even the chief of staff position, are more popular than

---

* This happened most recently when the director circulated a memo seeking the services' opinions on the Reagan administration's decision to break the SALT II treaty limits. The JCS agreed, then disagreed, then agreed again, going through the "flimsy, buff, and green" procedure no less than six times. The result was the presentation of a "green" document the size of the New York City telephone directory. The final decision, a fraction of the size, was issued on red-striped paper.

the choice combat commands. For the Army, command of American troops in Europe is considered the prize; for the Air Force, the premier combat assignment is in Omaha, as head of the Strategic Air Command. In the Navy, command of the Sixth and Seventh fleets is often more highly prized than even the position of Chief of Naval Operations.

Surprisingly, however, competition for the top spots on the JCS is fierce, a fact that can best be explained by one Army colonel's analogy to his service in Europe. "The closer we got to the Elbe River [dividing the two Germanys]," he said, "the more alert we became, the more ready for action. We were the first line of defense against a Warsaw Pact invasion. Here [at the JCS], the closer you get to civilians, the closer you get to making real policy. NATO is the first line of defense for America, the JCS is the first line of defense for the military." While operational commands make the best use of military training ("Give me a destroyer squadron at war," one naval officer said. "That's what I'm trained for"), it's the chance to make policy, not just carry it out, that is tempting for any military professional. In essence, a JCS staff assignment can be an intoxicating experience, allowing an officer to have a significant, if indirect, impact on American foreign policy.

A JCS assignment is also extremely demanding: twelve- to fourteen-hour days are common for most officers, who are also under the constant eye of their services' top officers. And the twenty-four-hour shifts during international crises, while rare, are at once draining, frightening, and exhilarating. While many military crises are readily apparent to the public — the invasion of South Korea, the Cuban Missile Crisis, the 1968 Tet Offensive — at other times, the nation's command establishment spends sleepless nights in response to events that, at first glance, seem somewhat less apocalyptic.

In September 1949, when an American B-29 on patrol in the northern Pacific registered higher than normal levels of radiation, for instance, the JCS staff scrambled to find out whether the Soviets had detonated their first atomic bomb. Officers then worked around the clock to determine just what kinds of atomic capability the Soviets had and spent weeks trying to assess how they planned to use them. Eventually, the studies sparked by the Soviet explosion involved every major JCS office; the JCS ordered papers on every aspect of American military readiness, including budget proposals to build a new bomber to counter the Soviet threat. Such secret crises create what one officer called a "schizophrenic" environment, in which JCS officers are not only prohibited from telling their families the reason for the long hours but even have to "pretend nothing [is] happening."

While international crises are physically draining and the JCS's secret crises are emotionally exhausting, it's the unknown, unre-

ported, everyday incidents of JCS service that are cited as being the
most frustrating and "nerve jangling," such as attack alerts that prove
to be command post exercises (operations to test military readiness) as
well as those that could signal the beginning of a world war. When the
alarm bells sound at Cheyenne Mountain, warning of a Soviet missile
launch, field commanders react with practiced restraint "in order to
think clearly," one said, "and to keep from rushing to respond to what
might turn out to be a false alarm." But all over Washington tele-
phones ring, and the JCS staff is alerted to the possibility of an attack.
Over the years, such alarms have made Pentagon career personnel
jaded observers of their own system, but for a field-hardened combat
commander serving his first stint at the JCS, the voice of a Pentagon
duty officer coming over the phone at three in the morning ("Sir, we
have an incident here") can be a jarring experience.

There are other differences. Where a field commander is at the end
of the "weapons pipeline," a JCS officer is at its tip. It's not unusual
for an officer to walk into the Pentagon's E Ring — the building's out-
ermost hallway, which houses the JCS offices — on any given morning to find it filled with an assortment of new weapons and a cohort of
salesmen. The weapons manufacturers go to amazing lengths to sell
their hardware: JCS officers arriving for work one morning found a
fully assembled Navy fighter interceptor in the courtyard. But the
manufacturers are just one small part of the JCS environment. A
number of officers are on call day and night to escort members of Congress, their constituents, foreign dignitaries, and military officials
from other nations through the Pentagon maze. The attendant briefings, discussions, lectures, talks, and ceremonies often take weeks or
even months of preparation.

A JCS staff assignment therefore makes new demands on former
field officers and provides a superheated environment that rewards
tact, patience, and an ability to compromise. JCS officers are so competitive because they soon realize that their services' programs almost
totally depend on their abilities to sell them. "It's not just promotions
that are at risk in the Pentagon," one officer pointed out. "It's the programs of your service, weapons programs, strategies, budget priorities, sometimes the future of the nation." In addition, the tense JCS
environment is insular, the result of policies that demand absolute
secrecy on sensitive military matters, a demand so significant that it is
everywhere apparent, in every document, every memo and every
flimsy, buff, and green. "In the field I expected to be told everything,
every last detail," one former Pentagon Army aide reported. "In the
Pentagon the rule was, if you aren't told, you don't need to know."

There is one rule of the JCS system that is more important than any
other, more daunting than any structural maze, more significant than

any ritualistic procedure, more demanding even than the JCS's obsessive need for secrecy, a rule so secret, in fact, that it has never been put into writing. The JCS is bound by an unwritten code of conduct that reflects well-worn and clearly understood JCS traditions. In many ways, this code is more diligently followed than any written law, imbuing the JCS with its own language and traditions. Members of the JCS refer to each other by rank, not name, a formality that is followed throughout the command ring. Descriptions of a fellow officer are often preceded by "honorable" and "patriotic," words that are used regardless of the depth of service conflicts over budgets, issues, or personalities.

The code dictates that while unquestioning loyalty to one's service and commander is not a requirement for assignment to the JCS staff, criticizing one's service and commander to others, especially to those in other services, is absolutely forbidden. In addition, criticism of civilian officials and policies is kept behind closed doors and is virtually unheard publicly.

But no rule is more deeply respected and strictly followed than that prohibiting one military officer from questioning the patriotism of another. While disagreement with civilian policies, even with those dictated by the president, can lead to dismissal and forced retirement, questioning the patriotism of a fellow officer can lead to exile from the community of the high command. This rule is so deeply and universally believed that few officers have ever considered breaking it. For those who have, the punishment of lifelong exile has been swift, certain, and merciless. The rule also applies to everyone who serves on or with the staff of the JCS, from the noncommissioned aide to the career colonel or brigadier general, even to the four-star chiefs of staff themselves and, in one well-known instance, to a five-star general.

MacArthur's dismissal not only sparked the public storm the JCS had predicted, it also led to a public questioning of the American strategy in Korea and the JCS's role. Congressman Joseph W. Martin, the powerful House minority leader, even hinted that the chiefs would stand in the dock with Truman when it came time for impeachment. Nevertheless, all four chiefs were at National Airport when MacArthur returned to Washington on April 19, 1951, just days after he was fired; they were joined by more than 12,000 well-wishers who had come to show support for the general.

Two weeks later, on May 3, 1951, the Senate Armed Services Committee began hearings on MacArthur's relief from command, with the general the first and primary witness. During his three days of testimony, MacArthur reviewed his position on the war in Korea. To nearly everyone's surprise, he took great care to assure the committee

that his views were fully in accord with those held by the JCS. "I want
to say that the relationships between the Joint Chiefs of Staff and
myself have been admirable. . . . If there has been any friction between
us, I am not aware of it," he said. Then, true to form, he went ahead to
point out key disagreements that he in fact did have with the JCS and
the frictions that had developed over the course of his command in
Korea.

Citing a memorandum issued by the JCS the previous January as
evidence, MacArthur said that the nation's military leaders had
adopted sixteen courses of action he had used to guide his decisions
while in command in Korea. Actually, the JCS memo explicitly
described the options as "contingent," and while several of them had
been considered by the Truman administration, it's clear that the JCS
had never intended the points as directives. Nevertheless, MacArthur
said he agreed with the sixteen points and had molded his strategy to
conform with JCS wishes. He added that it was his understanding that
these recommendations had been later "disapproved" at a higher
level, the clear implicaton being that the Secretary of State (and retired
head of the Army), George C. Marshall, had had a hand in overruling
the strategy developed by the JCS. MacArthur continued his defense
by proudly noting that the conditions he had set for a cease-fire in
Korea included the defense of Formosa and the American refusal to
seat mainland China in the United Nations, but that both proposals
had also been "disapproved" by Marshall.

When Marshall was called to respond, he denied that he had ever
overruled the JCS, stating that it was the policy of the United States
"to deny" Formosa to the communists and that there had been "no
deviation from the policy whatsoever." But, unlike MacArthur, Marshall refused to become embroiled in a personal battle, thereby invok-
ing the unwritten code governing the conduct of those serving in the
high command. "He [MacArthur] is a brother Army officer," Marshall
said, "a man for whom I have tremendous respect as to his military
abilities and military performances."

JCS Chairman Bradley, whose testimony followed Marshall's,
detailed what he believed was MacArthur's continual disregard for
JCS directives. It was clear, Bradley said, that the general disagreed
with stated military policy and advocated a strategy that, in his own
opinion, would "increase the risk of global war." But Bradley too
refused to engage the general in a debate. "I want to make it clear that
I would not say anything to discredit the long and illustrious career of
General MacArthur," he said, thus making it clear that while MacArthur felt free to criticize his "brother officer," Bradley did not. Even
Lawton Collins, MacArthur's most constant critic on the JCS,
declined to become involved in a contest of personalities. "I think he

is one of the most brilliant military leaders that this country has ever produced," he said. Unlike Marshall, Bradley, and Collins, MacArthur had not been above implying that the American high command, and Marshall in particular, followed a policy of appeasing communism, of not going all out to win the war in Korea. The JCS had lost the will to win, he said, and had been unwilling accomplices of a program of communist aggression.

A number of historians agree with this view. William Manchester, in *American Caesar*, pleads MacArthur's defense, citing a cable that Marshall sent to MacArthur on military operations in North Korea after his Inchon landing and the liberation of Seoul. The cable was marked EYES ONLY: "We want you to feel unhampered tactically and strategically to proceed north of the 38th Parallel"; clearly, it gave the general much latitude. Another cable followed, directing MacArthur to remain silent on the administration's agreement with his policy to march to the Chinese border: "We want you to proceed with your operations without any further explanation or announcement and let action determine the matter. Our government desires to avoid having to make an issue of the 38th Parallel until we have accomplished our mission."

MacArthur might have used this evidence to point up the practical inconsistencies in American military policy in Korea: he might have cited cables reflecting Washington's uncertainties, its inability to promote a policy of limited war, its belief that the Chinese would intervene (then wouldn't, then would), and its change of heart — that MacArthur should "proceed with operations" to defeat the North Koreans while stopping just short of the Chinese border. But MacArthur produced no cables, cited no policy papers, and launched no major defense of his own actions. Instead he appeared without notes, evidence, or aides. In the end, his three-day testimony turned into a lecture on American strategy that included a thinly veiled attack on "politicians," an insulting assault on America's European allies, and a characterization of limited war as "defeatism."

Many military officers agreed with MacArthur; they believed the United States was following an irrational policy in Korea, that containment of communism everywhere without a victory anywhere was a prescription for national disaster. But even his allies refused to come to MacArthur's defense. In fact, the unofficial military silence on MacArthur's dismissal began well before his testimony; it was best characterized by Eisenhower's statement to the General Motors chairman and future Secretary of Defense, Charles Wilson: "I assure you that I am going to maintain silence in every language known to man."

But MacArthur's disagreement with civilian policies had little to do with anyone's silence. While MacArthur was more than willing, as

Bradley said, to "rush us headlong" into a worldwide military confrontation with the Soviet Union, military officers had no fear of
being associated with anticommunism. Nor did they fear that MacArthur's reputation as an uncompromising warrior would somehow
have a negative effect on their own careers. In the end, they abandoned
MacArthur and allowed him to (in his own words) "fade away"
because he had violated probably the most important code of a military professional: he had questioned the patriotism of a fellow officer.

·During the hearings, MacArthur pointedly blamed Marshall for the
loss of China, which he called the "greatest political mistake we made
in a hundred years," and linked his colleague to the "defeatist" policies of the administration. MacArthur's argument left little doubt of
his opinion of his former commander, giving the undeniable impression that Marshall was not the patriot everyone thought. In some
quarters, MacArthur will never be forgiven.

In the years that followed, top Army officers often visited the old
general in his Manhattan apartment, more out of courtesy than necessity. They seemed to be driven by some kind of obsessive curiosity,
akin perhaps to the feeling that compels paleontologists to study the
habits of dinosaurs. Most found that MacArthur was out of touch
with national policy and was fighting battles that had already been
decided. Even William Westmoreland stopped by, in 1964, to "hear
what the gentleman might say" before taking on his new command in
Vietnam. "I like General MacArthur," he said afterward. "I had a very
fine relationship with him. But he was still very concerned about the
Chinese Communists. He was refighting the Korean war."

The firing of MacArthur is now seen by most military historians as a
struggle over civilian control of the military — though, in fact, civilian control was never very much in doubt (this despite Bradley's testimony that MacArthur's dismissal was a test case of obedience to
orders). MacArthur's battle was not simply waged against Truman, it
was also a conflict with the young JCS system, the very existence of
which MacArthur had often questioned. But the system survived, and
after MacArthur's dismissal its dominance was rarely challenged.
While the JCS might, and often did, defer to the wishes of a combat
commander, its position in Washington, as both a buffer with and an
intermediary between civilian leaders and military commanders, was
never again questioned.

The victory of the JCS was total: in its four years of existence, it had
become the dominant military command establishment of the nation,
more important than even an aging if heroic five-star general. But
more than that, its clear leadership marked the passing of a generation
of military leaders. When the seventy-one-year-old MacArthur
arrived at National Airport after his firing, it was his first visit to

Washington in more than fourteen years. That he was greeted by officers who could and did give him orders, though he outranked them, must have seemed a shock, perhaps even a humiliation. But the precedent was set: the days of the lone warrior who had nearly unquestioned power in the field had ended and a new command system put in place.

While the JCS was greeting MacArthur in Washington, General Matthew Ridgway was assuming full command of all U.S. troops in Korea. The JCS's decision to recommend Ridgway as MacArthur's replacement might justifiably be called one of the best command changes ever made by an armed forces staff — certainly it had a tremendous impact on America's war in Korea. Not only is Ridgway credited with saving Korea, he did it without the fanfare that might have accompanied a MacArthur-style victory. In fact, Ridgway was everything MacArthur wasn't: while MacArthur feigned sloppiness at every turn, a practiced informality that masked his martinet character, Ridgway showed up on the battlefield in neatly pressed greens. While MacArthur's signature was the slouch, Ridgway's was the sheaf of hand grenades that dangled from his right lapel. MacArthur always wore an officer's cap, while Ridgway liked to keep his ears warm — a necessity in Korea that MacArthur disdained. Most important, Ridgway told his troops what MacArthur told the press: that they were going to win, that they would not be abandoned, that officers who shirked their duties would be dismissed. (Duty, as defined by Ridgway, required commanders to be in the front lines with their troops.) He acted on his words, touring the battlefield and calling on enlisted men and officers alike to talk with him about their fight.

Ridgway was charismatic, but he was also ruthless: he dismissed four generals, then reached into the ranks to designate new commanders. The JCS gave him free rein in Korea, a sign of its confidence in his ability to rally the troops and turn the tide of the conflict. The result was that by mid-1951 the situation in Korea had stabilized: Ridgway had reinforced a defensive line girdling the waist of Korea, improved troop morale, and succeeded in containing the war. Because of this success, his stay in Korea lasted only one year, until 1952, when he was made Supreme Allied Commander in Europe. Finally, and logically, he was named the Army's chief of staff in August 1953, the culmination of a career of combat success. From West Point to Normandy and to Korea, Ridgway had been among the brightest stars in the constellation of officers that had won World War II and then proved that they could fight a limited war with limited strategic objectives.

But the military's brightest star was Dwight Eisenhower, the hero of America's cross-Channel invasion in 1944, the first Supreme Allied

Commander of the new Atlantic Alliance, and, in January 1953, commander in chief of all American forces, the head of the strongest nation in the world. Ridgway and Eisenhower, so similar in nature and tested in combat by German panzers, should have gotten along, but they didn't. Oddly, their falling-out was over the use and importance of nuclear weapons, of which neither had any experience and even less understanding. Questions involving the importance of these new weapons would become a pivotal issue in JCS history, an issue intensely debated during Ridgway's term as Army chief.

Eisenhower had come to office with a promise to end the war in Korea, which he had done by telling China that he was willing to use the atom bomb unless the war was resolved. The new president had been profoundly affected by the success of his threat and decided not only to adopt this strategy to keep the communists at bay, but also to make the threat of nuclear use — what his Secretary of State, John Foster Dulles, called "massive retaliation" against the communist aggressor — the core of his foreign policy. Eisenhower went even further, adopting a new defense budget philosophy and a national security policy to go with the threat. Dubbed "the New Look" by a group of Pentagon public relations experts brought in by Secretary of Defense Charles Wilson, the budget philosophy was based on the belief that nuclear weapons had made a strategy of massive retaliation believable and war impossible. So Eisenhower viewed nuclear weapons as an unusual blessing, a way of cutting government spending while protecting American interests.

He was asked repeatedly to define what he meant by the New Look in the first year of his administration, and he consistently argued that the advent of nuclear weapons had changed the way nations thought about war, adding that the armies he had led in Normandy were obsolete. "What do we mean?" he asked rhetorically during one press conference, then answered, "We mean this: We are not fighting with muzzle-loaders in any of the services." In other words, Eisenhower was committed to using atomic weapons against any threat to American security. In essence, the New Look reflected his belief that the nation could maintain a credible defense while cutting defense spending. By threatening the use of massive retaliation, Eisenhower claimed, the United States could actually reduce its reliance on more expensive conventional forces.

In addition, Eisenhower believed that the development of atomic weapons made a sneak attack on the United States impossible. The atom bomb, Eisenhower said, meant that the Soviet Union or any other communist nation would be unable to launch "a gigantic Pearl Harbor." While modestly claiming that the New Look wasn't really new at all — "to call it revolutionary . . . is just not true," he once said — he was proud that his new budget philosophy also made strategic sense, that it actually reduced the chance that the nation would have to send its young men into another war. "Now, our most valued, our most costly asset is our young men," he said during a press conference early in his administration. "Let's don't use them any more than we have to." Finally, he could point to the resolution of the Korean conflict as proof, the first proof, that the strategy he envisioned actually worked.

But his adoption of the New Look was only partly the result of his successful missile rattling (or bomber rattling, as the case may be) in Korea; it was also the result of the dilemma Eisenhower faced as Supreme Allied Commander in Europe after the war. His personal friendships with the Soviet military leaders notwithstanding, by 1948 he had cultivated a growing mistrust of Soviet motives, which was reinforced by the massing of 175 Soviet divisions in Eastern Europe just after the war. In 1951, two years after the formation of the North Atlantic Treaty Organization, Eisenhower attended the Lisbon NATO conference and learned that the military price of a successful defense of Western Europe was the deployment and provisioning of a 91-division force, a price that was simply too high. As the postwar Supreme Allied Commander, he attempted to fashion a nonnuclear solution by convincing the Europeans to bear the brunt of their own security, a faint hope considering that Europe was exhausted by the war, short on material, and politically divided. But, more significantly, Eisenhower was and had been a fiscal conservative all his life (he opposed the Navy's proposal for a new carrier *and* the Army's call for a new tank), and he knew that rearming Europe would be a costly venture. In effect, the Lisbon Conference spurred him to think about ways to prevent war without bankrupting the Western democracies.

By the time Eisenhower decided to run for president, in June 1952, he realized something had to give: either he had to dispense with his own fiscal philosophy and, he believed, bankrupt the nation, or he had to convince the Soviets he wouldn't hesitate to use the atom bomb. The choice he finally made was not only logical, it made perfect sense to him: the atom bomb made the threat credible and fiscal conservatism possible. In a letter to Charles Wilson, Eisenhower articulated his new views in stark terms, warning him that any leader "who doesn't clearly understand that national security and national solvency are mutually dependent, and that permanent maintenance of a crushing weight of military power would eventually produce dictatorship, should not be entrusted with any kind of responsibility in our country."

The New Look was much more than a domestic economic policy. In fact, it was a veiled critique of the military strategies adopted by the JCS during the Truman administration. Eisenhower believed Truman had been forced to react to communist aggression in a series of conflicts that not only embarrassed the United States but actually weakened national security. Korea was only the most obvious example; the United States had been placed on the defensive everywhere in the world — in Greece, Turkey, and Berlin — by minor military disruptions. The nation could not be responsible, Eisenhower said, for manning "a Roman wall," but must develop a strategy that kept local aggression from happening in the first place — a clear indication that Eisenhower believed Truman should have used the threat of atomic weapons at the beginning of the Korean conflict. Indeed, the heart of the New Look was strategic as well as fiscal, a rational policy of defense budget stability that ensured American nuclear dominance. On the eve of his election as president, Eisenhower was sure the military would agree with his philosophy.

But less than a year later, Matthew Ridgway, the new Army chief of staff, made it clear that he disagreed with Eisenhower and opposed the New Look. His first criticism came after the president had given his first budget proposals to the JCS in October 1953, just five weeks after Ridgway had taken his seat on the JCS. In 1953 alone, the chiefs told Eisenhower, they needed just over $37 billion to mount an effective defense against the Soviets, a fact not reflected in the proposed defense budget. The JCS was supported by Truman, who had announced just before leaving office that the military would need a total of $50 billion by 1954. The JCS had told Truman in 1951 that in three years the Soviets would not only have the hydrogen bomb, they would have the means to deliver it; 1954, the JCS said, was "the year of maximum danger."

But after a series of discussions on the Eisenhower budget in the tank, the chiefs decided to give the new philosophy a try; even Ridgway, who wasn't nearly as patient as his colleagues, decided to keep his disagreement with Eisenhower out of the public eye. In a November 1953 meeting at the White House, Ridgway pointedly reminded Eisenhower of JCS opposition to his defense budget proposals and emphasized that the JCS had maintained public silence even when the president decided to cut its $37 billion request for arms, a clear warning that the JCS, and especially Ridgway, wouldn't remain silent forever.

The Eisenhower budget was a bitter pill; the JCS's budget planners, used to dealing in larger figures, believed the $42 billion budget of 1952 would pave the way for even greater increases. In addition, top Truman administration officials recommended increases in defense spending of between $7 billion and $9 billion during Eisenhower's first year as president. But Eisenhower cut the figure to $36 billion and, during his late 1953 debate with the JCS, cut it again, to $34.5 billion. Unimpressed by Ridgway's arguments during his November White House meeting and with the JCS's silent decision not to publicize its disagreement with him in hand, Eisenhower successfully pressed Congress to pass his unprecedented defense cuts.

Although he had won the skirmish over the 1953 budget, Eisenhower had been disturbed by JCS disagreements, which led him to tell Defense Secretary Wilson that his policy toward military loyalty didn't differ all that much from his predecessor's: the chiefs could agree or they could leave, a message that was passed on to the JCS. But to make certain his views were followed — or perhaps fearing that Ridgway would put pressure on other administration officials — Eisenhower dictated a special memorandum to budget director Joseph Dodge in which he emphasized his view of the JCS's position on the budget. "We are no longer fighting in Korea," Eisenhower said, "and the defense establishment should show its appreciation for this fact and help us achieve some substantial savings — and without wailing about the missions they have to accomplish."

For Eisenhower, showing appreciation was critical to the military's acceptance of his new philosophy and placed a premium on military loyalty to civilian policies. Throughout his administration, he would seem almost obsessed by the notion that military disagreement over his budget proposals constituted disloyalty or, even worse, disrespect for the idea of civilian control over military affairs. In addition, he was angered by the fact that *his* chiefs disagreed with his policies. This view was the logical result of a series of decisions Eisenhower made in the earliest days of his presidency, when he stated that he would replace the Truman JCS with a set of officers more sympathetic to his own views. He was also persuaded by Republican arguments that the Truman chiefs, who seemed oriented toward a Europe First policy, were tied to the programs of the old administration. The president was never able to get it out of his mind that Ridgway's appointment had come with his express approval.

After Eisenhower's meeting with Ridgway in November 1953, the president realized he would not only be involved in a struggle over the defense budget with an increasingly skeptical Congress, but would also be faced with a battle from the JCS, where a recalcitrant and articulate Army chief wanted to increase conventional arms spending. Fortunately for Eisenhower, Ridgway's disagreement with the New Look could be countered within the JCS by its chairman, Admiral Arthur Radford, a New Look partisan and an Eisenhower loyalist.

Paradoxically, Radford was appointed chairman of the JCS the same day that Ridgway was appointed to head the Army, on August 15, 1953. But Eisenhower had first considered Radford for the position nearly one year earlier, during his November 1952 trip to Korea. Radford, who was then serving as commander of the U.S. Pacific fleet, impressed the president-elect with his concern for fiscal restraint and his agreement with Eisenhower's position on defense spending. In addition, Radford seemed well versed in Asian problems, was a dedicated but rational anticommunist, and was a strong proponent of naval aviation (he had experience as an aviator) to fight any future war — all characteristics that Eisenhower admired.*

But despite this favorable first impression, he hesitated to appoint Radford as JCS chairman, telling close aides he wasn't sure he could work with an officer who had been so instrumental in the removal of Louis Denfeld in 1949. Radford, as Eisenhower remembered, had not only embarrassed the former CNO as part of the Revolt of the Admirals, he had pressed questionable arguments against the Air Force's B-36 program and testified on the Navy's doubtful ability to wage an atomic conflict by deploying nuclear-powered aircraft carriers in world trouble spots. But Radford was supported by Ohio's Senator Robert Taft, who argued that the JCS needed someone who wasn't so concerned with defending Europe but had experience in the Far East. Eventually Eisenhower agreed, realizing that Radford's views on defense spending more than offset any shortcomings.

Radford was also well known in military circles as an innovative strategic thinker with an uncanny ability to pick out American vulnerabilities. While the military's attention was focused on Korea in 1952, for instance, Radford made a point of visiting Indochina, to confer with French officials on their war with the Vietminh, and ordered a team of naval experts to the area to study the feasibility of future naval deployments off Vietnam. This experience gave him a certain notoriety when Indochina became an American concern. His reputation as a strategist gave him credibility with civilian defense managers, who were awed by his suggestions for ways to deploy new weapons and by his faith that U.S. scientific knowledge ensured America's position as the world's premier military power.

Like Denfeld, Radford was a hero of the fight against the Japanese, commanding a group of carriers in the Pacific. But, unlike Denfeld, Radford had seen plenty of action during the war (his phrase "kill the bastards scientifically" had become a personal trademark) and was known throughout the Navy as a fighter, cut more in the mold of Halsey and Nimitz than the exiled CNO. Radford's experience in the Pacific was his ticket to higher postwar command, and he began by

---

* Radford was actually hoping that Eisenhower would make him CNO, a job he would have much preferred. He was still dissatisfied three years later, telling colleagues that he was little more than "a committee chairman."

serving on the JCS staff under Denfeld and by commanding the U.S. Pacific fleet. His fight for the supercarrier and his behind-the-scenes maneuvering against the Air Force's B-36 endeared him to his colleagues, who believed that as JCS chairman he would remain an effective advocate of increased Navy budgets. His appointment therefore received universal praise from the Navy officers on the JCS staff.

Radford cut a dashing figure in the Eisenhower presidency, where his simple but impressive uniform stood out against the more somber pinstripes of the New Look establishment. It didn't take long for him to have an effect. Within weeks of his appointment he had befriended Secretary of State Dulles, shook hands with members of the National Security Council, spent hours with Secretary of Defense Wilson (who was enthralled by his war stories), and endeared himself to Eisenhower by his forthright seconding of administration defense policies. White-haired, affable, articulate, Radford believed that strategic power could substitute for large armies; this was in accord with the New Look philosophy, as were his pithy, commonsensical arguments in its favor. Soon Radford had become one of the most outspoken advocates for the New Look, an unofficial ambassador from Eisenhower to the JCS.

But Radford wasn't Eisenhower's only ally. Joining him on the JCS was Air Force General Nathan Twining, an officer with a yen for new ideas tempered by a strong intuition that the United States would never be entirely safe from military attack, a position he repeated to Air Force officers who marveled at America's postwar military dominance. This seemingly contradictory attitude led Twining to a quick acceptance of the New Look: while the atom bomb wasn't an absolute guarantor of peace, he argued, it was certainly better than anything else. It was clear from the moment Twining was appointed to head the Air Force in June 1953, after Hoyt Vandenberg retired, that he was an Eisenhower ally. But, even more important, he was an Air Force partisan: he believed that American strategic air power had become the most important modern weapon as a result of his position as one of the Air Force's first pioneers.

A graduate of the West Point class of 1919, Twining transferred to the Army Air Corps five years later. In the 1920s, such transfers were considered foolhardy, almost eccentric: aviators were daredevils, the service's juvenile delinquents, their antics in the air frowned on by their staid, earthbound colleagues. Further, everyone knew that the Army Air Corps was a stepchild, an afterthought in budget battles, which left air units with the scraps left over from the Army's already measly pickings. Twining and a handful of other officers had changed all that, proving that air support for ground armies could be a decisive factor in battles.

Twining was Radford's foil: where Radford was ebullient, Twining was circumspect; where Radford was talkative, Twining was reticent. His bemused and silent glance, his disdain for anyone who did not believe that the Air Force was the *best* of all the services, a noble calling, made him a popular if somewhat mysterious figure on the JCS. Despite his military forbearance, Twining's arguments for the use of the bomb and its continued development and deployment were unassailable. Not only had he commanded the nation's strategic bombing campaign against Austria, the Balkans, and Italy in World War II, he had led the Twentieth Air Force in the Pacific at the end of the war, the command whose bombers dropped the first atomic devices on Hiroshima and Nagasaki.

In later years, what may well be an apocryphal story that made the rounds among Air Force officers says a great deal about Twining's character and beliefs. During one particularly stormy JCS session, an Army spokesman was arguing vociferously for a larger Army share in the defense budget and denigrating Air Force claims on the uses of strategic bombing. In the middle of the lecture, Twining turned to his vice chief and whispered the only argument he ever thought to use: "Ask him how many men the Army lost during the invasion of Japan."

Radford and Twining were a formidable pair, consistently dominating JCS debates on the New Look throughout Eisenhower's first year. While Radford was its most outspoken and public advocate, Twining's silent influence among Air Force generals, his consummate and hitherto unknown talent as a skillful infighter, were a necessary complement to the JCS chairman's confident and influential defense. More important, when the two men appeared in the tank to argue for Eisenhower's program, they were joined by a new CNO, Admiral Robert Carney, who joined the JCS on August 17, 1953. These three officers gave Eisenhower a three-to-one edge in JCS votes, the kind of influence he needed to rein in military spending. As JCS chairman, however, Radford had to take the lead in defending the president and the New Look to any remaining military skeptics.

The easy relationship between Eisenhower and Radford, whose position allowed him greater access to the administration's inner circles than Twining, was sealed for good on May 25, 1954, when Radford delivered a closed-door speech defending the New Look at the Naval War College in Newport, Rhode Island. "What does all this mean?" Radford asked rhetorically of the new, more austere budget figures. "It means that atomic forces are now our primary forces. It means that actions by other forces, on land, sea or air are relegated to a secondary role."

Radford reassured naval officers who feared that the New Look would mean budget cuts for every new weapons system and that cuts in armaments and manpower would eventually have as great an impact on the Navy as they did on the Army. On the contrary — or so Navy and Air Force officers believed, and as Radford's remarks implied — the New Look meant that there would eventually be budget increases for strategic weapons, that the Navy (and Air Force) would be given the job of developing a new set of expensive nuclear weapons, and that the two services would be "nuclearized." Finally, Air Force and Navy officers were relieved that the bitter feud between the two services of the late 1940s (which had only been resolved by the compromises at Key West and Newport) had been accidentally, though clearly, ended by Eisenhower's policy. The New Look meant that both services were given strategic missions involving the deployment of nuclear weapons, while the Army was relegated to the "secondary role" mentioned by Radford.

Ridgway, the JCS's lone dissenter, was predictably unimpressed by Radford's defense of the New Look and was convinced that increased defense spending was the only rational way to ensure the nation's military security. In fact, following Radford's Newport speech, Ridgway's defense of conventional deterrence and increased defense appropriations grew increasingly more strident. But Ridgway's position was not nearly as Army-oriented as it first appeared: the chief of staff disagreed not only with Eisenhower's austere defense budgets (which, he believed, might well result in a 50 percent reduction in Army forces) but with the strategy behind them.

Ridgway told his JCS colleagues that if the nation insisted on spending its funds on nuclear weapons, the Soviets were sure not to do anything to make the United States angry enough to use them. Instead, they were more likely to fund wars on "the periphery," in areas where the United States would have a difficult time deploying, let along supporting, a depleted conventional force. Moreover, Ridgway contended, the United States was preparing for the one war that was least likely to happen: a nuclear conflict that would destroy the Soviet Union. He said that the New Look's basic claim — that the United States would respond to Soviet aggression by launching a nuclear terror — was inherently incredible: if the United State used nuclear weapons in response to any but the most serious military threat, it would stand condemned in the international community.

Beginning in June 1954, Ridgway made a much more serious claim, one that resurrected Air Force and Navy doubts about Eisenhower's budget. Eisenhower, Ridgway argued, was not only in favor of cutting Army appropriations, he wanted to cut all service appropriations, a view he had adopted when he became convinced that America's nuclear superiority was enough to meet any threat. The Navy and Air

Force would eventually be disappointed by the New Look, Ridgway told JCS staff officers throughout the summer of 1954, when they discovered that Eisenhower's program didn't necessarily mean increased funding for strategic — that is, nuclear — weapons development.

Air Force and Navy staff officers pointed out that that increased strategic spending was inevitable, no matter what Eisenhower really meant: that even a modest nuclear force needed to be maintained, that eventually the United States would have to increase its military budget to buy more bombs and more bombers. The president had not realized this in October 1953, when he proposed overall cuts in defense spending, but the very logic of his strategic views — relying on the American nuclear arsenal — would eventually force him to increase spending for the Air Force and Navy in October 1954.

The views of the JCS staff were seconded by Radford and Twining, though it was later apparent that both men harbored unstated and nagging doubts about Eisenhower's real defense views. In fact, while they were pleased with their services' new roles as guarantors of Eisenhower's strategic vision — and defended the New Look solely on this basis — they realized that Eisenhower's initially modest defense outlays didn't necessarily mean an eventual long-term increase in the military budget. Through all of 1953 and into 1954, Radford and Twining decided to remain silent about their fears that what would be true for the Army would become true for the Navy and Air Force: that the real payoff for acceptance of the New Look was far less attractive than they had first thought, and that the New Look meant not only fewer divisions, but also fewer destroyer squadrons and air wings. Eventually, they believed, Eisenhower would increase the budget, and strategic forces would begin to receive the lion's share of higher defense outlays.

Still, the Ridgway argument had an impact, and by September JCS officers were waiting pensively to see just what kind of budget the president envisioned for the next fiscal year. When he sent his defense budget proposals to the JCS in October 1954, Twining and Radford finally realized that their worst fears were coming true: the defense budgets would get smaller, there would be fewer bombers, and, worst of all, Ridgway had been right all along. In budget meetings at the end of October, it was clear that Eisenhower's New Look didn't mean that the Air Force and Navy would be able to build the bombers and aircraft carriers they wanted. By November, the JCS had decided not only to oppose the Eisenhower budget but to do so publicly.

In retrospect, Twining and Radford's belated opposition is hard to understand. Ridgway had consistently maintained that Eisenhower's advocacy of the New Look was linked to his strong fiscal conservatism, that it wasn't dependent on service programs. The president wasn't posturing, Ridgway told his fellow chiefs, he really did believe that a strong national economy was the best defense against Soviet aggression. But while neither Twining nor Radford gets high marks for insight, neither does Ridgway. Although his explanation of the Eisenhower philosophy was correct, it was incomplete. It wasn't just that Eisenhower believed a strong economy was the best defense, it was that he believed the converse was also true, that overspending on defense actually weakened the nation. The question posed by the JCS as it looked over the new defense budget figures was, At what point did fiscal responsibility end and military irresponsibility begin? For the JCS, the new Eisenhower budget provided a clear answer: the military force levels the president envisioned were nothing less than irresponsible.

The defense appropriations Eisenhower sent to the JCS earmarked the Navy budget for a cutback from $11.2 billion to $9.7 billion, and while the Air Force received a slight increase, from $15.6 billion to $16.4 billion, no one "in the blue suits" (as those in the Air Force were then beginning to call themselves) thought it was adequate. But Army officers were even more outraged, noting that the Army was designated by Eisenhower to bear the brunt of his budget ax: not only was its budget cut from $12.9 billion to $8.8 billion, it would lose over 400,000 soldiers, reducing its strength from 1.4 million to 1 million men.

Radford, who had so eloquently defended the New Look to his Navy colleagues, realized he would have to lead the JCS's opposition, a position he didn't relish. But all the chiefs believed they had little to lose; it was doubtful that Eisenhower would abandon his reliance on nuclear deterrence for some other doctrine, no matter what they said about the New Look budget. This view was emphasized by Ridgway, who bitterly told his colleagues that reliance on the atom bomb was now assured, guaranteed by the reduced Army levels. Radford also realized that the JCS, specifically the Air Force and Navy, hadn't actually gained anything by its previous support of the president; the budget had been cut anyway. If the JCS kept pressing its point, Congress, which was already questioning Eisenhower's defense appropriation levels, might be forced to listen. So the Navy and Air Force joined the Army in opposing the New Look. At least to Radford's way of thinking, it failed to meet basic military needs.

At the end of 1954, Radford criticized the Eisenhower budget during congressional appropriations hearings, arguing that it did not adequately provide for an increase in strategic spending that was implied in Eisenhower's doctrine of massive retaliation. His testimony was softened, however, when Radford implied that he still believed in Eisenhower's basic philosophy, that it was the president who had erred. Radford was followed by the other chiefs, who made much the same point, though each made sure that his arguments were service-oriented. But the most outspoken criticism of the budget and the most public condemnation of the president's program of defense spending was made by Ridgway. He warned Congress that he could not be held responsible for the security of American troops with his "tiny army," a comment that made the front pages of the nation's newspapers and sparked widespread commentary that the president and his JCS were involved in an administration-splitting dispute.

Eisenhower responded angrily to the chiefs' open break with the administration, calling them to the White House for a meeting in December, a replay of his talk with Ridgway the year before. Eisenhower's personal liaison to the military, Andrew Goodpaster, a West Point graduate who was clearly marked for higher command, admitted that the meeting "was very tense," though "certainly nobody raised their voices." But while there was no outward sign of discord, it was also clear that Eisenhower wasn't going to give way on his budget proposals and that he expected the JCS to bring any of its disagreements over administration policy directly to him instead of to Congress.

"The president was very much against any public airing of administration disputes," Goodpaster said, "and thought that everything should be kept 'in house.' " In other words, if the chiefs didn't and couldn't agree with administration policy, they should quit. Actually, Eisenhower was stung by JCS criticism because he realized that it might undermine his New Look philosophy, and he felt betrayed by Radford. Above all, he told his aides, these men were his appointees, they were just as much a part of the Eisenhower team as any cabinet member; and not only were the chiefs appointed by the president, they were under his direct command. When a cabinet member didn't toe the line, the president fired him, a rule that, Eisenhower believed, went double for the military. Eisenhower told the members of the JCS that while he was always happy to hear about their disagreements, once the decision was made, it was their job to go along with it.

The December 1954 meeting marked an end to JCS support for the president's program of defense austerity. Never again would Radford or Twining defend an Eisenhower budget: Radford instead chose to push diligently for increases in specific strategic programs from within the administration, while Twining softened his public criticism of the president, saving his disagreements for their meetings. But for Ridgway, the December 1954 meeting was decisive. He believed his constant public criticism of the New Look placed him in an untenable situation: to make good on his argument, that his critique of the Eisenhower philosophy was being made for purely patriotic, not service, reasons, he realized he had little alternative to resigning from the JCS, ending a stellar forty-year military career.

Ridgway's refusal to serve a second two-year term increased congressional criticism of Eisenhower's defense posture and led to calls for a tougher defense policy against the Soviets. But Ridgway's dissent was only the public side of a much more volatile civilian-military debate on the New Look. In the end, it was this unpublicized and, at the time, extremely sensitive high-level debate over the use of nuclear weapons in support of the doctrine of massive retaliation that finally convinced Ridgway to resign.

While Radford had been one of the most consistent defenders of Eisenhower's New Look (and its implied austerity), he was still deeply disappointed by the president's December 1954 decision to cut defense spending. He had not only defended the New Look to his fellow Navy officers and JCS colleagues, he had publicly defended the president's policies. Radford found Eisenhower's philosophy compelling: it was modern, subtle, visionary, and took into account an entire class of new weapons. Just as Radford had understood the importance of aircraft carriers when others believed they would never be a significant factor in any conflict, so Eisenhower seemed to understand the strategic importance of nuclear weapons in an era when most people were refighting the battles of World War II. Most important, Radford was impressed by Eisenhower's views because they seemed to agree with his own military outlook. Although he was no longer convinced that the New Look meant increased strategic armaments — and eventually increased funding to buy more bombs, bombers, and aircraft carriers — he still believed that the president wouldn't hesitate to use nuclear weapons to defend American interests.

But history, and most especially the history of the JCS, speaks with a clarity unmatched by Radford's conviction: Eisenhower not only hesitated to use American military power, he actually overruled its use on a number of occasions. In three separate meetings with Eisenhower before the JCS's disagreement over his defense budget, the JCS chairman (as well as other members of the JCS and Secretary of State Dulles) argued strenuously for the preemptive use of nuclear weapons in defense of American interests in Asia. In each instance, Eisenhower rejected the advice of his top military and civilian advisers and took steps to dampen fears of a nuclear conflict. In each instance, Radford not only pushed the president to use the atom bomb, he actually promised officials of a foreign government that the United States would use the weapons, a promise that had not been approved by Eisenhower.

Radford first suggested that the president consider a nuclear strike in April 1954, when the French garrison at Dien Bien Phu, in Vietnam, was being pressed by a ragtag Vietminh army. The second time was just before the annihilation of Dien Bien Phu's garrison, when it was apparent that only massive American intervention could save the

French force from certain defeat. The third time came at the end of May 1954, when France told the United States that the Chinese air force was about to intervene in Indochina, tipping the balance decisively against the hard-pressed French forces, then fighting for their survival in the Mekong Delta in the wake of the Dien Bien Phu defeat.

Eisenhower never seriously considered using nuclear weapons during any of these incidents, even when Radford's arguments were seconded by Dulles (who had become a close friend and supporter of the JCS chairman) and the National Security Council. Eisenhower explained that if the United States attacked China, it would also have to attack the Soviet Union, a view that, according to later reports, "took Dulles' breath away."

In many respects, Radford's recommendation on using nuclear weapons at this time was even more deeply held than Dulles's position; he told Eisenhower that the United States would probably never again have the opportunity to gain a clear advantage over China, that the development of nuclear weapons and delivery systems would eventually give China and Russia nuclear parity, and that if the United States wanted a final victory, it should come now. But Radford was told that such an attack was out of the question. "I want you to carry this question home with you," Eisenhower said, looking directly at Radford during one White House meeting. "Gain such a victory, and what do you do with it? Here would be a great area from the Elbe to Vladivostok . . . torn up and destroyed, without government, without its communications, just an area of starvation and disaster. I ask you, what would the civilized world do about it? I repeat there is no victory except through our imaginations."

But the fourth time Radford pressed his cause, Eisenhower seriously considered the possibility. With the exception of the Cuban Missile Crisis, this incident marked the closest the United States has ever come to using nuclear weapons. The crisis came in February 1955, when the Chinese Nationalist leader Chiang Kai-shek warned the world that Communist China wanted to invade Formosa and that war could come "at any time." The JCS (with the exception of Ridgway) immediately told Eisenhower to launch an atomic attack against China in order to buttress the hard-pressed and demoralized Nationalist Chinese government. Radford's arguments to Eisenhower, which again found their way into the press, reflected the importance America placed on its interests in the Far East: they sparked a major international crisis, spurred a national war scare, and sent people scurrying to build bomb shelters.

At issue were Quemoy and Matsu, two Nationalist Chinese islands just east of the Chinese mainland, whose importance had been emphasized by Eisenhower when he publicly promised to defend them earlier in his administration. On January 10, the mainland Chinese threatened the two islands by launching preparatory bombing raids against the Tachen Islands, 200 miles northeast of Formosa. This aggression sent the American military scrambling; the JCS began immediate plans for the defense of Formosa; and Eisenhower asked Dulles to draft a congressional resolution giving him permission to deploy American troops in Formosa's defense. On January 21, Eisenhower met at the White House with Dulles, Secretary of Defense Wilson, and members of the JCS to go over the draft resolution. It was clear that most of those present believed that the United States would soon be involved in a war with China.

The meeting was uncomfortable, the residue of the bitter feud between the president and the JCS as well as the president's coolness toward the JCS after its earlier attempts to push for use of nuclear weapons. The JCS expressed disapproval of Eisenhower's resolution, believing the president wanted to use it as a pretext for giving up the Tachens. The chiefs' views were unambiguous: Eisenhower wasn't tough, wasn't willing to really defend Formosa — a point made clear when CNO Robert Carney argued that the Tachens should be defended, that it was "easier to defend the islands" than to evacuate them. In addition, he argued for deployment of the U.S. Seventh Fleet. Eisenhower said he appreciated the advice, but that he wasn't about to get the United States involved in a war with China if he could help it.

In fact, the president's view of the crisis was more practical than his statement to Carney implied, and took into account his many years of military experience. He just didn't believe, as he later told a number of aides, that the Navy could win a war with China alone, no matter what Carney said. Undeterred by Eisenhower's desire to stay out of war, the CNO pressed his point. It was better to make a stand at the Tachens than at Formosa, he said, and the Navy wasn't equipped for the kind of evacuation of the islands that Eisenhower was demanding. The president responded by saying that the decision had already been made, and when Carney expressed his views yet again, Eisenhower ordered him to silence, saying that the situation on the Tachen Islands had nothing to do with Formosa and that Carney should begin work on evacuation plans.

Nevertheless, the chief's intuitions about Eisenhower's real goal in seeking passage of the Formosa Resolution were essentially correct: the resolution was designed to head off a war with China, to convince the mainland Chinese that the U.S. policy to defend Nationalist China was not a bluff. The third week of January, Eisenhower presented the draft resolution to Congress, where it was summarily, and overwhelmingly, passed by the House. But it ran into problems in the Senate, where hearings began with the testimony of Ridgway, who was considered a supporter of the administration's plan.

But much to everyone's surprise and Eisenhower's chagrin, Ridgway decided to use the opportunity to once again open debate on the defense budget. He began by criticizing the New Look philosophy. In effect, he said, it might sound good to pass a resolution saying that the United States would defend Formosa, but as a practical matter it just couldn't be done; the military did not have the forces necessary to make such a defense successful. Ridgway's testimony was brief, but it had the desired effect: the next day, January 25, Eisenhower's anger got the best of him. The president told his Secretary of State to fire Ridgway and bring the rest of the JCS in line. Dulles was conciliatory. The move would just cause unneeded controversy, he told Eisenhower, and that was the last thing the administration needed. After a long conversation, the president grudgingly decided that firing Ridgway would create too deep a break with the JCS. Instead, he would talk privately with him.

Ridgway's testimony may have caused genuine surprise in the Senate, but the other members of the JCS knew that the Army chief looked on the nuclear option with disdain. The way to defend American interests, he had told his fellow chiefs during a series of meetings at the end of 1954, was by building a credible conventional deterrence. Otherwise, he said, the United States would, sooner or later, be forced to use nuclear weapons — if for no other reason than to show that the threat of their use was no bluff. Since he believed their use was out of the question, the only way left for the United States to defend its national security interests was for the military to develop tactics and weapons to fight nonnuclear wars.

The Formosa Resolution passed the Senate on January 28, 1955, but Ridgway's testimony had a significant impact on congressional opposition to Eisenhower's defense budget. In fact, while most members of the Senate were convinced that the United States should defend Formosa, they realized that the only way to do so was with nuclear weapons, a sobering thought for those who had supported the New Look in the belief that it would stop a war, not start one.

In February, as war hysteria in the United States mounted, Eisenhower dispatched Dulles to Europe for a round of talks on the crisis, hoping to convince the Europeans to support the American policy of a common defense of the island. But Dulles's arguments were largely rejected by America's European allies. In England, for instance, Winston Churchill argued for a cease-fire and negotiations, noting that Amercia's defense of Formosa could lead to a general war.

European caution was balanced by domestic pressures to settle the question through unilateral military action; once again, the charge was led by Admiral Radford. Radford, whose advocacy of nuclear weapons had failed three previous times, now believed the president had little choice. According to JCS officials who served with Radford and remember him as a reasonable man, he was nearly "beside himself with glee" that the United States would finally bring "the Asian question" to a conclusion.

By March, following Dulles's whirlwind tour of Europe and Asia, Eisenhower had additional problems. Not only was there increasing evidence that the Chinese were preparing for an air strike against Formosa, he feared that the Chinese Nationalist army would defect at first contact with the mainland troops. The Formosa Resolution had not short-circuited Chinese Communist designs on Quemoy and Matsu, as he had hoped. The nation was moving closer to a war Eisenhower desperately wanted to avoid; even more disturbingly, it was now apparent that such a war would involve the early use of the very weapons he had barred the JCS from using. Buffeted from all sides by pressures to commit American military might, Eisenhower turned to Goodpaster, sending him on a fact-finding tour to the Far East. Considering Goodpaster's background as an Eisenhower partisan, his reputation as an "egghead" (he had received a doctorate from Princeton in political science), and his deep, almost obsessive, concern with NATO readiness, his choice as the administration's envoy was fortuitous. Not only was he able to speak plainly to the president, he had become Eisenhower's primary supporter in military circles, a fact that resulted from the president's growing worries over Radford's calls for war. More important, Goodpaster understood that the president was searching desperately for a way to keep the nation out of a nuclear conflagration, and he was going to find a way to do it.

Goodpaster's tour of the Far East helped assuage Eisenhower's worries: the Nationalist Chinese, Goodpaster told the president, were improving their defenses. The United States would probably only have to provide logistical support to Formosa should the Chinese invade, and only become militarily involved should the Chinese air force be used. Eisenhower was pleased, not simply because he wanted to avoid a war with China, but because he had been telling the chiefs since the end of 1954 that Formosa's defense was predicated on the morale of Nationalist Chinese forces, a view that was now vindicated.

Unfortunately, CNO Carney rekindled the war scare before it barely had a chance to cool. On the evening of March 25, during a private dinner with reporters, he said that Eisenhower was prepared to intervene to defend Nationalist China, that war was nearly inevitable, and that he expected the war to break out "on April 15." It was an amazing performance, and one that again left Eisenhower in a state of rage with the JCS. On March 26, he called Dulles to complain about Carney's remarks, telling him that the JCS didn't understand "the meaning of loyalty." But his most critical remarks were reserved for Secretary of Defense Wilson, his longtime friend, whose laissez-faire style of running the Pentagon was becoming a problem. Eisenhower said that if Wilson couldn't control the JCS, he would take over the Defense Department himself.

"By God," Eisenhower raged at his press aide, James Hagerty, the same day, "this has got to stop. These fellows [on the JCS] don't realize they have a boss." Eisenhower singled out Carney and Ridgway for criticism, then told Hagerty he was going to meet with the JCS chairman: "I'm going to see Radford in half an hour, and I'm going to tell him to tell Carney to stop talking." Perhaps realizing his anger wasn't helping the situation, Eisenhower cooled off long enough to say that he thought Carney was wrong and that he "is going to look awful silly when April 15th comes and there is no incident, because honestly our information [from the Goodpaster trip] is that there is no buildup off those islands as yet to sustain any attack, and believe me, they're not going to take those islands just by wishing for them." Eisenhower then decided to deal with Carney publicly, challenging the press to take bets on Carney's date, a dare that did much to calm the nation's rising fears. Carney's bluff was called: by April 1 the war scare had all but disappeared, and by May the shelling of Quemoy and Matsu had stopped.

Two months after the Formosa crisis, in June 1955, Matthew Ridgway turned over his position to his old friend General Maxwell D. Taylor. His refusal to serve another term under Eisenhower was a testament to his frustration at his inability to effect changes in the administration's defense budget. When Ridgway left the military, he was convinced that American conventional capabilities were deteriorating and that the military's ability to affect foreign policy was nearly nonexistent.

In the years that followed, Ridgway's reputation as an Army partisan grew, and his currency as a "great General and great Chief of Staff" was indelibly burned into the memory of most Army leaders. Even now, they cite Ridgway as "the best of the crop" of the Army's high command. He is almost a legend, one of the few leaders who left an indelible impression on the JCS. But perhaps his most important legacy is his contribution to American military thinking, his view that the philosophy of "massive retaliation" that provided the strategic foundation for the New Look wouldn't work.

For Ridgway, the events of April and May 1955 were a vindication of this vision; he had been twice right: when he opposed the New Look as de facto disarmament, and when he criticized the Eisenhower philosophy as inherently incredible. In fact, he had been right three times, for he had discredited the belief that Eisenhower's faith in the deterrent value of nuclear weapons would be backed by his ready willingness to use them. As a result, the New Look had been gutted.

3

THE DEBATE

★ ★ ★ ★

As I reread these documents today, they convey an impression of innocent optimism which the next four years were to temper although, I am glad to say, not completely dispel. But at least no one could say that the new Chief of Staff did not know where he thought he wanted to go.

General Maxwell D. Taylor

IT IS AN AXIOM of military history that the final judgment of a society's armed forces and leaders must await the test of conflict. For this reason alone, the years that immediately followed the end of America's involvement in Korea have often been viewed as infertile ground for military analysis: these were the years of preparation, a quiet interlude between the end of one conflict and the beginning of another. The problem with the notion is, of course, that it's almost wholly false; while the U.S. armed forces were not involved in a major conflict, their leaders were engaged in a debate that eventually dictated the form of the nation's future wars. Thus, the seven years that followed the Korean War were among the most crucial in modern American military history.

After the Korean armistice was signed, the JCS rekindled the debate over the use and control of nuclear weapons. It faced a unique situation: while nuclear weaponry certainly had not made war obsolete, many officers firmly believed it had made a certain type of warrior obsolete. That the United States would deploy hundreds of thousands of troops in a highly sophisticated conventional conflict was unthinkable; the atom bomb was not only the ultimate insurance against defeat, it was also the ultimate deterrent to war. As long as the nation maintained its nuclear superiority, the deployment of entire mobilized armies would be unnecessary. The view had a logic of its own:

because nuclear weapons had made conventional wars unlikely, they also made conventional armies unnecessary. To prevent war, the United States would depend on its nuclear monopoly, responding to aggression by threatening the use of what was called massive retaliation.

The doctrine of massive retaliation reinforced the primary role of the Air Force and Navy in the deployment and use of nuclear weapons, a mission they were guaranteed by the Key West and Newport agreements. It's little wonder that Air Force and Navy officers were the chief proponents of the strategic doctrine, for it elevated what otherwise might have been viewed as a defense of narrow service interests into a defense of an accepted military strategy. The widespread acceptance of this strategy, however, marked an unprecedented threat to the Army. Within two years after the Korean War, it was in danger of being permanently relegated to a secondary position in the national defense establishment.

Army officers argued that in accepting the strategy of massive retaliation, the nation would become increasingly vulnerable to indirect threats, to limited wars waged in Third World nations by movements aligned with the Soviet Union. This possibility, Army officers maintained, undermined U.S. reliance on massive retaliation. Instead, the military should flexibly respond to Soviet aggression by maintaining a highly mobile conventional force. Such a force would constitute an unambiguous deterrent to Soviet expansion at the same time that it increased U.S. military options short of using nuclear weapons. By the time that Ridgway resigned as Army chief in 1955, this debate, massive retaliation versus flexible response, was becoming the most important military issue confronting the JCS.

When Maxwell Taylor arrived in Washington on the morning of June 23 to be sworn in as Army chief of staff, he carried four important documents in his briefcase. The first document reflected his views on the situation in Korea during his tenure as head of American troops in the last year of the war, the second was a critique of Eisenhower's military budgets, the third listed his personal goals and objectives in his new position, and the fourth was an analysis of America's ability to fight limited wars. It was this last document, "A National Military Program," that turned out to be critically important for the JCS; the new chief intended to present it to Eisenhower during their first meeting.

Taylor's National Military Program was a fundamental rethinking of the Army's combat doctrine, one that replaced a dependence on the deployment of large, division-sized units backed by massive firepower with smaller, more mobile combat units that relied on maneuver and surprise. This new vision reflected Taylor's growing conviction that the nation would be challenged by an increasing number of Soviet-backed Third World insurgencies, wars that demanded that the United States abandon its reliance on the threat of massive atomic retaliation. The program also reflected the general's belief that the Army needed to be modernized, outfitted with new weapons that would allow it to compete with the Air Force and Navy in nuclear weapons development and deployment — a view that would inevitably place the Army chief at odds with the other JCS members. Taylor's program marked a significant, though initially unacknowledged, shift in emphasis from Ridgway's own views: while both men agreed that the nation's, and especially the Army's, appropriations should be increased, they disagreed over just what form the increases should take.

The National Military Program not only served as an outline for the positions Taylor would advocate in his new role, it was also a valuable critique that he would use to force changes in a service still mired in the traditions of World War II. In this sense, it was the direct result of his experiences in Korea. Like other Army officers in the Far East, Taylor had been frustrated by the Korean assignment, commenting more than once to colleagues that the United States had fought the war incorrectly. He was particularly frustrated by commanders who made "exorbitant requests for firepower," a habit he believed was linked to "the Administration's passive attitude toward the war." He was convinced that the Korean fight, while not a total waste of men and material, had marked a clear regression in Army tactics. The Army was once again plagued by its old World War II problems, Taylor told his fellow commanders, when massive firepower had often served to cover a lack of command initiative.

Despite his preparation for the Army's top job — as shown by the four papers in his briefcase — Taylor realized he had been called to Washington prematurely, only when it became clear that Ridgway would never accommodate himself to Eisenhower's philosophy. But his colleagues weren't so sure that Taylor's appointment would solve Eisenhower's problems with the Army, despite the new chief's emphasis on a modern, more mobile Army. Like Ridgway, Taylor was known for his outspoken, pro-Army positions: he was convinced that the United States would be involved in limited wars, that America's response to foreign challenges should be more flexible, and that the Army's budget and manpower levels should be increased in case nuclear deterrence failed.

After being briefed by Ridgway, Taylor soon stopped at the White House, where Eisenhower and Defense Secretary Wilson were eagerly awaiting him. Both were anxious to learn whether he would cooperate with the administration's budget-cutting proposals. By all accounts, the meeting was cordial; the president knew Taylor from the European war and had admired his combat competence. In addition, his difficult command assignment in Korea, during a period marked by little battlefield movement and interminable negotiations, had also had a positive impact on the president; he believed the general's reputation would serve him well in convincing the Army to support the administration's budget. But Taylor was blunt with Eisenhower, saying that as chief of staff, he thought it was his job to promote Army interests and that, like Ridgway, he would oppose the budget if he thought it harmed the national security.

Surprisingly, Eisenhower reassured Taylor that he respected his views, saying that while he was certain there would be disagreements between civilians and the military, he was more than willing to listen to the military's point of view. Even so, he added, once he had made a decision, it was the military's job to maintain an agreeable silence and carry out his orders. As far as Eisenhower was concerned, that was the only question that mattered: whether as a good soldier Taylor was willing to follow the policy laid down by his commander in chief. Taylor, perhaps caught off balance by Eisenhower's affable reassurances, readily assented, saying that he was a defender of civilian control and a believer in strict obedience to orders.

He later emphasized that Eisenhower wasn't as concerned with the state of the nation's defense as he had hoped and that, "oddly, they [Eisenhower and Wilson] were not interested in my views on world strategy, but wished to be assured of my willingness to accept and carry out the orders of civilian superiors." But later historians have a different view, which downplays Taylor's implicit criticism of Eisenhower's disregard for his strategic vision and emphasizes Taylor's ready agreement with Eisenhower's demand for loyalty. Not only did Taylor agree to obey orders (hardly a significant concession, considering his professional background), these historians argue, he made an unprecedented pledge of public silence on those policies with which he disagreed. In fact, as one historian later noted, "it was clear from the beginning, that he would not speak out" on Eisenhower's budget cuts. In exchange, or so the story goes, Eisenhower agreed to include Taylor in all discussions on military matters, expanding his circle of advisers to include all the members of the JCS, not just its chairman.*

But the real story of the Eisenhower-Taylor agreement is far more complex. In fact, none of what Ridgway said about Eisenhower and the New Look during his briefing of Taylor extinguished his hope that

---

* Taylor never responded to these allegations, pointing out that his disagreements with the president's views were a matter of public record. But the record is clear in at least this sense: after Taylor was appointed Army chief, Eisenhower never held a meeting with the JCS chairman on matters affecting the military without Taylor's presence.

somehow he could change the president's mind on key parts of the nation's security policy, and he was confident that he would eventually convince the president to accept his new military program. Taylor had already decided that he would make his disagreements with Eisenhower, and his own views as an advocate of flexible response, the subject of internal administration debate. In addition, he believed he could be more effective working behind the scenes in Congress to gain significant budget increases than he could as a public critic of administration policy.

Not only was Taylor convinced that the sheer force of his views would win over administration skeptics, he was confident that he could fundamentally change the relationship between the military and the president. Whereas Ridgway had opposed the president publicly and lost, Taylor decided he would oppose the president privately — and quietly — by seeking out congressional allies. Where Ridgway had failed, Taylor would succeed: he would become the consummate political general.

At the outset of his term, Taylor identified a flicker of hope for the eventual acceptance of his program in the administration's Basic National Security Policy, the NSC's annual assessment of the nation's strategic status. "This year, 1955," Taylor later wrote, "it acknowledged for the first time the possibility that, as the Soviet nuclear weapons stockpile grew, our Communist enemies might be expected to step up local aggressions with reduced concern for provoking the United States. This possibility would require us to maintain mobile ground forces, suitably deployed with tactical nuclear weapons, able to deter local aggressions or to punish them swiftly as directed by the President if they occurred."

The "so there" tone of the Taylor argument — as well as his almost offhand reference to tactical nuclear weapons — is significant and marks a critical shift in the way he fought for Army budget increases and the adoption of a new strategic doctrine. Ridgway had put the same argument this way: "The belief seemed to prevail that it was enough to hold the threat of the A and H bomb over the head of a trembling world. No thinking soldier can accept this view. No honest student of military history could believe that the nuclear bomb alone was that key to quick and easy victory which mankind had sought since wars began." Taylor changed the view: he would hold the threat of the A and H bomb over the head of a trembling world, but only if it was the Army's bomb, only if it meant that the Army would achieve equal status with the Air Force and Navy in the development of new atomic strategies and weapons.

For the new Army chief, the task then was not merely to articulate his own strategic views or even to convince the president of the feasibility of a more flexible response, but to show that he could be as accommodating as Ridgway had been confrontational, even if it meant adopting some of the tactics of the Army's competitors. But he had to find allies in Congress who supported not only an increase in the administration's defense budgets but also the abandonment of massive retaliation. Taylor didn't have to look far.

Senator John F. Kennedy of Massachusetts was already known as one of Eisenhower's most vocal congressional critics, spurring Taylor to initiate firm, if brief, contacts with his staff members on the Senate Armed Services Committee. Kennedy anchored his criticism by pushing for a conventional arms buildup coupled with a more creative response to Soviet-backed Third World insurgencies. He described his views in one speech in words that were near copies of Taylor's: "Our reduction in strength for resistance in so-called brushfire wars, while threatening atomic retaliation, has in effect invited expansion by the Communists in areas such as Indochina through those techniques which they deem not sufficiently offensive to induce us to risk the atomic warfare for which we are so ill prepared defensively."

Taylor knew he could also count on support from an important group of strategic thinkers who were not only close to Kennedy but also the most public defenders of flexible response. The most prominent of the group was Paul Nitze, chairman of the State Department's Policy Planning Staff during the Truman presidency. He was best known in JCS circles for advocating a massive rearmament program predicated on a massive increase in conventional arms. In addition, he had argued that the United States should build a nationwide system of civil defense shelters, implying that America's nuclear monopoly was somewhat less than absolute, that the United States was, in Kennedy's phrase, "ill prepared" for a nuclear confrontation.

Joining Nitze was William W. Kaufmann, a highly regarded political science professor at Princeton who had helped develop the Air Force's doctrine of massive retaliation before abandoning it in the face of Soviet technological advances. Specifically, he argued that Soviet development of the H-bomb, and its likely progress in delivery systems, had radically undermined the massive retaliation theorists. Kaufmann discarded the idea of maintaining a "credible nuclear force" and suggested a radical departure in strategic thinking. Since it was becoming clear that the use of even one nuclear weapon might lead to national suicide, he joined Nitze in advocating a buildup in conventional forces.

Kaufmann's arguments were widely circulated in the Pentagon, on Capitol Hill, and among the nation's small circle of established military strategists. Codified in "The Requirements of Deterrence," a paper that was handed among the JCS staff at the beginning of Taylor's

tenure, Kaufmann's views provided a catalyst for congressional criticism of Eisenhower's military program and emboldened a new group
of strategists, including three Harvard professors close to Kennedy,
McGeorge Bundy, Arthur Schlesinger, Jr., and John Kenneth Gal-
braith. All three soon became influential critics of massive retaliation,
buttressing their arguments by pointing out that the postwar strategic
bombing survey showed that a massive air offensive — the kind advocated by the Air Force — actually failed to knock out the Germans'
warmaking capacity. While the bomb provided a more horrifying
weapon than the B-29, their attack on the hitherto unquestioned
assumptions of massive retaliation fueled doubts that the Eisenhower
strategy would actually work.

But Taylor's alliance with Kennedy, Nitze, Kaufmann, and other
proponents of flexible response, as well as his cultivation of important
administration critics on Capitol Hill — including the chairman of
the powerful Senate Subcommittee on Military Preparedness, Senator
Lyndon Johnson of Texas — failed to strengthen his position on the
JCS. While Taylor joined his colleagues in pushing for an overall
increase in military appropriations, he remained the lone JCS voice for
a conventional arms buildup. For his first twenty months, until mid-
1957, he remained isolated on the JCS, arguing vainly for increased
appropriations for the Army. At the same time, he kept his pledge to
the president, maintaining a studied public silence on his deep disagreements with the administration's policies.

Nevertheless, at the same time that Taylor was debating with his
JCS colleagues and contending with Eisenhower over the budget, he
was hammering out a shift in Army tactics that was to have a more
decisive impact on administration policies than any argument he
could raise in the tank. At the center of this shift was a "Pentomic
division" (Taylor admitted it was "a Madison Avenue phrase"), an
attempt to make certain that the Army was an equal competitor with
the Air Force and Navy for nuclear weapons. Paradoxically, it marked
a significant departure from the flexible response doctrine's usual
emphasis on conventional arms. According to Taylor, the Pentomic
division was seen as a new type of Army formation, one that included
atomic weapons as part of its standard equipment. "While it was true
that at the time the Army had only the cumbersome Honest John
rocket and the heavy eight-inch howitzer capable of firing nuclear
munitions," Taylor explained, "nuclear weapons were the going thing
and, by including some in the division armament, the Army staked
out its claim to a share in the nuclear arsenal."

Taylor supported an antiballistic missile defense program under
Army auspices — a kind of Strategic Defense Initiative for the 1950s.
He realized that the deployment of such a missile was years, even dec-

ades, away, but by supporting research on the project, the Army could compete in developing delivery systems for nuclear warheads with its competitors in the tank. By promoting an antiballistic missile system, Taylor was trying to outflank the Air Force and Navy, getting a jump on their missile programs that would make the Army the first, and therefore the premier, missile service in the nation. Fortunately, he learned that he didn't need to start from scratch; General James M. Gavin, his airborne colleague in World War II as well as his deputy chief of staff for research and planning, was involved in just such a project.

Gavin, a talented and highly respected field general, was developing a short-range missile for the Army in Huntsville, Alabama. He claimed it would not only make his service a competitor for increased defense dollars (and embarrass Air Force intellectuals who thought they had a monopoly on science), but might even put America in space. By mid-1957, with Gavin's Huntsville team clamoring at a chance to test its new Redstone rocket, Taylor's National Military Program was beginning to bear fruit. The launch of Redstone, coupled with Taylor's cultivation of well-known congressional and academic proponents of a conventional arms buildup, would, it was believed, neutralize the Army's opponents on the JCS.

It was a forlorn hope: while Taylor's advocacy of flexible response had inaugurated a debate over the role and mission of the Army, opposition to the doctrine dictated that its adoption would have to await the passing of the Eisenhower years. While the Army chief had won some important battles, he continued to be the only proponent of flexible response on the JCS. In large part, his retreat from public view, and his acknowledged frustration at being consistently outvoted in JCS sessions, was due to the formidable opposition sparked by his views. Led by Air Force Chief of Staff Thomas White, proponents of massive retaliation (many of whom had actually helped to formulate its basic tenets) continued to dominate JCS discussions on military strategy.

General Thomas Dresser White became Air Force chief of staff on July 1, 1957, an appointment that capped the stellar career of the most widely respected and talked about officer in the Air Force. White was promoted after Eisenhower decided to replace Arthur Radford, the retiring JCS chairman, with White's boss, Nathan Twining, a decision that continued the Army's three-to-one JCS voting deficit. More discouraging for Taylor and other Army leaders, White had served as Twining's vice chief during the critical first years of the New Look, taking credit for successfully defending a number of major Air Force strategic programs and even winning a few budget debates.

White's appointment marked the peak of Air Force influence in the Eisenhower administration. White was an intellectual giant whose quiet genius and familiarity with nuclear strategy so overpowered his colleagues that none dared argue with him. His reputation was particularly chilling for Taylor, whose arguments for increased spending on conventional arms were dismissed by White as outdated, hopelessly naive, and beyond debate. Most chilling of all, at least for proponents of flexible response, White was a strategic theorist who consistently failed to act like one, which meant that Taylor could not lord his wartime experience over him. White knew the face of war; he realized that, as he later said, it was "a brutal, deadly affair" and that "our enemy is a coarse, crooked megalomaniac who aims to kill us."

White is still remembered as one of the strongest Air Force chiefs, the service's first and most important military analyst, who is credited by his colleagues with pioneering strategic thinking and helping to establish the nation's first Cold War strategic bombing plan. Ironically, White's reputation as a thinker was gained at the expense of a broad combat background: throughout the early years of World War II, White had unsuccessfully lobbied Army Air Corps General Henry Arnold for a combat command, pleading with him and just about anyone who knew him for a transfer to a combat theater. But White was told that he was too valuable as one of the nation's chief air intelligence officers, making his transfer to the Pacific or Europe almost unthinkable. Finally, however, he was given command of the Seventh Air Force, serving during the air campaigns against Iwo Jima, Okinawa, and Japan.

After the war, White picked up where he had left off, as the Air Force's primary defender of "the atomic blitz" and a member of the vaunted Joint Strategic Survey Committee, the JCS's primary strategic planning group. He became the Air Force's most important nuclear war expert and a vocal advocate for Air Force claims to the premier role in defending the nation. White not only adopted the language of nuclear theorists, he expanded their views, arguing — along with Radford and Twining — that the New Look wasn't simply sound national policy, it made strategic sense. Studious, sometimes sarcastic, almost always impatient with long-winded colleagues, he responded to JCS staff fears that the Soviet Union was developing technology that would counter the atomic blitz by arguing that the doctrine of massive retaliation need only be expanded to be more effective: if the Soviet Union launched a first strike, the Air Force would be ready with more bombers and more bombs. While this view contradicted Eisenhower's budget dictums, White was convinced that adopting a program that expanded the Air Force's fleet of long-range bombers would still be cheaper than pouring money into conventional arms.

For all of this, White's reputation within the Air Force was built on his ability to compromise, a change from the arrogant irascibility that came to be the hallmark of other Air Force officers like Carl Spaatz and Henry Arnold. White is most often remembered as a conciliator, the one Air Force chief whose legacy of patience and an ability to keep the disparate Air Force commands working together has remained an example for his successors. White was efficient, unpredictably pulling essential reports defending the service from the nooks and crannies of the Pentagon on demand. JCS officers claimed that White had a photographic memory as well as the ability to engage intellectuals in erudite strategic debates.

White's message, then, was simple: he could bring the Air Force into the atomic age without becoming detached from the heart of the service; he could retain the fighters, the hard-bitten field commanders necessary to carry out a war plan, while using the Air Force's stable of theoreticians to defend service interests. But above all, perhaps even more important than his renowned efficiency, was his almost disarming patience, a firmness so deeply embedded that, as Air Force chief of staff, he once sat through a full thirty-minute tirade from the Strategic Air Command's Thomas S. Power without uttering a word of reprimand. In the end, White's detachment and patience shamed the explosive SAC commander, who stalked from the room, his argument rejected.

The Air Force officer who made White's theories come to life, who provided the impatient foil to White's even-temperedness, was General Curtis LeMay, who joined the JCS as White's deputy on the same day the Air Force chief was sworn in. By that time, LeMay's career had already become a legend. In early 1945, as a key air commander in the Pacific, LeMay had carried out one of the most unimaginably horrifying air campaigns in world history. In March 1945 alone his bombers leveled thirty-three Japanese cities, leading him to tell his superiors that at his current rate he could end the war on September 1; by then, there wouldn't be any targets left to bomb.

As head of SAC after the war, LeMay became the most widely known defender of massive retaliation. More accurately, LeMay believed in the Air Force and in the power of strategic bombing, a service loyalty that was so strenuously and consistently publicized that it made his defense of massive retaliation look like a mere debating position. He not only said that the nation didn't need a Navy or an Air Force, he even claimed that he would fight a nuclear war as he had fought the air war against Japan, by throwing everything against the Soviets from the outset, what he called his "knock-out punch." Throughout the late forties and early fifties, while Twining played the role of the silent but effective political infighter and White, the nuclear strategist, LeMay became a power all his own, the natural result of his total control of SAC. SAC is still the only military command that reports directly to the JCS and not to its own service. In many ways, LeMay was exactly the type of general the public always imagines: a pug-faced, cigar-chewing stump of muscle who doesn't look at you as much as peers at you, who grunts when he means yes, and who becomes explosively profane during even minor disagreements. Twining thought him plebian, mainly because he smoked cigars during dinner, but he needed LeMay and his expertise as a defense against critics of the Air Force.*

LeMay's vocal defense of the Air Force was needed most of all in 1957, when White realized that the Army was engaged in an all-out race with the Air Force in developing a new missile. He suspected that the Air Force was losing the battle, though it had gotten off to a head start by beginning the development of the Atlas missile when he was Twining's deputy. Even so, by mid-1957, White knew that the Atlas was nowhere near completion and had even fallen behind schedule, due primarily to the Air Force's decision to divert hard-won weapons money to building more bombers for SAC. Even more disturbing was a report to White from Air Force intelligence officers, who were claiming that the USSR was engaged in a crash program to produce an ICBM, a report with an end-of-the-world scenario that the Soviets could have as many as five hundred such missiles ready for final deployment within five to six years.

The final Air Force intelligence report, passed on to White on September 30, 1957, breathlessly argued that the Soviets were not only moving quickly to gain missile dominance, they had actually sketched a first strike strategy that would take advantage of their new technology. The Air Force study was complete with statistical summaries of Soviet production figures, including blueprints of missile plants. It went on to say that the USSR would have the means of launching a decisive first strike against the United States as early as 1963, targeting three nuclear warheads for each SAC base. It concluded that the Soviets' missile dominance would not only reverse America's nuclear monopoly and fatally undermine the Air Force's defense of massive retaliation, it would also make the nation vulnerable to a disabling first strike. For White, it looked as if defeat was just around the corner.

The CIA, however, disagreed with the Air Force report. The CIA

---

* LeMay's arrogance often got him in trouble. In 1949, he criticized Hoyt Vandenberg's bombing strategy as "too simplistic, and over optimistic." The comment nearly cost him his job. Air Force officers pointed out that Vandenberg was simply "plumping for the B-36." LeMay's remarks came back to haunt him. Vandenberg had been responsible for appointing LeMay commander of SAC, which made his remarks seem ungrateful. When his name was mentioned for the Air Force vice chief's job in 1952, the proposal was quickly dropped.

had been competing with the Air Force in trying to estimate Soviet military capabilities, though this task was supposed to be left solely in the hands of Army, Navy, Air Force — and JCS — intelligence officers. By the time White became Air Force chief, the CIA's reports were legendary, consistently denigrating military intelligence estimates by publishing figures that showed that the Soviets were not nearly as competitive as any of the services assumed. Its view of the 1957 Air Force estimates was no different; the CIA said that White's team of intelligence officers were overestimating Soviet capabilities, that even if the Soviets were able to develop the kinds of missiles the Air Force said they could, there was no evidence to show that they were doing anything about it.

White refused to accept the good news. He rejected the CIA's criticisms and accepted the Air Force report, telling his aides to come up with ideas to counter the Soviet threat. In addition, he told his staff to begin thinking of ways to make certain that SAC bombers were not caught off guard, including a program that envisioned underground housing for B-52s.* In fact, White argued, it wasn't the first time that Soviet capabilities had been underestimated. The United States had been caught off guard in 1949, when the Soviet Union exploded its first nuclear bomb, had been surprised in 1953, when the USSR had detonated a hydrogen warhead, and had been stunned by reports in 1955 that the Russians had developed a long-range bomber when everyone thought it couldn't be done. Given this history, the Soviets were bound to come up with an ICBM. Far better, White said, to go ahead with a missile program than to assume the Soviet Union would never develop a sophisticated warhead delivery system.

The one factor that White and his colleagues conveniently failed to mention in defense of their intelligence summaries was the well-known fact that the Air Force was already developing an ICBM. Any report that argued against Soviet capabilities argued not only against Soviet intentions (an article of faith in the Cold War era), but also against the Air Force's own interests. The bad news was actually good: the Air Force could now go to Eisenhower with a series of strategic proposals calling for a mammoth buildup in America's missile force, proposals that Eisenhower could hardly ignore in light of Air Force intelligence estimates that all but proved that the USSR was engaged in a crash program to build long-range missiles.

Even more significant, the Air Force report would help White regain his service's lead in missile development, a project of special interest

---

* White's deputy, LeMay, quickly sidetracked this proposal, arguing that it was too costly. In fact, the suggestion was insulting; LeMay pooh-poohed any notion that SAC, "his" Air Force, would be defeated by a Soviet surprise attack.

to him, for he had been diligently, though unsuccessfully, trying to untrack the Army's missile development program since it was first brought to the JCS's attention, when he was the vice chief under Twining. White's nemesis in missile development was Maxwell Taylor's old colleague James Gavin, whose service experience mirrored White's. Like White, Gavin had become a valued intelligence officer with an eye for detail and was one of the few generals who could legitimately compete with Air Force scientists in the field of nuclear delivery systems.

Gavin was eccentric and easy to anger, an officer who carried a grudge beyond any reasonableness. His combat competition with Taylor during the war, for instance, was carried over into the peacetime Army, with the result that the two men avoided any contact. Nevertheless, Gavin agreed with Taylor on a number of important points, including support for the flexible response doctrine and a quiet disdain for Air Force programs. While Gavin criticized what he called the administration's "Big Bomb" strategy, he also pressed openly for the development of long-range missiles — one of the few programs on which he and Taylor saw eye to eye.

Realizing that Gavin's interest in science might prove to be the Army's salvation during the waning years of the Eisenhower administration, Taylor gave his colleague almost total control of the Army missile program, stopping only long enough to read his detailed reports on the project's slow but certain progress. Throughout 1957, Gavin conducted experiments with unarmed rockets; his results brought convincing evidence that the Redstone was ready for deployment. These tests came as no surprise, for just a year earlier the Gavin team had issued a report stating that it had successfully designed a missile that could travel a distance of 3,355 miles at an altitude of 684 miles.

Successfully testing a rocket was only the first of many hurdles in the long process that would lead to a missile's deployment, a fact that Gavin learned when the Air Force lodged a stiff protest with Defense Secretary Wilson, arguing that the Army's missile research was intruding on Air Force prerogatives. Wilson agreed, telling Gavin that the Army's new missile would not be allowed to have a range in excess of 200 miles. This decision was tantamount to telling the Army to redesign the Redstone, scrapping everything that Gavin and his team had learned. It so angered Gavin that he broke his habit of silent disdain for such folly by telling Wilson that the Soviet Union, not the Air Force, was the real competitor in the missile race and that service feuds shouldn't be allowed to get in the way of the nation's security. Moreover, Gavin said, he was certain that the Soviet Union had developed a midrange missile and would soon launch a space satellite that would make irrelevant Air Force arguments over just who controlled what.

By September, it was clear that each of the three services was involved in the missile competition. While the Army had been developing the Redstone in Huntsville and the Air Force had been putting together the first ICBM, the nation's official satellite program, known as Vanguard, was being developed under the joint control of civilian scientists and the Navy, which planned to launch a satellite at the end of 1958. But none of the programs was fast enough to beat the Russians. Just days after the Air Force had given White its intelligence summary on Soviet missile capabilities, Gavin told the Army Scientific Advisory Panel that reliable intelligence reports indicated that the Soviet Union would launch a satellite within the next month; he characterized the event as "a technological Pearl Harbor." On October 4, 1957, Gavin's intelligence reports were confirmed: the Soviet Union announced the launch of Sputnik.

Within twenty-four hours of Sputnik's launch, the JCS missile skirmish exploded into a full-fledged service war: Army staff officers serving with the JCS accused their Air Force counterparts of putting service interests ahead of the nation's security, contending that the Army could have beaten the Russians by as much as two months by putting Gavin's Redstone rocket into space. Within forty-eight hours, these accusations became part of JCS history. Three days after the launch — a short span of time by JCS standards — the military chiefs held two special sessions on the Soviet achievement, pitting Army missile experts against Navy and Air Force officers.

Inevitably, the shouting match, which JCS Chairman Twining hoped would be confined to the tank, began to spill into the press. Twining, who had turned out to be a much more conciliatory JCS leader than his predecessor, worried that the service rivalry would mushroom into another embarrassing public debate over the administration's budget program. In particular, he feared that the publicity would ruin the unofficial truce he had engineered with Eisenhower. Like Taylor, Twining had promised Eisenhower that he would maintain a public silence on JCS disagreements with the administration, hoping that the courtesy would result in an increased defense budget. Twining also sensed that the administration was prepared to consider such a step.

Under public pressure to respond to the Soviet space launch, Eisenhower was as disturbed by newspaper reports of the JCS disagreements over the missile program as Twining. The president told Twining he would conduct an official assessment of the American missile program during a high-level meeting of civilian defense officials at the White House on the morning of October 8, to be followed by a private meeting with Secretary of Defense Wilson. In addition, Eisenhower said, he would use the two meetings to decide which service should go forward with a missile program, resolving the service feuding before it got worse.

Eisenhower began the meeting on the eighth by asking his civilian assistants whether the Army's report — that the Soviets could have been beaten — was true. The Assistant Secretary of Defense for Research and Development, Donald Quarles, said that the Army claim was not only true, its characterization was actually conservative; there was evidence that Gavin's Redstone rocket could have been launched as early as 1955, a full two years before Sputnik. Quarles outlined each service's program and recommended that the president allow each service to continue its missile research and development, rewarding the winner with the sole right to continue the nation's missile program.

When Eisenhower and the Secretary of Defense met privately later in the morning, Wilson was far more circumspect in his advice than Quarles, dismissing the Soviet launch as "a neat scientific trick." The soft-spoken secretary disagreed with his assistant secretary and emphasized that service competition had actually stood in the way of missile development, ominously adding that "trouble is rising" among the services over who should control American missiles. As in the past, talk of JCS disagreement enraged the president. He lashed out against the JCS, telling Wilson that he was fed up with the military's constant bickering, criticizing the high command for its inability to agree on programs that would benefit the nation, not just individual service interests. Eisenhower wondered aloud just when the services would stop competing. What the United States ought to do, he said, was "abolish" the services "and go to task forces under Defense." His anger seemingly cooled by the outburst, he then told Wilson that the Army should immediately go forward with the Redstone rocket and get a satellite into orbit as soon as possible.*

Eisenhower immediately called a meeting at the White House with the JCS. The service heads brought their files, filled to overflowing with charts, memos, and programs on missile development. Eisenhower told them to put away their files, he had already made his decision. Rather, he said, he wanted to give them a "seminar" on service

---

* Eisenhower lost his temper more often with the JCS than with any other branch of the government, but this outburst was by far the worst. Frustrated at attempts to bring the JCS into line, he thereafter confined his comments to jaundiced and sometimes bitter musings that "I might have to relieve them all" and that their privileged access to Congress constituted "legal insubordination."

rivalries. He told the JCS that service competition wasn't helping the nation and that the JCS officers had to learn how to agree, adding that the most recent fight was just one in a long series of service disagreements. Taylor ignored Eisenhower's plea, arguing that the Army's development of the Redstone rocket had been hampered by the Air Force, which had tried to block it. Twining responded to Taylor by citing the Key West and Newport agreements, which, the JCS chairman said, dictated that the Army should have no missiles with a range of more than "200 miles."

Eisenhower, by this time clearly exasperated by the chiefs' inability to see his point and certain that his seminar had failed, quickly sputtered his disbelief at Twining, then just as quickly issued his decision. Not only would the Army be allowed to continue development of the Redstone, he said, there was good strategic reason for it to have missiles that could be placed "farther back from the battle area." Eisenhower said that he not only expected the services to resolve their differences, he expected them to follow the example he had set as Supreme Allied Commander in Europe. His lecture was sprinkled with wartime anecdotes on how teamwork had not only helped to win the war, but ensured that there was enough credit for everyone who had a hand in the project.

In many ways, Eisenhower's talk with the JCS in October was his last plea for military unity, a desperate attempt to convince the service leaders to cooperate for the good of the nation. And at least for a short time on October 8, 1957, the members of the JCS agreed, telling Eisenhower they understood the need for cooperation, that in the wake of the Sputnik launch the American military needed to stop its service rivalry. They would attempt to put aside their disagreements for the good of the country, the chiefs said.

But the launch of Sputnik had a much greater impact on the administration than even Eisenhower was willing to concede. While it sparked a crisis at the JCS, it spurred a much more serious internal administration debate on the nation's nuclear strategy, on the defense budget, on service missions, even on détente with the Soviet Union. Yet this growing internal questioning did not have the desired effect on Eisenhower that the JCS was convinced was necessary to persuade him that a military buildup was essential. In fact, Sputnik had the opposite effect: now that it was clear the Soviet Union had both developed the bomb and found a way to deliver it, Eisenhower openly doubted whether the United States should proceed with a strategic weapons buildup. It was time, he told his assistants, for the country to come to an agreement with the USSR; he even proposed a unilateral nuclear weapons freeze as a possible first step.

"Just what are you going to do with all those bombs?" Eisenhower asked Twining soon after the October 8 meeting. The president was hoping for an answer, not simply because he was searching for more ways to cut the budget (though he was), but because he was genuinely puzzled by the military's need for more weapons, a need he was more certain than ever would eventually undermine America's economic strength. If the United States was to engage in a full-fledged competition with Russia in space, the money had to come from somewhere, even if it meant cutting nuclear weapons development, which Eisenhower said he would consider since the nation already had more than enough bombs to deter Soviet aggression. Twining was unimpressed by the president's question and equally blunt in his answer: while he said he agreed on the need to retain a large number of nuclear weapons, he said that the Air Force wouldn't be happy until it had one hydrogen bomb "for every aircraft plus a sizable reserve."

Frustrated by his attempts to gain JCS agreement on his defense program, under attack in Congress by a reinvigorated Democratic party, questioned by a resurgent academic community convinced by the arguments of the flexible response strategists, and faced with a sullen and critical national press, Eisenhower turned to corporate managers for advice, going so far as to call H. Rowan Gaither of the Ford Foundation to a meeting in the Oval Office. Gaither had been appointed by the president to head a committee to study the national defense, and Eisenhower believed its findings would vindicate his view of America's defense establishment. Confident of his position and comfortable with the group of some of the nation's most important business leaders — men who had helped elect him and who formed his most important block of support — Eisenhower met with Gaither and members of his committee on November 6, 1957. But a surprise awaited the president, shattering his confidence in Gaither. As Eisenhower's biographer Stephen Ambrose described it, the Gaither study "practically predicted the end of Western Civilization." The Soviets had 1,500 nuclear weapons, 300 submarines, 4,500 bombers, a sophisticated air defense system, an operational ICBM, and a strong economy, Gaither said. The Soviet GNP was growing, and the country was preparing for war. Gaither ticked off the reasons for his pessimistic view: the Soviet Union had bomb shelters, America didn't; the USSR was getting stronger, the United States was getting weaker; and Sputnik was only the latest in a long list of American failures. "Do something," Gaither pleaded.

Eisenhower stared at the group from his high-backed chair, saying that while he found the report "sobering," he couldn't agree with its conclusions. The American people might question, the JCS might argue, the press might take up the cudgel and attempt to force him to admit that his program of fiscal responsibility had failed, but he refused, he said, to turn the country into "a garrison state." The only thing the president said that he agreed with was that the United States would have to "carry the load" of the defense of the Western alliance into the near future. Moreover, he said, the prospects for peace were not as dim as Gaither supposed. If we waited long enough, remained vigilant enough, and refused to subvert the national purpose to military expediency, Eisenhower argued, the Soviet Union would eventually "change internally."*

When the Gaither Report was leaked to the national press the following week, the JCS realized that there was little hope for a sizable defense increase before the elections of 1960. In fact, the most it could hope for was that congressional pressure would force the administration into a series of budget compromises that would provide a modest increase in military appropriations. With this in mind, and following Taylor's belief that the military needed to gain political allies in its quest for more funding, the JCS made certain that by the end of 1957 the necessary groundwork had been laid to ensure that the administration's defense policies would come under congressional scrutiny. The president might be able to ignore the Gaither Report, but it would be much more difficult for him to ignore political pressure.

Emboldened by Eisenhower's weakness in the wake of the Sputnik launch, the JCS's public disagreement, and the Gaither Report, the Senate Armed Services Committee's Subcommittee on Military Preparedness decided to hold hearings on the administration's defense policies in December. Chaired by Lyndon Johnson, a 1960 presidential hopeful, it called members of the JCS to testify and aired the disputes that had been symbolized by JCS division on major strategic questions. Once again, a Senate hearing became a public forum for JCS criticism of Eisenhower. Johnson's witness list included the top military minds in the nation, most prominently the Army's chief, Maxwell Taylor, and the head of its missile program, James Gavin.

Johnson's questioning left little doubt of his own views; he wanted to know whether the military thought there was "a missile gap" — that is, if the Soviet Union actually had more missiles than the United States — and if there was, whether that gap could be closed. Both Gavin and Taylor took the lead in criticizing Eisenhower's budget priorities, implying that smaller defense budgets had handicapped scientific and military research. Both officers confirmed that the budget,

---

* This meeting with Gaither is the most accurate description of the president's beliefs that historians have. But Eisenhower's argument was hardly new; in fact, the president's words echoed the argument used by Winston Churchill in a conversation they had had at the end of World War II. Churchill told Eisenhower that Soviet military strength would remain the most significant challenge to peace over the next fifty years. But Churchill was optimistic; if the United States and its allies remained strong and "waited," the Soviet Union would become less of a threat.

at least in their view, had contributed to the embarrassment of falling behind the Soviet Union in missile technology. Taylor expanded on this point by openly questioning the advisability of the doctrine of massive retaliation and argued for an increase in the Army's budget in order to expand American conventional capabilities.

Johnson, who had already spoken to Taylor a number of times, prodded him, nodding approval of his major points, making it clear that he himself also had doubts about using nuclear arms as the sole deterrent to communist expansion. But despite Johnson's prodding, Taylor remained cautious: he refused to criticize the president openly and he deflected Johnson's suggestions that the military command structure should be reformed. "Undoubtedly there are areas in which it seemed to me improvement should be sought," he said, though he quickly added that he wasn't in a position to recommend specifics. "I think it takes time and observation and more wisdom than I presently have to come forward with these points."

Gavin, still angry and frustrated by the launch of Sputnik and disgusted with Air Force intransigence on the Army's missile program, was not nearly as modest; he criticized the administration for "wrong decisions" on the missile program. In addition, he pointedly resurrected the JCS's bitter missile debate, implying that the Air Force (which Gavin didn't name) bore the major responsibility for the U.S. failure to beat the Russians into space. Gavin told Johnson that the Army's missile program had not only been sidetracked three different times by the administration in the preceding three years, but that the Army had been mishandled, "made impotent," by administration policies. The result was that the Army was incapable of fighting future, nonnuclear wars. Gavin's strident criticisms surprised the committee. It knew the Army was a traditional opponent of Eisenhower's defense program, but it hadn't realized just how divisive the administration's internal debates had become. What followed was even more surprising.

"I don't believe in next year's budget," Gavin said forcefully, his voice shaking in anger. "I think what really is needed now is a competent military staff of senior military people working directly for the Secretary of Defense" — implying that the JCS was filled with incompetent officers incapable of making independent, service-neutral decisions. "I would have them, and again this is entirely my personal opinion, take over the functions of the Joint Chiefs of Staff," he concluded. "I would have the military staff organized to handle operations, plans, intelligence, and — in fact — break up the Joint Chiefs of Staff." Edwin L. Weisl, the subcommittee's counsel, leaned over to Johnson: "You have heard what the General testified to, Mr. Chairman." Johnson nodded. "I heard considerable."

Once again Eisenhower was outraged by the JCS's public airing of disputes and especially by Gavin's announcement, after his testimony, that he was leaving the military because of disagreements with administration policy. But this time the president kept his temper, deciding that he would take a new tack with the JCS. He decided to ignore the JCS's testimony and to punish Gavin by making him head of the American Army in Europe, a move that initially puzzled the military and that Gavin characterized as "playing some sort of game with me."

In fact, Eisenhower knew exactly what he was doing. After his testimony, Gavin was a pariah in JCS circles: he had not been satisfied with simply criticizing the president but had gone on to criticize the president's critics and imply that all JCS officers were incompetent (he hadn't even bothered to omit Taylor's name). By letting it be known that he was considering appointing Gavin to head the U.S. Army in Europe, Eisenhower was exacting his final revenge. JCS officers were enraged that an internal critic would actually be rewarded for his views. Not surprisingly, Gavin turned down the assignment, emphasizing that he would be glad to stay in the Army even "as a private if it were to be the kind of Army that I wanted it to be."

Despite his criticism of the JCS, the retirement of Gavin further embittered Army officers against the administration and once again isolated Taylor as the military's leading defender of flexible response. Yet Gavin's parting comment, that he would be glad to serve if it were to be his kind of Army, underestimated his own and Taylor's impact on administration policy. While Army manpower levels hadn't been increased in eight long years and budget increases had been modest or nonexistent, by the end of his last term as Army chief of staff, Taylor admitted that the strategy of massive retaliation actually "bore some resemblance to the strategy of Flexible Response." In many ways, the evolution of the two doctrines into one overriding strategic view was predictable, especially considering the Soviet Union's development of the atom bomb and a delivery system to go with it.

But this melding didn't resolve Taylor's major problem. In the wake of Gavin's bitter condemnation, the chances that Eisenhower would finally increase the Army's budget became almost nil. By early 1958, Taylor was forced to admit that his National Military Program, which had been predicated on his belief that Congress would eventually eviscerate Eisenhower's budget philosophy, had failed. In essence, he realized that in the absence of an outright war — which would mean a full conventional mobilization — the U.S. military, and especially the Army, was incapable of defending the nation against other kinds of conflicts, particularly those in the Third World. What was needed to meet this threat was a new kind of warfare, one that would allow the United States to respond to regional and local threats without committing large numbers of American troops and without soaking up badly needed Army appropriations. In essence, Taylor was looking for a response to Soviet aggression that would be cheap as well as effective.

In his last two years on the JCS, Taylor came up with two solutions. First, he directed a group of Army officers to begin a series of experimental exercises using helicopters in airborne assaults, an idea from his service in Korea. But, most important, he began to review Army programs designed to upgrade the training of its special "unconventional" paramilitary units for possible use in "the gray areas," in peripheral conflicts where American interests were being challenged by Soviet proxies. By deploying these specially trained forces, Taylor thought, the United States might be able to defend democracy's principles without bankrupting its arsenal. He had ignored these units throughout his tenure because, as a regular army officer, he had a natural inclination to dismiss the value of units trained in exotic tactics. Now, just months before his own retirement, when it was almost too late to do anything about it, he began to rethink his position.

Taylor's decision to review Army counterinsurgency programs came as a distinct and distasteful surprise to the JCS. While it had inherited a military tradition that celebrated the citizen-soldier, the Minuteman statue in Lexington had, over the years, become little more than an icon, a nostalgic symbol of the days before the republic had a military. Even in the midst of its Revolution, Americans struggled to learn the traditional way to fight a war, to transform humble volunteers into professional soldiers, to build a sophisticated and professional army. The effort had worked: the United States had built the most formidable military establishment in world history, albeit one that emphasized conventional military tactics. To change those tactics now, many JCS officers felt, would be needless, perhaps even dangerous.

In one sense, however, Taylor's suggestion might have been predicted: having lost the decade-long battle for a role in the deployment and use of nuclear weapons, the Army needed to find a mission to recoup its position as the premier service. Curiously, though Taylor promoted the counterinsurgency doctrine, he failed to identify it as an integral part of the flexible response doctrine. While there's no easy explanation for Taylor's oversight, it might be best seen as an officer's natural reaction to the suggestion that the military get involved in the dirty business of spying, a role the JCS had implicitly rejected during its long competition with the Office of Strategic Services (OSS).

Unconventional warfare tactics based on a systematic program of military intelligence-gathering were first initiated in the modern era by the OSS during World War II. It did not then have the imprimatur of heroism that it later gained, mostly in hindsight, for organizing and supplying partisans in occupied countries, operating a network of informers in hostile environments, and generally providing strategic intelligence on enemy military movements and plans. Instead, the OSS was a technical intelligence bureau, a semi-independent branch of the military under only the nominal direction of the American joint chiefs. This position meant that OSS intelligence and paramilitary operations competed with similar service operations throughout the war.

The overlap between service missions and OSS operations caused a number of command and control problems and led to disagreements over whether the OSS was as useful as its defenders claimed. At least some of the problems resulted from its policy of taking "untrained" civilian analysts and putting them in officers' uniforms, arising from the military's need for nonmilitary intelligence expertise. The policy caused resentment among regular army officers; MacArthur, for instance, refused to have OSS officers in his presence and even barred them from his theater of operations. Military professionals complained that OSS officers were "irreverent" and "flouted both authority and standard operating procedures." The complaint, the OSS officers responded, was laughable; intelligence-gathering was both intellectually demanding and dangerous and should not be hamstrung by "standard operating procedures." OSS operatives, as they proudly called themselves, bragged that not only was their organization "unorthodox," so were they. After all, their commander, Colonel William Donovan (later promoted to major general for his wartime exploits), was known as "Wild Bill" and had a penchant for providing "unconventional solutions" to strategic problems.

Despite his *nom de guerre*, Donovan had a practical grasp of how the military should use unconventional tactics to win conventional contests. The OSS became a reflection of his personal belief that the military's mission could be aided by his "all-encompassing concept" of psychological warfare, which included training in intelligence, propaganda, and special operations. It helped that Donovan was a close associate of Franklin Roosevelt's and could call on the president whenever the Army brass gave him too much trouble. In fact, as special warfare aficionados still argue, if it hadn't been for the regular Army and Navy officers, Donovan and the OSS could have done much more: the organization was consistently victimized by military procedures or, as one OSS historian said, by the "hesitant, skeptical, indifferent, and even antagonistic" views of top officers. After the war, these officers succeeded in undermining the OSS mission and America's unconventional forces, and its wartime spy network was dismantled.

The elimination of the OSS was the result of three separate but closely linked events: military demobilization, the efforts of the high command to bring it back under military control, and President Truman's mistrust of "cloak and dagger" tactics. None of this came as a surprise to Donovan or the OSS hierarchy, which was painfully aware of the adverse opinions and outright disdain of many military officers. *The War Report of the OSS*, the command's official history and analysis of its World War II mission, states that "an agency engaged in secret and unorthodox activities is peculiarly susceptible to difficulties in its relations with other agencies and departments of the government. Secrecy inevitably creates a psychological attitude of distrust and suspicion on the part of others. In many instances, this attitude is aggravated by the clash of established procedures and regulations which the performance of irregular and unorthodox activities often entails."

Truman's decision to dismantle the OSS left military intelligence operations in disarray. In much of occupied Germany, for example, commanders were left without essential information in the immediate postwar period, a disadvantage they attempted to remedy through civilian reconstruction experts. "I wouldn't say the situation was desperate," Lyman Lemnitzer, a major general serving on the Strategic Survey Committee, later admitted, "but there's no doubt, we were very short on intelligence officers. They were gone, just gone. We had to rebuild from the bottom up." With Soviet power growing and the division of Europe an accomplished fact, Truman was eventually forced to bury his mistrust, and, in 1947, he agreed to the creation of the Central Intelligence Agency, to coordinate the intelligence activities of government departments and to direct intelligence collection activities. Although the OSS was dead, fears of increased Soviet power meant that its mission wasn't; by the end of 1948, one third of all CIA employees were former OSS operatives, and clandestine activities were growing.

Despite its earlier views of the OSS, the Army continued to show an interest in intelligence activities, primarily through its reliance on psychological warfare experts from Eisenhower's European command staff. Though the military's Psychological Warfare Branch was undermanned and virtually isolated from command decisions immediately after the war, a number of officers continued to push for an increased military role in intelligence activities. This role was effectively ended in November 1947, however, when the three service secretaries of the Defense Department and the Secretary of State decided that covert activities should be handled by the State Department. Intelligence-gathering and analysis, on the other hand, would be the responsibility of the new CIA. This initial decision was reversed after Secretary of State George Marshall told Truman that he didn't want his depart-

ment associated with covert activities. The decision, Marshall told a
number of his colleagues, was strictly personal; like other former and
current officers of the regular Army, he harbored deep suspicions of
nonconventional warfare tactics and those who conducted them. The
services had a similar view: the JCS wanted oversight and knowledge
of the CIA's covert activities but didn't want to be responsible for running them.

In the summer of 1947, Truman acceded to Marshall by issuing
NSC-4 ("Coordination of Foreign Intelligence Activities"), giving the
State Department responsibility for monitoring foreign intelligence-
gathering activities, and NSC-4A, giving the CIA responsibility for
actually running covert activities. NSC-4 and 4A were followed by a
further expansion of CIA operations (NSC 10/2), to include responsibility for covert operations involving economic, political, and paramilitary warfare. Despite these new powers granted the CIA,
however, the military continued to conduct psychological warfare
training both before and during the Korean War, with little thought to
creating units with a special emphasis on intelligence-gathering to aid
its conventional arms. Apparently unconcerned with duplicating what
had already been decided in NSC-4 and NSC 10/2, the service chiefs set
about creating special units in each service, designed to support conventional combat operations.

By late 1947, the JCS was considering providing special operations
training at its service schools, a move that culminated in the publication of JCS 1807/1, a memorandum to the Secretary of Defense suggesting that the military establish a special agency "for conducting
guerrilla warfare." It dictated that such warfare be "supported under
policy direction of [the] NSC" and that "agencies for conducting guerrilla warfare can be established by adding to the CIA's special operations functions the responsibility for supporting foreign resistance
movements and by authorizing the Joint Chiefs of Staff to engage in
the conduct of such operations." The memo made it clear that the military was still divided on the use of special units. On the one hand,
military leaders still retained their distaste for the "unorthodox
methods" of Donovan's OSS; on the other, it was clear to a number of
strategists that special units would be essential in the struggle against
"communist subversion."

JCS 1807/1 is a confusing document, a vivid reflection of the Joint
Chiefs' attempt to grapple with the issue of covert activities and special warfare capabilities without really coming to terms with the fact
that such activities were not just unconventional, but well outside the
military's traditions. "The United States should provide itself with
the organization and means of supporting foreign resistance movements in guerrilla warfare," the JCS argued, but then curiously added
that "a separate guerrilla warfare school and corps should not be estab-

lished." For many, the JCS was simply mincing words; by showing an interest in "special warfare" techniques, the JCS meant "covert activities," whether it wanted to say so or not.

An Army memo to the Secretary of Defense on June 2, 1948, on the subject of covert operations added to the confusion. It complained that the CIA's reading of NSC 10/2, turning over control of covert *paramilitary* operations to the agency, "appear[s] to infringe upon the JCS responsibilities." The Army complained that the CIA believed that simply because it used military "operational methods" in conducting covert paramilitary operations, that made the CIA "the sole agency to conduct such operations." There is a certain abrupt quality to the memo, as if the JCS realized that its failure to come to terms with paramilitary operations and its continued distaste for the "cowboys" of the CIA had backfired. The military, the memo implied, had lost an important Cold War weapon and now wanted it back, or at least wanted a hand in what was already a fact. The nation's top officers seemed intent on staying away from military intelligence-gathering operations at the same time that they attempted to tie the military to an undefined (at least in 1948) hand in covert operations. Documents NSC-4, NSC 10/2, and JSC 1807/1 stand as contradictory signposts on the military's road to the establishment of special warfare units. The only thing the JCS could agree on was that the military needed to keep an eye on the CIA, not just to guard against overlapping operations (even though there weren't supposed to be any), but to provide assistance in covert operations training. With this in mind, in late 1949, the JCS set up the Joint Subsidiary Plans Division, to "coordinate detailed military plans" with other agencies of the government.

The JSPD's creation wasn't the only step the military took to make sure it was included in intelligence activities. Though the military, and the JCS in particular, remained ambivalent about covert and paramilitary operations, a small but dedicated core of combat officers kept alive the idea of forming units trained in special operations. One such officer was Brigadier General Robert A. McClure, a leading figure in "psyops" during World War II and later a director for Information Control for the U.S. Army in Germany.

McClure returned to Washington in 1950 and was immediately made chief of the Army's new Psychological Warfare Division as a result of his contact with like-minded military leaders who saw an increasing need for psychological and special warfare capabilities. One of McClure's first assignments was to find psyops experts from Army commands who had dispersed after the American victory. His second job was to provide basic psychological warfare materials ("training circulars, program schedules . . . and estimates of logistic requirements") for psychological warfare planning.

McClure convinced the Army high command to reactivate New

York's 301st Radio Broadcasting and Leaflet (RB&L) Group, which was soon retrained and shipped to Germany in November 1950 to serve in the Special Plans Branch of the European command. In addition, he established a seventeen-week course at Georgetown University, to train a new core of psychological warfare experts. But by far his most important move was convincing the JCS that special warfare units and other unconventional Army warfare functions should fall under his exclusive command in the new Special Operations Division. To make his point, McClure recruited a number of special operations veterans from World War II and used them to help sell top Army leaders "on the need for rapid organization of unconventional warfare capabilities."

The biggest hurdle was to convince key members of the JCS that special warfare unit training was an absolute necessity. McClure argued strenuously that such training should go forward at a school specifically designed to teach not just psychological warfare techniques but special operations tactics. Eventually he succeeded; by mid-1950 he had convinced the Army Deputy Chief of Staff for Operations and Administration, General Maxwell Taylor, of the need for special training. In fact, McClure's presentation was so convincing that Taylor wrote a memorandum favoring acceptance of the program, giving a hint of his own growing conviction that special warfare units could be used in unconventional environments. "In consultation with General McClure," Taylor wrote to the director of the Army's Organization and Training Division in March 1951, "please develop the Army responsibility for guerrilla and antiguerrilla warfare within the field of G-3 interests." This memo was the first official recognition of the value of special operations by any of the services. It also contained the seeds of the JCS's later emphasis on counterinsurgency, for it was Taylor who gave counterinsurgency its first impetus and its first claim to Army-wide acceptance.

There were still a number of obstacles to overcome before McClure's dream of the establishment of a special warfare school could become a reality, not the least of which was convincing the Army chief, Lawton Collins, that such activities would be strictly military and would use already active regular Army units. Collins suggested upgrading and expanding the Army's Ranger units, a program that McClure considered too traditional. His response to Collins was given by Lieutenant Colonel Russell W. Volckmann, one of his original psyops recruits and a chief organizer of the Philippine resistance to the Japanese occupation during the war. Volckmann briefed Collins on McClure's ideas during a special conference at Fort Benning, Georgia, at the end of 1951 and laid out a program for a new special warfare school, which would include training in guerrilla warfare, sabotage and subversion, evasion and escape, ranger "and commando-like operations," long-range and deep penetration reconnaissance tactics and missions, and psychological warfare. Volckmann said that special forces operations should not be left in the hands of a "civil agency" — a clear slap at the CIA — and that "delegation" of such training in the six areas was "unsound, dangerous, and unworkable."

The JCS approved McClure's plan in late March 1952; the headquarters of the new Psychological Warfare Center and its new 10th Special Forces Group was officially activated at Fort Bragg, North Carolina, on May 29. But the center languished, due primarily to the beginning of the Korean conflict as well as to the austere defense years under Eisenhower, and eventually McClure left the Army. According to Alfred H. Paddock, Jr., who has written the most comprehensive study of the Army's special warfare unit during its formative years, the blame for lack of interest in the unit during the Eisenhower years is placed on the Army, which was "hesitant and reluctant" and which "failed to cope with concepts and organizations of an unconventional nature." Paddock's conclusion is also a paradox: while McClure and his followers in the Army succeeded in establishing the foundation for the later emphasis on special warfare, they could not have done so without Taylor's help.

Ironically, while Taylor had found McClure's arguments compelling when he was a three-star general, he failed to become an advocate for unconventional warfare operations until the very end of his service on the JCS. Even then, as he later admitted, he failed to understand "the full significance of the threat of Wars of National Liberation" and how special paramilitary units could be used as a defense against subversion. While Taylor had ordered a reemphasis on special operations during his last year as Army chief of staff, most of the paramilitary training activities the JCS monitored were civic action programs that he had helped initiate while in command of the Eighth Army in Korea. These were hardly the kinds of military initiatives he later became identified with, counterinsurgency programs designed to defend Third World nations against subversion.

The last eighteen months of the Eisenhower administration were marked by a complete change in the JCS. Just two months before the election, Twining retired. His replacement was Army General Lyman Lemnitzer, the first Army chairman since Omar Bradley. In addition, General George Decker took over as Army chief, finally giving the JCS's most overlooked service a 2–2 vote in JCS decisions. Twining's legacy had been firmly established by the growth of SAC and his defense of massive retaliation. While Twining — who is now mentioned by JCS officers only in passing — did not have as significant an impact on the JCS as his two predecessors, Bradley and Radford, his quiet but constant advice to Eisenhower on JCS matters and American military capabilities had placed him in high esteem with the president.

JCS leadership of the Air Force and Navy was left in the able hands of General Thomas White and Admiral Arleigh "Thirty-Knot" Burke, both of whose terms bridged the Eisenhower-Kennedy transition. The stability of this leadership during Eisenhower's last years spurred both services to a last desperate attempt to increase the defense budget: both White and Burke pushed Eisenhower to increase budget outlays for technological improvements in the nation's defense in late 1959, expensive projects to which both services were committed. White was particularly interested in the development of a new class of strategic bomber, the B-70, and in upgrading and increasing the numbers of ICBMs. Burke wanted another aircraft carrier for the Navy, to comple-ment the development of its new nuclear-powered submarine.

Eisenhower vetoed both ideas and, in what had by then become a traditional response to JCS claims for increased budget appropria-tions, upped the ante: not only would he not approve increases in the defense budget, he actually wanted to withdraw troops from Europe because "we never intended to keep them there permanently." Eisen-hower also contended that the United States should leave the defense of the Mediterranean to the British and French. In time of war, he said, deployment of the American Navy in the Mediterranean would lead only to its inevitable destruction. When White ignored the president's wishes on the B-70 and testified, in early 1960, for congressional approval of the bomber, Eisenhower had his last fit of anger at JCS dis-loyalty, telling Secretary of Defense Thomas Gates that discipline had "been lost" in the military.

But Eisenhower's most even-tempered and poignant response to JCS demands came in the last months of his presidency, during an address at Washington's Gridiron Club. Describing his first day as president, Eisenhower told the hushed audience that some of his first visitors were members of the JCS, who wandered into the Oval Office even before he had begun to hang pictures or put down his own carpet. One by one, the chiefs told the president that while the armed forces needed more money, each of their services was particularly hard hit. When they finally left, Eisenhower said, he wandered to the window looking out on the South Lawn and said to himself, "My God, how did I get into this?"

The most significant change at the JCS occurred with comparatively little fanfare. On July 1, 1959, Maxwell Taylor retired, intent on fading into civilian life as one of the nation's most respected military leaders. As a young commander, he had led an elite division against the Ger-mans in Europe. As a commander of the Eighth Army in Korea, he had successfully presided over an increasingly unpopular and seemingly endless war. As Army chief of staff, he had privately incurred the anger of the president but succeeded in bringing about a change in the nation's tenuous massive retaliation strategy. At the end, he had even succeeded in convincing Eisenhower that a small increase in military appropriations was probably necessary.

On the eve of his retirement, Taylor was a wizened if highly respected spokesman for the military, a man whose honesty was above question and whose integrity had not been sullied by his opposition to the nation's "first hero" and popular president. Still, Taylor had been "soured" by his experience as chief of staff. In *Swords and Plowshares*, his autobiography, he reflected on his JCS years: "For the sword to be an effective instrument of foreign policy, its forgers must have some understanding of the purposes to which it may be put and, hence, know something of the future goals of national policy and the obstacles to them which may have to be resolved by military force." Taylor believed the reasons for his frustrations resulted from the inability of "civilian leaders" to provide "explicit guidance" on the threats to the national security. Eisenhower had not provided the guidance, nor had Secretary of Defense Wilson or his successor, Neil McElroy. It was with these frustrations gnawing at him that Taylor decided to "carry to the public the important issues which I had supported in the privacy of government." The result was *The Uncertain Trumpet*, an unvarnished and extremely popular attack on Eisenhower's New Look, which accused the outgoing president of sacrificing security concerns to the budget. Taylor advocated a strong buildup in conventional forces, a more balanced response to the Soviet threat, and a return to a conventional force strategy.

"If we are to assure that the disastrous big war never occurs," Taylor wrote, "we must have the means to deter or to win the small wars." In 1960, his book was viewed as a crucial argument for adopting the flexible response doctrine. It was not only widely read, it was also greatly admired, especially in circles where the discredited massive retaliation theory of the Eisenhower administration was in disrepute. In November 1960, Democratic leaders, fresh from their victory over Richard Nixon, embraced Taylor's book as the bible of their new, more creative, strategic philosophy.

For Kennedy, the new president, Taylor's critique not only made perfect sense, it elevated the retired JCS chief to new heights. Taylor wasn't one of those Eisenhower holdovers, like JCS Chairman Lemnitzer, he was a "sophisticated" general, a military man unlike any Kennedy had ever met. After all, when Taylor left the military, he became head of Lincoln Center and was seen at many of the major cultural events of New York society. Furthermore, the young president liked the retired general and valued his views. It wasn't surprising, then, that Kennedy decided to contact Taylor on April 21, 1961, three months after he had taken office and just two days after an invading force of Cuban exiles had been repulsed at the Bay of Pigs. Taylor later admitted that he believed Kennedy's call probably had something to do with the Cuban fiasco, but it wasn't until he was seated in the Oval Office the next day that he learned that Kennedy wanted him to head an investigation of what had gone wrong at the Bay of Pigs.

"He assured me," Taylor wrote in *Swords and Plowshares*, "that he was taking all the blame himself, but he must learn why he had failed." Kennedy's committee was composed of CIA head Allen Dulles, CNO Arleigh Burke, and Attorney General Robert Kennedy. Taylor set about his job by interviewing the administration's top decision-makers, including members of the JCS and its new chairman. Nevertheless, it wasn't until well after the publication of the Taylor Report that the truth about the Bay of Pigs operation began to emerge, though even now the events of that time remain murky. More ambiguous still is the role Taylor played.

Though military leaders didn't realize it at the time, Kennedy's appointment of Taylor to assess the Bay of Pigs failure ended the ten-year argument among the services and gave flexible response theorists a seal of presidential approval. While the nation would continue to rely on nuclear weaponry to deter large-scale Soviet aggression, both Kennedy and Taylor were convinced that the United States was on the verge of engaging the Soviets in a series of "twilight struggles," which would test America's willingness to engage in long and bitter wars for the hearts and minds of the world's underdeveloped countries. The massive retaliation–flexible response debate, which had characterized the Eisenhower years, had dictated the form of the nation's future war. The years of preparation, of quiet interlude, were ending. The test of conflict, the final judgment of the military that Taylor envisioned, was about to begin.

4

COUP D'ÉTAT

His [Maxwell Taylor's] general feeling was that air power
was not much good. I had trouble with that all the time I
was there. It would drive me practically crazy. He was a
little insulting about it, I thought. It took a lot of will
power to keep from letting him have one.

Curtis LeMay

FOR FOURTEEN YEARS, the JCS had been involved in a series of escalating battles with the nation's civilian leaders over a growing list of
military and foreign policy concerns: from intervention in Indochina
to the size and scope of the military budget, from the use of nuclear
weapons to the building of a supercarrier. These continual confrontations, however, had little to do with the military's belief in civilian
control: Truman's dismissal of MacArthur was endorsed, even abet-
ted, by the JCS, and while there was outspoken opposition to Eisenhower's austere military budgets, no one on the JCS doubted a
president's right to promote his own philosophy.

Instead, the confrontations of the 1950s were a reflection of the JCS's
inability to gain a voice in the inner councils of government, to be
involved in the actual formulation of foreign policy initiatives. In
large part, this inability was the direct result of the JCS's failure to
agree on common military policies. During the Truman years, the JCS
had been unable to resolve the service feud over the control of nuclear
weapons without publicly embarrassing the administration. Truman
was forced to castigate the chiefs for their lack of "a united front to
these questions." This same lack of unanimity occurred when Truman
insisted on maintaining a modest military budget during a period of
increasing Soviet aggression, which sparked a restrained, but visible,
JCS protest.

The most critical clashes, however, occurred during the Eisenhower

years. At first the JCS welcomed Eisenhower's election, believing that
if anyone would willingly accept military advice, it would almost certainly be one of America's most renowned former commanders. But
the chiefs were to be bitterly disappointed: not only did the president
consistently reject the views of those supporting flexible response, his
actions reflected only a ritual endorsement of massive retaliation. The
JCS's belated reaction to Eisenhower's challenge to military doctrine
in the name of fiscal austerity was the result of not only its unwillingness to believe that a former war hero would adopt an avowed antimilitary stance, but also its failure to draft a coherent military view that
took into account each service's opposition. By the end of the Eisenhower administration, the JCS was virtually paralyzed by its internal
disagreements.

The JCS's inability to influence the military and foreign policy positions of two presidents in succession presented it with a profound
dilemma. Because the 1947 act had not given the JCS an official role in
determining foreign policy (an apparently purposeful move on the
part of Congress), it was not politically tied to any administration.
While the intent of Congress was to make certain the JCS could give
objective military advice (regardless of who was president), the effect
of the act was to cut the JCS out of the foreign policy decision-making
process altogether.

The practical impact of the legislation was even more pernicious:
Congress unintentionally made certain that JCS advice, even on
purely military matters, would be virtually ignored. After all, as Eisenhower himself pointed out, how could the JCS present military solutions to foreign policy problems with which it had no familiarity?

Eisenhower answered that question himself, in 1958, by promoting a
series of reforms that would have actually given the JCS a greater voice
in running the military. By stripping away its purely administrative
duties, Eisenhower believed he could end service competition and promote military unification. Although there were no guarantees that
these reforms would have given the JCS greater participation in shap-
ing policy, they would have meant that the military would speak with
one voice. Eisenhower's implicit response to military complaints that
their advice was ignored was elegant: it wasn't that the military was
ignored, he said, it was that each service was ignored; the military was
unable to voice a unified position.

Ironically, the failure of Eisenhower's reform proposals made
his criticisms all the more valid. The individual services could not
only not agree on just what kind of military the nation should have,
they even disagreed over whether it needed reform. Once again, the
civilian-military confrontation over policy was transformed into a
debate on civilian control of the military. By unifying the three serv-

ices, reform critics argued, the principle of civilian control might be fatally undermined — a position that, for purely service reasons, actually gained the support of a large number of JCS officers.

The failure of Eisenhower's reform proposals meant that when Kennedy became president, he inherited a military establishment that was a disorganized confederation of ossified service bureaucracies locked in a debilitating competition with each other for more money, bigger weapons, and greater influence. The JCS remained a committee of military advisers that not only had little influence on major foreign policy decisions but had little influence in determining important military questions.

Despite this clear breakdown in the nation's foreign policy structure, the JCS attributed the civilian-military conflicts of the 1950s to simple differences in military and political philosophies. The solution was not to reform the system, as Eisenhower had supposed, but to make it work, to build a stronger relationship between military and civilian leaders. One way to do this, the JCS thought, was to forge a personal link between military leaders and the White House, then to buttress that relationship by making the JCS's military advice indispensable in the formulation of foreign policy.

For this reason, Kennedy's election had a profound impact on the JCS: for only the third time since World War II, it had an opportunity to work with an entirely new set of civilian officials. Not only would there be a new White House foreign policy team, a new set of Defense officials would be appointed. The new president's call to Maxwell Taylor and his appointment as the head of a task force investigating the Bay of Pigs incident gave the JCS its opportunity to find out whether better military-civilian relations would actually result in enhanced JCS influence.

The Kennedy administration's effort to overthrow Fidel Castro by supporting an invasion of Cuban exiles, now known as the Bay of Pigs incident, was originally conceived during Eisenhower's last year by the covert action branch of the CIA. The program actually began in January 1960, when the CIA station chief in Caracas, an old OSS hand known as Jake Engler,* was given the job of developing a detailed operation to create an upheaval in Cuba that could be carried out without overt American involvement. Engler's plan contained all the elements of a classic CIA covert operation: sophisticated paramilitary

---

* "Engler" had been involved in the successful operation to replace the left-leaning government of Guatemala in 1954 with the pro-American Guatemalan leader Castillo Armas. For good measure, Engler decided to promote a plot to kill Castro. The plot was dropped when it became apparent that many of the leaders around Castro were, in the words of CNO Burke, "even worse than Castro."

training units, special infiltration squads, and logistic and military aid
from surreptitious Cuban support groups. Perhaps most important,
the operation was self-contained: it would be monitored by the CIA
without interference from the JCS. Engler even put together a small
CIA team to run the project and in March 1960 reported on his progress through channels to CIA director Allen Dulles.

Engler and his small staff of covert operations experts recommended
that the United States train and deploy Cuban exiles against the Castro government, sparking an internal uprising that would lead to
Castro's downfall. By using Cuban nationals, Engler felt, the United
States could legitimately claim that the anti-Castro movement was
indigenous, and at the same time deny any involvement with it —
what is still called "plausible deniability" — should the invasion fail.
In mid-March, Dulles broadened Engler's plan and presented it to the
Washington Special Group as "A Program of Covert Action Against
the Castro Regime." The Washington Special Group, also known as
the 5412 Committee (from NSC 5412/2), was the most important covert
action committee in Washington and was responsible for reviewing
covert action programs before passing them on to the NSC and the
president. After a long discussion about the need to get rid of Castro,
the committee approved the Dulles-Engler operation and passed it on.
While the NSC didn't give the plan its official imprimatur, it clearly
approved of measures that would replace the Castro regime with a
pro-American government. Finally, Dulles went off to see Eisenhower
to garner what he was convinced would be final approval for the
operation.

But although Eisenhower showed an interest, he told Dulles he
couldn't approve the plan until he saw a list of its components, pointing out that such details were important in the success of two previous
covert operations, in Iran and Guatemala. In fact, Eisenhower admitted to Dulles, he just didn't think the plan would work, a reflection of
his belief that Castro was too entrenched and had taken careful steps
to solidify his support among the Cuban people. Nonetheless, Eisenhower said, he was willing to give it a try if Dulles could come up with
answers to a number of key questions: Who was going to carry out the
plan, when would it be conducted, what were the chances it would
succeed, and, predictably, how much would it cost?

While Dulles was surprised by the president's initial skepticism, he
was reassured when he recalled that Eisenhower's final approval of the
Iran and Guatemala operations had also been preceded by doubts and
lengthy discussions. Eisenhower had been excruciatingly careful in
mapping out the details for the earlier operations, fearful that the
United States would eventually be identified as the responsible party
— something that he wanted to make doubly sure didn't happen in

any operation against Cuba. Eisenhower's instructions to Dulles forced him to rewrite his program, outlining each step from materials provided by CIA covert operations experts.

With a final plan completed just a few days after Dulles's initial meeting with Eisenhower, the CIA director retraced his steps: he not only had to go back to Eisenhower, he had to resubmit the plan to the 5412 Committee and then to the NSC. But it wasn't surprising that everything went smoothly this second time around — despite Eisenhower's characteristic caution — especially considering the administration's continuing alienation from the new Castro government and the belief that Cuba now posed a threat to the national security. Finally, on March 10, 1960, the NSC considered Dulles's proposal and, while not stating explicitly that it would approve it, said that some kind of covert action against Castro was plainly necessary. Four days later, the 5412 Committee reconsidered the same plan and approved it, and three days later, Eisenhower himself signed off on it.*

From the outset, the CIA used military assets to train its Cuba Brigade, including National Guard units and shipping and arms proprietaries — a necessity considering that the operation was to be "eyes only"; that is, that even in the higher reaches of the American government few knew what was going on or why. During the last months of the Eisenhower administration, CIA operatives began to recruit and train Cuban exiles for the invasion, garnered the willingness of Alabama and Arkansas authorities to recruit American pilots as trainers for Cuban flyers, and purchased freighters to carry arms, ammunition, and men onto the shores of Cuba. The CIA's far-reaching recruiting program would not have gone unnoticed in the 1980s, when the press and official Washington have been particularly sensitive to such news, but in the early 1960s the government was apparently more insulated from the eyes of prying reporters and even from the unwanted questions of people who didn't have a need to know, with the result that covert operations were truly covert. Inevitably, however, word of the agency's operation came to the attention of a number of top government officials, including the chairman of the JCS, General Lyman Lemnitzer.

Lemnitzer was a lean and soft-spoken Army professional who spent most of his career arguing that the United States "should forget all this third world stuff and concentrate on Europe." In essence, he was the

---

* Dulles apparently resubmitted his plan of covert action against Cuba in reverse order, taking the plan to the NSC before he took it to the 5412 Committee. Apparently the method of resubmission was not as important as the fact of it. In addition, NSC officials remained uncertain whether the Dulles plan was the *final* plan; members of the group said later that they believed it was a draft plan. Oddly, it seems that most NSC members approved the plan and then promptly forgot about it.

military's leading "NATO-ist," a term used to describe officers who believe that the defense of Western Europe is central in defending America's security interests, that the greatest threat to the United States is from Soviet conventional arms, and that the next war will be fought on the battleground of the last. In this sense, Lemnitzer had a far different outlook from Maxwell Taylor's, though he made it to the top of the Army in much the same way as the former Army chief.

Lemnitzer was not only a fighter but also a politician, as adept at delicate diplomatic maneuvers as he was at plotting combat strategy. As a result, he was promoted swiftly up the military ladder and rewarded by important command assignments in the waning days of World War II. In 1945, for example, he was chosen by the American high command to communicate with Soviet forces in Czechoslovakia, making certain that American bombers didn't overshoot German targets, unloading their bombs on unsuspecting Soviet soldiers. Lemnitzer's assignment was a great compliment to his diplomatic abilities, especially because the Soviet General Staff refused to reveal the location of its units to anyone, even the Americans. That Lemnitzer not only succeeded in heading off a potential disaster but actually befriended a number of Soviet generals — in the end convincing them of America's good faith — made his promotion to flag rank, and then to JCS chairman, a virtual certainty.

Lemnitzer first discovered that the CIA was actually going forward with a Cuban operation from the Navy, whose own network of intelligence professionals had been running across CIA operatives mysteriously looking for ships up and down America's East Coast in late 1960. This intelligence was duly reported up the chain of command, until it reached the commander in chief of the Atlantic fleet (CINCLANT), Admiral Robert Dennison. When Dennison heard the story, he immediately sent his own officers on a search of Atlantic ports to gain more information and then decided to call the JCS chairman. Dennison was breathless: "Lem, I want to tell you a story."

But Lemnitzer, who had been hearing rumors that the CIA was broadening its original anti-Castro plan since just after the March 10, 1960, NSC meeting, which considered the Dulles report, didn't want to talk to Dennison. The chairman believed that the NSC meeting was the end of the plan, at least as far as he was concerned. Indeed, if Eisenhower hadn't informed the JCS that the plan was going forward, let alone telling them the details, then there was probably a good reason for it. In any event, Lemnitzer was convinced that the CIA's final operation — whatever it was — would probably fail. But none of this impressed Dennison, who protested Lemnitzer's lack of concern: if there was something going on involving Cuba that the JCS chairman didn't know, then it was his duty to find out. Dennison was adamant; a major foreign policy operation that involved the military was being launched by the administration without the cooperation, or even the knowledge, of the nation's military leaders. He finally convinced Lemnitzer to "nose around" and discover what he could.

But Lemnitzer didn't exactly "nose around": as a signal to the CIA that he knew what was going on, he dispatched an assistant to the agency with orders that Dennison should be briefed; after all, the Cuban operation would take place in Dennison's area of command. But within weeks Lemnitzer's briefing request was sidetracked, as were his innumerable subsequent demands that the agency provide information on what CIA operatives were doing in America's shipyards — a series of events that left Lemnitzer frustrated and even more puzzled. As it turned out, Lemnitzer wasn't the only one who had questions.

Admiral Arleigh Burke, the JCS's Chief of Naval Operations, had also been picking up reports that the CIA was planning a large-scale operation against Castro and that the JCS wasn't being included. Sensing that the CIA's plan had grown too fast and gotten too big, Burke sent out his own spies to spy on the CIA spies. Present at the original NSC meeting that had considered the plan, Burke had been the most outspoken advocate of overthrowing Castro and had signed on to the general NSC prescription for "some kind of operation" against him. In late 1960, though, Burke wasn't certain that the final Dulles plan should go forward, especially considering that a new president was about to be inaugurated. In addition, like Lemnitzer, the CNO also harbored doubts that such an operation could work, doubts that he shared with his JCS colleagues, including Air Force Chief of Staff Thomas White and Army Chief of Staff George H. Decker.

Following Kennedy's inauguration, JCS skepticism about the Cuban operation was causing consternation among the Little Chiefs, who were pushing the JCS chairman to warn Kennedy that the CIA's covert operation might not work and that, at the very least, the JCS should review the plan to see if it was feasible. Finally, Lemnitzer ordered his staff to conduct an internal study of anti-Cuban covert operations in order to detail what operations could and *could not* overthrow Castro. To run the study, Lemnitzer chose Brigadier General David W. Gray, chief of the Joint Subsidiary Activities Division ("the ash and trash" section, so called because its unused classified papers were routinely discarded in "burn bags"), the office the JCS had established back in 1948 to keep an eye on the CIA.*

* Lemnitzer told Gray to produce a report that would have the status of a "White Paper," that is, a study that would not be part of the flimsy, buff, green, red-striped variety. By keeping the Gray report out of the normal JCS system, Lemnitzer was hoping to keep it secret, perhaps because he knew the report would not give a favorable assessment of any attempt to overthrow Castro.

Lemnitzer's choice of Gray was fortunate. He was a meticulous and compulsive worker who kept detailed notes on every meeting and was considered one of the Army's leading experts on covert operations. That Gray was thorough was almost beyond question: Pentagon lore had it that reading his notes of a meeting often took longer than the meeting itself. In the case of the planned covert operation against Castro, however, Gray had only the bare outline of the initial CIA plan, as approved by the NSC, and was forced to work from scratch. Nevertheless, after only two weeks, Gray presented an analysis of the operation that came to the same conclusion as Lemnitzer and Burke had: any anti-Castro action, especially the kind of covert operation hinted at by the CIA in its NSC presentation, was bound to fail unless it had the full support of the Cuban people or, at the very least, was backed by the promise of American military intervention. In other words, while Gray was firmly convinced that Castro was anti-American, he believed that if the United States wanted to overthrow Castro, it had to deploy American troops.

In essence Gray, like Lemnitzer, was part of a by now well-worn and oft-stated military tradition: if the United States wasn't willing to go all the way in its attempt to overthrow Castro, it would be better not to go at all. Moreover, Gray concluded, the very fact that the United States wasn't willing to go all the way was clear evidence that the administration's heart wasn't in the operation to begin with — the most convincing reason of all, Gray felt, just to drop the whole thing.

On January 22, 1961, two days after Kennedy took office, Lemnitzer ordered Gray to present his conclusion and his own pessimistic feelings about covert operations to the new administration at an NSC meeting at the White House. Gray followed Lemnitzer's direction — he had little choice — but not gladly; he felt his remarks wouldn't be welcomed by the NSC, for the new Kennedy team considered itself distinctly more activist than its tentative predecessor. Indeed, the general might have had a crystal ball, for after the moment of discomforting silence that followed his thirty-minute briefing, it was clear that the NSC not only doubted his abilities, it doubted his loyalty to the new administration's more aggressive anticommunist policies. The Kennedy team told Gray that not only was the CIA operation already well under way, everyone was committed to seeing it succeed.

But Gray's briefing raised enough doubts among Kennedy insiders that, six days later, the president directed Lemnitzer to evaluate the CIA plan once again, but this time by conducting a study in cooperation with the agency itself, by learning everything he could from the CIA's operatives who were responsible for carrying it out. Lemnitzer turned the job over to his director of the JCS, Army General Earle

Wheeler, who in turn told Gray to take four paramilitary and intelligence experts, one from each service, over to the CIA for a full briefing. According to later reports, Wheeler decided to put the JCS's assessment into Gray's able hands once again because he knew Gray was not only the CIA's most loyal supporter in JCS circles, he was also its most outspoken critic. On the one hand, Wheeler had often heard Gray argue that the CIA could be an effective adjunct to U.S. military operations, especially when the agency put its mind to gathering intelligence, something it was rather good at. On the other hand, in true regular military style, Gray had often criticized the agency's penchant for cloak-and-dagger operations that were better left in the hands of professional military officers. Most important, however, as head of the JCS's ash and trash section, Gray knew more about intelligence operations than any other JCS staff officer, which not only made him the best man for the job, it made him (at least in Wheeler's eyes) the only man for the job. For the JCS, Gray's assessment was a clear test of the CIA's credibility: if the agency could sell its plan to the military's most detail-minded general, it would probably work; if not, the plan was probably flawed and should be terminated. In fact, Gray's assignment was seen not only as a litmus test of the CIA's ability to run a purely paramilitary operation with minimal official military support, it was seen as an assessment of the credibility of covert operations themselves, which the JCS had wrestled with since at least 1948.

Unfortunately, Gray's meeting with the CIA's planners was closer to a scene from a James Bond novel than to an official briefing. Not only was it held outside agency headquarters at the CIA's insistence, the six operatives who met with the general wouldn't tell him their real names (Gray later said that they were so secretive, he probably wouldn't have believed them in any case). In addition, the operatives sent told Gray that they didn't know the exact details of the plan, only its general outline, adding that they had purposely decided not to bring any briefing papers to the meeting for fear of a security breach. That the CIA insisted on being so surreptitious, even melodramatic, irritated the military officers accompanying Gray; they were already insulted by needless JCS instructions emphasizing that what they learned was to be kept absolutely secret. It was clear to Gray and his fellow officers that what they feared the most, that the CIA would become the major player in a drama of its own making, had already happened. But Gray had an even more frightening theory: the CIA didn't show up with any briefing books or plans because there weren't any; no one had ever bothered to put one together from the original draft Dulles had proposed to Eisenhower.

But despite his disquieting meeting, Gray went back to the Pentagon and wrote out the plan that he gathered from what the CIA agents had said. The result was a 125-page paper that concluded that the center-piece of the CIA plan — an invasion of the island using anti-Castro Cuban exiles — could succeed *if* (and Gray thought it was a pretty big if) it had air power, and *if* (again, a pretty big if) it had naval supporting fire, and then only *if* (the biggest if of all) there was an internal upris-ing against Castro that coincided with the landing of the Cuba Brigade.

The volcanic Wheeler, whose stressful job as director of the JCS had shortened his notoriously short temper, was dumfounded when he saw Gray's report. Called to the general's office, Gray stood uncom-fortably before Wheeler's desk at the Pentagon in mid-January as the head-shaking director leafed through the voluminous paper. He stared at Gray, his mouth a tight line of anger, his dark eyes flashing irrita-tion. What were the numbers? Wheeler asked after a long, uncomfort-able silence.

Gray said he wasn't sure and waited for Wheeler to erupt.

What were the chances of success? Wheeler asked. His tone was harsh and edged with sarcasm.

Gray couldn't say. By now, he knew that Wheeler was fighting to control his boiling irritation.

Well, were the chances good?

Gray was silent.

Was the chance of success "fair"? Wheeler asked, and this time there was a tinge of exasperation in his voice.

"All right," Gray said finally, nodding. The chance the CIA's para-military operation would actually succeed was "fair."

By this time Wheeler, who knew and liked Gray despite the lack of details he seemed to have come up with, was at the end of his fuse. He asked Gray what he meant by "fair."

Gray shrugged his shoulders and remained silent.

"Thirty in favor and seventy against?" Wheeler finally asked.

"Yes," Gray answered.

After this meeting, Gray presented his findings to the JCS on Jan-uary 31 at a special session in the tank. The JCS ordered that an official paper on the operation, incorporating Gray's report, be sent to the president — a paper that the JCS decided was too classified to be com-mitted to the red-striped "official" file. The JCS report, a lukewarm endorsement of the CIA plan that included many of Gray's ifs, was sent to Kennedy on February 3 as JCSM-57-61. JCS Chairman Lem-nitzer, Gray — in fact, the entire JCS — were "on board" the more activist Kennedy team — but just barely.

Obviously, the chiefs knew that JCSM-57-61 was hardly the kind of endorsement the president wanted. Because of the lack of detail, the paper noted that its favorable appraisal of the operation's success was based on "second- and third-hand reports" — in other words, on

Gray's interview with six shady CIA men who didn't bother to bring along briefing papers to a meeting designed to make a final evaluation of the invasion plan. Under the circumstances, then, the attitude of the JCS, and especially of Lemnitzer, was hardly constructive, which would later be noted by Kennedy's political allies. Indeed, there is much to be said for this critical view. The JCS never really believed the plan would work, though there's little evidence that its skepticism reflected its hopes that the operation would actually fail.

General David Shoup, the commandant of the Marine Corps, told aides, for example, that he hoped the CIA's plan would work despite its enormous problems, thus saving the JCS untold time and trouble in coming up with a straightforward military plan that would be both overt and violent. Yet Shoup was particularly disturbed that the CIA was going to launch an operation with such little prospect of success, and he openly scoffed at the CIA's military expertise in JCS meetings. He told his colleagues that Kennedy's approval of the CIA's plan was a slap at the military, evidence that "we are wasting our time" in setting up divisions, running an Air Force and Navy, that it could all be done by recruiting mercenaries and depending on "popular uprisings."

Shoup is still considered an oddball by many of the Marines who served with him and an embarrassment to gung-ho Marine officers, for whom patriotism is almost a religion. Shoup was patriotic, but he disdained patriotic talk, especially among those in the Kennedy administration who exhibited what JCS staff members were beginning to call the can-do attitude. In fact, he was a military pragmatist, telling the JCS staff that the United States couldn't do everything, everywhere. A Medal of Honor recipient for heroism at Tarawa, Shoup studied and wrote poetry, recited quips and British literary anecdotes, counseled soldiers to "read the classics," and during the Vietnam War said that United States involvement was evidence of "imperialism."* "That man was crazy," one former JCS officer says. "Absolutely crazy. But brilliant." Shoup was also a stickler for the law, reciting passages of the Constitution to his more militant colleagues.

Lemnitzer remembers Shoup as "a real thinker" and laughs when he recalls how Shoup presented opposing points of view. "He was very sarcastic," Lemnitzer says now, "but a good soldier. He couldn't stand stupidity." And for Shoup the CIA plan was the height of stupidity.[†]

---

* Shoup's outspoken opposition to the war made him extremely unpopular among his fellow officers, views that were exacerbated when Shoup's quotes started appearing on antiwar posters, at least a few of which appeared surreptitiously on Pentagon walls during the height of the conflict.

† The most critical member of the JCS was Arleigh Burke, the most outspoken in his opposition to Castro and the most vocal proponent of attempts to overthrow him during NSC meetings. In fact, according to reporter Peter Wyden, Burke thought the CIA's work was "weak" and "sloppy."

CNO Burke agreed with Shoup but refused to express his doubts outside the tank. A critic of the CIA, Burke told his staff that the agency
had no faith in military operations and wanted to conduct the Bay of
Pigs operation alone in order to teach the military a lesson, something
that Burke told one officer he was personally looking forward to. As
far as he was concerned, there was nothing to dislike about the CIA's
plan because Gray's interview with the CIA's planners showed clearly
that there *was* no plan.

Burke, Lemnitzer, Shoup, and to a lesser extent Thomas White considered launching a last-minute effort to warn the new president that
the CIA's operation wouldn't work, that it might prove a major
embarrassment to the nation. But, in the end, they let the Gray report
stand: after all, if Kennedy couldn't identify a backhanded endorsement when he saw one, there wasn't anything the JCS could do
anyway — the CIA had not even formulated the plan with JCS
approval, a fact well known to the president. That the JCS had not
been included in the initial planning is central to understanding why it
refused to articulate its opposition at the last minute: the plan could
succeed or fail on its own, with the responsibility laid squarely at the
feet of the CIA. If the operation turned out to be a disaster, as the JCS
believed it would, it would stand as an incontrovertible argument for
conducting future operations with the cooperation of the American
high command. The JCS also believed it was simply too late to make a
stand against the CIA or the Bay of Pigs operation: the Cuba Brigade
was set to hit the beaches inland from the Zapata Peninsula on the
south side of the island in April.

In the early morning hours of Monday, April 17, 1961, the CIA's brigade
of Cuban exiles hit the beach at the Bay of Pigs. This invasion force,
ferried to Cuba by the freighters the CIA had purchased in 1960, was
escorted by seven U.S. destroyers and the aircraft carrier *Essex*, but no
American soldiers went ashore. According to the plan, the Cuban
nationals would need little U.S. help because guerrilla groups in the
hills beyond the landing zone would confuse Castro's forces by igniting a popular uprising. In addition, specially trained Cuban para-
troopers would blow up the bridges leading from Castro's military
camps to the beaches, giving the exiles time to gain a foothold on the
island. Most important, the invasion would come as a complete surprise, catching the communists well back from the beaches, tying
them down with the uprising planned for Cuba's urban areas.

For a time after the initial landings it looked as if the invasion would
succeed: Castro's response was sluggish, and opposition was sporadic.
But within twenty-four hours all of that had changed: not only did the
exiles fail to destroy the small Cuban Air Force, their own control of

the air over the beaches became tenuous — a factor that hampered, and eventually doomed, the entire operation. But even more disappointing was the failure of the Cuban people to support the invasion; Castro's own forces remained strong, confident, and well disciplined. By the second day the exiles' chance for surprise, for control of the air, and for gaining the support of the people was slipping away. And by Wednesday morning, the third day, it was clear the operation was failing.

One of the first indications that things weren't going well was the failure of support aircraft to make planned drops of ammunition to the Cubans holding the beachhead on the first day of the invasion, a failure that Gray had warned of in his January 22 NSC paper. But the most significant misstep during the entire invasion was the failure of the exiles to knock out Castro's jets before the Cuba Brigade hit the beach. In fact, Cuban brigade commanders were under the impression that the United States had committed itself to supporting a number of important air strikes, launched from Nicaragua against Cuban installations, that would destroy the network of roads leading to the beaches, as well as give the attackers a chance to move inland once they had secured their landing zones. At the insistence of NSC planners, the air raids were to look as if they had come from the beaches themselves — any sign that the raids were supported by the United States would ruin the operation.

But to the JCS it looked as if the administration was splitting hairs. What good would it do for the United States to be able to deny having had anything to do with the invasion, CNO Burke asked one JCS staff member, if the invasion failed? Regardless, there had to be air strikes in order for the invasion to succeed, no matter how much the United States suffered in the court of world opinion. Once again, Gray was at the center of the storm; he was dispatched by the JCS to monitor the operation and make certain that the necessary air support was available. Gray had argued for the need for air supremacy and, just before the invasion, had vainly pleaded with Kennedy aides that he be allowed to give the president a full military briefing on the issue. Gray wanted to make sure that the president was committed to supporting the forces on the beach with air strikes, a tactic he thought essential if the Cuba Brigade was to have even a slim chance of victory. Unfortunately, Gray's plea for a general discussion was ignored just when it was most needed. As a result, within a few hours of the Monday morning landing, when fears were rampant that the United States would come under scathing criticism at the U.N., Secretary of State Dean Rusk told the CIA he had decided to cancel the air strikes.

At CIA headquarters, Marine Colonel Jack Hawkins, the one officer grudgingly dispatched by the JCS to help the CIA train the Cubans in amphibious operations, couldn't believe Rusk's order and pleaded with CIA officers to persuade Rusk to reconsider. But arguments went unheeded; Rusk had talked to the president twice by telephone, the officers said, and Kennedy had agreed with him. In desperation, Hawkins called Marine Commandant Shoup at his quarters in downtown Washington. Close to tears, Hawkins said that the cancellation of the air strikes meant that the operation would almost certainly fail; the commandant should intervene to get the air strikes reordered. But he wouldn't do it, telling Hawkins that such intervention was out of his hands, that things had "gone too far."

Gray's response was much the same. "There goes your operation," he told Jake Engler by telephone after learning of Rusk's decision. At the Pentagon, JCS Director Wheeler called Lemnitzer at his official residence on Generals' Row at Fort Myer. Lemnitzer's reaction wasn't nearly as low-key as Gray's, perhaps because the JCS chairman had never believed, as Gray did, that Kennedy would do everything necessary to make sure that the operation succeeded. According to reporter Peter Wyden, when Wheeler said that Kennedy had decided the invasion would succeed without air strikes and that the United States had to be sensitive to international pressure, Lemnitzer flew into an uncharacteristic rage, shouting that the president's decision was "absolutely reprehensible, almost criminal." But, like Shoup, he knew that it was too late, that Kennedy wouldn't change his mind.

Late on Tuesday evening, with the situation at the Bay of Pigs getting worse by the hour, Kennedy decided to call his first crisis management meeting. This rare late-night meeting in the Oval Office brought together the administration's top officials: Vice President Johnson, Defense Secretary McNamara, Secretary of State Rusk, NSC Director Rostow, as well as JCS Chairman Lemnitzer and CNO Burke. It was the first time that any members of the JCS were able to fully articulate their doubts about the Cuban plan. Indeed, while Lemnitzer and Burke had attended NSC meetings on the operation, their unofficial status had made them hesitant to speak out. Then, too, the NSC's response to the Gray report on covert operations had had a chilling effect on the JCS's efforts to warn the administration about the CIA's plan. In the more relaxed and unofficial atmosphere of the Oval Office, Lemnitzer and Burke were less fearful about their status as Eisenhower holdovers and more certain than ever that Kennedy's can-do philosophy had its drawbacks. Still, the two JCS members made it clear that they were willing to go all out to save the CIA's plan, even if it meant deploying American troops.

The meeting began with a report on the dire situation at the Bay of Pigs, a sober assessment that apparently convinced the president the plan had failed. With that completed, Kennedy said he wanted advice

Above: General George C. Marshall and Admiral William Leahy prepare to meet with the British Chiefs of Staff Committee, 1943. *Department of Defense*

Left: The JCS's first days: CNO Louis Denfeld precedes Chairman Omar Bradley and Air Force Chief Hoyt Vandenberg en route to a European conference, 1948. *National Archives*

John F. Kennedy poses with the JCS during his first week in office: Shoup, White, Lemnitzer, Kennedy, Burke, Decker. *National Archives*

Left: Kennedy and "the Inevitable General," William C. Westmoreland, at West Point. *U.S. Army*
Right: Maxwell Taylor (*right*) greets tennis player General "Big" Minh during a tour of Vietnam. Ambassador Henry Cabot Lodge is behind Taylor. *U.S. Army*

Defense Secretary Robert McNamara with the new JCS chairman, Maxwell Taylor. *National Archives*

Above: Taylor's chiefs in the tank: Earle Wheeler, Curtis LeMay, Taylor, George Anderson, David Shoup. *National Archives*

Left: John Paul Vann (*center*) with American advisers in Vietnam, 1963. *U.S. Army*

Left: Planning the bombing: Lyndon Johnson with Curtis LeMay and Earle Wheeler at his Texas ranch, late 1964. *White House Photo*
Right: General Harold Johnson during his trip to South Vietnam, February 1965. *National Archives*

After the Ia Drang: Admiral John McCain, JCS Chairman Wheeler, Robert McNamara, and General Harry Kinnard (*pointing*) inspect captured NVA arms, December 1965. *Department of Defense*

Left: General Earle Wheeler answers a question on war strategy, 1966.
National Archives
Right: Earle Wheeler is greeted by William Westmoreland and Ellsworth Bunker at Tan Son Nhut, February 1968. *Department of Defense*

LBJ's surprise speaker: Creighton Abrams argues for the Vietnamization of the war during a meeting with the wise men, March 1968.
National Archives

Secretary of Defense Clark
Clifford. *Department of Defense*

Creighton Abrams and Admiral Elmo Zumwalt, Jr., in South Vietnam,
1969. *National Archives*

on how to handle the rising tide of international indignation and the clear sense among the diplomatic corps that, despite American denials, the invasion was supported by the United States. Kennedy's remarkable question took everyone by surprise, with the result that his request was pointedly ignored. Rostow argued that the Cuba Brigade, now pinned by Castro forces to a tiny beachhead, could still be saved, but only if the president would agree to the release of jet tactical fighter support from the aircraft carrier *Essex*. Burke quickly agreed, pointing out that the United States could not afford to have the operation fail, that since most of the international community was now certain that the United States was supporting the invasion anyway, the president should go all the way and ensure that it succeeded. Burke told Kennedy that he should release the fighters aboard the *Essex*, noting that the exiles themselves were convinced that such support could turn the tide of battle.

The president, taken aback by this seemingly unanimous view, shook his head firmly, saying he would not approve the use of the Navy fighters. Undeterred, Burke renewed the argument in stronger tones, recommending that the president approve the dispatch of a naval destroyer to provide supporting fire to the brigade on the beach. When Kennedy shook his head again, Burke made his last suggestion, that unmarked fighters from the *Essex* could run missions over the beach to gain intelligence on the plight of the brigade. Perhaps, Burke said, pushing his privilege as a presidential adviser to the limit, the sight of unmarked fighters would improve the brigade's morale. By this time Kennedy was obviously angry. "Burke, I don't want the United States involved in this," he snapped. Burke snapped back: "Hell, Mr. President, but we *are* involved." Kennedy, glowering at the rebellious CNO — who had once again earned his sobriquet for headlong attack — stuck by his guns: the United States would not intervene, and the decision was final.

By the next day, it was clear the invasion had failed. The Cubans were stranded on the beaches, and it turned out that much of the early resistance had broken down: ammunition for the stranded brigade had not been delivered, the competence of Castro's fighters (and their high morale) was beginning to take its toll, and there had been no uprising among the island's populace. At the Pentagon, Lemnitzer wasn't surprised, especially considering the lack of military support for the brigade. He sensed, as he said later, that Kennedy "never really had his heart in it — you could tell from the very beginning. He had a 'go' date and he postponed it and had another round of meetings, and then he set a new date." General Gray was even more disenchanted. He admired the president, but viewed his failure to call in supporting air strikes the one decision that sealed their fate. Burke told aides that the

Cuban invasion was "a fiasco," the best evidence possible that military operations should be kept in military hands.

At the White House, Kennedy's views were quite different, swinging from puzzlement over the assurances of the normally conservative Allen Dulles that the operation would succeed to anger and even bitterness over the JCS's failure to warn him earlier that it couldn't succeed without full military support. Kennedy told his top aides that there were weak spots in his administration and that the Bay of Pigs incident proved that one of them was the JCS. In particular, he was angry that in the aftermath of the invasion, the JCS had made sure to stay out of the line of fire and was virtually unmentioned in national news reports. But during a 10:00 A.M. press conference at the State Department on April 21, the Friday after the invasion, Kennedy refused to point fingers, taking full responsibility for the incident: "I am the responsible officer of the government."

But Kennedy wanted to make certain that the Bay of Pigs catastrophe would be the last of his presidency (which was only ninety days old). What he needed, he told aides, was first-rate advice from a high-ranking and respected officer, advice that, in light of the Bay of Pigs, he doubted he could receive from the JCS. With that, he picked up the phone to call Maxwell Taylor. The call came as a surprise to the retired Army chief, who had settled into New York's Lincoln Center, "learning," as he wrote, "another new job and acquiring some experience in the ways of architects, construction engineers and opera buffs." Nevertheless, Taylor realized in the week before the Bay of Pigs attack "that something out of the ordinary was going on in Cuba" and that a "blow up" might occur at any moment. Like the rest of the nation, he was startled by the news that an invasion of Cuban exiles had failed, that the failure was being blamed on the new president, and that a covert military operation in support of the anti-Castro exiles had, in all likelihood, been bungled. In essence, while Taylor might have been surprised by Kennedy's call on the afternoon of April 21, he jumped at the chance to once again serve in government.

The president briefed Taylor on the Bay of Pigs operation the day after his State Department press conference. Kennedy's biographers say that the president spoke in calm, almost neutral tones, saying that while he wouldn't engage in any recriminations over the failure, he wanted to ensure that his top foreign policy officers understood what had gone wrong and what needed to be done to make certain such a fiasco didn't happen again. Taylor described the meeting in stark terms, likening it to those days in 1944 just after the German counteroffensive that shattered the 101st Airborne's position in the Argonne forest: "I sensed an air which I had known in my military past — that of a command post that had been overrun by the enemy. There were

the same glazed eyes, subdued voices, and slow speech that I remembered observing in commanders routed at the Battle of the Bulge or
recovering from the shock of their first action. In this instance, the latter was a more accurate analogy because this new administration had,
indeed, engaged in its first bloody action and was learning the sting of
defeat."*

Taylor's job was fairly simple, Kennedy said, and would only take
him away from Lincoln Center for two months, three at the most. The
charter that the president gave to the Cuba Study Group (which
included Taylor, Allen Dulles, Burke, and Robert Kennedy) was
explicit. "It is apparent that we need to take a close look at all our
practices and program in the areas of military and paramilitary, guerrilla and anti-guerrilla activities which fall short of outright war. I
believe we need to strengthen our work in this area," Kennedy said.
He pledged that the resources of his administration and the cooperation of each of its agencies would be made available to Taylor, adding
that "in the end what I want is your own report, drawing from past
experience, to chart a path towards the future."

Taylor later remarked on the "interesting" subject of Kennedy's
mandate, including "the almost passing mention of the Bay of Pigs."
Kennedy wanted more than a critique of the failed operation, he
wanted a plan for reinvigorating antiguerrilla military activities based
on the failure of the Cuba invasion. Put another way, Kennedy didn't
need to be told what had gone wrong at the Bay of Pigs: the invasion
had failed because the United States had not made a commitment to
training for the kind of paramilitary operations that would have made
it succeed. Kennedy thought the military had been intransigent, symbolized by the JCS's failure to warn him that they had little faith in the
CIA's plan. At the end of his meeting with Taylor, Kennedy once again
voiced his puzzlement over the Bay of Pigs failure. "All his advisers
had assured him that it was the right thing to do and that it had a good
chance of success," Taylor said. "Why had they all been wrong? What
was the cause of failure? He assured me that he was not looking for a
scapegoat."

The sixty-year-old general whom Kennedy chose to "take a close
look" at America's guerrilla and antiguerrilla activities is not only one
of the American military's greatest heroes but also one of its greatest

---

* Taylor should probably be forgiven this obvious hyperbole. While numerous histories of the period confirm that Kennedy and his advisers were shocked by the failure, it's
clear that Kennedy took it with his characteristic, almost cold calm. Also, Taylor didn't
have firsthand knowledge of how commanders of the 101st looked during the first days of
the Battle of the Bulge, since he was in Washington at the time.

enigmas. While Maxwell Davenport Taylor's seemingly effortless rise through the upper ranks of the U.S. Army is a model of what it takes to become a general, it is also a symbol of the necessary and unmerciful shift in command requirements that took place after World War II. America's conflict with Japan and Germany required commanders who were not only fighters but who could grasp an entirely new set of military tactics — strategic bombing, armored warfare, airborne combat, and amphibious assault. The postwar period, on the other hand, rewarded officers who mastered a new set of political tactics — compromise, accountability, patience, and tenacity. Taylor was one of those few officers who succeeded in making the adjustment, whose talents in peacetime were as great as those he had mastered in war.

A 1922 graduate of West Point, Taylor became a student at the Command and General Staff College while he was only a lieutenant, an assignment that is still considered a necessity for any ambitious officer. On the eve of World War II, Taylor won a spot on Army Chief of Staff George Marshall's planning team in Washington, a plum assignment that brought him under the watchful eye of the one man who could make or break his career. Taylor also had some unexpected assignments: he taught modern languages (French and Spanish) at West Point and was posted to Tokyo, probably his most important promotion, where he was tutored in Japanese and Chinese for two years. While in the Far East, he was given the enviable task of observing the Japanese Imperial Army's vicious conquest of Manchuria. In all of this he proved to be exceptionally proficient, and he caught the eye of the immensely knowledgeable General Joseph Stilwell in China and became friendly with Matthew Ridgway, who had also made it into Marshall's "little black book" of names marked for higher command.

There is something uncommon, even unique, in Taylor's career. In essence, Taylor was able to balance his desire for traditional assignments with his ability to identify, and be identified *with*, an innovative new tactic. This ability, to forecast changes in tactics and win assignments to take advantage of those changes, is a key to promotion. Those Navy officers of the 1930s who had enough vision to see that the aircraft carrier would become the maritime weapon of the future, for instance, were promoted more quickly than their classmates on battleships and were rewarded with the highest combat commands. Those Army officers with the same vision — the appreciation that America's next war would likely be an air war — could see that assignment to airborne units held the best chance for fast promotion. Ridgway could see this, as could Taylor, who made certain not only that his steady promotions coincided with the rise of "the airborne mafia," but also that he was one of its most outspoken defenders. His defense of airborne tactics was so well known, in fact, that when he served as superintendent of West Point just after World War II, the cadets began calling their school "the 101 Ranch," a compliment to Taylor's sure-handed management as well as to his ability to ensure that his combat colleagues were given important positions at the school.

In retrospect, Taylor made all the right moves, serving in a valued, even critical, command during the war and taking steps that would brand him as an intellectual in an Army of combat officers, a background that would serve him well when the military needed managers more than fighters. In one sense, he had been extremely lucky — lucky that he had met Ridgway, lucky that he won assignment to Marshall's staff, lucky to have graduated from West Point when MacArthur was its superintendent. For all of this, Taylor was a talented, though hardly brilliant, officer whose success at straddling two command eras — from wartime fighter to peacetime manager — set him off from his colleagues.

Taylor also had the foresight to make sure that his political beliefs were as well balanced as his career: while he criticized Eisenhower's defense budgets in the 1950s, he guarded against allowing his ringing condemnations to reach the public. In fact, he had eschewed any kind of notoriety on the subject, reserving his public criticism of Eisenhower for his own retirement and his memoir, *The Uncertain Trumpet*. Nevertheless, Taylor's critique of massive retaliation was clearly argued and extremely effective, so effective, in fact, that many believed that the Army chief, like Ridgway, had left the service in disgust over Eisenhower's philosophy.

But there was nothing transparently sinister in Taylor's promotion to the Army's top spot or even in his recall to Washington in the aftermath of the Bay of Pigs. Of all the four-star officers who served the nation after World War II, Taylor was certainly one of the most qualified and experienced to consult the young president. His ascent had been the result of personal ambition — a trait he shared with thousands of World War II commanders — as well as nearly forty years of command success. Taylor had steadied his lost troops in the darkness of Normandy on D-Day, then steadied them again on the Cotentin Peninsula and again in the race across France to the Rhine. In fact, this "steadiness" is what Taylor became known for, it was the adjective used again and again by friends and colleagues in describing what his superiors, his equals, and his troops found most compelling in his character. In later years, it was this steadiness, "even aplomb," as one colleague put it, that was his most prized trait.

In the final analysis, it was this steadiness, combined with a disquieting ability to make the best of a bad situation, that made Taylor the nation's most respected military adviser throughout the 1960s. In essence, he was the first of the new generals, men who had been schooled by warfare but also *schooled*, who were as comfortable in Washington's political circles as on the battlefield. Taylor and many of his colleagues had gained invaluable experience as commanders in the wars of the future, in the limited wars that Taylor — and Ridgway and Gavin — were certain would be continually ignited between Soviet proxies and the United States as the Cold War heated up. With this in mind, Taylor was the first person Kennedy called when it was clear the American attempt to overthrow Castro had failed and that an assessment was in order.

The Cuba Study Group interviewed more than fifty witnesses who had had a major role in conducting, participating in, and giving advice about the Cuba Brigade's invasion, including American trainers in the camps in Central America, as well as the director of the CIA, the Secretary of State, CIA planners who had put together the operation, and the JCS. Taylor's classified report was duly presented to Kennedy on June 13, 1961, not quite two months from the day the Cuba Brigade had landed at the Bay of Pigs.

In his memoir, Taylor listed four deficiencies in the operation, including "inadequacy" of air support, "failure" of the brigade to break into guerrilla units, "the responsibility of the Joint Chiefs of Staff for the military deficiencies," and "contradictions in the understandings and attitudes of senior officials involved in the operation." But in the end, despite Taylor's admission that the JCS never saw the CIA's final plan until April 15 and believed the operation could not succeed without a "popular uprising," it was the JCS that came in for the harshest criticism. "Piecing all the evidence together," Taylor later said, "we concluded that whatever reservations the Chiefs had about the plan, about the propriety of having the CIA continue to conduct a military operation of growing complexity, or about the erosion of military requirements by political considerations, they never expressed their concern to the President in such a way as to consider seriously a cancellation of the enterprise or the alternative of backing it up with U.S. forces."

He went on to note that the civilian officials he interviewed felt the chiefs "had been insufficiently forthright in expressing their reservations." It was a startling and, considering what history says of the JCS's actual doubts, an almost unbelievable conclusion. For perhaps the only time in history, a presidential task force concluded that a military operation had failed because it had *not* been opposed. "Our group," Taylor said later, "concluded that whatever their handicaps — and they were many — the Chiefs had certainly given the impression to their colleagues of having approved the plan and of having confidence in its feasibility." This criticism was an inadvertent reflec-

tion of the JCS's actual role in formulating a major foreign policy operation: not only wasn't the JCS informed of the operation, it remained a
passive outsider during its most formative stages.

The report stung Kennedy, who told Taylor he felt "let down" by
the advice he had failed to receive from the JCS. The report, Taylor
said in his autobiography, "hung like a cloud" over the White House
until May 27, 1961, when Kennedy ran into Taylor outside the West
Wing. The president said that he was on his way to the Pentagon for a
meeting with the JCS in order to, as Taylor later described it, "clear
things up." Kennedy stood facing Taylor in the open air of a Washington spring day with the shining white of the president's official residence gleaming behind him in the late morning sun.

Did Taylor have any recommendations before the meeting? Kennedy asked. "By pure luck," Taylor reported, "I had a working paper
of my own in my pocket which bore precisely on the subject on his
mind — the responsibilities of the Chiefs to the President in all
aspects of the Cold War." Taylor's description suggests that his good
fortune at having run into the president at precisely the moment he
was going to visit the JCS might have been more than coincidence, a
fact that Taylor himself noted by gauging the president's reaction: "I
think that he was a little shaken and perhaps made a little suspicious
by the readiness with which I produced my paper, but in any case he
took it, rushed off to the Pentagon, and, as I learned later, used it
extensively in his discussion with the Chiefs." If Kennedy was "a little
shaken," the JCS was downright hostile. Although Lemnitzer has
refused to comment on the meeting, a JCS officer close to him says
that Lemnitzer told him the JCS greeted Kennedy's lecture, that military advice should be unfiltered, with "icy silence."

The JCS had a similar view of Taylor's critique of its role in the Bay
of Pigs incident. While Arleigh Burke had served on the Cuba Study
Group, the final report was, as Kennedy directed, Taylor's own, and
while there wasn't much that the JCS necessarily disagreed with, the
Taylor memo on JCS-civilian relations angered members of the JCS
and its staff. In fact, after Kennedy's meeting with the chiefs, JCS staff
officers called Taylor an outsider, someone who not only criticized the
American high command after the fact but who was unfamiliar with
the JCS's machinations in this particular case. JCS staff members also
said that Taylor's own relations with civilian leaders, particularly during the Eisenhower years, were hardly a talisman of openness. Indeed,
from May 27, 1961, to this day, the military's opinion of Taylor has
remained open to question.

Taylor is still hailed as "America's greatest General," "a brilliant
tactician," and a "selfless commander" by officers who served with
him. Veterans of the 101st Airborne Division in World War II

remember him as "an easy soldier. One of us. You know, the kind of guy who worried whether you were hungry or cold." Even among four-star commanders, Taylor is remembered for his energy and imposing stature. For many, he is the man who "made them [civilian leaders] listen." But the compliments are almost always preambles to periods of confused silence, an almost palpable sense that behind all the fine words there is a feeling that Taylor's ambitions drove him more than his good sense. "Just who did Maxwell Taylor serve?" one general asked bitterly. "Just who did he think he was serving by writing that [Bay of Pigs] report on the chiefs? Did he really believe he was helping the country?"

Many officers have interpreted Taylor's report as an attempt by him to push his own views on flexible response with Kennedy. Moreover, many Army officers believe that Taylor wanted to recast the role of the JCS, making it an important participant in the conduct of U.S. foreign policy. Since the JCS then played only an advisory role, its influence was almost solely dependent on whether the president relied on its advice, a fact mentioned by Taylor in defense of his critique of the JCS under Lemnitzer. "With the opportunity to observe the problems of a President at closer range," Taylor said, "I have come to understand the importance of an intimate, easy relationship, born of friendship and mutual regard, between the President and the Chiefs. It is particularly important in the case of the Chairman, who works more closely with the President and Secretary of Defense than do the service chiefs."

Taylor's conclusion is all but explicitly stated: Lemnitzer was not as close to Kennedy as Taylor, did not have the easy relationship the president had developed with the former Army chief, and did not work as closely with Kennedy as McNamara. For Taylor, then, the main vulnerability for Kennedy — as he had shown in his report — was that he did not have a JCS chairman who agreed with his program. But the only test of the conclusion is to ask the chairman himself, Lyman Lemnitzer, whether Taylor's reflections have any basis in fact. Lemnitzer is currently the unofficial lobbyist for NATO in the Pentagon. Lemnitzer is highly respected, even loved. His office, just off the Pentagon's "NATO corridor," is served by one secretary and a military aide. The general writes letters, attends briefings, gives lectures, and at every opportunity pushes the military to show more concern for what he calls America's "primary allies." On the walls of his office are photographs of the American presidents he has known and served. Even at eighty-eight he shows only the most obvious signs of age. And, like most retired commanders in their seventies and eighties, he feigns deafness, especially when it is clear that he has heard a pointed but distasteful question.

Lemnitzer is hesitant to describe his views of his old friend Maxwell Taylor. When asked about their relationship he launches into a monologue on a totally different subject. Does he resent Taylor's investigation and view of the chiefs' role in the Bay of Pigs operation? The former chairman smiles, passing off the question. "Taylor?" He swivels in his chair and gazes out onto the Pentagon courtyard, filling the room with silence. "I didn't even know where General Taylor was at the time," he says after a long pause. He lurches his chair forward, leaning out over his desk. "Out of retirement, yes. I had no problems with Taylor, not that I know of. For the simple fact that the Joint Chiefs of Staff were not involved. *We were not involved.* It was not our operation. I can't believe it when people lay it on the Joint Chiefs of Staff. They can't understand that we couldn't have a major role to play." He is animated, remembering when he returned for a Pentagon ceremony only to find that the Bay of Pigs operation was going forward despite the JCS's reservations. What does it mean when the CIA becomes involved in military operations? "That they have to be small operations," Lemnitzer answers. "And that they have to . . . have to . . ." He swivels again in his chair and shakes his head. "Maxwell Taylor," he says. "He wasn't even here."

In fact, Taylor's role as Kennedy's most important military adviser started from the moment he returned to Washington to assess the Cuban operation. Kennedy often turned to him for advice on nonmilitary matters and included him in discussions on world events. Taylor became one of the few Kennedy confidants outside the president's circle of longtime friends. After he had completed his Bay of Pigs report, Taylor was offered the job as head of the CIA.

But he told Kennedy he was unsuited for the job, arguing that he did not have a broad background in intelligence operations and was unfamiliar with the inner workings of the CIA. He was more comfortable in uniform, he said, and his expertise was in military, not intelligence, fields. Nevertheless, Kennedy wanted to retain Taylor in some capacity and had a series of discussions with the general on the subject. Finally, with no job suited exactly to his specific needs or experience, the president decided to name Taylor his chief military representative, or MILREP, in which position he finally became an official member of the Kennedy administration.

Taylor was sensitive to claims that he was using his growing personal friendship with Kennedy to promote his own career, so he took care to consult with Lemnitzer on the subject. Apparently the JCS chairman had no objections to Taylor's new position. "Fortunately, General Lemnitzer . . . was a friend since cadet days at West Point," Taylor wrote. "I told him that I did not view my responsibilities as competitive with the Chiefs and did not intend to serve as a White House roadblock to their recommendations. . . . In turn, Lemnitzer promised to do all he could to prevent anyone from driving a wedge between us, a trend already visible in some of the press comment on my appointment." With Lemnitzer's assurances in hand, Taylor began to define a role he knew was unprecedented in the history of military-civilian relations. In effect, he was a military adviser outside the chain of command, somewhere between the JCS and the president. Indeed, Taylor's one sure area of expertise undermined his promise to Lemnitzer that he wouldn't stand between the JCS and the president.

In an administration that prided itself on its new vision for the nation, Taylor was a useful addition, proof that a Democratic president appreciated military prowess and depended on military advice. Taylor was, in the words of David Halberstam, "a *good* general, a romantic," the "cultured war hero." Halberstam also called him "more than a little vain," a characteristic that came out in his long disquisitions on military theory, tactics, and history and his own experience as a combat general. In fact, Taylor could be downright tiresome, though many of Kennedy's aides, at least initially, reveled in his pithy anecdotes.

Painfully aware that Taylor's new position could cause friction between the JCS and the White House as well as between Taylor and McNamara, Kennedy decided that his MILREP could be most useful studying and sizing up America's ability to respond militarily in a number of international hot spots. Taylor was therefore sent on a number of junkets, first to Indochina to report on the twin insurgencies in Laos and South Vietnam, then to Europe to report on NATO readiness. He went to South Vietnam for most of October 1961 at the head of a team of high-level American officials that included Walt Rostow. Taylor and Rostow had been given specific instructions, which emphasized that Taylor should find out what "course of action . . . our Government might take at this juncture to avoid a further deterioration in the situation in South Vietnam and eventually to contain and eliminate the threat to its independence."

Taylor's first stop in monsoon-ridden Vietnam was Saigon, where he had a number of discussions with South Vietnam's premier, Ngo Dinh Diem. Describing him as secretive and "somnolent," Taylor commented that he made his points "by soft-voiced indirection" — an obvious indication that Taylor not only didn't like Diem, he didn't trust him. On the other hand, his visit with South Vietnamese Major General Duong Van "Big" Minh gave him confidence in South Vietnam's military leadership. Minh was not only "friendly and congenial," he later wrote, he had "the additional credit point of being a formidable tennis player." During his long discussions with Minh,

Taylor was treated to complaints of Diem's corruption, the general unhappiness of the South Vietnamese officer corps, and the need for American aid.

Taylor returned to Washington with a full report for the president on the worsening situation in Southeast Asia. In essence, the Taylor-Rostow report was the first of its kind of the thousands that would be written over the next fifteen years; it was the first step in committing American resources to the salvation of the Diem government. Its final recommendations reflected Taylor's concern that South Vietnam's military was only "60 to 70 percent" combat-effective and that the Diem government was badly divided, its intelligence poor, its hold on the nation's villages in serious doubt. Despite this somber judgment and the fact that Taylor obviously found Minh a more honest judge of South Vietnam's potential troubles than the country's leader, Taylor didn't recommend Diem's replacement or the deployment of American troops, but suggested that the United States send a "logistical task force" to South Vietnam to bolster its army's morale. In addition, Taylor and Rostow emphasized the country's need for increased economic aid to help repair the ravages of the worst flooding on the Mekong River in more than a century.

On November 6, 1961, Taylor met with Defense Secretary McNamara and Secretary of State Rusk to review his report. McNamara and Rusk were cordial, agreeing with Taylor's views and with his recommendation on the Diem government and his more significant call for assigning a logistical task force to the country. But within a week, both officials changed their minds. On November 7, 1961, McNamara and the JCS filed an official memorandum with the president outlining U.S. goals in Indochina that diverged from Taylor's views. In fact, the JCS and McNamara decided to go beyond Taylor's call for a task force and asked the president to increase the number of advisers in South Vietnam. The following week, Rusk also had second thoughts about Taylor's recommendations, saying simply that he agreed with the JCS's views and not mentioning Taylor's at all.

The initial American policy for Vietnam was thereby set, instituted under John Kennedy's signature as a National Security Action Memorandum on November 15, 1961. Accordingly, the United States increased its advisory role to the South Vietnamese forces, including the eventual deployment of 16,000 military advisers to train the Army of the Republic of Vietnam. Both McNamara and Rusk considered the deployment of a logistical task force as too chancy; by increasing its advisers, the United States would still be committed to helping the South Vietnamese fight the Vietcong themselves. No one overlooked the implication of Taylor's recommendation: by sending a logistical task force (or any kind of task force at all), the United States would be deploying regular, rifle-toting American troops, something neither McNamara nor Rusk was yet willing to do.

Frustrated by McNamara and Rusk's silent but effective disagreement, Taylor flew off to Europe, where Kennedy was hoping his appearance would help allay the growing controversy among NATO partners over the U.S. commitment to use tactical nuclear weaponry in the case of war. But again, Taylor was unable to use his position as Kennedy's closest military adviser to advantage. He was unable to assure the West Germans that the United States was wedded to a "forward defense" (the Germans feared the United States would give ground in any Soviet conventional attack), and he was unable to convince NATO to increase its spending on conventional arms. As a compromise, Taylor recommended that Kennedy allow France access to nuclear weaponry through a multinational NATO force. In addition, Taylor told Kennedy that the United States should push its NATO allies to undertake their own assessment of Western Europe's conventional capabilities. As earlier, Taylor's recommendations were sidetracked by McNamara and Rusk. But this time neither secretary was courteous in forwarding his disagreement, and Taylor's advice was unceremoniously vetoed. By now, Taylor was getting the message. "The experience . . . reminded me of the impotence of a presidential adviser in tilting with policies originating in and supported by the bureaucratic power bases in State and Defense," he admitted.

In fact, Taylor's ill-defined role as the president's MILREP was proving to be as great a frustration to him as his position as Army chief of staff under Eisenhower. Even Kennedy noted his unhappiness and began a series of discussions with him in order to find out what new position he thought he could fill. Interestingly, at the time that Taylor's frustrations were coming to a head, General Lauris Norstad, the Supreme Allied Commander in Europe (SACEUR), planned to retire due to differences over the administration's European missile policy. In addition, Lemnitzer was ending his first term as JCS chairman, a term marked by growing disagreements with Kennedy and McNamara.

With Norstad's job opening in Europe, Kennedy offered Taylor the appointment as SACEUR in early July 1962. The president thought it was the perfect assignment and hoped that Taylor's experience as a commander on the Continent and his recommendations on NATO would dampen the growing divisions among America's European allies. Surprisingly, Taylor turned Kennedy down, saying that he had spent enough time overseas "and wished to have the opportunity to discharge neglected responsibilities to my family at home." Military officers still do not believe this episode, shaking their heads in wonder at Taylor's "nerve" in turning down his commander in chief. Their feelings are clear: an officer does not turn down a suggestion from the president of the United States — unless, of course, that officer is Maxwell Taylor.

On July 19, 1962, Kennedy acceded to Taylor's wishes and announced that he was transferring Lemnitzer to the post of SACEUR. Taylor was brought out of retirement and appointed as the new chairman of the JCS. Earle Wheeler, the no-nonsense JCS director, who had presided over the JCS staff's darkest days after the Bay of Pigs, was named to succeed the retiring George Decker as the Army chief of staff.

The new JCS lineup was a mix of old Cold Warriors and New Frontier managers. Joining Taylor were Marine Commandant David Shoup, CNO George W. Anderson, Jr. (who had taken over for Arleigh Burke in August 1961), Air Force General Curtis LeMay, whose long climb to the top of his service had taken nearly a full decade, and the new Army chief, Earle Wheeler, who had never served in a combat command. Taylor's principal assistant was General Andrew Goodpaster, who had been Eisenhower's military assistant (a position in no way comparable to that of Taylor as MILREP; the last thing Eisenhower needed was military advice) before taking command of a division in Europe. Goodpaster and Taylor worked well together, primarily because they both believed that the JCS needed an overhaul.

Goodpaster remembers Taylor as one of the first real JCS reformers, a chairman who took initiatives that he couldn't have taken as Army chief during the Eisenhower years or as Kennedy's military representative. Indeed, Taylor had long been an advocate of command reform. From the moment he took over as chairman, in fact, he began to put some of his ideas into practice, streamlining JCS procedures and cutting down on the paperwork. While he later criticized Ridgway, the former Army chief, as "a great centralizer," it was Taylor who took the first initiatives to cut away JCS red tape, thereby diminishing service battles over the budget and weapons programs. "The 'flimsy, buff, green' sequence hampered operations," Goodpaster said during an interview on the period, "so we decided to not allow rewriting of papers [and] just appended disagreements." It was a major, if unofficial, reworking of the system, and it put most of the staff's decision-making privileges directly into the chairman's hands.

But most of Taylor's reforms were started outside the JCS system, including one that the general had been planning since his earlier stint on the JCS. Frustrated by the Army's lack of command initiative during Korea, Taylor pushed Wheeler to approve a new conventional warfare doctrine using helicopters as mobile assault vehicles for the quick insertion of combat troops in counterinsurgency wars. Taylor, who had first proposed the idea when he was Kennedy's military representative, believed the JCS was moving too slowly. But Wheeler didn't need Taylor's prodding; he was already being pressured to approve the creation of new airmobile divisions by a number of top Army officers, including one who was becoming a definite nuisance.

Since the mid-1950s, General Hamilton H. Howze had been arguing for the adoption of a new training and doctrine system organized around just the system Taylor advocated. In fact, while Taylor was fighting budget battles with Eisenhower, Howze almost single-handedly fashioned the air assault concept by scraping together helicopters and leftover troops for special training sessions. Short and wiry, Howze was an anomaly, an officer who climbed the ladder even though he didn't, and wouldn't, get along with the Army high command. One colleague put it succinctly: "Hamilton Howze was a royal pain in the ass. He was sending these memos to McNamara and Wheeler would get hold of them and he'd say, 'Now what the hell does this guy think he's doing?' So there was some animosity there, going to the point of just letting Howze hang out there with some of his ideas."

Howze "hung out there" until mid-1962, pushing abrasively for air-mobility, for organizing all Army units around the helicopter, and denigrating those who thought the helicopter was too vulnerable to ground fire to be useful in combat. Put simply, top Army commanders not only disliked Howze, they didn't think his idea would work. But Taylor, using his influence with the Kennedy administration and seeing the jungles of Vietnam as a potential American battlefield, told Wheeler and the rest of the Army to give Howze's idea a chance. Predictably, Taylor, Wheeler, and Howze ran into immediate opposition from the Air Force chief. In early 1962, LeMay told his fellow chiefs that he didn't believe the Army should have any helicopters: the Army walked on land, the Navy sailed on the sea, and the Air Force owned the air.

The Army–Air Force showdown came in mid-1962 when Taylor suggested that the 101st Airborne commander and Howze disciple, Harry Kinnard, defend airmobility before a special meeting of the JCS at Fort Benning, Georgia. Kinnard stood in the well of an amphitheater with his pointer and sandboards and explained how airmobility would "extend the envelope" of combat missions for the armed forces in the new "wars of national liberation."

"The real question in counterinsurgency," Kinnard said, "is, How do you get those guys in there? You just can't walk into a jungle in the Third World. And we knew Vietnam was just around the corner.

"I can remember the front row of Air Force generals taking copious notes," Kinnard says. "They were just waiting to jump all over me. At the end of my talk they really went after me. I looked over at the generals in the Army and they were looking at their hands. I could tell right away that if we were going to win the battle to get helicopters, I was going to have to carry the ball." Kinnard won the debate when an Air Force officer scoffed at the idea that helicopters could control a larger battle area than a jet in combat situations. Kinnard pulled rank, stating that more than just the role of the helicopter was at issue, his personal reputation was "on the line." Kinnard said he knew about battle, he'd "been in some." It was a purposeful, almost unseemly reference to his combat experience as an intelligence officer with the surrounded 101st Airborne at Bastogne, waiting for the Army Air Force to break through the impenetrable winter skies. If helicopters had been there, Kinnard all but said, the Army might have saved itself a lot of trouble and quite a few lives. The row of Army officers smiled. Taylor had picked the right man for the briefing; Kinnard had silenced the Air Force.

Kinnard's lecture decided the issue of airmobility for the JCS: the Army could use helicopters for battlefield maneuvers while the Air Force, at LeMay's insistence, would retain its mission of close-in tactical air support. The official decision to train a number of combat divisions in airmobile tactics was made in February 1963 by JCS Chairman Taylor, who gave Kinnard command of the Army's 11th Air Assault Division. Kinnard had followed Taylor by becoming identified as a leading proponent of a new tactical doctrine, a sure sign that he was on his way to the top of the Army. At Taylor's express order, he moved quickly to establish his new command and prove that he could make work on the battlefield what had worked on the sandboard at Fort Benning. Kinnard immediately culled his division for the unit's top NCOs for special training. In the words of a 11th Air trooper, "They just took some of us out in a field and put us on helicopters and flew us around. When the helicopters landed, we jumped out. They made us do it again. And again. Then they started firing shells at us. We did it day and night. Then we went back and trained the rest of the division. That son-of-a-bitch never slept." But the deployment of airmobile divisions was only one of Taylor's innovations.

Following Taylor's 1952 commitment to General Robert A. McClure, which established a special forces center, the Army's support of counterinsurgency programs had languished, the natural result of Eisenhower's budget program and the JCS's missile and nuclear weapons competition. Now, with Taylor as JCS chairman, Kennedy's dream of building up a sizable special forces contingent was well within reach. Working from recommendations he had made as Kennedy's MILREP, Taylor decided to upgrade special forces training immediately, making sure to accede to the president's wishes that counterinsurgency experts be rotated through South Vietnam and that Army colonels eligible for flag rank spend some time in Indochina.

These policies were controversial in the Army, though few officers carried enough clout to disagree openly with the JCS chairman's new counterinsurgency program. In some circles, especially among those with experience in Indochina, this new emphasis on guerrilla training was greeted with open and unusually vocal criticism. Some counter-insurgency officers believed that deploying special forces units to Vietnam was a half measure, that Kennedy, Taylor, and Vietnam commander Paul Harkins were wrong in believing that South Vietnam's political problems could be solved by exotic military strategies carried out by beret-clad patriots. But just as this debate about America's role in Southeast Asia was beginning to heat up, the JCS was faced with a new crisis, which taxed each member's ability to get along with the new chairman. On October 14, 1962, a U-2 spy plane spotted a Soviet missile on the ground in Cuba; two days later, Taylor was summoned to the White House for a series of meetings on what came to be known as the Cuban Missile Crisis.

When Taylor went to the White House for the first executive commit-tee (EXCOMM) meeting on the deployment of Soviet nuclear missiles in Cuba, he had been JCS chairman for just barely two months. While he had wielded considerable influence in the Kennedy administration since the Bay of Pigs incident, skepticism about his abilities (and his apparent responsibility for the transfer of Lemnitzer) was put aside in the hope that as JCS chairman, he could forge a new military-civilian consensus on foreign policy. Even Curtis LeMay was optimistic that Taylor's well-traveled access in Kennedy's inner circle would mean a change in JCS fortunes. But within days of the White House meeting of the EXCOMM, the high-level group designated by Kennedy to advise him during the missile crisis, it became apparent that JCS views were an afterthought for the president — and for Taylor as well. In fact, the Cuban Missile Crisis was decisive in setting the JCS mem-bers, even Earle Wheeler, against their own chairman in a series of remarkable incidents that ultimately characterized Taylor's tenure as head of the military.

Beginning on October 16, 1962, Kennedy met with the EXCOMM biweekly to plot a strategy leading to the removal of Soviet nuclear missiles from Cuba. Taylor, the only military man on the committee, was designated to represent the views of the other chiefs, who were informed of the crisis within hours of the first meeting. Put simply, the JCS meetings paralleled Taylor's White House meetings in order to keep the JCS up to date on the administration's plans as well as to per-mit the chiefs to hand out orders for the deployment of American forces. Each JCS member was given full operational command author-ity by the chairman, with control over his service to make certain that

Kennedy's wishes were carried out: Earle Wheeler monitored U.S. Army troop deployments, George Anderson communicated directly with CINCLANT Admiral Robert Dennison, and Curtis LeMay passed instructions on to SAC commander Thomas Power.* In each case, the system worked according to design, an acquittal of the JCS's power to command (not just influence) the military establishment.

Paradoxically, however, the work of the JCS was marred by a number of internal disputes that centered on Taylor's personality and the growing skepticism that, as a Kennedy partisan, Taylor was adequately representing the different views of each service. It was clear to JCS staff members, in particular, that Taylor enjoyed his power in the administration. "I have just come from a secret meeting with the president," Taylor reportedly said at the outset of one JCS meeting, a remark that made Wheeler wince. In addition, Taylor's method of polling the JCS members irked LeMay, who thought that Taylor's habit of asking JCS opinions and then giving his own (which just happened to agree with the current thinking of Kennedy's foreign policy managers) was clear evidence that Taylor was setting himself up as the sole spokesman for the military point of view. Moreover, by October 17 — only the third full day of the crisis — it was clear that he was becoming more reticent in reporting EXCOMM actions to the military commanders.

The JCS's quickly growing mistrust of Taylor was soon brought into the open. During a meeting on October 18, JCS members demanded that Taylor schedule a meeting with Kennedy within twenty-four hours to make sure that their position, which was by no means unanimous, could be presented to him in person. Clearly, as far as the JCS was concerned, Taylor was abusing his role as a JCS messenger. But Taylor claimed he diligently reported his colleagues' views to the president throughout the crisis and characterized the JCS's meeting with Kennedy as his own idea: "Following each EXCOMM meeting, I returned to the Pentagon, reported to the Chiefs the events of the meeting, and set in motion any actions devolving on the Armed Forces from the decisions taken. When these decisions did not accord with the Chiefs' views, I was always cross-examined to see whether I had

---

* Kennedy was fearful that LeMay would publicize the growing crisis soon after he learned the Soviets had deployed the missiles. But he wanted the JCS aware of the problem. Since LeMay was out of town Kennedy was particularly sensitive to telling him why he was being recalled. He asked Taylor how he could get him back without telling him the country was on the verge of a world war. Taylor, who understood LeMay's sensitivities, told Kennedy that he would tell LeMay that funds for the B-70 bomber were being canceled and that he ought to get back to Washington right away. The ploy worked: LeMay burst into his vice chief's office with the words "Who in hell is it that's trying to stop the B-70?"

been sufficiently vigorous in defending their position. Occasionally, in the face of obvious skepticism as to the quality of my efforts, I would turn on them and offer to arrange for them a meeting with the President to present their views directly. I do not recall their seeking such a meeting (at which I promised to hold their coats), but on October 19, at my suggestion, the President invited them to meet with him and thus offered them the opportunity to give full expression to their individual opinions.''

It's impossible to judge the accuracy of the JCS's views of Taylor's actions during the Cuban Missile Crisis; not only have JCS documents on the period been classified, they would probably give an insufficient picture of what Taylor actually said, let alone thought, in the privacy of the Oval Office. Nonetheless, his protests offer at least some indication that there was trouble between the chairman and other members of the JCS from the very beginning of the incident. Also, JCS members were nearly unanimous in their belief that they were not being represented, which is at least indirectly borne out by the later reflections of EXCOMM participants. According to these officials, most of whom have written extensively on the Cuban Missile Crisis in biographies of Kennedy, the JCS was unanimous in advocating stern military measures against Cuba. But the views weren't even close: Anderson favored a naval quarantine, as did Wheeler. Only LeMay favored a full military response, in stark isolation from his colleagues. Even Taylor commented on the later, false depiction of the JCS as ''hard-nosed warmongers during the crisis, clamoring for air strikes and invasion and rejecting the more moderate proposals.''

With the extremely dangerous situation in Cuba resolved by the Soviets' agreement to remove their missiles — the result of what LeMay characterized as ''a trade with Khrushchev . . . he'd take his missiles out of Cuba, we would take our missiles out of Turkey and Italy'' — the situation between Taylor and his colleagues grew worse. In fact, the Cuban Missile Crisis was a peripheral issue for the JCS, a piercing light that simply illuminated their real problem, a resolution to the less volatile but certainly more vexing situation in Vietnam. Throughout November 1962, the JCS continued to debate America's involvement in Vietnam, with the relationship between Taylor and his associates becoming more and more strained. At issue was the type of commitment each of the chiefs advocated in dealing with the Vietcong insurgency. The JCS members felt that Taylor, and only Taylor, had any influence on administration thinking, a problem that they attempted to remedy by forcing Taylor to detail their positions on the war. It was, perhaps, a hopeless task, especially considering the chairman's commitment to the doctrine of flexible response, his formation of airborne assault units, and, finally, his agreement with Kennedy that counterinsurgency units could successfully defeat any guerrilla army.

"We in the military felt we were not in the decision-making process at all," LeMay told his biographer, Thomas Coffey. "Taylor might have been, but we didn't agree with Taylor in most cases, so we felt that the president was not getting . . . unfiltered military advice." For LeMay, Taylor's influence with Kennedy gave him almost sole access to the corridors of power, an unprecedented position for a JCS chairman, even one who stood in the shoes of the immensely influential Arthur Radford.

The most important aspect of the Vietnam issue for LeMay as well as the other chiefs was the policy of "gradualism," the belief that by matching U.S. responses to Vietcong and North Vietnamese actions in Indochina, the United States could eventually convince the communists that their hope to conquer the South would never be successful. There are a number of myths about the Vietnam War, but none is so widely believed as the one that supposes America's involvement was unremarkable, unconscious, and even unintended, that somehow the United States was drawn into the conflict much as a Sunday hiker is unwittingly drawn into quicksand. Vietnam, so it goes, was a "quagmire": once in, it was almost impossible to get out. This view is a natural adjunct to gradualism, the belief that Vietnam was a mistake because the United States became involved slowly, not that it became involved at all.

The one man who would most probably disagree with the quagmire theory was John Paul Vann, perhaps the best-known colonel in American history. Vann was the 1963 equivalent of Colonel Kurtz, the Brando-tinted character of *Apocalypse Now* who decided to fight the war himself. More properly, Vann was the disenchanted colonel of *Go Tell the Spartans* or even the alienated and treasonous general of *Twilight's Last Gleaming*, who took over a missile silo in an attempt to blackmail the president into "telling the truth about Vietnam." (Burt Lancaster, the compelling antihero of *Seven Days in May*, played both characters, having a yen, it seems, for such roles.) In 1963, Colonel Vann was both protagonists: he was disenchanted with the war (frustrated by his mysterious inability to imbue South Vietnamese troops with a fighting spirit), and he had a rare obsession for telling the truth.

Both of these characteristics came out in Vann just after the Battle of Ap Bac in South Vietnam's Mekong Delta in January 1963. Ap Bac was originally intended to be a model of what U.S. counterinsurgency training could accomplish when coupled with the new airborne tactics imported from Washington. Over Vann's objections, a confident South Vietnamese commander decided to attack a Vietcong unit in a three-pronged airborne assault at Ap Bac on New Year's Day. Eventually it had to be postponed to January 2, primarily because the American helicopter crews were hung over from their New Year's revelries. But the delay didn't help: Vann watched helplessly as the South Vietnamese were summarily defeated by a guerrilla group they outnumbered ten to one, suffering more than 60 killed and 100 wounded. Further, the South Vietnamese commander refused to follow Vann's advice during each step of the battle, a particular insult given Vann's knowledge that the ARVN (Army of the Republic of Vietnam) general was a crony of Premier Diem's and unsuited for any command, let alone the command of an entire division.

For Vann, who had been watching such fiascos for more than a year, Ap Bac was the final piece of evidence. "A miserable fucking performance, just like it always is," Vann said after the battle, a view that he contrasted, in sniggering tones, to General Paul Harkins's comment that the battle was a victory. Vann's view — that South Vietnam's political problems had to be solved before there was any hope of military victory (and his more private view that America needed a new Vietnam commander) — was widely repeated among members of the JCS staff, especially when the colonel told colleagues that he would take his case for a full U.S. review of its commitment to the high command.

In July 1963, Vann received Army clearance to return to Washington to present the JCS with a complete briefing on the war, which reportedly criticized JCS decisions to deploy large numbers of advisers trained in counterinsurgency techniques without providing the political foundation for their success. In essence, while Vann was, in Stanley Karnow's phrase, "the apotheosis of the American for whom the anticommunist struggle had become a crusade," he wasn't willing to fight any losing battles. Eventually, he thought, the United States would be forced to fight the Vietcong itself unless the South Vietnamese government made a commitment to training a professional army void of corruption.

When Vann reported to the Pentagon, he was told his briefing had been postponed but would be rescheduled. Within a week, it was postponed yet again. Finally, as Vann sat in the outer office of the Army chief of staff on July 8, he was told his briefing had been summarily "taken off the agenda," canceled by none other than the JCS chairman himself. A general met Vann in the hall shortly after he learned the news. "He was enraged," the general said later. "He said he was getting out. He said we couldn't win the war."

The result of Taylor's cancellation of the Vann briefing was an open war in the JCS. The chiefs concluded that Taylor was protecting his good friend Paul Harkins, the U.S. commander in Vietnam, whose reputation for competence was widely and openly questioned by Taylor's Army colleagues, one of whom told the JCS chairman that Harkins was "just plain stupid." The change in the JCS's agenda even angered Curtis LeMay, who had been watching the American buildup in Vietnam with increasing mistrust. His suspicions had originally been aroused when he pushed Taylor to appoint a high-level Air Force commander to help Harkins run the air war in South Vietnam, a request that Taylor (and Harkins) consistently rejected. In fact, LeMay was so maddened by Harkins's handling of the air war that his remarks on the general, and on Taylor's support for him, grew increasingly strident, even insulting.* During one JCS meeting just after Taylor canceled Vann's briefing, LeMay called Harkins an "idiot" — a remark that was met with glowering silence by the chairman. By late summer, LeMay was in the habit of reading Harkins's glowing reports on the situation in Vietnam to his JCS staff, punctuating them with his own pithy sarcasms: "oh, wonderful," "marvelous."

But Taylor ignored LeMay's criticisms as well as internal Army barbs that he had silenced the talented Colonel Vann. "I know Vann and saw him in operation in Vietnam," Taylor said of the incident. "I had a very high regard for him, as a matter of fact. I don't recall this particular visit; and certainly, I know I never muzzled anybody. When we had anyone of experience coming back from Vietnam, we tried to pick their brains completely clean before allowing them to return. There was no feeling of complacency anyplace in the Pentagon that we had the full story. In fact, we knew we didn't have it."† Taylor's remarks shocked those who served with him on the JCS staff. "He's lying," one general said simply.

With the Vann incident still reverberating through the JCS staff, the chairman became involved in yet another internally divisive argument. Unfortunately, JCS criticism of Taylor's position on administration proposals to replace South Vietnam's Premier Ngo Dinh Diem were probably unjustified. Not only did the chairman act with laudable restraint, he convinced the JCS that Diem's replacement would be a mistake, a position he took repeatedly in meetings with Kennedy. Indeed, through all of 1963, Taylor steadfastly opposed any attempt by

---

* Harkins learned of LeMay's criticisms and told friends that the Air Force chief actually attempted to bring him up on charges of "military incompetence." While there's no evidence that LeMay tried to have Harkins removed as U.S. military head in South Vietnam, it's certainly not impossible. LeMay hated Harkins and considered him a Taylor crony.

† Vann finally ended up back in Vietnam as a civilian official, and the Vietcong put a price on his head — the most telling testimony to his effectiveness. A fellow general gained an AID appointment for Vann over the heads of civilian officials, who wanted to see the former lieutenant colonel banned from Indochina. Vann died in a helicopter crash in South Vietnam in June 1972.

administration officials to support an anti-Diem coup, lining up with the pro-Diem forces of Lyndon Johnson, Robert McNamara, and CIA Director John McCone against Ambassador Henry Cabot Lodge, George Ball, and Averell Harriman. But Kennedy's decision was to leave the matter in the hands of Lodge, with the proviso that the coup should be engineered by "responsible leadership." On November 1, 1963, Ngo Dinh Diem was unceremoniously assassinated and stuffed into the back of an armored personnel carrier.

"This was a tremendous mistake," General Bruce Palmer, who served on the JCS staff, later reflected. "We should have never done that." Taylor's JCS colleagues were shocked by the coup. It reinforced the already bitter relationship between the chiefs and their chairman, whom they blamed for not pushing their position with the president — a criticism that, as they pointedly remarked to the chairman during one meeting, he had made of the deposed Lemnitzer. While the chiefs agreed with Taylor's view that an anti-Diem coup would damage the American position in Vietnam, they resented his inability to influence administration policies.* In the end, they believed that Taylor's access had been bought too dearly with results that were too meager.

When John Kennedy was assassinated on November 22, 1963, three weeks after Diem, Lyndon Johnson moved quickly to dampen JCS infighting. He dispatched Taylor on a worldwide fact-finding mission, which gave the new president access to other members of the JCS, who were outspoken in their criticism of Taylor. In particular, LeMay urged Johnson to engage the JCS in a discussion of U.S. war aims in Vietnam, a view that was seconded by the other chiefs (including even Wheeler), who believed Taylor was having an inordinate influence on administration policy. But, even more important, Johnson seemed to get along with the chiefs, especially the cigar-chomping LeMay, better than he had with Taylor. On several occasions, Johnson shared long talks with LeMay over drinks, regaling him with Texas stories and listening with amusement to his arguments for more money for the Air Force. Nevertheless, it came as a surprise when Johnson decided to reappoint him to the JCS. Like his predecessors, LeMay had irritated the president by his incessant calls for increased spending on Air Force

---

* Taylor's characterization of the Diem murder was downright weird. In his autobiography, he linked it with the reporting of David Halberstam, who had criticized the general in *The Best and the Brightest* for his treatment of Vann. "I certainly know his subversive work as a reporter in attempting to overthrow the Diem government which he certainly contributed to by the manner of his reporting," Taylor said. He then went on to detail his views on the proper role of the press in American society. "We're always the victim of a sensation hunting press," he told the interviewer. "We were terribly neglectful of our national interest in not imposing either censorship or something comparable in Vietnam."

bombers and had had a number of notorious run-ins with Secretary of Defense McNamara. But Johnson's next step was even more surprising. When Taylor returned from his inspection in the spring of 1964, Johnson named him ambassador to South Vietnam, a job that Taylor said "was about the last job I would have chosen." His judgment, at least in this last case, proved to be one of the most accurate he had ever made. When asked by reporters why he had been chosen, the retiring JCS chairman gave the only answer he could: he said he was expendable.

5

THE WAR OF
THE CHIEFS

★   ★   ★   ★

I can't tell you how I feel. I'm so sick of it . . . I have
never been so goddamn frustrated by it all . . . I'm so sick
of it.

> General John McConnell,
> on the Vietnam bombing

IN EARLY JULY 1964, the JCS staff stopped to catch its breath. For
almost four years, since Kennedy's inauguration, it had been in a constant state of tension, the spare routine of running the military on a
daily basis interrupted by the tumult of mounting international tensions. The increasingly dangerous state of affairs began when the
Soviet Union sent arms shipments to its allies in Laos; it was fueled by
the failure of the Bay of Pigs, exacerbated by the Soviet threats against
Berlin, and finally brought to a head by the near holocaust of the
Cuban Missile Crisis. Even so, the crisis atmosphere at the JCS might
have abated after October 1962 but for the continued personal sniping
between Curtis LeMay and Maxwell Taylor over even the most mundane policies. Their growing animosity finally erupted over Taylor's
cancellation of Colonel Vann's briefing in July 1963.

But even in late 1963, with the Vann incident a memory and the
worst international incidents seemingly consigned to history, the JCS
couldn't gain even a minor respite from the almost triphammer flow
of bad news. On November 1, word came of the murder of South Vietnamese Premier Diem, which was followed and overshadowed by the
assassination of President Kennedy. Even so, just when JCS officers
believed that nothing else could possibly happen, within three months
there was yet another South Vietnamese coup, this one aimed directly
at Taylor's good friend and tennis partner General Duong Van "Big"
Minh. The affable Minh was removed from Saigon's presidential pal-

ace by the tanks of Major General Nguyen Khanh on January 31, 1964, an act that met with widespread American support when it was learned that some members of Minh's entourage were pushing for a negotiated settlement of their conflict with the Vietcong.

But even this incident failed to end the almost unimaginable series of internal upheavals the JCS had endured. On July 3, 1964, Army General Earle G. Wheeler succeeded Taylor, becoming the nation's sixth JCS chairman. As usual, the change touched off widespread comment on the relative merits of the new appointee, and JCS staff officers jockeyed for position, lining up as either Wheeler loyalists or critics. Nevertheless, most officers believed that Wheeler's appointment finally marked an end to their time of troubles and returned the JCS to the status quo: the United States had agreed to a neutral solution in Laos, the Soviet Union had been humbled by the Cuban Missile Crisis, and Europe was quiet for the first time in nearly twenty years. Even in Vietnam, the pro-American government of General Khanh seemed to be making headway against the spreading insurgency, going so far as to reassure Washington that the new South Vietnamese government was as interested in punishing North Vietnamese aggression as the United States.

Wheeler's promotion was the respite that everyone had hoped for, a seemingly welcome change from Taylor's more complex, fast-paced days. Indeed, it was symbolized by a transition in JCS leadership that was much less volcanic than those of an earlier era, in part because it took almost no one by surprise. Not only was Wheeler well known on the JCS staff (he had served as director under Lemnitzer, then as chief of staff under Taylor), his promotion seemed to indicate that the JCS would take a much less active role in the councils of government; Wheeler did not have Taylor's insider touch, and he had made few friends among those in Lyndon Johnson's inner circle. More significantly, it was well known among the JCS staff that the president actually mistrusted the high command, an attitude that wasn't lost on JCS officers, who commented that such feelings were rarely in evidence when Johnson was a senator.

Indeed, for most of the JCS staff, Wheeler symbolized a clear break with the past. According to one Marine colonel, the appointment meant "an end to the age of heroes," closing the curtain on the careers of those officers who had served in highly visible combat commands during World War II and Korea. There's good cause for such a view: after all, for the JCS's first seventeen years, it had been dominated by officers who were often as well known to the public as the presidents they served.

The first JCS chairman, retired five-star General Omar Bradley, was viewed as a military titan, an officer whose already considerable stature had grown in the years since his retirement. The same could be said for Admiral Arthur Radford, though perhaps not to the same degree. The third chairman, Air Force General Nathan Twining, was remembered fondly for his even-tempered manner and his conciliatory stance on divisive issues. His successor, General Lyman Lemnitzer, was from the same mold, and while his two-year term was cut short by his assignment to Europe, his experience during World War II had already guaranteed his place in military history. The same was true of Maxwell Taylor, the 101st Airborne's most renowned Screaming Eagle, whose controversial role as the fifth JCS chairman could never diminish his place as one of America's foremost combat commanders.

Unlike any of his predecessors, Wheeler clearly lacked any combat experience whatsoever, a fact that spurred Air Force and Navy JCS staff officers to disparagingly reflect that "Bus [as he was called] had never heard a shot fired in anger." Other comments were even more critical; for the JCS Marine colonel who commented on the passing of the age of heroes, Wheeler was "the Army's highest-ranking sycophant," who won promotion primarily because he always agreed with programs that were popular with his superiors. With Vietnam the most important issue facing the nation, Wheeler was almost universally viewed as Taylor's mouthpiece to Lyndon Johnson, a buffer between the abrasive chairman and the politically savvy president. That Wheeler would have a minor military role as JCS chairman himself was universally accepted; all the important military decisions — or so JCS staff officers said at the time — would be made either in Saigon or in the White House. Wheeler was strictly a manager, an officer who was not only inexperienced at running a war, but actually incapable of doing so.

This view was a predictable reaction to Wheeler's nondescript career. A 1932 graduate of West Point, Wheeler's service was notably unspectacular: he spent his first twenty years in the Army as a trainer and staff director before finally winning his first command assignment in 1958, as head of the 2nd Armored Division, a promotion that many officers viewed as an afterthought, clear evidence that Wheeler had failed to win major combat leadership roles in both of his generation's major wars. For some, his lack of a combat command was a simple matter of bad luck, but for others it was a sign that the new chairman was a perfect "horse holder," an officer who was more satisfied with being in command of a staff (his assignment on three different occasions) than in command of fighters. For those who disparaged the JCS system as a career-ending assignment, Wheeler was a lightning rod of discontent, living proof that the "get along, go-along" road to high command bred mediocrity and that the real action was in the field — in this case, Vietnam.

Nevertheless, a small but important minority on the JCS viewed the short-tempered and near-sighted Wheeler in starkly different terms, believing that he would simply refuse to continue his career as a "desk general" and would actually move quickly to exert the power that went with his new rank. Wheeler might well typify the new style of military officer, these JCS staff members claimed, although such officers were indispensable and were a necessary balance to the over-weening and universally resented can-doers of McNamara's Pentagon — that group of civilian statisticians the Defense Secretary had brought in from the Ford Motor Company (where he had served as president) who were becoming known as "the whiz kids." In such a fervid political environment, the pro-Wheeler officers said, the military didn't need heroes as much as it needed bureaucratic infighters, and Wheeler was among the best.

Wheeler's most outspoken critics, who were convinced that the new JCS chairman would need help with his assignment, were mollified by the fact that three JCS members were holdovers. Curtis LeMay, in his fourth year as Air Force chief, was as wily and suspicious as ever. LeMay was also the JCS's resident expert on strategic bombing, a significant credential for those who believed that the real solution to America's problems in Indochina rested on the Air Force's ability to bring the North Vietnamese to the negotiating table. Admiral David L. McDonald had only served as CNO for one year, but his experience as a naval aviator (during the Battle of Leyte Gulf) as well as a combat commander (as head of the Sixth Fleet in the Mediterranean) gave him clout with the Navy that Wheeler would seemingly never have with the Army. Even the Marine Corps commandant, General Wallace Greene, who attended JCS meetings when Marine policies were being decided, was widely viewed as having more military influence than Wheeler. The hard-nosed Vermont native had been in the front line during a number of particularly violent island battles against the Japanese in World War II, a marked contrast to Wheeler's experience as a trainer of Army recruits in Georgia during the same period. JCS officers believed that when it came time to send in the Marines, Wheeler would be forced to defer to Greene's judgment.

The only new JCS member was Army General Harold K. Johnson, who was unexpectedly promoted over a number of other senior commanders and took the oath as Army chief of staff the same day that Wheeler was sworn in as chairman.* Even so, most JCS officers didn't

---

* In fact, Johnson's promotion stunned the upper command ranks of the service. The head of U.S. troops in Korea, the abrasive Hamilton H. Howze, was under the impression that he was next in line for the position. He promptly resigned and left the Army, a move he later characterized as "the biggest mistake of my life."

expect Johnson to be a Wheeler ally — the two were as different as any Army officers could possibly be: Wheeler was the product of Washington staff positions, Johnson, of the Bataan death march. In addition, Johnson was an Army outsider, a flag rank officer who had spent most of his career following in the footsteps of his classmates of 1936, West Point's "Class of the Stars." No one at West Point expected Johnson to succeed, and there was open surprise when he did. Paradoxically, his experiences at West Point had a much more negative impact on his character than his four-year nightmare as a prisoner of the Japanese, making him forever suspicious of officers like Wheeler, whom he characterized as "aristocrats." In fact, there was always a nagging feeling among the JCS staff, especially among career officers, that Johnson's stellar service record was the result of a carefully nursed resentment of those whose West Point record, Johnson believed, dictated their inevitable rise through the ranks.

One such Johnson classmate was William C. Westmoreland, who had taken over as head of the U.S. Military Assistance Command in Vietnam (MACV) six months before either Wheeler or Johnson was promoted at the JCS. Dubbed "the inevitable general" by his classmates — implying a less than wholehearted affirmation of his abilities — Westmoreland was well trained and self-confident, a welcome change from the more tentative attitudes of his predecessor, Paul Harkins. Nevertheless, the JCS harbored doubts about Westmoreland's command ability. In fact, JCS officers believed that a number of other top officers were more capable of fighting the kind of counterinsurgency war the Vietnam environment demanded. Unfortunately, none of the chiefs — who shared the views of the staff — could intervene to untrack the appointment. They were all painfully aware that Westmoreland had been hand-picked for the assignment by the martyred Kennedy, who had been impressed by Westmoreland when they first met in June 1962 and had pushed him as Harkins's replacement in the weeks before his assassination.*

In addition to these practical command problems, however, it was also clear that the chiefs felt uncomfortable with Westmoreland, a feeling they had difficulty putting into words. It came down to this: Westmoreland was aloof, almost distant with his colleagues; he had a difficult time making and keeping friends, and he actually alienated many officers in his own service by surrounding himself with a reti-

---

* As West Point superintendent, Westmoreland prevailed on Kennedy to increase the number of cadets, something Eisenhower had refused to consider. In addition, Kennedy's 1962 West Point commencement speech (about counterinsurgency warfare) impressed Westmoreland; he said it reminded him of Maxwell Taylor's comments in The Uncertain Trumpet. "Throughout my days as superintendent, I had an intuitive feeling that eventually I would go to Vietnam," he later wrote.

nue of public relations–minded aides. Obviously, some of the
doubters were jealous of his seemingly effortless rise through the
Army's command ranks, but others believed he was too focused on the
rise of his own star, his own place in history, to fight a patient, low-
key conflict against an elusive, highly motivated enemy.

But these undefined feelings weren't enough to pit the JCS against
Westmoreland or his policies. Although he wasn't the JCS's first
choice for the job, he was clearly one of the Army's most respected
commanders among civilian leaders, and he outranked most of the
other choices. Then, too, the JCS was confident he would never over-
step his bounds (like MacArthur) or demand complete control over
Vietnam policy (that wasn't his style). Moreover, it was simply too
late; Westmoreland was there, in Vietnam, and had been on the job
since January. Therefore, in July 1964, JCS officers, especially Wheeler
and Johnson, swallowed their inheritance of Westmoreland without
protest, though they swallowed hard.

So it was that on the eve of America's most important military challenge since World War II, the nation's highest-ranking officers represented the most diverse and divided group of policy-makers in the
JCS's history. For the first time since World War II, the JCS chairman
was virtually unknown to most of the American public, his wartime
record filled with unwarlike experiences. Army chief Johnson was the
closest thing the JCS had to a professional skeptic, an officer whose
dedication to integrity — and hatred of absolutes — was heightened
by his deep mistrust of easy solutions and inevitable generals. Both the
supremely confident LeMay and the circumspect naval aviator,
McDonald, viewed the Vietnam conflict as an Army affair.

Nor were the nation's military problems confined to the four thin
walls on the tank. While Westmoreland wore several rows of hard-
earned combat medals, none had been won by fighting half-starved
revolutionaries or by maintaining impeccable press relations. To make
matters worse, his civilian cohort was Maxwell Taylor, whose reputation with the JCS — even with Lyndon Johnson — had already been
tarnished by his controversial JCS chairmanship. The situation at the
JCS was fraught with danger. While few JCS officers believed that
Wheeler could manage the war in Vietnam, even fewer believed Westmoreland and Taylor would make a successful command team; while
they agreed on almost everything, it would be impossible for two generals to manage one war. The common wisdom was simple: the real
turmoil was bound to occur in Vietnam, not in Washington. Wheeler,
Johnson, LeMay, and McDonald would manage the military, while
Westmoreland and Taylor managed the war.

Indeed, at least for four weeks, this vision was borne out by events:
while Westmoreland and Taylor continued to train the South Viet-

namese Army and deal with a shaky military government, the JCS confined itself to mundane activities. Wheeler and Johnson settled into their new jobs, their only contact with Vietnam coming in planning for possible American troop deployment (then a purely theoretical consideration) or in monitoring naval intelligence activities, grouped under the code name Operational Plan 34-Alpha (OPLAN 34-A). But on August 2, an American destroyer assessing the impact of South Vietnamese raids on North Vietnamese installations (part of OPLAN 34-A) reported that it had been fired on by North Vietnamese patrol boats in the Gulf of Tonkin. The next day, another incident was reported: a destroyer said it had spotted twenty-two enemy torpedoes. On August 4, Lyndon Johnson ordered air reprisals against North Vietnam. The only thing left was congressional approval for these actions. On August 6, Congress provided it: the House of Representatives passed the Tonkin Gulf Resolution unanimously, and the Senate followed suit with only two dissenting votes.

When Lyndon Johnson decided to retaliate against North Vietnam, the JCS was ready. Beginning on August 2, within hours of the reports from the Navy's commander in the Pacific, Admiral U. S. Grant Sharp, Wheeler directed key JCS officers to begin drafting bombing proposals to present to the president and his top foreign policy team. Wheeler also took unambiguous military steps on his own to ready U.S. forces for rapid deployment to South Vietnam: he upgraded American capabilities, placed U.S. troops in the Pacific on full alert, ordered the deployment of additional fighter-bombers to South Vietnam and Thailand, and convened a special meeting of the JCS to consider additional measures to be used against the North Vietnamese. Wheeler also approved Admiral Sharp's decision to ready U.S. air power in the Pacific by ordering the aircraft carrier *Constellation* to steam into the South China Sea, where it would be joined by the U.S.S. *Ticonderoga.* By the time of the second incident, on August 3, Wheeler had the JCS's plans ready for review by the president, plans that designated specific military targets in North Vietnam that the JCS believed the United States should bomb.

On the evening of August 4, after Lyndon Johnson had been convinced that a second attack on American naval warships had taken place, he approved the JCS's plans.* This first target list, presented to Johnson for the JCS by Defense Secretary McNamara, designated five targets: four North Vietnamese patrol boat bases and a large oil depot. Stooped over his dining room table in the White House living

---

* Historians are now certain that the second attack never occurred and that the first was a reprisal for South Vietnamese raids on North Vietnam's coastal installations.

quarters, Johnson studied the maps of North Vietnam with the help of McNamara, gave his approval for the strikes, and then went on national television to announce his decision. Johnson said the U.S. strikes were in retaliation for North Vietnam's attack on U.S. warships and pledged that any future aggressive acts by North Vietnam would be met "with positive response." As Johnson spoke, just before midnight on August 4, U.S. warplanes were already in the air over North Vietnam. In all, U.S. fighter-bombers flew sixty-four missions against the five targets within six hours — an attack the White House described as "limited in scale."

In the Pentagon, JCS officers grouped themselves around a bank of television sets to listen to Johnson's announcement, then began to monitor the effects of the air strikes. Earle Wheeler, his elbows balanced precariously on his knees, his flitting eyes rising up over his glasses — a characteristic during times of great tension — listened to reports that the fighter-bombers were on their way to their North Vietnamese targets with apparent nonchalance. Although he was relieved, almost pleased, that the United States had finally taken action to oppose the worsening situation in Indochina, he was also deeply worried that the Tonkin Gulf raids of August 4 were a prelude to greater American involvement in Southeast Asia. In particular, Wheeler feared not only that American flyers had not gained the tactical surprise necessary to make the air attacks a success — in which case he would soon be answering questions in front of an explosive president — but that the United States would face a barrage of international criticism for its actions.

Wheeler was hardly a squeamish officer — his years at the JCS had inured him to such posturing — but he worried that such protests would have an undue impact on Johnson and his advisers and might even dampen the U.S. willingness to deal firmly with North Vietnam. Most of all, Wheeler feared that the American attacks would fail to convince the communist leaders that the United States had resolved to defend the South and that the actions on the late evening of August 4 would fail to end North Vietnam's policy of helping the Vietcong insurgency in the South. Eventually, he then thought, more and larger air attacks would be needed, and in the end, U.S. troops might have to be deployed to Southeast Asia to meet the threat. In fact, that evening Wheeler was certain that the United States should expand its attacks on the North, pummeling its modest industrial plant and strategic military assets with an air offensive that would make its leaders negotiate an end to the insurgency.

The entire JCS agreed with Wheeler on this point; within days of the successful completion of the air raids (two U.S. planes were downed in the attacks), it convened to draw up an expanded target list for Ameri-

can bombers. One week after the Tonkin Gulf raids, the JCS was pressing McNamara to recommend a series of military escalations in Indochina, including the interdiction of North Vietnam's supply lines in
Laos and the deployment of a logistics team to aid the South Vietnamese Army — the same recommendations Maxwell Taylor had made
one year earlier. Arguing that it was important that the United States
"not lose this momentum [gained from the air raids]," the JCS added a
curious note of caution that reflected its fears that civilian leaders
would not be willing to press the American advantage: "Failure to
resume and maintain a program of pressure though military actions
. . . could signal a lack of resolve."

Despite this plea, the administration decided to end its punishment
of North Vietnam by initiating a "holding phase," a pause in military
activities designed, as *The Pentagon Papers* states, to "avoid actions
that would in any way take the onus off the Communist side for [the
Tonkin] escalation." It was just the kind of action, or inaction, the JCS
had feared. By early September, JCS members were pressuring
Wheeler to present the military case for escalation in Indochina
directly to the president, bypassing McNamara (the JCS's usual messenger) if necessary. In all, the JCS wanted Wheeler to recommend that
the administration approve the targeting of ninety-four North Vietnamese industrial and military installations for destruction by U.S.
fighter-bombers. In fact, as some JCS members argued, the situation in
South Vietnam (as reflected in memos from Taylor) could only get
worse, which meant the bombing would have to be resumed eventually anyway.

Unfortunately, Wheeler was hardly in a good position to argue for
escalation. In fact, after his stunningly successful spurt of activity in
the wake of the Gulf of Tonkin incident, he fell into his practiced bad
habits. In essence, he seemed to become the desk general his JCS
detractors always thought he would be, deferring most decisions and
arguments to McNamara. This attitude was particularly frustrating to
JCS officers, who were in a state of near euphoria after the air raids,
and brought Wheeler under fire from other JCS members, especially
from Curtis LeMay. Ever the partisan of unrestrained air power,
LeMay engaged Wheeler in a series of discussions on America's
involvement in Vietnam throughout September and October, telling
him that he should be more argumentative with the president and
press for a full air campaign against the North Vietnamese during
White House meetings on the war. Wheeler was dubious; not only did
Johnson mistrust the military and especially the JCS, he said, but most
of LeMay's arguments were actually being promoted by McNamara.
Exasperated, LeMay said he would agree to the next best thing: the JCS
should send Johnson a series of memos on possible military alternatives, a view that Wheeler finally accepted.

In essence, LeMay's discussions with Wheeler convinced the members of the JCS to push Johnson into approving a major air campaign. LeMay's position on the war, described ever after as the most bellicose of any of the chiefs, was actually well argued, even elegant, and appealed to Wheeler and Harold Johnson. Both men endorsed LeMay's concept after they realized his contentions weren't so much pro–Air Force (which they always suspected) as they were pro-Army. The point is significant, because the reasons for LeMay's willingness to go to war over Vietnam are still widely misunderstood. His plan, LeMay told Wheeler, was intended to save the nation from the heartache and tragedy of a full-blown conventional ground conflict, which LeMay knew neither Wheeler nor Johnson wanted. In fact, LeMay said, the worst alternative facing the United States in September and October of 1964 was that a lack of U.S. response to North Vietnamese aggression would inevitably result in a worsening military situation and the concomitant inevitable deployment of U.S. units to save South Vietnam.

This was just the argument that Wheeler had tried to explain to JCS staff officers on the night of the Tonkin Gulf raids. Hearing it now from LeMay, Wheeler thought it made sense; the chairman went one step further, telling JCS staff officers that the deployment of U.S. troops in South Vietnam would mean that the United States had already begun to lose the battle. At that point, Wheeler implied, it would be all or nothing; the United States would commit itself to a full-scale war and full mobilization or it would decide to let South Vietnam fend for itself. LeMay made the same point with a less convoluted argument. "I don't remember that it ever came before the Joint Chiefs that we ought to send ground troops in there to fight," he said later. "I would certainly have been dead set against it. As far as I know, every military man I've ever heard of advised against it."

Other military leaders agreed with LeMay, though in the end they advised a different approach to the North Vietnamese. Ambassador Taylor, who spent his days in Saigon making vain attempts to shore up and reform the badly disorganized and corrupt South Vietnamese government, suggested to Lyndon Johnson that the United States respond to Vietcong attacks by engaging in "reprisal bombings"; that is, by matching U.S. air bombings to North Vietnamese and Vietcong actions in the South. But Taylor included a cautionary proviso, saying the South Vietnamese government could not stand up to a full-scale North Vietnamese attack; therefore he believed that Johnson should approve something less than a full bombing campaign aimed at strategic targets around Hanoi and Haiphong. Admiral Sharp, in command of U.S. Pacific forces, took the same position as Taylor, arguing that the United States had no choice but to punish North Vietnam for acts of terrorism committed in the South. The implication was that U.S.

actions should be guided by North Vietnamese and Vietcong actions; like Taylor, Sharp was in favor of a graduated system of reprisals against the North.

The JCS rejected both Taylor's and Sharp's strategy, instead endorsing LeMay's air campaign in a series of memos to Lyndon Johnson during the lull that followed the Tonkin incident. In one other notable case, the JCS also disagreed with the position of the MACV commander, William Westmoreland, who advocated deploying U.S. troops "to provide security for U.S./GVN operating bases." The JCS chose a third strategy, one it agreed would be more effective than either the Taylor/Sharp strategy of graduated response or the Westmoreland strategy of deploying troops. Instead, it unanimously urged that the president approve "prompt implementation of more serious pressures using U.S. air capabilities," a view that reflected a series of compromises worked out in October. These compromises, codified in JCSM 955-64, were an elegant mix of three courses of action: first, Air Force and Navy aircraft should bomb targets in Laos and North Vietnam, including military installations in Hanoi and Haiphong; second, the president should approve an airlift of Marine security battalions to major installations in South Vietnam and evacuate American dependents; last, the United States should take the military steps necessary to "lessen the possibility of misinterpretation by the DRV [North Vietnam] and Communist China of U.S. determination and intent."

But the JCS's recommendations were important for what they didn't recommend as well as for what they did. Specifically, the JCS explicitly and strongly rejected Taylor's and Sharp's strategy of reprisal: "The Joint Chiefs of Staff do not concur with a concept of 'tit-for-tat' reprisals nor with Ambassador Taylor's recommendation that the United States and the Government of Vietnam [GVN] jointly announce such a policy which ties our actions to equivalency." In essence, the JCS's recommendations reflected a stunning consensus among the nation's top service officers on just what kind of war the United States should wage in Vietnam, a point made clear by JCS officers privy to high-level discussions at the Pentagon throughout October. According to these JCS officers, Harold Johnson surprised LeMay during one particularly exhaustive discussion by agreeing that the United States should fully commit itself and all resources to the defense of South Vietnam, then adding a characteristic afterthought — that we should commit everything or nothing at all. Later LeMay, who apparently understood only the first half of Johnson's statement, portrayed this position in terms typical of his acerbic humor: "We should stop swatting flies and go after the manure pile."

But in each case the president and his top foreign policy advisers deferred a final decision on the JCS's plans, thereby effectively vetoing any strong follow-up to the August 4 Tonkin Gulf reprisals. With the election fast approaching, Johnson wanted to make sure that any military action didn't detract from his peace-oriented campaign against the Republican candidate, Barry Goldwater. But Johnson had other reasons as well. While the JCS — indeed, the entire government — had greeted the Tonkin Gulf reprisals with relief, even with celebration, the JCS staff's early August euphoria had worn off by early November, even in the wake of LBJ's landslide victory over Goldwater, because the raids had clearly had little impact on North Vietnam's leadership. Furthermore, the political situation in South Vietnam was actually getting worse: Buddhist rioting continued to plague the government, along with incipient uprisings sparked by dissatisfied, power-hungry ARVN generals. In essence, Johnson deferred a decision on Vietnam not because he wanted to win a major victory over Goldwater, but because he simply didn't know what else to do.

In fact, by early November, it was clear to Johnson that the United States didn't have a clear plan for waging and winning the war in Vietnam. Nor was he satisfied with the JCS's endless arguments for an all-out air campaign against the North; for a man with supreme confidence in America's ability to pass out good will (to bring, as Johnson later said, the Great Society to Southeast Asia), the vision of American bombers in full flight over North Vietnam was a horrifying prospect. Somehow, he told his top aides, the North Vietnamese had to be convinced that the United States was committed to a noncommunist state in the South — and they had to be convinced through actions somewhere short of outright war.

Just days before his reelection (*The Pentagon Papers* puts the date as November 1), Johnson asked Assistant Secretary of State William Bundy to draft a strategy that would bring North Vietnam to the negotiating table, that would convince the communists that the United States was committed to defending South Vietnam and was willing to go to war (if necessary) to get its way. For Johnson, Bundy seemed the only official with the background and knowledge to make the assessment: he had been one of the president's closest advisers since Kennedy's death and one of the few who valued Johnson's political acumen. In fact, Bundy was Johnson's mind reader, fashioning elegant political compromises from the dust of controversy and transforming sticky foreign policy problems into public relations victories that made the president look statesmanlike, even prophetic.

In the Pentagon, Bundy's position on the war was well known; if anyone could be held solely responsible for the American program in Vietnam up until November 1964, it was Bundy. When he recommended the escalation of covert operations against the North Vietnamese coast, for instance, the president listened with interest and approved the move. When Bundy formulated a response to the attacks on American warships in the Tonkin Gulf, LBJ ordered air strikes — suspending them after one day on Bundy's recommendation. When Bundy argued passionately against a declaration of war on North Vietnam and advocated instead a resolution of Congress (what became the Tonkin Gulf Resolution), Johnson bought the argument, thereby saving himself from a short-term, potentially embarrassing, pre-election political headache. Clearly Bundy, whom a later historian would describe as a "lean patrician with a lockjaw accent," was the adviser of choice for the president, accumulating enormous prestige as the State Department's resident intellectual on Vietnam.

But perhaps he understood Johnson too well: when he convened a National Security Council Working Group to undertake a full study of American policy in Vietnam during the first week of November, he presented U.S. options with an eye toward Johnson's own notions about what was desirable in Vietnam, not what was possible. In essence, he took it as a given that the United States needed to step up the pressure on North Vietnam, but not to a level where its allies, particularly Communist China, would enter the war. As *The Pentagon Papers* accurately notes, "The NSC Working Group approached its work with the general assessment that increased pressures against North Vietnam would be both useful and necessary," a view that immediately eliminated the JCS argument for a full air campaign. Of course, Bundy had also purposely eliminated one other option: that the United States should do nothing at all.

The JCS's representative on the NSC Working Group was Vice Admiral Lloyd Mustin, an ambitious and knowledgeable Navy officer who had won the trust of the JCS for his objective, honest political assessments. More important, he was one of the few JCS officers privy to the politics of the tank. He realized that the JCS wanted to have a bigger role in determining U.S. policy in Southeast Asia than it had hitherto been allowed and that it was obstinately opposed to gradual escalation, as advocated by Taylor and Sharp. But from the outset of the Working Group's meetings, Mustin and the JCS were frustrated by Bundy's handling of the process and realized that the administration foreign policy officials had eliminated the only two options that made any sense: get in and win or stay out.

Over a period of three weeks, Mustin diligently argued the JCS's position with Bundy and other top officials. By mid-November, these debates had been reduced to a disagreement between Mustin and Harold Ford of the CIA. Ford argued that the stability of the South Vietnamese government was central to understanding what was at stake in the war. More to the point, he said, North Vietnam was willing to engage the U.S. in a long-term "test of wills . . . over the course of events in South Vietnam." In effect, he argued that Hanoi was willing to take a calculated risk that the United States would eventually tire of its commitment to South Vietnam, that it was only a matter of time before the United States decided that waging an undeclared war against a poor Third World country wasn't worth the price of international condemnation. In addition, Ford said, the North Vietnamese were willing to wage a conflict for an indefinite amount of time by countering America's strategy of responses with low-key but effective guerrilla actions.

Mustin criticized the CIA assessment as too negative and pressured Bundy and others in the administration to take "early and positive actions" to convince North Vietnam that its strategy couldn't succeed. In fact, Mustin said, echoing LeMay's arguments, the CIA had the argument backward: instead of working to buttress the South Vietnamese government in order to make it better able to defend itself, the United States should take stern actions against North Vietnam to make that defense needless. Although Mustin's view took liberties with the JCS's literal position, it reflected the JCS thinking: as long as there was an insurgency in the South, it would be almost impossible to build a stable government there. Or as LeMay would later state, "The argument was, 'Look, we can't go north until we get some stability in the south.' I never understood this argument, but that was the one that was advanced. And my point was that we're never going to have any stability in the south unless you went north."

By the end of November, it was clear that Mustin and the JCS had lost the debate: while the CIA's assessment was toned down (it seemed to imply the United States could never win), the JCS's position that the United States should "go north" was firmly vetoed. The Working Group options were issued to a list of ten "principals," appointed by the president, who would make a final decision after Thanksgiving, when Johnson returned from a Texas vacation.* *The Pentagon Papers* later summarized Bundy's proposed courses of action: "Option A was essentially a continuation of military and naval actions currently underway. . . . Option B augmented current policies with systematic, sustained military pressures against the North and a resistance to negotiations unless we could carry them on while continuing the bombing. Option C proposed only a modest campaign against the North as compared with option B and was designed to bring the DRV to the negotiating table."

Just after Bundy issued these three proposals, Taylor returned to

---

* The principals were JCS Chairman Earle Wheeler, John McCone, Maxwell Taylor, Walt Rostow, McGeorge Bundy, George Ball, Dean Rusk, Robert McNamara, William Bundy, and President Lyndon Johnson.

Washington. He could not have come at a better time for those who advocated graduated response and who believed stability in South Vietnam was necessary to winning the conflict. During a whirlwind series of meetings that began on November 27, Taylor met first with the Bundy Working Group and then with the ten principals. To each group, Taylor presented a bleak assessment of the South Vietnamese government's capabilities.

Two days later, the principals officially rejected Wheeler's continuing advocacy of a sustained bombing campaign against North Vietnam, what some officers at the JCS were beginning to call the "quick war" solution. In effect, while Bundy had rejected Mustin's argument during meetings of the Working Group and the principals had rejected Wheeler's arguments at the end of November, Taylor had been decisive in tipping the balance. In fact, the final recommendation was a restatement of Annex I of Taylor's report, "Suggested Scenario for Controlled Escalation." The key word was "controlled." In effect, Bundy proposed a "middle way," the deployment of just enough American troops to avoid a disaster, but not enough to pose a threat to North Vietnam. The deployment would save South Vietnam without threatening the North with total defeat. In the words of a later historian, Bundy's recommendation avoided the pitfalls of "either quitting or brutal escalation" — a compromise that Johnson accepted wholeheartedly.

But this was just the kind of advice that Wheeler had wanted to avoid. On December 1, he returned to the Pentagon after a White House meeting that officially endorsed Bundy's second option as American policy in Vietnam. The decision was a deeply felt, bitter disappointment. In the words of one JCS officer, the Bundy plan meant that the United States "was going to war — kinda," a view that LeMay affirmed by telling the JCS staff that the administration's decision was ludicrous, which he repeated again and again as time went on. "You can't get a little bit pregnant," he said. "Once you get into this, you're into it." The decision had other ramifications for the military: when Admiral Thomas Moorer, a JCS deputy chief, referred to the Vietnam conflict as a "dirty little war," he was reprimanded by civilian officials for his use of words. "I thought they were mad because I used the word 'dirty,' " he said. "But that wasn't it at all. They were mad because I used the word 'war.' "

The momentous decision of December 1 had an immediate practical impact on the work of the JCS. From that time, the chiefs spent most of their efforts concentrating on the war in Indochina. Monday mornings were given over to a review of the situation with Secretary of Defense McNamara. It was continued during a shorter session on

Monday afternoons, with top JCS officers present. While Taylor and Westmoreland attempted to manage South Vietnam's response to the mounting insurgency, Chairman Wheeler bore the responsibility for the final military approval of air strikes against the North from his desk in Washington — strikes that were resumed in early February after detailed JCS planning. These first strikes, code-named Flaming Dart, were followed by sustained bombings of strategic targets (Operation Rolling Thunder) at the beginning of March. Wheeler's oversight of the air strikes was constant. The development of targets, the impact of the bombings, deployments of men and matériel, and assessments of Vietnamese morale became Wheeler's primary concern.*

Throughout early 1965, bleak military intelligence reports continued to cross Wheeler's desk, including one that indicated a total of nine North Vietnamese Army (NVA) regiments deployed in South Vietnam, with another two regiments poised inside Cambodia, ready to strike east and cut the nation in half. Reports from Saigon emphasized the worsening situation; it was doubtful, according to Westmoreland and Taylor, that the South Vietnamese Army could defeat the Vietcong and North Vietnamese. In addition, the large military base at Danang, with its full complement of U.S. advisers, trainers, support staff, and equipment, was in danger of being overrun by twelve VC battalions, numbering 6,000 men, in the immediate area. Eventually, Westmoreland told Wheeler, the Vietcong and NVA would respond to American air strikes by launching a raid against U.S. assets in the South, and while ARVN morale had been raised by the Flaming Dart and Rolling Thunder raids, it was clear that U.S. bases were in danger. On February 24, 1965, Wheeler received a cable from CINCPAC with Westmoreland's request that two Marine Battalion Landing teams be deployed to Danang to protect the base. The message, Wheeler realized, was urgent: the Marines were needed immediately, "before the tragedy," the Pacific commander said. Within minutes, Wheeler passed the message to McNamara, who approved the deployment. On March 6, the Marines landed in Vietnam.

The public record of March 1965 seems unambiguous: the JCS favored an uncompromising military solution to the Vietnam problem and quickly endorsed Westmoreland's call for troops. Furthermore, at every opportunity over the next several months, until the end of August, the JCS endorsed the deployment of increasing numbers of

---

* Despite this enormous responsibility, Wheeler was not the primary target officer. Beginning in early 1965, Lyndon Johnson took an obsessive interest in the U.S. air campaign, taking on the final responsibility for actually choosing targets. In fact, the White House situation room, not the tank, quickly became the nation's most important target selection center.

American soldiers to buttress the teetering South Vietnamese regime, thereby tying itself to the philosophy of graduated response it had attempted to undermine earlier. But the story of the events from March to August 1965 are far more complex than most military professionals are willing to admit. The belief that the JCS consistently and unanimously supported America's commitment to the tottering regime of South Vietnam might be comforting, but it isn't supported by the evidence.

In fact, even before the first administration debates on the war, and certainly well before Westmoreland pushed for the first deployment of troops to Southeast Asia, the JCS had been questioning the American policy in Indochina. The ostensible result of the debate — a consensus in favor of a large-scale air campaign *without* U.S. troop deployment — actually covered deep doubts among JCS members. In fact, by early 1965, at least one of the chiefs, Harold Johnson, openly wondered whether the American military even belonged in Indochina, a view that was exacerbated by Westmoreland's request for troops. For more than six months, he had been trying to persuade the JCS to adopt an either-or position, saying that the chiefs should tell Lyndon Johnson to "either get into this thing and win, or not go in at all." At the beginning of March, the Army chief was called to the White House to meet with the president — an opportunity, the general believed, to exchange views on the situation in Vietnam and to express his growing hesitation over American policy. Outfitted in his full service uniform, he looked forward to the meeting, which he believed would be cordial. But Lyndon Johnson was in a foul mood, frustrated by the war even in its earliest days and obsessed by the intransigence of Ho Chi Minh.

According to later accounts, the encounter was filled with tension. The president questioned Johnson closely for almost an hour, but remained dissatisfied with the replies. "You don't have any answers, do you?" Lyndon Johnson angrily asked. When General Johnson didn't respond, the president pointed his finger at him. "Well, go get some," he said. Within twenty-four hours, Harold Johnson was en route to Saigon to make a firsthand assessment of the situation. Appropriately, he spent his first day in the war zone closeted with Taylor and Westmoreland. The normally ebullient commander, his combat fatigues neatly pressed, his face scraped clean, painted a grim picture: the South Vietnamese Army was disintegrating, and more American troops than those deployed at Danang would be needed to save the country. Taylor was more circumspect: things were bad, but he wasn't sure that a large commitment of American troops would provide the answer.

The next morning, Johnson decided to go beyond the official briefings and take his own tour of the country. He visited major American installations near Saigon, then took a helicopter to a special forces camp outside Pleiku, in South Vietnam's Central Highlands. There, with the triple-canopied jungles rising around him and running west into the forbidding territories of Cambodia, Johnson told the American commander that "when the North Vietnamese come, they will come right at you," an amazingly prescient statement in light of later events. The commander was confident. "We're ready, sir," he said. Johnson stared him down. "No you're not," he said.

Johnson returned to Washington on March 12 with even greater misgivings about the American policy than he'd had earlier. On the fourteenth, he gave the Secretary of Defense twenty-one specific recommendations on handling the war, agreeing with Westmoreland that the situation in South Vietnam was deteriorating and stating, surprisingly, that the United States should commit combat troops to the defense of South Vietnam. But Johnson was unwilling to take most of the major steps suggested by the MACV commander. Specifically, the Army chief wasn't convinced that the United States should be the sole guarantor of South Vietnamese independence; instead, he recommended that the United States invoke the "SEATO treaty," to assure "allied participation" in the conflict. Moreover, he attempted to determine the course of battle, advising that the SEATO force be used as a "counter-infiltration cordon" against the NVA.

But Johnson's primary recommendation took the form of a veiled criticism of American policy-makers and Westmoreland's policy of escalation. "In order for the USG [U.S. Government] to evaluate his requests properly when submitted," Johnson wrote, "a policy determination must be made in the very near future that will assure the question: What should the Vietnamese be expected to do for themselves and how much more must the U.S. contribute directly to the security of South Vietnam?"

He implied that this central question had yet to be fully addressed by American policy-makers. But neither McNamara nor the president took the hint: at the bottom of the report, McNamara scribbled his own chilling answer to Johnson's question: "Policy is: anything that will strengthen the position of the GVN [Government of Vietnam] will be sent." In essence, he gave Westmoreland a blank check in Vietnam despite Johnson's misgivings. But in private, Johnson was even more skeptical than his report implied, a view reinforced by comments he made during several executive sessions of the JCS. Johnson questioned not only America's commitment but also the quality of American military leadership, singling out the special forces for particular criticism.

In later years, he summarized his views by describing the Green

Berets as "fugitives from responsibility" and a "new gimmick" that President Kennedy had mistakenly "latched onto." "These were people that somehow or other tended to be nonconformist," Johnson said. They "couldn't quite get along in a straight military system, and found a haven where their actions were not scrutinized too carefully, and where they came under only sporadic or intermittent observation from the regular chain of command." He also told his colleagues he had doubts that the American bombing campaign would convince the North Vietnamese to end their support of the southern insurgency.

Johnson's position became the most outspoken, and the most public, of that of any of the chiefs. And after his trip to Vietnam, he became obsessed by the conflict. "He kept saying, 'isolate the battlefield, isolate the battlefield.' He'd tell anyone who would listen," one former JCS staff officer remembers. Thomas Moorer has vivid memories of Johnson's agony. "When the Vietnam thing started," he said later, "Johnson vowed he would personally write the parents of every soldier killed in combat. And he did it, you know. He sat down at the end of every day and went through the personal files of the soldiers and wrote their parents. But he couldn't keep up; there were just too many dying. Some weeks he would try to write two hundred or more letters. In the end he just couldn't do it, he thought it was such a waste. It ripped him up. I could see it in his face." But Johnson had other qualities that were beginning to convince JCS staff officers that he was destined to be one of the greatest, if least remembered, Army chiefs in JCS history.

Unlike many of his West Point classmates of 1933, Harold Johnson wasn't picked for command; he graduated 232nd in a class of 347 and "did an awful lot of gambling." The view that he was one of the class's least likely future generals clearly embittered the new lieutenant, who was assigned to the Philippines, one of the Army's least romantic posts.* Johnson later dismissed these feelings, saying simply that he was part of the "class mafia, those whom no one would have chosen to succeed." As for the success of his classmates, many of whom later rose to high command, Johnson shrugged it off; they were simply "in the right place at the right time." But Johnson wasn't: when World War II started, he was flung into full combat against the Japanese on Corregidor and then became part of the Bataan death march, which had a profound and lasting impact on him. "God was close and very real," he said later. The road was littered with beheaded Filipinos.

---

* Johnson's language instructor at West Point was Maxwell Taylor. Earle Wheeler and General John McConnell (who served as Air Force chief after LeMay) were one year ahead of him. William Westmoreland, Johnson's deputy Creighton Abrams, and General Bruce Palmer graduated in 1933.

In a prisoner of war camp, he staved off hunger by playing poker with a Filipino prisoner (Johnson returned after the war to pay the man the $1,098 he was owed), and when the Americans drew near, he was put in the hold of a ship with 688 others bound for Formosa, a torturous trip. Johnson was then shipped to Japan and finally to Korea, where he was liberated in September 1945. "I have looked upon that period as a prisoner of war as a great laboratory of human behavior," he later reflected.* In the following years promotion came slowly; officers who had had combat commands during the war were promoted ahead of Johnson, who remained a part of the class mafia. Still, his journey up the military ladder was constant: he was given a combat command in Korea, where he became an acknowledged and outspoken critic of America's overuse of massive firepower. In 1960, he became commandant of the prestigious Command and General Staff College, a job he later said he preferred to the more glamorous position of superintendent of West Point, where William Westmoreland was meeting John Kennedy and becoming the inevitable general.

But while Westmoreland garnered the Army's most prestigious assignments, Johnson's views were more widely circulated and respected. By 1960, Johnson's outspoken opinions of how the military should be structured provoked widespread comment and controversy. "At the time I went to Leavenworth [the home of the General Staff College]," Johnson said later, "the dominant element in all the force at that time was the Strategic Air Command [SAC]. There was the assertion made that SAC deterred war. I had a little bit of trouble with that assertion because I'd served in Korea and the Army had taken some 33,000 casualties over there, killed in action . . . it was hard to see why so many Army people had died if SAC, in fact, had deterred war."

He also had a jaundiced view of tactical air support of Army troops, a view he expressed as a ditty that soon made the rounds in Vietnam: "If you *want* it, you can't get it. If you *can* get it, it can't find you. If it *can* find you, it can't identify the target. If it *can* identify the target, it can't hit it. But if it *does* hit the target, it doesn't do a great deal of damage anyway." Thus it is perhaps not surprising that by April 1965, Johnson was not only the Army's leading tactician but one of its best-known skeptics, an officer who believed that deploying troops should be the nation's last resort in a conflict and undertaken only if civilian leaders are willing to make "an irrevocable commitment."

Through the end of March and into April, Johnson pushed his col-

---

* As General Bruce Palmer, a retired Army deputy chief, later said, Johnson "made a Christian out of me with a single phrase" during a meeting of the chiefs in 1967. When Palmer swore, Johnson looked right at him and said, "General, I'd appreciate it if you didn't take the Lord's name in vain in my presence."

leagues to join him in attempting to convince the president to call for a full military mobilization, and he directed his staff to draw up a proposal for him to take to the White House — a political tactic as much as a military necessity. One of Johnson's chief aides, Edward C. Meyer, drafted the proposal. "The basis of it was that the war could not be won without calling up the reserves. It would show the American people we were serious," Meyer recalled.

In May 1965, Johnson's plan was formally presented to the chiefs, who quickly endorsed it. In fact, Chairman Wheeler, apparently undeterred by the president's veto of the earlier JCS recommendation, for a massive air campaign, had continued to press McNamara for a full U.S. commitment, which would revive the JCS's "quick war" scenario. The Army chief's proposal fit well with Wheeler's own thinking; it would not only mean that the United States had a chance of winning the war, it would send a clear message to North Vietnam's leadership, something that neither Flaming Dart nor Rolling Thunder had accomplished. The JCS immediately asked for a private meeting with the president. "Johnson went to the president," Meyer said, "and LBJ listened to the argument. And LBJ leaned across the table to General Johnson and he said, 'General, you leave the American people to me. I know more about the American people than anyone in this room.' "

Despite the president's almost rude dismissal, Wheeler and the rest of the chiefs continued to argue for mobilization in the administration's upper foreign policy echelons. In particular, Wheeler and Johnson continued to push their viewpoint with McNamara, who, they realized, had more influence with Lyndon Johnson. McNamara was willing to be pushed; like Wheeler, he was uneasy with Bundy's and Taylor's middle way, and Wheeler's adoption of the Johnson plan — declare a national emergency, mobilize the reserves, get in, win, and get out — was an elegantly simple (and cost-effective) plan. Finally, tentatively, McNamara agreed.

The administration's primary critic of mobilization was NSC adviser McGeorge Bundy, who was convinced that the American people wouldn't tolerate an expanded conflict. He also wasn't convinced that full mobilization, a phrase that dropped from McNamara's lips during one meeting with the president in early July, could convince the North Vietnamese to negotiate an end to the war. Bundy said that calling up the reserves was tantamount to a declaration of war, something that he and his brother William wanted to avoid. Meanwhile, McNamara went to Saigon with Wheeler, a journey that turned out to be the last bit of evidence the secretary needed to convince him that the JCS was right; the South Vietnamese government and army were near total disintegration, the nation in chaos.

Just one day after McNamara's return, on July 22, 1964, Lyndon Johnson called a high-level meeting to discuss America's options. McNamara was low-key, careful to take the stridency out of the JCS's arguments: McGeorge Bundy was right, he told the president, a national mobilization was tantamount to a declaration of war, but the situation in Vietnam was critical and would get worse without American troops. At this White House meeting, McNamara and the JCS, including the new Air Force chief of staff, John McConnell (who had taken over from the contentious LeMay), made their most convincing case for mobilization. Once again Harold Johnson, the JCS's key mobilization advocate, bore the brunt of Lyndon Johnson's cold stares.* After one exchange between the president and his civilian advisers, LBJ turned to Johnson and posed a question: "Are we in agreement we would rather be out of there and make our stand somewhere else?" General Johnson's answer was swift. "The least desirable alternative is getting out," he said. "The second least is doing what we are doing. Best is to get in and get the job done."

"What is your reaction to Ho's statement he is ready to fight for twenty years?" the president then asked.

"I believe him," Johnson said. Later reports suggest that he believed he was in a test of wills with the president, that he might even be fired.

The discussion turned to the reserve call-up. "Gerald Ford has demanded the President testify before the Congress and tell why we are compelled to [call] up the reserves," LBJ said, turning to McNamara. "Indications are that he will oppose calling up the reserves."

McNamara smiled. "I think we can answer most of the questions posed," he said confidently, and with that, Lyndon Johnson ended the meeting. He left the distinct impression, especially among members of the JCS, that he had decided to mobilize the nation for war.

Afterward, a jubilant and apparently victorious Wheeler met with Harold Johnson and told him to get the Army ready: the 1st Air Cavalry would be deployed to Vietnam immediately, and other units would follow. The president would go on television to tell the American people that the nation was mobilizing for war. Johnson immediately called Major General Harry Kinnard at Fort Benning, Georgia. "Get ready," Johnson said over the Pentagon's secure phone lines. "You're going to Vietnam."

"When?" Kinnard asked.

"Now."

There was silence on the other end of the line.

---

* In addition to the chiefs, NSC director McGeorge Bundy, the president's friend Clark Clifford, Robert McNamara, McNamara's assistant Cyrus Vance, and the president's aide Jack Valenti attended the White House session.

"Don't be so happy," Johnson finally said.
In fact, Kinnard was ecstatic.*

When Harry Kinnard heard that the nation was going to war in Vietnam, the man the new Air Cav soldiers called "that son-of-a-bitch" was ready. This was his chance, his first opportunity to show that the Army helicopter could be a decisive wartime weapon, that the Army's newest combat doctrine, airmobility, would actually work on the battlefield. A member of the West Point class of 1939, Kinnard took an important command position in Europe soon after graduation. In December 1944, as the chief intelligence officer for the encircled 101st Airborne Division at Bastogne during the Battle of the Bulge, he made the initial assessment that American tanks would sooner or later come to the rescue. "All we have to do," he said, "is hang on." The 101st's commander wasn't about to do anything else, but he was pleased to hear that his closest aide agreed. The day after Christmas, soldiers at the eastern edge of Bastogne reported three American tanks in the distance. Kinnard hurried to the edge of the American lines. When an American tank pierced the 101st perimeter, a young colonel came forward, smiling at Kinnard. He gave a lackadaisical salute and said, "Hello Harry."

The man in the lead tank of the first relief column was Colonel Creighton Abrams, later commended by Patton himself as probably the only American tank officer who compared favorably to himself (coming from Patton, an amazing admission). Now, as Kinnard's troops awaited transport to Vietnam, Abrams was trying to figure out where Westmoreland should deploy the general's newly designated 1st Cavalry Division (Airmobile). Looking at situation maps in the Pentagon, Abrams (like Harold Johnson before him) decided the NVA would enter Vietnam through the Central Highlands. The 1st Air Cav would be deployed to Pleiku while Johnson — who was ordering his staff to plan a full mobilization — readied the deployment of the reserves. Wheeler's plan — to fight a quick war without a drawdown of American forces elsewhere — was becoming a reality. But Johnson's orders on reserve mobilization were premature.

After his meeting with the JCS and his top foreign policy advisers on July 22, Lyndon Johnson decided he would review the JCS position in the less pressured environment of the presidential retreat at Camp David. Within hours of his arrival, he called three of his most trusted aides, Clark Clifford, Supreme Court Justice Arthur Goldberg, and

---

* "Your job, Harry," Johnson said in the same conversation, "is to keep them from cutting the country in half. You've got to go in there and stop them, because if they can do that they've got it won."

Robert McNamara, to go over the mobilization option yet again. Not surprisingly, McNamara was its most outspoken defender, stridently repeating the arguments he had used at the White House. But even he began to soften in the face of Clifford and Goldberg's firm opposition: both men contended that such a radical step was unnecessary.* Goldberg was the most intransigent, telling the president he would withdraw his planned resignation from the Supreme Court (he was slated to become ambassador to the U.N.), because mobilization would mean a full-scale war.

Goldberg's words chastened the president, who had rarely seen the judge so exercised. Finally, after a full day of talks, the president gave in and agreed that a reserve call-up wasn't necessary or even advisable. But he said he wanted one more White House cabinet session on the issue before making a final decision. This debate, on July 26, turned out to be a replay of earlier discussions: once again, Wheeler pushed the president to pick the quick war alternative, saying that mobilization was the best way to assure victory in Vietnam. But this time Johnson quickly dismissed Wheeler's argument: he announced he was reversing his previous decision. He would not call up the reserves, though he added (perhaps as a salve) that he agreed with McNamara's assessment of the situation in South Vietnam. In essence, Lyndon Johnson announced that he favored the strategy of graduated response: the United States would escalate military actions in Indochina, moving to a full complement of up to 200,000 combat personnel, with the possibility of increasing that number to 600,000. Across the table from the president, Wheeler sat silently, apparently stunned by the sudden reversal. Treasury Secretary Henry Fowler broke the silence: "Do we ask for standby authority now to call the reserves but not actually call them?"

"Under the approved plan, we would not ask for such authority now," the president said. Two days later, he announced his decision to the nation during a midday televised news conference. The United States would increase its Vietnam commitment from 75,000 to 125,000 men, and more combat soldiers would be sent "as requested." The draft would be doubled, but it was not necessary to call up the reserves now, the president added. At Fort Benning, Harry Kinnard — who had not been informed of the president's change of heart — gathered his top commanders to watch the president. The men of the 1st Air Cav

---

* The jockeying for position continued well after LBJ's meeting with the JCS. Undersecretary of State George Ball and Clark Clifford had an influential role in rallying the antimobilization forces. In a remarkable statement at Camp David, Clifford told Johnson, "If we lose 50,000 men there, it will be catastrophic for the country. . . . I cannot see anything but catastrophe for our nation in this area."

were "on knife's edge — ready to go." When the president came on, the room broke into applause.

"We all sat around the television watching the president and he activated the 1st Air Cav and then went off. I have to tell you, I was just stunned," Kinnard said later. "I didn't know what to think. There we were . . . we were going into a war without a national emergency. You have to understand what that meant. It meant that my guys whose enlistments were up would not go, but that was 50 percent of my command." In effect, half of the 1st Air Cav would be going into combat without airmobile training. At the Pentagon, Johnson was almost desperate. After the speech, he closed the door of his office and put on his best dress uniform. When he emerged, he ordered his driver to get his car; he was going to talk to the president, he told his staff. On the way into Washington, Johnson reached up and unpinned the stars from his shoulders, holding them lightly in his hands. When the car arrived at the White House gates, he ordered his driver to stop. He stared down at his stars, shook his head, and pinned them back on. Years later he reflected on the incident, regretting his own decision. "I should have gone to see the president," he reportedly told one colleague. "I should have taken off my stars. I should have resigned. It was the worst, the most immoral decision I've ever made."

By November 1965, just sixty days after the 1st Air Cav had finished deploying to South Vietnam's Central Highlands, it was involved in a brutal running battle with NVA regulars in the Ia Drang Valley. As Kinnard's grim reports came in, Wheeler was convinced that Harold Johnson's earlier recommendation — that the United States should "go in rapidly and win it" or not go in at all — was essentially correct. Kinnard's airborne soldiers, denuded by Lyndon Johnson's refusal to call the reserves, were being decimated by two NVA regiments. While the NVA's attempt to cut South Vietnam in half failed, the battle for the Ia Drang (characterized ever after as a victory) shook the upper echelons of the Army.*

In Washington, Harold Johnson read Kinnard's battle report with keen interest, noting that the NVA's campaign had opened with an attack on the Plei Me special forces camp near Pleiku, the same camp he had visited back in March. He had thought then that the special forces team there was vulnerable; now he knew the NVA had made the same judgment. But, more important, Johnson realized that the Ia Drang marked a turning point in the war; from then on, the United

---

* The gravity of the situation was highlighted by Westmoreland's visit to Kinnard after the immediate end of the battle. Participants in the battle say that Kinnard was wrong to describe the engagement as a victory. In particular, the military took special care to leave certain embarrassing aspects of the engagement out of official histories.

States was committed to defending South Vietnam despite the president's rejection of JCS arguments to get in, win, and get out. In fact, the Ia Drang engagement so disturbed Johnson that he decided to make another trip to Vietnam, in December 1965, to obtain a firsthand assessment of the situation. In particular, he seriously doubted that Westmoreland's conventional strategy for dealing with the Vietcong and NVA (which had come to ruin in the Ia Drang) would work. As earlier, Johnson decided the only way he could get answers was by visiting selected commanders in the field after receiving a glowing briefing from MACV headquarters in Saigon.

"During Christmas of 1965, Harold Johnson came over to Vietnam and made a tour," Edward Meyer, then a lieutenant colonel, remembered. "He got some colonels together without Westmoreland and he went around the room and he asked each of us why the war was being handled the way it was and whether we thought it was right. And there weren't too many of us who would criticize Westmoreland. But finally a lot of us did. We just didn't think we could do the job the way we were doing it. And Johnson nodded his head and left the room." Johnson's doubts about Westmoreland were heightened even more by firsthand reports on the Ia Drang situation, including one from Kinnard, who told Johnson he had pleaded with Westmoreland to redeploy the 1st Air Cav. "Use their [North Vietnamese] tactics," Kinnard reportedly told Westmoreland at the end of the battle. "Put us in Thailand and have us interdict the Ho Chi Minh trail. Seal off this battlefield." Johnson learned that one commander had pleaded with Westmoreland to "end the big unit war"; he later told the Army chief that "we're just not going to win it doing this." Other top commanders recommended that the United States take the fight to North Vietnam, an option Johnson knew was out of the question.

After his return to Washington, Johnson was involved in the detailed monitoring of the situation in Vietnam, which included quizzing returning commanders on American strategy and leadership. But Johnson's best advice came from the Army's vice chief of staff, the outspoken Creighton Abrams. Beginning in mid-1966, he began to question the Westmoreland "big unit" conventional strategy, arguing that the South Vietnamese should carry the burden of the war. Abrams's widely circulated contention on American overinvolvement, Johnson knew, was becoming more and more acceptable to frustrated combat commanders. Obviously, Johnson's incessant questioning of Westmoreland's tactics veiled his larger doubts on the war itself, doubts that were so deeply felt that the Army chief realized that in order to change America's view of the war, he would have to change the American commander. "Again in 1966 Johnson approached me personally and asked me what I thought we should do," Meyer remembered. "I was surprised he asked and took it to mean that he didn't think there was much chance we could win it the way we were doing it. And I said that there was a lot of agreement, the Americans should let the ARVN do the fighting . . . eventually we would have to let them do it anyway, so the sooner the better."

Still, Johnson wasn't prepared to recommend Westmoreland's replacement; the long-held JCS tradition of allowing a field commander to make battle decisions was too deeply ingrained. Instead, he decided he would slowly work to make Abrams Westmoreland's top deputy, a move he first suggested in mid-1966. In addition, Johnson decided that the JCS should be more forceful in arguing its position in its disagreements with civilian leaders, a contention he first articulated during a series of JCS meetings in June 1966. According to several JCS officers at these meetings, what bothered Johnson the most about the growing civilian-military tussle over war strategy was the government's habit of putting the best face on the war. In particular, he disdained the shameless public relations campaign to sell the war to the American people, a tactic that embittered him against the president and McNamara. By mid-1966, according to these JCS officers, the Army chief was so disenchanted that he was openly calling the Department of Defense the Department of Deceit.

Not surprisingly, Wheeler also harbored doubts about the American commitment, though for far different reasons than his Army chief. While Johnson was beginning to believe the United States should turn over responsibility for the war to the ARVN and push for a change in strategy, Wheeler advocated an increase in U.S. troop deployments. In fact, he approved every new troop request submitted by Westmoreland. With the possibility that 110 NVA battalions would be deployed in South Vietnam by mid-1966, the JCS chairman argued that the United States might need more than 500,000 soldiers to meet the threat, a figure that made administration officials uncomfortable. But Wheeler's strategy did not mirror Westmoreland's. While Westmoreland continued to provide Washington with reports that he was making progress, and was apparently buoyed by the big unit battles of late 1965 and early 1966, Wheeler knew the war could not be won without the nation's irrevocably committing itself to South Vietnam's defense.

In essence, Wheeler continued to work tirelessly for full mobilization, crafting a policy that made troop increases look incremental but brought the administration inevitably closer to full mobilization. In retrospect, this unstated strategy was one of the most elegant and astute political maneuvers in JCS history: by agreeing to an ever-larger commitment of U.S. forces, Wheeler realized he was slowly moving closer to the upper limit of U.S. troop availability; when he reached that upper limit, he believed, Lyndon Johnson would have little choice but to mobilize the nation. The JCS chairman even had a timetable. Taking increased troop deployments in early 1966 as a gauge, he knew the Army would start scraping the bottom of the manpower barrel in late 1967 or early 1968 (and the war still wouldn't be won). Throughout most of 1966, Wheeler was confident his strategy would work. Not only were American troop levels in Vietnam being consistently increased, McNamara remained an invaluable pro-mobilization ally.

But in August 1966, the CIA issued one of the most comprehensive and damaging assessments of the war the JCS had ever received. Entitled "Memorandum: The Vietnamese Communists' Will to Persist," the report argued that the U.S. bombing campaign against North Vietnam was failing and that the North Vietnamese had built "the most formidable air defense system in the history of modern warfare." The price of admission to the skies over Hanoi, it said, was the highest in military history, higher even than the one exacted by Germany over Berlin during World War II. The report went on to point out that the North Vietnamese were "tough and dedicated communists" who were "willing to take enormous casualties." Even the title of the report was a slap at the military. For more than two years, Westmoreland (with JCS concurrence) had been arguing that all the United States needed to do was "persist" in its current strategy, using the word that had come to characterize MACV's optimism. Now, the CIA was saying, North Vietnamese will power, its ability to persist, was greater than America's.

Wheeler initially believed the CIA report would reinvigorate McNamara's call for mobilization and convince Lyndon Johnson that the Bundy-Taylor strategy of graduated response was bankrupt, that it not only wasn't working, it could never work. To Wheeler's amazement, however, "The Will to Persist" had just the opposite effect, destroying McNamara's morale and, with it, his support of the JCS's position. In fact, the result of the CIA study was far worse than Wheeler could have ever imagined. In late August, McNamara said that he had shown the CIA report to Lyndon Johnson, who quickly read it, then slapped it down on his desk. Johnson looked up at McNamara and barked out his orders: "Hell, don't show this report to anyone. Put the clamps on it. If this gets out, it will destroy the morale and spirit of our armed forces."

The president's response, as well as his continued effort to hold down U.S. troop commitments and North Vietnamese bombing targets, was the subject of a number of important JCS discussions that continued well into 1967. While all the chiefs agreed that it was now too late for withdrawal (and that the United States should, therefore, make its commitment "irrevocable"), they couldn't agree on a strategy in selling their views to the administration: whether they should continue to push for full mobilization and an increase in the number of bombing missions over North Vietnam, or whether they should publicly break with Lyndon Johnson's support of the graduated response strategy. So, while American troop levels increased in Vietnam (and were expected to reach 470,000 by the end of 1967) and the tempo of fighting reached a new crescendo, the JCS failed to mold a strategy that would allow it to take control of the war.

In one sense, the chiefs were powerless: they were mistrusted by administration insiders as uncompromising hawks, whose advocacy of full mobilization bordered on the irrational, and by Westmoreland supporters as incessant worriers, who failed to take MACV's glowing reports at face value. Finally, however, after nearly nine months of indecision, the JCS received two pieces of good news that helped settle the internal disagreement. The first piece came in May 1967, when Abrams was finally made Westmoreland's deputy in Vietnam, an appointment Harold Johnson had been pushing for more than a year. It came at a good time for the Army chief, who was becoming more and more embroiled in the civilian-military debate, which had triggered a number of uncomfortable meetings between him and McNamara. Given his continued doubts about the Westmoreland strategy, the Army chief realized that the JCS needed someone in Vietnam who was willing to file something other than glowing reports of American victories.

The second piece of good news came in June, when Mississippi's Senator John Stennis said he had decided to hold hearings on the war that would feature testimony from the JCS. Stennis wanted his hearings to balance those being conducted by Senator William Fulbright, who headed the increasingly antiwar Foreign Relations Committee. While it was clear that the Stennis hearings might turn into a bloodletting, the JCS believed they would provide a public forum for military doubts on the war's conduct. More significantly, at least for Wheeler, they provided a way for him to get McNamara to "take off the clamps" on the situation in Vietnam. The secretary's testimony, scheduled for the end of August, would finally spell out what the JCS had thought all along — that the administration should approve the expanded JCS list of air targets and prosecute the war to its fullest by mobilizing the reserves. But even if it didn't happen, Wheeler thought, at least the administration would be forced to make a clear decision on the war, even if it was that the United States should withdraw.

The nation's high command, and especially the JCS, was greatly respected by Stennis; in the two years since American troops had landed in Vietnam their testimony had been applauded, their sacrifices praised, their opinions valued, and their programs greeted with approval by the hawkish senator. The views of his subcommittee were legendary. *The Pentagon Papers* later described its members as "defenders of 'air power' " who had "often aligned themselves with the 'professional military experts' " against "unskilled civilian amateurs." It wasn't a popular position. While Fulbright's Foreign Relations Committee grabbed headlines by questioning America's involvement, Stennis's committee continued to support JCS calls for increased military pressures against North Vietnam. At no time was this support more evident than during the hearings on the war in August 1967.

Praising the JCS for its opposition to what he called "the doctrine of gradualism," in the hearing's opening days, Stennis listened closely as the JCS publicly castigated the administration for failing to listen to its advice. The criticism was pointed. While Wheeler refused to say that the war was being lost, he made it clear that the administration's failure to increase pressure on North Vietnam might mean that it couldn't be won. In addition, he told Stennis that there was unanimous agreement among commanders at the Pentagon that air interdiction of supplies to the Vietcong would fail unless the United States closed the North Vietnamese port of Haiphong. If U.S. civilian leaders were serious about winning the war, Wheeler said, then they must take steps against North Vietnam that included approval of the full JCS target list. But he also implied that even this action would not be enough, a clear indication to administration foreign policy decision-makers that he was still interested in full mobilization. In essence, the JCS's cigar-chewing chairman, the Army's "leading sycophant," the officer who most represented the new breed of desk general, savaged the administration: the war wasn't being won and couldn't be won until North Vietnam's support of the southern insurgency was broken. Moreover, the Johnson-McNamara policy was doomed to failure unless the military was allowed to "go to the source," to stop the flow of supplies to North Vietnam.

On August 25, McNamara responded to Wheeler's charges. For subcommittee insiders, the secretary's testimony was the culmination of months of work, a fragile strategy designed to expose the unacknowledged breakdown of the military-civilian consensus on Vietnam policy. They were not disappointed. McNamara smiled confidently as he took his seat, nodded at the frowning senators, opened his file folder, and began to speak in his cool, professorial style: "I welcome this opportunity to discuss with you our conduct of the air war in North Vietnam." Then, in clipped phrases, he outlined America's policy to end North Vietnamese aggression and "to assure the people of South Vietnam the freedom to choose their own political and economic institutions." McNamara was initially modest, saying that the nation's civilian leaders clearly understood the military point of view. The military was right, he admitted; no air campaign could by itself completely shut off the flow of supplies from North Vietnam. Nevertheless, he added, the administration's bombing policy would eventually bring victory. It was part of an overall campaign designed to end the southern insurgency and would be successful when coupled with "an effective counter-insurgency campaign in South Vietnam."

But then McNamara took the offensive, attacking the JCS claim that an expanded air offensive against North Vietnam could help bring an end to the war. He reviewed the military's target list, arguing that most targets had already been bombed and that only 57 of 359 targets "have not yet been authorized." This bombing, he added, represented 85 percent of the targets on the JCS list. Halfway through his testimony, McNamara looked up and paused, purposely emphasizing his next statement: "There can be no question that the bombing campaign has and is hurting North Vietnam's war-making capability." There was silence in the hearing room, a palpable sense of tension. "A selective, carefully targeted bombing campaign, such as we are presently conducting," he reiterated, "can be directed toward reasonable and realizable goals. This discriminating use of air power can and does render the infiltration of men and supplies more difficult and more costly." His words were almost a shout. While Johnson's policy might be debatable, he was saying, its impact wasn't; it was working. The North Vietnamese were buckling. America was winning the war in Vietnam.

The JCS was stunned. Not only had McNamara ignored the CIA's report, he had dismissed the most important JCS contention: that a successful conclusion could only be gained by shutting off supplies to the North, not to the South. Moreover, as Wheeler had told the committee, the effectiveness of the U.S. bombing campaign was not a matter of opinion but the most important statistical measure of American progress in the war. If the U.S. air campaign was working, as McNamara said, why were shipments of men and arms to South Vietnam increasing? In other words, McNamara had lied. What Wheeler and his fellow officers had told the subcommittee might be discomfiting, but it was also transparently provable: the U.S. strategy *wasn't* working, the North Vietnamese *weren't* buckling; America probably couldn't win by continuing the graduated escalation policies of Bundy and Taylor.

While the testimony had been, as one general remembered, "a particularly stormy session" that opened deep wounds between "the Wheeler chiefs" and their Secretary of Defense, the impact actually went far deeper. McNamara's testimony broke the unofficial contract between civilian leaders and military officers that, by necessity, exists in every democratic society: members of the military pledge they will obey civilian authorities without question; in return, civilian leaders pledge that those orders will not lead to the useless sacrifice of military life.

The highest-ranking officers now believed that they had been betrayed by their civilian leaders, that the war could not continue without an irrational loss of American lives, and that, given McNamara's bad-faith defense of a clearly discredited strategy, there was little reason to hope for an eventual American victory. On one level, JCS officers believed that to continue the war under current conditions would be immoral: it would lead to a useless sacrifice; but on another level they believed that the crisis had more practical consequences: it actually convinced a large number of America's three- and four-star officers that the military itself must have a greater voice in determining U.S. policy. The change in attitude was fundamental; it marked an unprecedented break in American military tradition. After 1967, the JCS would work slowly, but certainly, for a role in determining U.S. foreign policy.

Within hours of the testimony, Wheeler realized he would have to act quickly to expose McNamara's lie, if only to tie the JCS's clear break over civilian policies to a well-publicized and controversial event. More important, he realized that in order to convince the American people that the tenuous consensus on the war between the nation's elected leaders and its military officers had been shattered, he would have to convince all the JCS members to make their break public. For Wheeler, it was paramount that the public event be an unambiguous and shattering message to Johnson and McNamara, that it shift public debate from an argument over the scope to an argument over the type of American involvement in Vietnam. In effect, Wheeler believed that the JCS had a unique opportunity to convince the American people to pressure Lyndon Johnson to make an unambiguous stand in Vietnam — or get out.

On the late afternoon of August 25, Wheeler presented his plan to the rest of the JCS. The meeting was unprecedented. Not only did it not take place in the tank, Wheeler barred all JCS aides and did not allow anyone to take notes. His instructions to his staff (who lived in continual fear of his temper) were exact: the JCS would accept calls from the president but from no one else. His next step was even more unusual. When the chiefs convened in his office, he asked each of them to pledge that what they were about to discuss would be kept strictly secret as long as any of them remained alive; they agreed. Facing his colleagues from a chair pulled in front of his desk, Wheeler said that he believed they should resign "en masse" during a press conference to be held the next morning. The chiefs weren't shocked; the idea had come up during informal discussions over a period of three months. Now, though, the talk was serious.

This meeting was so unusual, so outside normal practice, that it was immediately noticed throughout the Pentagon. The JCS staff, pressed by the increasing demands of the war, was particularly curious, even troubled. While the chiefs were friendly, they were hardly close. None of them, with the possible exception of Wheeler and Johnson, knew each other socially. Nor was the chairman the type who, as one JCS officer subsequently noted, talked off the record. If he wanted a special session of the chiefs, they could always meet in the tank; Wheeler valued procedure. As the sun set on a humid August night in Washington a new duty shift came on, and JCS officers waiting for their bosses decided to go home. The new watch was briefed on the current military situation before taking their posts. There was nothing unusual to report; all land, sea, and air forces were on regular duty at Defense Condition Five, the lowest state of readiness. Only in Vietnam did American soldiers fight and die.

The unofficial meeting of the JCS lasted from late in the afternoon into the very late evening. When the chairman and the service chiefs left the Pentagon, Washington had been dark for many hours. "We knew something was up," one officer commented years later. "Things were just too quiet. People seemed to just hang around, as if waiting for the final word on what McNamara had said."

Finally, in the mid-1980s, the story began to emerge. Although none of the chiefs went back on his pledge of silence, aides began to talk openly about civilian-military disagreements over the nation's policies in Vietnam and about what one JCS officer calls "the command crisis of 1967." Some of them even speculated on what might have happened "if only" the secret agreement "had stuck."

There was no vote. The chiefs discussed McNamara's testimony matter-of-factly. Moorer said he hadn't been surprised, only disappointed that the administration had not changed its position on JCS targeting. McConnell, whose daily reports on the air war over North Vietnam were beginning to sicken him physically, said he would agree to whatever anyone else wanted. They were a team, he said, and he would do anything to help his flyers. Johnson was the most outspoken proponent of resignation, saying that the military was being blamed for a conflict over which it had little control. The discussion went on for three hours before agreement was reached. Wheeler said they would call for a press conference early the next day, Saturday, to make the announcement and explain the reason behind it. The headlines would be about McNamara's testimony and the apparent administration consensus on the war. With that, the members of the JCS filed out for the evening.

Less than five hours later, early on August 26, Wheeler returned to the Pentagon from his quarters at Fort Myer, knowing that the sweltering day ahead would be anything but typical. The sixty-one-year-old Army general, plagued by the onset of a heart illness that he knew would eventually kill him — he had been experiencing chest pains for the last week, he told one close friend — was exhausted. But it wasn't his health that plagued him; he had spent an almost sleepless night grappling with his sense of loyalty and his military oath. Although he had pushed his colleagues to resign, now every instinct he had told him it was the wrong thing to do and he changed his mind. When he walked into the Pentagon, he knew he faced one of the most difficult tasks of his career: he had to persuade his colleagues that their decision of the night before would not work. Again, Wheeler called for a meeting in his office at eight-thirty. The same rules, he said, would be in effect: no aides, no notes, and a pledge of absolute secrecy.

Wheeler began with a startling statement: "We can't do it. It's mutiny." He then reviewed the events of the previous day, recalling McNamara's statement, the JCS reports on Vietnam, and the probable effect of a group resignation. Johnson stood fast, arguing that the chiefs should resign because it was apparent to him that "no one was really paying any attention" to their recommendations. "If we're going to go to war, then we had better be honest with the American people," he added. Wheeler then decided to turn the discussion around, to raise the points that had kept him awake. "This is mutiny," he said again. "If we resign they'll just get someone else. And we'll be forgotten. Twenty-four hours from now there will be new guys sitting in our places and they'll do what they're told." Wheeler added that as military men they had dedicated their lives to their country, to carrying out the orders of their civilian leaders. "All our lives we've been told to obey orders, we've been schooled in it. We've been told to give our lives for our country. Now, we're going to throw all of that away." Johnson responded by raising other arguments. The war was being lost, he said, and the military would "take the fall." Wheeler pleaded with him. "Give it some time," he said. "You never know, maybe we can pull it out."

In the years that followed, the pledge would remain virtually unbroken. Wheeler died, his silence intact. He made only one slip, during a dinner conversation with a colleague while the war was still raging, when he said he would like to tell the story, but in the form of essays on the breakdown of civilian-military relations during the Vietnam era. Johnson, on the other hand, told one group of veterans that the chiefs had "considered the possibility," and he told several aides, largely because, pledge or no pledge, he believed the story needed to come out. Before his death, he sat down with a close friend and told him about the incident. Vietnam, he said, "has ruined my career."

On the other hand, McConnell, who was near despair over the loss of his flyers, refused to speak of the incident. Uncertain about the impact of mass resignation and a close friend of the president, he consistently refused to talk about the meetings to either friends or aides. Moorer was more circumspect: he admitted years later that "we considered resigning," but retracted his statement in subsequent interviews. Finally, he feigned loss of memory over the incident, only to grudgingly imply that the action hadn't been official. "We considered it," Moorer said, "but never in the tank."

6

WHIZ KIDS
AND WISE MEN

★   ★   ★   ★

The Chairman of the Joint Chiefs has a difficult job living with his civilian bosses, the Secretary of Defense and
the President, striving to convince them in terms they
can understand of matters that he views as military
necessity and, in General Wheeler's case, within the concept of one thing at a time.

General William C. Westmoreland

IN THE TWENTY YEARS after the August 26, 1967, meeting of the JCS,
the reputation of Wheeler grew to such a degree that he soon was considered one of the most important and influential officers in JCS history. Indeed, he is now considered one of the greatest officers to have
served in the postwar era by an astonishing number of the military,
including officers who had only indirect contact with him. Among the
general public, however, Wheeler's name is virtually unknown. He is
rarely included among the pantheon of American military heroes —
men like Patton, MacArthur, Eisenhower, and Bradley — or even
among those who had tremendous influence as postwar strategists,
such as Arthur Radford, Thomas White, and Matthew Ridgway. Nevertheless, officers who knew Wheeler agree that his influence on the
JCS, as well as his legacy, has had a profound influence on civilian-
military relations. In essence, they say, his actions in August 1967, and
in the three months that followed, fundamentally altered the military
tradition of deference to civilian rule.

There seems no easier way to put it. While the JCS had argued,
sometimes persuasively, for the adoption of its own policies during
debates on major international questions for twenty years, it had
never done so with the stridency of Wheeler and his colleagues during
the Vietnam War. While the August 1967 incident is the best example
of this attitude, it's not the only one; in the months that followed, the

JCS would, if anything, be even more outspoken in its opposition to administration policy in Vietnam. In essence, Wheeler's argument of August 26 — that resignation was "mutiny" — was really the beginning of the debate over what policy the United States should follow in Vietnam, not the end. The JCS decided to initiate a series of moves that, it hoped, would lead the president to adopt the strategy he had clearly rejected: to mobilize the reserves, embolden the nation, and win the war. More significantly, Wheeler decided to demand an entirely new role for the JCS, transforming it from a planning body responsible to the Secretary of Defense to an organization of officers answering to the commander in chief.

Surprisingly, it was Wheeler's argument against resignation that has won him the greatest respect among military men. This viewpoint seems universal, held by Wheeler partisans as well as the few remaining detractors. For partisans, the chairman's argument symbolized the triumph of reason, constituting absolute evidence that military officers comply with civilian rule. Even among his detractors, those who strongly disagree that the resignation of the JCS would have been "mutiny," Wheeler is still described as "one of the great chiefs," an officer whose talents might be questioned but whose loyalty remains beyond doubt. In fact, Earle Wheeler is perhaps the only JCS chairman widely viewed as a martyr to the cause of military-civilian unity; he sacrificed his own career rather than embarrass the president and, in the words of Army Colonel Harry Summers, "was killed by the war in Vietnam just as certainly as if he had died in combat."

But while military professionals agree on the pivotal role played by Wheeler, others, including prominent civilian policy-makers in the Johnson administration, view the events of August 1967 far differently. It isn't so important, they argue, that the JCS's basic proposition on the war turned out to be right but that American (nonmilitary) foreign policy experts turned out to be wrong. In other words, the United States was losing in Vietnam not because it failed to adopt the right tactics but because it failed to make the correct political judgments. It failed to understand the inherent weakness of South Vietnam, failed to assess adequately the persistence of North Vietnam and the Vietcong, and, perhaps most important, failed to estimate public opposition to the war properly.

For Wheeler, however, the discussion over what went wrong in Vietnam and why (the subject of incessant internal administration debate) was pointless; the United States was committed in Vietnam despite the failures. The only question for Wheeler was whether the United States would make up for the failures by making an irrevocable commitment in Vietnam. It's clear now, as perhaps it wasn't then, that this fundamental difference in approaching the problem contributed significantly to the deterioration of civilian-military relations during the Vietnam era. The breach reflected more than a division of opinion; throughout the U.S. command establishment, officers were beginning to believe that administration policy was negligent, even criminal, and that, as General Bruce Palmer said, "it was clear that Lyndon Johnson's heart just wasn't in it — that he was looking for a way out."

The breach was total: in the immediate aftermath of the JCS's secret meeting, Wheeler insisted that he be included in the president's Tuesday luncheons with McNamara on Vietnam policy and strategy. Fearing the worst, or perhaps sensing just how close members of his administration had come to open rebellion, Johnson readily agreed. But the JCS meeting had more practical, everyday consequences: after his Senate testimony, JCS members could hardly bring themselves to speak with McNamara. Official meetings between the JCS and the Secretary of Defense degenerated into cold, formal affairs punctuated by stiff, uncomfortable silences. They were ruled by an icy cordiality that conformed strictly with the requirements of courtesy, but no more.

In one sense, the JCS's resentment of McNamara was more the result of years of pent-up rage over his aloof management of the military establishment than his shifting position on the war or his bad-faith testimony. Indeed, for the JCS, McNamara's deceit over Vietnam was simply the last in a series of bitterly disappointing incidents. Not only had McNamara misled the nation on Vietnam, he had grafted a new, hopelessly complex, and universally reviled weapons procurement process (called the Planning, Programming and Budgeting System, or PPBS) onto the JCS's flow chart. In addition, he established an Office of Systems Analysis manned by a retinue of management experts headed by cost-analysis expert Alain Enthoven, the most prominent and widely denigrated of McNamara's "whiz kids."

It was Enthoven's assignment to cut duplication from the military budget or, as he described it, "to motivate the Joint Chiefs of Staff to hunt for deadwood without being prodded." The deadwood, as Enthoven saw it, was apparent everywhere. The military was victimized by its confusion over missions, hampered by poorly designed weapons, hamstrung by its inability to define clear objectives, and caught in a morass of overspending — all evidence of JCS "inefficiencies." From the beginning of McNamara's term as Defense Secretary, Enthoven was granted almost total control of the Pentagon budget and JCS weapons programs — with predictable results.* By late summer 1967,

---

* Enthoven's notable success in weeding out costly weapons programs made him an immediate JCS enemy. During their tenure, McNamara and Enthoven "phased out" four weapons programs: the Skybolt missile system, the sea-based ABM system, the B-70 strategic bomber, and research on the nuclear plane. In addition, he "phased out" the Jupiter, Thor, and Atlas missile projects and the Army's ground-based air defense system.

Enthoven had joined McNamara as a JCS pariah, a man so widely criticized by the military that his appearance in the Pentagon's command
ring was greeted with almost open derision. Even now, high-ranking
officers remember the era bitterly. "This guy Enthoven used to be a
pretty good friend of mine," General Harry Kinnard said. "I think I
understood what he was after. But he ended up just playing with figures. He turned out to be a liar, moving figures around a spread sheet
that would tell us whether the weapons were any good. In the end he
probably cost us lives." That's just what the JCS claimed, citing Enthoven's espousal of a dual-purpose aircraft as the best example.

When the Air Force told McNamara that it wanted to produce a new
high-tech jet named the TFX, he vetoed the idea. In addition, he canceled the Navy's newest fighter, the F6D Eagle Missileer; producing
one kind of jet for one service and another kind for another was just a
waste of money, he said, an argument quickly seconded by Enthoven.
Instead, McNamara proposed that the Air Force and Navy design a
high-performance jet fighter that could be used by both services, that
could carry out long-range bombing missions for the Air Force, and
that could fly off the deck of an aircraft carrier for the Navy. Air Force
and Navy design experts told McNamara and Enthoven that it
couldn't be done, that each service needed a different fighter because
each had a different mission.* But McNamara prevailed, and soon the
new dual-purpose F-111 ("the McNamara fighter") was in service, flying missions into Laos from bases in Thailand. The only problem was,
the F-111 didn't work; not only wasn't it an effective dual-purpose aircraft, Air Force pilots considered it a death trap. According to one Pentagon official familiar with the program, "The F-111 had a bad habit of
plowing into hillsides." The F-111's problems were compounded by the
shameful performance of the F-111B, the Navy's version. It was never
even given its final test run, probably because at 70,000 pounds, naval
aviators were more concerned about sinking aircraft carriers than
actually landing on them.

This was no laughing matter. During 1967, America's year of decision in the Vietnam War, Air Force pilots were saying that McNamara's decision on the F-111 had cost the lives of just over fifty Air
Force pilots, a high price for cost efficiency. The F-111 fiasco proved
that the Army wasn't the only service that had suffered from McNamara's programs; the war (which was supposed to be mostly an Army

---

* When CNO George Anderson, an experienced aviator, clashed publicly with McNamara over the TFX cancellation in 1963, he was quickly made ambassador to Portugal,
thus having one of the shortest terms in JCS history. For bothering to disagree with
McNamara, Anderson was given a medal for his "consummate knowledge and understandings of international relations."

show, anyway) had hurt everyone on the JCS. In August, Air Force Chief McConnell and CNO Moorer, both disgusted by the F-III fiasco, had also had their fill of McNamara. The low-key McConnell was incredulous that the clipboard-strutting secretary could appear so calm in the midst of chaos, convincing the Air Force chief that McNamara probably didn't have any idea of what was happening in Vietnam. Moorer knew better, telling his colleagues that McNamara's studied grace under pressure was a pose that hid an almost obsessive fear of failure.

Indeed, it's one of the paradoxes of JCS history that the Air Force and Navy, the two services most at odds during the JCS's first twenty years (the Revolt of the Admirals is only the best remembered of these clashes) were unanimous in their castigation of McNamara. The attitude of Lieutenant General Glen Martin, a colleague of McConnell's and a JCS officer with experience in Vietnam, typified Air Force attitudes toward McNamara. Serving in top commands during Vietnam, Martin was responsible for briefing McNamara during one of his early trips to Saigon. With pointer in hand, the general expertly ran through his talk, coming at last to what he considered one of the most important military questions of the war: the control and use of tactical aircraft in support of Army combat missions. "Now sir, we should talk about the related tactical air requirements," Martin said, but McNamara waved him off impatiently. "That's peripheral, peripheral," he said and, clipboard in hand, stalked out of the briefing. "It was *critical*," Martin later said. "It wasn't peripheral."

The frustration shown by Martin's remarks permeated the entire Air Force command with the JCS. When McConnell related McNamara's testimony on the positive impact of the air war to Vice Chief John D. Ryan at the end of August (a conversation that almost caused McConnell to break his vow of silence to Wheeler), the former LeMay understudy reportedly sputtered in disbelief. For Ryan, any civilian leader who didn't have the courage of his convictions wasn't worth defending. In later years, the normally reticent Ryan would talk openly and bitterly to other Air Force officers about his years on the JCS, as both vice chief and chief of staff, and would cite this dissembling as the major reason America's Vietnam strategy failed.* The whole Kennedy team, but especially McNamara, Ryan thought, had

---

* Ryan was considered one of the Air Force's major air power strategists in 1967, an able successor to Curtis LeMay and John White. He was also one of the military's leading critics of the can-do spirit that permeated the New Frontier–Great Society national leadership. While other officers praised Kennedy for his understanding of the military, Ryan remained a critic. When told by a fellow officer that it was actually Robert Kennedy, *not* the president, who had "pulled the air power" during the Bay of Pigs, Ryan commented, "I'm not surprised."

brought on the war but had then been unwilling to fight it, a lack of inner courage that, he believed, characterized many of their foreign policy failures.

These Air Force attitudes also held true for the Navy. When Moorer joined the JCS in July 1967, he was already widely known as an outspoken McNamara critic, though he rarely expressed his disdain as openly as the Air Force's Martin or Ryan. Instead, the crafty Pearl Harbor veteran was content to work behind the scenes to undo many of McNamara's policies. Moorer was especially critical of McNamara's weapons philosophy, particularly of his handling of the F-III debate, which Moorer said was a "first-class fiasco." So, in August 1967, just weeks after he took over as CNO, Moorer moved to circumvent McNamara's cost-efficiency program by ordering naval planners to come up with a new, "high-performance, swing-wing, long-range fighter bomber" that could be used on aircraft carriers. In doing so, he proved that he was undeterred by what had happened to previous Navy chiefs who went up against the Secretary of Defense: "I knew exactly why they fired [former CNO George] Anderson," Moorer later reflected. "They wanted me to shut up and go along with the F-III. It was a bust. I wasn't frightened by them. I just worked along until we got the F-14. That's my baby, that's the Moorer fighter. I'm responsible for it. In the end they didn't scare me, and we got what we wanted."

It's not surprising, then, that at the same time that Wheeler and his chiefs were deciding not to resign, running commentaries on the man they opposed were standard fare in the military's command circle. In fact, the JCS's disgust with the Secretary of Defense and his "whiz kids" was so open that in any other, less volatile time its actions might easily have been considered insubordinate. Not only was Harold Johnson ridiculing the Pentagon as the "Department of Deceit," Wheeler constantly modified the secretary's full name into a more suitable description of JCS feelings, calling him Robert "Very Strange" McNamara, which brought smiles to the frustrated and overworked JCS staff.

It was clear to the JCS that the "McNamara revolution" — which the former president of the Ford Motor Company had promised would transform the unwieldy Pentagon bureaucracy into a smoothly functioning and rational defense organization — had been gutted by the Vietnam War. Indeed, at least as far as the JCS was concerned, the worsening situation in Vietnam was the natural result of McNamara's arrogance; wars could not be run like corporations or managed by civilian experts who openly styled themselves "defense intellectuals." If nothing else, the JCS could take comfort in knowing that McNamara's bottom-line mentality was being checkmated by pajama-clad guerrillas half a world away whose desire to persist had transformed the secretary's desire for good management into a parody of bad strategy. But even this comfort, gratifying though it was, could not take the place of a clear strategy, one that Wheeler, in particular, began to chart within hours of the JCS meeting of August 26.

For more than two years, since the end of July 1965, Wheeler had been pressing government officials to mobilize the reserves and commit the nation to a full war in South Vietnam. Indeed, his arguments had been so persistent that by the time the JCS testified before the Stennis subcommittee, the views were greeted with dismissive resignation by most members of the administration. It was clear Wheeler would never win the argument; not only had the president specifically ruled out calling up the reserves, almost all his top aides were hopeful that the war could be concluded without a full U.S. military commitment. So Wheeler decided to take an entirely different tack. Although he was still committed to a reserve call-up, he decided to remain silent on its merits. This time, Wheeler told his Army chief, Harold Johnson, he would let the war itself act as the catalyst for administration policy.

The chairman was more confident than ever that his new tactic would actually work. Not only was he certain that Westmoreland would need more troops, he realized the nation had reached what administration officials were beginning to call the Plimsol Line — the point at which further call-ups would automatically trigger a full-scale American mobilization. In August 1967, the United States had 490,000 men committed to the defense of South Vietnam, with another 35,000 ready for ʋuty in accordance with a presidential directive on what Pentagon officers referred to as the Program 5 deployments. The grand total of U.S. troop deployments, Wheeler knew, would soon reach the 525,000 level. The figure is significant. For several months, the JCS staff had been telling the chairman that anything beyond 525,000 troops would place the United States in an untenable military readiness situation. According to JCSM 218-67, the country was actually reaching what General Johnson called "the bottom of the barrel"; at some point, JCSM 218-67 said, the United States would be forced to activate the reserves or fight the war with the troops it had.

Wheeler wasn't satisfied. JCSM 218-67 only mentioned "estimated" troop needs, not actual figures. As a result, Wheeler demanded a new study from the JCS staff that would answer a series of detailed questions on troop deployments. First, Wheeler wanted to know, just how many troops "above and beyond the 525,000 limit" would need to be called in order to trigger national mobilization? Second, how many troops would the United States actually need in order to reconstitute the strategic reserve; that is, in order to win the war in Vietnam while maintaining U.S. force levels in other parts of the world? And last, what political impact would a call-up have, and what mechanism had to be established for such a call-up to occur?

It would be four months before the JCS staff realized the full import of Wheeler's obsession with "the arithmetic" of Vietnam, but to his colleagues, the reason for a new study seemed all too clear. Not only was the chairman intent on forcing the administration to make a decision on the war, he was willingly becoming involved in a brutal, though unpublicized, political conflict over the question of mobilization that would once again pit the JCS against the administration. Those who realized the change in the chairman's tack have since commented that this tactic not only reflected a last attempt to win in Vietnam, but involved Wheeler, and the entire nation, in a vicious psychological dilemma. The only way that Johnson would call up the reserves, Wheeler realized, was if the situation in Vietnam got worse, not better. In fact, in order for Wheeler to win in Washington, America had to lose in Vietnam. Inevitably, the dilemma this posed for Wheeler, who considered himself a suave and sophisticated patriot, was bound to take its toll: in the first week of September, Wheeler suffered a heart attack, the first of many that would eventually kill him.

Wheeler's mild heart attack placed the JCS in a quandary. While Harold Johnson, who took over for the chairman, understood Wheeler's strategy, it was clear that he did not have the same relationship with the president that Wheeler had so diligently cultivated. So, instead of pushing the president to change American policy, Johnson undertook yet another study of America's command arrangements in Vietnam. Having succeeded in placing Creighton Abrams as Westmoreland's deputy, Johnson initiated another round of discussions on Westmoreland's strategy. In particular, he was interested in determining whether Westmoreland's overall strategy of engaging NVA and Vietcong units in battles of attrition was actually working. Again, he received advice from a close circle of trusted colonels, mostly West Point graduates who had been to Vietnam and were now on the JCS staff.

Perhaps predictably, Johnson was again treated to a critique that only deepened his doubts of Westmoreland's capabilities. Still, he didn't make any move to replace Westmoreland with Abrams, though clearly he believed that Abrams's strategy, of turning the war over to the South Vietnamese themselves, would eventually be forced on the American government. In fact, the historical record of Johnson's views seems unambiguous: for perhaps the first time in his career, the veteran of Bataan was indecisive. Having decided that Westmoreland should be relieved, Johnson wouldn't take the necessary steps. In the end, two deeply held beliefs probably influenced him to forgo recommending Westmoreland's replacement. First, he was convinced that his position in Washington dictated a hands-off policy in Vietnam, and second, there was the nagging doubt that even with a new commander, the United States still might not be able to win the war.

The hands-off policy, an old military tradition, was reiterated by Edward Meyer, one of the most frequent participants in Johnson's sessions on the war. "Once you start tampering with that tradition," Meyer reflected, "you have a hell of a mess, like we did for a while in the Civil War. You just can't take it upon yourself to overrule the man who is fighting the battle. You just can't do it. So when pressure came from Westmoreland to let him do it the way he wanted, that he was in the position to know, the Joint Chiefs said, 'Well, all right. Maybe he's right.'" The fact that Johnson was operating under such strictures didn't make him feel any more comfortable with the way the war was going, a point that was brought home by his attempt to deal with troop deployments in Wheeler's absence.

It was this attempt that caused Johnson to bump up against his own doubts about replacing Westmoreland. Although Abrams's argument appealed to Johnson, it seemed to him that Westmoreland's big-unit strategy had at least minimal validity. The NVA was beginning to deploy in ever-larger formations, with battalion, regiment, and even division-size units being spotted in the far northern parts of South Vietnam. Nevertheless, the war was being fought: at besieged Con Thien, in northern South Vietnam, Air Force General William W. Momyer was battering the Vietcong with 830 B-52 flights that resulted in 2,000 casualties, transforming the Vietcong-held hills into "a tortured landscape of crater and ashes."

Also, for Johnson — as for Wheeler — it was simply too late in the war to reverse American tactics. Not only was Johnson caught by his own agreement to abide by the hands-off policy, he was trapped by his own ill-advised optimistic statements on the war. While Johnson had been one of the JCS's most vocal doubters about the American involvement in Vietnam and clearly the most outspoken advocate for a reserve call-up, he had tempered his own instincts by continuing to put the best face possible on American progress. In fact, at the same time that *The Pentagon Papers* said that the JCS was making troop recommendations "in a resigned tone" and describing "the rate of progress to have been and to continue to be slow," Johnson was telling the press that he believed the United States could be out of Vietnam in eighteen months.

He knew better: as acting chairman, he was faced with the bitter truth. Pushed by the increasingly embattled McNamara to make a quick decision on which units could be sent to Vietnam in compliance with the president's approval of the Program 5 deployments, Johnson began to scrape the bottom of the nation's manpower barrel. The pressures became almost intolerable, pushing him into eighteen-hour days and endless meetings. Not only was he required to carry out the duties of the chairman, he also had to make crucial deployment decisions that were becoming impossible to make.

There were no easy choices. In addition to the maw of Vietnam, Johnson was given explicit instructions by the Secretary of Defense to make certain that enough troops were left in the United States to see to what the JCS euphemistically called "domestic security require- ments." What it meant was that Johnson didn't dare deploy a sizable number of U.S. troops to Vietnam because of the very real threat of widespread domestic disorder. It was an impossible task, a two-front war that was symbolized by Johnson's refusal to deploy two remaining brigades of the 82nd Airborne to Vietnam, choosing instead to begin deployment of the 101st. The choice was not insignificant. When West- moreland had pleaded for the immediate deployment of the 82nd Air- borne during the summer, the JCS had turned him down, one of the few times it disagreed with such a request. The 82nd couldn't be deployed, the JCS told Westmoreland, because it was already engaged in combat operations in downtown Detroit, in barricaded ghetto buildings in the midst of one of America's worst race riots. Now, in late September, Johnson was forced to make the same choice. The 82nd would stay at home (it had experience with inner-city uprisings) while the 101st, one of the last major CONUS (continental U.S.) units, would be slowly sent to Southeast Asia.

In addition, Johnson was receiving pressure from Lyman Lemnitzer, the U.S. commander in Europe and former JCS chairman, to put an end to the ceaseless pillaging of U.S. troops in West Germany. He felt the need for more troops in Vietnam "was downright frightening, we were stripped to the bone." The situation was reminiscent of that faced by the JCS during Omar Bradley's tenure, during the Korean War. In fact, according to Lemnitzer, the situation was actually worse: the U.S. Army in Europe was "damn near nonexistent. Vietnam was eating up everything." Johnson's solution satisfied no one; in addition to "accelerating" deployment of the 101st Airborne, he decided to "marry" ready units with equipment taken from reserve stocks held in Europe.

Faced with these conflicts, the acting chairman decided to take a desperate step, indicating to McNamara that he would "deploy units to South Vietnam in substandard readiness condition in personnel, training and/or equipage." For a man who was writing more than two hundred letters a week to the parents of those killed in the war, the decision to deploy untrained troops was a galling prospect. On Sep- tember 10, Johnson produced his recommendations at a subdued meet- ing of the JCS. After studying the figures, the chiefs, flanked by their three-star aides, remained uncharacteristically silent. Finally, Johnson punctuated the deathly stillness with his own two-word commentary: "Cannon fodder." The deployments were approved after Johnson met with the president on September 12 and duly instituted as JCSM 505-67 under McNamara's orders on October 5, 1967.

Fortunately for Johnson, his stint as acting chairman was cut short by the return of Wheeler, who returned to his duties just as McNamara was approving the JCS's recommendations. Still, Wheeler was unable to pursue a full slate of activities. "He looked terrible," one aide remembered, "as if he would rather have been anywhere else." CNO Moorer remembered him as "a very sick man." Clearly, Wheeler was pushing himself, concerned that the troop deployment plan he had initiated, which he believed would inevitably force the president to mobilize the nation, would be derailed.

To make sure such a derailment didn't occur, Wheeler took a formative role in writing the JCS's newest study on the war. Officially released on October 17, just a week after his return, JCSM 555-67 bears his unmistakable imprint. Ostensibly written in response to questions posed to Harold Johnson by the president during the chairman's absence, the memo is one of the most far-reaching and detailed plans for total war ever put forward by the JCS. Not only did it reiterate its position on expanding the list of North Vietnamese bombing targets, it argued that U.S. forces should mine North Vietnam's harbors. Moreover, it recommended that all bombing restrictions over Hanoi, apparently including those for residential districts, be lifted. JCSM 555-67 is the clearest articulation of the JCS's position on the war that has yet been made public. Not only did it go further than any other previous memo, it even included actions that the chiefs themselves realized the president would never approve.

These unprecedented recommendations were hardly accidental. In fact, they were a purposeful attempt by Wheeler to give Lyndon Johnson one last chance to change his war strategy. For Wheeler's purposes, JCSM 555-67 was perfectly timed. Not only was Wheeler convinced that the recommendations represented the best military strategy, but in early November he had just received word that McNamara would be resigning. This news was greeted with relief by the chiefs, though hardly with the jubilation that might have been expected. In the two months since his Senate testimony, McNamara had become an almost pathetic figure, hounded by his doubts about the war and by his clear loss of faith in a policy he had once endorsed. The distinct chill that greeted his arrival at JCS meetings confused and saddened him, serving finally to convince him that he no longer enjoyed the trust of the military.

More important than McNamara's resignation, however, the release of the JCS memo just happened to coincide with the president's most important year-end conference on the war, a review scheduled to take place during the regular Tuesday luncheon at the White House. This fact, Wheeler knew, gave the JCS's position added importance. With McNamara's resignation just months away and Johnson under fire by his own party in Congress, the administration's policy-making apparatus was clearly in chaos and therefore vulnerable, Wheeler believed, to JCS arguments. He viewed the meeting as an unprecedented opportunity to make one last pitch on the military's position on the war.

The October 17, 1967, meeting at the White House lasted from 1:00 P.M. until late in the afternoon and once again proved disappointing to the JCS. While it sampled opinions on the war from a wider array of experts than had hitherto been included in such strategy sessions, Target Tuesday, as it came to be known, found the president more committed than ever to the philosophy of graduated response adopted more than thirty months earlier. In addition, while McNamara's recommendation, which now included a "pullback" in Vietnam, was studiously ignored by the president, his previous defense of graduated response was ably articulated by Secretary of State Rusk. Once again, the president came down on the side of increasing pressures on North Vietnam, but not to the degree recommended by the JCS; the bombing target list would be expanded and the Program 5 deployments would be accelerated, but that was all.

While the president's response wasn't unexpected, the JCS was disappointed by the administration's continuing arguments in favor of a policy that wasn't working. But the chiefs also realized that their position had been harmed by their own optimistic progress reports, which they felt they were forced to make as a result of their inability to convince the administration to adopt a more aggressive strategy. While the JCS had been arguing for full mobilization ever since the United States actually became involved in South Vietnam, it had failed — or been unable — to argue the *other* side of the argument convincingly: that if the administration was unwilling to make a full commitment to Vietnam, it should make no commitment at all. In fact, by November, the JCS found itself in the position of going along with increased deployments of troops under the belief that at least some deployment was better than none at all — the exact opposite of Harold Johnson's position.

This paradox caused enormous pressures on the JCS system itself, in which officers were becoming openly divided on American strategy, an issue that had hitherto been the sole province of the chiefs, their top aides, and the military command in Vietnam. By mid-November, the factionalization of the JCS staff was obvious, with a small coterie of pro-Westmoreland officers faced off against a larger group, who believed the war might actually be lost. Westmoreland's appearance in Washington on November 19 didn't help: the general gave a stirringly optimistic address to the National Press Club, telling the reporters that the war in Vietnam was being won, that the American forces were on the edge of victory.

The speech sparked bitter recriminations among JCS staff officers who had been to Vietnam and realized that Westmoreland's big-unit strategy was failing to win the all-important "war of the villages." But to the small group of supporters, the general's words were a welcome respite from the ceaseless round of civilian-military infighting. More important, they posed a dilemma for Wheeler; while he supported Westmoreland's right to make decisions in Vietnam, the commander's words undercut Wheeler's argument for full mobilization. Then, too, while the United States had reached the bottom of the manpower barrel, with nearly 525,000 troops serving in South Vietnam, it appeared that Wheeler was just plain wrong about the need for mobilization. To all appearances, the United States wouldn't need more troops in Vietnam; it wasn't losing and wasn't going to lose. In fact, it soon appeared that Westmoreland was right — the United States was starting to win the war.

By the beginning of December, four NVA divisions were ranged against the American position inside the Marine base at Khe Sanh, in the far northern reaches of South Vietnam. The American position, at the edge of the demilitarized zone, was tenuous, but it was clear to Westmoreland that the North Vietnamese were dangerously exposed, leading him to suggest that the United States was on the verge of winning its most decisive engagement against the North Vietnamese. He acted quickly, shifting nearly one third of all American combat soldiers to the defense of the base and its approaches. The strategy seemed sound: while the Marines resented digging into static positions, their defense of the base resulted in enormous enemy losses. Westmoreland promised there was more to come, stating publicly that he would make the defense of Khe Sanh "the greatest battle" of the war, a Dien Bien Phu in reverse.

Lyndon Johnson was not nearly so optimistic. As a former member of the Senate Armed Services Committee, he vividly remembered the military descriptions of the Viet Minh's superhuman effort to overrun the French base of Dien Bien Phu just thirteen years earlier. He had become obsessed by the Viet Minh's ability to master the complex logistical problems necessary to win a decisive engagement against a major power. Now he was just as intrigued, spending hours in the White House situation room stooped over a map of the Khe Sanh base. His attention to detail, to the military side of the war, disturbed his aides; the situation room was becoming the nation's map room, an inner sanctum for a president whose abilities to manage his own administration were the talk of Washington. At the center of the tableau was a detailed photorama of Khe Sanh: its perimeter was marked in blue, with red pins for known NVA units. Johnson's obsession with the battle became almost manic; throughout December he demanded minute-by-minute details of the battle. By early January, Johnson's worries over the battle reached a fever pitch that resulted in a shouting match with Wheeler.

Johnson wanted statistics and more statistics, saying that the information he was getting wasn't complete. Ammunition wasn't getting through to the Marines, Johnson said, and he wanted to know why. He besieged the JCS with questions: Was this the right strategy, could the Marines pull it off, would the weather over the base clear, who was in charge of the units on the east perimeter, why weren't the South Vietnamese helping more? The questions were endless, detailed, demanding; for Johnson, Khe Sanh was the litmus test of the nation's ability to hold back the rising communist tide. Wheeler moved to reassure Johnson, showing him Westmoreland's reports comparing Khe Sanh to Dien Bien Phu; the Americans had more firepower than the French had in 1954, they were in a better position, morale on the base was good, there was no reason to suspect that the NVA would overwhelm the garrison. It wasn't enough. Even after the weather cleared and enemy activity dropped off — just when it seemed almost assured that Khe Sanh would hold — Johnson had one more bout with his JCS chairman, shouting out his most elemental fear.

"I don't want any god-damn 'Din Bin Phoos,' " Johnson said on the afternoon of January 28, his words edged with panic. He demanded that Wheeler order his colleagues to provide assurance that the American forces inside the base would not be overrun, that the JCS guarantee a victory *in writing*. The next day, Wheeler came back with a memo signed by each of the chiefs, saying that they approved of Westmoreland's Khe Sanh plans. Wheeler was confident; not only would Khe Sanh hold, he said, but the drop in Vietcong activity in South Vietnam had buoyed flagging JCS spirits. Then Wheeler once again pushed his three-year argument, telling the president that with Khe Sanh safe (the JCS had guaranteed it), it was time to put the pressure on North Vietnam, time to break its hold on the rest of the South. But Johnson remained unconvinced. If Westmoreland was winning — indeed, had actually won at Khe Sanh, as Wheeler claimed — then North Vietnam would ask for a further round of negotiations. After such enormous losses, it would be impossible for it to recover. With that, Johnson stalked imperiously from the situation room, the Khe Sanh guarantee clasped firmly in his hand.

Wheeler was exhausted by the president, by the war, by the seemingly interminable debate on U.S. strategy that continued to divide the administration. "I'm sick of this niggling," he told one aide. While Khe Sanh seemed safe, a clear American victory, Wheeler was still frustrated by the ambiguity engendered by the American strategy. Khe Sanh might turn out to be a victory, but he didn't believe it would be a decisive, war-ending victory. There was also the chilling thought that Khe Sanh would only be a prelude for further NVA actions; while enemy activity in the South had fallen off, there was no sign the North Vietnamese were any more willing to negotiate an end to the war than they had been in 1965. The chairman clung to the belief that mobilization, and only mobilization, was the way to escalate the war beyond the point where North Vietnam could pay a price. All that he needed was a spark, an event that would trigger one last debate over the American involvement. For once, the war cooperated.

In the early hours of January 31, 1968, the Vietcong and their North Vietnamese allies launched attacks throughout South Vietnam that coincided with the celebration of the Tet holidays. The attacks mesmerized the American public and threw the JCS into a whirlwind of activity. In Saigon, the American embassy was besieged by a Vietcong squad that blew a hole in the compound wall and shot the Marine guards. Throughout South Vietnam, American soldiers were attacked in barracks, at airfields — wherever there were large numbers of troops. In Cholon, the populous Chinese suburb of Saigon, house-to-house fighting, punctuated by hand-detonated bombs, threw the people into a panic. Even Westmoreland's headquarters was shelled, and in Hue, the ancient imperial capital, the citadel was captured. Only at Khe Sanh were things relatively quiet, though the Special Forces camp at Lang Vei, just up the highway, was overrun by NVA troops, who deployed tanks for the first time in the conflict.

While the JCS was shocked by the strength of the offensive, Westmoreland later claimed that the onslaught hadn't surprised the intelligence experts at MACV headquarters in Saigon at all, a view that is still much debated in the military. In fact, it wasn't so much that the attacks were a surprise that stunned the MACV, it was that the Vietcong had struck everywhere, at once, and in force. Indeed, the enemy showed surprising strength, especially in view of reports that its ranks had been thinned by nearly three years of war.

According to later reports, the one thing that saved Westmoreland, and the JCS, from a classic military rout was the fact that MACV aides had been warned of such attacks as early as mid-December by a group of CIA operatives in a small office in downtown Saigon. This official CIA field report, dutifully passed on to Washington, noted that the "war has reached a turning point" and cautioned that the NVA and

Vietcong were planning a number of key military moves "on or before Tet." In Washington, CIA director Richard Helms received the report and passed it on to his specialist for Vietnam, George Carver. "Carver wrote a memo on the report," a military specialist later said, "and made Helms sign it. In effect, the memo said, 'This is a lot of bull.' So no one at the White House paid attention to it." But at MACV, intelligence analysts not only took the report seriously, they continued to gather corroborating evidence. By mid-January they were certain there would be some kind of offensive, probably just before the Tet holiday. But by the end of the last week of the month, with no attack in sight, everyone was starting to breath a little easier.

The optimism was premature: on January 30, just twenty-four hours before the Vietcong attacks on Saigon, enemy units in northern South Vietnam started the offensive early, apparently confused over the exact timing of the event. "Thank God they did," one American commander said later. "It gave us twenty-four hours to prepare. We knew it was coming. It's a damn good thing. We might have lost Saigon." The Tet Offensive arrived with all the force of an explosion in Washington, where officials had been promoting the illusion of progress in the war. Only Westmoreland seemed optimistic, sticking to his view that Khe Sanh would remain a focus of NVA attention. "In my opinion this is a diversionary effort to take attention away from the north, an attack on Khe Sanh," he said on February 1. For exhausted JCS officers following the rising tide of the Vietcong wave, Westmoreland's statement was laughable. "We could never quite figure out what the hell war he was fighting," one officer said later. "They had taken Kontum, Pleiku, attacked Quang Tri. They actually held Hue and here was this guy talking about Khe Sanh. It was eerie."

Inevitably, JCS officers learned to ignore Westmoreland's reports, especially when the first South Vietnamese counterattack against NVA emplacements in Hue was turned back with bloody losses. The United States dispatched Marines to Hue and began a costly, block-by-block battle to retake the Vietcong stronghold. It was the worst urban warfare since World War II, a particularly vicious fight that became an obsession for JCS staff members on all levels. Still, despite the intensity of the continuing offensive, the JCS started to realize that the Vietcong wave was beginning to crest, that while the U.S. forces were badly stunned, their recovery was now certain. In a few weeks, JCS officers predicted, U.S. and South Vietnamese forces would go over to the offensive, regaining the battlefield initiative. This was false bravado; the Vietcong continued to strike at sixty-four district towns, literally scores of smaller outposts had been overrun, and five of South Vietnam's six major cities were under withering attack. The JCS also realized that the number of American casualties from Tet was staggering, putting increased pressure for troop replacements on JCS planners, who were already hard-pressed to find men for the war.

To make matters worse, the JCS soon saw that Westmoreland's effort to retake Hue, a city that was becoming a symbol of America's combat inefficiency, was being bungled. In fact, the handling of the attack was so confused that Westmoreland himself, in an apparent and controversial fit of frustration, appointed Creighton Abrams to handle the Marine counterattack, which angered Marine commanders responsible for the Hue operation. "My God, Westmoreland hated the Marines," a retired colonel, William Corson, said. "That bastard damn near crapped his pants when the Vietcong hit, so he blamed the Marines." Others see it differently. "Abrams's appointment was clearly one of the best decisions Westmoreland made," one frustrated Army lieutenant colonel said. Whatever the final judgment, Westmoreland's decision to put an Army commander in charge of Marine troops led to service divisions that are still apparent.

More disturbing still, when the Marines began to fight their way into the city, they ran into resistance from three NVA regiments that were supposed to be at Khe Sanh.* This intelligence took the last bit of optimism out of the MACV command, where it slowly became apparent that the United State had suffered "a Dien Bien Phu in reverse," not the North Vietnamese. Inevitably, the intelligence found its way to Capitol Hill, where legislators who had defended the war on the grounds that it not only could be won, but actually was being won, were embarrassed by reports on the Tet fighting. Even the normally hawkish Senate Armed Services Committee began to question America's strategy, focusing its anger on Westmoreland's seeming inability to blunt Vietcong and North Vietnamese attacks. This new skepticism culminated in a hastily called Armed Services Committee hearing on February 5. Committee members quizzed Wheeler on replacing Westmoreland, a clear indication that many of them believed a change was necessary. Despite his own doubts, Wheeler defended his MACV chief, cautioning the committee against interpreting the offensive in the worst light. But the damage was done. In the wake of the hearing, confidence in Westmoreland had eroded to such a degree that Wheeler was forced to cable his Vietnam commander in order to allay his fears

---

* Abrams's actions in Hue vindicated Harold Johnson. Abrams brought order out of chaos. "Anyone who brings in nonessentials is interfering with the conduct of the war," he said, limiting all supplies coming into Hue to "beans, bullets, and gasoline." By the second week of February, he had mounted a house-to-house counterattack. But it wasn't until February 26 that Hue was retaken. In Saigon, the fight to pacify the city was led by General Frederick Weyand, who was probably responsible for saving the city when he convinced Westmoreland to pull his troops back into the city on January 10, three weeks before the Tet attack.

over his sudden replacement, saying that "all of us, including the Commander in Chief, repose complete confidence in your judgment."

In private, however, Wheeler had been outraged by the Tet surprise and by reports coming into the JCS that morale at American headquarters in Saigon was at an all-time low; apparently Washington wasn't the only place where Westmoreland's actions were being questioned. By the second week of February, Westmoreland's confident victory statements were beginning to sound hollow. While the initial Tet attacks had been repulsed, there was still fighting in the center of Saigon, and Hue was still under control of the Vietcong. Worse yet, the offensive had forced American troops back into the cities. No one knew what was going on in the countryside, though everyone assumed that NVA units had moved in to set up new bases. As far as Wheeler was concerned, things had gone from bad to worse. It was no longer a question of whether the United States would make a full commitment; Tet meant there was now little choice. With this in mind, he sent a barrage of cables to Saigon, hoping to push Westmoreland to give a more realistic picture of the fighting.

The first cable went out on February 8 and was followed by a more stridently worded missive the next day. In both, Wheeler pushed Westmoreland to ask for more troops to meet the Vietcong-NVA threat. "If you need more troops ask for them," Wheeler said in his first cable. He also hinted that Lyndon Johnson was open to increasing the number of troops, implying that Westmoreland ought to make the request regardless of whether they were necessary, an argument Wheeler attempted to explain in yet another tiresome bow to military tradition. "Please understand that I am not trying to sell you on the deployment of additional forces," he lamely added in his second cable. Westmoreland didn't take the hint; by return cable he said he might need another division in April, but no sooner. Finally, it occurred to him that Wheeler was inviting him to ask for more troops, apparently because the Tet Offensive had softened Washington's position on new deployments. Westmoreland made "a firm request" for more troops on February 11, couching the request in language that could only have pleased Wheeler and his colleagues: "A setback is fully possible if I am not reinforced."

As if to convince the JCS that its commander knew how to take a hint, Westmoreland sent off another cable on February 12, just in time for a meeting between McNamara (who was due to retire in three weeks) and the JCS: "I desperately need reinforcements. Time is of the essence." That's what Wheeler was waiting for. With McNamara's agreement, the JCS immediately released one Marine regiment and one Airborne brigade, the last troops available for deployment, to South Vietnam. They brought the American commitment to just under the 525,000 limit set by the president. Surprisingly, however,

Wheeler and his colleagues decided not to overplay their hand, placing the onus of added U.S. reinforcements, and the inevitable reserve call-up that they would trigger, in the hands of Johnson's foreign policy advisers. Indeed, the JCS refused to endorse any further deployments during its February 12 meeting with McNamara.

The message the JCS thus conveyed was unmistakable: without a "reconstitution of the strategic reserve," the United States simply couldn't afford to send more troops to Westmoreland, regardless of how serious the situation became. In JCS parlance, Johnson had been "sandbagged," approving a troop deployment that might have been good for Westmoreland but that was definitely bad for the United States. This point was made clear on February 13, when the JCS told McNamara that "the 82nd Airborne Division represents the only readily deployable Army division in the CONUS-based active strategic reserve." The JCS then issued an even darker warning: "The impending reduction of this division by one-third to meet approved deployments establishes an immediate requirement for its prompt reconstitution which is possible only by the callup of Reserve units." In other words, the JCS said, it was okay to send added troops to Vietnam as long as the administration realized that in doing so they were stripping the country of any internal protection, a chilling prospect for a president faced with the specter of burning cities.

This warning was taken seriously by the administration. Not only did McNamara huddle with the JCS over how further troop deployments to Vietnam could be met ("They can't be," Wheeler said bitterly during one such meeting, on February 14), he closeted himself with Johnson in a series of White House meetings on the same topic. Predictably, Johnson said he could only make decisions on Vietnam reinforcements when he knew what was going on in Saigon, thereby conveying his doubts about Westmoreland's response to the Tet attacks. Johnson wasn't yet willing to make the most logical choice, to accede to JCS requests for a "minimal callup" of the reserves, without a firsthand report from Wheeler himself. McNamara passed Johnson's orders to Wheeler on February 22, and within hours he was on his way to meet with Westmoreland.

When he arrived in Saigon on February 23 for his fourth visit to the war zone, the pressures of the war and his recent heart attack were plainly visible. Stepping off an Air Force jet onto the tarmac of Tan Son Nhut airport, he went through the usual ceremonial trappings with less than wholehearted animation. In fact, according to Westmoreland, the chairman looked as if he were "near the point of exhaustion." This description, however, tells only part of the story, for Wheeler was also making it clear that his support for Westmoreland was much less than total. Wheeler was abrupt, almost cruel, in dismissing Westmoreland's apparently heartfelt greetings. Indeed, within minutes of his arrival, he said that he wasn't interested in an optimistic report; he said he'd read Westmoreland's cables carefully and added that "I just don't believe them." NVA and Vietcong mainline forces had penetrated the American combat shield around South Vietnam's cities, and Wheeler wanted to know why. He noted sarcastically that the president also "just happened to be curious." In essence, Wheeler wasn't only exhausted when he reached Saigon, he was damned mad, a fact overlooked by Westmoreland in his own recollections.

In *A Soldier Reports*, Westmoreland goes out of his way to criticize Wheeler, implying that his judgment was impaired by his illness and had been influenced by newspaper reports that Tet looked like "the worst calamity since Bull Run." The retired general continues to emphasize this point. "You have to understand General Wheeler was a sick man, he really was," Westmoreland said. "He came to Saigon and he looked just terrible. Very pale. Dying. He was a dying man. I knew he wasn't going, really, to last much longer." But Westmoreland's characterization is not supported by the evidence. Indeed, Wheeler was not in the best of health, but he was nowhere near the point of physical collapse, a fact supported by the breakneck round of meetings he had with Westmoreland and his staff over a period of five days. Not only is Westmoreland's description unflattering, it's particularly ungracious; Wheeler had defended him for three years and had most recently been forced to reassure the JCS's primary allies in Congress that Westmoreland was still the man for the job.

It's now almost certain that Westmoreland had more to be worried about than the continuing nationwide attacks on American troops. When Wheeler stepped off the plane in Saigon, General William DePuy, the JCS's resident expert on counterinsurgency, came down the steps after him, a clear signal to Westmoreland that Wheeler's visit had as much to do with him as it did with the Tet Offensive. DePuy, whose name had been brought up as a possible Westmoreland successor, had come along at the recommendation of Harold Johnson, who wanted another firsthand report on Westmoreland. While the cards weren't stacked against the commander, DePuy — a friend of Westmoreland — was now considered a Westmoreland critic, an outspoken advocate of altering America's strategy from the big-unit battles of the previous years to small-unit engagements.*

---

* DePuy served the JCS in his official role as Special Assistant on Counterinsurgency and Special Activities (SACSA), a position created by Maxwell Taylor in 1963. The SACSA was the JCS's official "ambassador" to the CIA. DePuy was a well-known military theorist and combat general who endorsed the idea that the United States could fight and win Third World struggles.

Irritated by the pomp and circumstance of his arrival, Wheeler told Westmoreland after a preliminary briefing that he would like to get some rest. He settled into a guest villa, hours after his arrival, and suddenly the serious nature of the Vietnam situation made itself plain. Just sixty seconds after Wheeler went to bed, a nearby Vietcong mortar unit opened up on him (spurring JCS staff officers to say later that he "had finally become a combat general"). Wheeler returned to headquarters to ask Westmoreland a series of embarrassing questions on American intelligence capabilities in Indochina. Wheeler was reaching the end of his rope. It was clear that American troops were "under siege," he told Westmoreland, a view he repeated when Westmoreland greeted him the next morning. While this first meeting began with a discussion on the fighting then being waged around South Vietnam, Wheeler soon turned to Westmoreland's call for more troops.

He began his discussions on the question of reinforcements on the afternoon of his arrival, bombarding Westmoreland with arguments in favor of using the opportunity presented by Tet to make an unprecedented request for an increase in the American commitment. This was the "hard sell," as one of Westmoreland's aides later described it; Wheeler wasn't just trying to find out whether Westmoreland needed more troops, he was telling him he needed more troops. To Westmoreland, this sudden attention to reinforcements was strange, even suspicious; after all, the NVA was on the run and the Vietcong all but destroyed by their failed attack on South Vietnam's cities. Clearly, as he had indicated in his early post-Tet cables, the Americans needed reinforcements, but certainly not on a permanent basis. The next morning, February 24, Wheeler gave Westmoreland his argument: McNamara was leaving the government and a pro-war Secretary of Defense, Clark Clifford, was coming on board. Yes, Tet was a victory, Wheeler said in exasperation, but here was a chance to make the victory stick.

"General Wheeler came over there and he was actually begging me to ask for more troops," Westmoreland said. "Really, just begging me. And he told me the president was ready to call up the reserves, and if that were to happen how many men would I need, how many men would I use. And that was when I said well, we could use another 200,000." Wheeler wasn't satisfied; 200,000 "just isn't the right number," he bluntly told Westmoreland on the twenty-fourth. Troop deployments and dispositions had to be studied, plans put into effect, a full assessment made and then presented to the president. He needed to know exactly how many troops were going to be needed in Vietnam and what they were going to be used for. To make his point even clearer, Wheeler named the possible units that could be sent to Vietnam, indicating the total number of troops such a reinforcement would involve. Chastened by the suddenly volatile chairman, West-moreland went back to his headquarters to study the problem. "Well, Wheeler and I talked about it," Westmoreland says now, "and came up with the troop dispositions, and I said I wanted them in three incre-ments. Well, the total came to 206,000, and that's the figure he took back to Washington."

While Westmoreland has never admitted it, 206,000 was the exact figure Wheeler had brought with him from Washington, the figure that resulted from the study he had ordered his staff to complete in answer to the question of just how many troops it would take to "trig-ger" a reserve call-up. In fact, it's likely that Wheeler convinced West-moreland that that was exactly the total number of reinforcements he needed. When Westmoreland returned for another round of discus-sions on the night of the twenty-fourth, he had finally taken Wheeler's hint. The conversion was total; to capitalize on the victory of Tet, Westmoreland said, he needed immediate reinforcements totaling 206,000 troops. "I was convinced," he later gushed, "that with addi-tional strength and removal of the old restrictive policy, we could deal telling blows — physically and psychologically — well within the frame of the reservists' one-year tour. The time had come to prepare and commit the Reserve."

It's almost as if Westmoreland were claiming he had waited for pre-cisely that moment to make the decision. Why, it wasn't Wheeler's idea at all, it was Westmoreland's. "Wheeler came over and Westy didn't know what was going on," a former Westmoreland aide claimed. "Westy didn't really need any more troops, and told Wheeler that maybe just a few thousand more would do it and that we had the Vietcong destroyed and the NVA on the run. And really, after Tet we were in very good shape. But Wheeler insisted on it and told Westy to go ahead and ask for more. Westmoreland said the optimum was 200,000 and Wheeler said he couldn't ask for a round number. He told Westy to ask for 206,000." The aide claims that either Westmoreland was "blind or he refused to admit" that Wheeler used him to fight the war on the only battleground that counted, at least in 1968 — in Wash-ington, against Lyndon Johnson.

"Well now, some of us knew what was going on and told Westy to really study the thing, but he loved command, so he just went ahead and asked for 206,000. Well, that was the number that would trigger the call-up of the Reserves and mean really that the country was going to war," a retired general says now. "So when Westmoreland says he just didn't know what Wheeler did, he's being less than honest. He's really giving Wheeler the benefit of the doubt, but he knows what hap-pened, whether he admits it or not. Fact is, asking for those troops wasn't his idea, it was Wheeler's."

Wheeler returned to a rain-drenched Washington on the morning of February 28 and immediately went to the White House for a special breakfast meeting. He had been in Saigon only four days, but he brought back with him a plan for the final strategy for winning the war as well as an assessment of the situation in Saigon. Seated around the dining room table with Wheeler were Lyndon Johnson, Clark Clifford (who would take office the next day), Robert McNamara, Dean Rusk, Vice President Hubert Humphrey, Maxwell Taylor (who had completed his stint as ambassador to South Vietnam), Richard Helms, and Walt Rostow. Wheeler painted a grim picture of the toll taken by the Tet Offensive. The situation was bleak, Wheeler said, with the NVA "operating with relative freedom in the countryside." American troops had pulled back into the cities, the South Vietnamese Army was shaken, and Khe Sanh was still threatened. Defeat had been averted, he admitted, but the United States had been lucky. "In short," he said, looking up at Johnson, "it was a very near thing."

The room was suddenly quiet, sobered by Wheeler's words. Johnson leaned across the table, his eyes studying the chairman in anticipation. Reaching into his briefcase, Wheeler presented his recommendation that the United States commit an additional 206,000 troops to the fight. Specifically, he recommended "a major reinforcement of more than 3 divisions and supporting forces totaling in excess of 200,000 men" and asked for a "call-up of 280,000 reservists to fill these requirements and flesh out the strategic reserve and training base at home." Wheeler then returned to his office to await the president's reaction, leaving only when it was apparent that Johnson would save the decision for another day. As at an earlier time, the JCS offices were "deathly still"; the top military commanders realized they had played their last card in their campaign to grasp the reins of the nation's war policies.

Wheeler had come full circle, from the "deskbound" general who had never seen combat to the vicious infighter who, in February 1968, had not only wrested control of the war from his commander in the field, from Westmoreland himself, but who was now attempting to wrest the future of the conflict from the hands of the civilian foreign policy apparatus. It was a bold gamble, but Wheeler and the rest of the JCS thought it was a gamble they had to take.

Wheeler's call for an additional 206,000 troops had all the subtlety of a high-megaton blast. Indeed, while he had pushed for mobilization a number of times in the previous three years, his February 28 arguments left little doubt about what he believed Lyndon Johnson should do. Yet within twenty-four hours the president had decided to defer the decision, instead telling Clark Clifford to convene a task force to study the troop recommendations. In effect, the meeting of the task force amounted to a simple reconvening of the group of "principals" put together by William Bundy in 1964. As before, Clifford was to find answers to three basic questions on the war: What course should the United States take, how would the enemy respond, and what were the implications of accepting Westmoreland's troop requests?

Intent on resolving the crisis, the famous Washington lawyer set about his task with tireless efficiency. "I spent sixteen years as a prosecuting attorney," Clifford remembered. "I know how to ask the hard questions. Regardless of my feelings on the war at the time, the president had directed that those questions be asked." Within hours of being given his assignment, Clifford began his own whirlwind tour of the military; unlike McNamara, however, he didn't go to Vietnam but into the heart of the Pentagon, asking hard questions of officers outside the chain of command. Clifford's tour is still the stuff of legend. He "walked the halls of this place all hours of day and night," one retired officer remembered. "All he did was ask questions." Finally, he went to see Wheeler, whom he described as "an old friend whom I had known for some years." Not surprisingly, Wheeler was wary, sensing that his own strategy was backfiring.

Clifford reconstructed his interrogation of the JCS chairman for the July 1969 issue of *Foreign Affairs*. "Would 206,000 [more] men do the job?" Clifford asked. "There is no assurance that they would," Wheeler answered.

Q: If not, how many more might be needed — and when?
A: No one can say.
Q: Could the enemy respond with a buildup of his own?
A: Yes, he could and probably would.
Q: Could bombing end the war?
A: Not by itself.
Q: Would a step-up in bombing decrease American casualties?
A: Very little if at all. The United States has already dropped a heavier tonnage of bombs on North Vietnam than in all theaters of war during World War II. Yet, during 1967, some 90,000 North Vietnamese made their way to the South and, in the first weeks of 1968, were still coming at three to four times the rate of a year earlier.
Q: How long must the United States go on carrying the main burden of combat?
A: The South Vietnamese are making great progress, but they are not yet ready to replace American troops in the field.
Q: What is the plan for victory?
A: There is no plan.
Q: Why not?

A: Because American forces operate under three restrictions: The President has forbidden them to invade the North, lest China intervene; he has forbidden the mining of Haiphong Harbor, lest a Soviet supply ship be sunk; he has also forbidden pursuing the enemy into Laos and Cambodia because that would widen the war, geographically and politically.

Q: Given these circumstances, how can we win?

A: The United States is improving its posture all the time, the enemy can not afford the attrition being inflicted on him; at some point he will discover there is no purpose in fighting any more.

Q: Does anyone see any evidence that four years of enormous casualties and massive destruction through bombing have diminished the enemy's will to prevail?

A: No.

The spare tone of Clifford's questions and Wheeler's blunt answers have led to speculation that the JCS chairman resented Johnson's appointment of Clifford to make major decisions on the war. That, Wheeler thought, was his job. But Clifford rejected the notion. "I'm sorry if you get the idea that General Wheeler was sullen, or somehow didn't think the questions should be asked," he said. "I didn't get that impression at all. I was doing my job, and he was doing his." Nevertheless, Wheeler's meeting with Clifford was a grueling recitation of America's problems in Vietnam, a clear delineation of the critical dilemmas faced by the JCS in running the war. It was also one of the most significant meetings between a Secretary of Defense and a JCS chairman. Afterward, Clifford concluded that the United States could not win the war in Vietnam and must begin to disengage, an opinion he put in writing and passed on to the president on March 4.

While the Clifford document seemed to have something for everyone, including a partial reserve call-up to meet threats to U.S. security worldwide, it was clear that the new secretary believed the United States had failed to meet its goals in Vietnam. Lyndon Johnson wasn't so certain; while the war was costly, he tended to believe Westmoreland's optimistic statements of continuing progress. Or maybe he wanted to believe them. Unwilling to make an all-out effort, convinced that the United States could wage the conflict according to the gradualist principles laid down by Taylor and Bundy, though by now also convinced that the American people would reject an interminable conflict, the president was torn between Clifford's surprising antiwar views and his own feelings that America could eventually win. Finally, at Clifford's urging, the president decided he needed new advice from a Senior Informal Advisory Group of trusted public figures, or "wise men," to pass judgment on America's commitment in Indochina.

The group that met for the first time at the State Department on the evening of March 25 included some of the most astute political figures in the nation, a group that was also composed of a number of officials who had originally drafted America's policy on Southeast Asia.* Treated first to a lecture on the South Vietnamese government by foreign policy expert Philip Habib, the wise men were given six hours of background information. What they heard was a devastating indictment of American policy, which had corrupted a government, sewn discord among allies, and led to worrisome problems among the military. The goal of American arms, to pacify South Vietnam and allow a stable government to rule, was in shambles. This meeting was only the first and most formal round in a series of debates that would pit America's elder statesmen against a disbelieving president.

When they reconvened at the White House on the morning of March 26, the shift in views on the war was immediately apparent. George Ball, who led off the discussion, reiterated his long-held skepticism about American efforts. It was soon clear his views had suddenly become a majority opinion. Douglas Dillon, Arthur Goldberg, Matthew Ridgway, and Cyrus Vance agreed with him, saying that a decisive victory was probably beyond reach. Only Maxwell Taylor and Abe Fortas stridently disagreed; both said the United States was making slow progress, that Johnson should hang on. When the group broke for lunch, the president announced that there would be a surprise luncheon speaker; he had invited deputy MACV commander Creighton Abrams to talk about the war, paying special attention to the quality of the South Vietnamese Army.

The group soon learned that Abrams was a tough talking, brutally honest, and steady officer, as incapable of withholding his own opinions as he was at censoring his own earthy phraseology. By almost all accounts, he gave a brilliant presentation, portraying the Vietnamese Army as "damn near nonexistent" and ending his lecture with the opinion that turning the war over to the South Vietnamese would mean turning the entire country over to the communists. Still, the United States, he said, should plan for the day when the South Vietnamese were capable of defending themselves. Under such a plan, American troops must provide security or, as he put it, "the environment in which the South Vietnamese can take on the enemy." In addition, Abrams told the group what Army Chief of Staff Harold Johnson had claimed since 1965, that there was a direct relationship between the American presence and South Vietnamese morale. Abrams's implica-

---

* The group included Dean Acheson, George Ball, Omar Bradley, McGeorge Bundy, Arthur Dean, Douglas Dillon, Abe Fortas, Arthur Goldberg, Henry Cabot Lodge, John McCloy, Robert Murphy, Matthew Ridgway, General Maxwell Taylor, and Cyrus Vance.

tion, taken to its most logical conclusion, was startling: if the United States trained the South Vietnamese and started to disengage, there was actually a better chance that South Vietnam could be saved than if America remained in the country.

Abrams's presentation had a powerful impact. In particular, some of the more experienced diplomats began to argue for a "complete turnaround" on the war and suggested that the president start searching for "a way out." This attitude was carried over into the afternoon session, which witnessed some of the most renowned pyrotechnics of the entire war. Seventy-four-year-old Dean Acheson, a former Secretary of State, began by saying that the nation's military leaders were trying to win in Vietnam when it had been apparent for some time that that was impossible, alluding to the morning's presentation. Acheson was suggesting that it was the military that had gotten the country into the war, that the JCS had somehow convinced the president to undertake the challenge.

Seated across the table from Acheson, Wheeler, clearly enraged, snapped back that Vietnam was "a different kind of war," that there couldn't be "a classic military victory," and that Vietnam was a test of "staying power." Acheson responded by calling Wheeler "disingenuous," which brought the temperamental chairman out of his seat and nearly across the table. He knew when he'd been called a liar, but before he could reply, the president stepped in to end the exchange.* Acheson sat grimacing at Wheeler, his deftness in raising hackles among the military in order to bring out what he believed was their traditional appeal to force proven yet again.

The president took one last poll before dismissing the wise men, stopping only to listen at length to Omar Bradley, a former JCS chairman, who quizzed others about their perceptions. More interested in the facts than ever, Bradley's intuition told him that the military position on the war was probably correct. But he wavered, nodding his head at a restatement of American prospects, that even under the best of circumstances the fighting could go on for another two or three years. He turned to Johnson and said, "Maybe we ought to lower our sights." It was the first crack in the military edifice, and while the

---

* Wheeler believed ever after that he had been set up for the exchange by Acheson, which was confirmed when William DePuy told him that Acheson had invited him to his Georgetown home for a briefing before the March 25 and 26 meetings. In fact, Acheson believed Vietnam was a huge mistake, a position he began to take after watching his son-in-law, William Bundy, struggle with the war. Just months before, Acheson had been Johnson's guest in the White House, where he slept in the situation room — with its huge Khe Sanh photorama. The next day he told Walt Rostow: "You tell the president — and you tell him in precisely these words — that he can take Vietnam and stick it up his ass."

president continued his poll around the table, it was clear that Bradley's comment had turned the tide of optimism. Over the next few
days, Johnson began the same questioning process that had spurred
Bradley's shift on the war. Finally, perhaps inevitably, he realized that
the wise men were right: America wasn't winning and couldn't ever
win. He would accept Clifford's proposal to send 12,500 more troops as
a stopgap measure, but that was all.

There was another change. In the midst of his meetings with the
wise men, Johnson decided the United States needed a new commander in Vietnam, a viewpoint that was sealed by Abrams's unintentionally bleak lecture on how a new strategy might be able to break the
stalemate in Southeast Asia. Westmoreland would return a hero, Johnson told his aides, but above all he must return. If there was to be a
turn in the war, a reopening of channels of negotiation, a deescalation
of the conflict, and a new strategy for ensuring South Vietnam's independence, then Abrams should be in command. After March 26,
Abrams was given the go-ahead to institute his new policy. In addition, a new peace initiative would be made to North Vietnam, including a full halt to the bombing of the North. But the reserves would not
be called, the nation would not be mobilized.

There was yet another surprise, though Johnson didn't tell the wise
men what he had in store. Days later, the president addressed the
American people, talking to them "of peace in Southeast Asia and
Vietnam." He said he would try to find a way to end the Vietnam War,
that he would not seek another term as president. Three years and
twenty-three days after American troops had landed at Danang, Johnson finally made his most important decision on the conflict. At the
Pentagon, the chiefs were subdued. CNO Thomas Moorer wondered
whether the United States could survive a morale-sapping pullout.
John McConnell agreed. While the air war that hounded him was coming to an end, he didn't think the United States could save South Vietnam without it. Surprisingly, Harold Johnson was optimistic. The
United States had decided on a new strategy, and his faith in Abrams
made him believe that the war might yet be won. Then, too, the Army
chief would no longer have to struggle with writing letters to the
mothers of dead American boys, more than five hundred in the previous week.

Wheeler was alone in his thoughts, apparently reflecting on the
events of the previous eight weeks and preparing for his last months of
service under a new Secretary of Defense. Wheeler wasn't certain he
could get along with Clifford, especially in light of the secretary's role
in changing the administration's view of the war. Clifford was also
sensitive to Wheeler's concerns, taking immediate steps in the wake
of Johnson's announcement to put the JCS chairman at ease. Clifford

went out of his way to tell Wheeler that he knew exactly what role the JCS had played in forcing Johnson to make a decision on the war, and while he didn't disagree with it, he let it be known that during his tenure, such political infighting would not be allowed. The secretary was solicitous of Wheeler, mindful of the emotional destruction the war had wrought on him. "The first thing I did was, I told General Wheeler that we were all in this together," Clifford says now. "Vietnam wasn't the president's war, it wasn't the chiefs' war, it wasn't my war. It was an American war. Our first responsibility was to the American people. I tried to impress on General Wheeler that regardless of our personal opinions, we had to do what we thought was right for the nation."

When Johnson's March peace initiative was accepted by North Vietnam in April 1968, the president dispatched seventy-seven-year-old Averell Harriman to open peace talks with the North Vietnamese in Paris. As a former Assistant Secretary of State for Far Eastern Affairs under Kennedy, Harriman had opposed American intervention in Vietnam and worked behind the scenes in running what came to be known as the State Department's "peace shop" throughout the early 1960s. However, his outspoken views made him some well-known enemies, including Johnson, who took him out of the line of fire (and the decision-making process) by making him Undersecretary of State. Harriman's opposition so irritated the president that at one point he told friends that he wouldn't trust the aging diplomat to "take out my garbage." Finally, Harriman had had enough. After all the years of openly predicting disaster in Vietnam (as early as 1964, Harriman told a friend that eventually Johnson would have to negotiate and that "I'm the only one he can send"), he relegated himself to the role of involved bystander, lobbying administration insiders to push Johnson to the negotiating table. Now, after nearly five years on the outside, Harriman was back on the inside; he believed he had been vindicated.

The JCS was skeptical about the peace mission. After fighting the North Vietnamese for three years, it doubted that its adversary would settle for anything less than certain victory. The North Vietnamese would, the JCS thought, be as intransigent at the peace table as they had been in the rice paddies and highlands of Southeast Asia, thus pushing the administration into a desperate attempt to resolve the war on North Vietnam's terms, which would be interpreted as an American defeat. Once again the JCS was torn, divided by its desire to win the war on the battlefield and its belief that the war probably couldn't be won. Even so, it was unanimous: the Paris talks should result in a negotiated peace.

Accompanying Harriman to Paris were Clark Clifford (who provided the jet for the trip), diplomat Cyrus Vance, and General Andrew Goodpaster, the official military representative. Johnson had chosen the members of the delegation as much for their different views as their prestige, hoping the diversity would satisfy the various factions of the administration. But, in fact, it resulted in the same kind of debate that had been waged in the administration's inner circles. There were troubles from the very beginning: during the trip to Paris, the delegation held a heated debate on its negotiating position.

"Now it's our job to end this war," Harriman told his colleagues soon after their departure, "to get the best terms we can, but to end the war." Goodpaster, seated across from Harriman, shook his head. "That's not my understanding," he said, and he reviewed Johnson's instructions: the delegation was to negotiate with the North Vietnamese, but "not in any way [to] compromise the 'maximum pressure' being put on North Vietnam by American troops." Harriman, a longtime critic of Goodpaster's friend Maxwell Taylor and a man viewed with suspicion by the American high command, was adamant. "That's not right, General," he said politely but firmly. "I think it's clear what our position is — what the president ordered."* Clifford attempted to dampen the conversation by taking a seat between the two men, but Goodpaster peered around him, fixing Harriman with his gaze. "No sir," Goodpaster said. "The president would not want us to endanger American lives. We have not been instructed to end the war on the 'best terms we can.'" "We're going to end this war," Harriman responded angrily. "That's what the president said we should do." Goodpaster tried to get in the last word. "Sir," he said acidly, "that is not what the president said. Those are *not* our instructions."

By the time the negotiating team landed in Paris, the Goodpaster-Harriman split had destroyed whatever consensus it might have presented to the North Vietnamese. Fortunately, the split never became public, largely because it soon became apparent that the North Vietnamese were much less willing to end the war than the Americans had been led to believe. By June 1968, it was apparent that the U.S. government was as divided as ever; the Goodpaster-Harriman argument was really a symbol of the civilian-military split over Vietnam policy. In addition, Harriman's antiwar intransigence, which was deeply resented by Goodpaster, reignited the JCS's mistrust of Johnson, whom they now believed would do anything to engineer a U.S. withdrawal from Vietnam.

---

* Harriman's dislike of Maxwell Taylor, for instance, was ferocious. "He is a very handsome man, and a very impressive one, and he is always wrong," Harriman said when Kennedy appointed him MILREP. Later, Harriman dismissed Taylor's recommendation that a logistics team be sent to Vietnam. "You were wrong about wanting to send the 82nd Airborne into Rome [during World War II]," he said, "and you've been wrong about everything since."

In particular, Harriman's apparent willingness to change Johnson's instructions to the delegation forced Goodpaster to take an unusual step to make sure the military's position didn't change. While Harriman communicated with the president on the progress (or lack thereof) in the talks throughout the summer, Goodpaster stayed in constant communication with Earle Wheeler, telling him as much about Harriman's activity as America's chief negotiator as he did about the intransigence of the North Vietnamese. He kept Wheeler informed on the delegation's continuing arguments over American policy in Vietnam and reiterated what he thought to be the president's major point, that the opening to North Vietnam did not mean an end to American combat efforts. "Don't let anyone tell you that we're supposed to stand down [in Vietnam]," he told Wheeler at one point. "You're supposed to keep the pressure on."

Goodpaster's report came at a particularly bad time for Wheeler, who was faced with some major changes of his own. On July 3, 1968, Harold Johnson was replaced as Army chief of staff by William Westmoreland, who believed that he had not been given a chance to prove that he could win in Vietnam. Almost perceptibly uncomfortable with his new role, he sat through his first JCS meetings without uttering a word, allowing Wheeler, Moorer, and McConnell to take over. In effect, Westmoreland's inaction placed a greater burden on Wheeler, who was concerned that the Army needed a stronger hand than Westmoreland was able to give. Wheeler also feared that Westmoreland would not be able to carry out his duties because of his worries about Vietnam, and he nearly had to order him to appoint Bruce Palmer as his aide. Westmoreland didn't like Palmer and he resented Wheeler, finding it hard to believe that the JCS chairman could give him orders.

But the appointment of Palmer proved to be a wise choice. Within weeks of his swearing in as Army chief, Westmoreland decided that his talents required him to make frequent visits to Army bases, resulting in his frequent absence from JCS meetings. "I thought it important to be seen by the troops," Westmoreland explained, "where my presence could be seen as a real boost to their morale." But the judgments of JCS officers during the Johnson-Westmoreland transition are not as kind. They began laughingly to refer to "the inevitable general" as "the indispensable general," a nickname that Wheeler had to order them to stop using on several occasions. But Westmoreland wasn't the only problem. At the end of the long, hot summer of 1968, Wheeler had to deal with an increasingly serious morale problem on the JCS staff, the natural result of the military's failure to take a larger role in prosecuting the war. In fact, according to Palmer, the JCS had a bad case of "the disbeliefs."

"You know part of the military's job is to assess their military policies in the light of the public's thinking," Palmer said later. "And really, we never could believe the American public would not want to fight that war. It's hard to imagine that in retrospect because not many *military* people were in favor of fighting in Vietnam." In an effort to rebuild the JCS's shattered confidence, especially among the higher echelon, Wheeler held a number of dinners at his home at Fort Myer that included officers of different services and ranks. This action was unprecedented; it was one of the few times a JCS chairman actually tried to break down the traditions of service and status in an attempt to reforge military views on the Vietnam War. In addition, he wanted to give the officers a chance to speak freely outside the restraining environment of the Pentagon.

Surprisingly, one of Wheeler's key allies in this effort was Clark Clifford. By the fall of 1968, he was still considered by much of the JCS the one civilian official responsible for changing Johnson's mind, the man who had pushed the president away from mobilization. Still, he had gained a grudging admiration, for he had proven himself more adept at dealing with the military, even when he disagreed with them, than McNamara ever had. Clifford's method of handling the JCS was far different: not only did he ask the JCS for its opinions (McNamara rarely did), he gave them the credibility the JCS thought they deserved. Clifford was honest, straightforward, hard-working, realistic, and respectful, everything the chiefs thought McNamara wasn't. Perhaps even more important, when Clifford wanted to talk with the chiefs he requested a meeting — a stark contrast to McNamara, who often showed up in the tank uninvited. The weekly meetings with the new secretary were formal but less strenuous than those with McNamara, devoid of the embittering arguments over bombing policy that had characterized the darkest days of the war. Clifford's policy was purposeful. "I knew the chiefs were extremely disappointed with the way things had turned out," he later said. "That they had wanted to take a stronger stand in Vietnam. So at least in part my job was to help allay that disappointment, to get us working together. I wanted to do this not only because it would be good for the country, but because frankly I was *very* disturbed about the future. We had an opportunity to extricate ourselves from this terrible war and very little time to do it."

In fact, as Clifford admits, the clock was ticking; after Richard Nixon's nomination as the Republican standard-bearer in August, Clifford and Harriman pushed Johnson for a more reasonable negotiating position with the North Vietnamese in Paris. Both men were convinced that Nixon's election would be a disaster for the country, leading to four more years of war and causing further strains in civilian-military relations. Clifford reiterated these views to Wheeler in September and October 1968, pushing him away from his hard-line stance on the war toward one that could accommodate a diplomatic solution. Wheeler wasn't willing to be convinced, though by November he was willing to concede that Nixon's "secret plan to end the war" probably didn't mean an acceptance of the JCS's long-held position on mobilizing the reserves. But Clifford's arguments went much deeper; not only did the secretary argue that Nixon's policies wouldn't mean a greater prosecution of the war, he claimed they were actually antimilitary, warning that four more years of war without either a full commitment or a full withdrawal would be disastrous for the nation. Further, Clifford argued, Nixon's policies might actually jeopardize the gains the military had won, bringing commanders even further into a domestic debate on the war, forcing them to follow the orders of a new president who insisted on trying out old policies.

Nevertheless, Wheeler and most of his staff were relieved when Nixon won the close election, primarily because they believed that a change in national leadership was at least better than continuing along the road charted by Johnson. But when Nixon appointed Melvin Laird as his Secretary of Defense, the JCS was skeptical. While the chiefs had had long experience in dealing with Laird — he had served nearly all of his sixteen years in the House as a member of the Subcommittee on Military Preparedness — they knew he wanted to get the United States out of Vietnam as quickly as possible. Strangely enough, this knowledge was communicated to the JCS by none other than Clifford, who had been having off-the-record conversations with the secretary-designate throughout the transition period — a time that Clifford later called "a farce."

"Transition? There was no transition," Clifford said. "Not once was I asked for my opinion on the war, on the Pentagon, on dealings with the JCS. I was just never approached. They didn't give a damn about our experiences and how we handled them. It was apparent from the very beginning — we were the bad guys. I had the very real impression that here were people who didn't *want* to know what we thought." It was worse than that. Not only were Johnson administration officials "bad guys," the new Nixon team, led by national security adviser Henry Kissinger, believed they were actually enemies. Only Laird took the time to visit his predecessors at the Pentagon, making certain that word of these meetings, especially those with Clifford, didn't leak out to Nixon's highest officials. No one knows yet just how often Laird met with Clifford, but it is clear that the meetings not only had a profound effect on his thinking about American policy in Vietnam, but also influenced the way he decided to deal with the JCS.

Inevitably, Laird's meetings became common knowledge among Nixon's top staff, which poisoned both Nixon and Kissinger against the new secretary even before he took office. Oddly enough, according

to a retired JCS staff officer, Clifford's report to the JCS on his meetings with Laird came to the attention of Nixon by way of Andrew
Goodpaster, who was on temporary assignment as the new administration's military aide during the transition. He was on leave from
Vietnam, where, as a result of the breakdown in the Paris talks, he had
been Creighton Abrams's deputy. Working as the chief military transition figure wasn't exactly what the intellectual Goodpaster considered
a cushy assignment — he made it plain that he wanted to be back in
Saigon — but it was one at which he was particularly adept. Then, too,
Nixon trusted him, for he had served ably as an aide to Eisenhower.
Goodpaster did his current job almost too well, reportedly passing on
information that Laird was not only meeting with Clifford, but that he
was heavily influenced by what Clifford had to say. To top it off,
Goodpaster related his jaw-clenched argument with Harriman on Clifford's jet, yet another piece of evidence that there was a coterie of for-
eign policy officials (which now included Laird) who were plotting an
American withdrawal from Vietnam.

The Goodpaster report reinforced Kissinger's and Nixon's views of
the previous administration, and the NSC adviser noted darkly that if
Clifford had been talking with Laird, then it was imperative that the
White House make its control over foreign policy impregnable. Nixon
agreed, not only because he now distrusted Laird, but because he
wanted to make sure that all foreign policy decisions were made in the
White House. He even reportedly told Kissinger that they would
"have to keep an eye" on Laird, making certain their views on the war
were made clear to the military. Goodpaster served as an important
intermediary between Nixon, Kissinger, and high-ranking officers
(including members of the JCS), generally smoothing the predictably
rocky transition between administrations.* For the JCS, such courtesy
was invaluable; while Goodpaster was competing with certain JCS
officers (Deputy Chief Bruce Palmer, in particular), he was a trusted
combat commander whose inside knowledge of how the civilian
establishment worked comforted JCS officers who were fearful of any
change, even one with which they seemingly agreed.

Perhaps more important, Goodpaster served as an initial bridge
between the civilian and military establishments, showing as much
allegiance to the JCS as he did to the new president. In particular, he
let Wheeler know that Nixon was more willing to listen to the JCS
than Johnson, that he admired the military (and Wheeler), and that he

---

* For Henry Kissinger, whom Goodpaster introduced to Dwight Eisenhower, he was
one of "the new breed of military officers" and a man of "great honor and considerable
ability." The fact that Goodpaster agreed with Kissinger's view of the war and not Laird's
undoubtedly helped.

hoped that the general would stay on as JCS chairman. Wheeler was still skeptical. While he wanted good relations between the JCS and the new administration, he was physically worn out by his service during the previous five years and wanted to retire. The swearing in of a new president, he thought, would be a good time to initiate a change, a point of view that he communicated to the White House but that was diligently ignored. Wheeler was adamant, but he didn't have a chance to broach the subject until after Nixon had been inaugurated.

On January 21, 1969, just hours before the new administration's first National Security Council meeting, Wheeler went to the White House to tender his resignation. He met with the president privately in the Oval Office, perhaps one of the few times that Nixon ever met alone with a high government official outside his staff. After an exchange of pleasantries, including the traditional pledge of cooperation from the JCS, Wheeler said that he wanted to retire, that the new president deserved a JCS chairman of his own choosing. Wheeler's recitation of his role in the Johnson administration was probably unnecessary, but he went through it anyway, just to make certain that Nixon knew his position.*

He told Nixon that he had served the nation for five full years, well beyond the usual four-year term for a JCS chairman, only because Johnson had insisted that he serve until the official end of his presidency. Now, Wheeler said, it was time for him to retire; he had served his country well and well past the time for retirement of most Army officers. He then sat back, expecting Nixon's thanks for a job well done and agreement that it was time for a new man. But that's not the way Nixon saw it. He shook his head in disagreement and surprise. Hadn't the JCS chairman already been confirmed by Congress? he asked. Why would he want to resign? How could he be replaced?

According to colleagues to whom Wheeler later spoke, he didn't know whether to be suspicious or complimented. Apparently, it had never even occurred to Nixon that Wheeler would want to leave, that he would choose retirement over power. It was a notion so foreign to Nixon as to be beyond belief. But Wheeler had his reasons, which he repeated in increasingly insistent tones: not only had he served well past the time of other chairmen, he had actually served longer than any other individual, including Omar Bradley and Arthur Radford. To serve any longer, he told Nixon, would set a bad precedent. Again, Nixon disagreed, saying that he not only liked Wheeler personally, he admired the position he had taken on the war in Vietnam. Wheeler was one military man who had wanted to win the war, Nixon said,

---

* Wheeler became a comforting presence to Johnson during the last months of his presidency. Johnson even began asking Wheeler for advice on heart disease.

adding that he understood just how difficult it had been for him over the last several years. As for precedent, Congress had already settled that question by extending Wheeler's term another year. They could do it again. Wheeler wouldn't have any problems on that score; it was clear he deserved the job.

But if Nixon thought Wheeler was being polite, he was wrong. It wasn't so much that he didn't want to set a precedent, Wheeler said, he was tired. He needed a change, a rest, a chance to recover his health. He had been looking forward to retirement. Nixon wouldn't listen. He dismissed Wheeler's arguments with a wave of his hand, ready to go on to the next subject. Only when Wheeler continued to press his point, leaning impolitely over the president's desk, did Nixon finally understand that the JCS chairman was serious. Nixon, surprised by Wheeler's continued argument, launched into a long monologue on the problems faced by the nation because of the war. In effect, Nixon appealed to Wheeler's patriotism, telling him the nation had not passed its "moment of decision" in Vietnam and that his invaluable experience was desperately needed. He promised Wheeler his full cooperation and then, as a last resort, dangled the bait: his administration intended to take the military's advice on the war more seriously than the previous administration did, more seriously than either "Mr. McNamara or Mr. Clifford" did. Nixon uttered the names mockingly, his emphasis pointedly on the "Mr."

Wheeler must have been tempted by Nixon's offer and by his implicit promise that the war could be, would be, won; that in the end it would be a military victory, that at the very least Nixon and his appointees intended to see the war through to its conclusion. But he was not deterred. He believed that if he insisted on retiring, Nixon would have little choice. Wheeler put it to the president bluntly: he was dying, he said, and had served long enough; "Of course, sir," he reportedly said, "if you make it a direct order, I will do as you wish." Otherwise he was leaving. After a short pause, Nixon gave the order.

There is a picture of Wheeler taken just after this meeting. The mood is obviously upbeat; a new team with new solutions is in place. In the photograph, Wheeler is standing between Spiro Agnew and Richard Helms. Across from him is Melvin Laird. In the background is Henry Kissinger and Secretary of State William Rogers. It is a statement of the time: of all the men surrounding Wheeler, none had been as privy to the formation of military policy over the previous six years as he. None had his experience in formulating military policy positions, much less carrying them out. However, as many colleagues pointed out later, while no one in the new administration was as experienced as Wheeler, neither was anyone as jaded. None of them had suffered through the most agonizing moments of the war; none of them had been subjected to the crucible of Vietnam.

Kissinger, the beaming centerpiece of this tableau, might have written its caption. Although he later described Wheeler as "tall, elegant, calm" (but also as a man "deeply disillusioned" by Vietnam), his views of what ailed the military were hardly charitable. Wheeler, Kissinger said, stood as a symbol of the era, a military descendant of "Grant, Pershing, and Marshall" who had "never fully grasped that attrition is next to impossible to apply in a guerrilla war against an enemy who does not *have* to fight because he can melt into the population." He believed there was something decidedly weak about Wheeler, as if he had an infectious malady brought on by his years of experience with Johnson. He had "played into the hands of a civilian leadership" during the Johnson presidency, and the results were policies that "demoralized" the military by applying restraints.

Of course, Kissinger said, Wheeler, and the rest of the generals who had fought the war, had no one to blame but themselves for the failure of Vietnam; they had "brought on some of their own troubles. They permitted themselves to be coopted too readily. They accommodated to the new dispensation while inwardly resenting it." Kissinger made it clear that from the beginning of the Nixon administration that was going to change, that the military would be given wide latitude in advising the president, in formulating military policy. "In the final analysis," he wrote, "the military profession is the art of prevailing, and while in our time this required more careful calculations than in the past, it also depends on elemental psychological factors that are difficult to quantify."

Such judgments, and specifically Kissinger's appeal to "elemental psychological factors," would have undoubtedly brought a sardonic smile to Wheeler in early 1969; certainly he would have been disturbed by Kissinger's boundless confidence in the military's ability to continue waging a war in Vietnam. For Wheeler as well as the other members of the JCS, Kissinger's view would have been vilified as unworkable or even hopelessly naive. Not only had the Kissinger program of "prevailing" in Vietnam been tried and discarded, there was little optimism that the new president would take the steps the JCS had been advocating for almost four years.

In one sense, however, Kissinger's judgment was quite correct: the JCS had been coopted by the Johnson administration, as evidenced by its deep bitterness over taking the blame for designing a strategy that couldn't assure the victory it desired. In common military slang, the JCS had been "snookered," taken in by its own belief that civilian leaders would never purposely place American lives in danger without providing an unambiguous and overwhelming support for their deployment. But the JCS had learned its lesson well; it had not been as accommodating to this dispensation as Kissinger thought. In fact, the JCS had engaged in an administration debate that was at once vicious and decisive.

The JCS would continue to press for a resolution of the conflict in Vietnam by promoting its own position, even if that meant continuing the infighting that had characterized the last years of the Johnson administration. In the future, it would not be "coopted" as readily as in the past — as Kissinger was about to discover. The view of the members of the JCS on this last point was universal, a belief articulated not just by those disenchanted with America's involvement, but also by the JCS's most conservative, anticommunist, and increasingly powerful officer, CNO Thomas Moorer.

7

The problem in this town is that no one can keep a secret.
It's a goddamn shame if you ask me. You can't even conduct foreign policy without everyone and their mother
finding out what the hell is going on.

Admiral Thomas Moorer

IN THOSE FIRST, heady, almost buoyant days of 1969, Richard Nixon
and the new foreign policy team put together by Henry Kissinger were
supremely confident that they could not only manage the war, they
could also manage the public's distaste for the war. In fact, to admit to
anything less was simply "defeatism," a word used by the administration's top foreign policy advisers to describe the malady that they
believed infected the people and even seemed to plague the nation's
military leaders. As Kissinger himself would say, the military did not
have the "self-confidence" to carry out a program of American withdrawals from Vietnam (thereby assuaging public sentiment) while
escalating the conflict (and thereby winning the war). Most of the
members of the JCS, however, didn't agree with either Nixon or Kissinger. They were skeptical that the new administration could alter
American policy in South Vietnam to the degree necessary to force a
resolution of the conflict, and they believed that the issue had already
been decided publicly by the electorate's condemnation of Lyndon
Johnson.

Wheeler, for one, wasn't convinced that the new foreign policy team
understood the complexity of America's involvement in Indochina
and that, as a result, the JCS and the rest of the military would be
forced to suffer through its long learning process. Air Force Chief of
Staff John McConnell, entering the last year of his career, agreed:
unless the administration was willing to depart radically from past
policies, it was doubtful that any solution short of an all-out commit-

ment (a politically impossible option) would end the conflict. Ironically, even William Westmoreland, the JCS's most detached service leader, wasn't optimistic about the feasibility of a tougher strategy. Their views reflected not just a lack of faith in civilian authority but new doubts about America's involvement. Of all the chiefs, only CNO Thomas Moorer was absolutely convinced that the United States could still actually win the war with a tougher strategy, though he too questioned that "these new guys," as he called Nixon and Kissinger, had any idea just what that entailed.

Not surprisingly, Moorer's hawkish views made him the focus of the administration's plan for winning in Vietnam. Moorer seemed less bitten by the bug of defeatism than his colleagues, more willing to take the steps necessary to resolve the conflict on American terms. The administration's view was also reflected in the tank, where Moorer's opinions began to take on added importance during JCS strategy sessions on Vietnam. But it wasn't just his opinion that gave his views importance, it was also his status as the heir apparent to the ailing chairman. In late January 1969, it was obvious that Wheeler was definitely in his last term (and would therefore need to begin to turn over his duties to a successor); it was also obvious that the CNO would succeed him.

Wheeler's continuing illness placed strains on the JCS. In effect, the chairman was forced to share many of his responsibilities, especially with Moorer. By early 1969, the approaching transition in military leadership had taken on new significance; the new JCS chairman would be assuming his responsibilities in the midst of an unpopular and undecided conflict. Perhaps, however, Moorer's increased power on the JCS was more the result of Wheeler's decision to take time from his JCS duties to monitor the worsening morale of the troops still in Vietnam, where combat reports showed a critical drop in unit discipline. As Wheeler was learning, the Army's position in Southeast Asia was deteriorating to such a degree that commanders were admitting that many units were on the edge of outright rebellion. Coupled with his desire to acclimate himself to Nixon's foreign policy group, Wheeler made certain that Moorer played a larger role in JCS decision-making; his retirement was just seventeen months away, a comparatively short time in which to engineer a smooth transition. Moorer seemed perfectly suited to be chairman, especially since he seemed to agree with many of the new administration's policies.

Wheeler's willingness to play a less significant role in U.S. military policy was apparent to JCS staff officers, many of whom remained Wheeler partisans until their own retirement. More than any other person in its history, Earle Wheeler has come to epitomize the professional JCS officer. Dutiful, loyal, convinced of the essential rightness of the American vision, he nonetheless asserted what he believed were military prerogatives in the face of civilian policy, even when it meant placing his own reputation on the line. The bare facts of military history will show that Wheeler failed: his strategy calling for a full response to North Vietnam in 1965 was rejected, his questioning of U.S. deployment was ignored, his personal judgment was called into question, and, in the end, his arguments for full mobilization were firmly put aside. He was resentful, convinced that the military would be blamed for the failure of the nation's civilian-dictated policy in Vietnam.

It's a curious and twisted tale: in the midst of personal defeat and national humiliation, Wheeler significantly strengthened the role of the JCS, winning with his silence and loyalty what could never have been won with his resignation. More than any of his predecessors, Wheeler was willing to push JCS programs and policies, even to consider mutiny, to win a voice for the military in the back rooms of official Washington. While not as storied as "the romantic general," Maxwell Taylor, nor as comfortable with official Washington as Arthur Radford, Wheeler clearly had a better fix on his role than either. Even so, officers are unwilling to build myths. Wheeler was short-tempered and unfair, demanding that JCS staff officers eviscerate their personal lives in the name of their service. He was too loyal, his closest friends say, defending colleagues who later refused to do the same for him. Though filled with personal bitterness, he kept his own counsel, refusing to engage in recriminations against those who had decided a policy that he opposed. Nevertheless, the JCS and, more important, JCS officers are, in large part, the product of his service.

While it's difficult to call Wheeler a bona fide American military hero, he nonetheless set the standard for professional excellence in the postwar era. No JCS chairman who followed has been able to equal the great respect his name has engendered, nor would any JCS member so glibly threaten resignation, knowing that he refused the act under more serious circumstances. But if Wheeler set the precedent for military loyalty to civilian control in his refusal to resign, his actions also became the test of military silence in the face of civilian incompetence. Since Wheeler's tenure, it has been impossible for a JCS member to assent silently to policies with which he strongly disagreed. This was immediately apparent during the tenure of Wheeler's successor.

Thomas Moorer was the eleventh in a long and distinguished line of Navy chiefs dating from the early days of World War II, a man as acclimated to high command as any officer in JCS history. Heir to the traditions of King and Nimitz, whose strange personal habits and rough language he seemed to emulate, the balding, spit-and-polish former aviator was perhaps the most quintessentially professional Navy officer. Yet Moorer remained an enigma to most of his fellow chiefs, an officer whose blustery exterior and famous temper tantrums were viewed as fine dramas but little else. A hard-boiled conservative and fanatical anticommunist, he was well known throughout the JCS for his outspoken support of the war, his earthy, no-nonsense manner, and his intractable all-for-the-Navy position. If it hadn't been for Curtis LeMay, Moorer might well be remembered as the most partisan service leader in JCS history; his trust in the Navy's ability to fight and win the next all-out conflict was an article of faith. He was so partisan that he invariably portrayed the Navy's needs as America's needs while arguing that the most fundamental programs of other services detracted from the national security. As one colleague described him, "If it was a program that benefitted the Navy, he said it was for the good of the country; if it was for someone else, he said it was a waste of taxpayers' money."

On one level, Moorer was an almost transparent figure, a stereotypical officer whose solution to world problems was to apply overwhelming force, a position he had consistently advocated since becoming a member of the JCS in August 1967. But on another level, he was deeply disturbed by America's action in Vietnam, in part because the military's inability to defeat the Vietcong seemed to disprove so many of his theories. The enigma in his character, then, consisted mainly in his almost shocking and completely unpredictable view of the war. At one moment Moorer would denigrate civilians for failing to show "some guts on this whole thing," while at another he would wonder aloud "just what the hell we're doing there anyway." So while Moorer hated communists, he thought there was something distinctly distasteful in using aircraft carrier–launched jets to bomb Third World nations. Like the massive retaliation theorists who provided much of the thinking for his service in the 1950s, Moorer believed the United States should save itself for an all-out fight with the Soviet Union, believing with LeMay that the American military effort should be preserved to "go after the manure pile."

Indeed, everything in his training had prepared Moorer for that one final showdown between the American fleet and its Soviet competitor. After graduating from the Naval Academy in 1933, the Alabama native (and a football star) decided he would cast his lot with the Navy's aviation branch, a risky choice in the 1930s, with the battleship-dominated Navy. But on December 7, 1941, the Japanese attack at Pearl Harbor ended battleship dominance forever, transforming Moorer's shortsighted choice into a prescient and downright dangerous vision. When the Japanese bombed Hawaii, they not only shot up the harbor, they hit the naval air station, almost ending the young officer's life. Moorer survived and went on to fly reconnaissance missions off Australia, where he was shot down by a Japanese Zero in late 1942. Moorer was rescued, though his troubles had not ended: the ship that rescued him was torpedoed and he was forced back into the ocean. He remarked later that "my war had barely started and I had already been shot and torpedoed" — a bit of bad luck that became a badge of pride for him. Transferred to duty in the States after these close calls, Moorer stayed out of danger thereafter, though his exploits as a combat flyer were beyond dispute, especially in light of his early experiences in the South Pacific.

Moorer's career after the war could well be a symbol of how a Naval Academy graduate rises to the top: the young aviator served in the best commands and was sure to make contact with the right civilian officials to ensure his promotion. From the late 1940s, Moorer was considered one of the Navy's most talented and potentially most successful officers. He was not only competent but also a member in good standing of the Navy's most powerful clique, the officers who ran the aircraft carrier fleet. Perhaps the only real surprise is that he wasn't drummed out of the Navy for speaking his mind, which he did often — and apparently with little thought. Moorer was absolutely without tact, taking any and every opportunity to call a fellow officer who disagreed with him "a dirty bastard" or "an unshaven peacenik," a phrase he used with disarming frequency during the height of the Vietnam War.

Moorer's gruff partisanship is now legion and has made him one of the most feared and controversial figures in the Navy's two-hundred-year history. "I guess you could call Moorer and Radford the old guard," said Eugene Carroll, a retired admiral and leading critic of his former colleague. "Both of those guys are just pure Navy. Hell, they'd rather bomb Omaha [home of SAC] than Moscow. They just absolutely hate the Air Force; they spend every minute they can trying to fight the Air Force. They did everything they could to circumvent the joint system. It's become a tradition in the Navy." Carroll's description brought a heated reply from Moorer, whose response stands as proof that he has earned his reputation as an irascible Navy patriot. "That's just bullshit," he said angrily. "What the hell would that pacifist know about anything?"

But perhaps Moorer's staff knew him better than anyone, even better than those who served with him in 1969, when he first became a powerful, if controversial, figure on the JCS. Indeed, despite his almost insulting mannerisms that bordered on a cold elitism (junior officers who failed his assignments were publicly criticized as "fools" and "idiots"), Moorer was loved by his staff as few other CNOs. According to a contemporary, now retired, the JCS staff officers would present Moorer with a birthday cake and card every year — a highly unusual event on the Pentagon's command ring — out of sheer respect for the man they called "the boss." "Now just what the hell is going on?" Moorer angrily asked when a troupe of JCS officers began singing "Happy Birthday" to him in 1970. When he realized that it was a celebration in his honor, he became embarrassed. "Oh well, shit, thanks," he said.* This deep respect, surprising as it was, also led to other anomalies. While Moorer is shaped like a bottle of port, no one ever thought to parrot his grim manner (as they had that of other JCS officers) or mimic his Bull Halsey hands-on-hips stance when chewing out subordinates. It might be done to other chiefs, but never to Moorer.

There were other puzzles. While members of the JCS realized that the CNO was an intelligent and savvy political infighter (second only to Wheeler), they also realized that he was modest about his personal strengths; he enjoyed playing the role of the simple naval aviator who "just liked to fly" and disparaged his appointment to the JCS by saying that it took him away from his real job of "fighting commies." Nothing could be further from the truth. According to officers who served with him, Moorer thrived on his role as head of the Navy, loved the intrigue of the JCS office, and "got an unforgettable look on his face every time he talked to the president, like he just worshiped the idea of being around real powerful people." It now seems certain that Moorer took great pride in passing himself off as a simple southern boy who just wanted to do his job, a ploy that he worked with particular pleasure on the intellectuals of the Nixon administration.

To Kissinger, for instance, Moorer was an affable "country bumpkin" who only knew how to obey orders, a quality of almost atmospheric importance in the foreign policy wing of the White House. His apparent lack of intelligence was his most important quality; he was uninterested in foreign policy theory, so wasn't hamstrung by endless debates over what would work in Vietnam. Kissinger characterized Moorer's solution to the Vietnam War with nodding approval; the CNO — whom he took to calling Admiral Mormon — would bomb and bomb and bomb, he said. Kissinger's apparent approval of Moorer's position even showed up in the NSC adviser's memoirs, in which the CNO was described as an officer who didn't "really know all this new jargon about strategy and all that" but clearly understood

---

* During an interview for this book, Moorer was faced with a similar situation: a crowd appeared outside his office with a candle-decked cake in tow. Moorer turned to his secretary. "Oh shit," he said. "I suppose I have to do this now, right?" She nodded. "Well, okay," he said. When he went to the door, he acted surprised, touched, and complimented.

that "there isn't a country in the world who can take bombing for very long."

Kissinger, who was clearly the most powerful foreign policy spokesman (even Secretary of State William Rogers deferred to him), thought that Moorer's increasingly important role on the JCS was a bonus for the administration, especially since both he and Nixon believed that the United States had made a mistake in ending the bombing of North Vietnam in lieu of talks with the North Vietnamese in Paris. In fact, the new administration's "secret plan to end the war," trumpeted by Nixon during his campaign, turned out to reflect Moorer's own feelings: the United States should continue to up the ante in Vietnam by increasing military pressure on the North Vietnamese, including the mining of Haiphong Harbor, reinstituting the large-scale bombing of North Vietnamese cities, and returning to the offensive in the South. In addition, the JCS was considering recommending that the United States attack North Vietnamese troop sanctuaries in Cambodia, an undertaking that was becoming necessary in view of Nixon's and Kissinger's apparent hurry to begin some nominal American troop withdrawals from Indochina.

It's no wonder that Nixon's foreign policy experts were confident they could manage the war. Not only was the administration headed by a man who had vowed that the United States would not be defeated in Vietnam, the foreign policy apparatus was firmly in the hands of officials who were, as they themselves had said, more confident than their predecessors. Kissinger, in particular, was more than willing to reinvigorate the JCS, which he believed was badly shaken by the war, with a new sense of purpose, even if it meant using more hawkish officers (like Moorer) as a lever against those who advocated a faster disengagement. Not surprisingly, however, this overly simple us-versus-them view of foreign policy involved going over the head of the new Defense Secretary, a prospect that was all the clearer after the NSC meeting on January 21.

Of all the officials who gathered at the White House, the one who seemed as out of place as Earle Wheeler was Melvin Laird. The former congressman, whose name was most often mentioned by members of Congress who wanted one of their own in the White House, was one of the few foreign policy moderates in the new administration. Even-tempered, affable, obsessively patient, and a good listener, Laird quickly realized that his greatest detractor in the White House was Kissinger, who was busy telling aides even before the inauguration that Laird was "out to get me." In addition, Nixon had made it clear to Laird that the NSC staff would be responsible for establishing the administration's most important foreign policy (and military) positions and that its role as a filter for recommendations from Laird and

Rogers was paramount.* Laird viewed this "reorganization," as Nixon euphemistically called it, with skepticism; he believed the government ran best when it ran "by the book"; that is, the administration should follow the procedures in the 1947 National Security Act as well as those in the 1969 Defense Reorganization Act. Under the latter, the commandant of the Marines was included as a member of the JCS and the Secretary of Defense was made an official part of the national chain of command. Laird read between the lines, opposing Nixon's reorganization because he believed that the president wanted to do more than just streamline the decision-making process; he wanted to centralize it in his and Kissinger's hands. By placing additional responsibilities on the NSC staff, Laird believed, Nixon was actually giving it more power, which would freeze out the more traditional government bureaucracy from the foreign policy structure.

For Laird, the administration's strategy in Vietnam and its handling of the JCS were apparent from the beginning: the United States would follow the JCS's natural inclination to escalate the conflict in Indochina, punishing the North Vietnamese with increased bombing pressures while slowly bringing down U.S. troop levels. To do this effectively, Laird realized, Nixon, Kissinger, and their top aides would dangle the promise of victory before the military chiefs, using them as a foil for Laird's more moderate views. It was a delicate and extremely complex situation, and to deal with it the secretary had to come up with a strategy of his own, one that mirrored his own views on what the United States could and could not do in Vietnam. In essence, Laird had to win over the JCS. But this task, as he well knew, would be difficult, perhaps impossible.

The afternoon following the first NSC meeting, Wheeler walked from his office on the command ring of the Pentagon down a short hallway and into the tank. There, around a dark oak conference table, sat the four-star chiefs flanked by their three-star deputies and a phalanx of notetakers and aides. It was the first JCS meeting under the new administration, and Wheeler intended to discuss its policies as well as report on his interview with the president and review the material covered by the NSC meeting. Seating himself comfortably at the middle of the table, Wheeler began by nodding to the JCS director, seated

---

* Laird was not Nixon's first choice for the post. Nixon had wanted to appoint Washington's Senator Henry "Scoop" Jackson. But, under pressure from his Democratic colleagues, Jackson turned him down. Disappointed, Nixon turned to Laird. "You got me into this," he said. Laird didn't want the job but didn't think he should reject it. Eisenhower opposed Laird's appointment. "He's too devious," he said.

on his left, to review the agenda for the meeting. All this was done according to strict JCS protocol, even though the members of the JCS were impatient to hear just what Wheeler thought of the new president and his foreign policy team. The director, however, surprised everyone by stating that the agenda had been swept clean in anticipation of the appearance of the new Secretary of Defense. He then turned the meeting over to the chairman.

As was his habit, Wheeler began by cracking several self-deprecating jokes, including an aside that his meeting with Nixon meant that his colleagues "will have to put up with me for another year." The cool, offhanded manner of the announcement, Wheeler's bantering and wry style, his way of dismissing what everyone realized must have been a personal sacrifice, brought smiles of appreciation from his listeners. But then the chairman grew serious, saying that the new president "sends his greetings and good wishes, and believes the relationship between the civilian leaders of the U.S. government and the nation's Joint Chiefs of Staff is entering a new era of cooperation and understanding." Reading from his notes, he added Nixon's personal assurance that "the door to the Oval Office is always open for any of the chiefs," emphasizing Nixon's promise to listen to military opinions on foreign policy issues.

Repeating the director's announcement that Laird "will be joining us soon" for a "get-acquainted" session, Wheeler quickly reviewed the topics discussed at the NSC meeting. He said that the administration was "intent on solving this problem in Vietnam," beginning with "a full assessment of where we stand on the war." With that, Wheeler passed out the new administration's first major planning document, National Security Study Memorandum 1 (NSSM 1), written by Kissinger himself and entitled "Situation in Vietnam." It was the first of many foreign policy questionnaires handed out by the NSC, internal administration surveys intended to elicit opinions from the government bureaucracy on a number of sticky foreign policy issues. NSSM 1 was, Wheeler said, supposed to be "the basis for determining U.S. policy on the war for the next four years," a document of such importance that each member of the JCS "should be prepared to give detailed answers" to each of its seventy-eight questions on the situation in Vietnam.

Put simply, NSSM 1 asked the JCS to assess the tasks the military should be prepared to undertake in all aspects of its confrontation with the North Vietnamese, requiring a broad review of American strategy, the nation's force levels, and contingency plans if American policy failed. The members of the JCS were silent as they looked at this first study paper, perhaps because they sensed that "study memorandums," unlike "decision memorandums," would have little real impact on foreign policy; the JCS was being asked its opinion, nothing more.*

Wheeler returned to a review of his meeting with Nixon, keeping his voice level, never once betraying his feelings that the new administration had done little to prepare itself for many of the foreign policy issues that had arisen over the previous six years. Only once did Wheeler come close to betraying himself, saying that "the president obviously wants to make his policies much clearer than those of the Johnson administration and particularly those put forward by 'Mr. McNamara or Mr. Clifford.'" Wheeler snapped out the names just as Nixon had said them, then looked around and smiled before quickly going on, summing up by saying, "I'm sure we can all return the confidence placed in us by the president."

It was suddenly apparent to the members of the JCS that Wheeler wasn't as comfortable with Nixon as his words implied. As a number of aides later commented, his characterization of Nixon was almost a parody; he was disgusted with his veiled condemnation of the previous administration and its top officials, which meant that Nixon couldn't possibly appreciate the complexities of the Vietnam conflict. Others, however, couldn't be sure: Wheeler had given his report without batting an eye (except for when he quoted the president word for word), a formal recitation of civilian-military courtesy that was so ritualistic it was almost a sedative.

But, across the table, McConnell understood; he sat back in his chair after Wheeler finished and shook his head in disbelief. Behind him, his vice chief, John D. Ryan, stared back at Wheeler, a frown on his face; he was just as disturbed. It was one thing for a president to disagree with his predecessors' policies; it was another to hold his colleagues and competitors in such contempt. Of the two generals, however, Ryan was the more outraged by Nixon's disparagement of McNamara and Clifford. Ryan, a football great in the West Point class of 1938, was clearly in line for a new assignment — as McConnell's replacement as Air Force chief of staff — but Ryan was more outspoken, a "stronger chief," in JCS parlance. He had a pathological hatred for what politicians and journalists called "spin," a way of slanting a policy or story that skirted the truth without ever becoming a full-blown lie.

During his career in the upper reaches of SAC and on the JCS, Ryan had become known as a commander who expected the absolute truth in every matter — a quality he particularly prized during wartime because, as he said, "lives are hanging on our every decision." Not sur-

---

* In fact, National Security Study Memorandums (NSSMs) were intended to provide policy options, while the real decisions were made in National Security Decision Memorandums (NSDMs). The papers were initiated as part of a plan to allow the NSC to intervene directly in State and Defense policy-making procedures.

prisingly, by early 1969 Ryan had about had his fill with civilian policies on the war, for he believed they symbolized the ultimate lie: that
having decided to sacrifice American lives in a far-off conflict, civilian
policy-makers had been unwilling to take the steps necessary to make
the sacrifice worthwhile. According to JCS officers who served with
him, Ryan was so disturbed by these policies — most of which he
blamed on McNamara — that he had considered resigning his commission and returning to civilian life on a number of occasions. Now,
with a new administration firmly in place, it looked to Ryan as if the
policies of McNamara were about to be replaced with the same policies under Laird.

But Ryan wasn't the only JCS officer who had that feeling; throughout the two-month transition, the JCS staff had consistently questioned the president-elect's abilities not only to manage the Vietnam
War but to carry out the withdrawal of American troops without endangering the shaky South Vietnamese government. At first, the focus
was on Nixon himself, but eventually concerns had shifted to the Secretary of Defense. The JCS believed that Laird was too much of a politician to effect any lasting change in American policy. Indeed, it's
likely it would have preferred the continued leadership of Clifford,
even though he opposed the war, to that of the unknown and untested
Laird. After Wheeler's formal litany of welcome from the new president, these doubts resurfaced. Even Moorer, who welcomed a more
aggressive military stance on the war, smiled at Wheeler's characterization of Nixon and probably wondered if Laird had the back-
bone to prosecute an unpopular war. William Westmoreland and
Marine Corps Commandant Leonard Chapman, the other two members
of the JCS, had these same doubts. Chapman worried whether Laird
had had enough experience in handling the military, while Westmoreland feared Laird would not seek out his advice on specific operations.

But more important than any of these personal doubts, the JCS harbored a deep mistrust of any civilian manager, a bitterness that was
clearly left over from the days of McNamara. At the very worst, Laird
would turn out to be another "very strange" Secretary of Defense,
who — like McNamara — would not have the courage of his convictions on the war (no matter what they were), who would agree with
the JCS one minute in private and disagree with it the next minute in
public. Worse yet, the JCS feared that the new administration would
make the same mistakes as the last: it would prosecute the war without seeking popular support; it would say that the United States was
winning when it was not and that the strategy was working when it
was not; and it would think that the nation could withdraw from its
commitments without bearing the responsibility for its mistake. In
sum, with Laird taking over for the respected Clifford, the chiefs
feared a return to the days in which "critical" issues would once again

become "peripheral," in which military goals would be sacrificed to domestic politics. Most of all, their fears centered on Laird.

After completing his remarks on his meeting with Nixon, Wheeler left the tank for a moment and returned with Laird. It was an incredibly tense moment, especially considering that it had been more than eight years since the JCS had been formally introduced to a new Pentagon leader operating under the instructions of a new president. Amazingly, however, whatever doubts the chiefs harbored were dispelled from almost the very first moment the new secretary entered the tank. Making a quick circuit of the table, Laird shook hands with all of the chiefs and their assistants, making sure to stop for introductions to aides who had not reached flag rank.

In many ways, it was a performance the more savvy officers should have expected from a Wisconsin politician. "Hi, how are ya, I'm Mel Laird," he announced to each face. "Hi, General, an honor to see you again," he said to Westmoreland, who beamed. Then, shaking hands with Wheeler, Laird seated himself at the head of the table and nodded to everyone. Unexpectedly, there was silence in the room as he looked from one chief to another, apparently waiting for permission to speak. Only after Wheeler nodded to him, giving him the floor, did he begin his remarks. Laird opened with an apology: "Well, I want to say first of all that I want to thank you for inviting me here today, and I'm sorry to take this time to interrupt your work" — at which point, one JCS officer remembered, "I goddamn near fell off my chair." Laird laughed a bit, embarrassed, then continued. "I know that you're busy and have a lot of things to think about, one of which probably has to do with figuring out just what kind of policies the president is going to come up with." Laird then thanked the chiefs for taking the time to draw up briefing papers on various issues (written by JCS "Indians") that he had used during the transition period to familiarize himself with military issues. He noted that he had met many members of the JCS when they had testified on Capitol Hill and had always "respected each of your views. We cooperated then," he said, "and I'm confident that we can cooperate now."

Opening the single folder in front of him, Laird launched into a review of the administration's policies on the war, on military readiness, and on weapons procurement (a thirty-minute monologue that sent JCS aides scrambling for memos to give their chiefs). When Laird was finished, he said he hoped to meet often with the JCS and that a spirit of cooperation between military and civilian leaders could be initiated. As he rose to leave, he again made a point of shaking everyone's hand, then left some papers for Wheeler, gave one last wave, and walked out of the room. Following the predictable stunned silence, there was an almost palpable sense of relief around the table as well as a chilling realization that an enormously self-confident and adept politician was in control. Laird had accomplished in a few minutes what most officers believed would take years to gain: he had won the trust of a disenchanted high command that was more than willing to mistrust any Defense Secretary, regardless of his policies.

It was no less than a revolution in civilian-military relations, a commentary on what officers prize above all else. In the history of the JCS, the Laird introduction of January 22, 1969, stands out as the primary example of just how a civilian leader can both dampen military mistrust and gain military allegiance for controversial foreign policy initiatives that run counter to traditional military beliefs. But the lesson is a paradox, a reversal of predictable nonmilitary views of what officers think and respect. The paradox entails nothing less than looking at the JCS as a body of officers whose rise to high command means that they have become as acclimated to compromise and consensus as any civilian in elective office. Indeed, the Laird meeting proves the point: of all the secretaries who have served at the Pentagon, Laird remains among the most respected, not because he agreed with military programs and policies (he very often didn't), but because he was willing to compromise on JCS positions and accord the chiefs the respect they thought they deserved. Perhaps Laird, with eight terms in Congress under his belt, could not have acted any other way; nevertheless, his intuition to treat members of the JCS as intelligent political equals rather than warmongering subordinates worked wonders in transforming the Pentagon from a battlefield to a demilitarized zone.

The evidence is compelling. In the early years of the Vietnam conflict, McNamara agreed with the JCS's position but was universally mistrusted because of his elitist attitude, his habit of breaking in on their meetings, and his feeling that he knew what was best for the country. His attitude was particularly galling to those members of the JCS who had spent untold hours in the holds of Japanese prison ships, regardless of whether they agreed with him. Clifford realized this and tried to reassure the JCS that its opinions mattered, but he had only a short time and could only accomplish the most cosmetic changes. Laird was different; when Wheeler went to him the first week after the inauguration, Laird asked him to make recommendations to help change the organization of the Department of Defense, a task for which only Laird was responsible. From the beginning, then, he went out of his way to signal the chiefs that theirs was a team effort, that he would earn their respect, not just demand it.*

---

* Laird told Wheeler that he had four goals: to end the American involvement in Vietnam, to end the draft, to cut the defense budget, and to repair civilian-military relations. In addition, he said that he thought McNamara had served too long as Defense Secretary and that he would serve only four years. Laird repeated his belief so often that it is now known as the Laird Rule.

These good relations were reinforced by Laird's appointment of top aides who would carry on the everyday management of the Pentagon; in effect, the whiz kids were shown the door and replaced by a team of officials "prized for their political and bureaucratic savvy," according to a Pentagon official at the time. At the top of the list was the industrialist David Packard, the new assistant secretary, who was put in charge of defusing the vicious bureaucratic fights in the Pentagon left over from the McNamara days. Packard, as wise politically as Laird himself, made it his job to work closely with the chiefs, the Pentagon agencies, and top Pentagon bureaucrats whose relations with the military has suffered from McNamara's obvious dislike of military advice, a view that had infected Defense civilian officials. In the words of one high-ranking officer, "Packard told the civilians to mind their manners." But Laird's most important step was his informal agreement with Wheeler, and later Moorer, that all service communications with the White House would be routed through his office and that, in exchange, he would fight for service programs within the administration.

With enormous experience in dealing with the defense budget from his time in the House, Laird knew that while military outlays had to be cut, it would be impossible to ask the JCS to volunteer such cuts in their most important weapons programs. So he told the JCS that instead of unilaterally cutting (or expanding) the budget himself (a practice made famous under McNamara), he would enlist them in the process; he would even lobby the president to approve new weapons, but only as long as the JCS understood it had to be selective. More important, Laird said that he would force the JCS to choose between its desire for newer and better weapons and an increase in monies earmarked for the costly involvement in Vietnam. Laird's message was hardly subtle, but it was honest: if the JCS wanted new weapons, it had to support his push for a faster withdrawal from Southeast Asia; the military could continue to fight in Vietnam (and forget about any new weapons) or it could get the weapons and hope to do better next time. In effect, the JCS would have to juggle its desire to win in Vietnam with its desire to modernize its forces.

The second part of the Laird-JCS agreement was put in writing: Laird promised that the individual services would once again be put in charge of designing their own force structures and would be responsible for dictating what weapons they believed were essential to carrying out the nation's foreign policy goals. As a result, the Office of Assistant Secretary of Defense for Systems Analysis — which had been headed by the hated Alain Enthoven and his whiz kids — was left vacant, its role downgraded, and its service responsibilities returned to the services. Packard was directed by Laird to speak personally to the JCS, primarily to reassure them that while the Office of the Secretary of Defense would still rely on the kinds of statistical studies popular with the systems analysts, they would no longer be the sole factor in determining who got what. The payoff for Laird was immediate: he had gained the JCS's support of his program for an early withdrawal from Vietnam without threatening the new spirit of cooperation between the JCS and himself — which was tested within two months of his appearance in the tank.

If Nixon and his top foreign policy advisers were confident that the United States could manage and eventually win the war in Vietnam, the results of NSSM 1 should have convinced them otherwise. Passed on to the NSC in mid-February, NSSM 1 contained some of the most pessimistic predictions on the war's outcome in the four years of America's involvement. At the current rate of progress, the JCS said, the United States could not expect to pacify South Vietnam for another eight years. That was an optimistic view; civilian CIA officials believed it might take another ten years, and only then with the continued full commitment of U.S. and allied ground troops. Such judgments would have been enough to paralyze the Johnson administration, but for Nixon they were only proof that the United States had to design a policy that would short-circuit the pessimists' predictions, a policy that linked pressure on Hanoi with threats to North Vietnam's major allies.

Nixon's strategy was first made apparent in mid-March, when the new president decided to launch a series of air raids on North Vietnam's sanctuaries in Cambodia. Not surprisingly, the raids were the result of a recommendation made by the MACV commander, Creighton Abrams, and JCS Chairman Wheeler, who had received evidence that the NVA's major political and military office for the war was just across the border in Cambodia. But Kissinger was skeptical. He wasn't sure that the U.S. bombing program in Cambodia would actually destroy the North Vietnamese headquarters complex, and he worried that it might in fact spread the war farther west, into Norodom Sihanouk's nominally neutral Cambodia. Fortunately for the JCS (who remained convinced that the sanctuaries had to be attacked), one of the military's most pro-Vietnam officers was serving on Kissinger's staff, a man who not only had experience in Vietnam but who was also proving to be an indispensable support of JCS actions in the White House.

When the JCS needed someone on the inside to argue its position, it learned to rely on the good offices of Lieutenant Colonel Alexander Haig, a man with impeccable government contacts (he had been an aide to Cyrus Vance and Joseph Califano), a silver star winner in

Vietnam (he had participated in secret, extremely dangerous ground operations just across the Cambodian border), and an officer who was clearly on his way to the Army's top spot (he had served as deputy superintendent at West Point). In mid-March, Haig pushed Kissinger to approve the JCS's plan to bomb the Cambodian sanctuaries, arguing that such a program would take the pressure off the increasingly hard-pressed U.S. ground forces in Vietnam. Kissinger, anxious to persuade the president that he was a hawk on Vietnam, let himself be convinced, but insisted that the Cambodian raids be kept secret.

Like Kissinger, Laird had initially opposed the Cambodian strikes, telling Wheeler that they would "do the one thing we don't want to happen, they will expand the war." But Wheeler had been adamant. Here was a chance to wipe out the entire NVA headquarters, to change the entire face of the war, to make it easier for American forces to leave Indochina. In a series of high-level Pentagon meetings over a period of two weeks, from the end of February until early in March, Wheeler had cajoled Laird with promises that the strikes would be "of short duration" and would accomplish in one act what the JCS had been advocating for four years. To Wheeler's amazement, Laird had not only listened closely, he had begun to concede the military necessity of the proposed program. His willingness to be convinced by Wheeler resulted in the decision to hit NVA concentrations in Cambodia.

After a meeting with Nixon in the Oval Office on March 15 that resulted in the approval of the strikes, Laird and Wheeler returned to the Pentagon to begin choosing targets and sending out orders. Wheeler was ecstatic. It appeared that Laird's promise to listen to the JCS and support them with the president was more than just a ploy to gain trust. Like the JCS, Laird seemed intent on taking whatever steps were necessary to win the Vietnam War — or at least to allow U.S. troops a decent interval between withdrawal and the final NVA onslaught. But in many ways, Laird's surprising immoderation on what came to be called the "menu bombings" of Cambodia (military acts that involved the JCS in a clear violation of the law) was just the kind of political ploy that Wheeler had feared. Within days of the American B-52 strike in Cambodia, Laird presented Wheeler with a memo advocating a large-scale American troop withdrawal from South Vietnam, a not very subtle way of saying that now that he had backed the bombings, Wheeler could repay the debt by backing American troop withdrawals.

Laird's political methods had other uses. Having reinforced the JCS's initial trust of him during the bombing debate, the secretary gave it another lesson in political infighting in April, this time tutoring the chiefs in the fine art of being underhanded with the president.

When the North Koreans downed an American EC-121 espionage plane on April 14, Laird told Wheeler to swallow his opposition to the president's call for immediate retaliation by agreeing that the United States should immediately launch reprisals against Kim Il Sung's North Korean regime. Laird — who by this time had clearly taken Nixon's measure — counseled the JCS to act in its traditional role but to argue that such a reprisal was tactically infeasible until U.S. air assets could be gathered in the area.

So it was that in the forty-eight hours after the attack, Wheeler became the administration's most outspoken advocate of striking North Korea despite his own fears that such retaliation would begin a new war on the Korean peninsula (the last thing the JCS wanted). Much to Wheeler's amazement, the ploy worked; by the time the United States had deployed enough aircraft carriers off Korea to launch a strike, the crisis had passed, and the political momentum for a military response had evaporated. This approach — to claim the military was unable to respond because of logistical considerations and that the American military behemoth had spawned an unwieldy command system — came in handy during future crises, especially when the JCS remained uncertain about the impact of civilian policies.

But more important than either the Cambodian bombing decision or Laird's tutorial on how to deal with the president was an incident that had a decisive impact on how the JCS dealt with Nixon and his top advisers. In mid-April 1969, Wheeler was given a clear portrait of just what they really thought about the military. Following the EC-121 incident, Kissinger reportedly approached Wheeler with a suggestion that the NSC and the JCS cooperate in sharing foreign policy and military information outside the government's usual lines of communication. In a meeting at the White House, Kissinger hinted to Wheeler that while the president (and Kissinger) believed Laird could not be trusted, they believed the JCS could be. In fact, Kissinger said, Nixon hoped the JCS reciprocated the feeling and "trusts us over here." Within days, the president himself reiterated Kissinger's point, saying that he hoped Wheeler would be "frank" in his appraisal of Laird's views. For Wheeler, the president's unaccountable concern could mean only one thing: the White House wanted the JCS to issue orders without Laird's knowledge, in the apparent belief that the secretary was soft on Vietnam and therefore could not be trusted.

Wheeler later told a colleague that any doubts about the president's hints were made clearer in a meeting with Kissinger in May. He again approached Wheeler with hints that Nixon wanted a "more wide open policy" on Vietnam, a policy that, he explained, the Secretary of Defense "doesn't seem to agree with." Kissinger intimated that Wheeler's support "in this matter" was "certainly appreciated," and that a means had to be found to "communicate the president's concern directly to the men in the field" — a euphemism. He meant that White House officials wanted to run the war without passing orders through Laird. Indeed, Wheeler soon realized that the White House was not only intent on bypassing Laird in the chain of command, it wanted to obtain information on Laird's programs at the Pentagon. At first, Wheeler put this down as typical bureaucratic infighting, believing that Nixon and Kissinger feared that Laird was diluting White House instructions because of his own doubts on Nixon's policy in Vietnam. But eventually he realized that they actually suspected Laird was undermining their own policy, which Wheeler found astounding. When he didn't respond to these veiled suggestions, Kissinger and Nixon dropped the matter but continued to search for a way to circumvent Laird.*

That May, with the controversial Cambodian bombing decision and the frightening Korean incident behind them, the JCS finally turned to Laird's call for a study of American troop withdrawals. It was like pulling teeth; while the JCS realized that America's effort in Vietnam had been a disaster almost from the very first, back in March of 1965, the prospect of actually withdrawing troops forced it to face the failure of its efforts. Regardless of Nixon's adamant refusal to engage the United States in a unilateral withdrawal of troops and his bellicose public statements that the United States would take whatever steps were necessary to ensure South Vietnam's continued survival, the JCS realized its commitment to a military victory was finally at an end. This was the most bitter pill the chiefs had ever had to swallow; the prospect of a "drawdown" in U.S. forces, they believed, would inevitably be interpreted as a failure in military policy.

Laird was sympathetic but tough. The question, he told the JCS, was not whether U.S. forces could save South Vietnam but whether the South Vietnamese could save themselves, whether his program could accomplish what the JCS had to realize was the intent of its decision to intervene in Vietnam from the very beginning. Indeed, Laird told the increasingly ill Wheeler on several occasions that the JCS had never intended to maintain a permanent military presence in South Vietnam anyway, so the sooner the withdrawals could begin, the better off the

---

* The White House didn't have to search too far. A former student of Kissinger's at Harvard, Lieutenant General John Vogt, passed on information to Kissinger about what Laird and the JCS were doing while serving as the JCS director. In addition, in May 1969, Kissinger reportedly ordered Haig to wiretap the phone of Colonel Robert Pursley, Laird's military assistant. When Pursley confronted Haig over the problems between the White House and the Department of Defense, according to reporter Seymour Hersh, Haig waved a "green binder notebook" at the colonel. "We started keeping notes right away on you," he said.

military would be. It was time to rebuild the military, Laird said, time for the United States to begin meeting its other worldwide commitments. In this sense, the EC-121 incident gave him a perfect example of just the kind of disaster-in-the-making the continued presence of American troops in Vietnam could cause: the truth was that the United States could not have fought the North Koreans even if it had wanted to — the troops just weren't available.

If the U.S. goal was to make South Vietnam an independent state, secure from its neighbor to the north, Laird told the JCS, the U.S. military had to begin to turn the war over to the South Vietnamese Army.* Nor, as Laird said, was the United States prepared to fight the war the Army still believed would eventually be fought — against the Soviet Union, in Europe. Or, as Wheeler himself might have argued, Lyndon Johnson's decision against mobilizing the reserves for an all-out fight in Vietnam had sealed the debate; the question now was just how fast the JCS could extricate the United States from its mistake. Laird's strategy of dealing with the JCS was thus a reversal of McNamara's classic cost-effectiveness ploy and played on the military's worst fears — that the United States would have to fight everywhere, at once.

The debate over troop withdrawals that began in May continued for more than thirty days of hard bargaining between the JCS and Laird. Anxious to meet the deadline imposed by Nixon for announcing withdrawals — which coincided with his meeting South Vietnam's Nguyen Van Thieu in Honolulu — Laird incessantly badgered the JCS to come up with a full list of troop redeployments that would mean the immediate return of 25,000 men to the United States.

But this initial midsummer withdrawal was only the beginning; Laird pushed the chiefs to draw up a list of further redeployments, at times angering them with his insistence that they plan far into the future for the withdrawal of all American troops in Indochina. At the beginning of one particularly memorable session, Laird actually ordered the chiefs to closet themselves in the tank until they had come up with a full schedule of withdrawals, a marathon session that lasted three full days, leaving the JCS officers at once exhausted and exhilarated. Laird refused to rest. In each debate with the JCS, he laid out its only option: agree to a schedule of accelerated withdrawals or come up with a smaller budget; bring the boys home or cut outlays for new weapons. He was bludgeoning the JCS, ironically employing the same

---

* Laird took credit for the term that corresponded to the doctrine, but in fact "Vietnamization," inculcated as official American policy in April 1969 (in NSSM 36), was first used by Creighton Abrams during his talk with Lyndon Johnson's "wise men" in March 1968.

"carrot and stick" approach adopted by Kissinger and Nixon in dealing with North Vietnam to force concessions from a recalcitrant military staff.

Surprisingly, Wheeler — at one time considered one of the most
intransigent pro-mobilization voices in the JCS — allowed Laird to
push the JCS without much visible protest. Indeed, while Wheeler privately complained to aides that the administration was withdrawing
from Southeast Asia faster than was militarily safe and that the NSC
was actually the home of a group of "secret doves," he was once again
torn by America's seeming inability to force a military resolution.*
Slowed by heart disease, frustrated by his ceaseless attempts to fashion
a workable military strategy that would leave South Vietnam free of
North Vietnamese troops, Wheeler hoped that the administration's
backchannel negotiations with North Vietnamese officials in Paris
would be coupled with an escalation in the U.S. air war. In essence, he
allowed Laird to push his JCS colleagues because he realized that
bombing was the only hope for an American victory.

Indeed, in November 1969, with only eight months left as JCS chairman, Wheeler was slowly becoming convinced that the United States
had to accelerate the training of the South Vietnamese Army in order
to be able to withdraw at the earliest opportunity — by the end of 1971.
The papers, reports, and combat assessments that crossed his desk
every day made him realize he had little choice: not only were American troops in danger in South Vietnam (their strength slowly being
stripped away by Laird's push for early withdrawal), the Army was
facing a grave internal crisis. At the beginning of November, Wheeler
learned that racial incidents among American troops in Germany had
reached almost epidemic proportions. More disturbing still, unit commanders in Europe were beginning to report that some troops were
publishing antiwar GI newspapers, a practice that Wheeler believed
went hand in hand with the increased use of heroin on Army bases.
Nor was the Army the only service affected; naval officers began to
report a disturbing increase in racial incidents "below decks," which
many officers feared could become a full race war on Navy ships on
war footing in the South China Sea.

Still, the situation among Army troops in Vietnam was the worst, as
Wheeler learned on November 13, 1969, when the *New York Times*

---

* Wheeler reserved his most bitter words for NSC assistant Morton Halperin, a hold-
over from the Johnson years. Haig apparently fed Wheeler's animosity, telling the chairman that Halperin had "undue influence" on Kissinger and Nixon. Halperin was
eventually the subject of administration wiretaps, instituted at Kissinger's direction by
Haig himself. Haig later told one reporter that he would not apologize for the wiretaps,
adding that he ordered them because he believed that "anybody who was against the war
was an enemy of the state."

reported that eighteen months earlier, a company of American soldiers — Charlie Company, 1st Battalion, 20th Infantry — entered My Lai, a small village in the Son My district of South Vietnam, and indiscriminately murdered more than 350 men, women, and children. The My Lai massacre was the most appalling atrocity in American military history and shook the upper echelons of the military establishment. The JCS acted quickly to investigate the matter, appointing General William Peers (whom Westmoreland once called "a dynamic commander") to head a commission to determine who was responsible for the massacre and whether the "rules of engagement" in Vietnam were clearly understood by all American forces. Shaken as it was, the JCS — and Wheeler in particular — realized that the massacre was simply a public manifestation of a problem that went much deeper. In Vietnam, Wheeler realized, the U.S. Army was beginning to disintegrate.

"In 1965, the United States had the best Army in the history of the world," Harry Summers, a retired Army colonel, said, "but by the end of 1968, things were really starting to fall apart. I went back to Vietnam [for another tour as a combat officer], and the whole thing had changed. I couldn't believe it. And it just got worse. It's almost as if there had been two armies, one that existed in 1965, and one that existed three years later — after Tet." Summers wasn't the only one who noticed the change: at the same time that Wheeler was debating the mobilization question with President Johnson, in March 1968, the first of a series of disturbing reports on racial incidents, drug use, and poor morale among the American troops in Vietnam were beginning to reach the Pentagon. The JCS initially believed that the vast majority of the incidents represented isolated disciplinary situations that resulted from poor leadership, but eventually the sheer number of cases forced it to change its views.

Most disturbing of all were confirmed incidents of soldiers in the war zone who refused to fight, turned on their officers in open rebellion, or even deserted. The first and most significant incident after Tet occurred in Nha Trang, where an American enlisted man entered a bar and severely wounded two officers with a shotgun, then calmly walked out to the cheers of his comrades. In midsummer 1968, four months after the end of Tet, one entire platoon of the American Division refused to obey a direct order to engage a small unit of NVA regulars; the unit melted back into the jungle. In I Corps, in northern South Vietnam, a group of black soldiers formed a Black Panther brigade, elected their own officers, and decided to run the war themselves. By 1969, most American firebases in Vietnam were divided between "bloods" and whites, and racial incidents were increasing.

The statistical evidence was even more disturbing. In 1968, for instance, the Army concluded that there were sixty-eight "refusals to fight" in Vietnam, a number that actually increased *after* the United States announced its first troop withdrawals, in mid-1969. In addition, the JCS learned that "fragging" (the assassination of officers with explosive fragmentation grenades, or by other means) was reaching frightening proportions — more than 350 officers were assaulted by their own troops in the three years after Tet, a figure that far exceeded that of similar incidents during World War II. The statistics on the use of hard drugs were even more disturbing. According to *Crisis in Command,* the most authoritative study of the Army's problems in Vietnam: "The available data suggest that almost a third of the Army in Vietnam had used a hard narcotic at some time, while one in four U.S. soldiers used narcotic drugs worldwide." By any measure, then, the ability of the U.S. military to meet the nation's worldwide requirements at the end of 1969, when Wheeler was learning about the My Lai atrocity, was at its lowest point in the history of the republic.

This was not the JCS's finest hour — faced with the Army in a state of open rebellion, its officers demoralized and lacking in the most fundamental training for the kind of combat they would face in Vietnam, the JCS decided to leave the solution to these problems (and the policy of Vietnamization) in the hands of the able but still very human Creighton Abrams.* The JCS's decision, to go slowly in rooting out the dissenters and disenchanted in the military, might have been ill advised, but it was hardly unexpected. Its penchant for internal conflict aside, the JCS was, and is, a traditionally conservative group, a committee of officers whose marriage to tradition, including its delegation of combat authority, is well nigh legendary. But in Vietnam this tradition had a devastating impact; faced with policies that dictated that the United States would fight the war with officers who were either on hand or could be trained quickly, the JCS instituted procedures that resulted in the promotion of men without even the most fundamental leadership skills.

The results were clear from at least 1968 (if not earlier) until the very end of the war. Indeed, at least in one fundamental sense, the actions of U.S. troops in combat reflected almost exactly the views of the JCS. When the JCS and its key subordinate commanders were convinced the war could be won, the military performed remarkably well (considering the circumstances), but it failed miserably as doubts about the

---

* Officers who served with Abrams say that his task was almost impossible. Not only did he have to deal with a disintegrating Army, he had to follow explicit instructions to turn over the war to the Vietnamese as soon as possible. How explicit were these instructions? Lyndon Johnson put it best: "General, I want every Vietnamese who carries a peter to be in uniform and to be in this war effort, and I want us to get out as fast as we can."

war began to be made public. Indeed, the disintegration apparent in all the services in Vietnam when Abrams assumed command had started at the top and filtered down, a conclusion that military commanders still have difficulty accepting.

Fortunately, Abrams was the one officer with the ability and courage necessary to deal with the problems around him, which he believed went far deeper than anyone at the JCS was then willing to admit. In the short term, however, there was little he could do to remedy the larger problems; in fact, during the last part of 1968 and throughout 1969 the news only got worse, the discipline problems more critical. Abrams's solution was to draw back, to temper his well-known habit of instituting harsh wartime discipline ("We just ought to shoot those troublemakers," he noted with disgust after reading one unit report) by applying soothing words coupled with standard pep talks to combat noncommissioned officers in the field.

But he was unwilling to take the same steps when it came to his own staff or the military's top combat commanders. From the first moment of his command, Abrams decided he would wage the Vietnam War in a totally different manner from his predecessor. To the MACV command headquarters staff in Saigon ("these sycophants," he called them), he gave new and explicit orders, dispatching intelligence analysts, "bean counters," and military aides (the notorious "spear carriers" or "horse holders," who were generally loathed by the enlisted man) into the field. He instructed his staff to "stop talking to the press," and he ended Westmoreland's practice of "showing the colors" to the public. The tone was set during his first briefing, when he showed up in rumpled combat greens without his medals and told a brigadier general that he would "bust you all the way to civilian" if he ever talked "off the record" to reporters again.

On one particularly memorable morning in sweltering Saigon, Abrams once again "laid it on the line" to his commanders, making explicit his view of those in Vietnam without a rifle. Puffing on a cigar, he leveled his eyes at the eagles and stars arrayed around the conference table. "Gentlemen," he said, "we had a very sad thing happen this week. The finest division commander we've ever had in Vietnam — happened to be a Marine, but nevertheless the finest division commander we've ever had — made a mistake. That fine division commander had a friend, and that friend was a member of the press, and that commander took that newsman in his helicopter on his final rounds, and he trusted that friend, and he confided in that friend, and the next day he found himself in the headlines. That commander has been embarrassed, and this command has been embarrassed, and, gentlemen, with regard to the press, that magnificent commander forgot just one thing: *They're all a bunch of shits.*"

At another briefing, an Air Force general told Abrams that his service could redeploy its forces to the United States by 1976. Nineteen seventy-six? Abrams slammed the table with his hand. "Bullshit! Bullshit! Bullshit!" he screamed, then told the Air Force officer, "You're five years late. Five years!" More important, though, Abrams stopped sending glowing combat reports to the JCS in Washington, deciding instead to "tell them what the hell is up over here, whether they like it or not." After settling in at MACV headquarters, Abrams made sure his messages were short, accurate, and included numbing accounts of the problems faced by the military. What went for the JCS went double for troops in the war zone, a fact that became apparent in his unusual manner of inspecting the troops. In one case, he reportedly surprised some Seabees in Saigon by bursting into their barracks in the middle of the night, calling their commander to task for not setting a guard, and cashiering him on the spot. In another case, however, Abrams showed incredible compassion. During a "skull session" outside Danang in 1970, a group of disgruntled enlisted men were in the midst of a shouting match with their battalion commander when a sergeant noticed Abrams standing unobtrusively in the background. The group came to attention. "Keep going," Abrams said, and walked away.*

By the end of his first eighteen months as MACV commander, even the most hard-core, antiwar soldiers began to notice subtle changes. While the high incidence of fragging, desertion, and drug use continued, Abrams's efforts to segregate offenders from combat-ready units and to establish policies that would move officers back into the field with their troops began to yield modest results. Other changes were even more radical. American advisers training ARVN troops were given new instructions: to get the South Vietnamese into fighting form and to do it at an almost breakneck pace. "Kick them," Abrams told the advisers. "Kick their asses. They've got to fight, they've got to fight." His admonition was tied to his incessant pleas with the Thieu government that they increase their call-up of South Vietnamese youths, that they replace corrupt field commanders with ones certified as "real bastards" by Abrams, and that they plan and maintain a presence in each of South Vietnam's most important provinces to offset the social revolution begun by the Vietcong.

---

* Army courier Phil Scott remembers Abrams after meeting him accidentally. Deciding one night to take a walk by his house ("just to see it"), Scott came across "one old warrant officer." Scott and a companion laughed at the white-haired "lifer," joshing him and throwing off a "half-assed salute." The "old warrant officer," Scott learned, was none other than Abrams himself, who laughed at the men's embarrassment when they realized whom they had saluted. He stopped and talked with the men and made Scott feel that "for a brief moment" he was "back in Detroit talking to my grandfather. There he was all by himself with no guards, no ass-kissing colonels running after him, just him, by himself carrying the load of the war."

It's now apparent that Abrams was following his own personal agenda, apart from the battle over American troop withdrawal being waged in Washington. While Abrams's strategy was never codified or put into the official records, the clues he left for historians are clear. In addition, he took steps, especially after Nixon announced that the United States would bring home an additional 200,000 soldiers from Vietnam in April 1970, to insert himself in the withdrawal debate. Surprisingly, Abrams took every opportunity to oppose the additional removal of troops, believing that he would be gaining valuable time to train the South Vietnamese Army. Then, too, Abrams was confident that his policy changes in Vietnam, including those that relegated the least dependable U.S. units to noncombat duties, would keep the military (and South Vietnam) from total collapse. For Abrams, the Vietnam situation in April 1970 represented a classic two-front war; to his commanders Abrams was the ultimate "kick ass" pusher, telling them to initiate steps to "get your men out of this war," while with Washington politicians he was the recalcitrant hard-liner, pleading for a few more months, a little more time. "Abe was in the grinder," one three-star aide at MACV recalled. "If we got out right away, the ARVN would probably just melt away. If we stayed too long, we would melt away. He ended up talking it both ways, assuring the soldiers that their commanders were dealing with the war and getting out, while telling them we still needed to fight."

Abrams also supported a still-controversial effort to destroy the Vietcong-NVA infrastructure in the South. In many ways, the intelligence program, using trained covert operators who disdained military leaders, contradicted his well-known distrust of cloak and dagger operations. But Abrams believed he had little choice; at the very least, the program (known as the Phung Hoang, or Phoenix program) would give American troops additional breathing space for a clean withdrawal.* Abrams was instituting a program that had been approved at the highest levels of the administration. Still, the tactic was clearly distasteful to him, an attitude he made clear in several widely repeated lectures to CIA operatives who reported to him on the program. During one briefing, for instance, Abrams demanded an "eyeball-to-eyeball" faceoff with a CIA operative in Vietnam after being told that one special forces unit was "operating independently."

"What do you mean, 'operating independently'?" Abrams reportedly asked. (The question was needless; he knew exactly what was

---

* The program resulted in the assassination of 50,000 to 100,000 rural leaders. Hailed as a success by CIA officials, it was despised by most regular military officers, who believed it was used as an excuse for South Vietnamese officers to kill political and business competitors. In later years, the program was used to exemplify the narrow "terror" tactics engaged in by the CIA.

meant.) The briefer told Abrams that the unit was being used to run CIA paramilitary operations that included "snatch-and-snuff" tactics — the practice of assassinating Vietcong-controlled village leaders as part of the Phoenix program. Abrams called in the CIA official and upbraided him for using American combat personnel to run intelligence missions without "authority from the highest command." Soon after, Abrams stepped up MACV efforts to wean the Special Forces from CIA operations, a project that he was convinced was essential if the military was to survive the Vietnam debacle. Indeed, according to Andrew Goodpaster, the deputy MACV commander, Abrams's belief that paramilitary units needed to be wrested from the CIA was the result of a JCS order that MACV "get these guys under control." Or, in the words of one Special Forces soldier, Abrams "cracked down on those of us who had gone beyond the pale, you know, [who] were fighting their own special war."

Unfortunately, Abrams's attempts to restrain the Special Forces were never fully successful, in large part because they continued to play a major role in South Vietnam's pacification efforts. In fact, they were absolutely indispensable in helping South Vietnam's attempt to win over its rural population. Nevertheless, Abrams did succeed in running some of the most egregious paramilitary commanders out of the combat theater, transferring them back to Fort Bragg in the United States or recommending their early retirement in dispatches to the JCS.* In several cases, he took extraordinary steps to see that certain Special Forces commanders were disciplined, especially when they had overstepped their authority. In 1969, for instance, Abrams ordered the arrest of a number of Special Forces officers for the murder of a South Vietnamese suspected of being a double agent, a move that shocked MACV commanders and the JCS. He was eventually (and predictably) overruled by Westmoreland, who ordered the prisoners freed and the charges dropped after CIA officers associated with the accused men refused to appear as witnesses.

Despite these setbacks, by the time Wheeler retired in July 1970, Abrams's timetable for turning the war over to the South Vietnamese was on schedule thanks, in large part, to a little-known admiral who had headed the inland Navy in Vietnam, the "brownwater Navy," since September 1968. Before this assignment, Admiral Elmo Zumwalt, Jr., had been a soft-spoken, self-effacing flag rank officer who was known more for his contacts with high Pentagon officials (including

---

* "When I went out there to serve with Abrams I found that this was one of our real jobs, to stay on top of what those people [in covert and paramilitary operations] were doing," Goodpaster remembered. "And to maintain effective control. Abrams was a man of strength and determination, and he was quite well up on this subject, so when he took over command that was one of the things he went after."

his patron, the indefatigable Paul Nitze) than for his shipboard prowess. Zumwalt was initially given the Vietnam post (and his third star) at the recommendation of CNO Thomas Moorer, who worried that the bushy-browed admiral was becoming a Pentagon competitor, a view reinforced by Zumwalt's own recollection. As he later wrote, it was "Moorer's way of getting rid of me: *Promote the son of a bitch and nobody will ever hear from him again.*"

It was one of Moorer's few mistakes. Within a year, Zumwalt had patched up relations between the Navy and MACV (Zumwalt's predecessor in Vietnam and Abrams had not been on speaking terms), and he told Abrams that he would have the South Vietnamese Navy ready to take over the job of patrolling Vietnam's thousands of miles of inland waterways "in three years." It was music to Abrams's ears. Not only did Zumwalt's aggressive training of the South Vietnamese accord with his own policies, it gave American soldiers a chance to draw back from their dangerous exposure in the Mekong Delta to the relative safety of American enclaves in South Vietnam's largest cities. Abrams was so impressed that when Laird made his first official tour of the war zone, Abrams told him to consider Zumwalt as the next CNO. Laird passed the advice on to Navy Secretary John Chafee: "When you're making nominations for the next CNO, give me three names, but make sure Zumwalt is one of them."

So it was that when Moorer finally began his long-awaited tenure as the nation's seventh JCS chairman, Zumwalt became the twelfth CNO, a promotion that the new chairman openly opposed.* The sometimes parochial Moorer, who apparently had a hard time believing that anyone but Navy fliers was really Navy, was horrified by the prospect of a nonaviator in the spot he had once filled, telling aides that "this guy is nothing but trouble." As it happened, Zumwalt was more trouble than Moorer could ever imagine. Not only had he gotten the Navy involved in combat operations in Vietnam, thereby breaking the five-year Navy tradition of keeping Vietnam "an Army show," he had begun to make remarks about the morale problems plaguing the service. Predictably, there were immediate problems between Moorer and Zumwalt on the JCS, which were exacerbated by Zumwalt's criticism of Moorer's hawkish views; to Moorer, Zumwalt was a "peacenik" because, as Zumwalt admitted, "I didn't believe the U.S. should be in Vietnam in the first place."

There were even more significant problems, at least as far as the new

---

* Nixon approved Zumwalt's appointment without comment under the mistaken belief that Laird could never make a good appointment. But Kissinger's NSC deputy, Haig, was infuriated. "Laird can't do this," he reportedly said when told of Zumwalt's promotion. Moorer had a different reaction. After learning of the appointment, he went back to his office, closed the door, and kicked his waste can across the floor.

chairman was concerned. For years admirals, including Moorer, had treated the Navy as a personal fief, perpetuating customs that were rarely questioned by civilian managers. Zumwalt set out in Vietnam to change all this, which was well known to the more conservative Moorer. Zumwalt, as one retired naval officer delicately phrased it, "had a bad habit of mingling with sailors of differing views." He meant to say that Zumwalt was color blind, an unprejudiced commander of the new Navy, a reformer who realized that the Navy could no longer operate according to "nineteenth century regulations and primitive traditions." Moorer, enraged, told friends that Zumwalt was trying to "blacken the Navy," a comment that only spurred the CNO to suggest even more radical changes in Navy procedures.

Though Moorer did not know it at the time, Zumwalt's promotion inaugurated a new era in JCS history, one that involved the reform of outdated military policies — an inevitable result of the critical demoralization that all the services suffered during the Vietnam War. Zumwalt was indeed the first of a long line of military reformers, but it's likely that he had inherited many of his more radical ideas from Abrams, the stern regular army disciplinarian and follower of George Patton. "If it had been any other war, Creighton Abrams would have been anyone's nominee for president," Zumwalt said. "He was a great man, one of the greatest men in the history of our country."

He might have added that Abrams was the one flag rank officer who believed that the tragedy of Vietnam — in particular, the destruction of the American Army — needed to be immediately addressed by high-level reforms enacted by the JCS. For eighteen months during his service in Vietnam, Zumwalt discussed his ideas with the supportive Abrams, ideas that eventually became a catalyst for widespread military change. Unfortunately, however, the nascent reform movement envisioned by both Zumwalt and Abrams had to, perhaps inevitably, be postponed. First, Moorer — locked in a vicious feud with Nixon's foreign policy gurus from the day he became chairman — had to accomplish his own goal of extricating America from Vietnam on terms that would ensure, in Nixon's phrase, "peace with honor."

By July 1970, it was clear to Moorer that the president mistrusted not only the military (and the JCS) but just about everyone else in his administration, including the Secretary of Defense. This attitude, however, didn't come as a surprise: Wheeler had repeatedly warned Moorer that top administration officials would attempt to circumvent the normal chain of command and that they were dedicated to making foreign policy decisions without anyone's advice or, to use their term, "interference." But Wheeler's warnings were unnecessary; Moorer had actually been a willing accomplice to the Kissinger-Nixon ploy to bypass Laird before his promotion.

When Wheeler had fallen ill in mid-April, the CNO had stepped in eagerly to replace the chairman. For a naval officer and now an acting JCS chairman who enjoyed hair-raising experiences, the timing could not have been better. Norodom Sihanouk had just (on March 18) been overthrown as head of Cambodia, and Nixon was mulling over ways to protect the new regime of Lon Nol from the apparent threat posed by the NVA in their sanctuaries in eastern Cambodia. On April 22, 1970, the president convened a special NSC meeting on the problem of the sanctuaries. Moorer (as the ranking JCS member) and Laird presented their arguments for an invasion of the area by South Vietnamese troops. But, as Moorer then almost certainly realized, Nixon had already been in touch with Abrams about just such a possibility, using a backchannel link that effectively bypassed both Laird and the JCS.* The backchannel system, housed in the Pentagon's underground Relay Center, was under twenty-four-hour civilian guard that had instructions directly from Kissinger that specifically denied access to the Secretary of Defense.

Using the Relay Center, Nixon pushed Abrams to approve the Cambodian invasion, which enraged Laird and his top military aide, Robert Pursley.† When U.S. troops invaded Cambodia on April 30, Laird and Pursley complained bitterly that Abrams had somehow been manipulated into approving the U.S. forces, though neither could figure out how. This White House policy of bypassing Laird, first used by Kissinger and Nixon to initiate the April-May 1969 Cambodian incursion, remained the unstated policy of administration insiders — who eventually included Moorer. Unlike Wheeler, Moorer readily agreed to the ploy, apparently because he believed that Laird was not as dedicated to ending the war on American terms as either the president or the national security adviser. Then, too, Moorer still distrusted the "new guys" at the White House and wanted to be able to check up on the NSC on his own. His subsequent actions — setting up a separate line of communication into the White House (in effect, a spying operation run by the JCS chairman on his own government) — was an all too natural by-product of the administration's obsession with security.

---

* The JCS had access to all military messages sent and received by the Pentagon, but apparently it didn't initially realize that some messages were being sent without its or Laird's approval. Westmoreland, for instance, has noted that many of the military decisions of this period came as a surprise to him, as if they were coming from the bottom up, a distinct reversal of the normal chain of command.

† Kissinger set up another channel to bypass Laird in communicating with the JCS, passing messages to Haig to give to Moorer during regular JCS-NSC liaison meetings. Setting up such channels became as politically tricky as the reasons they were set up in the first place. Eventually Kissinger didn't trust Haig (who didn't trust Moorer), who had already decided he didn't trust anybody.

Indeed, no matter how much Moorer wanted to believe Kissinger's assurance that he, and not Laird, would be privy to every policy decision made by the president, he decided that certainty was far more important than trust. More important, he realized that the growing power of Haig (now a brigadier general) could cause the Navy potential problems — and already had. Haig's role on the NSC, for instance, ensured that Army weapons programs were brought immediately to the president's attention, access that even Moorer, as JCS chairman, could never assure. In addition, by September, Haig's aura was clearly expanding, taking in far too many anti-Navy JCS officers whom Moorer saw as competitors. Even Kissinger joked about Haig's parochial service views, believing him almost transparently naive in so baldly pushing for Army programs. Moorer knew better, thinking that Haig was in almost constant contact with Westmoreland, his former MACV commander and now Army chief of staff, who took every opportunity to praise his abilities to his JCS colleagues.

To resolve this growing problem, Moorer asked Admiral Rembrandt Robinson, an NSC assistant, to keep his eye on both Haig and Kissinger. By now, however, the political machinations between the NSC and the JCS were almost byzantine. Kissinger mistrusted Haig as well as Laird; at one point he told Zumwalt that Robinson (not Haig) would be passing messages to the JCS. Unfortunately for Kissinger, whose penchant for underestimating "country bumpkin" Moorer had reached epic proportions, Robinson's allegiance was to the JCS, not to the NSC. The Moorer-Robinson connection — what amounted to a JCS spy ring in the heart of the American government — began in September 1970, when Robinson received his first batch of classified NSC material from a Navy yeoman and NSC stenographer, Charles E. Radford.*

Robinson had picked his contact with studied acumen: the twenty-seven-year-old Radford was an ambitious Navy careerist whose primary goal in life was to become an officer. He was soon an indispensable part of the Haig team. His loyalty to Haig was unquestioned, and he was a properly deferential "gofer" whom Haig and Kissinger grew to trust. His access meant that he could easily copy important NSC documents for Robinson. These documents, including some of the most sensitive "eyes only" material produced by Nixon's

---

* Yeoman Radford also kept some of the most sensitive documents to himself, selectively leaking them to the columnist and investigative reporter Jack Anderson. The leaks caused consternation at the White House, where the usual suspects once again became subject to wiretaps, though almost every shred of evidence suggested that the leaks came from the NSC staff. Apparently Haig was simply unwilling to believe that anyone in the Navy, let alone a Navy man who wasn't even an officer, would spy on him.

inner circle, gave the JCS critical insight into the Nixon administration's increasingly secret foreign policy.

That September, for instance, the JCS learned that the administration was in an uproar over the impending election of Chile's Salvador Allende and was considering a number of responses — including his overthrow. In December, the JCS learned that the administration was putting pressure on South Vietnam's Premier Nguyen Van Thieu over American troop withdrawals; it had a file of secret documents stolen by Radford during Haig's trip to meet Thieu in Vietnam. Again, in March 1971, Radford stole hundreds of documents that gave a detailed accounting of Haig's high-pressure tactics intended to force Thieu into greater efforts to effect improvements in the South Vietnamese Army. In addition, Haig was pressuring Thieu to agree with core parts of the American negotiating strategy to end the war — an approach that Moorer angrily characterized as "browbeating" after seeing some of Radford's documents. In July 1971, in his most dangerous mission, Radford accompanied Kissinger on his globe-trotting foray to China and actually stole documents from Kissinger's briefcase. Finally, in September 1971, during yet another trip to Southeast Asia, Radford rifled Haig's briefcase, forwarding documents on Haig's discussions with Thieu to Moorer.

While it's not clear just how Moorer used the documents, there's little doubt that their theft reinforced JCS fears that the administration was moving too quickly to a full withdrawal of American troops from Vietnam. Indeed, Moorer's continued skepticism toward Nixon's claim that the United States was committed to the survival of South Vietnam (a claim the president made repeatedly during NSC meetings in 1971 and 1972) almost certainly came from Moorer's knowledge that the administration, in the person of Haig, was arguing just the opposite point to Nguyen Van Thieu. In fact, Moorer continually cautioned Nixon and Kissinger that the North Vietnamese could not be trusted to abide by any negotiated settlement, a view that hardly endeared him to officials engaged in secret negotiations in Paris.

Moorer's strident position on the war and his open disbelief of Nixon should have made Haig and Kissinger suspicious that many of their secret foreign policy positions — and their talks with Thieu — were being leaked. But it wasn't until mid-December 1971, when information from NSC documents appeared in print, that Radford's role was uncovered. The administration responded immediately: Radford was called to the Pentagon for a series of interrogations that inevitably bared the JCS spy ring. Under any other circumstance, the story would have turned into a government-shattering scandal — the Pentagon's chief investigator said that it reminded him of a scene from *Seven Days in May* — but everyone involved was intent on making sure that the spy ring wasn't made public.* So the scandal was hushed up by Haig and Kissinger, who were placed in the delicate position of having to tell the American people why their own military wasn't privy to major foreign policy information. Only when the incident was later investigated by the Senate Armed Services Committee did it become apparent that almost every top official in the Nixon administration — Laird, the JCS, even the Secretary of State — was barred from any role in determining U.S. foreign policy. It was still firmly in the hands of the president, his caustic NSC adviser, and a one-star general.

Surprisingly, the Radford spy scandal actually seemed to enhance Moorer's stature among top administration officials; in part, it was the natural result of Kissinger's and Haig's fears that the JCS chairman had knowledge that could be used against them. But, far more important, the incident proved to Kissinger and Haig that Moorer was more like them than they had imagined. Not only was he not a country bumpkin, he was actually an adept, if manipulative, insider. And in the months that followed, he proved to be even more of a sophisticated insider than either Kissinger or Haig. By March 1972, Moorer had not only recouped his trust with the president, he proved to be a valuable ally, one of the few administration figures willing to take whatever steps were necessary to bring the deteriorating Vietnam situation to a quick, though painful, resolution.

For the increasingly embattled Nixon, Moorer was the perfect loyalist: he was a figure whom Nixon, with his well-known obsession for military heroism, could emulate, and he was as mistrustful of communists and as committed to their downfall as the president. At no time was this more apparent than at the end of March 1972, when the North Vietnamese launched their Easter offensive, sending more than 100,000 men rolling across the DMZ into South Vietnam. Moorer was one of the few in the administration who pushed the president to step up the pressure on North Vietnam. Just days after the offensive began, on April 3, Moorer told Nixon that he should immediately order the mining of Haiphong Harbor, escalating the war so that North Vietnam "finally pays a price." The JCS, Moorer announced at a meeting at the White House, "is 100 percent behind me on this; we have to go after them." It was advice that Nixon wanted to hear, even though a full-scale American response might ruin the U.S.-Soviet summit scheduled for May.

---

* While Moorer refused to discuss the Radford spying incident, his characterization of the Nixon administration's desire for a full withdrawal of Vietnam leaves little doubt about his own position. (According to Moorer, pushing for early withdrawal "was downright dangerous.") Nor would he discuss some of the other titillating information passed on by Radford, including reports that Haig was a heavy drinker — a report that made the rounds of the Pentagon and was later used against him.

Richard Nixon's NSC: Earle Wheeler, Richard Helms, Henry Kissinger, William Rogers, Spiro Agnew, Melvin Laird (behind Agnew), and an unidentified official. Wheeler has just been ordered by Nixon to continue as JCS chairman. *White House Photo*

Before meeting with the South Vietnamese leadership: Nixon, Rogers, Laird, Wheeler, Abrams, McCain, Kissinger, Lodge, and Bunker. *National Archives*

President Jimmy Carter tours the Air Defense Command with (*from left*) David Jones, Zbigniew Brzezinski, JCS Chairman Brown, and SAC commander Richard Ellis. *U.S. Air Force*

General Edward C. Meyer introduces the XM-1 Abrams tank during a press conference at the Chrysler tank plant in Lima, Ohio, 1980. *U.S. Army*

David Jones and Caspar Weinberger at ceremonies welcoming the new Defense Secretary to the Pentagon, January 22, 1981. *Kate Patterson*

Left: JCS Chairman John W. Vessey, Jr. *Army Times*
Right: The first JCS chairman, Omar Bradley, in retirement during ceremonies honoring his service. *U.S. Army*

General P. X. Kelley at
a press conference.
Kate Patterson

John Tower and John Stennis, 1981. *Kate Patterson*

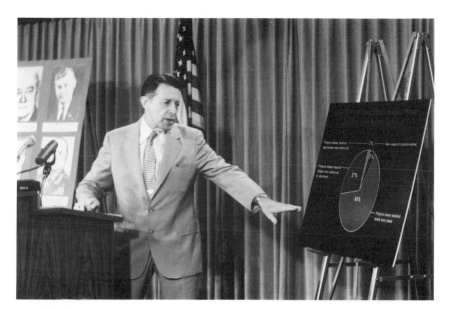

Caspar Weinberger briefs the press, September 1985. *Department of Defense*

CNO James Watkins with Navy Secretary John Lehman. *Kate Patterson*

Ronald Reagan at the Pentagon ceremony honoring Douglas MacArthur. Behind Reagan are Lew Allen, Edward C. Meyer, William Small, and P. X. Kelley. Mrs. MacArthur and Mrs. Reagan look on. *Department of Defense*

Left: JCS Chairman William Crowe. *Kate Patterson*
Right: Bruce Palmer talks about "the war of the chiefs," December 1985. *Vince Finnigan*

But Nixon did not want to jeopardize the summit, so he spent most of April ordering the JCS to unleash B-52 sorties against the communist positions ringing Quang Tri City, in northern South Vietnam. The JCS watched the communist offensive with increasing concern: while the South Vietnamese Army was fighting well, it wasn't winning the victories promised by Vietnamization. In fact, by the end of April it was clear that the offensive might swamp the government forces in all of northern South Vietnam. Moorer was beside himself with anxiety, fretful that Nixon wouldn't make good on his pledge to save the South Vietnamese. According to Moorer, the JCS was so persuaded that mining Haiphong Harbor would resolve the situation that it was "ready to walk out the door unless Nixon did it." Its position, according to Moorer, was the result of the chiefs' unanimous decision on May 5. "I'm telling you plain," he said more than fifteen years later. "We thought we had a real chance to break their backs — we weren't going to throw it away like Johnson did [during Tet]."

On May 7, Moorer reiterated the chiefs' position to Nixon and the NSC. With reports on the deteriorating situation in Quang Tri lying before him, Moorer made an eloquent plea for a "full-scale operation against Haiphong," using MacArthur-esque phrases to punctuate his views. Paraphrasing him, one former JCS aide said that he pleaded with Nixon to "let us make these bastards pay for the American blood they've spilled." Counting on the president's respect for tough talk, Moorer silenced the more circumspect members of the NSC (including Laird) by saying that the JCS "thinks we've let them get away with this long enough and I agree." He reportedly continued his tirade in the face of growing opposition by Laird, who attempted to interrupt him, apparently in order to caution Nixon against taking any steps that would ruin the summit. Moorer snapped back at Laird in a particularly memorable incident that he recalled with fondness: "Hell, someone had to say something. Here we'd been taking it for so long. If we hadn't done something, we'd still have men in prison there."

On May 8, Nixon made the decision the JCS had advocated for more than seven years, announcing publicly that he was not only mining Haiphong Harbor, he was also throwing down the gauntlet on America's negotiations in Paris by offering the North Vietnamese a new proposal that would allow a cease-fire in place and by amending the South Vietnamese constitution to give the Vietcong's Provisional Revolutionary Government a role in any postwar government. While these concessions enraged Moorer and the rest of the JCS, the chairman believed his position was vindicated; the Soviet Union did not cancel the proposed summit, and North Vietnamese attacks on the South ground to a halt. Perhaps more important, at least for Moorer, the JCS's argument had convinced Nixon that the JCS chairman should be reappointed for another term — the last bit of evidence Moorer needed that Nixon was willing to overlook the Radford spying incident. As it happened, he would depend increasingly on Moorer's expertise over the next two years. This was his vindication, his legacy — Moorer had finally convinced the nation's civilian leaders to follow military advice.

Moorer's July 1972 reappointment as JCS chairman came as a surprise to those officers who continued to believe, with some justification, that his habit of spurring controversy would undermine his status as an effective chief. But, at least in purely military terms, Moorer is considered a success, though not nearly in the same way as Wheeler. Paradoxically, Moorer — the dogmatic and unrepentant anticommunist — is remembered as the JCS chairman who presided over the last days of America's most devastating foreign adventure. Indeed, while he continued to push Nixon to ever higher levels of military activity (including an air blitz against Hanoi that finally brought the North Vietnamese to an agreement leading to a full American withdrawal from Indochina), he remains an enigma to even his closest colleagues.

More startling still, Moorer's last two years seem oddly out of place in America's postwar history, a feeling that has as much to do with the personality of Moorer as it does with the era in which he served. Nixon's own feelings about Moorer, buttressed by his obsessive and sometimes downright weird love for the movie *Patton*, now seem strangely accurate. Moorer was not only a real military hero, he was more like Patton than anyone will ever admit. Like Patton, he acted the role of the chivalrous warrior-knight caught in the twentieth century. Moreover, he was as incapable of compromise as his predecessor, and he had the same obsession for battle, for rooting out enemies. Intent on cursing a president one minute, Moorer would show almost obsequious loyalty the next, and although he didn't affect learning or enrichment (as Patton did), his understanding of what it took to motivate men in battle — in the field or in the Pentagon — bespeaks an intelligence not plainly visible. Also, those who served him loved him, and still do.

"I'm a patriot," he said. "I've put my life on the line. I didn't see you there." This statement is Moorer's best response to critics who cite his role in the Radford spy scandal, his push to mine Haiphong Harbor, and his argument to bomb Hanoi to bring the North Vietnamese back to Paris as evidence that he actually failed as a JCS chairman. According to traditional military standards, Moorer should be considered a major success: as JCS chairman, he convinced the president to adopt policies in Vietnam that the military had been advocating for seven years. He accomplished what Wheeler — perhaps the most legendary JCS chairman — hadn't: he put in place military strategies that were designed to win a war. Still, somehow, Moorer's success hasn't been enough to ensure him a place beside the other great postwar military leaders.

The paradox is apparent at every level, a symbol for the real problems faced by the military at the end of the Vietnam War. Using a kind of military shorthand that has become popular with JCS officers — a pithy way of understanding difficult military problems that often gives rise to wishful might-have-beens — it's possible to understand Moorer's tenure by applying the metaphor used to explain Westmoreland's failure as head of MACV. According to the shorthand, Westmoreland "fought the war in reverse." This is incredibly accurate and disproves the theory that common notions are often wrong. Westmoreland deployed the Americans in big-unit battles against an elusive foe, when he should have been fighting a guerrilla war. Abrams made the same mistake. He began to fight a small-unit guerrilla war when the North Vietnamese were invading with division-size units. Hence, the war was fought in exactly the opposite manner in which it should have been engaged.

Similarly, for two years, Moorer acted like a JCS chairman, like the leader of a military establishment that could deftly respond to his every wish, that was as vigilant and ready to defend democracy and American ideals as it had been under Omar Bradley or Arthur Radford. The only problem is that Moorer led a military establishment that had ceased to exist, which was as apparent to Abrams as it was to CNO Zumwalt. In essence, from the time Moorer began his second term, his actions were out of step with the real needs of the military; what it needed wasn't a tougher stand against North Vietnam or even better weapons but a complete, top to bottom overhaul.

From the moment that Abrams became Army chief of staff, in October 1972, the JCS became involved in assessing the debacle of Vietnam, which made Moorer's role as the JCS's leading advocate for a tough anticommunist approach increasingly beside the point. Abrams knew then what Moorer could hardly bring himself to admit years later: that Vietnam had effectively destroyed American combat readiness; it had not only eviscerated the Army but caused untold tensions between the services and between officers and the personnel they led. In fact, Vietnam had gutted the military, inflicting wounds that, Abrams knew, would take years to heal. He realized that the problems were daunting. While military manpower strength was down — the natural result of the drawdown in force strengths due to the American withdrawal from Vietnam — the smaller number of men didn't make the situation any easier. In effect, Abrams feared that any attack on U.S. forces might result in "a bug-out," a retreat that would be the residue of Vietnam.

The figures were frightening: Abrams knew that by 1971, the Army had been stripped of ten full combat divisions — not because they had been demobilized, but because the equivalent of 250,000 men were absent without leave. The 1973 figure, while lower, was just as disturbing: all commands reported that 100,000 soldiers in uniform were actually not in uniform — the equivalent of three divisions, about what it would take to respond to an invasion of South Korea. "The morale, discipline and battleworthiness of the U.S. Armed Forces are, with a few salient exceptions, lower and worse than at any time in this century and possibly in the history of the United States," Colonel Robert D. Heinl, Jr., wrote during the last years of the Vietnam War. But the palliative, the end of the war itself, did not end the problems. In Europe, the incidence of drug abuse, racism, and insubordination was out of control.

As Army chief, Abrams continued the leadership programs he had begun in Vietnam and endorsed stateside policies that were intended to liberalize the Army's regimented traditions. More than ever, he wanted to make certain that officers continued their daily contact with subordinate commanders, a practice he had noticed lacking in Vietnam that he believed was directly responsible for the Army's disintegration. In addition, Abrams dredged up an Army War College study of leadership that had been ordered by Westmoreland; it stunned even the jaded Abrams: "The Army rewards system focuses on the accomplishment of short term, measurable, and often trivial tasks, and neglects the development of those ethical standards which are essential to a healthy profession."

The situation in the Navy wasn't much better: the U.S.S. *Constellation* had been the scene of bitter racial incidents beginning in early 1973, and they proliferated throughout the service the following year. Zumwalt acted swiftly to dampen the incidents, but not in the manner dictated by Nixon or Kissinger, both of whom wanted the black sailors dismissed for "mutiny." Kissinger even went so far as to threaten Zumwalt with summary dismissal, passing off the racial incidents as inspired by a few malcontents, a view that Moorer endorsed. Zumwalt ignored both men and began a program that made black sailors feel a part of their own service; it included "making books, magazines and records by and about blacks available in commissaries," according to Zumwalt. In addition, he hired black support personnel at naval bases and jumped qualified black officers in rank.

Further offending the Navy's more traditional officer cadre, the CNO even lectured JCS officers on racism, which so enraged Moorer that he refused to speak to Zumwalt for three weeks. The situation was made worse by the CNO's isolation; Zumwalt was forced to face the ire of the chiefs and the JCS staff officers almost daily. He was changing the face of the military, some of his colleagues claimed, tampering with decades of tradition that had made the American fighting force the best in the world. When Abrams arrived, Zumwalt had at least one other supporter, but it wasn't nearly enough. Nixon openly questioned the reforms and Kissinger confronted the CNO with Nixon's concern that he was being too permissive. Zumwalt remained undeterred, though he realized that many of the reforms he envisioned would only increase the president's mistrust. He appointed "gripe boards" to air racial problems, and the resulting recommendations were contained in "Z-grams" that eliminated "Demeaning and Abusive Regulations." Eventually, Nixon's continual questioning of the reforms and his denigration of such permissiveness got the best of the CNO, an otherwise patient man. "Nixon was the closest we have ever come to fascism," Zumwalt said.

Nor was the Air Force, the service most forgotten in talk of reform, immune to problems. At the height of North Vietnam's Easter offensive, the straight-backed chief of staff, John Ryan, learned that his colleague General John LaVelle had been falsifying bombing reports, carrying out strikes over North Vietnam that had not been approved by the JCS. LaVelle was relieved of his command, busted to lieutenant general, and shipped back to the Pentagon, where he reportedly pleaded to Ryan that Moorer himself had told him to "bend the rules a little" in launching the strikes. His pleas were useless, though Ryan undoubtedly knew that Moorer (and probably the president himself) shared responsibility for the false reports. "Why are you doing this?" LaVelle asked Ryan during their last meeting in the Pentagon. The two had been close throughout their careers, but Ryan didn't bat an eye. "You lied," he said, and dismissed the general. Ryan realized that the Air Force, like the Army and Navy, was in need of a complete overhaul that emphasized training, readiness, and understanding.

Over the next decade, the nascent reforms sparked by Abrams, Zumwalt, and, to a lesser extent, Ryan during their JCS tenures would start to take hold among the military, though it's difficult to argue that all the changes they envisioned have supplanted the traditions of two hundred years of military history. In some cases, the reforms they believed were necessary have yet to be enacted. This is far more true for the Navy than for the Army, in part because the Navy's problems went far deeper and in part because Abrams himself was far more conservative (and less willing to undertake the kind of revolutionary overhaul initiated by Zumwalt) than any of his successors. Still, fired by the crucible of Vietnam, the Army, Navy, and even the Air Force, the most progressive of the major services, began the slow process of reassessment that resulted from the Vietnam debacle.

But the reforms envisioned by a number of key officers even before the last American soldier left Vietnam were not confined to a study of what went wrong with arms in the field. Even among the chiefs and the JCS staff, the problems caused by the Vietnam War sparked a review of traditional military policy and a wide-ranging study of what went wrong in Vietnam and why. Not surprisingly, however, the JCS review of itself wasn't the result of any well-intentioned internal study but rather the by-product of an accidental and bizarre sequence of events that were ignited by Westmoreland's strange postwar habits.

In mid-1970, fully two years after his return to serve on the JCS, Westmoreland began a serious personal study that involved collecting, reading, and cataloguing every cable, order, and study conducted on the war by the JCS. "Westmoreland's little hobby," as JCS officers characterized it, became a personal obsession, a search for redemption that struck most officers as "chilling." For more than a year, until Abrams succeeded him as Army chief, Westmoreland spent long nights locked in his office at the Pentagon poring over military files brought to him by JCS assistants, reconstructing the command decisions that had led to the American commitment. When he retired, he turned over his voluminous file to Abrams and told him it was "pretty interesting reading."

When Abrams received the documents, he reportedly spent hours going over them, as Westmoreland had done. In late 1973, just months after the final withdrawal of American ground troops from Vietnam, Abrams decided to make these documents an official part of the JCS record and ordered JCS officers to begin compiling a complete "command history of the war in Vietnam." The resulting four volumes are among the most closely guarded documents of the JCS. According to JCS officers and a handful of historians, the secret, chronological history is officially titled *The Joint Chiefs of Staff and the War in Vietnam.* In addition, it contains an "annex," a description of how the officers in charge of the study organized the avalanche of JCS documents and reached their conclusions.

The history is tucked safely away in the office of the chairman of the JCS, available only to interested members of the JCS upper echelon. Its dusty pages contain the last and most significant secret of America's involvement in Vietnam, the final recommendation of JCS officers who spent days reviewing the high command's decision-making process. Their most important conclusion, according to one officer who has seen the study, is a startling indictment of civilian-military relations, albeit a simple recounting of what the military considers the most important lesson of the Vietnam conflict, a recommendation apparently written by the chiefs of the Wheeler era. They concluded, according to this Pentagon official, that the JCS "should publicly recommend the President seek a declaration of war before again agreeing to deploy American troops in combat." The history reportedly also concludes that U.S. officers were apparently hampered in convincing civilian officials that their Vietnam strategy would work because top officers have traditionally been barred from any involvement in foreign policy decisions.

Over the next fifteen years, the report's conclusions were tested again and again. Slowly, but certainly, the military's highest officers became convinced that the tragedy of Vietnam might have been averted by a fundamental change in the government's mechanism for deciding policy. JCS officers now claim that Vietnam proved that those who argue that the military is a tool for civilian policy-makers, that officers should not have a role in determining policy, do so at their peril. The lesson of Vietnam, whose final act was yet to be staged, was not that the military might disobey orders but that it might obey them too well. On a more practical level, the lesson for the JCS was a stark condemnation of civilian policies during the Vietnam era: the nation could no longer afford to ignore military advice, could no longer bar officers from a greater role in deciding the nation's policies. That, after all, had been tried, and the United States had suffered the greatest military defeat in its history.

8

POLITICS

We didn't have a tough time getting defense increases
through the Congress, we had a tough time getting the
increases past the people. After Vietnam the American
people were just sick of the military. They didn't want to
hear about defense spending.

Admiral James Holloway III

MELVIN LAIRD KEPT his promise: when Nixon was inaugurated for
his second term as president, in January 1973, he retired. In following
his own rule that a Defense Secretary should serve no more than four
years, the eternally optimistic Laird left a legacy of accomplishment
clearly unequaled by any of his predecessors. Laird had presided over
one of the most difficult military operations in American history —
the withdrawal of a nearly shattered 500,000-man Army from a tenuous, even desperate, position on a battleground 13,000 miles from the
continental United States. And he had used his considerable political
talents to begin closing the chasm of misunderstanding that had
opened between military and civilian leaders during the eight years of
the Vietnam conflict.

Nevertheless, Laird remains an anomaly: he is overshadowed by his
more activist, controversial, and famous predecessors, Robert McNamara and Clark Clifford, as well as by his seemingly more sophisticated successors, James Schlesinger, Harold Brown, and Caspar
Weinberger. Of all of them, Laird is remembered the least, though he
clearly succeeded the most. The key to his success might well be his
stiff-backed, purposeful silence, his assiduous belief in practicing a
Pentagon version of Eisenhower's "hidden hand" presidency. Ever the
politician (he was the only Defense Secretary to be appointed from
Congress), he brought the art of compromise into a military establishment that had become a willing participant in the art of confrontation.

When he left, JCS officers were hard-pressed to say exactly what he'd done, yet they noted that his effects seemed everywhere apparent. Laird's term paralleled that of JCS Chairman Moorer, the one four-star officer least remembered by history for either his tact or his adept handling of the give-and-take of everyday Washington. They were true opposites: where Laird sought consensus, Moorer preached single-service parochialism and styled himself the consummate insider, the one officer capable of taking on the sleazy political operators of Nixon's inner circle. He went even further, on occasion sniping at Laird for his intransigence on Vietnam troop withdrawals, on his constant attention to defense budget cuts, on what Moorer interpreted as his plotting with the Army ("the Laird-Abrams axis") against the other services.

Moorer rarely failed to provide the JCS consensus that Laird required to sell his programs, however, which indicates that either he understood Laird's program far better than the record seems to indicate or, more likely, he realized that a unanimous JCS strengthened the military's bargaining position on everything from Vietnam to the budget. Perhaps most important, Moorer was finally able to acclimate himself to Laird because the JCS chairman was simply unwilling to engage the JCS in the kind of open civilian-military warfare that had caused such havoc during Wheeler's tenure.* Not only was Moorer a convinced hawk on Vietnam, he realized that the open divisions between civilian and military officials at the height of the Vietnam conflict, in 1967, had come dangerously close to igniting the nation's first major civilian-military crisis, something that he — much to his credit — desperately wanted to avoid.

When Laird retired, it was clearly the end of one era and the beginning of another, which was signaled by the appointment of Elliot Richardson as the new Defense Secretary. Richardson, a Boston intellectual with extensive diplomatic experience, was perceived by the JCS as an administration insider, a moderate Republican who could be expected to deemphasize the Pentagon's past troubles in Vietnam while pushing Congress to approve unpopular but (Richardson thought) necessary strategic weapons budget increases. His first step with the JCS was designed to win its loyalty; within weeks of his appointment, he

---

* There are three examples of Moorer's adept handling of the JCS: Moorer convinced Zumwalt to forgo a statement saying the Navy only had a 50 percent chance of defeating the Soviets at sea. Second, he arranged a truce between the Army and the Marines over the withdrawal from Vietnam, convincing the Army to let the Marines leave first; and last, he convinced his colleagues to soft-pedal their concerns over the growth of Soviet military power, arguing that such a position could be used to drive a wedge between the services.

asked Congress to double outlays for the construction of the Navy's newest weapons system, the Trident submarine.

The JCS greeted the controversial Trident request with open approval and viewed Richardson's outspoken advocacy for newer and better weapons as an act of courage: the new secretary had not only asked for more money for a weapons system during a time of mounting public exhaustion with military problems, he had upped the ante, requesting that Congress appropriate a whopping $1.7 billion to fund the program. Not even the politically savvy Laird would have made such a request; his initial $977 million Trident budget had been cut by just over $200 million the year before. Not surprisingly, Richardson's request worked magic with the JCS, who had been fearful that a new Defense Secretary would bring havoc to the predictable universe of Laird's Pentagon. Furthermore, the JCS (especially the Navy) was pleased that the administration's post-Vietnam defense plans apparently called for a wide-ranging program of military rebuilding, a revitalization of weapons programs the JCS believed the United States needed to keep the military at rough equivalence to that of the Soviet Union.

Richardson went out of his way to ensure that the JCS was brought into the Defense Department's major decision-making process, promising that his predecessor's practice of close consultations with the chiefs would continue. Not only would the JCS be a part of major budget decisions, Richardson announced, the military's weapons programs would be given a high priority in Nixon's second term. The reassurances had an impact: although Moorer had only one year left as chairman, Richardson went out of his way to befriend the eternally suspicious admiral, listening closely to his claim that the long conflict in Southeast Asia had left the country less capable of providing military competition to the Soviets. What Moorer (and the rest of the JCS) had in mind, however, was a wish list that Richardson doubted he could sell to Congress.

In early 1973, with only 30,000 American combat troops left in Vietnam, Moorer said that the United States was faced with a dangerous strategic situation that could only be met by a massive infusion of defense dollars. Moorer ticked off the military's needs: the Navy wanted a new submarine and a third nuclear-powered aircraft carrier. The Air Force had reinitiated its seemingly endless fight to win approval of a new long-range bomber (the "low insertion" B-1) to replace the aging and vulnerable fleet of B-52s, a surprising number of which had been lost in the skies over North Vietnam. The Army needed a new main battle tank, an all-purpose behemoth that could cost more than $4 billion to develop, as well as a new troop carrier. There were bound to be other expenses as well, including unpredictable costs for maintaining the voluntary force that replaced the draft (which Moorer privately doubted could work). JCS officers also felt that the Soviet Union's missile strength meant that the nation would have to find a way to fund and deploy more of the new generation of intercontinental ballistic missiles, the Air Force's newly developed MIRV'd (multiple warhead) Minuteman IIIs. In all, the bill would be staggering.

Richardson was undaunted. While it was unlikely that the JCS would get all the weapons it wanted, he told the chiefs that he would do his best to balance strategic needs with the antimilitary mood on Capitol Hill. In addition, he told Moorer, he would hold the JCS responsible for rational budget figures — not wish lists — to make his job easier. Richardson's operating style made his transition one of the most comfortable in JCS history. The military was not only pleased that the new secretary would fight for its programs, they were certain that the destructive competition between the White House (in the person of Kissinger) and the Pentagon could finally be brought to an end. Unfortunately, this cooperative approach was short-circuited by the stunning revelations of the Watergate scandal, which was first made public just months after Richardson's appointment. Under mounting pressure to appoint new cabinet officials whose commitment to public service was unquestioned (and with few options), Nixon decided to name the scrupulously honest Richardson as John Mitchell's replacement as Attorney General. To replace Richardson, Nixon first offered the Defense job to David Packard, Laird's former deputy, who turned it down. In increasingly dire political straits, the president turned to the professorial James Schlesinger, a Kissinger competitor and the head of the CIA.

The May 1973 appointment of Schlesinger threw the JCS into yet another debate over just how he would view the chiefs. By now such discussions — the perhaps predictable residue of the bad feeling of the McNamara-Wheeler era — were rituals, as much a part of JCS tradition as the meetings in the tank. Predictably, Schlesinger's appointment was viewed with suspicion (an attitude that seemed to greet every high-level defense appointment) and as evidence that Nixon was desperate to end the scandal that threatened his presidency. In fact, Schlesinger was resented by the JCS; not only had it lost an ally in Richardson, it believed it had been victimized by Nixon's own bad judgment. Also, Schlesinger was hardly unknown; his feud with Kissinger over foreign policy issues threatened to reignite the Pentagon–White House competition laid to rest by Richardson as well as undo the internal defense budget commitments the JCS had so easily won from Richardson.

The JCS's attitude was not unjustified. In the course of twenty years, Schlesinger had won a name for himself as an outspoken and self-promoting defense strategist. A 1950 Harvard graduate, he began his career as an economics professor before moving on to the RAND Corporation, where his superior abilities as a strategic thinker resulted in his becoming director of strategic studies. His time at RAND clearly endeared him to the upper echelons of the Air Force, at least until 1969, when he was named assistant director of the Bureau of the Budget by Nixon. His service there and in the Office of Management and Budget was characterized by a number of run-ins with both Nixon and Kissinger over Pentagon weapons requests, which gained him valued allies at the Pentagon at the same time that it convinced JCS officers that he might be too fiery to transform the JCS's legislative goals into congressional victories.

There was something vaguely disturbing about Schlesinger, a sense that he was his own worst enemy — a view reinforced by his actions at the CIA after he was named its head in February 1973, replacing Richard Helms, just weeks after Richardson had become Defense Secretary. Schlesinger gutted the CIA, spurring a reorganization that resulted in the forced resignations and retirements of more than a thousand intelligence community employees. These actions were so controversial that he received numerous death threats, and his personal bodyguard had to be increased. Schlesinger also seemed to go out of his way to bare agency complicity in the administration's foreign policy disasters before a number of Senate committees, actions that sowed mistrust among top Pentagon officials. All of this was taken as a harbinger of future policies at the Pentagon; certainly it wouldn't have surprised the JCS to find Schlesinger forcing the same kind of changes in defense policy that he had undertaken during his short tenure at the CIA.

The JCS also doubted that Schlesinger's defense views would reflect military needs. While the new secretary had spent six years at RAND and spoken out publicly for an increase in defense spending ("It is time to stop the erosion of the real resources going to the national security," he had said in a speech six months before his appointment), there was little confidence among the JCS that he would remain an advocate for increased military appropriations, particularly in light of his actions at the CIA. The JCS believed that his personality would prove to be an insurmountable barrier to civilian-military understanding. Schlesinger was aloof, too self-confident, and seemingly taken with his own strategic prowess — all of which were obvious after his Senate confirmation. From the moment he took over, he made it clear that he was the Pentagon's resident expert on military strategy, an attitude that the chiefs, no slouches on such matters, found grating.

In one of his first meetings with the JCS, in July, the new secretary appeared in the tank with a prepared lecture on American defense capabilities. Striding to the lectern, he began a two-hour presentation on the problems facing the military, complete with flow charts, position papers, statistical studies, and color slides. The befuddled chiefs sat in stunned silence: it was a bit of typical showmanship that didn't offend them as much as convince them that Schlesinger was absolutely incapable of embarrassing himself. The lecture set the tone of this tenure: unlike any previous Secretary of Defense, Schlesinger was apparently without any redeeming administrative qualities and liked nothing better than clearing out his crowded daily schedule in order to engage in lengthy discussions with Pentagon strategists on such airy topics as throw weights, limited strikes, "nihilistic individualism" (a phrase he used at his swearing-in ceremony), and essential equivalence.* Sprinkling his monologues with long parenthetical comments on why the United States should mistrust the Soviets despite Nixon's yen for détente (the president had signed a strategic arms limitation agreement with the Soviet Union in May 1972), Schlesinger said he believed that the nation had to put Vietnam in the past and begin the long, slow process of rebuilding its strategic capabilities.

So the pipe-puffing, off-putting, well-educated, even elitist Schlesinger, who had a penchant for mumbling words between clouds of smoke, turned out to be just the kind of Secretary of Defense the JCS was afraid it would get — but, it soon realized, just the kind of secretary it needed. Within weeks of his confirmation, Schlesinger had dampened JCS fears that he would attempt to intimidate it or that he would replay his CIA experience. To make sure the military understood his position, he added these reassuring words during a September 1973 interview with the press: "There has been a fair amount of abuse in using the Department of Defense and the military services as a whipping boy for all the frustrations of Vietnam and all the idiocies committed by civilian leadership," Schlesinger said. "A democratic nation gets about the kind of military establishment it deserves, and if we continue to abuse these fellows and treat them this way, it is going to have consequences."

Moorer might have written Schlesinger's words. Embittered by America's apparent loss of prestige in Vietnam, in open revolt against Nixon's arms negotiations with the Soviets, and disenchanted with the growing Watergate scandal, he looked forward to his retirement with fond anticipation. In his last year as JCS chairman, Moorer main-

---

* The *Chicago Tribune*'s defense correspondent, Fred Farrar, wrote that the press listened closely to Schlesinger because "there was the feeling that one should pay attention because the speaker might later give a test on what he said." Other correspondents gave similar descriptions: "Besides being one of the worst-groomed men around, he is also brilliant, hard-headed, testy and determined to rebuild our defense establishment," columnist Nick Thimmesch wrote.

tained a studied silence, allowing other members of the JCS (Abrams in particular) to take on the administration's détente policies. The first public airing of the JCS's opposition to détente came in January 1974, during a speech Abrams gave to a group of officers. "The major military challenge to our global interests is the Soviet Union," he argued. "It is the only other truly global military power. And so we must gauge our ability to maintain freedom of action in terms of the Soviet Union. . . . This is not saber rattling. This is not warmongering. This is not some kind of idle scare tactic. It is the most reasoned, responsible position I know for having our military strength up to par."

For the JCS, the strategy of détente was misconceived, even dangerous. JCS officers argued that the United States was falling permanently behind the Soviets in a number of major military categories. In conventional weaponry, in particular, the longstanding Soviet superiority in numbers of tanks in Western Europe had actually been widened as a result of the U.S. commitment in Vietnam. To make matters worse, the American military had been forced to dig even deeper into its stockpile in October 1973, during a last-minute airlift of matériel to keep Israel afloat during the Yom Kippur War. The airlift, accounting for an outlay of $2.2 billion in highly prized military hardware, gutted what was left of the American stockpile of conventional arms, all but denuding (at least in the JCS's opinion) America's ability to blunt a Soviet conventional attack in Europe.

All of this was much on the mind of both Moorer and Schlesinger as they faced one of the most difficult summers in the nation's history. In April 1974, the worsening Watergate scandal was the subject of a number of off-the-record JCS discussions in the tank, according to a JCS general at the time. Interestingly, they had less to do with Nixon's fate than with the military's fears that Watergate could undermine the public's nascent but growing concern over the apparent weakness of American arms. The military could be thankful that both Laird and Schlesinger had remained outside the Nixon White House's corridor of power; in the weeks and months that followed, neither would be implicated in any of the public hearings on the scandal, and the JCS would remain untouched by the public condemnation of Nixon's illegalities. The JCS had much more on its mind than the constitutional crisis that seemed to envelop the nation; within a period of sixty days, beginning on July 1, 1974, almost the entire group of chiefs were retired or replaced, marking the most complete turnover of the JCS.

Schlesinger welcomed Moorer's retirement. Although he had a grudging respect for the former war hero and had learned to ignore his obvious impatience when he delivered his interminable strategic monologues, he wanted a JCS chairman who was more in tune with his emphasis on a strategic weapons buildup. At first, Schlesinger considered appointing Abrams, but the JCS had had its share of chairmen from the Army (four of the seven previous chairmen, for fifteen of twenty-five years), and, in July 1974, the former Vietnam commander was about to be hospitalized for cancer. In addition, Abrams's appointment would not have signaled the emphasis on strategic arms to which Schlesinger was firmly committed. Instead, he appointed Air Force Chief George S. Brown, the first JCS chairman from that service since Nathan Twining, at the end of the Eisenhower era.

Brown's appointment not only symbolized a decisive shift in JCS leadership, it also reflected Schlesinger's belief that the military should have a new, post-Vietnam agenda. No longer would the chairman be concerned with a faraway war; he would instead be responsible for reemphasizing the long-term goal of military readiness and the reconstruction of an American strategic response to the Soviet threat. In many ways, Schlesinger was making a perfect statement of the conservative belief that America had allowed itself to become obsessed by Vietnam and that, as a result, the long-term goal of providing a credible response to Soviet aggression had eroded. By appointing Brown, he also lowered the JCS's high public profile. Brown was an affable, capable officer who eschewed the aggressiveness of Taylor, Wheeler, and Moorer. His task was clear: to return stability to the armed forces and rebuild the nation's gutted arsenal.

Like his predecessor, Brown had seen combat in World War II, flying B-24 Liberator bombers over Nazi Europe throughout much of the conflict. Perhaps more important, especially for those officers for whom combat service was the litmus test of leadership, Brown was a survivor of one of the Air Force's most embarrassing military debacles — the 1943 American bomber strike against the Romanian oil refinery at Ploesti. After seeing the lead bomber of his group shot down over the refinery, Brown (then a major) led the surviving Liberators south across the Mediterranean, making a safe landing in Benghazi, Libya, a feat that resulted in a citation for heroism and the Distinguished Service Cross. Brown also served in Korea, where he commanded an American fighter wing, and in Vietnam, where he led the Seventh Air Force.

But Brown's experience went beyond combat commands; in 1974, Brown was known throughout the military as one of the few flag rank officers who specialized in developing nuclear warfighting strategies, which was very important to the Secretary of Defense. For the three years before his appointment, Brown had been head of the Air Force Systems Command in Washington, the focus of the nation's experiments, using sophisticated Air Force hardware, to find new ways to exploit America's technological edge over the Soviet Union. Just as important, he had experience with the JCS, serving as Wheeler's assistant from 1966 to 1968, two of the JCS's most tumultuous years. Brown's appointment was therefore a perfect fit for Schlesinger; the intellectual strategist who headed the Pentagon had found his equal, an officer who not only understood the intricacies of nuclear strategy, but also would welcome Schlesinger's meandering disquisitions on changes in America's nuclear capabilities.

A decade later, Air Force officers still remember Brown as one of the most intelligent leaders to have served on the JCS. For some, Brown was "a genius, one of the most intelligent men to have ever held the post." Even among his colleagues, who are normally chary with their acclamations, Brown's apparently gifted understanding of weapons and strategy is still held in awe: "He was a master at strategic development, at finding out what was needed, when it was needed, and how much it would cost," one Air Force officer remembers. Yet a retired general who served with him at the JCS recalls him as politically savvy. "He knew government so damn well," he says now. "He was just so damn effective. But I wouldn't call him an intellectual or a genius; he was very straightforward, a good man, a good man." With his colleagues, Brown worked as well as or even better than any of his predecessors. During the first months of his tenure, for instance, he made certain that each service head had as much time to speak on the JCS agenda as he wanted. It meant that meetings in the tank went on far longer than anyone wanted, but the chiefs were satisfied.

Brown's appointment also gave Schlesinger a rare opportunity: to appoint a strong, strategically oriented officer as Air Force chief of staff. In fact, Schlesinger had been planning the JCS transition for over a year. According to one JCS officer familiar with this period, the Defense Secretary often conducted tours of military installations with an eye toward replacing the group of Moorer chiefs he had inherited with a group more to his own liking. High on his agenda was finding an Air Force officer who would understand the politics of defense spending well enough to mold the kinds of congressional compromises the Pentagon's legislative officials predicted would be forced on the service by a fiscally conservative Congress.

A year before Brown became JCS chairman, Schlesinger believed he had found an Air Force general who met his requirements. During a tour of European combat commands, he was impressed by the work of David C. Jones, head of the Air Force in Europe (who was in fact Brown's nominee for the top Air Force job). This view was reinforced when Schlesinger stopped off to visit Jones during a tour of Europe before a meeting of NATO defense ministers in the late summer of 1973. According to one of Jones's subordinates, the visit sealed Jones's appointment, but not because the two shared common policy concerns. According to Pentagon lore, Jones went out of his way to impress Schlesinger, apparently because he knew the secretary would determine his future. Just days before the visit, Jones ordered his staff to scour the files to determine Schlesinger's likes and dislikes. The men came up with an interesting bit of information: Schlesinger was an avid ornithologist, a man absolutely taken with birds and bird-watching.

"I'll never forget how Jones latched onto that," one staff officer says now. "He literally sent us out looking for books on birds, anything we could find. When Schlesinger showed up, Jones had his office lined with these things. Finally Schlesinger took an interest. 'Gee, I see you're interested in birds too,' he said. Well, that pretty much sealed it. Jones was Air Force chief of staff." While others say the story is apocryphal, a number of high-ranking officers swear by it, though some say that Schlesinger's obsession had nothing to do with birds. "I think it was cars," one says. "Something like that." There were undoubtedly other reasons for Schlesinger's decision. Articulate and intelligent, Jones had a reputation for leaving every command better than he found it. He was a stickler for organization, just the kind of skill needed by an Air Force chief, whose primary responsibility was to lobby successfully for newer and more expensive weapons.

Jones looked and acted the part of an Air Force general — a much more important quality for an officer who appears with frequency before congressional committees than many people will admit. In fact, Jones — tall, athletic, with a deep voice and just a tad bowlegged (a dead ringer for Burt Lancaster) — seemed the perfect choice. He was a good service manager and welcomed change, a quality he had earned primarily during his stint in Europe. "The most satisfying job I ever had was air commander of the U.S. Air Force in Europe," he admits. "I was able to change things there more than anywhere else. . . . I moved to headquarters from downtown Wiesbaden, where you could get it into an operational environment. . . . Moved Third Air Force out of London and got it under cover and built shelters for our Air Force so that we could survive an attack and came up with collocated operating bases we could put our forces on. George Brown gave me a free hand in Europe to do what I wanted to do."

Although Schlesinger didn't know it at the time, his appointment of Jones inaugurated the Washington career of one of the most important and controversial officers in JCS history. Schlesinger had wanted an officer who was at home in a collegial environment, an independent thinker who could juggle service desires with overall military requirements. What he got instead was a firestorm of criticism from many of Jones's fellow officers, most of whom claimed that Jones was the least independent thinker in Air Force circles, a follower instead of a leader, an officer who would do anything to get to the top. These criticisms have persisted to this day. "He's a very complex individual," General Edward Meyer admits ruefully. "It's hard to figure out sometime just what he has in mind." Others are even more critical, including a Navy admiral who served in the JCS's top ranks during Jones's tenure. "He just turned out to be a two-faced son-of-a-bitch," the officer said. "He was just two-faced. Real political. He would do anything to get to the top, that was apparent from the beginning."

Soon, Schlesinger was also able to name a new CNO, which gave the secretary almost a monopoly on the major JCS positions. On July 1, 1974, the same date that Brown and Jones joined the JCS, Schlesinger reached agreement with top Navy officers on Zumwalt's replacement, Admiral James L. Holloway III, who had a family history of naval success. His father, Vice Admiral James L. Holloway, Jr., a colleague of the great admirals of World War II, had been so successful that the younger Naval Academy graduate (1942) often suffered from charges of nepotism, as well as from comparisons. Nevertheless, it was the son who left the greater imprint on the Navy, balancing his own desires to see an increase in the total number of Navy carriers with a keen political sense of timing that kept each of the Navy's four "unions" (submarine, aviation, surface fleet, and administration) happy with his leadership. Holloway's political sense was the result of his own experiences. He had served in nearly every branch of the Navy: as an officer on a destroyer during the Battle of Leyte Gulf, as a trained aviator (he won his wings in 1946), and as captain of the first nuclear-powered aircraft carrier, the U.S.S. *Enterprise*, in 1966. In the end, it was his experience with nuclear power that probably tipped Schlesinger's hand in his selection as CNO.*

The appointment was greeted with widespread skepticism. It led to speculation that it was actually the result of the intervention of Admiral Hyman Rickover, the father of the nuclear Navy and one of the most powerful officers in naval history. Although Holloway denied that Rickover had anything to do with his promotion ("You can be sure that if he recommended me, I wouldn't have ever got the job," he said later), the rumor persists, undoubtedly because Rickover was indebted to Holloway's father. In 1953, a Navy promotion board bypassed Rickover in announcing thirty-nine new captains. It was an open, public slight, due in no small part to the Navy's own hidebound internal prejudices that worked against anyone who was Jewish. But

---

* Zumwalt had wanted Admiral Worth Bagley to succeed him, but Secretary of the Navy John Warner preferred Admiral Isaac Kidd. Schlesinger finally settled on Holloway, whom both Zumwalt and Warner approved.

jealousy was also involved, a fact noted in the early 1950s by James Holloway, Jr., the chief of Naval Personnel. Realizing Rickover's special talents ("He's got plenty of G-U-T-S," Holloway wrote in one memo), he helped the Secretary of the Navy to manipulate the promotion regulations to ensure Rickover's ascendence. According to one JCS officer, Rickover never forgot the kindness of the Holloway clan.

Rickover was initially pleased by Holloway's promotion, for he thought that the new CNO would give his proposals for revitalizing the Trident submarine program a fair hearing, which he believed he had been denied under Zumwalt. The Trident program was Rickover's dream: a new generation of faster, quieter, more powerful, and deadly submarines to meet the growing numbers of Soviet undersea launchers. The longer submarine, the result of ten years of breakneck work, was the core of a program that envisioned the eventual deployment of an "underseas long-range missile system" (ULMS), which would make the United States the ruler of the ocean. In fact, Trident was a monster, displacing 18,700 total tons and packing a terrific nuclear wallop of twenty-four missiles with a range of 4,000 miles. These new missiles balanced the apparent vulnerability of the nation's aging, land-based missile system; after the Minutemen had sponged up a Soviet first strike, the theory went, the Tridents would still be there to deliver the knock-out blow.

There were problems, however, most of them caused by Rickover. During the ten years since its inception, Rickover had changed the Trident again and again to make it faster, better, bigger, quieter — a tough goal when he insisted that it also be longer and heavier. By the early 1970s, when Zumwalt was CNO, naval submarine experts were openly questioning whether Rickover's changes actually meant that the Trident was as good as the admiral claimed. Every time Rickover made it bigger, it got slower, and every time it got slower, it became easier to spot, identify, follow, and, ultimately, destroy. This problem, as well as his natural inclination to slow the process of changes wrought by the powerful Rickover, caused Zumwalt to veto successive design modifications. When Rickover demanded that the submarine be even longer, Zumwalt pointed out that it was already costing too much (a staggering $780 million per copy), which meant the Navy would be forced to build far fewer Tridents than Rickover (or anyone else) wanted.*

---

* Rickover and Zumwalt continued their sniping well past the time that healing, humility, and history should allow. Zumwalt said that there are three villains in the world, the Soviet Union, the Air Force, and Hyman Rickover. Rickover implied that Zumwalt was not qualified to make technological decisions. Zumwalt told Rickover's biographers Norman Polmar and Thomas Allen that "Rickover is paranoid. And he has turned the world into his asylum."

Zumwalt's decisions were interpreted as a clear antisubmarine bias by Rickover, who reportedly looked to Holloway as the program's salvation. In particular, he wanted to convince Holloway to argue for a number of costly additions to the program in addition to an accelerated building schedule that would result in the completion of ten Trident submarines by 1980. Rickover reportedly believed that Holloway's appointment all but ensured the last of his most dearly held fantasies: that the United States would deploy a full fleet of nuclear-powered ships, not just submarines and aircraft carriers, but cruisers and destroyers as well. It would be an all-nuclear surface Navy, the first in the world.

But the new CNO had other plans. After taking another look at the budget figures, Holloway was convinced that Rickover's dream was a delusion. The U.S. Navy certainly could build such a Navy, but at an enormous cost. He understood that by realizing Rickover's goals, the Navy would be trading each nuclear-powered ship for two nonnuclear ships, which would be costly and impossible: he would have to either double the budget (a political impossibility) or halve the number of ships (which would be military suicide). Holloway didn't think he had much choice; Navy building projects were established under the secretary's defense guidance paper, which called for the Trident program to continue at a modest rate of construction. Holloway's decision to press ahead with his own shipbuilding program, designed to bring the Navy up to a 600-ship level, sparked a public attack by Rickover that many Navy officers viewed as a veiled criticism of Holloway. "In my opinion there has been no point in the past fifty years where the fleet has been in as poor condition as it is today," Rickover said just sixty days after Holloway's promotion. "The Navy is raising a generation of officers who believe that technical training is not essential and that they can rely on management techniques to make decisions." It was a slap at Holloway's leadership and the entire JCS system, a kind of initiation that Holloway realized he could come to expect from every part of his service, all of which would be dissatisfied with the grim budget facts put out by the Pentagon.

In time, Holloway built a reputation as an able JCS infighter, a veteran of some of the most controversial budget battles of the 1970s, which were waged constantly by the JCS after the 1974 turnover in JCS personnel. Like his predecessors, Holloway became known as an intransigent defender of the Navy's claim to a greater share of the budget than the other services, a position he proudly defended as in the national interest. "I wasn't alone in pushing for a constant budget," he said later. "We stayed pretty consistently at around 42 percent of total service outlays during my whole term. I don't think there was any disagreement with that by anyone [at the Defense Department]." In fact,

Holloway stridently disagreed with Schlesinger's view that the Navy should design a budget reflecting a "high-low mix" of Navy construction programs, a position inaugurated by Zumwalt. Instead, Holloway said, he would commit the Navy to building more aircraft carriers and more sophisticated cruisers to defend them. While Holloway's intransigence never led to an open break, Schlesinger realized he would be forced to shape a military establishment without the full cooperation of his CNO.

Schlesinger had been extremely fortunate: through a sheer coincidence in timing, his goal of revitalizing the military by ending its obsession with Vietnam was being made possible by a major transition in JCS leadership at the very moment the nation needed it most. He could now concentrate on rebuilding the military. His luck, however, didn't hold. The service competition implied in Schlesinger's mission of battling for increased defense dollars was continually postponed by a series of critical incidents that had a direct impact on the new JCS.

In July 1974, the country turned its attention to the Watergate scandal, perhaps the most critical constitutional struggle in its history. Although it was not directly involved, the JCS was implicated in the events surrounding Nixon's pending resignation. During the second week of the month, in one of the strangest incidents in JCS history, the chiefs were openly cautioned by civilian officials to follow only those orders passed through the U.S. chain of command.

The incident itself is easy to describe: in the course of a routine meeting with Brown, Schlesinger cautioned him to make sure that "any emergency order coming from the president" be shown to the other chiefs, "and the Secretary of Defense," before its execution. Schlesinger nodded knowingly, passing off the remark as a formal, yet unofficial, reminder. Brown was reportedly shocked, but nodded his agreement with Schlesinger's emphasis on following the chain of command. Not one to dismiss a warning, Brown dutifully called a closed session of the chiefs within an hour.

"I've just had the strangest conversation with the Secretary of Defense," Brown said. Brown's puzzlement was met with surprise and outrage by almost all the JCS members, who were insulted by the implication of Schlesinger's reminder. Holloway later observed that he didn't know whether to be complimented or not. But his colleagues were clearly offended. Schlesinger had told Brown that the military might actually be used by the president in an attempt to retain power, implying that the JCS would obey his orders without question or that it might somehow be used to effect a smooth transition from Nixon to his successor. Or perhaps, as some members of the JCS speculated, Schlesinger was attempting to ensure the military's complete neutrality should Nixon refuse to obey a congressional order that he be dismissed from office. The JCS was confused by Schlesinger's talk about strictly adhering to the chain of command precisely because it was uncertain what would be expected of the chiefs should a standoff between the president and Congress result from Nixon's impeachment and trial. The summer's events were unprecedented: never before had a sitting president so baldly attempted to circumvent the law. Nor had the nation ever undergone such a crisis while it was supporting a standing military establishment. The immediate result of Schlesinger's meeting with Brown contradicted the JCS's own deep offense: instead of considering their own actions, JCS members dismissed Schlesinger's words as no more than a bit of melodramatic byplay from a secretary obsessed with politics and the military. Fifteen years later, however, it's clear that Schlesinger's talk was far more important than anyone realized.

Meetings on what would be involved in removing Nixon from office actually began in earnest in early June, when a group of advisers to Vice President Gerald Ford met informally at the White House. Among them were two old friends of the new vice president's, Philip T. Buchen and Clay Whitehead, who had taken Ford in hand after his House staff had proved inept at managing his new responsibilities. At this meeting, Buchen and Whitehead confronted some of the more dangerous aspects of a presidential transition. Among other things, the group discussed the public steps Ford would have to take in order to reassure the public that despite the crisis the traditions of constitutional government would continue. The subject of whether Nixon would leave office willingly was touched on, skirted, then mentioned again before being dropped. Later that evening, during a walk down the White House driveway, Whitehead turned to Buchen and raised the subject once again: What would happen, he asked, if Nixon refused to leave office? What if Nixon called on the military to bail him out? Buchen's response was that every possibility, no matter how nightmarish, had to be considered. At that point, both men agreed to raise the question with Schlesinger.

The Defense Secretary mishandled his assignment. Instead of outlining civilian fears that the president might attempt to circumvent the wishes of Congress, he hinted that Nixon might actually order the military to intervene in a domestic crisis. The evidence seems clear: Schlesinger's talk with Brown led the JCS to believe that the civilian authorities worried that Nixon might issue an illegal command. The most unfortunate part of the incident was that the JCS apparently decided not to follow up on Schlesinger's comment. Were military officers required to obey the orders of a sitting president? More significant, were the chiefs being told to disobey an order from the president if they, or the Secretary of Defense, considered it illegal?

Fortunately, the drama of Watergate ended when Nixon decided to resign in early August. The JCS was relieved: Schlesinger's words of caution had been unnecessary, and no officer had been publicly tarnished by the Nixon White House. The military had, in fact, maintained a dignified silence during the crisis. The administration's earlier troubles with Moorer, the JCS's almost ingrained dislike of Haig, and the backchannel attempt to circumvent Laird during Nixon's first term could now be relegated to their rightful place, a small footnote to history. With Nixon out of office, the nation enjoyed a respite from the crisis atmosphere. For the JCS, however, the rest was short-lived.

In late August, JCS officers learned that Creighton Abrams was dying, a distinct tragedy not only for the Army but for every service. Increasingly unable to perform his duties due to the final stages of lung cancer, Abrams was confined to his bed at Walter Reed Army Medical Center. Nonetheless, in his last week of life, he made certain that his early 1974 agreement with Schlesinger — that the Army would be increased from thirteen to sixteen divisions — would be kept and that his successor would continue many of the rebuilding programs he had begun. The agreement to add three divisions had been dubbed "the golden handshake" by JCS officers, who realized that it would lift Army morale and commit the nation to future increases in conventional force strengths, which Abrams believed were necessary if the Army was to recover fully from the Vietnam disaster.* Just as critical, he elicited a pledge that the Department of Defense would develop a new Army battle tank (the Main Battle Tank, or M-1), which he believed would help America turn the tide of Soviet conventional superiority in Europe. Just as important, however, the M-1 tank represented the Army's high-tech response to the Air Force B-1 bomber and the Navy Trident programs.

Schlesinger, who admired the way Abrams handled the American withdrawal from Vietnam (he later called him "a genuine American hero"), not only willingly agreed to his last wishes, he appointed Frederick Weyand, America's last commander in Vietnam, as his replacement — the best assurance that his programs would be continued. Abrams's widely mourned death, on September 4, was a depressing finale to the events of August, stark evidence that the only constant within the four walls of the tank were the ripples of change that now seemed to flow over the JCS with increasing frequency.

Weyand's appointment meant that Schlesinger was now running the

---

* Abrams is best remembered by former JCS officers for his keen attention to improving morale at the Pentagon, which had gotten so bad that before his appointment, the staff had started a GROW (Get Rid of Westmoreland) campaign.

Pentagon with an almost entirely new set of JCS chiefs (the exception was Marine Corps Commandant Robert E. Cushman, Jr.). The changes went far deeper than anyone would have imagined, for as new chiefs came on board, they brought with them a new set of personal deputies and trusted aides. By the end of September, the JCS corridor of the Department of Defense had undergone such a massive turnover in personnel that fully 40 percent of its officers had fewer than three months of experience with the JCS.

The Secretary of Defense was counting on the JCS to provide the major impetus for Congress's acceptance of defense increases despite the nation's post-Vietnam bias against the military. He also realized that the new group of JCS officers were more acceptable military spokesmen than many of their predecessors or even, to be blunt, than he. Continually spurned by Stuart Symington, one of the more powerful members of the Senate Armed Services Committee, and by Congressman George Mahon, head of the House Appropriations Committee — both of whom had ungraciously taken credit for a $5 billion cut in the military's 1974 appropriations bill — Schlesinger hoped that Brown's low-key affability would help him win a $14 billion spending increase for the Defense Department's newest (fiscal year 1977) military budget.

In fact, Schlesinger was not only mistrusted by many members of Congress, he was dismissed as a prig by the very politicians he needed to influence; they considered him snobbish, pedantic, and intolerant of the political considerations that went into approving a defense buildup. To his credit, Schlesinger realized that his erudite speaking style tended to irritate people. It was perhaps because of this trait that Schlesinger pushed Brown to be more outspoken during major appearances at Senate and House budget hearings. Even so, the attributes of the likable Brown, as Schlesinger no doubt knew, could not be solely counted on to sell a budget figure of $117 billion. The figure, proposed by Schlesinger during a time of high inflation, appeared to be the epitome of fiscal irresponsibility, which meant that Congress was less willing than ever to sit through his dull lectures on strategy. In the end, it was Brown's job to clear the path, reassuring Congress that Schlesinger really was a good manager, really did understand all the problems that Congress faced, and really was concerned with the political unpopularity of major defense spending increases. With Brown leading the way, Defense Department budget experts opened discussions with the staff of the House Committee on Armed Services on the FY 77 budget in October 1974.

At first everything seemed to go well. Brown was articulate and convincing, and Congress seemed to listen more closely to the Pentagon's arguments. More important, congressional staff members found that

JCS papers on new appropriations were well argued and detailed; not only had the JCS and each service done its job (the result of Schlesinger's open budget process in meetings with the service heads), there also seemed to be a new air of trust between the Hill and the Pentagon. With Ford's administration less than a month old and Watergate behind it, Congress was more willing to hear that it was time to rebuild the nation's defense. Even within the JCS itself a more positive attitude seemed to prevail, as if its officers realized they had just emerged from a long dark tunnel. The chiefs also gained confidence from their belief that while a massive defense buildup was out of the question, a more modest increase clearly wasn't.

This newfound confidence suffered an unpredictable blow, at the hands of George Brown, the low-key JCS chairman. On October 10, in responding to a question during a seminar at Duke University, Brown said that "Jews own, you know, the banks in this country, the newspapers. You just look at where the Jewish money is in this country." The remark stunned the JCS, angered Ford, and depressed Schlesinger, who believed his best weapons lobbyist had just made the most incredibly stupid remark of his life. Both men called on Brown to apologize for his statement publicly (which he promptly did) and even considered replacing him as chairman. But soon both Ford and Schlesinger realized that the anger had cooled and that Brown's apparently heartfelt apology had satisfied the public.

JCS officers, including Brown's closest colleagues, remain puzzled by the chairman's remark. Not only did they refuse to believe that Brown was anti-Semitic (they had never heard him make such a remark), some even speculated that his outburst was proof that he was, as one Air Force commander noted, "possessed. It was like he wasn't doing the talking at all." The incident had a devastating impact on the JCS, which realized that the chairman was now even less capable than Schlesinger of carrying the budget fight to Capitol Hill. Even more damaging, Brown's own role clearly suffered; after his public apology, Brown decided to assume a less activist role, leaving many of his colleagues to carry on the budget fight alone. A four-star general who knew the JCS chairman at this time described the impact of the event on Brown: "The affair at Duke grated on George, really followed him the rest of his life. George was somewhat different after the Duke affair, became somewhat different."

While Brown realized that his statement implied a straightforward anti-Semitism at the very top of the military establishment, he told close friends that he wasn't anti-Semitic. All he was trying to do, he told JCS officers, was point out that the United States was heavily committed to the military survival of Israel at the one time in American history when the nation was least capable of giving military aid to anyone. During the Yom Kippur War, the United States had cleared the shelves for Israel, shipping off needed conventional stocks to assure a key ally's survival. This reprovisioning of Israel so angered some JCS officers that they believed Congress owed them a program of one-for-one weapons replacements. The possible validity of this point of view was never discussed during Brown's tenure, in all likelihood because Brown himself had closed the door by his remark at Duke.

Brown's misstep seemed to seal the fate of the Pentagon's proposed budget increases. As 1974 ended, the Ford administration made it clear that it would accept lower defense budget figures from Congress, reflecting the growing consensus that the nation could not afford defense increases. Throughout January and February 1975, Schlesinger and the JCS continued their lobbying activities with dimming hopes. Still, there was a bright side: for the first time since 1965, the JCS was lobbying Congress without having to consider the fiscal constraints of a foreign war. Although no one was satisfied with what looked like a modest defense bill (in the $110 billion range), JCS officers realized that whatever they received would all be earmarked for building a military force at home.

As if to make this point even clearer, the JCS was faced with its final Vietnam crisis just as it was beginning to plan its final budget position for the fall 1975 congressional hearings. On March 1, North Vietnam's General Van Tien Dung opened an NVA offensive by attacking the small town of Ban Me Thuot in South Vietnam's Central Highlands. By March 4, Ban Me Thuot, the key to central South Vietnam, was in danger of being overrun, and by the end of the month, the hinge on which South Vietnam's defense rested started to swing back, slowly and inexorably. On March 25, Secretary of State Kissinger held a hastily called meeting of the top military and foreign policy advisers at the White House to draw up a plan to deal with the mounting crisis. There was a "sense of panic" among White House officials, one officer remembered. In particular, Kissinger was "just bothered as hell that this was happening, berating Congress for 'letting it come to this.' "

However Weyand, Abrams's soft-spoken and highly respected successor as commander of MACV, remained calm. "We don't know really what's happening," he reportedly told Kissinger. "There's only one way to find out." With that, he suggested that the United States send a high-level mission to Saigon to "assess the needs of the South Vietnamese" and to "develop solutions, or options." Weyand, who had begun his career as an intelligence officer, picked Erich Von Marbod, the Pentagon's logistics expert, and intelligence guru Theodore Shackley, who had been the agency's top man in a number of tight situations (for instance, the Miami station chief during the Bay of Pigs operation), to accompany him. Weyand trusted Von Marbod to give him a calm assessment of the deteriorating situation, with an eye toward retrieving American assets should it become apparent that South Vietnam would fall. It was a good choice; Weyand had a tendency to be too optimistic about Saigon's chances for survival, a viewpoint not shared by Schlesinger.

Upon their arrival in Saigon, it was apparent to all three men that ARVN would not hold back the communist offensive, that the fall of the nation was inevitable. Moreover, top intelligence analysts in Saigon told Weyand that American intervention was the only way to save the Saigon government — an option that, Weyand knew, was highly unlikely. Eventually, inevitably, the NVA rolled south, overrunning the ARVN positions, province capitals, and even Saigon, which fell on April 30, 1975. The North Vietnamese immediately inherited a cornucopia of American military hardware, though not nearly to the degree they might have had Weyand not directed Von Marbod to begin a crash program of airlifting the most valuable weapons out of the South.*

Still, the final "beans and bullets" count gutted the American military's Far East operations, including more than 70 jet fighters, 550 tanks, and enough matériel to reprovision an entire military establishment. The Vietnamese became the dominant power in Southeast Asia largely because of what they had captured from the Americans. In reality, however, the final toll was mild compared to the impact the fall of South Vietnam had on the officer corps and on Weyand. "South Vietnam was going to be Abe's [Creighton Abrams's] gift to the United States," one former Army officer said in retrospect. "Weyand was going to make sure that was Abrams's legacy. And he thought he could do it if only he had a little more time, just one more shot of aid, just start the bombing and stop them in their tracks. When Saigon fell, I just think it took it out of Fred, just drained him really."

The administration's respect for Weyand was so great, however, that when Brown considered retiring in June 1976, President Ford wanted to make the Army chief the new JCS chairman. While some Army officers now claim that Ford actually made the decision, Holloway denied the appointment was ever offered. "It just never happened," he said. Weyand is still mentioned as one of the Army's most highly respected officers, coming close to the depth of feeling the

---

* Just before the fall of Saigon, Von Marbod returned to Saigon to extricate American military equipment. According to Defense officials, his "psychologically brutal" tactics saved thousands of weapons: "In essence, Von Marbod went to the South Vietnamese and said, 'You've lost it. You can give the weapons to us or you can give the weapons to those assholes. Now, who's it going to be?' " Von Marbod reportedly won an agency commendation for his work.

Army has for Abrams. "Fred Weyand was a tremendous officer, but I think that he wanted out, especially after Vietnam," said Colonel Harry Summers. "He just had tremendous respect for Abrams, and after his death and the fall of Saigon he thought it was time for someone else to take over." Ford's final decision not to promote Weyand meant that Brown would continue on the job for another two years, into what Ford thought would be the first years of his only elected term in office. Instead, in November 1976, Brown realized that he would be leading the military during the first two years of the term of President Jimmy Carter and his Secretary of Defense, Harold Brown.

As the JCS assembled for its first official meeting with President-elect Jimmy Carter, in December 1976, it was clear that none of them was looking forward to the occasion. There was an air of suspicion among the chiefs, an almost palpable feeling that Carter didn't appreciate their views. The JCS attitude was predictable: Carter had campaigned on a pledge to make the Pentagon more efficient, a phrase the JCS interpreted to mean that he was interested in cutting the defense budget. He had even promised that he would cancel production of the B-1 bomber and pursue an arms control agreement with the Soviet Union.

For George Brown and David Jones, both of whom had been involved in early plans to design a new long-range, low-flying bomber, Carter's pledge meant that one of their most important programs was dead even before they could argue its merits. Holloway was just as disturbed. Carter had continually played on his broad experience in a number of unrelated fields, one of which was nuclear power. He even went so far as to cite his time as a student of Rickover.* His obsession with nuclear power bothered Holloway, who feared that Carter was more interested in submarines than aircraft carriers. For Bernard Rogers, Weyand's successor, the election of Carter was also bad news. Although he had been getting reports that the president-elect favored strengthening NATO, he also learned that Carter didn't think that increasing the Army's budget was the way to do it. Instead, Carter wanted to push America's European allies to increase their own defense budgets, an idea that brought instant yawns to officers who had been trying to do the same thing from the day NATO was established.

The meeting with Carter was worse than anyone could have imag-

---

* When Rickover heard that Carter had named him as one of the influences in his life, he sent aides scrambling to find out just who Carter was and when he had served. The admiral, a man with a talent for instant recall, couldn't remember. Carter took the title of his autobiography, *Why Not the Best,* from a statement of Rickover's when Carter met him for the first (and only) time before his election.

ined. After greeting each of the chiefs and their deputies personally, Carter sat smiling through a briefing on the nation's worldwide military posture, complete with graphs, maps, pointers, charts, slides, and memos. It was a typical JCS production, not only a shameless attempt at impressing the new commander in chief, but also a transparent endeavor to win his support for pending weapons programs. According to former Assistant Secretary of Defense Lawrence Korb, such briefings often leave civilians with the feeling that "Ivan is just around the corner, somewhere in the next corridor." The Carter briefing was more of the same. The president-elect was told that the Soviet Union outnumbered the United States in launchers, warheads, battlefield nucs, bombers, fighters, divisions, tanks, and amphibious vehicles in a welter of major strategic areas that, it was implied, spelled doom to the free world. As the lights in the room went up, Brown summarized the briefing, detailing the budget figures the JCS had put forward as minimal requirements to meet the national security needs laid out during the previous year. He noted that during the last two years of Ford's tenure, Congress had increased defense appropriations that reflected increased Soviet defense outlays, but he added that in the military's opinion, the increase would have to continue if the United States was to meet its worldwide obligations.*

Nodding in apparent agreement, Carter thanked the JCS and promised that he would study the figures provided him. He went on to say that he believed the briefing would set a precedent of good civilian-military relations for his term in office; the words were ritualistic and formal, just as at the beginning of every administration. Carter reassured the JCS that its commitment to maintain a ready defense was appreciated by him, his aides, and by the American public. He then asked a number of specific questions about the briefing, focusing on the JCS claim that the Soviet Union was gaining a military edge. At the end, there was a surprise. "By the way," Carter asked, "how long would it take to reduce the numbers of nuclear weapons currently in our arsenal?" Brown was taken aback, apparently uncertain about what Carter meant. Was he asking how the JCS believed the United States could reach nuclear equivalence with the Soviet Union, or if it was possible for the United States to negotiate arms limitations that would bring the Soviet numbers down to U.S. levels? Not wanting to appear hesitant, the JCS chairman broke the question down into all categories. "No, no," Carter said. "I guess I want to ask what you

---

* Gerald Ford won approval of two defense increases before leaving office, including a fiscal year 1978 budget that called for $123 billion in defense outlays. Donald Rumsfeld, who succeeded James Schlesinger as Defense Secretary, proved a capable lobbyist in getting the package passed.

think it would take to cut the missiles, how we could cut the number of missiles." Again, Brown was baffled. Did the president-elect mean to say that the United States was going to cut the number of its missiles unilaterally? "What would it take to get it down to a few hundred?" Carter asked.

"That did it," one JCS aide said. "It brought down the house. You could hear a pin drop." Another defense analyst described Carter's questions: "The inquiry alarmed the chiefs, putting them on notice that they were dealing with a very different commander in chief." The portrait is understated; in his first meeting with the JCS, Carter let it be known that one of his major priorities would be to negotiate deep cuts in U.S. and Soviet strategic arsenals at the same time that he was cutting the defense budget, a proposal the JCS thought unrealistic, even naive. After the meeting, the JCS chairman approached the new Secretary of Defense, Harold Brown, arguing that cuts in the U.S. nuclear arsenal would not only be difficult to effect, they might be downright dangerous. The JCS, he argued, had committed itself to building a military force in line with the policies set out in the Ford administration's last Defense Guidance, which indicated that the United States needed to upgrade its strategic capabilities. The chairman's plea was useless; Carter had been elected on a program of cutting defense spending by as much as $7 billion; it was one campaign promise he wasn't going to abandon.

This first meeting between the JCS and Carter set the tone for military-civilian relations for his administration, a tone that soon grew into a major debate on just what kind of forces the nation needed. While there was a wide division over central military and foreign policy questions, the differences never reached the open breach they had during the Johnson era. Instead, the military's mistrust of the president's foreign policy set the stage for a bitter internal administration debate over defense priorities that culminated in the election of Ronald Reagan. In his first year, Carter announced a series of initiatives that were to increasingly estrange the JCS from its civilian superiors; they not only involved the status of U.S. overseas commitments, but actually led to the cancellation of some of the military's most highly prized weapons programs.

In one of his first acts, Carter directed Bert Lance, the head of the Office of Management and Budget, and Harold Brown to come up with the promised $7 billion in defense cuts from an already inflation-ravaged budget. It wasn't an easy task. Brown believed that defense cuts should be more modest, and neither he nor Lance could agree on just which programs should be trimmed. Finally, after nearly three days of around-the-clock negotiations, they earmarked $3 billion in cuts they believed they could sell to the military, cuts that left many expensive weapons programs in place. Although Carter eventually accepted this more modest proposal, he continued to pressure Brown to designate wide-ranging cuts in defense spending in line with his own promise to cut Pentagon waste. For Carter, cutting weapons programs seemed the easiest way to deal with Pentagon weapons cost overruns, continuing complaints about poor production and performance, weapons duplication, and increased costs in dubious weapons add-ons — called "chrome plating."

Carter was convinced that weapons duplication was costing at least $50 billion per year, a problem he blamed directly on the JCS. In large measure, his concerns were justified: the eternal service rivalry was fueling the number of weapons requested in the immediate aftermath of Saigon's fall, when the services began pressing Congress for increased appropriations for big-ticket systems: Patriot, Stinger, Sidewinder, Sparrow, and Phoenix missiles, nuclear-powered aircraft carriers, Aegis cruisers, F-15 fighters, AH-64 helicopters, M-1 tanks, and MX missiles. The military's promotion of these weapons systems sparked administration efforts to streamline the procurement system. One of the leading critics of the system was John Kester, an assistant to Harold Brown. "With the blessing of the [JCS]," he noted at one point, "the country continues to buy four independent tactical air forces, one for each service. Civilians still have to wrestle the Army and Air Force so that the tanks of one will fit inside the planes of the other."

Carter was convinced that the Defense Department needed the overhaul that Kester advocated, but he also knew that large cuts would undermine civilian-military cooperation. With this in mind, Bert Lance and Harold Brown began the budget-cutting process by reassuring the JCS that the services would be treated equitably. Regardless, each service was convinced it would suffer the most. The Army, for example, believed that it would fare the worst because it had the furthest to go in recovering from the Vietnam years. In particular, Army staff officers claimed that they would be unable to develop their newest wonder weapon, the Bradley Fighting Vehicle. The highly touted personnel carrier, which cost $1 million per copy, was the Army's dream machine, a necessary replacement for the M-113 armored personnel carrier, with mounted guns, missiles, and heavier armor. Army leaders also believed that Carter's cuts would endanger the M-1 "Abrams" tank, envisioned as a high-tech successor to their aging but legendary Pattons. Not only did the Abrams cost more than the Patton (some $560,000 per copy, compared to the Patton's $250,000), the M-1's major contractor, the Chrysler Corporation, was nearly bankrupt.

The orphaned feeling among the Army's highest ranks was reinforced on May 12, 1977, when Carter signed Presidential Decision 13, announcing that the United States would withdraw its combat forces from South Korea, a decision the president made in line with his own belief that the deployment was a drain on the budget and that the United States should not defend nations with poor human rights records. In signing PD 13, Carter shocked Army commanders, who had been pressing for personnel increases in order to make up for the Army's lost ground as a result of the Vietnam drawdown. The Carter policy was greeted with derision by Army leaders, including the U.S. commander in Korea, General John W. Vessey, and his deputy, Major General John K. Singlaub. Vessey's exile and Singlaub's subsequent transfer and resignation — following a Carter reprimand — soon became a cause célèbre for Army commanders, who initiated congressional actions to slow the pace of the Army's withdrawal.

Carter's next decision, a month later, was even more controversial. Carter had long believed that the Air Force's B-1 bomber program was too expensive to be retained as part of the Pentagon's defense budget. On June 30, he officially canceled the project, despite his earlier (May) signal to the JCS that he would consider retaining the bomber as part of the American arsenal. His announcement therefore surprised both the JCS and top Air Force officers, who had made retention of the B-1 one of their primary goals. Within twenty-four hours of Carter's decision, the JCS "issued a strong protest to the president through channels," according to several Air Force officers, implying that the military would continue to lobby Congress for appropriations to keep the B-1 alive despite his decision.

While Carter's moves to cut the Pentagon budget and withdraw troops from South Korea were vociferously opposed by the JCS, his decision to end the B-1 program was by far the most controversial defense decision he made as president, even though terminating B-1 funding would have an impact only on the Air Force. The decision turned the JCS against the president completely and ignited open opposition to administration policies on the part of JCS officers. According to Air Force officers, the JCS exhibited more than the usual dismay over the cancellation, apparently because it was made against the wishes of Carter's own Secretary of Defense. Harold Brown, who had served as one of McNamara's top scientists in the early 1960s, told Carter in May that he believed the B-1 program should be continued, albeit with a scaled-back production schedule. In addition, the Office of Management and Budget recommended that the B-1 be used as a bargaining chip in the approaching arms reduction negotiations with the Soviet Union, a ploy that made perfect sense to the JCS's own team of arms reduction experts.

Carter soon realized that the B-1 decision was more controversial than he had intended. Pro-defense Republicans on Capitol Hill used the issue to criticize him for being soft on the Soviets, and they mounted a public campaign to undercut his other defense initiatives. Nor was Carter the only administration figure affected; JCS staff officers began to question Brown's leadership as Defense Secretary, accusing him of mimicking the policies he had promoted during McNamara's regime. Brown's response, that he had urged Carter to continue funding the program at a reduced rate, didn't help: JCS officers were not inclined to believe him, especially when they recalled his 1962 recommendation that McNamara eliminate funding for the B-70, the Air Force's dream bomber of the 1960s.

The controversy over just what Brown had told the president was only the beginning of the B-1 debate. Within thirty days, Air Force Chief of Staff David Jones was under fire from his colleagues, who had expected him to resign in protest over the decision. "That thought never occurred to me," Jones said later. "Why should I put myself up on this pedestal and say that I have all the answers for this nation?" He was forced to respond to claims that he had turned on his own service, that his desire to be JCS chairman (George Brown would retire in 1978) outweighed his commitment to increases in the defense budget. Jones remains embittered by the claims. "Here we have a leader elected by the American people, and during his campaign he said he was going to stop the B-1," Jones argues. "And the American people voted for him. Who am I to step above that?"

Jones's defense left Air Force officers, even those on his staff, contemptuous of his leadership. With little thought to Carter's rationale (the nation's bout with inflation had ravaged the program, pushing the Air Force to admit that each B-1 would cost some $75 million), Jones's Air Force assistants began planning ways to circumvent the president's wishes, including a behind-the-scenes lobbying campaign on Capitol Hill that came within three votes of overturning the decision. "Carter's decision on the B-1 was just a disaster for him," one retired Air Force officer admitted. "It really made him a lame duck with us [on the Air Force staff] long before his other decisions made him a lame duck with the American people."

But it was Carter's handling of the Navy's commitment to a force built around nuclear-powered aircraft carriers that led to open revolt. As with the other two services, the series of events that led to the break began in May 1977. "The Revolt of the Navy," as it is now called, began when Harold Brown decided he would back Carter's cutbacks in Navy shipbuilding programs. Carter vetoed the Navy's move to add another mammoth carrier and cut naval construction to no more than twelve to fifteen ships per year. He also denied funds for two additional programs, the nuclear cruiser and the submarine-launched cruise missile. Navy officers decided to oppose the cuts on Capitol Hill, hoping to gain approval for programs in Congress that they couldn't hope to win in administration circles.

Within a year, members of the House Armed Services Committee were publicly opposing Carter's decision to build a smaller fleet, using Navy studies that showed the service was increasingly vulnerable to the growing Soviet threat. Unlike Denfeld in the Revolt of the Admirals, Holloway led the fight to retain the Navy's most important project, the construction of a 90,000-ton aircraft carrier, the one program officers believed was necessary for the Navy to reach the 600-ship level, a long-term goal. It was the one policy from which every other followed: if Holloway could win approval of the carrier, he knew he could win approval to build an entire aircraft carrier task force. Holloway and his colleagues in the Department of the Navy eventually won their point, but not without cost. While the House Armed Services Committee voted to approve the construction of a new carrier (at a cost of $2.1 billion), which was interpreted as a slap at Carter's defense program, no one expected the president to do what no other president had dared: he not only vetoed the carrier bill, he mounted an intense anti-Navy campaign against the Navy on Capitol Hill and in the Pentagon. It was costly, though successful. Although the Navy failed to gain the necessary two thirds of the votes to override the veto, it had embarrassed the president and fueled the anti-Carter defense lobby gathering steam for the 1980 election.

By early June 1978, it was clear that Carter and Defense Secretary Harold Brown would have the opportunity to appoint a new JCS chairman; it would be a chance for Carter to convince the military that during the next two years of his administration, he would recoup some of his early, ill-advised weapons decisions. In particular, Carter wanted to make sure his new arms negotiating position with the Soviet Union, a continuation of the SALT talks begun under Nixon, was endorsed by the JCS. He also wanted to reassert his hold on the presidency by appointing JCS officers that he and Brown considered loyal to administration goals. Therefore, when George Brown retired, Carter appointed David Jones as JCS chairman on June 21, a promotion that many Air Force officers interpreted as Carter's way of rewarding Jones for taking the heat on the B-1 cancellation. Jones's promotion also allowed Carter to name the military's most widely respected scientist, General Lew Allen, as the new Air Force chief of staff. The appointment it provided the Defense Secretary with a like-minded scientist, at ease in the world of sophisticated missiles, and it showed Congress that Carter would move forward on one of the nation's most expensive and increasingly controversial strategic weapons, the highly accurate MX missile.

Allen's appointment was a concession by Carter to congressional arms control hard-liners, who believed that the MX should be used as a bargaining chip in SALT negotiations. It was Carter's way of admitting that he now accepted the hard-liners' position, especially after his initial SALT II proposal (canceling the MX in exchange for a 50 percent reduction in Soviet SS-18s) had been dismissed as a propaganda ploy by the Soviets. The problem with the MX was that it was an example of the one problem it was intended to solve: just as Soviet missiles would be vulnerable to its reputed accuracy, the MX would be vulnerable to Soviet missiles with advanced targeting systems. The problem, as most arms negotiators in the administration realized, was not with the building of the MX but with its "basing." The MX was being built not just to increase Soviet vulnerability but to replace the still-vulnerable Minutemen; putting the MX down in Minutemen holes, as Allen well knew, just wouldn't solve that problem. Of course, Allen was the kind of officer who could be given the problem and come up with a solution — at least with a better solution than those that had already been thought of — including one that proposed putting the missile deep underground and letting it corkscrew its way to the surface. JCS officers referred to this as the DUMB option, an acronym for "deep underground missile basing."

Allen was a welcome addition to the JCS. The bespectacled scientist and West Point graduate was not only the most learned missile expert in JCS history, he was also one of the most even-tempered chiefs, a welcome counterpoint to Jones's often fiery personality. His appointment was greeted with relief by JCS officers, who knew they would soon be facing tough decisions on such esoteric subjects as missile deployments, throw weights, and basing modes. In Allen, they had a general who could stand toe-to-toe with Harold Brown himself, acknowledged since the days of McNamara as the Pentagon's foremost scientist. Allen also proved to be a good compromiser, defusing JCS debates by long but quiet discourses on the effects of "EMPs [electromagnetic pulses] and verification" and by reportedly doodling at odd times in the midst of bitter feuds over weapons priorities.

If Allen was the JCS's scientist, then Admiral Thomas B. Hayward, who took over as CNO on July 1 was the JCS's pilot — a reversal of roles for the two services. Hayward had won his wings in naval aviation during the late 1940s; he flew combat missions over Korea in the early 1950s, and by the mid-fifties he was considered one of the service's premier jet pilots. He was also one of the few CNOs known for his polite approach to JCS problems. "The man was a gent," one naval officer remembered. "Just a real good guy. He always took an interest in what his fellow officers were doing." The promotion of Jones and the appointment of Allen and Hayward gave Carter the high-tech military staff he wanted, a necessity if he was to negotiate an arms limitation agreement with the Soviets that could also be sold to Congress. The new JCS reaped immediate benefits for Carter in other ways: when the administration opened its long debate on the details of the strategic arms limitation package it would present to the Soviets, it also undertook a study of the vulnerability of Allen's MX.

The JCS conducted a number of high-level discussions on the MX basing problem throughout 1978, but in the end it was Allen who finally hit on what he thought was the only commonsense approach. If the MX was vulnerable because the Soviets knew where it was, then the United States should hide it by playing a "shell game" — building twenty-three hardened shelters in the desert for each missile. Even if the Soviets launched a massive attack against the MX, large numbers of Soviet missiles would destroy each other (what JCS war planners called "fratricide") instead.

At least partly as a result of Carter's actions on the MX and his promise that he would not trade off the new missile unless he gained a similar concession from the Soviet Union, the president's relations with the JCS began to improve. Carter also realized that JCS members could be valuable allies in gaining Senate ratification of an arms control agreement with the Soviets. He was helped as well by the JCS's new roster, which contained a less fiery cast of characters. While Jones was hardly the most patient JCS chairman, he also wasn't crippled by embarrassing statements, like his predecessor. The addition of Allen and Hayward also had an impact. They were able to argue military positions without engaging in political battles with the president's congressional opponents, which helped win over Carter on the key question of retaining the controversial MX missile system during arms control talks.*

There was only one more change that Carter and Harold Brown thought would strengthen their support on the JCS, and they finally got their chance. General Bernard Rogers had served well as Army chief of staff, emphasizing readiness, U.S. capabilities in Europe, and the debilleting of Army troops to make the service more attractive to potential recruits, but he had remained at odds with Brown over the administration's new attention to strategic problems. Carter's call for greater support for his programs from the military seemed to have had little effect on Rogers, who continued to lobby Congress for budget increases. "He came up here and just banged away," one House Armed

---

* When Carter and Brezhnev signed the SALT II agreement in June 1979, the MX was retained under a proviso allowing each nation to develop and deploy a new ICBM. According to JCS officers, the president made only one mistake: he appointed Army General Edward Rowny as one of the chief negotiators. Rowny resigned in protest when the SALT II treaty was signed and campaigned against its ratification.

Services Committee staff member recalled. "The country wasn't in the mood for a military buildup, but he couldn't have cared less. It was a personal thing." Inevitably, Rogers grew tired of fighting both Carter and Brown and was frustrated by the public's apathy toward the military. By the beginning of 1979, he thought he could do a better job as the Supreme Commander in Europe, which seemed to fit his talents as a diplomat as well as his background as a Rhodes scholar with broad experience in several European commands. Most important, he was obsessed by what he believed was America's inability to reinforce Europe swiftly in the case of a Soviet conventional attack on NATO forces, a problem he had become increasingly aware of during his time on the JCS.

In 1978, Rogers directed the first in a series of REFORGER (Return of Forces to Germany) operations, to test U.S. capabilities to reinforce the Seventh Army in Europe. Operation Nifty Nugget, as it was called, included airlifting major portions of U.S.-based combat troops (some 17,000 in all) to Europe within forty-eight to seventy-two hours, along with their equipment and supplies. Nifty Nugget was, as Rogers himself later admitted to a large group of officers named by the JCS chairman to assess the operation, a first-class disaster. A high-level defense official who is still involved in assessing U.S. military readiness remembers Nifty Nugget, and Rogers's reaction, in chilling terms: "We really busted our tails to make that thing work, and it was beautiful. The operation was well planned, wonderfully managed — the whole bit. And the troops came out of those big cargo planes and then the planes with the supplies landed. Rogers was there, waiting for the tanks and troop carriers, and the ramp came down and the plane was empty. Absolutely empty. Well, Rogers went crazy. Here we'd been spending billions to build bombers, and when it came down to it we didn't have the guns and ammo to fight the war that was most likely to happen." Carter's decision to transfer Rogers to Europe was made in part to meet the Army's criticism that Nifty Nugget proved that the budget cuts of the previous two years had actually harmed NATO's standing. In addition, it was politically comfortable, Rogers would be out of Harold Brown's way, yet many of the reforms he had initiated as Army chief would be carried over to the European command.*

Rogers's successor, the sturdy and outspoken Edward C. Meyer, was picked by Carter to carry on Rogers's programs in the "new Army" in

---

* Rogers's impact on NATO was so pervasive that JCS officers began calling Europe "Mister Rogers' neighborhood." In addition, Rogers reportedly began carrying a little black book with the names of young commanders who impressed him — a tradition started by George Marshall and continued under Maxwell Taylor. Marshall's book contained Taylor's name, and Taylor's book contained Rogers's.

June 1979. Like Rogers, Meyer was seen as a leader among the new generation of more progressive commanders, who were committed to broadening Creighton Abrams's first tentative steps to building a new Army. Years later, Meyer discussed Rogers's move to "the new Army," noting the difference between the World War II generation of military leaders and the four-star commanders who served under Carter and Reagan. His comments also reflected just how far his service had come since the time of Abrams's nascent reforms. "I have heard that Abrams was quite a great general, and it's true that he pulled us through Vietnam after Westmoreland," Meyer said, "but I wonder really whether anyone who fought in World War II could understand or run the army that we have now. Really, we have an 'unmarried' army. They're not married to their barracks, or units; they have cars and houses and families, and it's totally different. Twenty years ago only 6 or 7 percent of our NCOs had families. Now it's more than 30 percent. That's one hell of a change. So our job in the 1970s was to figure out a way to keep our cohesiveness while reflecting the basic people we had to work with. It's just a different army now, and the World War II guys would have a hard time acclimating themselves to it. Frankly, I just don't think they could have built or commanded the army we have now."

With Meyer's promotion, Carter and Brown had a new JCS in place, one they believed would carry them through the final months of the first Carter administration and well into the first two years of a second. In early November, however, Carter was faced with the gravest crisis of his presidency — when the American embassy in Tehran was stormed by a group of Iranian Revolutionary Guards, who immediately took fifty-three Americans hostage. Although Carter claimed he would solve the impasse peacefully, the JCS was told to assemble a special rescue planning staff within forty-eight hours of the incident.

Surprisingly — at least for defense analysts, who have since spent considerable time assessing the JCS actions that followed the embassy takeover — the Joint Chiefs were ill prepared to handle the crisis. This lack might have been predicted, at least to those on the JCS staff who had seen the military's (and particularly the Army's) desire to distance itself from its own Special Forces units, which had caused Harold Johnson and Creighton Abrams such problems in Vietnam. Nevertheless, planning for a rescue attempt went forward under the leadership of the JCS chairman. Within a month, Jones, with the help of Meyer, had planned a rescue operation, chosen a force, and begun its training. The force, reportedly chosen at Meyer's recommendation, was the long-forgotten and extremely controversial Delta Force unit stationed at Fort Bragg, North Carolina. The unit was under the command of Colonel Charlie Beckwith, a Vietnam Special Forces expert who had been exiled to Fayetteville, along with his commanding officer, General Robert Kingston, by the heavy hand of Abrams. Unfortunately, the unit had only been in existence for two years, hardly enough time to become acclimated to the kind of operation Jones and Meyer had in mind.

While Delta Force operated under the auspices of the Special Forces, it was clear that Beckwith and his cohorts believed their team was even more "elite" than the Army's elite — or any other service elite, for that matter. It was not simply a "special operations unit," it was also conceived of as an intelligence operation, a military unit of *all* services that was a cut above the Special Forces. Even so, there were problems with Beckwith and his unit from the beginning. Lines of communication and funding were confused, and Beckwith had problems explaining some of Delta's more byzantine accounting techniques to the JCS command, though these "eccentricities," as Beckwith called them, were apparently designed to win Delta autonomy from the Special Forces. In addition, Beckwith clashed with officers at Fort Bragg over the use of base facilities and equipment. Eventually, however, Delta Force was approved by the JCS as an elite antiterrorist unit, and Beckwith took steps to maintain the unit's secrecy. In the course of two years, he fleshed out Delta with personnel, equipment, and training.

When Beckwith was contacted by Jones, he was told that an ad hoc group of specially selected planning officers on the JCS staff had decided that a helicopter rescue offered the best chance of success; Beckwith agreed. The JCS plan was incredibly complex, owing in part to the large distances involved. Six C-130 transports would fly Beckwith's team from Egypt to Oman for refueling and then into Iran, where they would rendezvous (at "Desert One") with eight Sea Stallion helicopters from the U.S.S. *Nimitz*, stationed in the Arabian Sea. The rescue team would transfer to the helicopters and fly to a location outside Tehran ("Desert Two"). They would move into the city by van and truck, then storm the embassy and free the hostages. Helicopters waiting at the embassy compound would take the hostages to an airstrip just south of Tehran, previously secured by a group of Rangers airlifted into Iran for that purpose. There they would be met by a number of C-141 Starlifters. The rescuers' helicopters would be destroyed and the hostages flown to safety.

But the attempt failed when only five of the original eight helicopters arrived at Desert One; one had turned back to the *Nimitz* due to a mechanical failure, and two had been forced down by a sandstorm. Carter acceded to Beckwith's wishes and ordered the mission aborted. In the process of leaving Desert One, another helicopter collided with a C-130, and eight members of the team were killed. This failure was not only a military embarrassment but a deeply felt humiliation for JCS officers, who went so far as to tell Carter that they believed it had a 60 to 70 percent chance of success. Inevitably, a series of unseemly charges, countercharges, and personal recriminations among those involved in the attempt made their way into the press.

Beckwith, for instance, alleged that the Marine helicopter pilots were not sufficiently trained for the mission, a point he had omitted when assuring his superiors that he was fully prepared to go into Tehran. Soon after, it was revealed that Beckwith had called members of his team "cowards" upon their return, which eventually became public knowledge. The recriminations were not restricted to those who had participated in the raid; in a public speech in Washington, D.C., CNO Hayward criticized his colleagues and said that the JCS should take the blame for the failure. It had made a serious mistake, he said, in not studying past special operations missions, a comment that was seen as a personal criticism of David Jones.

Nevertheless, Jones convened a "special review group" led by the hard-nosed former CNO, James Holloway. This appointment, especially in light of Hayward's criticism, stunned the JCS staff; it looked as if Jones had confused objectivity with self-flagellation. Holloway could hardly be expected to be nice to the Air Force or Army, or to Jones. Holloway, though, took no pleasure in his task, knowing that his findings would likely be as controversial as the mission itself. His public report recommended that the JCS establish a separate advisory panel on such operations and designate a "permanent special operations force." But the classified version of the Holloway findings reportedly recommended that the rescue mission had failed, in part because of the "informal chain of command," a clear criticism of Jones's insistence that Desert One remain a JCS operation. The call for a permanent special operations force irritated Army officers, who had been trying to stop the establishment of such a command ever since Harold Johnson had dubbed the Special Forces "fugitives from responsibility." Holloway's recommendation, however, should not have come as a complete surprise. The panel was composed of special operations experts who had been pushing for the creation of such a task force, even "a separate command," for a number of years.

The failure of the rescue operation spelled doom for Carter, whose hard-pressed administration had been forced to retreat from a number of major programs, the most important being his desire to streamline the Department of Defense and cut back on military waste. Clearly, the people believed (and still largely believe) that Carter's defense program failed, the invasion of Afghanistan by the Soviet Union standing as final proof that Carter himself didn't understand the true nature of the military threat posed by the Soviets. The military agreed with the electorate's own judgment: just before the November 1980 election, only 1 percent of all officers indicated in a public opinion survey that they believed Carter should be reelected.

The military's final judgment of his presidency has yet to be determined: while officers may have preferred Reagan in 1981, there's now a strong sense that Carter's program of defense cuts was outweighed by his honesty. In particular, JCS officers cite Carter's handling of the botched Iran rescue mission. "Carter didn't intervene," one Army officer noted. "He listened to what Beckwith had to say, he asked for his recommendation, and when Beckwith said it couldn't be done, Carter followed his advice. He could have said, 'Go, go get 'em and don't come back alive.' It might have even led to his reelection. But instead he took the heat." The implicit message is that a more pro-military president (such as Johnson or Nixon) might not have been so honest. The irony is that Carter rejected the legacy of his predecessors: he was not nearly so bellicose or willing to expend American lives as Johnson nor as duplicitous as Nixon. In fact, he was open to JCS arguments that he change his policies, that he be more realistic in his expectations. As a result, he accepted Allen's and Jones's arguments for deployment of the MX; in return, the military endorsed his SALT II arms limitation agreement.

The last two years of the Carter presidency saw a slow rise in defense outlays — a result of Carter's purposeful decision to bargain arms agreements from a position of military strength, a philosophy the JCS was responsible for instilling. Despite this, Carter's defense program fell victim to the JCS's bungled rescue operation in Iran. As a result, the JCS would finally get the kind of president they had always wanted. When Ronald Reagan was elected overwhelmingly, the vast majority of JCS officers looked forward to his administration with keen anticipation. Not only would they be getting the kinds of weapons they had only dreamed of before, they would be getting the first peacetime, pro-defense president in their history.

9

PROTRACTED
WARFARE

★　　★　　★　　★

The public doesn't seem to understand that the military
is probably the largest body of moderates in the nation.
We generally tend to be between the two extremes.

General David C. Jones

DEPENDING ON WHOM YOU TALKED WITH in Washington at the
end of 1980, Caspar Weinberger — a former California legislator and a
Harvard alumnus (magna cum laude, 1938) — was either the incarna-
tion of the Second Coming or a double for the devil himself. On the
one hand, Reagan's appointment of "Cap the Knife" (a sobriquet
earned as Nixon's director of the Office of Management and Budget)
as Secretary of Defense was greeted with relief by liberals; they
believed that he would bring efficiency to a military establishment
still reeling from the Iran hostage rescue operation. On the other hand,
the appointment shocked conservatives, who believed that Reagan's
landslide election meant that the defense budget would be increased
and that the United States would begin taking a harder line with the
Soviet Union. Basically, everyone had expected the new leader of the
conservative revolution to appoint one of its many true believers, a
group that did not include Weinberger, to be Secretary of Defense.

Even before Reagan's inauguration, the head of the defense transition team, William Van Cleve, lobbied Congress to keep Weinberger
from naming Frank Carlucci, Carter's CIA director, as his top assistant. It was a particularly brutal and unusually public contest, one that
seemed to portend things to come. When Van Cleve, a hard-line conservative, broke with Weinberger over Carlucci's appointment, the
secretary designate unceremoniously fired the ambitious Van Cleve

and named William Howard Taft IV, another moderate, as his replacement. The move further enraged conservatives, but Reagan simply told Weinberger to make whatever changes at the Pentagon he thought necessary.

The early jockeying for position in the new administration had little perceivable impact on the JCS. It had learned to mistrust first appearances (especially when it came to predicting relations with a new Defense Secretary), and its history had taught that even the most pro-military Defense Secretary could cause problems. The JCS had welcomed the appointment of Robert McNamara, for instance, because he was a good manger, then fought with him for eight long years on precisely that point. The chiefs had also been wrong about Melvin Laird; there wasn't a politician around who could take on the services and win, they had said back in 1968, yet that's just what Laird had done. In all, the JCS had seen fifteen Defense secretaries by 1980, and almost every one had turned out to be a surprise. In fact, contrary to popular political notions, the JCS had had its best relationships with those secretaries who seemingly mistrusted the military (like Clifford and Laird) and their worst relations with the hawks (like McNamara).

At first Weinberger's critics had their way; in the wake of Van Cleve's firing, congressional conservatives successfully pressured Reagan to name a number of anti-Soviet defense experts to top Pentagon positions to balance Carlucci and Taft. Reagan's new appointments included Richard Perle, a former aide to Senator Henry Jackson; Fred Iklé, who became Undersecretary of Defense for Policy; and a new Secretary of the Navy, John Lehman. All three were well-known pro-defense conservatives with similar backgrounds. Perle (dubbed "the Prince of Darkness" by the JCS staff) had helped design the 1974 restrictions on arms control negotiations that undermined Kissinger's move to strengthen détente; Iklé was a former defense analyst with the RAND Corporation; and Lehman was a rising young anti-détente conservative who had joined Perle in a defense consulting business during the Carter years.

With this new, but divided, defense team in place, Weinberger made his first, and by now traditional, trip to the tank on January 15, 1981. Like each of his predecessors, Weinberger hoped that this meeting would result in a close alliance between his office and the JCS. At first, it looked as if his hope would become reality; like Laird, Weinberger made sure to shake hands with each of the chiefs and their three-star deputies, to be precise, almost deferential, in his comments, and to invite the military leaders to be full partners in the new administration. Seating himself at the end of the conference table, Weinberger began the meeting on a formal note: "I have been asked to convey the regards of the next president of the United States and to assure you that this administration is committed to a strong defense." He then said he hoped that the JCS and his office would "find some common ground on the important issues that face the nation" and reassured those seated around him that "you will have full access to my office and to the president."

In a clear break with tradition, this meeting was attended by many of the new Pentagon appointees as well as a number of high-level assistant secretaries. In all, this first civilian-military meeting of the Reagan administration was witnessed by more than forty major Pentagon officials (a "full tank," as JCS officers say), a few of whom were holdovers from the Carter administration. The inclusion of officials besides the chiefs was alternately described as a "good sign," suggesting that there would be close relations between the civilian and military leaders, and a "bad omen," because it showed that Weinberger would not rely solely on the JCS for military advice. But the most important people in the room were clearly the members of the JCS. On Weinberger's left was the commandant of the Marines, Robert H. Barrow, flanked by his top military assistant. Next to Barrow was the Air Force chief of staff, the "father of the MX," Lew Allen. On Weinberger's right was Army Chief of Staff Edward C. Meyer, and next to him CNO Thomas Hayward. At the other end of the table was David Jones, beginning his third year as JCS chairman.

After Weinberger had pledged his cooperation with the military, Jones expressed confidence that relations between the JCS and the new civilian leaders would be "cordial and cooperative" and said that the JCS looked forward to working with Reagan. Unstated was the fact that all the JCS members had not only been appointed during Carter's presidency, they had also supported a number of Carter's more controversial foreign policy initiatives. The JCS had unanimously endorsed the ratification of the SALT II treaty, which Reagan had roundly criticized, and it supported Carter's decision not to fund the B-1 bomber. That Reagan publicly castigated the Carter administration for being naive about Soviet intentions wasn't lost on the chiefs, who were fearful that the topic might sour their first meeting with Weinberger. "In a lot of ways we were lame ducks," Meyer later reflected. "We had been there under Carter. So this was a new start. We didn't really know what to expect."

After Weinberger and Jones completed their ritual opening and response, many officials expected the meeting to be adjourned, for the hard work of hammering out a new defense policy would take place in smaller, more private, groups. Instead, Weinberger surprised everyone by launching into a detailed summary of the administration's foreign policy goals. In disarmingly specific terms — and much to the horror of his top assistants — he noted that the administration was commit-

ted to "defense growth" and "more defense dollars" to meet "the
growing menace of Soviet expansion." The United States would take
the offensive, he said, would make certain that the Soviet Union
understood that "we are a very real competitor."

Jones nodded, then smiled, anticipating that the new secretary
would soon finish his review. But "he went on and on," as one participant later commented, "saying that 'the United States is in a very poor
position vis-à-vis the Soviet Union' " and that the "situation would be
remedied immediately." With Jones continuing to nod in agreement,
Weinberger said that one of the first tasks of the JCS was to "close the
window of vulnerability," a term reflecting Reagan's campaign claim
that the Soviet Union was outstripping the United States in strategic
missile systems. Weinberger noted that if the nation did not begin a
massive strategic arms buildup soon, it would be "in grave peril."
Finally, Weinberger curtly and somewhat self-consciously nodded to
Jones for his response.

Taken aback by Weinberger's monologue, Jones said that he understood the administration's view and that he welcomed the secretary's
detailed analysis of the issues facing the JCS. For some of those in
attendance, it was clear that while Jones was growing more uncomfortable by the minute, he was also doing his best to accommodate
Weinberger's apparent need to bring any JCS disagreements with the
Reagan program into the open. Though Jones privately doubted that
the country faced a growing "window of vulnerability," he wanted to
make it clear that he didn't disagree with the new emphasis on
rebuilding American defenses. He wanted to make certain that Weinberger understood that the military supported the continuation of a
number of key weapons programs, noting the need to review funding
for the B-1, increase funding for the Navy Trident program, and
increase monies for Army readiness.

"Good," Weinberger said. "Now then, I suggest we get right to
work, and in that vein I have a proposal for your consideration." He
peered down at his papers, grabbed a pen, and looked back up at Jones.
Along the walls of the tank, a number of the new defense officials
began to look around uneasily. "I suddenly wondered if I should
leave," one later said, ruefully. "I wasn't cleared for this kind of discussion." Weinberger outlined his proposal. "Since we are required to
remedy our vulnerability in the strategic area," he said, "I suggest we
resolve the MX basing debate and the vulnerability of the rest of our
ICBM force here and now." The members of the JCS and their three-
star deputies were stunned. During the last years of the Carter administration, the nation had been debating the complex problem of hiding
the MX, of finding a "basing mode" that would make America's newest, heaviest, and most accurate missile "survivable." It was the kind

of knotty technical problem that wasn't going to be resolved in one short meeting.

"You want to discuss this now?" Jones reportedly asked. "Yes," Weinberger said. "At least we can get some initial ideas out on the table." Jones nodded agreeably, though reluctantly, as Weinberger took the floor. "I think one of the things we can do with our MXs is deploy them on ships," he said forcefully. "You know, we can do it with the cruise missile, why not with a Regular missile?" One of the deputy chiefs mouthed the phrase regular missile? Around the table the chiefs were starting to smile, at first in silent amusement and then, when it became apparent that the Secretary of Defense wasn't joking, in almost audible mirth. Weinberger didn't notice. "It's simple," he said. "In time of war, the ship's company just rolls the missiles off the decks of the ship, and gravity takes care of the rest." Weinberger rolled his hand over, then put it upright, the fingers together, pointing straight in the air, to show what he meant. "We move the ships around, you see, and they can't take the missiles out. The missiles right themselves in the water and blast off for the Soviet heartland."

The room was dead silent. The Air Force's Allen had turned to face Jones, his hand over his mouth, his eyebrows up, questioning. According to one civilian official at the meeting, no one seemed more surprised than CNO Hayward, who look straight at Weinberger in apparent disbelief, his jaw slack. Jones was "the most calm"; "he just kept looking down at the papers in front of him, leafing through them, like he was taking it very seriously." Jones nodded, looked down at his papers once again, then up at his colleagues before taking his own informal poll of Weinberger's proposal. "Well," he asked, "does anyone at this table support this idea?" The room remained embarrassingly silent. As one of the new assistant secretaries, Lawrence Korb, later described it: "Weinberger was sitting there looking as if he had just proposed something that would save America from the communist hordes, and the silence seemed to indicate they all agreed with him." Weinberger nodded in "a mix of pride and affirmation," according to another onlooker, and waited for the accolades.

Jones, in what must have been one of the most courageous acts of his long career, finally looked straight at Weinberger and said, "Well, I think this is the kind of idea that *Reader's Digest* would like." The comment startled the other chiefs, some of whom had to turn away to keep from laughing. There was open laughter from the back of the room. Weinberger stared at Jones, his anger apparent. "That happens to be where I get my medical advice," he said, and with that he put his papers back in his folder and stalked angrily from the tank. It had been one of the most embarrassing incidents between a new Secretary of Defense and the nation's military leaders, a meeting that rivaled some of the most bitter and tension-filled early moments of the McNamara regime.*

Weinberger's first meeting with the JCS ignited a vicious, though unpublicized, intergovernmental squabble, pitting Jones (and the other JCS lame ducks) against an increasingly hostile secretary in a competition to determine just who would design U.S. military policy. Within weeks, Weinberger convened a high-level meeting of government analysts at Washington's National Defense University to thrash out the new administration's military policies. But Weinberger apparently wasn't as interested in drafting a policy as he was in getting back at Jones for embarrassing him in front of almost every top official in the Pentagon. Not only wasn't the JCS invited to the conference, Weinberger also made it clear that he preferred receiving his military advice outside the JCS.

"Weinberger just hated Jones," Meyer later recalled. "Really despised him. That [the appointment of an outside strategy group] did it for me. I'd been in the Army all my life and knew a hell of a lot more about strategy — what forces we could commit where — than any group of nonmilitary people. So I almost resigned. I didn't because, really, the group was just set up to get Jones. And it was powerless, but really, that told me where Weinberger was coming from." The personal animosity between Weinberger and Jones soon became the talk of the Pentagon. "Jones just thought Weinberger was as crazy as you could get and tried at every turn to add some rationality to Weinberger's proposals," one former civilian defense official noted. "This isn't to say, mind you, that Jones tried to circumvent Weinberger. Jones was a good soldier and was totally loyal because that's what he'd been trained for. When Weinberger went up to the Hill, Jones supported him a hundred percent. It was something Weinberger could never understand, and so Weinberger hated him even more." Weinberger, in fact, wanted to get rid of Jones within weeks of taking over as Secretary of Defense and asked his civilian aides again and again to look into the possibility of pushing Jones to retirement. "When's his time up?" Weinberger asked one aide. When told it wasn't until 1982, he said, "Are you sure? Are you sure he won't retire?"

Despite Weinberger's almost public disdain for Jones and his early snub of JCS members, the chiefs decided they could learn to live with

---

* Weinberger next suggested that the MX be put on Air Force bombers. When this idea was spurned, he revived the "dense pack" theory, saying the MXs should be put next to each other in the desert. He liked the idea that incoming missiles would destroy each other during descent ("Just like bumper cars," one JCS officer noted). Eventually, fifty MXs were purchased, though a basing system to make them invulnerable continued to elude the Secretary of Defense. In 1983, the Scowcroft Commission decided they should be put in old Minuteman silos.

their new civilian boss, especially considering his effective advocacy
of increased defense spending. Soon after taking office, Weinberger
had set in motion the largest defense buildup in JCS history: the military would get not only its coveted MX but also a revived B-1 bomber
program, approval of a 600-ship Navy, and modernization of Army
weapons. Weinberger's victory had been effortless. After winning a
series of budget skirmishes with the apocalyptic wunderkind David
Stockman, the thirty-four-year-old director of the Office of Management and Budget, to increase defense spending by $32 billion, Wein-
berger went on to sell his program to a pliant Congress.

It was only the beginning: the full price tag for the buildup
amounted to a whopping $100 billion increase. In all, the Reagan revo-
lution in the Department of Defense accounted for more than $330 bil-
lion in real growth in military spending from 1981 to 1985, with one
quarter of the increases earmarked for modernization of three strategic weapons programs: the MX, the B-1, and the Trident II submarine
missile. Another quarter was set aside for procurement and research
and development. The chiefs' response to these increases was overwhelmingly positive; nearly all the JCS members had been advocating
just such a buildup since the end of the Vietnam War. Not all the JCS
officers, however, were pleased; even at this early point in the Reagan
era there were some disquieting and surprising notes of caution.

A number of JCS budget officers, for instance, were concerned that
Weinberger's massive budget increases would actually make it more
difficult for the military to defend budget increases into the 1990s. The
belief that defense growth should be slow but constant reached into
every part of the military. No one was more cautious than Jones himself, who was put in the unenviable position of having to defend what
he called "real growth" instead of "getting roller-coastered" by the
unwieldy outlays proposed by Weinberger. While Jones suppressed his
doubts and told Congress he agreed with the increases, his comments
on the buildup betrayed his fear that it would only be temporary. "I
testified . . . that I supported the defense increase because we had so
many requirements we needed to meet," Jones recalled later, "but that
the most important thing was to be able to sustain substantial growth
over the long term. I would rather have had moderate growth that
could be sustained than sharp growth that could not be sustained."

By mid-1981, the anti-Weinberger members of the JCS staff were
forced to admit that the new secretary had been able to accomplish
what none of his predecessors had even come close to realizing. They
were amazed by Weinberger's considerable ability to sell the administration's defense program to a suddenly agreeable Congress. Weinberger's avalanche of public appearances, his calm television
demeanor, and his apparent facility with defense issues (which he, in

fact, lacked) convinced Congress (and an initially reticent Reagan) that the Pentagon needed more money. JCS officers have been attempting to account for Weinberger's success ever since. The explanation might well rest in the pessimist's criticism of Weinberger; after all, the secretary was a talk show host (running a successful public affairs program on Los Angeles television for nine years), and he was a "quick study," asking aides to brief him on complex strategic issues only hours, and sometimes minutes, before appearing in a public forum.

These infallible public instincts served Weinberger well. Although he lacked a clear strategic vision and was not concerned with the daily management of the Pentagon (leaving it to his talented deputy, Frank Carlucci), he was able to use his considerable skills as a lobbyist and public relations practitioner as the Defense Department's most potent weapons advocate. With an uncanny talent for remembering numbers and complex arguments coupled with his disarming characteristic of ignoring criticism by repeating his major points, Weinberger was able to quickly forge a consensus on defense spending unequaled in military history. His strategy for dealing with Congress was almost maddeningly simple: he consistently overestimated Soviet capabilities while portraying America's military establishment as undermanned and underfunded.

On the other hand, this hard-charging style had its drawbacks. While Weinberger was able to win his defense spending increases during his first two years in office, he did so by sacrificing his relationship with the JCS. It's not that the JCS would have disagreed with his program of increases, it's that he took its point of view for granted, a slight so seemingly minor that it might not have made any difference had he had the personal characteristics of Laird or even Schlesinger. Within the first year of his tenure, most of the chiefs began to believe that he was everything the pessimists had said he would be — secretive, private, humorless, single-mindedly loyal to his own programs and policies. Eventually, even predictably, Weinberger's infallible public instincts were overmatched by his private failures, and his failure to gain the trust of the JCS would undo the defense increases he had so easily won.

Determining just what kinds of weapons the military should purchase and how much they should cost is one of the most complex and significant responsibilities of the JCS. With the possible exception of recommending the deployment of U.S. combat troops overseas, the annual wrestling match with the Pentagon budget represents the most volatile event in each JCS member's tenure. More politically charged than almost any other decision, more unwieldy than even the incredible labyrinth represented by the flimsy, buff, green procedure, the budget gives the JCS a unique opportunity to establish weapons and readiness priorities and to participate in molding the structure of the U.S. fighting forces. The JCS's budget procedure might well be a textbook on public policy-making: the system is designed to mesh national security goals, laid out by the nation's civilian leaders, with weapons and personnel designed to meet foreign threats, using forces structured by the JCS and led by the regional unified commanders.

In reality, however, the Pentagon's textbook procedure has evolved from the original budgeting system, one that purposely institutionalized service rivalry, put in place by McNamara in 1961. Called the Planning, Programming Budgeting System (or the PPBS in Pentagon shorthand), the process is designed to reconcile the services' competing desires with the overall military policy goals. It begins when the chiefs submit a Joint Strategic Planning Document to the Secretary of Defense, a paper that gives detailed recommendations on what military forces the JCS thinks it needs to defend the country. In fact, it's a military "wish list," an idealized statement of what forces the JCS would deploy to meet every military contingency, no matter what the cost. Using this document, the Secretary of Defense submits his initial Defense Guidance to the Defense Resources Board, the Pentagon's civilian-controlled budget committee, which is responsible for resolving interservice budget disputes and making final recommendations. The Secretary of Defense is central to the process; as the head of the Pentagon, he holds absolute veto power over any final decision by the resources board.

After resolving major service disputes, the Defense Resources Board submits a final Defense Guidance to the JCS, a planning document that gives a realistic and detailed assessment of just how much federal money Pentagon officials believe will be available to the JCS for programming military force structures. At this point, the real work begins. Using the Defense Guidance as their primary planning document, the individual services actually design, or "program," their service budgets, putting their final recommendations in a Program Objectives Memorandum (POM). The debates over the weapons and personnel to be included in the POMs involve weeks of intense study and argument, for the credibility of the final recommendations of each service rises and falls on the quality of research, the depth of argument, and the assessment of threats presented by service budget officers. The process is brutally competitive: the JCS evaluates each service's POM in detail, submitting its final budget report in a Joint Program Assessment Memorandum.

In theory, the Secretary of Defense is given full power to decide which specific requests will be accepted and passed on to the president for inclusion in the administration's final budget. In practice, however, the system is a hodgepodge of compromises, wish lists, unilateral decisions, and military logrolling that reflects political realities. Critics argue that, in effect, the JCS's budget process actually rewards service parochialism, exacerbates weapons cost overruns, causes service mission duplication, leads to poor service coordination, and, in the end, costs the taxpayer money. Dina Rasor, the head of Washington's Project on Military Procurement, agrees but points out that these budgeting problems became critical during the Weinberger era. "Procurement has totally corrupted the officer corps and everyone knows it," Rasor recalled. "Every once in a while we get a good soldier. But the problem is that every time one of these guys raises the problems plaguing the system, they don't go anywhere. So now what we have are K mart men — soldiers who spend their time shopping." A surprisingly large number of high-level defense officials who participated in the Reagan administration's budget process during the first two years of the Weinberger buildup agree with Rasor. They say that defense procurement under Weinberger became "a circus," that "it was grab what you could while the grabbing was good."

Such apparent gluttony was initially welcomed by the chiefs, who had traditionally been forced to fight for each of their programs under successive administrations. Under Truman, JCS arguments for a defense buildup had been short-circuited by the Korean War. Eisenhower's administration was dedicated to fiscal austerity. Under Kennedy and Johnson, the JCS saw its defense programs eviscerated by the maw of Vietnam. The Nixon and Ford chiefs faced public distaste for military programs, which dictated cuts in appropriations. Only during the last two years of the Carter administration was the JCS able to win approval of modest increases.

Reagan's election signaled the first time in JCS history that the military high command was able to promote a defense increase without large-scale opposition from any segment of the public or government; it had what the Army's Meyer called "our window of opportunity." The chiefs were able to initiate the defense buildup they had advocated since the end of the Vietnam War, and they started to plan a more rational system of defense procurement that would institutionalize the "slow but steady growth" envisioned by Chairman Jones. Unfortunately, the JCS officers soon learned that their plans for sustained growth were being victimized by Weinberger himself, who actually told them that he was less concerned with their budgetary plans than with each service's weapons programs. Budgeting thus became a secondary priority for Weinberger, a point he made clear soon after taking office. During the first week of February 1981, Weinberger told the services that while he would review their budget documents, they were "not to feel constrained by outside budget pressures" but "to give priority" to military programs they thought the nation needed. In effect, Weinberger threw out the JCS's budget planning documents and, with them, the entire PPBS system.

This same hands-off JCS budget policy began to dictate service budget programs; according to JCS officers, each service's POMs during Weinberger's first two years were "packed with everything you can think of" — what one naval officer imaginatively described as "greasing our POMs." The new policy wreaked havoc on the Pentagon's already chaotic defense procurement system. Service wish lists took the place of Joint Strategic Planning Documents, with budget plans "no more than POMs that were stapled together, one right on top of another." Weinberger's emphasis on service budget documents over the more rational, if flawed, JCS planning documents had other, more fearful, consequences, with services pushing peripheral weapons programs at the expense of manpower and readiness priorities.

There was another, more political, drawback to the buildup. Although the services could purchase the weapons previously denied them, it was clear that this newfound freedom also meant that they were forced to accept what was given, a disconcerting turn of events for JCS officers trying to structure forces to meet actual threats. If the budgeting process didn't mean anything — and it was becoming increasingly clear throughout 1981 that it didn't — then it was also clear that the Secretary of Defense could reorder military priorities as he saw fit, without the advice of the JCS. "Anyone can write up a wish list," one JCS budgeting officer said at the time. "There's nothing difficult about it. The elegance of a realistic PPBS system, for all its faults, is that it made the military choose. It made us careful. We're just not careful anymore; it's a binge."

However, the almost total eclipse of JCS influence on defense procurement policies during Weinberger's first months was only partly due to the secretary's eccentric method of deciding Pentagon budget priorities. Weinberger's admittedly few defenders pointed out, for instance, that determining just how much the military would spend and how it would spend it had as much to do with an administration's view of military strategy as it did with its view of the budgeting process. Accordingly, Weinberger's decision to consistently ignore the JCS in the budget-making process was more the result of a fundamental disagreement over the military strategy adopted by Reagan than it was a reflection of Weinberger's personal quirks. Weinberger abandoned the PPBS method not only because it undermined the administration's belief that the United States was falling behind the Soviet Union in the production of modern strategic systems, but also because it empowered the lame duck chiefs who had unanimously endorsed the SALT II treaty.

In this sense, defense budgets represent fundamental political philosophies and are symbols of strongly held political beliefs. Since the passage of the National Security Act of 1947, each administration has attempted to put its own stamp on the defense budget as a way of reordering priorities. The election of Kennedy in 1960, for instance, marked a sharp shift in priorities that emphasized the administration's concern that the U.S. military should be able to respond more effectively to the threat of Third World counterinsurgencies. Although Kennedy's budgets represented only a minor increase in defense spending over Eisenhower's budgets (discounting the Vietnam buildup), the subtle shifts in each service's budgets actually amounted to a significant redirection of national strategy: more total dollars were given over to Special Forces training and deployment than under any previous administration, though the shift represented a nearly minuscule percentage of the total defense appropriation. Similar subtle budget shifts occurred under Ford and Carter: the Ford administration emphasized naval modernization; Carter emphasized increased funding for NATO readiness.

There is a precise relationship between military strategies (the Ridgway-Taylor flexible response doctrine being the most obvious case) and defense budget priorities. More important, the existence of this relationship is fundamental to understanding the role of the JCS in determining military policy. The promotion of a flag rank officer to a service chief might appear to be mere happenstance, but in reality each president has molded the JCS to suit his own strategic philosophy. Eisenhower picked Arthur Radford as JCS chairman because he agreed with the doctrine of massive retaliation. Kennedy replaced Lyman Lemnitzer, a "NATO-ist," with Maxwell Taylor, whose own flexible response doctrine fit more easily with Kennedy's interest in fighting counterinsurgencies. The same held true for Nixon, who felt most comfortable with the hawkish Thomas Moorer, and Carter, whose brainy Defense Secretary got on well with the equally brainy George Brown and, later, the intense David Jones. In each case, the nation's civilian leaders had been able to gain JCS acceptance of each administration's strategic philosophy.

But in August 1981, just five months after Weinberger had won passage of his $32 billion defense increase, it became clear that the relationship between the administration's strategic views and the JCS had suffered perhaps the most critical collapse since 1967. The last week of August, Weinberger issued his fiscal year 1984 Defense Guidance, which shocked the JCS. For one thing, it failed to lay out a detailed budget plan for the new administration; for another, it reflected a defense strategy that few, if any, JCS members agreed with. Weinberger's budget wasn't a defense guide at all but a strategy statement that told the JCS to design forces that could "prevail" in a "protracted nuclear conflict," which administration officials envisioned might stretch over many months.

It was one of the most controversial ideas the JCS had ever seen. In a series of meetings throughout the fall, JCS members debated Weinberger's Defense Guidance, attempting to mesh its wide-ranging recommendations — Weinberger told the JCS to plan forces that could meet a Soviet conventional threat anywhere in the world as well as forces that would participate in Third World conflicts — with their own views of what kind of defense buildup was needed.* One result was a JCS document that detailed the kinds of forces the JCS believed were needed to meet Weinberger's ambitious program, an exercise in one-upsmanship that angered the Defense Secretary. In a document completed at the beginning of September, the JCS said it could meet the goals in the Defense Guidance by increasing Army divisions (from 16 to 23), by building 9 more aircraft carriers (from 15 to 24), and by nearly doubling the number of Air Force tactical wings (from 24 to 44).

This tongue-in-cheek response did not, however, result in outright opposition to the administration's defense plans, though it is now clear that two of the chiefs, Jones and Meyer, considered making public their doubts about the administration's more aggressive and expensive military strategy. Only Meyer decided to raise, albeit obliquely, the prospect of a clear military-civilian break over national military strategy during a public address on the Reagan program on September 24. His words were measured, cautious, and well crafted, the sole public hint that there were high-level disagreements. "There has, and was, and continues to be a differential between the strategy we've announced for the nation and the capabilities of the forces we have to respond to that strategy," he said. He noted that failure to address the "differential" could result in "the president and the leadership of our nation proposing ways in which they will go about national security without the military strength to back it up." Nevertheless, neither Jones nor Meyer decided to actually break with the proposed strategy, preferring instead to debate its merits in administration circles.

The first such debate took place just as the JCS finished its meetings on the August Defense Guidance. At the end of September, it became involved in an internal Pentagon debate over whether it should endorse what Weinberger called "a strategic modernization program"

---

* The Defense Guidance institutionalized what has come to be known as "horizontal escalation," a doctrine designed to defend Western interests by aggressively responding to a Soviet attack. As the Guidance itself noted, "Counteroffensives will be directed at places where we can affect the outcome of the war. If it is to offset the enemy's attack it should be launched against territory or assets that are of an importance to him comparable to the ones he is attacking."

that would close the "window of vulnerability" that Reagan claimed existed between U.S. and Soviet nuclear forces. Throughout September, Weinberger had pushed the JCS to agree on an across-the-board buildup of strategic nuclear systems, the centerpiece of which would be the MX missile. Under normal circumstances, the JCS might be expected to endorse such a proposal, but after the August Defense Guidance was issued, the JCS had begun to rethink its initial glee at Weinberger's program of increased defense spending. While the chiefs eventually endorsed the modernization plan (their decision coming just days before its formal announcement, on October 2, 1981), they did so hesitantly, realizing that it would cost close to $100 billion.

The JCS's hesitation led to immediate problems for the defense budget on Capitol Hill. Even the normally pro-defense chairman of the Senate Armed Services Committee, John Tower of Texas, castigated Weinberger for presenting a program that would leave other, nonstrategic programs underfunded. "The impression has been left that many important aspects of the president's strategic modernization agenda are as yet undefined, are undergoing continuing review, or are subject to debate and confusion within the executive branch," he said. Nor was the situation helped by the details of the plan, which included increased funding for the MX missile, the revival of the B-1 bomber, research funds for an experimental and undetectable "Stealth bomber," increased appropriations for a fleet of cruise missiles, funds for the Trident D-5 submarine missile, and even funding for an expanded civil defense program.

The JCS was even more fearful that the Weinberger buildup would overwhelm other budget considerations. Specifically, the chiefs were increasingly concerned that it would threaten combat support functions, drawing down funds for the military's low-profile but essential programs designed to improve readiness, command, control, communications, transport, supply, reinforcement, and military living conditions. Still, criticism of Weinberger's program and the administration's strategic views behind it remained firmly locked within the four walls of the tank. The JCS was not yet ready to break publicly with either Weinberger or Reagan over the budget, perhaps out of fear that it would mean an end to some of the services' more cherished weapons programs.

The JCS's silent hesitation even survived one of Reagan's more controversial statements on nuclear war. During a talk with reporters on October 16, Reagan hypothesized a limited nuclear conflict confined to a European battlefield: "I could see where you could have the exchange of tactical [atomic] weapons against troops in the field without it bringing either one of the major parties to pushing the button." The statement sent shudders through the Pentagon's military command ring, where JCS opposition to the administration's strategy was growing. Reagan's statement of October 16 was followed by an even more controversial discussion by Weinberger, who was asked on a national television show whether he believed a nuclear conflict could be isolated. "It is possible that with nuclear weapons there can be some use of them," he said, "in a connection with what is up to that time war solely within a European theater."

Still, the JCS refused to be critical until Reagan himself had taken steps to institutionalize the strategy as part of American defense policy. The first break came in February 1982, when the president directed the NSC to conduct a major study of defense strategy that would provide an assessment of U.S. nuclear capabilities. The study, under only nominal NSC direction, was actually undertaken at the urging of Pentagon hawks, who viewed the JCS as an impediment to a major weapons buildup. Reagan appointed the Pentagon's Undersecretary of Defense for Policy, Fred Iklé — a former official at the RAND Corporation and a "bona fide expert on nuclear strategy and arms control" — to head the study. Over the course of four months, the Iklé group met regularly to discuss U.S. nuclear options, even though, according to JCS officers, there was never any real doubt about what it would finally recommend.

The group's findings were issued that May as part of a "top secret strategy directive" to the JCS. Known thereafter as NSDD 32, the broad strategy paper instructed the JCS to draw up contingency plans to win a protracted nuclear conflict. For JCS Chairman Jones, NSDD 32 was the symbol of everything that was wrong with the administration's defense policies: not only were Reagan and Weinberger sacrificing steady, long-term defense spending goals for dubious, short-term gains, they were also ignoring the expertise of the military, a policy that convinced Jones he needed to disagree publicly. Within days of receiving the Reagan directive, Jones was telling defense reporters that he didn't believe the United States could prevail in a nuclear conflict: "If you try to do everything to fight a protracted nuclear war, then you end up with the potential of a bottomless pit." He was blunt: "We can't do everything. I personally would not spend a lot of money on a protracted nuclear war."

Jones's harsh words marked the first real public break between the military and the civilian hawks. Already considered one of the most controversial chiefs and condemned by many of his colleagues as a "real manipulator," Jones won himself yet another set of formidable enemies, including a group of powerful retired officers who had already had a profound impact on the administration's military policies. During Reagan's first year, it became generally acknowledged among JCS officers that the president's policies were heavily influenced by a group of retired naval officers, "Reagan's Admirals," which included an unlikely but allied pair of former CNOs — Moorer and Zumwalt. These unofficial advisers had first met in 1976 to form the Committee on the Present Danger, a bipartisan, conservative group of defense analysts in Washington who believed the United States was becoming increasingly vulnerable to an expansionist Soviet military policy. Within three years, the committee became a formidable pro-defense lobbying group with a broad network of Washington contacts.

Joining Moorer and Zumwalt were former Johnson official Eugene Rostow, Henry Fowler, a former Secretary of the Treasury; David Packard, Laird's Deputy Defense Secretary and an old strategic guru; and Zumwalt's patron, Paul Nitze. The committee's program for rearming the United States reads like the introduction to Nitze's 1952 NSC paper, which warned of an imminent Soviet military buildup. The U.S. opposition to Soviet expansion is more than a simple competition, the group's literature reads, it involves a last defense of the free world against Soviet expansionism, with its avowed internationalist strategy of undermining U.S. security interests worldwide. There's little doubt that the committee's members were valuable in selling Reagan's program of defense budget increases. During his first term, the president appointed a number of committee members — Jeane Kirkpatrick, Kenneth Adelman, and George Shultz — to major administration positions. More important still, as a longtime member of the committee, Reagan was significantly influenced and impressed by the pro-defense arguments presented by the former military officers in its ranks.

While Jones knew that the Committee on the Present Danger and "Reagan's Admirals" were playing a significant part in the administration's decision-making process, he seemed powerless to formulate a strategy that would reassert the JCS's role as the nation's primary strategic body. After his critical remarks, designing such a strategy seemed impossible; Jones had made enemies of Reagan's closest allies and was only months away from retirement. In just sixty days, however, the JCS chairman took two steps that eventually destroyed the stranglehold that defense conservatives maintained in the administration's inner circles. First, he gained a stunning and unexpected JCS victory by reversing a critical administration arms initiative. Second, he ignited a bitter feud over the question of military reform, an issue that was to become a bloody, four-year battleground that pitted Weinberger and a group of influential defense conservatives against a coalition of officers and reform-minded civilian analysts.

By the time NSDD 32 was released, the administration had already been through some of its most vicious debates over the value of engaging in any arms negotiations with the Soviet Union. The first round of this debate, over whether the United States should deploy Pershing II missiles as a counter to Soviet missiles in Europe, was won by administration moderates, led by Secretary of State Alexander Haig and his assistant, Lawrence Eagleburger. This victory was the result of Reagan's early endorsement of Haig's "dual track" strategy, requiring the United States to deploy the Pershing II missiles as a way of wringing arms control concessions from the Soviets. Reagan's decision was a major victory for the State Department and a clear defeat for the anti–arms control cabal in the Pentagon.

It was a symbol of those times that Haig and Eagleburger were considered moderates: both were nuclear arms experts and had served under Kissinger on Nixon's NSC. Haig had gained his experience as head of U.S. troops in NATO, a command he had taken over from the highly respected Goodpaster.* Eagleburger had made his career as a Washington insider, a diplomat who knew all about arms control but was bored by the excessively detailed explanations of nuclear strategists. By the time Reagan took office, Eagleburger was the State Department's leading expert on the intricacies of dealing with U.S. allies in Europe. Both men believed in conducting ongoing arms control negotiations, an almost unheard-of position during the early Reagan days.

On the other hand, the administration's most influential defense conservatives, Perle and Iklé, were convinced that the Soviet Union was on the edge of a strategic "breakout," a massive technological breakthrough that would give them nuclear superiority. "Their philosophy of arms control is real simple — they sit down across from the Soviets and say, 'We win, you lose, sign here,' " noted retired Admiral Eugene Carroll. His description fit Perle — thoughtful, self-assured, intellectually daring — perfectly. His idea of a good arms control agreement was one that would provide for a massive cut in Soviet weapons without a compensatory cut in the U.S. arsenal, what he called "supply-side arms control." Iklé had similar beliefs. Iklé, too, thought that the Soviet Union was on the edge of a technological "breakout," and he was the administration's expert on Soviet violations of previous arms treaties, an expertise he took pleasure in flaunting before members of the JCS.

These two groups dominated the administration debate over arms control throughout 1981 and 1982, which was primarily concerned with whether the United States should deploy its Pershing II missiles in

---

* When Haig took over the Army's top post in Europe, Goodpaster refused to attend the change-of-command ceremony. According to his former aides, Goodpaster considered Haig intellectually inferior, a feeling that may well be communicated by Haig himself. The Secretary of State once referred to Europe as "the vortex of cruciality."

Europe. The State Department's moderates favored deployment because they believed it would convince the Soviets to take a more serious stance on a full package of arms proposals. The conservatives, however, actually opposed deployment, arguing that the Pershing IIs were unnecessary in Europe and only added more targets for Soviet missiles. Both positions were transformed by West German Premier Helmut Schmidt's proposal for a "zero option," a tradeoff that would keep the Pershing IIs out of Europe in exchange for a cut in Soviet SS-20 missiles, which the Pershings were designed to counter.

Haig's response to Schmidt was surprisingly lukewarm. Fearful of being painted as a liberal on arms control, Haig only grudgingly endorsed the proposal as an "ideal," leaving the distinct impression that the United States would settle for something far less than the total elimination of all Soviet SS-20s. Seeing a chance to flank Haig's arms control position and at the same time embarrass the Secretary of State, Perle drafted his own paper on arms control for Weinberger. It was a deft political maneuver: he proposed that the United States forgo deployment of the Pershings in exchange for a Soviet agreement to dismantle all of its SS-20s, what he called the "zero only" option. The paper sparked an immediate debate between the Haig moderates and the Pentagon conservatives; the State Department argued that Perle's proposal should include elimination of only the largest Soviet missiles, while the Pentagon group wanted to eliminate every Soviet missile with a range in excess of 800 kilometers — not just the SS-20s, but three entire classes of Soviet missiles.

The JCS, a mere onlooker in the Haig-Perle debate to this point, finally became involved during a series of meetings at the end of 1981. Almost every JCS member (only CNO Hayward hesitated) believed that the military should support Haig's philosophy: it would be impossible to negotiate the total elimination of Soviet missiles from Europe; moreover, such elimination might actually be dangerous. U.S. conventional forces, the JCS contended, were critically outmanned and outgunned in Europe, a fact made clear by the shrill demands of the NATO commander, General Bernard Rogers, for more weapons, ammunition, and tanks. Nor were JCS members convinced that Perle's zero only option would leave other valuable weapons programs in place. Jones, in particular, saw no reason that Perle would be restrained from bartering away most of the American arsenal. If he was willing to throw all of the Soviet Union's East European missiles onto the bargaining table at Geneva, he might also include the U.S. military's high-tech fighters and long-range bombers.

Soon, there was an even better reason for endorsing Haig's proposal — at least for the JCS. In the late summer of 1981, Jones knew, Perle's zero only option had gained the support of Weinberger, which baffled

Jones. As he told his staff, it meant that Weinberger supported scrapping an entire missile program at the same time that the nation was in the midst of one of the largest defense buildups in American history, which Weinberger himself had helped to sell to Congress. For Jones, Weinberger's position was the height of hypocrisy; the JCS had been castigated by administration insiders for its support of strategic arms limitations during the Carter years because they provided no real cuts in the superpowers' nuclear arsenals. Now it was being asked to do the exact same thing: promote arms control while building an increasing number of strategic weapons. While Jones would never have supported Haig just to get back at Weinberger (it was bad enough that the JCS was in league with the man who had caused so much trouble for Moorer back in the early 1970s), he was willing to oppose Weinberger's endorsement of the Perle proposal because he knew the secretary had contradicted his own position on defense modernization.

Perle was enraged by the JCS's decision to support Haig's "zero plus" position and took immediate steps to force the JCS into the Pentagon's corner. According to reporter Strobe Talbott, Perle "had Weinberger lay down the law to General David Jones." It was blackmail: Weinberger told Jones to "get on board" the Perle proposal in order to present a united front — either that, or sacrifice one of the military's traditional and nearly sacred arms control positions, that U.S. strategic bombers and high-tech fighters would not be considered "negotiable weapons" during any Soviet-American arms talks. When the JCS still hesitated, Perle told Admiral Robert Austin, the JCS's representative on the arms control policy committee, that the administration would consider bombers as weapons "open to negotiation" if Jones and his colleagues continued to support Haig.

Embittered by Perle's blackmail, angered by Weinberger's easy agreement with "the Prince of Darkness," and now all but convinced that it was a pawn in the intramural contest pitting conservatives against moderates, the JCS believed it had little choice. After a series of meetings with Weinberger and Perle in December 1981, it knuckled under to the Pentagon's position, agreeing to support Perle's zero only option. Perle, never a gracious victor, was disdainful of the chiefs, commenting that they were "pushovers and patsies for whoever leans on them the last, the longest, and the hardest."

Stung by the concession, JCS Chairman Jones continued to search for a way to align the military's moderate views of arms limitations with similar views held by arms control experts in the State Department. Eventually, he believed, the Pentagon would have to concede that its arms control strategy contradicted its plans for nuclear modernization, but until the administration actually developed strategic plans, the policy contradiction wouldn't be apparent. Finally, in May

1982, Jones got his chance: by issuing NSDD 32, he realized that the administration had inadvertently tipped its hand. By ordering the JCS to develop plans that would make the United States victorious in a protracted nuclear conflict, the administration was admitting that its nuclear modernization plan could be dismantled before it became a reality. In the words of one JCS member, "We were being told by our commander in chief to be ready, on a moment's notice, to destroy all the Soviet Union — everything, everywhere, of any conceivable consequence, of time-urgent value. At the same time we were supposed to climb on board the [arms] reductions bandwagon."

In other words, the JCS was being asked to endorse two contradictory proposals, a nuclear modernization program that would emphasize the deployment of new strategic systems and a strategic arms reduction proposal (called START) that advocated building systems that might eventually be dismantled. While Perle, Weinberger, and even Haig might argue that modernization helped to get the Soviet Union to the negotiating table, Jones realized that Perle's program meant that the JCS would be unable to carry out the recommendations in the Weinberger Defense Guidance. The JCS felt that Perle's proposal invited disaster: by accepting fewer warheads without a tradeoff in fewer targets, the American military would actually be conceding a measure of nuclear superiority to the Soviet Union. This time, Jones vowed, the JCS would not be blackmailed into changing its position. "Secretary Weinberger thinks we capitulated to Harold Brown by supporting him on SALT," he said, "so he thinks now all he has to do is make us capitulate to him on START."

Once again, the arms control moderates in the State Department sided with the JCS against Weinberger, Perle, and Iklé, arguing that under any new U.S. arms agreement, warheads had to be able to "cover all possible Soviet targets" — the ratio of warheads to targets had to be exact. "It was more than that," one JCS officer later reflected. "What the JCS was saying was that Perle either had to change his position on arms control or Weinberger had to change the Defense Guidance. I think it [the JCS strategy] was really a slap at the Defense Guidance. Jones wanted to send a message to Weinberger: 'If you want us to defend the world, then don't take a position that will negotiate away our weapons.'" Jones's strategy worked; an around-the-clock NSC meeting on the U.S. arms position in May 1982 not only affirmed the JCS's position, it also undermined the value of Weinberger's aggressive strategy. By the end of May, the administration had accepted the NSC's recommendations on the new U.S. arms reduction position, giving the JCS its first arms control victory in the Reagan administration. Reagan's START proposal accepted a ceiling of 5,000 ballistic warheads, 2,500 ICBM warheads, and 850 launchers. There

were more controversial proposals as well. To meet the levels designated by the Americans, the Soviets would have to agree to reduce
their SS-18 (their heaviest missile) force by two thirds, their SS-19 force
by more than half, and eliminate their SS-17s. More critical, however,
at least from the JCS point of view, the JCS-State proposal allowed the
military to retain its most important new strategic system, the MX
missile.

After nearly eighteen months of struggle between the State Department's arms control moderates and Perle and his Pentagon conservatives, the administration's final policy had ended up being almost
solely dependent on the JCS's position on missile cuts. Much to Perle's
chagrin, the lame duck JCS had become an indispensable player in the
arms control debate, as important to Reagan's attempt to spur a new
arms control exchange with the Soviet Union as either Haig or Perle.
The fact that the Soviet Union abruptly walked out of the Geneva
START talks just months after Jones's arms control victory does not
detract from Jones's impact on the process. Jones's victory reasserted
the JCS's role as one of the nation's primary arms control players. JCS
officers later speculated that the U.S. position on arms reduction was a
secondary concern for the chairman; Jones, they said, was interested
not only in reasserting JCS power but also in undermining the Weinberger and Perle influence in administration circles, an essential step
in building a reasonable consensus on arms control.

Some of Jones's flag rank colleagues saw the chairman's decision to
oppose Weinberger and Perle as a courageous act, a tacit admission
that, in the words of Meyer, "Jones knew that deterrence is all we
have, that it couldn't be sacrificed to politics," and that "there had to
be a way to bring the administration back into the mainstream of arms
reductions." But for others, mostly flag rank officers who believed
that Reagan never had any intention of bargaining in good faith,
Jones's decision to "play politics with nuclear weapons" was far worse
than "all show and no substance," it betrayed the JCS's role as
defender of the national security. Jones "is the most manipulative bastard, cynical, self-aggrandizing man I've ever met," one three-star
officer observed in the wake of Jones's victory. "He put his own position out there, but he didn't believe a word of it." Now retired, Jones
is much less outspoken in his own defense. "I don't want to get into
personalities; that's one thing I have to make sure not to do," he said
in 1986. "I just thought that there had to be some way to stabilize the
nuclear buildup. If we continue to show mixed signals [in the Reagan
administration], we're going to pay a price."

Through the first five months of 1982, at the same time that Jones and
the rest of the JCS were taking steps to assert their central role in
determining the administration's final arms control position, the JCS

chairman and Army Chief of Staff Meyer were also engaged in a bitter feud with Weinberger over a series of legislative programs that, if enacted, would change the face of the military forever. The Jones-Meyer initiatives were designed to strengthen the office of the JCS, end service budget disputes, increase the power of unified commanders, and, most important, give the JCS chairman a greater role in determining policy by making him a member of the NSC. The military reform issue bared the full impact of the Jones-Weinberger struggle over defense policy and represented the most critical civilian-military split since the days of Earle Wheeler.

Jones had first launched the campaign for military reform during the last years of the Carter administration, when he spoke at length on the subject with Defense Secretary Harold Brown. While nothing came of these discussions, Brown told Jones to make whatever internal reforms in the JCS system he thought necessary. But they weren't enough. "We were able to make some marginal changes," Jones later noted, "but because it [full JCS reform] needed concurrence of all services and all chiefs, the changes were at the margins. So then I concluded Admiral Mahan was right when he said no military service could reorganize itself, the pressure had to come from outside." Jones made a second attempt to gain official endorsement for reform in the early days of the Reagan administration, but again the changes he recommended were sidetracked. The major obstacle in 1981, however, wasn't the JCS system but the new Secretary of Defense. "Weinberger was opposed to it," Meyer said later. "But I told him that he would lose, that he had better get out in front of it because actually it wouldn't hurt him, it would strengthen his position. But he couldn't see that, or wouldn't admit it."

Frustrated by the lack of support and fearful that he would be unable to initiate any changes in the JCS before he retired, Jones decided to promote his ideas from within by establishing a JCS committee in March 1981, just sixty days after Weinberger said that reform was out of the question. Jones appointed five officers and one civilian to a Special Study Group to assess "the effectiveness of the JCS organization and its procedures" and recommend changes in its operation.* But the real campaign for change was ignited by Jones himself, in March 1982, when he published a critique of the organization in a national management magazine. This article, "Why the Joint Chiefs of Staff Must Change," anticipated the Special Study Group's find-

---

* The Special Study Group comprised General William V. McBride, USAF (ret.), General Walter T. Kerwin, USA (ret.), Admiral Frederick H. Michaelis, USN (ret.), General Samuel Jaskilka, USMC (ret.), Lieutenant General Charles A. Corcoran, USA (ret.), and William K. Brehm, former Assistant Secretary of Defense. With the exception of Brehm, it was the same team Jones had chosen as analysts for the REFORGER exercise Nifty Nugget.

ings. "Without stronger and better support for the Chairman," Jones
wrote, "the work of the Joint Chiefs is likely to remain too dispersed,
diluted, and diffused to provide the best possible military advice or to
insure the full capability of our combatant forces."

Weinberger was enraged by the article, which he believed would
undermine his authority and indirectly spur congressional questioning of defense budget increases. He was even more enraged, however,
by Jones's ability to bring his proposals into a public forum, a goal the
JCS chairman accomplished by convincing the House Armed Services
Committee to hold hearings on military reform in April 1982, just days
after the Special Study Group published its recommendations for a
wide range of reorganization proposals. At least part of the reason the
House decided to go along with Jones's plan was its growing concern
that Weinberger's program of budget increases was doing little to
resolve what many House members considered the military's inability
to formulate a command structure able to respond to an international
crisis. Many members of the committee were also privately beginning
to doubt that the Weinberger buildup was actually buying the nation
extra security.

"I think the problem in the Reagan budget is simply that people are
going to think that now we're prepared militarily simply because
we've bought into the MX missile and the B-1 bomber," House Armed
Services aide Arch Barrett said. "And the truth is that we're not prepared." His views were endorsed by many of the committee's most
influential members, including one of its most powerful voices, Les
Aspin of Wisconsin. He was not only unsure that the buildup
increased preparedness, he was also beginning to believe that it sacrificed readiness. By April 1982, he was willing to support Jones's proposals and had decided to write his own reform proposal as well, one
that would begin by cutting back the topheavy Weinberger Defense
Department. Jones's article was embraced by the House committee as
a way of kicking off a broad debate on everything from military
reform to Defense Department *reorganization*, two often inter-
changeable words that eventually came to imply a complete overhaul
of Defense. The fact that a JCS chairman had taken the lead in promoting reform also reinforced congressional arguments that the move had
"come from within," that it wasn't a political ploy aimed at undermining Weinberger.

Jones's task was formidable: although congressional leaders were
convinced that the military needed a general overhaul, the long process of gaining passage of such legislation was by no means assured.
Jones needed to do more than just write an article, convene a Special
Study Group, or convince House Armed Services Committee leaders
to call a hearing; he needed allies. In the highly charged political

atmosphere of Washington, it's almost always more important to gain a consensus on an issue than it is to become a principled lone warrior. In Jones's case, it was all the more important; Weinberger's opposition to any type of reform could prove almost insurmountable. Fortunately, Jones's concern had piqued the curiosity of Meyer, the outspoken Army chief.

Meyer, a bright West Point graduate with a stellar record as a combat commander, had had personal experience as a JCS infighter: he had been a close associate of General Harold Johnson during the Vietnam years and had served two terms as Army chief. He had also experienced the sometimes stormy relationship between civilians and military officers at first hand: his 1979 comment that the United States was fielding "a hollow Army," for instance, had so angered Carter that Brown had called Meyer to his office and demanded a public apology. Meyer, remembering Johnson's experience as Army chief ("I think Vietnam just killed him, really"), told Brown that he would resign or be fired, but he would not retract his statement. "You know, we have a responsibility to the Congress, too; we don't just serve at the behest of the Secretary of Defense," he said. Brown backed down and the statement stood — a valuable lesson for Meyer, who wasn't about to be intimidated by Weinberger's opposition. He supported Jones from the very beginning. Not only did he push his own reform proposals during a number of notably chilly JCS meetings in late 1981, he also wrote an article on reform that came out the same week as Jones's.

Jones and Meyer made a powerful pair. They were respected on Capitol Hill as the most influential members of the JCS, officers who represented two major services and who, with a combined twelve years of service in the Pentagon, symbolized the essence of military leadership. All they had to do was to convince powerful civilian leaders — except, of course, Weinberger — that a broad legislative program of military reform was in the national interest. For that, House committee members realized, Jones and Meyer needed the support of Washington's civilian establishment, including some of the most respected national security thinkers in the nation. Fortunately, and quite by accident, committee members learned just before the April hearings that the new Franklin D. Roosevelt Center for American Policy Studies, a Washington think tank, had begun an independent assessment of the nation's defense establishment.

The Roosevelt Center's study was headed by two well-known insiders, Barry Blechmann and Doug Bennett, who were attracted to the issue because they realized it was bound to be one of Washington's hottest topics. If the fledgling center could take the lead in studying the issue, they thought, it would both provide an invaluable public service and give the new group increased visibility. The center's willingness to undertake this study was a definite plus for Jones and Meyer, giving their recommendations the imprimatur of credibility they would have lacked had the proposals won the support only of reform-minded officers.

That military reform was a hot topic was apparent from the first day of the House hearings, April 21, 1982. It was a full-court press: Aspin had made the issue a top priority of the 97th Congress. The lead was taken first, however, by the low-profile House Armed Services Investigations Subcommittee, on which Aspin purposely played a secondary role to pro-reform Richard White and Dan Daniel — a bit of political engineering designed to keep the volatile issue from becoming a cause célèbre for the expected anti-reform forces, already being marshaled by Weinberger. As expected, Jones and Meyer were the first officers to testify. They emphasized the central role of the JCS in the defense establishment and recommended changes in its structure.

"I believe we have to increase the role of the chairman so that he is the provider of military advice concerning interservice capabilities and requirements and the provider of advice on operational matters," Meyer said. He advocated the passage of revolutionary legislation that would give the JCS chairman added power while dampening the role of the Secretary of Defense in actual military planning. During one incautious moment, Meyer even took a slap at Weinberger: "We are doing the best we can, sitting around that table. But you must remember that as you look at the Armed Forces today — I don't care which of the services you look at — each one of us sees very severe shortages, either in people or in modernization or in the ability to be able to carry out the tasks we have been directed to perform." The observation passed without comment, though it must have come as a distinct shock that the Army's chief believed that the Weinberger buildup had failed to increase military readiness.

Jones followed Meyer with recommendations that were even more radical, including a detailed rewriting of the 1947 National Security Act that named the JCS chairman as the "principal military adviser to the President, the National Security Council, and the Secretary of Defense." What Jones envisioned was nothing less than an end to the collegial, consensus-driven Office of the JCS; the JCS chairman, served by an independent joint staff and a deputy chairman, would be solely responsible for "oversight of the unified and specified commands." Jones ended with a clear warning. "I am convinced we will reorganize," he said. "The question is whether we do it with foresight in a measured way or whether we will do it after some crisis or conflict when we find we don't have the right organization."

The testimony of Meyer and Jones brought howls of protest from the Pentagon, including a comment from Secretary of the Navy John

Lehman that "the Russians will be happy to hear about this," a remark that was to be repeated with vicious regularity until well into Reagan's second term. Other reactions were just as strident; Weinberger told aides he would fight the proposal "with everything I have" and reportedly ordered his top deputies to begin organizing the opposition. It wasn't difficult: within weeks a coterie of Navy officers, including former CNOs Thomas Moorer and James Holloway, had organized a large group of retired officers to speak out against the reforms. "I don't think it's any secret that I strongly opposed this thing," Holloway noted later. "It all came out of an article Davey Jones did in '82 — that was the beginning of it. He backed reform, and I absolutely opposed what he was proposing."

Moorer was just as strident. "As soon as I heard it I couldn't believe it," he said. "This Jones character — just take a look at his record. Every time he's had a command he's tried to reorganize it. It's the most self-serving proposal I've ever heard. It won't do anything. It wouldn't have solved the problem in 1967 or 1973 and it won't solve the problems now." In April 1982, Moorer's and Holloway's arguments had a numbing impact on congressional reform proponents. Moorer scoffed at the idea that the JCS chairman should sit in on NSC meetings. "What if the president doesn't want him there?" he said. "That's meaningless, just a piece of fluff. If the president doesn't want the chairman of the Joint Chiefs there, he'll convene an NSC meeting and call it a prayer breakfast." Holloway was more tactful, giving House subcommittee aides a detailed analysis of Jones's proposal that dampened its growing support. "Adding a deputy chairman just adds another layer," he said. "The collegial group works and works well. All you're going to do is give the unified commanders another layer of administrators."

This opposition had the desired effect. While Aspin and his allies in the House continued to hold hearings, it was clear that it would no longer be possible to pass a comprehensive reform package in the 97th Congress. By June, Aspin had other problems; not only was Jones on the verge of retirement, his Senate colleagues were unwilling to take even the most elementary steps to push the legislative initiative. The newest obstacle was the chairman of the Senate Armed Services Committee, John Tower, who was unwilling to offend Weinberger, reportedly because he believed he had a better chance of succeeding Weinberger as Defense Secretary if he didn't oppose the administration.

Even more critical was the collapse of the reform study. The Roosevelt Center was unable to keep going because of organizational problems and personality conflicts. Its demise meant that proponents of reform lacked a forum for further study outside the government. It was a heavy blow: Jones and Meyer realized that passage of military reform now meant engaging in a lengthy political battle. When Jones retired, in June, his worst fears seemed to be realized: JCS reorganization and military reform would not come "with foresight" but only "after some crisis or conflict." In the end, reform would come not through legislation but after one of the worst debacles in American military history.

At the beginning of June 1982, the Army's vice chief of staff, General John W. Vessey, Jr., went home to Garrison, Minnesota, intent on easing into a well-deserved retirement. He had built a reputation for stalwart honesty and service loyalty and was considered one of the best officers the Army had ever produced, with a command record unrivaled by any of his colleagues. Vessey enlisted in the Army because, as he noted, "they told me I could ride a motorcycle." Instead, he ended up as a common foot soldier in the 34th Division, facing the German Wehrmacht in North Africa and Italy. In May 1944 he was made a lieutenant without fanfare or choice: he was one of the few combat soldiers left alive in his unit on Anzio beach in Italy. "It didn't seem like the right time to protest," he later said.

The new officer stayed in the military through the Italian campaign, then through two tours with the famed 3rd Armored Division in Germany, where he was promoted steadily. In Vietnam, he served with the 25th Division and afterward commanded the 4th Infantry Division before being named deputy chief of staff for operations and plans (one of the "little chiefs") at the JCS. In the late 1970s, he served as commander in chief of American forces in Korea before being promoted to serve as Meyer's vice chief in July 1979. His career, his commands, his experience, and his rise to a spot just below the Army's top officer had been nothing less than astonishing; he was the soldier's soldier in the truest sense: from buck private to four-star general in forty years.

His career, however, had been marked by one notable failure. In 1977, just after Carter announced that the United States would be withdrawing troops from South Korea, Vessey's deputy commander in Korea, General John Singlaub, had publicly criticized this decision. This action led to a public reprimand, a transfer, and, eventually, Singlaub's forced retirement. Vessey supported Singlaub, seconded his criticism of Carter, and waited for the inevitable call from Washington. Although it never came, Army officers — and Vessey himself — were convinced that his loyalty to Singlaub probably cost him the Army's top job. The appointment of Shy Meyer as Army chief in June 1979 seemed to confirm that view; Vessey was appointed vice chief, but everyone knew his career was over. "I came back [in 1977] to talk to Carter about it because I knew we had to try to modify his proposal," he recalled. "But I opposed the move so I had to say something, even though I knew it would cost me, or really, I thought it would cost me. I guess it did in 1979."

Vessey had few regrets. "I had had a good career, much better than I had thought," he noted, "so I was ready for retirement. I had everything planned out." What he hadn't planned and couldn't have predicted, however, was the phone call he received from Reagan just days after his return to Minnesota, asking him to succeed David Jones. Vessey's promotion caught everyone by surprise. JCS staff officers in the Pentagon were open-mouthed, and they greeted the news with something approaching outright glee. Unlike Jones, Vessey was respected by his colleagues; he was not only an experienced combat officer, he also knew what it was like to serve in the ranks. Nor was he viewed as being as openly political as his predecessor, which meant he would be able to repair the strained relations between the JCS and the Secretary of Defense. Most important, however, the staff was looking forward to working with a chairman who had the endorsement of a new and popular president.

When Vessey took office, he faced some immediate problems. The JCS was undergoing yet another transition: within thirty days two of the three remaining lame ducks would be replaced. On July 1, Admiral James Watkins was scheduled to replace Hayward as CNO and General Charles Gabriel would be replacing Allen as head of the Air Force. Although welcome, the changes provided Vessey with his first problem, of ensuring that the transition in JCS leadership provided continued stability on the staff. Thankfully, he could count on the continued cooperation of General Robert Barrow (in his third year as head of the Marine Corps) and the Army's Meyer. Meyer, in particular, could be counted on to give some needed advice: while he was put in the potentially uncomfortable position of serving with a chairman who was once his deputy, he openly supported Vessey and believed that the appointment was "just a brilliant move."

Vessey would need all the help he could get: in addition to presiding over a JCS transition, he was faced with monitoring an increasingly volatile situation between Israel and its PLO enemies in Lebanon, the first military confrontation facing a JCS chairman since Jones had tried to rescue the American hostages in Tehran in 1980. Unfortunately, the Israeli-PLO confrontation was far more serious, especially when — just days into Vessey's tenure — it threatened to escalate into a full-scale war. As the administration looked on in growing discomfort, Israeli units were ordered past the Letani River and into the southern suburbs of Beirut, where they threatened PLO strongholds and the three Palestinian refugee camps of Burj el-Barajneh, Sabra, and Shatilla.

For the JCS, it looked as if the Israeli Defense Force (IDF) had pulled off yet another first-class military victory: the race from the Litani to Beirut had taken them over some of the most hotly contested ground in the Middle East and to the very edge of complete victory over the PLO. The victory, however, had not been gained without a loss. As the Israeli armored units arrived at the outskirts of Beirut, international opinion and pure military good sense provided a necessary pause; no one wanted to think what might happen to the IDF in Beirut, no one — least of all the Reagan administration — wanted to preside over a back-alley bloodbath that might forever end any hope of a Middle East peace settlement. Working behind the scenes, Reagan's Middle East envoy, Robert McFarlane, finally came up with a way of dampening the confrontation. In July, he convinced the PLO and the Israelis that the United States could serve as a trusted guarantor of the PLO's withdrawal from Beirut. By deploying U.S. Marines, the Israelis could be assured of increased security for its northern border, while the PLO would benefit by U.S. protection for its civilians in Beirut's refugee camps, whom they considered vulnerable to attacks from Israel's Lebanese allies, the Christian Phalange.

The JCS watched with fascination as the hitherto nearly invincible IDF hesitated just outside Beirut. Almost one decade earlier, JCS chairman Moorer had just about single-handedly bailed out the Israel military with a sudden airlift of badly needed weapons that were in short supply in the United States. The airlift had caused consternation among the U.S. military, who believed that America's support of Israel had unnecessarily denuded U.S. conventional defenses — leading, it was thought, to George Brown's embarrassing remarks when he was the JCS chairman. Although much had changed (the United States was not in the same condition in 1982 as at the end of the Vietnam era, in the early 1970s), top-ranking officers were still disturbed that Israel's rush to Beirut would lead to another call for U.S. support. McFarlane's plan to deploy Marines to Beirut confirmed that fear but did not spark a break between the JCS and the administration.

In August, Reagan announced that Marines would be deployed in Lebanon to act both as a buffer between the IDF and the PLO and as protectors of the Palestinian civilians in the refugee camps. Reagan's decision had the full, though hesitant, approval of the JCS, primarily because Reagan and Vessey had talked at length about the Marines' rules of engagement while in Beirut and had gained assurances from Israel that the PLO would not be attacked while leaving. Under no circumstances, Reagan told Vessey, would the Marines be caught in a PLO-Israeli crossfire. Even more important, Reagan promised the JCS that the Marine unit would only be in Beirut as long as it took to carry out its mission — in any event, no longer than thirty days.

Reagan's assurances were critical in winning JCS approval. "Every one of the chiefs was opposed to it," Vessey said. "Shultz [Haig's replacement as Secretary of State] was for it, McFarlane was for it. But we knew the president wanted to send them in, and we knew why. There really wasn't much choice." The JCS wasn't alone in its opposition. Weinberger, who was locked in a personal power struggle with George Shultz, also opposed the deployment, believing the Marines' Beirut mission placed them in an untenable combat situation. His views were seconded by NATO's Bernard Rogers, who visited Washington to confer with the JCS in an attempt to iron out the Marines' rules of engagement. In fact, Reagan's plan had come as a distinct shock to the JCS, who thought little could be accomplished. The JCS not only disagreed with McFarlane's assessment of the situation in Lebanon, they also believed that American troops would become a convenient new target for Arab-Israeli enmity, regardless of Reagan's assurances.

Nevertheless, the deployment went ahead. After coming ashore in Beirut on August 25, 1982, the Marines presided over the PLO's departure for seven nerve-racking but uneventful days. By September 1, the JCS had begun to relax. The Marines were not being subjected to the crossfire that everyone had feared; in fact, they were actually welcomed by PLO civilians and Shiite militia as neutral liberators, the only troops that stood between the PLO and their traditional enemies. Nor did civilians in the refugee camps seem in any particular danger. The hot war in Lebanon had suddenly begun to cool, and Israel and the Phalange seemed content to allow the PLO to withdraw graciously. By the end of the first week of September, the JCS was pushing the president to pull the Marines out of Lebanon; while the presence of American soldiers had seemed to calm fears of a general war, it was no use pressing their luck — the JCS still feared that the Marines would become the target of contending Lebanese factions.

The JCS's position probably helps explain Reagan's surprising announcement (made with JCS concurrence) that the United States would withdraw its troops before the agreed-upon thirty-day period. On September 10, therefore, the Marines began their redeployment to Navy ships off Lebanon's western coast in apparent violation of the administration's pledge to the PLO, a move that was immediately criticized by the PLO's leadership as exposing its refugees. JCS staff members discounted the PLO's claims; for the first time in nearly three weeks, the American military could rest easy that none of its combat units was serving in an exposed area. Reagan had not only been right about the value of using U.S. forces to calm Middle East fears, he had also kept his pledge to the JCS. But on September 14, Lebanon's president and the head of the Christian Phalange, Bashir Gemayel, was assassinated.

Within hours, the IDF pushed into West Beirut in an apparent

attempt to subdue the Phalange's greatest military threat, Lebanon's
Shiite militia. This movement brought a swift international response,
with Reagan leading the way by charging that Israel had reneged on its
earlier agreement to stay out of the city. The IDF finally pulled back,
on September 17, but it was clear to the JCS that Lebanon's civil conflict had not been calmed and that it might again be asked to approve a
deployment. On September 18, militiamen of the Phalange entered the
Palestinian refugee camps of Sabra and Shatilla and killed seven
hundred men, women, and children. The massacre shocked the world
and renewed the administration's debate over the U.S. role as guarantor of the Israeli-PLO settlement. During the next five days, the JCS
and high-level presidential aides argued over U.S. responsibility for
the massacre and Reagan's insistence that the Marines return to Beirut
as a "peacekeeping force."

The JCS had little choice but to agree with the president. Although
he had not officially ordered the redeployment of the 32nd Marine
Amphibious Unit (MAU) into the war-torn city (couching his views in
the form of a "request"), JCS members realized that it was only a matter of time before the request was transformed into the proper, unde-
batable form. The five-day argument was one of Vessey's most trying
times, his first real lesson in consensus-building. According to JCS
officers, Vessey had a particularly difficult time keeping the JCS's
arguments against deployment from developing into a mud-slinging
match between contending JCS factions. At the center of the controversy was the newest JCS member, CNO Watkins. His position was
baffling. Although he had initially agreed that deploying the Marines
was a bad idea, he had wavered after the massacre.

JCS officers say that Watkins's sudden willingness to support
deployment was the natural result of his own political beliefs and his
lack of experience on the JCS staff. Occasionally the otherwise taci-
turn CNO could turn into a rabid anticommunist, transforming his
superpatriotic views into concrete national security recommendations
that surprised and dismayed his staff. At one JCS meeting, he suddenly burst out with the view that the U.S.-Soviet competition was "a
holy war" — bringing open stares from his suddenly silent colleagues.
Watkins also seemed strangely confused by the JCS environment;
although he had served as Vice CNO for two years before his assignment to command the Pacific fleet, it was clear to his colleagues that
JCS debates on national security issues made him impatient. This was
especially true of the debate over whether to continue arguing with
Reagan about the Marine deployment in Lebanon. If that's what the
president wanted he should just order it, Watkins reportedly said.
Why ask anyone's opinion? "You take a guy like Jim Watkins, who
never served in a joint command, and you bring him into the Pentagon

and he doesn't know what he's supposed to do," one two-star admiral reflected. "Watkins never really wanted to be there. He just looked across the table at those other guys, the Army and the Air Force guy, and it was like they were from another planet as far as he was concerned."

Watkins's uncertainty notwithstanding, Vessey succeeded in keeping the JCS firmly and unanimously opposed to Reagan's plan, but at the end of their fifth day of deliberation, the JCS members began to doubt that their opposition would change the president's mind. In the end, Vessey himself took the responsibility for selling the president's plan to the JCS, a position he has since defended by citing Reagan's own commitment. "We knew the president wanted to send them in, thought it was something we should do," Vessey noted. "It was his decision. It's easy to second-guess it now, but he had good reasons for doing it. There are a lot of people who say we should have walked out on this one, but the president is the commander in chief, and the military is here to serve the nation's elected representatives. It's not that we decided to go along with it — we obeyed our orders."

On the evening of September 23, the JCS dispatched the requisite deployment plan to the head of the Marine unit aboard naval warships in the Mediterranean. The 32nd MAU would secure and hold the Beirut International Airport in cooperation with units from U.S. allies deployed in the area. "The argument was that they were supposed to be a presence," one Pentagon official noted. "But all the military guys said that it looked like another Vietnam; they would be surrounded by hostile forces without rules of engagement being made clear. The Joint Chiefs considered it as just another act of real civilian arrogance, fueled by the belief that simply because they're American soldiers everyone is supposed to be frightened of them. But that just didn't happen. After they'd been there for a month [in November 1982], there were discussions in the tank, real controversies and arguments."

The arguments were spurred by reports from the Marine commanders that the airport in Beirut was militarily indefensible, that it was "a mini Dien Bien Phu" surrounded by high mountains, perfect positions for artillery sightings by Lebanese Moslems who were no longer willing to view the U.S. troops as peacekeepers. Despite JCS concerns, the chiefs endorsed a number of administration decisions that made them even more vulnerable. In November, the White House decided to provide training for the Christian-dominated Lebanese army, which virtually assured that the Marines would come under fire from Druse units positioned in the Chouf Mountains, just east of the airport. In December, the administration decided to ship arms to the Lebanese Army, which further added fuel to Druse claims that the United States had taken sides against them. Finally, in March 1983, long after the JCS had learned to live with the U.S. deployment, the Marines took their first casualty. "The whole thing was just a disaster," Meyer recalled. "It just kept getting worse and worse. By April, I think it was, I knew we were in real trouble."

The trouble came in the form of tragedy: on April 10, the U.S. embassy in Beirut was destroyed by a terrorist bomb that killed sixteen Americans, including the head of the CIA's Middle East division, Robert Ames. If there was any remaining doubt among JCS members that the Marines were involved in a combat situation, the bombing erased it. "Beirut was a very complicated place, a dangerous place for us to have been," Vessey reflected later. "It came down to this: we had made our decision and we weren't going to go back on it, so basically we stuck ourselves between the Israelis and the Arabs and we got shot at. But the Marines weren't the target; the American people were the target." In the wake of the bombing, a number of high-level U.S. officials were dispatched to Beirut to assess the Marines' increasingly vulnerable position.

One of those sent was Noel Koch, the Deputy Assistant Secretary of Defense for International Security Affairs and one of the Pentagon's most respected intelligence officers. Accompanying him was Lawrence Eagleburger, who had stayed on at the State Department despite Haig's resignation. The two men flew to Europe, where they were joined by a number of high-ranking officers from the European command before flying into Beirut to inspect the Marine position on the ground. "It's not as romantic as it sounds," Koch recalled. "We went in there ostensibly to bring back the bodies from the Beirut embassy bombing, and we got to squirreling around with some heavy breathers from the Lebanese armed forces and some special ops types who were out of harm's way. We went in to check out the barracks at the airport, and really, it was all fucked up. That's when we knew something had to be done."

According to Koch, the intelligence team found that the Marines were virtually unprotected and had taken none of the necessary steps to protect their already vulnerable position. "It was just deplorable," he said. "They were unprepared for what they found in Beirut. Anyone could have walked in the back door. They had no idea what they were doing — they were in deep trouble." Eagleburger, equally surprised, recommended to Marine Colonel Geraghty, the commander on the ground, that additional steps be taken to secure the Marine barracks. According to Koch, Geraghty's response — spit out in apparent anger at Eagleburger's implied criticism — served as convincing evidence that disaster was on the way. "Don't make the mistake of telling us Marines how to suck eggs," Geraghty said. "The Marines know how to suck eggs better than anyone in the world." For Koch, Geraghty's decision to ignore their advice meant that "someone, somewhere up the line, would have to do something."

When Koch returned to Europe, he immediately sent a six-page memo to Weinberger on the Marines' vulnerability to terrorist attack, explicitly warning of an impending tragedy at the Marine compound at the airport. "I said, 'You've either got to get them out of there or protect them,' " Koch claimed. The memo also ended up on Vessey's desk with other, similar reports. "I don't know what happened to those reports, but I can speculate," Koch said. "There was a lot of bad feeling between the JCS and the special operations folks at the time — basically, Vessey just thought it was beneath him to listen to people like me. His hatred for special operations made him almost psychotic. That man turned out to be a loser all the way around." Koch hesitated before giving his final assessment. "The JCS just resents civilians telling them anything, so they took my report and they threw it in the wastebasket." Koch continued to search for a way to head off what he called "my feeling that somehow this was going to turn out bad" throughout the summer of 1983, but to no avail.

"No one likes to hear the bad news," Koch said. "John Vessey didn't want to hear it, no one at the JCS wanted to hear it." As the environment around the Beirut airport became increasingly violent and the Lebanese civil war in the Chouf Mountains began to heat up in the late summer, the JCS considered issuing amended rules of engagement orders to the Marine detachment, then reconsidered it in light of Reagan's continued insistence that the U.S. troops were peacekeepers. By September, JCS officers became increasingly concerned about the Marines' apparent vulnerability. The amphibious unit was tied down in a "shooting gallery," and Marine noncoms were required to receive permission from their officers before they could even load their weapons. It takes only a few seconds to load an M-16, but on a Sunday in October, those few seconds made all the difference in the world.

10

S E M P E R
F I D E L I S

★   ★   ★   ★

> The Marine Corps, Mr. Chairman, is proud of many
> things, but nothing more than the way we take care of
> our own.
>
> General P. X. Kelley,
> October 31, 1983

AT 6:22 A.M. ON October 23, 1983, a large yellow Mercedes truck
rumbled down Beirut's main airport highway and turned left into the
four-story Battalion Landing Team headquarters of the 24th Marine
Amphibious Unit. Eighteen seconds later, five thousand pounds of
high explosives were detonated by the two members of a Shiite revolutionary group who were driving the truck. The headquarters folded up
like a house of cards, killing more than 225 Marines. Within a week,
the official death toll would be put at 241, one of the single worst disasters ever suffered by the American military. FBI agents later interviewed by a task force set up to investigate the incident characterized
the detonation as "the largest non-nuclear explosion in history," a
thundering roar that collapsed thousands of tons of concrete and steel
into a pile of smoldering rubble.

The week that followed provided a critical test of Vessey's ability to
defend military interests. The JCS chairman was judged by his capacity to deflect the criticism aimed at his combat commanders, by his
power to dampen traditional service competition, and by his ability to
forge disparate plans for a response to the bombing into a common
program. Beirut and its aftermath were Vessey's crucible, combining
in a series of short but significant episodes the tests that had faced a
number of his predecessors over a longer period of time. Perhaps most
important, Beirut helped to determine whether the JCS system was

capable of handling the crisis or whether its very structure should be overhauled in an effort to avoid future tragedies.

News of the disaster in Beirut reached the White House situation room within minutes, at approximately thirty-five minutes after midnight on Sunday morning. The duty officer monitoring the secure communications link with Lebanon in the basement of the White House followed standard procedure, asking first for confirmation of the bombing, then for casualties. The first call, to the national command center's operations room at the Pentagon, confirmed that officers on duty with the JCS had also received the news and had alerted the chairman. The duty officer then called McFarlane, the administration's new national security adviser, who had been at his position for just one week. According to later reports, McFarlane ordered NSC officers to mount extra duty at the White House to monitor the situation. In all, he was on the telephone for two hours, informing official Washington of the bombing. Just before 2:30 A.M., he called the president at Camp David to tell him the news and to suggest an early meeting of the NSC, which they agreed should be set for 8:00 A.M.

After learning of the disaster, Vessey spent most of the night on his secure phone link to the commanders on duty at the national command center. Then, in the early morning, he went to the Pentagon to get the latest reports from Lebanon himself. Within minutes of his arrival, he learned that well over 200 Marines had been killed, that security measures at the Marine headquarters had been lax, that the suicide bombers had belonged to a radical Moslem sect, and that the group probably received its weapons, and instructions, from Iran. Vessey also knew what others were only beginning to guess — that the American military was again facing a major crisis, its worst since Vietnam. He knew there was little he could do to respond on the ground: the backup for the destroyed Marine battalion was on its way to the Far East; another U.S. task force heading for Lebanon was still in the western Atlantic. But Vessey took what steps he could: he made certain that aircraft off Lebanon were on full alert and that the Marines elsewhere in Beirut tightened their security. After discussing the situation with NATO commander Bernard Rogers in Europe, Vessey penned a recommendation to the president, suggesting that the Marine commandant, General P. X. Kelley, go to Beirut to conduct a firsthand study of the situation.

One hour before the NSC meeting was scheduled to begin, Vessey reportedly reviewed classified reports from military intelligence operatives in Beirut, part of the web of unofficial information-gathering operations under JCS control. The number of operatives had been increased after the bombing of the Beirut embassy the previous April. They had been sending "eyes only" reports to the JCS, detailing the increased anti-American militancy of Lebanon's various Moslem factions since June, and had even cultivated a number of Shiite militia officers. In mid-July, the tenor of these reports began to distress Vessey so much that, according to a colleague, he asked the president to "expand the Marines ROE [rules of engagement]" at a meeting in the Oval Office. These orders directed that the Marines could "use only the degree of military force necessary to accomplish the mission or reduce the threat." In other words, they could fire only if fired upon and even then only if they had received permission from their commanders.*

Vessey, who had initially determined the rules of engagement with Rogers (and had them approved by Weinberger), had told the president he should give the Marines greater latitude in responding to suspected threats. But Reagan refused Vessey's request for political reasons; the Marines were peacekeepers, he said, in Lebanon to calm a volatile military situation. While he acknowledged that the troops needed to be protected, he said he was convinced that any upgrade in their ability to respond to threats would only worsen the situation. According to military intelligence officers, Vessey's meeting with the president led him to warn Kelley to order the Marines to beef up security, but the warning had either been ignored, come too late, or, as Vessey suspected, would not have been effective in stopping the kind of terrorist act for which the Shiites (and others) were known.

With a stack of reports tucked under his arm, Vessey emerged from the Pentagon into the gray autumn morning of Washington, called for his driver, and was driven the short distance to the White House. For the first time in anyone's memory, the normally stoic and almost formidably cool chairman was visibly shaken. Four years later, just one year after his retirement, Vessey's remarkable stoicism was once again betrayed during an interview at Fort Myer, just minutes from the Pentagon. Vessey spoke in somber, regretful tones, shaking off a personal emotion that was still painfully obvious. His response to questions about the bombing were blunt and subdued and he shook his head in wonder that it had happened at all. "Yes, I was surprised," he said. "Stunned, I guess. The real question is, did the military people do everything in their power to prevent the casualties?" He hesitated for a moment before going on. "Well, they weren't prevented . . . were they."

---

* The different rules were a source of bitter debate among JCS officers. Marine guards at the embassy were ordered to have their weapons loaded while Marines at the airport were ordered to have them empty. JCS officers believed the reason for the disparity was that Marines at the embassy were guarding civilians, whereas those at the airport weren't.

At the NSC meeting on October 23, with almost all the top foreign policy officials in attendance, Vessey reviewed the incident and the military forces available for a response. According to Vessey himself, the meeting was unusually formal, the result of the almost palpable tension caused by the divisions the deployment had created among administration officials. Weinberger sat through the briefing without comment. He didn't need to tell any of those who supported the deployment that he had been adamantly against it; his silence was his testimony. According to an NSC aide, Reagan, on the other hand, was "outright stunned" by the bombing, as if he couldn't understand why anyone would doubt America's good intentions.

The president was reportedly exhausted by the catastrophic events. After receiving McFarlane's call, he had monitored military and intelligence reports through the early morning, becoming increasingly depressed by the disaster. Nor had he been allowed to rest in the short time before the NSC meeting. His attention turned to the CIA's latest report on the increasingly disturbing situation on Grenada, where American students were in apparent danger of being taken captive by the pro-Marxist government that had overthrown and executed Prime Minister Maurice Bishop. At 7:00 A.M., McFarlane informed Reagan that the JCS had finished preliminary plans for an invasion of the island, designed to overthrow Bishop's successors. Reagan agreed that the United States should be prepared to intervene, but said he would delay any final decision on intervention until the end of the NSC meeting.

For those at the meeting, the bombing was not only a "major disaster" but a morale-shattering blow to Reagan's activist foreign policy. As the most vocal supporters of this policy, Shultz, McFarlane, and CIA director William Casey were concerned that the Beirut debacle would be used by administration foes to attack Reagan's Middle East peace program. More critical still, it could open a new debate on defense spending, on support for the administration's policy in Central America, even on Reagan's arms control strategy. McFarlane was the most visibly affected: when Vessey finished his nearly thirty-minute briefing, McFarlane questioned him about his findings. "How could this have happened?" he reportedly asked. "Were people asleep, for God's sake? Didn't they even know it was coming?"

Vessey told McFarlane only those things he had confirmed: reports from Lebanon were still sketchy, but it was clear there had been no warning that a terrorist attack was on the way. While the Marines had come under increasing pressure in recent months, including sniper attacks from Shiite neighborhoods surrounding the airport, there had been little reason to believe that such attacks would end in the suicide bombing of the Marine barracks. Nor, Vessey added, was the United

States in a good position to launch an immediate military response. The available Marine units in Beirut were still vulnerable to the same kind of attack, and an immediate response against suspected terrorist strongholds might worsen the situation. Whatever forces were available in the eastern Mediterranean should be used to cover the medical evacuation of those wounded by the bombing. As an afterthought, Vessey added that the deputy commander in chief of the European command was being dispatched by Rogers to inspect the Beirut site. His trip, Vessey said, would be followed by one from Kelley.

McFarlane wasn't satisfied with Vessey's answers and pressed the chairman for more details. It was a moment of great truth for the national security adviser, a former Marine officer whose love for his service was well known in the White House. Above all, McFarlane was considered blunt, honest, and compassionate (his interest in the Vietnamese people during his time there was nearly legendary) as well as a man whose broad government experience (as an aide to Henry Kissinger and Senator John Tower) was a welcome change from that of his predecessor, Bill Clark, who lacked fundamental foreign policy skills. Patient and thoughtful, McFarlane had finally gotten the drift of things in the administration, learning in one short week that in order to be heard he had to be loud. He could now glower and curse with the best of them, a trait he used to good effect by turning his level stare on Vessey, at the other end of the room. "I'd like to know what happened — how this could happen," McFarlane reportedly said, his voice rising in anger. "Somebody has got some questions to answer."

Vessey's short response was a repetition of his previous statement: the possibility of terrorist action had always been present in Beirut, but no amount of preparation could have stopped the bombing. This straightforward reply to McFarlane's obvious criticism leaves the distinct impression that Vessey was unwilling to get into a debate over the deployment itself. It was McFarlane, after all, who had thought it was a good idea, it was McFarlane who had suggested it to Shultz, and it was McFarlane, not Vessey, who had sold it to the president. Four years later, Vessey dismissed the deep administration divisions over the Beirut deployment by implying that Reagan and his aides, as well as the JCS, were simply unaware of the Marines' vulnerability. "We all thought the airport was the best place for the Marines to be," Vessey remembered. "Sure it was open ground, sure the Marines were vulnerable to shelling, but we all thought — 'Well, here, at least, they can see what's coming.' " He also downplayed the deep divisions that resulted from the bombing. "We were shocked, really, that it had happened. Everyone was shocked. There is a feeling of being helpless in these situations, and I think we had that feeling."

The portrait of NSC unanimity implied by Vessey's comment is wide of the mark: the McFarlane-Vessey exchange was only the beginning of the harsh warfare that erupted inside the administration as a result of the bombing. Shortly after McFarlane's outburst, Weinberger deflected the growing clamor against Vessey by indelicately reminding the president that the administration would be called by Congress to testify on the bombing. He further observed that "as Secretary of Defense" he would "have to provide the administration's point of view." Reagan responded by noting that important congressional leaders would be briefed on the Beirut situation at the White House that same afternoon — which didn't palliate the Defense Secretary. "We'll need better information than we have now," he reportedly said, and he suggested that the president ask the Senate leadership to postpone any hearings "for a few days until we know what's going on."

While Vessey was being questioned by McFarlane, JCS officers were dealing with the increasingly complex problems posed by the bombing. At a midmorning conference in the Pentagon, each service's planning officers were attempting to determine whether to recommend that Navy forces off Lebanon respond to the attack. Soon after the meeting of service planners began, however, JCS officers in attendance had put aside the question of military retaliation and become engaged in a bitter debate over Vessey's leadership. According to Defense officials who were privy to these discussions, Army officers loyal to Vessey were forced to defend him to Navy officers who were embittered by his agreement to send the Marines into Beirut in the first place. Now, they said, their service would have to pick up the pieces. Unfortunately, this angry exchange paralyzed JCS activities at the very moment that commanders in Lebanon were most in need of overall direction.

The service debate that was fracturing the JCS staff in Washington was being played out in a far more dangerous environment in Beirut, where Marine and Air Force officers were arguing over which service should be credited with treating the wounded. Marine officers were dumbfounded to learn that sixteen of the most critically wounded soldiers would be placed on an Air Force C-130 transport bound for West Germany. This decision — made by NATO medical officers — stunned the civilian officials monitoring the situation at the Pentagon. They pleaded that the wounded be taken to the naval hospital in Naples, which was closer, but they were powerless to stop the transfer. A second argument between the services broke out after the C-130 was airborne.

After receiving orders from medical officers at NATO headquarters to bypass Naples and fly to the Ramstein Burn Center, doctors on board learned that the aircraft would be rerouted yet again. The NATO officials had been overruled by a higher-ranking Air Force officer who wanted the wounded treated at Wiesbaden, an Air Force hospital.* Despite the pleas of the doctors on the C-130, the Air Force officer refused to rescind the order. "It was an idiotic decision," one defense official remembered. "The Wiesbaden facility had only one operating room." As a result, when the C-130 landed at Wiesbaden, eight of the sixteen most critically wounded Marines were put on Blackhawk helicopters for the trip back to Ramstein, where they should have gone in the first place. "There were two soldiers who went into cardiac arrest on the way over, but they recovered, thank God, or it would have been a major disaster," one military medical expert recounted.

While the JCS staff was involved in a divisive debate over military leadership and the services were competing for glory in the skies over Europe, Vessey remained closeted with the NSC at the White House. The meeting lasted until almost noon, then was reconvened an hour later. With the exception of one short afternoon break, when Vessey, Weinberger, and McFarlane briefed congressional leaders, the top policy-making body of the administration stayed in session from eight in the morning until nearly eight that night. It fueled speculation that officials were busy planning an immediate military response, including probable air attacks against terrorist strongholds.

"Beirut — sure, we discussed Beirut for a while," Vessey later reflected. "But, you know, there really wasn't much we could do. As I remember, most of the time was taken up with a discussion of the situation in Grenada." In fact, a discussion of what military steps should be taken to respond to the Beirut debacle wasn't even on the afternoon agenda, nor did Vessey suggest one. Instead, the NSC discussed actions to resolve the burgeoning crisis in the Caribbean. Vessey was still at center stage, briefing the president on the JCS plan to launch a military invasion of the island. A twenty-one-ship naval task force was in the area, the JCS chairman said, and intelligence reports showed that Grenadian leaders were not expecting U.S. military action. JCS planning for an invasion had been going on since October 21, even though the president had held off a final decision until the United States had gained the support of other Caribbean nations. With that support firmly in hand, the NSC reviewed the JCS's plans, then made its recommendation: the JCS would order the Beirut-bound aircraft carrier task force to divert to Grenada. The invasion was scheduled for Tuesday morning.

---

* The result of the Naples-Ramstein-Wiesbaden debate meant that the most critically wounded Marines were transported the farthest distance. Most of the other wounded were taken into Beirut for care. None of the wounded were transported to nearby Israeli military hospitals. Weinberger had ruled out that option in an early morning discussion with Israeli officials, saying that such a transfer would be too politically charged.

With its plans for the Grenada invasion in place, the NSC finally adjourned. When Weinberger returned to the Pentagon, aides briefed him on the situation in Beirut, including revelations about the service battle over the Marine wounded.* Enraged and convinced that swift punishment was in order, the secretary wanted to dismiss the Air Force's deputy medical commander in Europe (who had ordered the C-130 to Wiesbaden), but he was dissuaded by military officers, who believed such an action should await the report of a Pentagon team appointed to assess the military's medical readiness program. Weinberger's aides, however, gave him their initial judgment: the medical foul-ups in Europe and the eastern Mediterranean were clearly the result of service rivalry, the desire of Air Force officers to make sure that their hospital received credit for taking care of the American soldiers.

When Vessey returned to the Pentagon, he was brought up to date on the status of the bombing and told that Kelley was already on his way to Europe. Vessey then began to put the finishing touches on the JCS plan for the invasion of Grenada, which had to be in its final form when he met with the president the next evening. With a twenty-one-ship aircraft carrier task force headed for the Caribbean, Vessey issued orders to increase the readiness of the 82nd Airborne Division in preparation for a Tuesday morning airdrop. He then met with key JCS operations officers to check the status of a number of special operations teams that were ready to infiltrate the island. Concerned that the smallest detail could stain the operation's expected success, Vessey quizzed JCS officers on every detail of the preparations. In light of the events in Beirut, he wanted to make sure that the sudden deployment of U.S. forces, known as Operation Urgent Fury, lived up to its name.

On the morning of October 25, elements of two Ranger battalions parachuted onto Grenada's Point Salines airstrip, captured more than 100 of its Cuban defenders, and freed a lone group of American students. Later, a brigade of the 82nd Airborne Division captured the airport barracks and gained control of the road linking the airstrip with St. Georges, Grenada's capital. That same day, more than 250 Marines assaulted the airport at Pearls by helicopter before being ordered to rescue the island's governor general near Point Salines. Boarding amphibious craft, they landed at Grand Mal Bay, fired a few shots at

---

* The October 23 feud was not without precedent. "When the Army decided to relocate some of its hospitals on the Czech border, the Air Force objected," one JCS officer said. "When the Army insisted, the Air Force just came in and made the Army hospital an Air Force hospital. The hospital will be overrun on the first day of the next war, but now the Air Force can say they have more hospitals than the Army."

the Cubans surrounding the governor general's house, and then, on Wednesday morning, rescued him. Army and Marine units freed a second group of students, captured Richmond Prison in St. Georges, and cut off the escape of its defenders. The 82nd Airborne then occupied the capital, freed the last group of Americans, and captured the Calivigny barracks. Urgent Fury ended when Navy aircraft attacked Fort Frederic, a mountain redoubt overlooking the capital. Late on October 27, the U.S. commander for the area reported that "all major military objectives" on Grenada were in the hands of the United States.

JCS officers claimed that Urgent Fury was a textbook example of how the units of different services could act together in pursuit of clearly defined national objectives. In fact, the U.S. units were poorly coordinated and ill prepared for the invasion. The failure extended to every unit: when a group of Delta Force commandos failed to take the airport on the morning of the invasion, Ranger units had to make an unexpected parachute assault on the island. The subsequent failure of the Rangers to subdue the airport's defenders meant that the airborne landing on the afternoon of the twenty-fifth was unexpectedly contested. The Marines who landed at Pearl were ordered to make an amphibious assault on Grand Mal Bay because a SEAL (Navy special operations) team had failed to rescue the governor general; the assault took twenty-four hours, against light resistance. Even more critical, intelligence officers failed to locate the U.S. students on the island. The last group wasn't rescued until the third day of the invasion. It's now clear that the Cubans could easily have shot the students had they desired. In addition, some students later said that they only felt in danger when U.S. units launched an assault to free them.

Urgent Fury wasn't a disaster, but it wasn't the clear victory that Reagan had hoped for in the wake of the Beirut bombing. Planned and executed by the JCS, it was yet another example of how the services failed to cooperate in running tactical operations.* According to one JCS officer, the planning was "chaotic and embarrassing," which was borne out not only by Urgent Fury's operational details but also by the almost otherworldly stories that surfaced after the invasion. The problems actually began before the first American landed on the island. On the afternoon of October 22, Army and Navy staff officers argued bitterly, trying to determine which service should be responsible for actually capturing the island. The solution, in typical JCS fashion, was

---

* The president gave the JCS control of Urgent Fury because he believed the military had been hamstrung during the Iran rescue mission. In fact, the JCS had full responsibility for the Iran mission, which retired CNO Holloway later cited as one of the reasons for its failure. "I was critical of General Jones," he said. "He did not accept joint planning. He turned his back on the system. The JCS just ad-hoc'd it all the way. That's why it failed."

simple: the island was literally split, with half going to the Army and the other half to the Marines. "They cut it up like a pie and really botched the whole operation," one former Pentagon official said. "The result was easy to see, command and control, communications, planning and operations — it was just a disaster. Hell, we haven't had a successful military operation since Korea. Grenada should have been a walk."

There were other planning glitches. Army officers wanted the highly regarded Delta antiterrorist team to be responsible for the clandestine operation before the landing, but the Navy wanted its SEALs to get the job. Once again, the island was divided in half: Delta would come ashore at Point Salines, the SEALs would secure a heliborne landing zone for the Marines. Both units performed deplorably (Delta was pinned down by the Cubans; some SEAL teams drifted helplessly out to sea), hampering the military's regular combat operations and delaying the final conquest of the island. Service competition plagued every aspect of the assault. Army helicopter pilots were unable to evacuate wounded soldiers because they had never been trained to land on Navy ships. According to one JCS assistant, "The Navy didn't believe the Army should have helicopters in the first place."*

As a result of Urgent Fury, the highly regarded mobility of Army assault troops (who aren't trained to land on aircraft carriers) was called into question. Defense analyst Richard Gabriel pointed out that as many as 20 percent of all the helicopters used were downed by small arms fire, a shattering indictment not only of the helicopter but also of how the United States plans to fight its future wars. The Army's newest helicopter, the A-64 Apache, has been plagued by mechanical problems, but its difficulty on Grenada probably had more to do with pilot training. Of the twenty helicopters downed, four were lost during midair collisions; most of the others were brought down by fire from World War II–vintage rifles. This experience reinforced the belief among the Army's helicopter pilots that "helicopters don't fly, they crash."

JCS officers responded to criticisms by noting that Urgent Fury was planned and executed in just six days; officers of the 82nd Airborne reinforced the defense by noting that they had received their orders just hours before "mounting up" and that, "considering all the

---

* Communications problems during the invasion led to a number of embarrassing incidents. One episode involved a platoon leader in the 82nd Airborne who was forced to use a pay phone to call Fort Bragg for air support. The officer at Fort Bragg used a direct communications link to contact offshore naval vessels to provide the fire. Apparently no one had bothered to coordinate service radio frequencies.

glitches, we did damn good."* Of the defenders, Vessey was the most outspoken. "We put that thing together with just forty-eight hours of planning," he said. "Anyone who thinks there's not going to be screwups is wrong. Sure, there were lessons to be learned, but the number one lesson is that people make mistakes. But we took two airfields from four thousand–plus potential enemy forces in just three minutes. We have tremendous flexibility, tremendous mobility, we accomplished our mission." Of all the criticisms, the most damaging came from civilian officials, who claimed that Urgent Fury was ordered to divert attention from Beirut.

Vessey angrily rejected that hypothesis. "We didn't go into Grenada because of Beirut," he said. "We went into Grenada because of the situation on Grenada. We did it for good, legitimate reasons." Nevertheless, Urgent Fury helped push the Beirut bombing off the nation's front pages and dampened public and congressional criticism of both Reagan's Middle East policies and of the military's inability to defend American interests in Lebanon. For Weinberger, the apparent success of Urgent Fury was welcome news. He was scheduled to answer questions from the Senate Armed Services Committee just five hours after the Rangers parachuted into Point Salines.

Weinberger made the most of his opportunity. When the committee was brought to order by John Tower on the morning of October 25, the invasion of Grenada, not the Beirut bombing, was the first item of business. As was his custom, Weinberger began by speaking in a matter-of-fact tone, shrugging off the senators' suggestions that the U.S. action on the island was unnecessary, unilateral, or costly. The portrait he gave was of modest but sure success, making certain to finish by confidently saying that the U.S. troops would not remain on the island any longer than was absolutely necessary. "If all goes well," he said, "and this resistance I mentioned to you is overcome and these various points are secured — again, two airports, Fort Ruppert, and the medical school have been secured already — then I would very much hope in a matter of days we could leave and leave the island in the hands of the Organization of Eastern Caribbean States and the multinational group that has gone in, too." His description was glowing, almost exuberant.†

---

* One of those who helped the 82nd "mount up" was none other than Vessey himself, who flew to Fort Bragg on the twenty-fourth. Officers there describe with pride how, in the dead of night, he stripped off his coat to help in the back-breaking labor of loading a C-141 transport.

† Weinberger was stretching the truth; not only had the Army and Marines not overcome resistance at "two airports, Fort Ruppert, and the medical school," as he reported, they were having difficulty overcoming the "light resistance" of a handful of Cuban construction workers billeted at the Point Salines airstrip.

Weinberger was far less confident answering questions about the Beirut incident, though he remained as composed and self-assured as ever. After the first several minutes of his testimony, however, it was clear that while he was willing to defend the military from charges of incompetence, he was unwilling to lay the blame for the bombing on civilian officials. In answer to a question from Georgia's Sam Nunn — whether the Marines had permission to "take whatever steps were necessary to protect their own security" — he said that the Marines in Beirut were "free to return fire and take necessary steps to protect themselves." It's hard to believe that Weinberger could have been misinformed on this point: his words were in direct contradiction to statements made by a number of Marine officers in Beirut, who complained that they were hampered by the established rules of engagement. Nunn let the answer pass, choosing instead to ask the same question of General Bernard Trainor, the deputy commandant of the Marines.

Trainor was far less categorical in his answer than Weinberger, saying that the Marine unit in Beirut was "in the operational chain of CINCEUR [commander in chief Europe, Bernard Rogers]." But Nunn wasn't satisfied. "Who was the top person in military uniform whose duty it was to make sure that the base was secure? . . . What was the order of responsibility for security at that base?" he asked. Trainor responded, "Now, that would be for all practical purposes the battalion commander who commanded the battalion landing team there, who was under the command of the 24th MAU commander." This answer was technically correct, but committee aides later learned that although the Marine commander was "for all practical purposes" responsible for base security, he could not dictate his unit's rules of engagement. As the committee was just beginning to understand, the Marines had been nearly defenseless — their weapons unloaded, their ability to respond to an immediate threat subject to approval by higher officers. The ultimate responsibility, according to commanders now embittered by the controversy that followed the Beirut experience, was with the president, who decided to put the Marines in Beirut and then refused to protect them.

Fortunately for Weinberger, the invasion of Grenada, the general unfamiliarity of the senators with the Marines' rules of engagement, and a desire to question Kelley upon his return from Beirut cut short the October 25 session. As a result, the questioning of Weinberger did not take on the importance the committee had hoped for, and he was excused without the kind of bitter exchange on military policy to which he was normally subjected. "We just didn't have enough information," one committee aide explained. "The Beirut thing was a disaster, but we only had a feeling that something was wrong." The committee's feeling was clear in Tower's response to Trainor's claim that nothing could have been done to stop the attack. "I think you can see the concern of this committee," Tower said, "that we didn't do everything, to the extent possible, to at least minimize the risk or the attempt of an action such as this being successful. I think you should know of our great concern about that as we await further information."

The further information that Tower wanted was scheduled to come on October 31 from Kelley, at that point one of the most highly respected Marines ever to have served on the JCS. Spare, almost proletarian in appearance, he symbolized the breed of "new Marines," officers who had made a point of understanding something other than their own service. What made Kelley unique was his experience in an unusually large number of non-Marine assignments. In the early 1960s, he was the military liaison with the British Royal Marines, serving successively in Aden, Borneo, Singapore, and Malaysia. He attended the Air Force War College at Maxwell Air Force Base and for two years served as the Chief, Southeast Asia Branch, of the Plans and Policy Directorate of the JCS, which brought him into contact with large numbers of officers from other services. Of all the Marine officers of the 1950s and 1960s, Kelley was perhaps the best prepared to take on joint responsibilities; it's almost as if he had been groomed for the top Marine job at the JCS. He was one of the first commanders of America's Rapid Deployment Force and one of the first to realize that it was a major step on the ladder to the top. By October 1983, on the eve of his testimony to the Senate committee, the JCS staff was betting that Kelley would become the first Marine JCS chairman.

Appearing with Kelley was NATO's Rogers, making it a parade of stars. Both men had had extensive experience in testifying on Capitol Hill, both had been briefed by military aides on the testimony of Weinberger and Trainor, and both had prepared rational, low-key, and articulate defenses of the Beirut deployment and the Marines' rules of engagement. According to JCS officers, they were expecting a tough session, especially during the closed morning meeting, but no one predicted anything out of the ordinary. Although important senators were angered by the bombing, the long-term pro-military tradition of what had once been the Stennis committee would undoubtedly hold sway. The generals would be questioned closely but treated with deference, as befitting a committee that not only gave the military the benefit of the doubt but was also now controlled by conservative Republicans.

However, the hearing turned out to be one of the most combative since the dark days of 1967. This startling turn of events was brought on by Kelley himself, who insisted on beginning his testimony with a hectoring monologue on military capabilities. Almost immediately afterward, more than forty minutes into the session, he was asked to weigh the Marine mission against its cost. He was clearly being baited by insulted committee members, though he didn't have the insight to see it. He answered that he wasn't capable of an assessment and shied away from suggestions that the deployment called for special military plans. "Our troops in Europe are vulnerable also to terrorism on a day-to-day basis," Kelley said angrily. "What we need, in my opinion, is a national policy which says that we make extraordinary efforts to run down the perpetrators and we hold the host country responsible for their actions. . . . We in the military can only do so much against that kind of attack."

Suddenly, almost inexplicably, the atmosphere of the hearing room grew tense, combative; Kelley's reference to "a national policy . . . to run down the perpetrators" of terrorist incidents was viewed as an explicit criticism of policies promoted by the nation's elected leaders. Kelley was criticizing civilian officials for exposing U.S. soldiers to attack at the same time that he defended military actions by arguing that such attacks could not be stopped. Is this what he had told Reagan when he implicitly endorsed the deployment of the Marines, or was he an officer with a can-do spirit who only disagreed with civilian policies when they failed? He could not have it both ways. If he believed civilian policies needlessly endangered American lives and didn't serve the national purpose, then why was he still in uniform?

Perhaps, as committee aides later speculated, Kelley didn't understand that he was tangling with some of the most sophisticated questioners in the Senate, politicians whose facility for drawing out embittered witnesses was legendary. One of the most effective was the Michigan Democrat Carl Levin, who had a habit of lobbing queries with the same deft touch as a knuckleballer spins horsehide. The pitch is almost always slow and almost always a strike. Peering over his glasses from behind the table, Levin delicately, skillfully, but imperiously drew out Kelley's own deep and bitter feelings. His first question implied that the general had purposely failed to give the committee a copy of his testimony in an attempt to cover up the facts of the bombing.

Levin: "General, did you indicate that the statement you made is or is not classified?"

Kelley: "My statement, sir, is not classified."

Levin: "Will copies of that be made available?"

Kelley: "Sir, I have never in my entire life worked for so many masters as I have in the past week."

Committee aides present later insisted that Kelley had raised his voice, that his answer to Levin was a hiss of disrespect. They also argued that Kelley did not say "masters," as he later claimed, but that he had tripped over his own true feelings. "Sir," these aides claim Kelley said, "I have never in my entire life worked for so many bastards as I have in the past week." Levin threw Kelley a life preserver.

Levin: "Did you say masters?"

Kelley: "I said masters. I did not say the other word, Senator. I never have. If you want to, of course, you may see this statement, which was being literally massaged in the car coming over. I just do not have a further prepared statement."

If Kelley ever had a chance to become the first Marine JCS chairman, it ended that morning. He had been rude, defensive, resentful, even disrespectful of congressional leaders and had, in one of the few times in JCS history, publicly questioned the intelligence of the nation's civilian leaders. One Armed Services Committee counsel described the public afternoon session in much the same terms. "Kelley was very highly regarded up here," he said. "People just flocked to the committee hearing to listen to him. He was the new Patton, and senators really wanted to show him some respect. After all, how do you denigrate someone who's been under fire all his life. But Kelley blew it — he was way overemotional. He just opened his mouth too far. He was very defensive. [Senator William] Cohen and Nunn just devastated him. Took him apart. You know, in a few moments even moderately intelligent witnesses know that they should keep their mouths shut, that they've gone too far. But not Kelley, he just kept on going."

The JCS was embarrassed, even angered, by Kelley's testimony and immediately tried to repair the damage. "We got several calls," one Armed Services staff member said. "They were just all over themselves with providing information. They let us know that Kelley was up here pretty much on his own hook. They didn't agree with everything he had to say."

After Kelley's testimony, the full implications of the disaster in Beirut started to come out, and Congress began to gather forces for a fight over military reform. The reform movement, stagnant for a year, was given new impetus by the events of October 1983, and official opposition to a complete review of military command arrangements began to evaporate. The JCS system was the focus of these initial efforts, but eventually the entire military establishment was being poked, pulled, and probed for soft spots. Eventually, Congress would mold far-reaching reform legislation, but it was all made inevitable by tragedy in Lebanon. Before Beirut, as one aide later noted, the military reform movement didn't have a chance of winning; after Beirut, it couldn't lose.

By November 1983, legislative proposals calling for JCS reorganization were gaining momentum. While the bombing in Beirut and growing questions about the Grenada operation were the most significant prods, the unambiguous divisions on the JCS were also important. The bombing had significantly undermined the traditional respect Congress had for the JCS, and JCS staff officers were still debating just who was to blame. The criticism was directed pointedly at the JCS leadership, where Vessey's tenure was coming under increasing fire. High-ranking officers (including a number of longtime colleagues) gave the chairman low marks for his lack of leadership during the week of crisis in October.

Military critics cited a number of different reasons for their harsh judgment. Although Vessey opposed Reagan's plan for Lebanon, he had failed to come up with an alternative, thereby ceding the argument to White House hard-liners. Once the Marines were deployed, Vessey failed to persuade civilian leaders that they were vulnerable, a reflection of his lack of experience in government and evidence that his official position carried little real power. He had failed to deflect public criticism of his combat commanders, seemed unaware of the traditional service competition that plagued every operation, and failed to present a unified plan for a military response to the Beirut disaster. "John Vessey had the potential of being the best, the very best chairman in the history of the country," said Meyer. "But he just didn't do it. You know, in many ways he was a big disappointment. He came in there with high hopes but didn't do very much."

JCS staff officers were making similar comments about Meyer's replacement, General John Wickham. Like Vessey, Wickham had been welcomed by those who believed that the JCS could benefit from the leadership of an officer whose combat record was considered one of the best in the service. But although Wickham had been a stellar combat leader, his peacetime résumé was the butt of military jokes. While in command of the 101st Airborne Division at Fort Campbell, Kentucky, for instance, the teetotaling Wickham barred liquor from the base, despite the protests of a number of subordinate commanders. When he issued the order anyway, Fort Campbell's officers took matters into their own hands, smuggling beer onto the base so their men could enjoy themselves in their off hours. Wickham also required subordinates to join the Association of the United States Army (AUSA), a lobbying group in Washington led by retired Army officers. "I've already joined the Army, sir," one noncommissioned officer reportedly told Wickham. "Isn't that enough?" "No," Wickham said. "This is your Army, you ought to take an interest."

At the end of 1983, JCS staff morale had plummeted. Vessey's leadership was under fire, Wickham's abilities were being widely questioned, and Kelley's military judgment was all but discredited. Reform proponents, however, gained little solace from the crisis. While the effectiveness of all three officers was questioned, the leaders of the reform movement realized that a broad legislative program could not be initiated without their consent. When coupled with the anti-reform bias of CNO Watkins, JCS opposition to reform constituted a formidable barrier to congressional action. Only the Air Force chief of staff, Charles Gabriel, could be counted on to support reform.

Like many of those he succeeded, Gabriel came from a combat aviation background that was combined with broad experience on the JCS itself, where he served as deputy chief of staff for operations, plans, and readiness under Lew Allen. Outspoken and at times painfully blunt about the problems facing the JCS, he was the only JCS member who had publicly endorsed many of the reformers' most important proposals. He was a strong advocate of increased joint service training and had even suggested that it be a requirement for receiving flag rank. He noted many of the drawbacks of the JCS system that had plagued his predecessors: the infighting that marked its deliberations and its inability to have an impact in civilian policy-making circles. He also had strong ties to pro-reform legislators on Capitol Hill, who provided many of the arguments he could use in attempting to sway his colleagues. Inevitably, these ties made him an indispensable back-channel communicator to reform opponents on the JCS.

Reform advocates and opponents were beginning to line up by the end of 1983. The advocates included a group of public policy analysts known for their expertise on defense issues. But leadership of the movement centered on a group of retired officers led by David Jones and Edward Meyer, who could count on growing disenchantment with military leadership in Congress. While pro-reform legislators did not yet control key committee positions, which would ensure legislative success, they clearly outnumbered their more conservative, anti-reform colleagues. The opposition was led by Weinberger, whose position had actually been enhanced by the Beirut bombing; he let it be known that he had opposed the deployment of the Marines, then was seen as a courageous defender of military interests after the bombing. His views were endorsed by four of the five JCS chiefs and "Reagan's Admirals," an influential group of retired military leaders who had the ear of the president.

Congressional reformers were counting on the results of an outside report of defense organization issues being conducted by the prestigious Washington, D.C., Center for Strategic and International Studies (CSIS). This report, the product of CSIS's Defense Organization Project, was the responsibility of defense analyst Philip Odeen. As Odeen himself conceded, however, giving the report a CSIS imprimatur involved a certain risk. The Washington think tank was the home of some of the best-known names in defense policy formulation, including James Schlesinger, Jeane Kirkpatrick, Alexander Haig, former NATO ambassador William Lynn, and R. James Woolsey, who served as Undersecretary of the Navy. To make matters worse, CSIS was the philosophical center of the anti-reform opposition, a group that included the titular leader of the Reagan Admirals, retired JCS Chairman Thomas Moorer.* Despite Moorer's bias, Odeen could not exclude him, since such a decision would ruin the study's claim to impartiality.

By late 1983, Odeen had convened members of the project, established working groups on specific issues, and structured a year-long agenda of meetings that touched on every major area of the defense establishment. The report would include recommendations for JCS reform and reorganization proposals for "the Office of the Secretary of Defense, the military departments, the joint military structures, and the defense industry." Because of the wide range of topics, reform became a dominant concern of the defense establishment. At the beginning of 1984, it began to play an increasingly important role in congressional and administration decisions on defense and foreign policy issues. Military reform was suddenly one of Washington's most talked-about political topics, one of the few broad-based initiatives that both promised to ignite the long-smoldering debate over defense spending and raised the question of the quality of military advice.

While it's a common failing of representative democracies to transform public policy issues into personal struggles, a question of who will win and who will lose, the defense reform debate remained relatively free of such personal attacks. While Weinberger continually characterized it as a tacit critique of his capabilities — and a typical Washington turf battle — reform advocates refused to be drawn in. They realized their efforts could be sidetracked by an open struggle with the secretary, and they knew there was much more at stake. And although they perceived glaring deficiencies in the daily management of the Pentagon, they were quick to note that such deficiencies reflected organizational weaknesses.

By downplaying their differences with Weinberger, the JCS, and the Reagan Admirals, Odeen, House aide Arch Barrett, and Senate aide Jim Locher challenged opponents to make the case for the status quo, to prove that the American military was well enough organized to win not only the next war but any conflict of the previous three decades. History was on the side of the reformers, a point made by a number of

---

* During an interview on this issue, Moorer said that Odeen accused him of trying to have funding for the project killed, an accusation he rejected. "They [Odeen and his allies] had the deck packed. They say I tried to get money out of the hands of CSIS for this report, but the fact of the matter is that they told me to keep my mouth shut, tried to keep me from writing a dissent."

commentators early in the debate. This viewpoint was critical to the reformers' position that military reorganization was essential. One such comment, by defense analyst Jeffrey Record, is typical of the arguments for reform. "Not since the Inchon landing has a significant U.S. military venture been crowned with success," he noted at an early stage. "On the contrary, our military performance since September 1950 suggests that we as a society have lost touch with the art of war."

By March 1984, the Defense Organization Project had made substantial progress in studying the need for change in the military's command structure, in defense planning and resource allocation, in the congressional budget process and in procurement. The group's progress and the broad base of support it had gathered from retired officers and former high-level defense officials, including study co-chairs Andrew Goodpaster and Melvin Laird, worried the Secretary of Defense. "Weinberger was going nuts," Locher noted later. "He could see that we were gaining momentum on the study, that we were getting some attention. There were some hurdles left."

In particular, House and Senate aides wanted to break up the nearly unanimous opposition to reform among members of the JCS. After a series of meetings with the chiefs, however, it was clear that reform legislation would have to go forward without their approval. Looking elsewhere, reform advocates turned to other Pentagon officers. To their amazement, they discovered that higher-ranking two- and three-star officers secretly supported JCS reorganization. The depth of this feeling among flag rank officers on the JCS staff was related by a congressional aide, who remembered one notable meeting with an Air Force general. "It was pretty weird really, this meeting," he said. "We went to this general and he just laughed at us, said that he could never support reform, that Weinberger would never support reform. Then he took off his coat, made us put away our notebooks, and started talking — almost like he had taken off his stars. He told us OSD [the Office of the Secretary of Defense] was a mess. So that's when we figured it out — we had to get these guys out of uniform."

These meetings between congressional reform advocates and JCS officers had a significant impact on the fight. While Vessey, Wickham, Watkins, and Kelley were publicly opposed to reform, they kept a low profile on the issue. Reformers speculated that the JCS's near silence during this part of the debate was the direct result of pressures from the JCS staff. There was also speculation that JCS members were taking Weinberger's warnings literally. The secretary's public claims that the military should not have a larger role in the councils of government contained an ironic consequence. By raising the specter that reform would embolden military disagreement with civilian policies, Weinberger had inadvertently silenced his most effective political

asset: barring their opposition to the debate in the name of his defini-
tion of military loyalty.

Locher discovered a parallel group of unknown reform supporters at
the NSC, where McFarlane was secretly advocating a program of military reorganization. "McFarlane turned out to be one of the really
important people on this whole thing," a colleague of Locher's
reflected, "but McFarlane couldn't be identified with it — it was just
too dangerous." McFarlane, this aide said, refused to publicly support
the legislation because of his fragile relationship with Weinberger, but
he did promise advocates that he would work behind the scenes to put
together a comprehensive reform package. "It was the Beirut thing,"
one defense analyst acknowledged. "McFarlane was just sick about
what happened in Beirut, and he blamed the JCS. His attitude was, 'If
they don't want reform, it must be the right thing to do.' "*

By late November 1984, Barrett's and Locher's strategy was gaining
an almost unstoppable momentum. While they had failed to garner
the absolute support of the JCS or the White House, they had succeeded in dampening JCS and White House opposition. The
November elections, meanwhile, had removed John Tower, an opponent of the reorganization. His replacement as the Armed Services
Committee's ranking Republican, Barry Goldwater, not only supported the legislation, he considered it the one package that could be
his legacy. By the end of the year, reform proponents were confident
that they could win a congressional vote on a variety of proposals,
including one that would give the JCS chairman greater power over
the services and a more influential role in determining U.S. foreign
policy.

These hopes were buoyed in February by the release of the Defense
Organization Project report, which gave reform advocates their first
major public victory: it endorsed a program that called for nothing less
than a complete overhaul of the military and civilian defense establishment. Signed by six former Secretaries of Defense (McNamara,
Clifford, Laird, Richardson, Schlesinger, and Brown), it recommended
that the JCS be transformed from a collegial body of powerful service
officers to a group of military commanders answering to a senior
chairman. The report specified that the chairman "be made the principal military adviser to the president" and that he be given "full
authority over the Joint Staff." It also recommended that "unified and
specified commanders should be given greater authority over the service components within their commands and a larger institutional role

---

* McFarlane's bitterness about the Beirut disaster was made clear to one Senate aide in
late 1984. "He called it a planned failure," the aide said. His statement shocked the aide.
He seemed to be hinting that the JCS had purposely "botched the deployment because
they didn't agree with it."

in the allocation of defense resources." These recommendations stunned the opposition, who realized the report marked a clear reform victory.

The JCS staff, especially those three- and four-star officers who had been involved in earlier discussions on the issue, interpreted this first public reform victory as a clear defeat of traditional service prerogatives. If the CSIS recommendations became law, the influence of the individual service chiefs would be significantly dampened. The chiefs themselves, however, maintained their aloof silence. While a number of officers have speculated that this silence symbolized an unknown internal struggle between the Vessey chiefs and Weinberger, it's more likely that outside political pressure — from officers on the NSC — played a major role. Congressional aides claim that McFarlane's NSC aide, Admiral John Poindexter (who was lobbying for the Navy's top job), was instrumental in keeping JCS disagreements under wraps.

In March 1985, House staff members decided that they needed to write reform legislation that would combine the CSIS recommendations with proposals put forward by important civilian and military defense experts. Gaining such advice, however, posed a delicate problem: many of the nation's top experts were members of the Defense Department, career civil servants and political appointees who owed their continued employment to Weinberger. Capitol Hill reformers presented their problem in blunt terms, telling a number of experts that the passage of reform legislation was a fait accompli, that Congress was set to vote on a series of proposals whether or not it received their recommendations. These surreptitious conversations (many of them conducted after hours) led to a number of high-level meetings between Weinberger's assistants and House aides in April 1985, held without the secretary's knowledge. "One full weekend was spent hammering out the bill with an assistant secretary of defense," a House investigator reflected. "We just got this phone call and the secretary said, 'Well, all right, if you're going to do this thing, you might as well do it right.' "

While these private discussions were being held, Senate aides were conducting similar sessions with the NSC, using hundreds of taped interviews with officers to show that there was widespread support for the initiative throughout the defense establishment. According to one Senate aide, the interviews were used in a last attempt to convince McFarlane to confront Weinberger on the issue.* Despite his convic-

---

* "The NSC got the Packard commission," a top Senate Armed Services defense expert later reflected. "McFarlane was the guy who got the president to appoint the commission, and after him it was Poindexter who made sure it did its work. They had really won the battle for us; they should take the credit."

tions, McFarlane refused, but he came up with a strategy that he believed would be more effective in neutralizing Weinberger's opposition. In April, he told Senate aides that he would convince the president to appoint a special commission to study defense reform, putting at its head a credible and highly respected pro-reform chairman. His proposal was received with great joy by members of the Armed Services Committee, especially after McFarlane reported that the president had agreed to appoint former Assistant Secretary of Defense David Packard as the chairman.

When Reagan announced the establishment of the Blue Ribbon Commission on Defense Management on July 15, 1985, Weinberger immediately endorsed the idea. According to reformers who had pushed for the special study, he believed his position as Defense Secretary made his views against reform impregnable. Senate aides say that they were counting on his arrogance, his belief that a special study would acquit his personal management style. The aides also believed Weinberger was comforted by the probability that the appointment of a committee meant that the controversy would be sidetracked, at least for the immediate future. Even the appointment of Laird's most notoriously cost-conscious assistant to head the study was welcomed by the secretary, who was apparently operating under the delusion that all Republicans believed in large defense budgets.

By the late summer of 1985, reform proponents could look back on nearly three years of slow but certain progress. After sparking a congressional debate, Jones and Meyer had convinced congressional aides to pursue the issue. The Beirut bombing and the continued questioning of the JCS leadership reinvigorated these efforts at the moment they seemed most likely to fail. The report of a highly regarded outside study group, the retirement of a Senate chairman opposed to the initiative, an unexpected alliance with the NSC, and, finally, the appointment of a presidential task force were symbols of the reformers' success. Still, congressional leaders, many of whom advocated a sweeping reorganization of the defense establishment, had failed to garner support for their position from the JCS.

While the JCS had maintained a proper silence throughout the debate, its opposition to reform, to a clearer and more influential role for JCS officers, was well known. The most important opponent was Vessey, who believed that the program outlined in the CSIS report gave unified commanders nearly dictatorial power over their own forces. He was also concerned that by increasing the JCS chairman's influence, reformers would be inadvertently including him as a combat commander. Eventually, he said, the two power centers — one focused on the JCS chairman, the other on unified commanders — would contend for military dominance.

Vessey would not change his position, even though a number of his two- and three-star colleagues attempted to convince him that it was time to compromise, ensuring that a number of his ideas were included in the final legislation. Even after warnings that the legislation would pass Congress without his input, he refused to listen to reform arguments. While Vessey's approval wasn't essential to the legislation's final passage, aides to the two Armed Services committees were disappointed not to have even implicit JCS approval. But just as congressional reform proponents were readying the first in a series of legislative packages, Vessey announced his retirement.

His decision surprised almost everyone, including Reagan. With six months left in his second term, Vessey told the president that "it [is] time for me to go." He was apparently exhausted by his responsibilities and by the mounting criticism of his leadership after the Beirut bombing and the invasion of Grenada, and he felt he had fulfilled his official duties. His retirement on October 5 brought to an end one of the most colorful military careers in recent JCS history. While Vessey's rise through the ranks served as proof that military prowess can be rewarded by prompt promotion, his failure as the military's top officer seemed to show that combat is not always an infallible teacher. It was a new era; Vessey's tenure was evidence that the JCS needed good managers even more than good soldiers.

The October 1985 appointment of Admiral William Crowe, Jr., to be the nation's eleventh JCS chairman was greeted with something less than the total celebration that had followed the appointment of his predecessor. Crowe was not unknown, but he certainly didn't cut the same figure as the steady, steely-eyed former farmboy from rural Minnesota who had learned how to command troops from inside the Anzio meatgrinder. Crowe's promotion seemed emblematic of the JCS's fate: civilian leaders were now rewarding politically astute desk-bound officers, relegating the more colorful and combat-wise service leaders to a life in the front lines. For some officers, the trend spelled doom. Here were military leaders in name only; the real decisions should be made from the shotgun seat of a jeep. For others, the appointment was reassuring. It didn't matter that Crowe wasn't a real commander because the JCS wasn't a separate military body with actual command authority.

Determining just which of these two points of view was accurate is one reason that military reform had caused such a divisive administrative struggle. The two views were really shadows of the real question: Should the JCS be the nation's premier military command body, in which joint officers were rewarded for their ability to fight a war ("in all elements, with all services, as one single concentrated effort," as

Eisenhower said), or merely the Secretary of Defense's top management team? Crowe's promotion seemed to resolve the debate. The apple-faced former submariner who, like Wheeler, had "never heard a shot fired in anger" was ostensibly named because of his lack of command experience, not in spite of it. A premium had been put on his ability to get along; he was viewed as a cooperative, modest, self-effacing commander who could be counted on to support the administration, an officer in the mold of Count Helmuth von Moltke, not George S. Patton.

In fact, Crowe became the most loyal chairman in JCS history: not only did he agree with Weinberger's position on everything from the budget to nuclear disarmament, he actually deferred to him in public, seconding his positions in Congress, nodding approval of his statements on the Soviets during NSC meetings, and defending his increasingly embattled tenure to his colleagues. For Congress, this loyalty was disturbing, then amusing, and, finally, even puzzling. George Wilson of the *Washington Post* castigated Crowe and his colleagues for this obsequious loyalty, writing that the JCS had "taken a dive" on a number of important issues. Senate aides castigated the chairman for "piling up the sandbags round Weinberger's office, just piling them up." House aides were even more outspoken: "It's damn embarrassing to see this guy — always one step behind Weinberger, following him around like a little dog." Even the House committee chairman, Les Aspin, got into the act. "Has anyone seen the JCS lately?" he asked during one hearing on disarmament policy. "Does anyone know what happened to them? Where did they go, anyway?"

In the minds of most members of Congress, the JCS had truly become, in Richard Perle's words, "pushovers and patsies for whoever leans on them the last, the longest, and the hardest." In many ways, however, this view was unjustified; there was one area in particular where Crowe ended up privately, but firmly, disagreeing with Weinberger. When it came to defense reorganization and JCS reform, Crowe was not the intransigent and outspoken opponent that Weinberger had wanted. When the admiral took over as JCS chairman, he was convinced that legislation mandating sweeping military reforms would have a negative impact on the JCS. The one part that was most disturbing to him was the provision for a vice chairman of the JCS, which he thought would actually prove damaging to the military decision-making process.

Within five months, however, it was becoming apparent to reform proponents that Crowe was beginning to moderate some of his opposition. While he was not in open, public disagreement with Weinberger, he was beginning to take a position that failed to mimic Weinberger's views. At least part of the reason for Crowe's change of heart, according to JCS staff officers, was his frustration with his colleagues who seemed unwilling, or unable, to make substantive policy decisions on even minor issues. Crowe was dissatisfied with JCS procedures that obscured the importance of the JCS as the nation's premier military leaders. Its tradition of seeking consensus had often hampered military advice, but during the Reagan years it seemed to be even more damaging, intruding into every decision made by the JCS staff. According to JCS officers, Crowe was particularly angered by an incident that seemed to epitomize this paralysis.

In early 1986, a flimsy paper arguing for the inclusion of skimmed milk in military stores was circulated in the offices of the JCS and then forwarded to a joint directorate. Several days later, however, a buff paper was recirculated; service action officers had been unable to reach a decision. Documents appended to the original statement had grown in thickness, reflecting the services' positions. The director of the JCS chose to make the decision on his own, which he then passed back to each service's action officer. These officers, however, failed to endorse the director's decision. The differences of opinion were startling: one service officer argued eloquently for the inclusion of skimmed milk on overseas bases, while each of the others took an opposite position. The divided opinions eventually ignited a debate among the three JCS deputy chiefs, who also disagreed. The debate was summarized on green paper and forwarded to the JCS for a final decision. Crowe was outraged. The most important military men on the planet would now decide whether skimmed milk should be offered to U.S. personnel overseas.

The skimmed milk debate was repeated as Defense Department lore, cited as proof by JCS officers that reorganization was long overdue, that the American high command had become prisoners of its own system, that the failure of American arms began not in Beirut or Grenada but at the very highest level of the Pentagon. According to JCS officers, Crowe and his colleagues "must have had dozens of meetings on the [skimmed milk] issue," including one in which Weinberger made a plea for the inclusion of skimmed milk in the diet of American soldiers. "I use skimmed milk on my cereal," Weinberger told the chiefs. The statement surprised Wickham. "Really?" he said. "I use two percent." Three months after the debate began, the JCS issued its decision on red-striped paper: military canteens were allowed to sell the product to their customers.

That the JCS decided military policy in every area wasn't a surprise. During the Reagan years, however, the importance the chiefs attached to being a part of even the most negligible debate had become an obsession. In the mid-1970s, the JCS reviewed nearly 15,000 separate policy papers each year, a considerable but manageable number. By

1986, however, the number of annual policy papers had risen to nearly 20,000. The JCS's desire to treat each service equally had resulted in paralysis. Worse yet, JCS officers feared, the practice had led to what they called "lowest common denominator leadership," the institutionalization of procedures that allowed the dissent of a single service to have a significant impact on military policy. Crowe was more than just disgusted by these procedures, he was convinced they could be changed. Holding a Ph.D. from Princeton, Crowe had written his thesis on military cooperation in the British joint system; he knew there was an alternative to a system that produced a blizzard of inconsequential policies.

By April 1986, Crowe had softened his position on military reform to the extent that he agreed with certain critical provisions of a reform bill being drafted in Congress. His tentative endorsement of the legislation — what one House aide called his "winking approval" — placed him in a delicate position vis-à-vis Weinberger. Crowe would have to maneuver carefully and quietly to make certain that the JCS influenced key reform provisions. He had to be especially careful not to alienate Weinberger, who, he knew, could make his tenure as JCS chairman miserable. His tentative opening led to a series of meetings between Capitol Hill reformers and high-ranking JCS officers. The two- and three-star officers said that while Crowe and his colleagues could not endorse the congressional proposals, they implied they would not publicly oppose them. The chairman would even work to modify Weinberger's opposition, they said. Most important, Crowe and his colleagues wanted to be sure that the provision mandating that the JCS chairman serve as a full member of the NSC remain a central part of the legislation.

These meetings put the finishing touches on the reform legislation, bringing the JCS into the process for the first time. The work of Gabriel, who had long served as a backchannel of communications between the Hill and JCS members, had paid off: the chiefs had not only softened their opposition, they suggested detailed changes that would clear up ambiguities in the legislation. The JCS acted just in time, according to Senate staff members; Barry Goldwater was ready to move forward to the passage of the bill at the beginning of May, even though the president's Blue Ribbon Commission had not yet issued its report.

The reform legislation put forward by Congress proposed nothing less than a complete organizational revolution. It designated the JCS chairman as the principal military adviser to the president and Secretary of Defense; the entire JCS membership had previously been given that responsibility. Under the act, the chairman, not individual JCS members, would be responsible for developing the military's strategic plans and budget proposals. The services would no longer have control over their own budgets. The chairman was given complete control of the JCS staff; joint service officers would no longer answer to each JCS member. The act also gave the commanders in chief of the unified commands the power to name their own subordinates, regardless of service, a responsibility previously given to the service chiefs. To make certain that the chairman's new powers were not undermined by individual service heads, Congress created a joint officer specialty. In effect, the act ended service parochialism by allowing the chairman to promote officers in the joint arena regardless of whether an individual chief agreed.

JCS staff officers told members of Congress that they had serious disagreements with certain aspects of the bill. In particular, they believed the act gave the unified commanders too much power. The fear of Vessey (and Crowe) was that the legislation would create unnecessary tension between a powerful chairman and the group of dictatorial unified commanders. JCS officers also worried that a proposed amendment repealing the Navy's independent operating authority would be met with overwhelming and open opposition. In addition, Crowe was still opposed to the creation of a vice chairman.

Although this opposition was significant, it wasn't enough to cause an irreparable break between the reformers and the JCS. In a last series of meetings in April, House staff members informed JCS staff officers that the legislation might become law without their support, something neither group wanted. While critical members of Congress knew that Crowe could not publicly endorse the legislation, they wanted his assurance that he would not publicly oppose it — this despite his disagreement with a number of its provisions. This last-minute gamble — that the JCS would remain silent in its opposition rather than be excluded from the legislative process altogether — paid off. When the bill reached the Senate floor on May 5, opposition was limited to a small group of Weinberger partisans.

In effect, Crowe cut a deal: in exchange for implicit JCS agreement, Congress accepted point 11 of Title II, which authorized "the JCS Chairman, subject to the direction of the president, to attend and participate in National Security Council meetings." The seat on the NSC was so important to the JCS that it was willing to abandon its opposition to reform.

On the evening of May 7, 1986, the Senate passed the most sweeping military reform legislation in the history of the nation by a stunning 95–0 vote and, in a surprise move, named it for one of its chief architects, Arizona's Barry Goldwater. Seated in a wheelchair, the senator wept in gratitude as his colleagues rose in unison to pay him homage. Goldwater, who was retiring after more than thirty years, was even more moved by the news that a special provision of the act established a Barry Goldwater Scholarship and Excellence in Education Program, with an initial endowment of $40 million. "Only Goldwater could produce this," one senator told his colleagues from the floor. "If anybody else had been the one who had been advocating this reorganization, every military man and woman at the Pentagon would have been down our backs as 'communist sympathizers.' " Finally, after struggling to his feet with the aid of crutches, Goldwater choked out a response: "Damn. The hell with it. When you get old, you get to the point where you can't say thank you. I'll just shut up and let you do what you want." After the session adjourned, Goldwater assessed the impact of the legislation. "It's the only goddamned thing I've done in the Senate that's worth a damn," he said.

One month later, in a ceremony in the Rose Garden, David Packard presented Reagan with the final report of the Blue Ribbon Commission on Defense Management, endorsing the changes enacted by the Goldwater legislation, while Weinberger looked on in apparent agreement. At the back of the crowd, those most responsible for the success of the reform package knew that Reagan's acceptance of the report was the final, absolute assurance that the Goldwater bill would become law. For some, Weinberger's smiling acceptance was particularly ironic. "It was an amazing scene," one Senate aide reported. "I kept thinking, 'We got you, you bastard, we got you.' "

The Goldwater-Nichols Defense Reorganization Act, signed into law by the president on September 20, ended forty years of service ascendancy. It was just such service ascendancy, reform proponents argued, that led to the dismissal of MacArthur, the resignation of Ridgway, the shock of Sputnik, the firing of CNO Anderson, the chaos of Vietnam, the national humiliation of Desert One, the Marine barracks massacre in Beirut, and the embarrassment of Urgent Fury. But the legislation's impact is likely to be far less public. Military reform was designed to end the "lowest common denominator" philosophy that characterized "ponderous and poorly written" JCS papers on often arcane subjects, that led to the establishment of "meaningless OPLANS," that involved the four-star heads of the services in a continual competition for congressional appropriations (and glory), and that sparked incessant internal power struggles that divided the JCS and, by extension, the military services.

The victors were straightforward in their characterization of the new legislation: the bill would end service parochialism and reinforce the concept of combined arms operations. The increased power of the JCS chairman meant that the military would be better managed. He could now present options to civilian officials that accurately reflected U.S. capabilities. The nation's military programs and policies would be designed by an independent staff of joint officers answering to a chairman; their policies would no longer be the product of a JCS committee beholden to the individual services. By making the chairman an official member of the NSC, Congress endorsed long-held JCS beliefs that civilian decisions on military questions had often led to disaster. The JCS chairman had the right to give advice not only when asked, but also when not asked. The nation's military leaders were no longer disqualified from being included in foreign policy discussions simply because they wore uniforms.

The passage of the reorganization bill was certainly a victory for the JCS, but, even more, it was a personal triumph for Crowe. The reform asserted the power of the JCS and reinforced the chairman's role as the nation's highest-ranking and most influential officer. The office had grown in stature, as had Crowe himself. This increased stature and Crowe's new role were symbolized by an incident that occurred at the beginning of the first formal session of the chiefs after the bill was passed. That morning, Crowe walked from his office down a short hallway to the tank. Trailed by an aide, with an agenda tucked firmly under his arm, Crowe hesitated for a moment before walking into the room, nodding to his colleagues. For the first time, the four-star chiefs of the services all rose to their feet as the chairman entered.

AFTERWORD

★　　　★　　　★　　　★

While the Goldwater-Nichols Defense Reorganization Act of 1986 guaranteed the JCS a voice in the councils of civilian government, it could never ensure that its advice would be heeded. As in the past, the effectiveness of the JCS would continue to be predicated more on the strength of its top officers than on a legislative mandate. As one Senate staff aide noted two years after the passage of the bill, reform did not inoculate the military against failure, inefficiency, or poor leadership. Nor could it ensure its influence in determining foreign policy goals; for that, the JCS would continue to rely on the final policy formulations of civilian leaders.

The JCS continued to battle the presidents it served. Within weeks of the bill's passage, Reagan met with Gorbachev in Reykjavik, Iceland, provoking the first confrontation between the JCS and civilian leadership since reform. Taking his cue from Weinberger, Crowe decided not to attend the summit as Reagan's military aide. Nor, White House officials assured him, would he be needed. Reagan, they said, would be holding nonsubstantive discussions with the Soviet general secretary. The outcome of the summit came as an unpleasant surprise: the president and his aides nearly bargained away 50 percent of all U.S. strategic missiles, setting aside the agreement only after it became apparent that the Soviet Union wanted a guarantee that the Strategic Defense Initiative would not be developed or deployed.

To make matters worse, Crowe was enraged that the chief of the Soviet General Staff, Marshal Sergei F. Akhromeyev, had stood just behind Gorbachev throughout his public appearances in Reykjavik. It was hard to miss the implication: the military held a place of honor in the Soviet government but was ignored in the United States. "What the hell is going on?" Crowe reportedly asked Weinberger the day Reagan returned from Iceland. The angry chairman decided it was time to make his own views known, even if they caused the administration public embarrassment. Over the next several days, he spoke with reporters on the JCS's opposition to Reagan's apparent willingness to negotiate major cuts in strategic weapons. Other high-ranking officers did likewise; General Bernard Rogers, the outspoken Supreme Allied

Commander, said that the proposed cuts gave him "gas pains."

Stung by the criticisms, administration officials spent the better part of the next two months attempting to sell the idea that they had gained a major victory in Iceland. In the end, however, the cost of their failure to consult with U.S. allies — and with the JCS — proved to be the most important lesson. Chastised by the military's dim view of his arms negotiations, Reagan assured the JCS that he would ask for advice before his next meeting with the Soviets. This almost public admission of failure was followed by a round of activity on Crowe's part, and he suddenly became a familiar figure on Capitol Hill.

Invigorated as much by his moral victory following Reykjavik as by his new status under the Goldwater-Nichols Act, Crowe began to take positions that angered Weinberger, his former patron. He even downplayed what everyone thought was the military's infatuation with the Strategic Defense Initiative. Asked to give a date for final deployment by Les Aspin, Crowe presented an indictment of the administration's optimistic forecasts. "It's not out in the parking lot, if that's what you're asking," he said. His dissent was infectious. "We were asked to agree to prepare for a nuclear war when we knew that a nuclear war was the least likely conflict we'd ever be faced with," a Navy admiral said in late 1986. "Then we were told to forget increasing conventional arms or adding manpower when that's precisely the one thing we needed to keep from using nuclear weapons. Then we were told we were going to get rid of nuclear weapons. Does that make any sense?"

Yet, within two weeks of the Reykjavik summit, Crowe faced another policy crisis. At the end of October, Reagan announced his support of legislation establishing a separate military command for special operations forces. The news was a blow to JCS members, who had lobbied vainly to get the proposal killed during Senate consideration. Crowe had even approached Sam Nunn with a final plea to allow the JCS to "deal with this on our own." Crowe's worries were justified; over a period of five years, the special operations forces had been plagued by a number of scandals, including allegations that a secret Army unit, the Intelligence Support Activity, had misappropriated funds. The scandals had become so worrisome that both Vessey and Crowe had been forced to institute strict accounting procedures for all special units. The worst problem, according to JCS officers, was that these units had been competing with the CIA in a number of intelligence operations.

Crowe had privately claimed that the JCS should be given new authority to discipline the special units, that the services were incapable of monitoring their operations. The forces, he reportedly told Nunn, were "out of control" and "poorly disciplined," a clear echo of Harold Johnson's warning in 1965 that the Green Berets were "fugitives from responsibility" who had "found a haven where their actions were not scrutinized too carefully, and where they came under only sporadic or intermittent observation from the regular chain of command." Crowe's plea fell on deaf ears, and at the end of October, Reagan signed a bill that gave special operations forces new credibility in the defense establishment. It was the JCS's second defeat since the Goldwater-Nichols bill. A worse crisis, however, was still ahead.

On November 5, 1986, Reagan announced that the administration had shipped arms to Iran in a covert mission run by the NSC. As the weeks passed, these revelations grew into a major scandal that forced Reagan to fire his national security adviser, Admiral William Poindexter, and his aide, Lieutenant Colonel Oliver North. North had already become known to JCS officers as "the highest-ranking lieutenant colonel in history." For Crowe, the Iran-contra revelations were an embittering experience, particularly since they seemed to mirror the JCS's Reykjavik experience. He told a House committee with considerable disgust that he had learned of the operation "inadvertently." This bitter admission reflected his own views that Senators Nunn and Cohen, who had pushed for the approval of the special operations command, had learned a valuable lesson.

As the Iran-contra scandal consumed Washington, the controversy surrounding the military began to fade. By early spring 1987, with Reagan increasingly besieged by claims that his administration had "privatized" foreign policy, the JCS began to effect the reforms enacted the previous autumn. Crowe seemed to become more articulate, more outspoken, more willing to disagree with his civilian superiors over military and foreign policy initiatives. Even during a series of military crises — in the Persian Gulf, in Central America, and in Moscow (where Marine guards were accused of consorting with female KGB agents), he cultivated his image as a tough but cool and articulate leader. Even in the midst of his most severe crisis — when an American warship mistakenly downed an Iranian jet in July 1988 — he proved resilient. Through controversy and crisis, through a season of mounting international tensions, the JCS chairman diligently and patiently managed the chiefs through the reform transition. In the process, he became one of its most outspoken advocates.

The passage of the Goldwater-Nichols Act had not altogether ended the tradition of controversy that had plagued the JCS. At the same time that Crowe was transforming the structure of the military, a series of unforeseen international incidents was placing enormous pressures on the JCS, almost as if the new civilian-military relationship was being purposely tested. The chiefs were forced to focus on a host of subjects, from disarmament to whether U.S. officers should be allowed to serve as NSC directors. They were quizzed on military policy, the effectiveness of U.S. weaponry, and on their relationship with civilian leaders. All of this was yet another test of the military's ability to overcome "the inescapable weak point in the structure."

Reformers remained optimistic. Although the reorganization was not yet a year old, the JCS was more confident than ever that it could handle the continuing crises that faced the nation. It would not, however, be an easy transformation: pockets of dissent continued to slow full reform, as a number of JCS staff officers postponed critical decisions to carry out the congressional mandate. JCS members themselves hesitated in designating officers to institute the legislation's provisions. It was only the presence of Crowe himself — with his new powers as JCS chairman — that broke the logjam. He was his own best example: after months of hesitation, he appointed a JCS vice chairman.

By the late summer of 1988, the transformation was nearly complete. In the wake of his exuberant and highly publicized national tour with the head of the Soviet Armed Forces, it was clear not only that Crowe had become one of the nation's best-known JCS chairmen, he was also one of its most powerful and was acknowledged as a central figure in internal administration debates on foreign policy questions. But the current impact of JCS reorganization, which has been acquitted by Crowe's abilities and by his growing cordial relations with civilian leaders, is but a partial measure of its effectiveness. We are left, in fact, with a sobering thought: the true test of military reform will come not in peace, but in war.

MEMBERS OF THE
JOINT CHIEFS
OF STAFF

★ ★ ★ ★

*Chief of Staff to the Commander in Chief of
the Army and the Navy*

Admiral William D. Leahy	1942–49

Chairmen of the Joint Chiefs of Staff

General Omar N. Bradley, USA	1949–53
Admiral Arthur W. Radford, USN	1953–57
General Nathan F. Twining, USAF	1957–60
General Lyman L. Lemnitzer, USA	1960–62
General Maxwell D. Taylor, USA	1962–64
General Earle G. Wheeler, USA	1964–70
Admiral Thomas H. Moorer, USN	1970–74
General George S. Brown, USAF	1974–78
General David C. Jones, USAF	1978–82
General John W. Vessey, Jr., USA	1982–85
Admiral William J. Crowe, Jr., USN	1985–

Chiefs of Staff, United States Army

General George C. Marshall	1942–45
General Dwight D. Eisenhower	1945–48
General Omar N. Bradley	1948–49
General J. Lawton Collins	1949–53
General Matthew B. Ridgway	1953–55
General Maxwell D. Taylor	1955–59
General Lyman L. Lemnitzer	1959–60
General George H. Decker	1960–62
General Earle G. Wheeler	1962–64
General Harold K. Johnson	1964–68

General William C. Westmoreland   1968–72
General Bruce Palmer, Jr. (Acting)   1972
General Creighton W. Abrams   1972–74
General Fred C. Weyand   1974–76
General Bernard W. Rogers   1976–79
General Edward C. Meyer   1979–83
General John A. Wickham, Jr.   1983–87
General Carl E. Vuono   1987–

Chiefs of Naval Operations, United States Navy

Admiral Harold R. Stark   1942
Admiral Ernest J. King   1942–45
Admiral Chester W. Nimitz   1945–47
Admiral Louis E. Denfeld   1947–49
Admiral Forrest P. Sherman   1949–51
Admiral William M. Fechteler   1951–53
Admiral Robert B. Carney   1953–55
Admiral Arleigh A. Burke   1955–61
Admiral George W. Anderson, Jr.   1961–63
Admiral David L. McDonald   1963–67
Admiral Thomas H. Moorer   1967–70
Admiral Elmo R. Zumwalt, Jr.   1970–74
Admiral James L. Holloway III   1974–78
Admiral Thomas B. Hayward   1978–82
Admiral James D. Watkins   1982–86
Admiral Carlisle A. H. Trost   1986–

Chiefs of Staff, United States Air Force

General Henry H. Arnold   1942–46
General Carl Spaatz   1946–48
General Hoyt S. Vandenberg   1948–53
General Nathan F. Twining   1953–57
General Thomas D. White   1957–61
General Curtis E. LeMay   1961–65
General John P. McConnell   1965–69
General John D. Ryan   1969–73
General George S. Brown   1973–74
General David C. Jones   1974–78
General Lew Allen, Jr.   1978–82
General Charles A. Gabriel   1982–86
General Robert T. Herres   1986–

Commandants, United States Marine Corps*

General Lemuel C. Shepherd, Jr.	1952–55
General Randolph McC. Pate	1956–59
General David M. Shoup	1960–63
General Wallace M. Greene, Jr.	1964–67
General Leonard F. Chapman, Jr.	1968–71
General Robert E. Cushman, Jr.	1972–75
General Louis H. Wilson	1975–79
General Robert H. Barrow	1979–83
General Paul X. Kelley	1983–87
General Alfred M. Gray	1987–

* Commandants, USMC, served as JCS co-equals since 1952, but only in matters directly affecting the Marines. Since 1969, commandants serve on the JCS and advise on all matters.

NOTES

INTRODUCTION

xiii "Civil-military relations": Palmer, *The 25-Year War*, p. 200.

xiii Colonel Casey is the movie's hero: *Seven Days in May*, Seven Arts Productions and Joel Productions, 1964.

xiv It holds regular meetings: Interview with General David C. Jones.

xiv The JCS comprises: Interview with General Bruce Palmer. In *The 25-Year War* (p. 21), Palmer describes the seating arrangement for JCS meetings in the tank: "The JCS seating arrangement has the chairman in the center of the long axis of the table with his back to the clock. The Air Force chief sits to the right of the chairman, and the director of the Joint Staff is on the chairman's left. Across the table the Army chief sits facing the director, and the chief of Naval Operations faces the Air Force chief. The commandant of the Marine Corps sits at one of the short ends of the table between the Air Force and Navy chiefs, while the secretary of the Joint Staff . . . holds down the other end."

xv They are responsible for overseeing: Defense 86, pp. 24–43 (figures have been updated to include the 1987 programs for Army and Navy units).

xvi While civilian secretaries: Barrett, *Reappraising Defense Organization*, pp. 18–25.

xvii "the inescapably weak points": Military History Institute (hereafter MHI), Interview with General Andrew Jackson Goodpaster, April 7, 1976.

I: AN ADMIRAL AND A GENERAL

1 "All members": Bradley memo, April 24, 1951, in Schnabel and Watson, "History of JCS," III: 542.

1 Joint Army-Navy Committee: JCS, "Concise History," p. 1. See also Larrabee, *Commander in Chief*, p. 17.

2 The Navy led the charge: Eisenhower, *Eisenhower at War*, p. 72.

2 Admiral Ernest J. King: Ibid., p. 84.

2 "joint coordinating body": JCS, "Concise History," pp. 2–3. See also JCS, "Evolving Role," pp. 2–4.

2 "war plans and strategy": JCS, "Concise History," p. 3.

3 Eisenhower's memo viewed the conflict: Eisenhower, *Eisenhower at War*, p. 81.

3 Operation Victory: Ibid., p. 73.

4 "conspired" to "expose the Navy": Ibid., p. 83.

5 Casablanca Conference: Ibid., pp. 6–7.

5 a "comprehensive reappraisal": Ibid., p. 7.

5 "the burden of detailed and routine matters": Ibid., p. 8.

6 "we did a better job": Interview with Admiral Thomas Moorer.

6 One effort was initiated: JCS, "Concise History," pp. 13–14.

6 JCS Special Committee on Reorganization: Ibid., p. 14.

6 committee headed by . . . Ferdinand Eberstadt: Ibid., p. 15.

7 a board of senior officers: Ibid., p. 18.

7 Navy witnesses argued: Ibid.

7 The Norstad-Sherman plan: Condit, "History of JCS," pp. 1–3. See also "Senate Report No. 239," June 5, 1947.

7 Not only did it officially name: National Security Act of 1947, pp. 61–63. See also U.S. Senate, "Defense Organization," p. 140.

7 Proponents of the bill: JCS, "Concise History," p. 23. See also Schnabel, "History of JCS," p. viii.

8 The act made no provision: JCS, "Concise History," p. 27.

9 Denfeld, a Naval Academy graduate: "Admiral Louis Emil Denfeld, U.S. Navy, Retired," Naval History Division, Washington, D.C. See also McHenry, *Webster's American Military Biographies*, p. 99.

9 Denfeld's predecessor: Larrabee, *Commander in Chief*, pp. 355–57.

9 He didn't take long: Korb, *Joint Chiefs of Staff*, p. 101. See also Condit, "History of JCS," p. 330.

9 "could establish offshore": Condit, "History of JCS," p. 160.

10 Just after Nimitz filed: Ibid., p. 174.

11 The military was split: Ibid., pp. 167–71.

11 "three Services": Ibid., p. 170.

11 At the beginning of the month: Ibid., pp. 173–76. See also MMH, "Functions of the Armed Forces and the Joint Chiefs of Staff," March 26, 1948.

12 "or have a field unit headquarters": Condit, "History of JCS," p. 175. See also U.S. Senate, "Defense Organization," October 16, 1985, pp. 435–37.

12 Within days: Ibid., p. 177.

12 "uncoordinated, and even conflicting requests": Ibid.

12 Once again, Forrestal: Ibid., p. 180.

13 In December, Denfeld: Ibid., p. 308. See also JCS 1952/1, December 21, 1948.

13 Denfeld's ploy worked initially: Condit, "History of JCS," p. 310.

14 The news came: Ibid., p. 311.

14 One week after Denfeld's: Ibid., p. 315.

14 In the office of the CNO: Interview with a retired Defense Department official.

14 He didn't care what: Condit, "History of JCS," p. 315. See also MMH, "Construction of 6A Carrier," May 26, 1948.

14 "The 1949 budget": Condit, "History of JCS," p. 315.

15 "called in those fellows": Ibid. See also MMH, "JCS to DJS," May 27, 1948.

15 In mid-1949, top Navy officers: Condit, "History of JCS," p. 329.

16 The changes had been suggested: U.S. Senate, "Defense Organization," p. 140. See also JCS, "Concise History," p. 30.

16 The opening shot of the B-36 debate: Condit, "History of JCS," p. 322.

17 Denfeld's honesty: U.S. House, *National Defense Program*, pp. 349–64.

17 They would testify: Condit, "History of JCS," p. 334.

17 True to form, the Navy: Ibid., pp. 339–49.

17 "Can the B-36 be intercepted": U.S. House, *National Defense Program*, p. 42.

18 "I fully support": Ibid., p. 349.

18 "A prime objective": Ibid., p. 456.

19 They had testified: U.S. House, *National Defense Program*, pp. 53–56.

19 "Integrity of command": Condit, "History of JCS," p. 343.

20 The U.S. military mission: Goulden, in *Untold Story of the War* (pp. 33–34), notes that KMAG commander Brigadier General William L. Roberts's glowing reports of ROK abilities were not held by every KMAG adviser.

20 It was a good thing: JCS memo, "Military Importance of Korea," September 23, 1947.

20 "In the face of": Schnable and Watson, "History of JCS," p. 47.

21 NSC-68 portrayed: Kaplan, *Wizards of Armageddon*, p. 140. See also Poole, "History of JCS," pp. 8–15.

21 "oversimplified issues": "Comments of the Bureau of the Budget," May 8, 1950; "Supplementary Budget Comments on NSC 68," May 8, 1950, in "Foreign Relations," p. 301.

22 The invasion of South Korea . . . not unexpected: Schnabel and Watson, "History of JCS," p. 26.

22 MacArthur initially disagreed: Ibid., p. 23.

22 "not within the capabilities": Ibid.

22 "sit by while Korea": Goulden, *Untold Story of the War*, p. 33.

23 "unless the Russians": "O.N.B. to Gen. Vandenberg, Gen. Collins, Adm. Sherman, and Adm. Davis," June 25, 1950, in Schnabel and Watson, "History of JCS," p. 61.

23 "To back away": Acheson, *Present at the Creation*, p. 375.

23 Present were Secretary of State Acheson: Schnabel and Watson, "History of JCS," p. 71.

23 a "complete defense" of the island: Ibid., pp. 405–6.

23 They included assessing: Ibid., pp. 72–73.

24 The official JCS history: Ibid., p. 79.

24 This characterization is inexact: Goulden, *Untold Story of the War*, pp. 66–68. See also Acheson, *Present at the Creation*, pp. 375–77.

24 It was an odd turnaround: Goulden, *Untold Story of the War*, p. 67.

25 "The Korean army is entirely incapable": Schnable and Watson, "History of JCS," p. 113.

25 "The decision had been taken": Ibid., p. 117.

25 "Korea is the wrong war": Ibid., p. 554; U.S. Senate, "Military Situation in the Far East," pp. 731–32.

25 Ridgway, an awe-inspiring general: Goulden, *Untold Story of the War*, p. 68.

26 After hesitantly agreeing: Manchester, *American Caesar*, p. 685.

27 "My confidence in the Navy": Ibid., pp. 686–87.

27 "Ask not for whom": Interview with a retired flag rank Army officer.

27 "I wish I had": Manchester, *American Caesar*, p. 687.

28 "an elaborate arrangement": Ibid., p. 692.

28 The JCS history: Schnabel and Watson, "History of JCS," p. 276.

28 "conduct the necessary military operations": Manchester, *American Caesar*, pp. 697, 698.

29 The evidence seems incontrovertible: Schnabel and Watson, "History of JCS," pp. 274–75.

29 "a matter of military necessity": Ibid., p. 275.

29 "hasty decisions": Ibid., p. 290.

30 "Men and material in large force": Ibid., p. 293.

30 "This is a very personal": Ibid., p. 296.

31 "We face an entirely new war": Ibid., p. 336.

32 When General Walton Walker: Goulden, *Untold Story of the War*, p. 424.

32 "changed the situation enormously": MHI, "Interview with General Harold K. Johnson," p. 42.

32 This outlook was reflected: Schnable and Watson, "History of JCS," pp. 408–9.

33 "As I have pointed out": Ibid., p. 411.

33 "Here is a posterity paper": Manchester, *American Caesar*, p. 745.

33 It cabled MacArthur: Schnabel and Watson, "History of JCS," p. 529.

34 Bradley favored: Ibid., p. 540.

34 George Marshall was called: Ibid., p. 543.

35 "I deeply regret": JCS 88180 to CINCFE, April 11, 1951.

2: FLIMSY, BUFF, AND GREEN

36 "These laborious processes": Eisenhower, "Special Message to Congress," p. 282.

36 Critics say . . . bureaucratic: Barrett, *Reappraising Defense Organization*, pp. 48–52.

36 The JCS chairman and a vice chairman: Defense 87. See also "HASC Unveils 'Revolutionary' New Pentagon Reorganization Bill," June 17, 1986.

37 The director of the JCS: Korb, *Joint Chiefs of Staff*, pp. 22–23. According to "Defense Organization" (p. 181), October 16, 1985, there are "roughly 750 military officers assigned to OJCS which includes the 400 officers on the Joint Staff."

37 These officers perform: Palmer describes the operations deputies: "In addition to attending the regular three-times-a-week JCS meetings with their four-star bosses, the director of the Joint Staff and the service operations deputies meet as a group several times a week. Known as the 'Operations Deputies,' this group of five three-star officers, chaired by the director, handles less critical or noncontroversial matters (*The 25-Year War*, p. 21).

37 In this sense . . . "dual hatted": Korb, *Joint Chiefs of Staff*, pp. 16–17.

38 In addition . . . "dual hatted": Barrett, *Reappraising Defense Organization*, p. 4.

38 JCS Memorandum of Policy 39: "JCS MOP 39," September 28, 1983.

38 According to the MOP 39: Ibid., pp. 6–8. See also U.S. Senate, *Defense Organization*, pp. 156–57.

38 The directive (or memorandum): Ibid., p. A-5, Appendix A.

38 It is summarized: Ibid.

38 Most issues are decided: Korb, *Joint Chiefs of Staff*, p. 24.

39 If the action officers: Ibid., p. 23.

39 These operations deputies: Palmer, *The 25-Year War*, p. 21.

39 After the JCS decides: U.S. Senate, *Defense Organization*, p. 157.

39 The process usually takes: Barrett projects the total staff strength at just over 2,700 people (*Reappraising Defense Organization*, p. 24).

39 In select cases: Interview with General David C. Jones.

40 The JCS meets: Ibid.

40 This tradition: Interview with Admiral Elmo Zumwalt, Jr.

40 "It's the kiss of death": Interview with a former JCS staff Army colonel.

41 "The closer we got to the Elbe": Interview with a former JCS staff officer.

41 A JCS assignment: Interview with Lawrence J. Korb.

41 While international crises: "War Games," *Defense Monitor*, 1984.

42 When the alarm bells: Interview with a JCS staff Army major.

42 "Sir, we have an incident here": Interview with a JCS flag rank officer.

42 The weapons manufacturers: Adde, "Solving the Puzzle Palace," October 13, 1986.

42 The attendant briefings, discussions: Interview with General Edward C. Meyer.

42 "It's not just promotions": Interview with a JCS staff officer.

42 "In the field I expected": Ibid.

43 MacArthur's dismissal: Goulden, *Untold Story of the War*, pp. 513–15.

43 Nevertheless, all four chiefs: Manchester, *American Caesar*, p. 786.

43 Two weeks later: Ibid., p. 795.

44 "I want to say that": Schnabel and Watson, "History of JCS," p. 560.

44 Citing a memorandum: Goulden, *Untold Story of the War*, p. 515. See also Schnabel and Watson, "History of JCS," pp. 550–51.

44 Nevertheless, MacArthur said he agreed: Goulden, *Untold Story of the War*, p. 551.

44 When Marshall was called: Ibid.

44 "He [MacArthur] is a brother": Ibid., p. 559.

44 "increase the risk": Ibid., p. 553.

44 "I want to make it clear": Ibid., p. 559.

44 "I think he is one of the most brilliant": Ibid., p. 560.

45 "We want you to feel unhampered": Manchester, *American Caesar*, p. 697.

45 Instead, he appeared: Goulden, *Untold Story of the War*, pp. 513–14.

45 "I assure you that": Ambrose, *Eisenhower: Soldier*, p. 511.

46 "greatest political mistake": Manchester, *American Caesar*, p. 802.

46 Even William Westmoreland: Interview with General William C. Westmoreland.

46 "I like General MacArthur": Ibid.

47 Ridgway showed up on the battlefield: Blair, *The Forgotten War*, pp. 561–62.

47 Ridgway was charismatic: Ibid., pp. 571–72.

48 Dubbed "the New Look": Ambrose, *Eisenhower, The President*, p. 171.

48 "What do we mean?": Ibid.

48 The atom bomb, Eisenhower said: Ibid.

49 "Now, our most valued": Ibid.

49 In 1951, two years after: Ambrose, *Eisenhower: Soldier*, p. 506.

49 In a letter to Charles Wilson: Ibid., p. 513.

50 The nation could not be responsible: Ibid., p. 505.

50 His first criticism: Ambrose, *Eisenhower, The President*, p. 172.

50 The JCS was supported: Ibid., pp. 86–87.

50 "the year of maximum danger": Ibid., p. 88.

50 But Eisenhower cut the figure: Ibid., p. 89.

51 Although he had won: Ibid., p. 90.

51 "We are no longer": Ibid., p. 144.

51 Paradoxically, Radford: JCS, "Concise History," p. 35.

51 But Eisenhower had first considered Radford: Ambrose, *Eisenhower, The President*, p. 30.

52 In addition, Radford seemed: Korb, *Joint Chiefs of Staff*, pp. 84–85.

52 Radford, as Eisenhower remembered: Ambrose, *Eisenhower, The President*, p. 90. Eisenhower even had Radford pledge that as JCS chairman he would be an advocate for "all the services, governed by the single criterion of what is best for the United States."

52 But Radford was supported by: Hoopes, *The Devil and John Foster Dulles*, p. 194.

52 Radford was also well known: Ibid.

52 "kill the bastards scientifically": Ibid.

53 This seemingly contradictory attitude: Ambrose, *Eisenhower, The President*, pp. 432–33.

53 A graduate of the West Point class: "Statement of Military Service of Nathan Farragut Twining," September 26, 1955.

54 During one particularly stormy JCS session: Interview with a retired JCS Air Force officer.

54 "Ask him": Ibid.

54 "What does all this mean?": "Modern Evolution of Armed Forces," May 25, 1954. See also Kaplan, *Wizards of Armageddon*, pp. 183–84.

55 On the contrary . . . the New Look: Kaplan, *Wizards of Armageddon*, p. 183.

55 Instead, they were more likely: Ambrose, *Eisenhower, The President*, p. 172.

56 Through all of 1953: Interview with a retired JCS Air Force officer.

56 When he sent his defense budget: Ambrose, *Eisenhower, The President*, p. 224.

57 The defense appropriations Eisenhower sent: Ibid., p. 223.

57 At the end of 1954: Ibid.

58 He warned Congress: Ibid., p. 234.

58 Eisenhower's personal liaison: Interview with General Andrew Goodpaster.

58 "The president was very much against": Ibid.

58 Eisenhower told the members of the JCS: Ibid.

59 Radford first suggested: Interview with a former JCS intelligence officer. That Radford made the recommendation is supported by almost overwhelming circumstantial evidence. For a discussion of this, see Prados, *The Sky Would Fall*, pp. 153–54, and Ambrose, *Eisenhower, The President*, p. 181.

60 Eisenhower never seriously considered: Ambrose, *Eisenhower, The President*, pp. 177–79.

60 "I want you to carry this question": Ibid., p. 206.

60 The crisis came in February 1955: Ibid., p. 231.

60 Radford's arguments to Eisenhower: Hoopes, *The Devil and John Foster Dulles*, pp. 266–68.

61 On January 21: Ambrose, *Eisenhower, The President*, p. 232.

61 The JCS expressed disapproval: Ibid.

61 "easier to defend": Ibid., pp. 232–33.

61 The president responded by saying: Ibid., p. 233.

61 The third week of January: Ibid.

61 Ridgway decided to use the opportunity: Ibid., p. 234.

62 The president told his Secretary of State: Ibid.

63 "beside himself with glee": Interview with a retired flag rank Navy officer.

63 Buffeted from all sides: Interview with Goodpaster.

63 Goodpaster's tour: Ambrose, *Eisenhower, The President*, pp. 238–39.

63 On the evening of March 25: Ibid., p. 240.

64 "By God . . . this has got to stop": Ibid., p. 241.

64 "the best of the crop": Interview with General Bruce Palmer.

3: THE DEBATE

65 "As I reread these documents": Taylor, *Swords and Plowshares*, p. 164.

66 The doctrine of massive retaliation: Kaplan points out that "from 1955 on, in JCS meetings and in public relations campaigns, the Army took a much more aggressive stance against the Air Force–Navy position" (*Wizards of Armageddon*, pp. 193, 195).

66 The widespread acceptance: Ibid., p. 196. According to Eisenhower, the Army was to be a garrison force, "the stabilizing thing after the big war, the force that pulls the nation together."

66 Army officers argued: Taylor, *Swords and Plowshares*, p. 165.

66 The first document: Ibid., p. 164.

66 Taylor's National Military Program: Ibid., pp. 164–65.

67 Like other Army officers: Ibid., p. 153.

67 "the Administration's passive attitude": Ibid., p. 137.

67 Like Ridgway, Taylor: Ibid., p. 156.

68 He later emphasized: Ibid.

68 "it was clear from the beginning": Biggs, *Gavin*, p. 87.

69 Not only was Taylor convinced: Interview with General Andrew Goodpaster.

69 At the outset of his term: Taylor, *Swords and Plowshares*, p. 165.

70 He described his views: Schlesinger, *A Thousand Days*, p. 310.

70 In addition, he had argued that: Kaplan, *Wizards of Armageddon*, pp. 140–41.

70 Joining Nitze was William W. Kaufmann: Kaufmann, "The Requirements of Deterrence," 1954.

71 All three soon became: Kaplan, *Wizards of Armageddon*, p. 195.

71 For his first twenty months: Ibid., p. 196. See also Taylor, *Swords and Plowshares*, p. 170. For a more complete treatment of Taylor's own views on his relationship with the JCS, see Taylor, *Uncertain Trumpet*.

71 "Pentomic division": Taylor, *Swords and Plowshares*, p. 171.

72 He claimed it would not only: Biggs, *Gavin*, pp. 88–90.

72 General Thomas Dresser White: "Statement of Military Service of Thomas Dresser White," April 28, 1955.

73 White was an intellectual giant: Ibid. See also Kaplan, *Wizards of Armageddon*, p. 216. During his career, White was responsible for directing the activities of a variety of Air Force offices: manpower, intelligence, plans, communications, atomic energy programming, and guided missile operations. He was the youngest man ever to graduate from West Point.

73 "a brutal, deadly affair": White, "Strategy and the Defense Intellectuals," May 4, 1963.

73 Finally . . . he was given command: Korb, *Joint Chiefs of Staff*, pp. 73–74.

73 Studious, sometimes sarcastic: Kaplan, *Wizards of Armageddon*, p. 244. See also Thomas White Papers, Library of Congress, Box 27, SAC folder, and Box 37, RAND folder; and Thomas Dresser White Papers, Office of Air Force History, Washington, D.C.

74 White's message: Thomas White Papers, Missile/Space/Nuclear folder, May 6, 1959, Box 26, Command Letters folder.

74 In early 1945: Larrabee, *Commander in Chief*, pp. 620–22.

74 By that time, LeMay's: Coffey, *Iron Eagle*, pp. 164–65.

74 He not only said: Kaplan, *Wizards of Armageddon*, p. 134.

75 Even more disturbing: Ibid., p. 161.

75 The Air Force study: "Estimate of Sino-Soviet Capabilities World-

Wide, '59–63 and Assessment of Dimensions of Soviet ICBM Threat to Security of U.S.," Thomas White Papers, Library of Congress, Box 6, McConnell Report folder.

76 Its view of the 1957 Air Force estimates: Kaplan, *Wizards of Armageddon*, pp. 158–59.

77 Gavin was eccentric: Biggs, *Gavin*, pp. 51–54.

77 His combat competition with Taylor: Halberstam, *Best and Brightest*, p. 477. Gavin was also disliked by Ridgway, who refused to appoint him to a combat command in Korea because, as his staff told him, Gavin wasn't sufficiently thankful to Ridgway for everything he had done for him during World War II.

77 Throughout 1957: Biggs, *Gavin*, p. 88.

77 It so angered Gavin: Ibid., pp. 88–90.

78 "a technological Pearl Harbor": Ibid., p. 90.

78 The president told Twining: Ambrose, *Eisenhower, The President*, p. 428.

79 The Assistant Secretary of Defense: Ibid.

79 "a neat scientific trick": Ibid.

79 "trouble is rising": Ibid.

79 He lashed out against the JCS: Ibid., pp. 428–29.

80 "Just what are you going to do": Preinaugural Papers (1957), pp. 546–47.

81 "practically predicted the end": Ambrose, *Eisenhower, The President*, p. 434.

81 "Do something": Ibid.

82 Johnson's witness list: Subcommittee Report, "Inquiry into Satellite and Missile Program," November 25, 1957–January 23, 1958.

83 Gavin told Johnson: Ibid., p. 42. See also Biggs, *Gavin*, p. 95.

83 "I don't believe in next year's budget": Biggs, *Gavin*, p. 96.

83 "You have heard": Ibid.

84 "as a private": Ibid., p. 97.

85 First, he directed a group: Interview with General Harry W. O. Kinnard.

85 But, most important, he began to review: Interview with General Andrew Goodpaster.

85 Taylor's decision to review: Interview with General Bruce Palmer. Others disagree with the assessment, saying that while Taylor reviewed the Army's paramilitary programs, he had "no special interest in them." Indeed, Taylor (in *Swords and Plowshares*, p. 202) credits John Kennedy with giving the initial impetus to the program.

85 Curiously, though Taylor promoted: Taylor, in *Swords and Plowshares* (p. 200), says, "It took some time for most American officials in Washington, myself included, to sense the full significance of the threat of Wars of National Liberation as President

Kennedy viewed it." Taylor is disingenuous; the JCS was hardly
unfamiliar with such "limited wars."

86 Instead, the OSS: Roosevelt, *War Report*, I: 16.

86 Military professionals complained: Weigley, *History of US Army*,
pp. 543–44.

86 Despite his *nom de guerre:* Ford, *Donovan of OSS*, pp. 91–110.

86 The OSS became a reflection: Brown, *Wild Bill Donovan*, p. 822.

86 "hesitant, skeptical, indifferent": Hymoff, *OSS in World War II*,
p. 341.

87 "an agency engaged in secret": Roosevelt, *War Report*, II: 255.

87 "I wouldn't say the situation": Interview with General Lyman
Lemnitzer.

87 Although the OSS was dead: U.S. Senate, "Select Committee to
Study Governmental Operations with Respect to Intelligence
Activities," Book 4, p. 28.

87 This role was effectively ended: Paddock, *U.S. Army Special Warfare*, p. 23.

88 The decision, Marshall told: Ibid., p. 52.

88 By late 1947, the JCS: MMH, "Study on Guerrilla Warfare,"
March 1, 1949.

89 "appear[s] to infringe upon": MMH, "Memorandum," June 2,
1948.

89 With this in mind: MMH, "The Military Organization for Psychological and Covert Operations," November 2, 1949.

89 One such officer . . . McClure: Bank, *From OSS to Green Beret*,
pp. 140–41.

90 Eventually he succeeded: Ibid., p. 140.

90 "In consultation with": MMH, "Summary of Major Activities of
OCPW . . ." April 7, 1953 (JCS 1969/18), March 17, 1952.

91 "hesitant and reluctant": Paddock, *U.S. Army Special Warfare*, p.
159.

92 The stability of this leadership: Ambrose, *Eisenhower, The President*, pp. 560–61.

92 "we never intended to keep": Ibid., p. 551.

92 "My God, how did I get into this?": Ibid., p. 563.

93 "For the sword to be an effective instrument": Taylor, *Swords
and Plowshares*, p. 175.

4: COUP D'ÉTAT

95 "His [Maxwell Taylor's] general feeling was": Coffey, *Iron Eagle*,
p. 423.

96 After all, as Eisenhower himself: Interview with General Andrew
Goodpaster. At one point, Eisenhower stated his belief that the
JCS should be politically loyal. The comment came in 1960, dur-

ing the controversy over the B-70. "I hate to use the word," he said, "but this business is damn near treason."

96 Although there were no guarantees: Gorman, "Toward a Stronger Defense Establishment," pp. 295–96. See also "Hearings on S. 84 and S. 1482," pp. 411–40.

97 Engler's plan contained: Wyden, *Bay of Pigs*, pp. 24–25.

98 "A Program of Covert Action": Ibid.

99 Four days later: Ibid., p. 25.

99 "should forget all this": Interview with General Lyman Lemnitzer.

100 In 1945 . . . he was chosen by the American high command: Ibid.

100 "Lem, I want to tell you": Wyden, *Bay of Pigs*, p. 79.

101 But Lemnitzer didn't exactly "nose around": Interview with Lemnitzer.

101 To run the study: Wyden, *Bay of Pigs*, pp. 86–88. According to one JCS intelligence officer, the JSPD was originally set up to act as a liaison office with the CIA "to monitor paramilitary operations."

102 Nevertheless . . . Gray presented an analysis: Interview with Lemnitzer. The final JSPD study was given a JCS code: JCSM 44-61.

102 On January 22, 1961: Wyden, *Bay of Pigs*, p. 87.

103 Unfortunately, Gray's meeting: Interview with Lemnitzer.

104 The result was a 125-page paper: Wyden, *Bay of Pigs*, p. 87.

104 The volcanic Wheeler: Ibid., p. 90.

104 After this meeting: Interview with Lemnitzer.

104 The JCS report, a lukewarm endorsement: Ibid.

105 "we are wasting our time": Wyden, *Bay of Pigs*, p. 90.

105 In fact, he was a military pragmatist: Interview with Colonel William Corson. There are varying views of Shoup. One JCS Army major said of Corson's description, "Shoup was no pragmatist, he was crazy."

105 Lemnitzer remembers Shoup: Interview with Lemnitzer.

106 A critic of the CIA: Interview with a retired JCS flag rank Army officer.

107 But the most significant misstep: Prados, *Presidents' Secret Wars*, pp. 204–6.

107 Once again, Gray was at the center: Interview with Lemnitzer.

107 Secretary of State Dean Rusk: Wyden, *Bay of Pigs*, p. 264.

108 "There goes your operation": Ibid., p. 266.

108 At the Pentagon . . . Wheeler called Lemnitzer: Interview with a retired flag rank JCS Army officer.

108 This rare late-night meeting: Wyden, *Bay of Pigs*, p. 269.

109 "Hell, Mr. President": Ibid., p. 270.

109 By the next day: Prados, *Presidents' Secret Wars*, p. 206.

109 "never really had his heart in it": Interview with Lemnitzer.

110 "I am the responsible officer": Schlesinger, *A Thousand Days*, p. 290.

110 "another new job": Taylor, *Swords and Plowshares*, p. 179.

110 "that something out of the ordinary": Ibid.

110 "I sensed an air": Ibid., p. 180.

111 The charter that the president: "Narrative of the Anti-Castro Cuban Operation Zapata," April 22–May 25, 1961, Part II.

111 "It is apparent that we need": Taylor, *Swords and Plowshares*, p. 184.

111 "in the end what I want": Ibid.

111 "the almost passing mention": Ibid.

112 A 1922 graduate": McHenry, *Webster's American Military Biographies*, pp. 429–30.

113 "the 101 Ranch": Interview with a retired JCS flag rank Army officer.

113 Nevertheless, Taylor's critique: Halberstam, *Best and Brightest*, p. 40.

113 In fact, this "steadiness": Interview with Lemnitzer.

113 "even aplomb": Interview with Colonel Harry Summers.

114 In his memoir: Taylor, *Swords and Plowshares*, p. 186.

114 "Piecing all the evidence": Ibid., p. 188.

114 "Our group . . . concluded": Ibid., p. 189.

115 The report stung Kennedy: Ibid.

115 "By pure luck": Ibid.

115 "icy silence": Interview with a retired JCS flag rank Army officer.

116 Even among four-star commanders: Interview with Goodpaster.

116 "Just who did Maxwell Taylor serve?": Interview with a retired flag rank Army officer.

116 "With the opportunity to observe": Taylor, *Swords and Plowshares*, p. 252.

117 "I didn't even know where": Interview with Lemnitzer.

117 After he had completed: Taylor, *Swords and Plowshares*, p. 195.

117 Finally, with no job suited: Ibid., p. 197.

117 "Fortunately, General Lemnitzer": Ibid.

118 "a *good* general": Halberstam, *Best and Brightest*, p. 40.

118 "more than a little vain": Ibid., p. 162.

118 Taylor was therefore sent: Taylor, *Swords and Plowshares*, pp. 227–44.

118 "somnolent": Ibid., p. 230.

118 "the additional credit point": Ibid., p. 234.

119 In essence, the Taylor-Rostow: Halberstam, *Best and Brightest*, p. 170.

119 On November 7, 1961: Ibid., p. 173. Halberstam calls this "a highly personalized memo."

119 Accordingly, the United States: Taylor, *Swords and Plowshares*, p. 248.

120 Frustrated by McNamara: Ibid., pp. 204–15.

120 As earlier, Taylor's recommendations: Ibid., pp. 214–15.

120 "The experience . . . reminded me": Ibid., p. 215.

120 "and wished to have the opportunity": Ibid., p. 252.

121 Goodpaster and Taylor worked well: Interview with Goodpaster.

121 Goodpaster remembers Taylor: MHI, "Interview with General Andrew Goodpaster," tape 4, section 4, p. 20.

121 Taylor pushed Wheeler: Interview with General Harry W. O. Kinnard.

122 Since the mid-1950s: Interview with General Hamilton H. Howze.

122 "Hamilton . . . a royal pain in the ass": Interview with a retired flag rank Army officer.

122 In early 1962, LeMay: Interview with Kinnard.

122 "The real question": Ibid.

123 Working from recommendations: Interview with Summers.

124 Beginning on October 16: Taylor, *Swords and Plowshares*, p. 264.

124 Each JCS member was given: Ibid., p. 269.

125 "I have just come": Interview with a retired flag rank Army officer.

125 "Following each EXCOMM meeting": Taylor, *Swords and Plowshares*, p. 269.

126 "a trade with Khrushchev": Coffey, *Iron Eagle*, p. 393.

127 "We in the military": Ibid., p. 422.

127 Both of these characteristics: Halberstam, *Best and Brightest*, pp. 202–3.

128 "the apotheosis of the American": Karnow, *Vietnam*, p. 262.

128 When Vann reported: Interview with General Bruce Palmer.

128 "He was enraged": Interview with a retired flag rank Army officer.

129 "I know Vann": MHI, "Interview with General Maxwell Taylor," section 4, February 16, 1973, p. 33.

129 "He's lying": Interview with Palmer.

130 "This was a tremendous mistake": Ibid. See also Perry, "Just for the Record," December 1985.

131 When asked by reporters: Taylor, *Swords and Plowshares*, p. 314.

5: THE WAR OF THE CHIEFS

132 "I can't tell you": Boettcher, *Vietnam*, p. 242.

133 Not only was Wheeler well known: Interview with Colonel Harry Summers.

133 "an end to the age of heroes": Interview with Colonel William Corson.

134 Wheeler clearly lacked: "Earle Gilmore Wheeler," Office of the JCS.

134 "Bus [as he was called] had never heard": Interview with a retired Marine colonel.

134 "the Army's highest-ranking sycophant": Interview with Corson.

134 Wheeler's service: McHenry, *Webster's American Military Biographies*, p. 474.

135 "the whiz kids": Kaplan, *Wizards of Armageddon*, p. 257.

135 Admiral David L. McDonald: "Admiral David Lamar McDonald," September 1967.

136 Johnson, of the Bataan death march: McHenry, *Webster's American Military Biographies*, p. 201.

136 Dubbed "the inevitable general": Interview with General William C. Westmoreland.

136 They were all painfully aware: Westmoreland met Kennedy when the president gave an address at West Point when Westmoreland was superintendent. Kennedy was very impressed with the general and spoke about him with Maxwell Taylor. When Harkins left, Westmoreland was the natural choice.

137 Although he wasn't the JCS's first choice: Interview with General Bruce Palmer. Many believed that General Hamilton H. Howze would be named commander in Vietnam.

138 Wheeler and Johnson settled: Karnow, *Vietnam*, p. 364.

138 On August 6: Ibid., pp. 365–66.

138 Beginning on August 2: Ibid., p. 369.

138 Wheeler also approved: Ibid., pp. 368–69.

138 Wheeler had the JCS's plans: *Pentagon Papers*, II: 199–200; III: 185.

139 "with positive response": Karnow, *Vietnam*, p. 372.

139 "limited in scale": Ibid.

139 Although he was relieved, almost pleased: Interview with a former JCS flag rank Army officer.

139 In fact, that evening Wheeler: Ibid.

140 One week after the Tonkin Gulf: Karnow, *Vietnam*, p. 397. See also *Pentagon Papers*, III: 189–91.

140 "Failure to resume": *Pentagon Papers*, III: 190.

140 "avoid actions that would": Ibid., III: 191.

140 In all, the JCS wanted Wheeler: Ibid., III: 132 (JCSM 746-64).

140 Ever the partisan . . . LeMay: Interview with a former JCS flag rank Army officer.

141 LeMay's position on the war: Coffey, *Iron Eagle*, pp. 428–29.

141 "I don't remember that it ever": Ibid., p. 429.

141 "reprisal bombings": *Pentagon Papers*, III: 241.

141 Admiral Sharp, in command of: Sharp, *Strategy for Defeat*, p. 49.

142 The JCS rejected: *Pentagon Papers*, III: 628–29.

142 "prompt implementation": Ibid., III: 208–9.

142 These compromises: Ibid., pp. 628–30.

142 "We should stop swatting flies": Coffey, *Iron Eagle*, p. 436.

143 Just days before his reelection: *Pentagon Papers*, III: 210.

144 "lean patrician with a lockjaw accent": Karnow, *Vietnam*, p. 344.

144 "The NSC Working Group": *Pentagon Papers*, III: 221.

144 Over a period of three weeks: Ibid., pp. 630–32.

145 Although Mustin's view: Ibid., pp. 628–30.

145 "Option A was essentially": Ibid., p. 221.

146 To each group, Taylor: Ibid., p. 240.

146 "either quitting or brutal escalation": Karnow, *Vietnam*, p. 324.

146 "You can't get a little bit pregnant": Coffey, *Iron Eagle*, p. 429.

146 "I thought they were mad": Interview with Admiral Thomas Moorer.

147 The public record: *Pentagon Papers*, III: 420–22.

148 In fact, by early 1965: Interview with General Edward C. Meyer.

148 "either get into this thing": Interview with a former JCS flag rank Army officer.

148 The president questioned Johnson: Ibid.

148 "Well, go get some": Interview with a retired Army colonel.

148 The normally ebullient commander: Interview with Westmoreland.

149 "We're ready, sir": Interview with a retired Army combat general.

149 On the fourteenth: *Pentagon Papers*, III: 429.

149 the "SEATO treaty": Ibid.

149 "Policy is": Ibid.

150 "fugitives from responsibility": MHI, "Interview with General Harold K. Johnson," January 22, 1973, p. 8.

150 "He kept saying": Interview with Meyer.

150 "When the Vietnam thing started": Interview with Moorer.

150 "did an awful lot of gambling": MHI, "Interview with General Harold K. Johnson," December 19, 1972, p. 20.

151 "At the time I went to Leavenworth": Ibid., February 7, 1972, p. 20.

152 "The basis of it was": Interview with Meyer.

152 "Johnson went to the president": Ibid.

153 Just one day: Kahin, *Intervention*, pp. 380–84.

153 "Are we in agreement": Ibid., p. 386.

153 "I think we can answer most": Ibid.

153 He left the distinct impression: Interview with a retired Army colonel.

153 Johnson immediately called: Interview with General Harry W. O. Kinnard.

154 "All we have to do": Ibid.

154 The man in the lead tank: Ibid.

154 Now, as Kinnard's troops awaited: Interview with Meyer.

154 After his meeting: Kahin, *Intervention*, p. 366.

155 Goldberg was the most intransigent: Ibid., p. 367.

155 But this time Johnson: Ibid., p. 390.

155 "Under the approved plan": Ibid., p. 394.

155 At Fort Benning, Harry Kinnard: Interview with Kinnard.

156 On the way into Washington: Interview with a retired Army colonel.

156 "I should have gone to see the president": Ibid.

156 the battle for the Ia Drang: Triplett, "Chaos in the Ia Drang," October 1986.

157 "During Christmas of 1965": Interview with Meyer.

157 "Use their . . . tactics": Interview with Kinnard.

157 But Johnson's best advice: Interview with a retired Army combat general.

157 "Again in 1966": Interview with Meyer.

158 By mid-1966 . . . the Army chief: Interview with a former JCS flag rank Army officer.

159 Taking increased troop deployments: For a detailed discussion of the numbers involved, see *Pentagon Papers*, III: 484; IV: 444, 527, 591, 385, 564.

159 "Memorandum: The Vietnamese Communists' ": Interview with General Bruce Palmer. This document was later released as part of the libel suit *Westmoreland* v. *CBS Inc., et al.*

159 "the most formidable air defense system": Interview with Palmer.

159 "Hell, don't show this report": Ibid.

161 "defenders of 'air power' ": *Pentagon Papers*, IV: 197.

161 Praising the JCS: U.S. Senate, "Hearings on the Air War in Vietnam," July–August, 1967.

161 "I welcome this opportunity": Sharp, *Strategy for Defeat*, p. 191.

162 "There can be no question": Ibid., p. 192.

162 The JCS was stunned: Interview with Palmer.

162 "a particularly stormy session": Ibid.

163 Within hours of the testimony: Interview with a former JCS flag rank Army officer.

163 When the chiefs convened: Ibid.

164 "We knew something was up": Ibid.

165 "We can't do it": Ibid.

165 He made only one slip: Interview with Palmer.

166 "we considered resigning . . . but never in the tank": Interview with Moorer.

6: Whiz Kids and Wise Men

167 The Chairman of the Joint Chiefs: Westmoreland, *A Soldier Reports*, p. 468.

167 Nevertheless, officers: Interviews with Thomas Moorer, Bruce Palmer, Elmo Zumwalt, Jr., Harry Summers, and others.

168 The JCS decided to initiate: *Pentagon Papers*, IV: p. 538.

168 For partisans: Interview with Palmer.

168 Even among his detractors: Interview with Colonel William Corson.

168 "was killed by the war": Interview with Summers.

168 It isn't so important: Interview with Clark Clifford.

169 "it was clear that": Interview with Palmer.

169 The breach was total: Karnow says Johnson "also invited General Earle Wheeler ... to participate regularly" (*Vietnam*, p. 510). Moorer says that Wheeler "insisted."

169 Official meetings between the JCS: Interviews with Moorer, General Harry W. O. Kinnard.

169 Not only had McNamara misled: Stubbing, *Defense Game*, p. 267.

169 In addition, he established: Ibid., p. 286. See also Kinnard, *Secretary of Defense*, p. 86, and Kaplan, *Wizards of Armageddon*, pp. 252–54.

169 ... cost-analysis expert Alain Enthoven: Stubbing, *Defense Game*, p. 264. See also Enthoven and Smith, *How Much Is Enough?*, pp. 52–61.

170 "This guy Enthoven": Interview with Kinnard.

170 Instead, McNamara proposed: Franklin, *The Defender*, pp. 187–200.

170 "The F-111 had a bad habit": Interview with a career Defense Department official. The first three F-111s used in Vietnam reportedly crashed due to mechanical failure. One crew member survived.

171 The low-key McConnell: Ibid.

171 Moorer knew better: Interview with Moorer.

171 The attitude of Lieutenant General Glen Martin: Office of Air Force History (hereafter AFH), "Interview with Lt. Gen. Glen Martin."

171 For Ryan: Interview with a retired Air Force general.

171 The whole Kennedy team: AFH, "Interview with General John Ryan."

172 "first-class fiasco": Interview with Moorer.

172 "I knew exactly why": Ibid.

172 Wheeler constantly modified: Interview with a retired flag rank Army officer.

172 Indeed, at least as far as the JCS: Interview with Moorer. See also White, "Strategy," May 4, 1963.

173 Although he was still committed: Interview with a former JCS flag rank Army officer.

173 "the Plimsol Line": *The Pentagon Papers* referred to the Plimsol Line as "a political sound barrier" (IV: 385).

173 In August 1967: Ibid., pp. 523–24.

173 The grand total: Ibid., p. 527.

173 According to JCSM 218-67: Ibid., pp. 431–32. This study was finished on April 20, 1967, the result of a strategic assessment by MACV intelligence officers and the U.S. Pacific Command. The recommendations resulted in what are generally referred to as Program 4 reinforcements.

173 First, Wheeler wanted to know: Interview with a former MACV intelligence officer.

174 Those who realized the change: Interview with Palmer.

174 So, instead of pushing the president: *Pentagon Papers*, IV: 528–29.

174 Again, he received advice: Interview with General Edward C. Meyer.

174 First, he was convinced: Ibid.

175 "Once you start tampering": Ibid.

175 The NVA was beginning to deploy: Interview with General William C. Westmoreland.

175 Nevertheless, the war was being fought: Momyer, *Air Power*, p. 303.

175 "a tortured landscape": Pisor, *End of the Line*, p. 53.

175 "in a resigned tone": *Pentagon Papers*, IV: 533.

176 What it meant was: Ibid.

176 When Westmoreland had pleaded: Perry, "The Fire Last Time," August 1987.

176 In addition, Johnson was receiving pressure: Interview with General Lyman Lemnitzer.

176 "was downright frightening": Ibid.

176 "deploy units to South Vietnam": *Pentagon Papers*, IV: 529.

177 The deployments were approved: Ibid., pp. 530–31.

177 "He looked terrible": Interview with a retired JCS Army officer.

177 "a very sick man": Interview with Moorer.

178 He viewed the meeting: Interview with a former JCS flag rank Army officer.

178 Target Tuesday: Karnow, *Vietnam*, p. 510.

178 This paradox caused enormous pressures: Interview with a former MACV intelligence officer.

179 Westmoreland's appearance in Washington: Karnow, *Vietnam*, p. 514.

179 Now he was just as intrigued: Pisor, *End of the Line*, p. 103.

180 Johnson wanted statistics: Ibid., p. 114.
180 The next day, Wheeler came back: Ibid., p. 118.
181 "I'm sick of this niggling": Interview with a retired JCS Army officer.
181 Westmoreland later claimed: Interview with Westmoreland.
181 According to later reports: Interview with Palmer.
181 "war has reached a turning point": Interview with Sam Adams.
182 "Carver wrote a memo": Interviews with a former MACV intelligence officer and Palmer.
182 "Thank God they did": Interview with Palmer.
182 "We could never quite figure out": Interview with a retired JCS Army officer.
183 In fact, the handling of the attack: Interview with Corson.
183 "That bastard damn near crapped his pants": Ibid.
183 "Abrams's appointment": Interview with a retired Army lieutenant colonel.
184 "If you need more troops": Karnow, *Vietnam*, p. 549.
184 "Please understand that I am not": Ibid.
184 "A setback is fully possible": Ibid., p. 550.
185 Indeed, the JCS refused to endorse: *Pentagon Papers*, IV: 542.
185 "the 82nd Airborne Division": Ibid.
185 "near the point of exhaustion": Westmoreland, *A Soldier Reports*, p. 465.
186 "I just don't believe them": Interview with a former MACV intelligence officer.
186 "You have to understand": Interview with Westmoreland.
186 DePuy, whose name: Interviews with a retired JCS Army officer, a retired army general, and Palmer.
187 He began his discussions: Interview with a retired flag rank JCS Army officer.
187 "General Wheeler came over there": Interview with Westmoreland.
187 200,000 "just isn't the right number": Interview with a retired flag rank JCS Army officer.
188 "Well, Wheeler and I": Interview with Westmoreland.
188 "I was convinced": Westmoreland, *A Soldier Reports*, p. 466.
188 "Well now, some of us knew": Interview with a retired flag rank JCS Army officer.
189 Seated around the dining room table: Karnow, *Vietnam* p. 551. See also *Pentagon Papers*, IV: 547.
189 Yet within twenty-four hours: *Pentagon Papers*, IV: 549.
190 "I spent sixteen years": Interview with Clifford.
190 "walked the halls of this place": Interview with a former high-ranking Air Force officer.
190 "an old friend whom I had known": Interview with Clifford.

190 "Would 206,000 [more] men": Clifford, "A Vietnam Reappraisal," July 1969.

191 "I'm sorry if you get the idea": Interview with Clifford.

192 The group that met: *Pentagon Papers*, IV: 591–92. See also Karnow, *Vietnam*, pp. 561–62.

192 The group soon learned: Interview with a retired intelligence official.

193 Seated across the table: Ibid.

193 "Maybe we ought to lower our sights": Ibid. See also Oberdorfer, *Tet*, p. 314.

194 In the midst of his meetings: *Pentagon Papers*, IV: 593.

194 At the Pentagon: Interview with a retired flag rank JCS Army officer.

194 Clifford went out of his way: Interview with Clifford.

195 "The first thing I did": Ibid.

195 Harriman's opposition so irritated: Halberstam, *Best and Brightest*, p. 376.

195 Accompanying Harriman to Paris: Interview with General Andrew Goodpaster.

196 "Now it's our job to end this war": Ibid.

197 While Harriman communicated: Ibid.

197 "Don't let anyone tell you": Ibid.

197 Westmoreland didn't like Palmer: Interview with a retired JCS Army staff officer.

197 "I thought it important": Interview with Westmoreland.

197 "You know part of the military's job": Interview with Palmer.

198 Wheeler held a number of dinners: Interview with a former flag rank JCS Army officer.

198 "I knew the chiefs": Interview with Clifford.

199 Strangely enough, this knowledge: Interview with a former high-level Defense official.

199 "Transition?": Interview with Clifford.

199 Oddly enough . . . Clifford's report: Interview with a retired Army officer and government official.

200 He even reportedly told Kissinger: Ibid.

200 In particular, he let Wheeler know: Interview with a retired admiral.

201 On January 21: Interview with a former flag rank JCS Army officer.

201 According to colleagues: The group includes General Bruce Palmer, among others.

202 He promised Wheeler his full cooperation: Interview with a former flag rank JCS Army officer.

203 Although he later described: Kissinger, *White House Years*, p. 34.

203 "In the final analysis": Ibid.

7: CRISIS

205 "The problem in this town": Interview with Admiral Thomas Moorer.

205 Wheeler, for one: Interview with a former flag rank JCS Army officer.

206 Ironically, even William Westmoreland: Interview with a retired Army general.

206 Of all the chiefs: Interview with Moorer.

206 The administration's view: Interview with a retired admiral.

206 Wheeler's continuing illness: Interview with Westmoreland.

206 Moorer seemed perfectly suited: Ibid. Westmoreland said, "If ever anyone deserved to be JCS chairman, it was Thomas Moorer."

208 He was so partisan: Interview with Admiral Eugene Carroll.

208 "If it was a program": Ibid.

208 The enigma in his character: Intervew with a retired admiral.

208 After graduating from the Naval Academy: "Admiral Thomas H. Moorer," September 4, 1974.

208 When the Japanese bombed Hawaii: Interview with Moorer.

209 "I guess you could call Moorer": Interview with Carroll.

209 "That's just bullshit": Interview with Moorer.

210 "got an unforgettable look": Interview with a retired admiral.

210 To Kissinger, for instance: Interview with a retired admiral. See Kissinger, *White House Years*, p. 36. Kissinger could never admit he was taken in by Moorer's affected naiveté, saying that Moorer "exaggerated the attitude of an innocent country boy caught in a jungle of sharpies."

210 Kissinger characterized Moorer's solution: Interview with a retired admiral.

211 In fact, the new administration's: Interview with Moorer.

211 "out to get me": Interview with a retired army general. See also Szulc, *Illusion of Peace*, p. 18.

211 In addition, Nixon had made it clear: Hersh, *Price of Power*, p. 71.

212 "He's too devious": Nixon, *Memoirs*, p. 339.

212 To do this effectively: Szulc, *Illusion of Peace*, p. 38, and interview with General Edward C. Meyer.

212 The afternoon following the first NSC meeting: Interview with a retired admiral.

213 He said that the administration: Interview with a retired flag rank JCS Army officer.

213 With that, Wheeler passed out: NSSM 1 was a Vietnam Situation Paper; NSSM 2 was conducted to determine what role the United States should have in the Nigerian Civil War; NSSM 3 was a defense paper on military forces assigned to the JCS. Each was intended to keep the military high command busy.

214 Only once did Wheeler: Interview with a retired admiral.

214 But, across the table: Ibid.

214 During his career in the upper reaches: Interview with a retired Air Force general.

215 Indeed, it's likely it would have preferred: Interview with General Bruce Palmer.

215 Chapman worried whether Laird: Interview with a retired flag rank JCS Army officer.

216 It was an incredibly tense moment: Ibid.

216 Amazingly, however, whatever doubts: Loory says that Laird's cooperation with the JCS led to their regular meetings in the tank. Stories began appearing that indicated the chiefs were "up" in the administration's esteem (Defeated, p. 108).

216 In many ways, it was a performance: Interview with a retired flag rank JCS Army officer.

217 Laird had accomplished: Stubbing concludes that "Laird treated the military chiefs with deference and respect" (Defense Game, p. 293).

217 Indeed, the Laird meeting: Ibid., p. 291.

218 These good relations: Ibid., p. 299.

218 At the top of the list: Ibid., p. 300.

218 "Packard told the civilians": Interview with a retired admiral.

218 More important, Laird said: Interview with Lawrence Korb.

218 The second part of the Laird-JCS agreement: Stubbing, Defense Game, pp. 302–4.

219 The payoff for Laird: Interview with Admiral Elmo Zumwalt, Jr. See Stubbing, Defense Game, p. 306.

219 At the current rate of progress: Hersh, Price of Power, p. 50.

219 Nixon's strategy was first made apparent: Ibid., p. 63. The bombings had been urged during the transition period by Wheeler. They were initially coordinated by Air Force Colonel Ray Sitton, who eventually turned over their monitoring to the White House, according to a retired JCS Air Force officer.

219 When the JCS needed someone: Ibid., p. 55. Ironically, Goodpaster had been instrumental in getting Haig his White House job. Later, in 1974, Goodpaster refused to attend the change of command ceremonies when Haig took charge of NATO troops in Europe. When Goodpaster was asked about his views of Haig, he said, "I don't want to talk about that man."

220 In a series of high-level Pentagon meetings: Interview with a retired admiral.

220 After a meeting with Nixon: Hersh (*Price of Power*, p. 63) implies the Laird-Wheeler meeting occurred after March 15, which disagrees with my date. He notes that Secretary of State William Rogers opposed the bombing.

220 Within days of the American B-52 strike: Interview with a retired flag rank JCS Army officer. See also Stubbing, *Defense Game*, p. 296.

221 When the North Koreans downed: Hersh, *Price of Power*, pp. 71–72.

221 In mid-April 1969: Interview with a retired admiral.

221 He again approached Wheeler: Ibid.

222 At first, Wheeler put this down: Interview with a retired flag rank JCS Army officer.

222 When he didn't respond: Ibid. See also Hersh, *Price of Power*, p. 466.

222 Laird was sympathetic: Stubbing, *Defense Game*, p. 297.

223 If the U.S. goal was to make South Vietnam: Ibid., p. 296. See also Nixon, *Memoirs*, p. 392, and Trask, *Secretaries*, pp. 37–39.

223 But this initial midsummer withdrawal: Stubbing, *Defense Game*, p. 297.

223 At the beginning of one particularly memorable: Interview with Zumwalt.

223 He was bludgeoning the JCS: Interview with Moorer.

224 "secret doves": Wheeler apparently picked up this description from Westmoreland (the first JCS officer to use the term), who mistrusted Laird. "The drawdown was too fast," Westmoreland said in an interview.

224 At the beginning of November: Interview with a retired flag rank JCS Army officer.

224 Nor was the Army: Interview with Zumwalt.

224 Still, the situation among Army troops: Peers, *Inquiry*, p. 25. See also Hersh, *My Lai 4*, p. 22.

225 "In 1965, the United States": Interview with Colonel Harry Summers.

225 The JCS initially believed: Interview with a retired flag rank Army officer.

225 Most disturbing of all: Heinl, "The Collapse of the Armed Forces," June 7, 1971.

225 The first and most significant: Interview with a judge adjutant general corps officer.

225 In midsummer 1968: Ibid.; interview with Palmer. Palmer suggests that the Americal's remote assignment in I Corps in north-

ern South Vietnam contributed to its poor morale and the cover-up of the My Lai incident.

226 The statistical evidence: Gabriel and Savage, *Crisis in Command*, pp. 43–46.

226 "The available data suggest": Ibid., p. 49. Gabriel and Savage's study provides an unprecedented and chilling look at this problem. They conclude: "No comparative modern Western population shows rates of hard-drug usage remotely resembling those of the United States Army in 1971."

226 The JCS's decision: Interview with a retired flag rank JCS Army officer.

227 Abrams's solution was to draw back: Interview with a retired admiral.

227 "We just ought to": Interview with a retired Army major.

227 On one particularly memorable morning: Zumwalt, *My Father, My Son*, p. 46.

227 At another briefing: Interview with Zumwalt.

228 "tell them what the hell is up": Interview with a retired Army major.

228 "Keep going," Abrams said: Interview with a judge adjutant general corps officer.

228 "Kick them": Interview with a retired Army major. Interviews with Palmer and Goodpaster yield a surprising judgment of Abrams's work; both believe that, given more time, he might have won the war.

229 In addition, he took steps: Szulc notes that Abrams and Moorer attempted to slow the withdrawal schedule (*Illusion of Peace*, p. 248).

229 "Abe was in the grinder": Interview with a retired three-star Army general.

229 Still, the tactic was clearly distasteful: Ibid. Prados, in *Presidents' Secret Wars*, points out that most Phoenix activities occurred during Abrams's tenure as MACV commander (p. 309).

229 During one briefing, for instance: Interview with an MACV intelligence officer.

230 Indeed, according to Andrew Goodpaster: Interview with Goodpaster.

230 Or, in the words of: Interview with Major Steve Trueblood.

230 Nevertheless, Abrams did succeed: Ibid. Included in that number was Colonel Charlie Beckwith, who played a role in reviving U.S. Special Forces in the late 1970s.

230 In 1969, for instance: Westmoreland, *A Soldier Reports*, pp. 484–85. A number of high-ranking JCS officers now claim that Abrams was not responsible for the arrest. The officers included the commander of the U.S. 5th Special Forces Group, Colonel Robert

Rheault (pronounced "row"), who calls it "that unfortunate incident."

231 Zumwalt was initially given: Interviews with a retired admiral and Zumwalt.

231 "Moorer's way of getting rid": Ibid., *My Father, My Son*, p. 41.

231 Abrams was so impressed: Ibid., p. 44.

231 After learning of the appointment: Ibid., p. 103.

231 The sometimes parochial Moorer: Interview with a retired admiral.

231 "I didn't believe the U.S.": Interview with Zumwalt.

232 "had a bad habit of mingling": Interview with a retired admiral.

232 "blacken the Navy": Interview with a retired JCS admiral.

232 "If it had been any other war": Interview with Zumwalt.

232 By July 1970, it was clear: Interview with a retired flag rank JCS Army officer.

233 On April 22, 1970: Ibid. See also Hersh, *Price of Power*, p. 187.

233 The backchannel system: Hersh, *Price of Power*, p. 182.

233 This White House policy: Ibid.

234 In addition, by September: Westmoreland (*A Soldier Reports*, pp. 510–11) notes that Haig's subsequent promotion was a "political move to make a man of rare ability and loyalty beholden to the president."

234 Moorer knew better: Interview with a retired admiral. Carroll expressed a similar belief, saying that "service interests probably dictated that line [of communications] as well."

234 To resolve this growing problem: Hersh, *Price of Power*, pp. 120, 258–59, 265–68. See also Westmoreland, *A Soldier Reports*, p. 512. Most reporters who covered this story disagree with my conclusion that Moorer shared some of his information with Laird.

234 Robinson had picked his contact: Hersh, *Price of Power*, pp. 258–59, 266.

235 That September, for instance: Ibid.

235 In July 1971: Ibid., p. 469.

236 Nor would he discuss: Interview with a retired admiral. See also Hersh, *Price of Power*, p. 468.

236 Moorer was one of the few: Interview with Moorer.

236 Just days after the offensive: Ibid.

237 According to Moorer: Ibid.

237 "I'm telling you plain": Ibid.

237 "Hell, someone had to say something": Ibid.

238 Moorer's July 1972 reappointment: Interview with a retired admiral.

238 "I'm a patriot": Interview with Moorer.

239 He realized that the problems: Interview with a retired flag rank JCS Army officer.

239 The figures were frightening: Sherman, "Army Blues," March 1, 1971.

240 "The morale, discipline": Heinl, "The Collapse of the Armed Forces," June 7, 1971.

240 "The Army rewards system": War College, "Military Professionalism," pp. 30–32.

240 Zumwalt ignored both men: Interview with Zumwalt.

240 Further offending: Interview with a retired admiral.

241 Zumwalt remained undeterred: Interview with Zumwalt.

241 "Nixon was the closest": Ibid.

241 "Why are you doing this?": Interview with a retired Air Force general.

242 In mid-1970: Interview with a JCS Army major.

242 When Abrams received the documents: Interview with a retired Army colonel.

242 According to JCS officers . . . historians: Information provided by Colonel George McGarigle.

242 The history is tucked: Interview with a JCS Army major.

242 They concluded . . . that the JCS: Ibid.

8: POLITICS

244 "We didn't have a tough time": Interview with Admiral James Holloway III.

245 They were true opposites: Kinnard (*Secretary of Defense*, pp. 146–48) called Laird "a skilled politician and master of bureaucratic maneuvering."

245 He went even further: Interview with Admiral Thomas Moorer.

245 Not only was Moorer a convinced hawk: Ibid.

245 Richardson, a Boston intellectual: Korb, *Fall and Rise of the Pentagon*, p. 96.

245 His first step: Interview with a retired admiral.

246 Not even the politically savvy: The drawback was that Richardson demanded that the JCS close down one third of all military bases. See Stubbing, *Defense Game*, p. 249.

246 Richardson went out of his way: Interview with a retired admiral.

246 In early 1973: Interview with Moorer.

247 To replace Richardson: Stubbing, *Defense Game*, p. 310.

247 In fact, Schlesinger was resented: Interview with a retired JCS admiral. See also Kinnard, *Secretary of Defense*, p. 166. Kinnard

says that apparently "the chiefs were initially skeptical of this professor character, with his big ego and analytical ability."

248 A 1950 Harvard graduate: Stubbing, *Defense Game*, pp. 310–14.

248 There was something vaguely disturbing: Ibid., p. 312.

248 In one of his first meetings: Interview with a retired Air Force general. See Stubbing, *Defense Game*, p. 315.

249 Within weeks of his confirmation: Stubbing, *Defense Game*, pp. 320–21.

249 "There has been a fair amount of abuse": Canan, *Superwarriors*, p. 235. This interview first appeared in *Time*, September 12, 1973.

250 "The major military challenge": Ibid., p. 95.

250 For the JCS, the strategy: Again, the critic was Abrams, who told one audience that the "Soviets had made great strides" in reaching military parity with the United States since the late 1960s.

250 The airlift, accounting for: Interview with a retired JCS admiral.

250 To make matters worse: Ibid. This admiral says that Schlesinger and Moorer disagreed about the airlift. Schlesinger opposed it; Moorer stood in favor. A retired JCS Air Force general says that the airlift went forward after Kissinger sided with Moorer. Other accounts disagree: reporters Marvin and Bernard Kalb (in *Kissinger*) say that both Moorer and Schlesinger opposed the airlift. Moorer has a simple but ambiguous defense. "I obeyed orders," he said.

250 Schlesinger welcomed Moorer's: Ibid. See also Kinnard, *Secretary of Defense*, p. 167.

251 At first, Schlesinger considered: Kinnard, *Secretary of Defense*, p. 167.

251 Brown's appointment not only symbolized: Ibid.

251 Brown was an affable: Interview with General David C. Jones.

251 Like his predecessor: USAF, "General George S. Brown," February 1978.

251 But Brown's experience: Canan, *Superwarriors*, pp. 236–39.

252 "a genius, one of the most intelligent": Interview with an Air Force general.

252 "He knew government so damn well": Interview with a JCS Air Force general.

252 High on his agenda: Interview with Lawrence Korb.

252 During a tour of European combat commands: Interview with Jones.

252 According to one of Jones's subordinates: Interview with an Air Force general.

253 Just days before the visit: Interview with a retired admiral.

253 "I'll never forget": Ibid.

253 "The most satisfying job": Interview with Jones.

254 "He's a very complex": Interview with General Edward C. Meyer.

254 "He just turned out to be": Interview with a retired admiral.

254 Nevertheless, it was the son: Interview with Admiral Eugene Carroll.

254 Holloway's political sense: USN, "Admiral James L. Holloway, III."

254 The appointment was greeted: Interview with a retired Navy officer.

254 It led to speculation: Interview with a retired admiral.

254 In 1953, a Navy promotion board: Polmar and Allen, *Rickover*, pp. 203–4.

255 "He's got plenty of": Ibid., p. 203.

255 Rickover was initially pleased: Interview with a retired admiral.

255 In fact, Trident was a monster: Franklin, *The Defender*, p. 304. See Stubbing, *Defense Game*, 304–6, and Canan, *Superwarrior*, pp. 164–67.

255 Rickover and Zumwalt continued: Polmar and Allen, *Rickover*, p. 479.

255 Zumwalt's decisions were interpreted: Ibid., pp. 411–12.

256 Holloway didn't think he had: Interview with Holloway.

256 Holloway's decision to press ahead: Ibid.

256 "I wasn't alone in pushing": Ibid.

257 While Holloway's intransigence: Stubbing, *Defense Game*, pp. 326–27.

257 During the second week: Woodward and Bernstein, *Final Days*, p. 215. See also Stubbing, *Defense Game*, p. 331.

257 "I've just had the strangest": Ibid., p. 332.

257 Holloway later observed: Interview with Holloway.

258 Among other things, the group: Woodward and Bernstein, *Final Days*, p. 215.

259 In late August: Interview with Colonel Harry Summers.

259 Nonetheless, in his last week: Stubbing, *Defense Game*, p. 324.

259 Just as critical, he elicited: Interview with a retired Army colonel.

260 The Secretary of Defense was counting on: Ibid. See also Kinnard, *Secretary of Defense*, p. 167.

260 In fact, Schlesinger: Interview with a retired Army colonel.

261 This newfound confidence: Korb, *Joint Chiefs of Staff*, p. 186.

261 "Jews own, you know": Canan, *Superwarriors*, p. 239.

261 JCS officers, including Brown's: Interview with an Air Force general.

261 "possessed": Interview with a retired JCS Air Force general.

261 "The affair at Duke": Ibid.

262 This reprovisioning of Israel: Interview with a retired Army colonel.

262 Although no one was satisfied: Stubbing, *Defense Game*, p. 329.

262 On March 1: Snepp, *Decent Interval*, p. 272.

262 There was a "sense of panic": Interview with a U.S. intelligence official. See also Snepp, *Decent Interval*, pp. 235–36.

262 "We don't know really": Interview with a retired Army colonel.

262 Weyand, who had begun his career: Interviews with a retired Army colonel and Summers. See also Snepp, *Decent Interval*, p. 237. Snepp says that Von Marbod found out about the Weyand mission and was the one to suggest that the Army chief put together "a team."

263 Upon their arrival: Interview with a U.S. intelligence official.

263 Still, the final "beans and bullets": Ibid.

263 "South Vietnam was going to be": Interview with Summers.

263 "It just never happened": Interview with Holloway.

264 "Fred Weyand was a tremendous": Interview with Jones.

264 There was an air of suspicion: Interview with an Air Force general.

264 For Bernard Rogers: Interview with a retired flag rank JCS Army officer.

264 The meeting with Carter: Interview with a retired Army colonel. See also Stubbing, *Defense Game*, p. 345. Stubbing says this meeting took place in December 1976.

265 "Ivan is just around the corner": Interview with Korb.

265 Nodding in apparent agreement: Interview with a retired Air Force general.

265 "By the way": Ibid.

266 "That did it": Interview with a retired Army colonel.

266 In one of his first acts: Stubbing, *Defense Game*, p. 343.

267 In large measure: Ibid., p. 350.

267 "With the blessing": Kester, "Revamp," in *Reorganization Proposals*, April 21–August 25, 1982. See also Kester, "Future of the Joint Chiefs," February 1980.

267 In particular, Army staff officers: Interview with a retired Army colonel.

268 In signing PD 13: Stubbing, *Defense Game*, p. 345.

268 Vessey's exile: Interview with General John Vessey, Jr., who says, "Well, I thought that was the end of my career."

268 Carter had long believed: Stubbing, *Defense Game*, p. 347.

268 Harold Brown, who had served: Ibid., p. 384.

269 Within thirty days: Interview with Jones.

269 "That thought never": Ibid.

269 Jones's Air Force assistants: Interview with a House Armed Services Committee aide.

269 "Carter's decision on the B-1": Interview with a retired Air Force general.

269 "The Revolt of the Navy": Stubbing, *Defense Game*, p. 353. See also USN, "Sea Plan 2000."

271 Allen's appointment: Interview with a retired admiral.

271 JCS officers referred to this: Interview with a retired Army colonel.

271 Allen was a welcome addition: USAF, "General Lew Allen, Jr.," September 1981.

271 If Allen was: USN, "Admiral Thomas B. Hayward." Interview with a retired Navy officer.

271 "The man was a gent": Interview with a retired Navy officer.

272 General Bernard Rogers: Interview with retired Army major.

272 "He came up here": Interview with House Armed Services Committee aide.

273 In 1978, Rogers directed: Interview with a Defense Department official.

274 "I have heard that Abrams": Interview with Meyer.

274 Although Carter claimed: Interviews with Jones, Meyer, and a U.S. intelligence official.

274 The unit was under the command: Perry, "I.S.A. Behind the N.S.C.," January 1987.

275 It was not simply: Beckwith and Knox, *Delta Force*, pp. 106–7. See also Ryan, *Iranian Rescue Mission*, pp. 1–2.

275 In addition, Beckwith clashed: Interview with a U.S. intelligence official.

275 Six C-130 transports: Gabriel, *Military Incompetence*, p. 87.

276 Beckwith, for instance: Ibid., p. 114.

276 His public report recommended: "Holloway Report," September 15, 1980. See also "The Holloway Report," September 15, 1980.

276 "permanent special operations force": Interview with a U.S. intelligence official. See also Perry, "I.S.A. Behind the N.S.C.," January 1987.

277 "Carter didn't intervene": Interviews with a retired JCS Army colonel and Meyer.

9: PROTRACTED WARFARE

278 The public doesn't seem to: Interview with General David C. Jones.

278 On the one hand: Stubbing, *Defense Game*, pp. 368–69.

278 Even before Reagan's inauguration: Interview with Lawrence Korb.

279 At first Weinberger's critics: Interview with a Senate Armed Services Committee aide.

279 Reagan's new appointments: Stubbing, *Defense Game*, p. 374.

279 "the Prince of Darkness": Interview with Korb.

279 At first, it looked: Interview with a retired admiral.

279 "I have been asked to convey": Interview with a retired JCS general.

280 In a clear break with tradition: Interview with a retired Army colonel.

280 After Weinberger had pledged: Interview with a Defense Department official.

280 "In a lot of ways": Interview with General Edward C. Meyer. See also Cimbala, *Reagan Defense Program*, p. 41, who notes that Carlucci, Jones, and Pustay (Jones's deputy) "formed an effective team, but they were always under suspicion for having somewhat liberal Democrat-style tendencies."

280 After Weinberger and Jones: Interview with a retired admiral.

280 Instead, Weinberger surprised everyone: Interview with a Defense Department official.

281 Jones nodded: Interview with a retired admiral.

281 "he went on and on": Interview with Korb.

281 He peered down: Interview with a retired admiral.

281 The members of the JCS: Ibid.

282 The room was dead silent: Ibid.

282 Jones was "the most calm": Interview with Korb.

282 "Weinberger was sitting there": Ibid.; interview with a retired admiral. Jones said he would not comment on any reports of this meeting.

282 "Well, I think": Interview with a retired admiral.

283 Weinberger next suggested: Interview with Korb.

283 Within weeks: Interview with Meyer. Defense analyst Thomas Gervasi reviewed this material in part for his work *The Soviet Estimate*. The Weinberger — "Team A/Team B" — approach paralleled one taken during the Ford administration in 1975. See Stubbing, *Defense Game*, pp. 12–13.

283 But Weinberger apparently wasn't: Interview with General David C. Jones, who did not refer to Weinberger by name.

283 "Weinberger just hated Jones": Interview with Meyer.

283 "Jones just thought Weinberger": Interview with a Defense Department official.

283 "When's his time up?": Ibid.

284 Soon after taking office: Stubbing, *Defense Game*, pp. 376–77.

284 Weinberger's victory: Ibid., p. 375.

284 In all, the Reagan revolution: Interview with Dina Rasor.

284 The belief: Interview with Jones.

284 "I testified": Ibid.

285 With an uncanny talent: Interview with House Armed Services Committee defense analyst Arch Barrett.

286 The JCS's budget: U.S. Senate, "Defense Organization," pp. 491–93.

286 It begins: Korb, *Fall and Rise of the Pentagon*, p. 86.

286 Using this document: U.S. Senate, "Defense Organization," p. 485.

286 In practice: Interview with Barrett.

287 "Procurement has totally corrupted": Interview with Rasor.

287 A surprisingly large number: Interview with a Defense Department official.

287 "our window": Interview with Meyer.

287 During the first week of February: Interview with a Defense Department official.

288 what one naval officer: Interview with Admiral Eugene Carroll.

288 "no more than POMs": Interview with a Defense Department official.

288 "Anyone can write up": Interview with a JCS Army colonel.

289 The last week of August: Ibid.; interview with a retired admiral.

289 Weinberger's budget: Talbott, *Deadly Gambits*, p. 255.

290 In a series of meetings: Interview with a Defense Department official.

290 One result was a JCS document: Ibid.

290 In a document completed: Ibid. Meyer would not confirm the existence of such a document. See Talbott, *Deadly Gambits*, pp. 66–67.

290 "There has, and was": Meyer, "Remarks," September 24, 1981.

291 Throughout September: Interview with Korb.

291 "The impression has been left": "Senate Panel," November 7, 1981.

291 "I could see where you could": "Interview," October 16, 1981. See also Stubbing, *Defense Game*, p. 385.

292 "It is possible": Stubbing, *Defense Game*, p. 385.

292 "If you try to do everything": Halloran, *To Arm a Nation*, p. 294.

292 During Reagan's first year: Interview with Carroll.

293 Joining Moorer and Zumwalt: Talbott, *Deadly Gambits*, p. 52. See also Stubbing, *Defense Game*, p. 17.

293 The first round: Talbott, *Deadly Gambits*, pp. 63–65.

294 "Their philosophy of arms control": Interview with Carroll.

294 These two groups: Talbott, *Deadly Gambits*, p. 65.

295 It was a deft: Ibid., p. 61.

295 The JCS, a mere onlooker: Interview with a retired admiral.

295 Jones, in particular: Talbott, *Deadly Gambits*, p. 66.

296 As he told his staff: Interview with a retired admiral.

296 Perle was enraged: Interview with Korb. See Talbott, *Deadly Gambits*, p. 67.

296 "pushovers and patsies": Talbott, *Deadly Gambits*, p. 68.

297 "Secretary Weinberger thinks we": Ibid., p. 253.

297 "It was more than that": Interview with a retired admiral.

298 "Jones knew that deterrence": Interview with Meyer.

298 Jones "is the most manipulative": Interview with Carroll.

298 "I don't want to": Interview with Jones.

298 Through the first five months: Interview with Meyer.

299 Jones had first launched: Interview with Jones.

299 "We were able to make": Ibid.

299 "Weinberger was opposed": Interview with Meyer.

299 establishing a JCS committee: Interview with Jones.

299 But the real campaign: Jones, "Why the Joint Chiefs of Staff Must Change," February 1982.

300 Weinberger was enraged: Interview with a House Armed Services Committee aide.

300 At least part of the reason: Interview with Barrett.

300 "I think the problem": Ibid.

300 Jones's task was formidable: Interview with Jones.

301 Meyer, a bright: USA, "Edward C. Meyer."

301 Meyer, remembering Johnson's: Interview with Meyer.

301 "You know, we have": Ibid.

302 "I believe we have to increase": House Hearings, "Reorganization Proposals," April 21, 1982, p. 5.

302 "We are doing": Ibid., p. 16.

302 Jones followed Meyer: Ibid., pp. 46–97.

303 "the Russians will be happy": Interview with Korb.

303 "I don't think it's any secret": Interview with Admiral James Holloway III.

303 "As soon as I heard it": Interview with Admiral Thomas Moorer.

303 "What if the president": Ibid.

303 "Adding a deputy chairman": Interview with Holloway. His reference to a "deputy chairman" is common; he means vice chairman.

303 The newest obstacle: Interview with a top Senate Armed Services Committee aide.

304 At the beginning of June 1982: Interview with General John Vessey, Jr.

304 He had built a reputation: Interview with Meyer.

304 "they told me": Interview with Vessey.

304 "It didn't seem like the right time": Ibid.

304 In 1977, just after Carter: Ibid.

304 "I came back [in 1977] to talk": Ibid.

305 Meyer, in particular: Interview with Meyer.
306 Working behind the scenes: Interview with a U.S. intelligence officer.
306 In August, Reagan: Gabriel, *Military Incompetence*, p. 118.
306 Under no circumstances: Interview with a JCS staff officer.
306 "Every one of the chiefs": Interview with Vessey.
307 His views were seconded: Interview with a Defense Department official.
307 Nevertheless, the deployment: Gabriel, *Military Incompetence*, p. 118.
307 On September 10, therefore: Ibid., 120.
308 The five-day argument: Interview with a Defense Department official.
308 His position was baffling: Ibid.
308 "You take a guy like Jim Watkins": Interview with a retired JCS admiral.
309 "We knew the president": Interview with Vessey.
309 "The argument was that": Interview with a Defense Department official.
309 The arguments were spurred: Gabriel, *Military Incompetence*, p. 123.
309 In December, the administration: Interview with Vessey.
310 "The whole thing was": Interview with Meyer.
310 "Beirut was a very complicated place": Interview with Vessey.
310 One of those sent: Interview with Noel Koch.
310 "It's not as romantic": Ibid.
310 "Don't make the mistake": Ibid.
311 When Koch returned: Ibid.
311 "No one likes to hear": Ibid.

10: SEMPER FIDELIS

312 The Marine Corps: U.S. Senate, "Lebanon," October 1983, p. 57.
312 At 6:22 A.M.: "Long Commission Report," *Congressional Record*, pp. 358, 365–367. See also Gabriel, *Military Incompetence*, pp. 131–32, Hammel, *The Root*, pp. 303, 386.
312 The headquarters: Hammel, *The Root*, p. 386. Hammel says 128 American servicemen were treated in the aftermath of the bombing — 83 at aid stations, 18 aboard offshore naval vessels, and 27 in local hospitals.
313 News of the disaster: Interviews with a U.S. intelligence official and General John Vessey, Jr. See "Lebanon: Anatomy," *Newsday*, April 8, 1984.

313 The duty officer then called: Interview with a U.S. intelligence official.

313 After learning of the disaster: Interview with a retired admiral.

313 Within minutes of his arrival: Interview with Vessey.

313 He knew there was little: Ibid.

313 After discussing the situation: Ibid.; interview with a Senate Armed Services Committee aide.

313 One hour before: Interview with a Senate Armed Services Committee aide. Some military intelligence information on the bombing was given to important Senate Armed Services Committee members within two weeks in an effort to deflect criticism of Marine security precautions.

313 The number of operatives: Interview with a U.S. intelligence official. In addition, Noel Koch detailed the security warnings that had been given to the JCS prior to the bombing.

314 "expand the Marines ROE": Ibid. Vessey declined to respond to this report, saying only that "the rules of engagement were approved by the officer in command, by myself, and by the Secretary of Defense."

314 "use only the degree": Interview with Vessey. The "Long Commission Report" (p. 367), however, notes that the Marine commander was instructed to receive "guidance from higher headquarters prior to using armed force if time and the situation allow." Nevertheless, Marines were to keep their weapons unloaded.

314 For the first time: Interview with a retired Army major.

314 "Yes, I was surprised": Interview with Vessey.

315 At the NSC meeting: Ibid. In our initial interview, he detailed the events of the day (though not of the meetings), but declined to speak about them during subsequent questioning.

315 Weinberger sat through: Interview with a Senate Armed Services Committee aide. Information on the NSC meeting comes from this source, a Defense Department official, an NSC defense analyst, and published reports, including Cannon, "Standing Fast," October 25, Cannon, "Reagan's Upbeat Mood," October 30, Hiatt, "Security Steps," October 24, and Oberdorfer, "U.S. Resources," October 24.

315 At 7:00 A.M.: Interview with a Defense Department official.

315 As the most vocal: Cannon, "McFarlane's Appointment," October 24, 1983; interview with a Defense Department official.

315 "How could this": Interviews with a Defense Department official and a Senate Armed Services Committee aide.

316 Above all, McFarlane: Interview with a Senate Armed Services Committee aide.

316 "We all thought": Interview with Vessey.
317 He further observed: Interview with a Defense Department official.
317 While Vessey was: Interview with a retired Army major.
317 The service debate: "Medical Readiness" (classified), April 18, 1984.
317 Marine officers were: Interviews with a retired Marine colonel and a Defense Department official.
318 "It was an idiotic decision": Interview with a retired Marine colonel. In the wake of the incident, according to this official, Defense Department employees at NATO headquarters were instructed to determine who gave the order to bypass Ramstein.
318 With the exception of: Interview with Vessey.
318 "Beirut — sure, we discussed Beirut": Ibid.
318 A twenty-one-ship naval task force: Hiatt, "U.S. Flotilla," October 25, 1983.
318 JCS planning for: Interview with Vessey. See Gabriel, *Military Incompetence*, p. 150. He reports that the "initial discussions concerning Operation Urgent Fury began almost a week before the invasion."
319 When Weinberger returned: Interview with a Defense Department official.
319 When Vessey returned: Interview with a retired JCS admiral.
319 On the morning of: Cannon, "Reagan's Upbeat Mood," October 30, 1983. See also Gabriel, *Military Incompetence*, pp. 156–57.
320 Late on October 27: Gabriel, *Military Incompetence*, p. 173.
320 Planned and executed: Interview with Vessey.
320 According to one JCS officer: Interview with an Army colonel.
321 "They cut it up": Interview with a retired lieutenant commander.
322 "We put that thing": Interview with Vessey.
322 "We didn't go into": Ibid.
322 The portrait he gave: U.S. Senate, "Lebanon," p. 4.
322 "If all goes well": Ibid., p. 8.
323 "free to return fire": Ibid., p. 11.
323 "in the operational chain": Ibid., p. 12.
323 "We just didn't have enough": Interview with a Senate Armed Services Committee aide.
324 In the early 1960s: "General Paul X. Kelley," July 7, 1983.
324 This startling turn of events: U.S. Senate, "Lebanon," pp. 47–57.
325 "Our troops in Europe": Ibid., p. 61.
325 Perhaps, as committee aides: Interview with a Senate Armed Services Committee aide.
325 "General, did you indicate": U.S. Senate, "Lebanon," p. 64.
325 Committee aides present: Interview with a Senate Armed Services Committee aide.

326 "Kelley was very highly regarded": Ibid. House Armed Services Committee aide Arch Barrett agreed. "Kelley was just an embarrassment when he was over here," he said. "We just couldn't believe it."

326 "We got several calls": Ibid. Kelley never learned his lesson. Soon after his retirement, he publicly suggested that the United States was being undermined because women weren't staying at home to raise families.

326 Before Beirut: Interview with House Armed Services Committee aide Arch Barrett.

327 "John Vessey had the potential": Interview with General Edward C. Meyer.

327 While in command: Interview with Lawrence Korb.

328 Only the Air Force chief of staff: Interview with a Senate Armed Services Committee aide. Even that was in doubt; Senate aides believed that Gabriel would withhold his approval until he saw a final proposal.

328 Gabriel came from : USAF, "General Charles A. Gabriel," September 1982.

328 But leadership of the movement: Perry, "Defense Reform," August 1987. See also Adde, "Where Are They Now?" January 1987, Hiatt, "Can Congress Quell Rivalry?" March 1986.

328 His views were endorsed: Interview with a Senate Armed Services Committee aide.

328 As Odeen himself conceded: Interview with Philip Odeen.

329 They realized their efforts: Interview with Barrett.

330 "Weinberger was going nuts": Interview with Jim Locher.

330 "It was pretty weird": Interview with a House Armed Services Committee aide.

331 "McFarlane turned out": Interview with a Senate Armed Services Committee aide.

331 These hopes were buoyed: CSIS, "Effective Defense."

331 The report specified: Ibid., p. 13.

332 These surreptitious conversations: Interview with a House Armed Services Committee defense analyst.

333 By the late summer: Interview with Barrett.

333 The most important opponent: Interview with Vessey.

334 "it [is] time for me": Ibid.

334 The October 1985: OJCS, "Admiral William J. Crowe, Jr.

335 "never heard a shot": Interview with Colonel William Corson.

335 In fact, Crowe: Interview with a Defense Department official.

335 George Wilson . . . castigated: Wilson, "The Chiefs Take a Dive," June 22, 1986.

335 "piling up the sandbags": Interview with a Senate Armed Services Committee aide.

335 "Has anyone seen": Aspin asked this question during subcommittee hearings on administration disarmament proposals. He later repeated it in 1986 in the wake of the Iran-contra scandal. He said then, "Everybody used to be scared of the chiefs when it came to making arms proposals. I'm wondering what's happening to the chiefs" (Wilson, "Rift Seen Between Reagan," November 25, 1986).

335 Within five months: Interview with Barrett.

336 In early 1986: Interviews with Korb and a Defense Department official.

336 "I use skimmed milk": Interview with Korb.

336 "Really?": JCS officers gave Wickham a new nickname after this incident, "two percent Wickham."

337 "winking approval": Interview with a House Armed Services Committee defense analyst.

337 The work of Gabriel: Ibid.

337 The reform legislation: Gruetzner, "DoD Reorganization," May 1987; Budahn, "DoD Overhaul," December 1986; Budahn, "Accord Reached," September 1986.

338 While critical members: Interview with a Senate Armed Services Committee aide.

338 On the evening of: Wilson, "Pentagon Reform Bill Sweeps," May 8, 1986. See U.S. House, "Goldwater-Nichols," September 11, 1986, and "Conference Report," *Congressional Record*, September 16, 1986, p. S 12658.

339 One month later: Blue Ribbon Commission, *Quest for Excellence*, June 1986.

339 I kept thinking: Interview with a Senate Armed Services Committee aide.

339 The victors were straightforward: Interviews with Generals David Jones and Meyer.

340 That morning, Crowe: Interview with a Defense Department official.

AFTERWORD

341 "What the hell is": Interview with a retired Army major.

342 Chastised by the: Interview with a Defense Department official.

342 "We were asked": Interview with a Navy admiral.

342 At the end of October: Budahn, "Special Forces," October 27, 1986.

342 Crowe had even approached: Perry, "I.S.A. Behind the N.S.C.," January 17, 1987.

342 The forces, he: Interview with a Senate Armed Services Committee aide.
343 "the highest-ranking": Interview with a Navy admiral. See Perry, "I.S.A. Behind the N.S.C.," January 17, 1987.
343 For Crowe: Wilson, "Rift Seen," November 25, 1986.
344 It would not, however: Interview with an admiral.

BIBLIOGRAPHY

BOOKS

Acheson, Dean. *Present at the Creation.* New York: W. W. Norton, 1969.

Adams, Gordon. *The Iron Triangle.* New York: Council on Economic Priorities, 1981.

Allman, T. D. *Unmanifest Destiny.* Garden City, N.Y.: Doubleday, 1984.

Ambrose, Stephen E. *Eisenhower, The President.* New York: Simon and Schuster, 1984.

———. *Eisenhower: Soldier, General of the Army, President-Elect.* New York: Simon and Schuster, 1983.

Art, Robert J., Vincent Davis, and Samuel P. Huntington, eds. *Reorganizing America's Defense.* Washington, D.C.: Pergamon-Brassey's, 1985.

Bank, Aaron. *From OSS to Green Beret.* San Francisco: Presidio, 1986.

Barrett, Archie D. *Reappraising Defense Organization.* Washington, D.C.: National Defense University, 1983.

Beckwith, Charlie A., and Donald Knox. *Delta Force.* New York: Harcourt Brace Jovanovich, 1983.

Beschloss, Michael R. *Mayday, Eisenhower, Khrushchev and the U-2 Affair.* New York: Harper & Row, 1986.

Biggs, Bradley. *Gavin.* Hamden, Conn.: Archon Books, 1980.

Blair, Clay. *The Forgotten War.* New York: Times Books, 1987.

Bletzz, Donald. *The Role of the Military Professional in U.S. Foreign Policy.* New York: Praeger, 1972.

Boettcher, Thomas D. *Vietnam: The Valor and the Sorrow.* Boston: Little, Brown, 1985.

Bradley, Omar. *A Soldier's Story.* New York: Henry Holt, 1951.

Brewin, Bob, and Sydney Shaw. *Vietnam on Trial.* New York: Atheneum, 1987.

Brown, Anthony Cave. *Wild Bill Donovan, The Last Hero.* New York: Times Books, 1982.

Brown, Harold K. *Thinking About National Security, Defense and Foreign Policy in a Dangerous World.* Boulder: Westview, 1983.

Broyles, William, Jr. *Brothers in Arms.* New York: Knopf, 1986.

Canan, James W. *The Superwarriors.* New York: Weybright and Talley, 1975.

Cimbala, Stephan J., ed. *The Reagan Defense Program.* Wilmington, Del.: Scholarly Resources, 1986.

Clark, Asa A., IV, and Peter W. Chiarelli, Jeffery S. McKitrick, and James W. Reed. *The Defense Reform Debate.* Baltimore: Johns Hopkins, 1984.

Clotfelter, James. *The Military in American Politics.* New York: Harper & Row, 1973.

Coates, James, and Michael Kilian. *Heavy Losses.* New York: Viking Penguin, 1985.

Cockburn, Andrew. *The Threat: Inside the Soviet Military Machine.* New York: Random House, 1983.

Coffey, Thomas M. *Iron Eagle: The Turbulent Life of General Curtis LeMay.* New York: Crown, 1986.

Dugger, Ronnie. *On Reagan.* New York: McGraw-Hill, 1983.

Eisenhower, David. *Eisenhower at War.* New York: Random House, 1986.

Enthoven, Alain, and K. Wayne Smith. *How Much Is Enough?* New York: Harper & Row, 1971.

Epstein, Joshua M. *The 1987 Defense Budget.* Washington, D.C.: Brookings Institution, 1986.

Fall, Bernard B. *Anatomy of a Crisis.* Garden City, N.Y.: Doubleday, 1969.

Fallows, James. *National Defense.* New York: Random House, 1981.

Ford, Corey. *Donovan of OSS.* Boston: Little, Brown, 1970.

Ford, Daniel. *The Button.* New York: Simon and Schuster, 1985.

Forrestal, James. *The Forrestal Diaries,* ed. Walter Millis with E. S. Duffield. New York: Viking, 1951.

Franklin, Roger. *The Defender: The Story of General Dynamics.* New York: Harper & Row, 1986.

Gabriel, Richard A. *Military Incompetence.* New York: Hill and Wang, 1985.

——— and Paul L. Savage. *Crisis in Command.* New York: Hill and Wang, 1978.

Gavin, James M. *War and Peace in the Space Age.* New York: Harper and Brothers, 1958.

Gibson, James William. *The Perfect War: Technowar in Vietnam.* Boston: Atlantic Monthly Press, 1986.

Goulden, Joseph C. *Korea: The Untold Story of the War.* New York: Times Books, 1982.

Graebner, Norman A., ed. *The National Security.* New York: Oxford, 1986.

Gravel, Mike. *The Pentagon Papers: The Defense Department History of United States Decisionmaking on Vietnam,* 4 vols. Boston: Beacon Press, 1971.

Hadley, Arthur T. *The Straw Giant.* New York: Random House, 1986.

Halberstam, David. *The Best and the Brightest.* New York: Random House, 1969.

Halloran, Richard. *To Arm a Nation.* New York: Macmillan, 1986.

Hammel, Eric. *The Root: The Marines in Beirut.* New York: Harcourt Brace Jovanovich, 1985.

Hammond, Paul Y. *Organizing for Defense.* Princeton: Princeton University Press, 1961.

Hart, Gary, and William S. Lind. *America Can Win.* Bethesda, Md.: Adler & Adler, 1986.

Hersh, Seymour M. *My Lai 4: A Report on the Massacre and Its Aftermath.* New York: Random House, 1970.

———. *The Price of Power.* New York: Summit Books, 1983.

Hilsman, Roger. *To Move a Nation.* Garden City, N.Y.: Doubleday, 1964.

Hoopes, Townsend. *The Devil and John Foster Dulles.* Boston: Little, Brown, 1973.

———. *The Limits of Intervention.* New York: David McKay, 1969.

Hymoff, Edward. *The OSS in World War II.* New York: Ballantine Books, 1972.

Isaacson, Walter, and Evan Thomas. *The Wise Men: Six Friends and the World They Made.* New York: Simon and Schuster, 1986.

Just, Ward. *Military Men.* New York: Knopf, 1970.

Kahin, George McT. *Intervention.* New York: Knopf, 1986.

Kalb, Marvin, and Bernard Kalb. *Kissinger.* Boston: Little, Brown, 1974.

Kaplan, Fred. *The Wizards of Armageddon.* New York: Simon and Schuster, 1983.

Karnow, Stanley. *Vietnam, A History.* New York: Viking, 1983.

Kaufmann, William. *The McNamara Strategy.* New York: Harper & Row, 1964.

Kinnard, Douglas. *The Secretary of Defense.* Lexington, Ky.: University Press of Kentucky, 1980.

———. *The War Managers.* Wayne, N.J.: Avery, 1985.

Kissinger, Henry. *White House Years.* Boston: Little, Brown, 1979.

Korb, Lawrence J. *The Fall and Rise of the Pentagon.* Westport, Conn.: Greenwood, 1979.

———. *The Joint Chiefs of Staff: The First Twenty-Five Years.* Bloomington, Ind.: Indiana University, 1976.

Kotz, Nick. *Wild Blue Yonder.* New York: Pantheon, 1988.

Kreisberg, Paul H., ed. *American Hostages in Iran.* Council on Foreign Relations. New Haven: Yale University Press, 1985.

Kruzel, Joseph, ed. *American Defense Annual.* Lexington, Mass.: Ohio State University and Lexington Books, 1986.

Larrabee, Eric. *Commander in Chief.* New York: Harper & Row, 1987.

Loory, Stuart H. *Defeated: Inside America's Military Machine.* New York: Random House, 1973.

Luttwak, Edward N. *The Pentagon and the Art of War.* New York: Simon and Schuster, 1984.

Maclear, Michael. *The Ten Thousand Day War.* New York: St. Martin's Press, 1981.

McCoy, Alfred W., with Cathleen B. Read and Leonard P. Adams II. *The Politics of Heroin in Southeast Asia.* New York: Harper & Row, 1972.

McHenry, Robert, ed. *Webster's American Military Biographies.* New York: Dover, 1978.

Manchester, William. *American Caesar.* New York: Dell, 1978.

Momyer, William W. *Air Power in Three Wars.* Washington, D.C.: U.S. Government Printing Office, 1978.

Moses, Louis J. *The Call for JCS Reform.* Washington, D.C.: National Defense University, 1985.

Mylander, Maureen. *The Generals.* New York: Dial Press, 1974.

Nalty, Bernard C. *Strength for the Fight.* New York: Free Press, 1986.

Newman, Aubrey. *What Are Generals Made Of?* San Francisco: Presidio, 1987.

Nixon, Richard M. *The Memoirs of Richard Nixon.* New York: Grosset & Dunlap, 1978.

Oberdorfer, Don. *Tet.* Garden City, N.Y.: Doubleday, 1971.

Paddock, Alfred H., Jr. *U.S. Army Special Warfare.* Washington, D.C.: National Defense University, 1982.

Palmer, Bruce, Jr. *The 25-Year War: America's Military Role in Vietnam.* Lexington, Ky.: University Press of Kentucky, 1984.

Parmet, Herbert S. *Jack: The Struggles of John F. Kennedy.* New York: Dial Press, 1980.

Patti, Archimedes L. A. *Why Vietnam?* Berkeley: University of California Press, 1980.

Pisor, Robert. *The End of the Line: The Siege of Khe Sanh.* New York: Ballantine Books, 1982.

Polmar, Norman, and Thomas B. Allen. *Rickover.* New York: Simon and Schuster, 1984.

Prados, John. *Presidents' Secret Wars.* New York: William Morrow, 1986.

———. *The Sky Would Fall.* New York: Dial Press, 1983.

Pringle, Peter, and William Arkin. *S.I.O.P.: The Secret Plan for Nuclear War*. New York: W. W. Norton, 1983.

Radford, Arthur W. *From Pearl Harbor to Vietnam*. Stanford: Hoover Institution Press, 1980.

Rasor, Dina. *The Pentagon Underground*. New York: Times Books, 1985.

Raymond, Jack. *Power at the Pentagon*. New York: Harper & Row, 1964.

Reichart, John F., and Steven R. Sturm, eds. *American Defense Policy*, 5th ed. Baltimore: Johns Hopkins, 1982.

Richelson, Jeffrey T. *The U.S. Intelligence Community*. Cambridge, Mass.: Ballinger, 1985.

Ridgway, Matthew B. *The Korean War*. New York: Doubleday, 1967.

———. *Soldier*. New York: Harper and Brothers, 1956.

Roosevelt, Kermit, ed. *War Reports of the OSS*, 2 vols. New York: Walker and Company, 1976.

Ryan, Paul D. *The Iranian Rescue Mission, Why It Failed*. Annapolis, Md.: Naval Institute Press, 1985.

Salinger, Pierre. *With Kennedy*. Garden City, N.Y.: Doubleday, 1966.

Schlesinger, Arthur M., Jr. *A Thousand Days*. Boston: Houghton Mifflin, 1965.

Schlight, John, ed. *Second Indochina War Symposium*. Washington, D.C.: U.S. Army Center of Military History, 1985.

Sharp, Admiral U. S. G. *Strategy for Defeat*. San Francisco: Presidio, 1978.

Sivard, Ruth Leger. *World Military and Social Expenditures*. Washington, D.C.: World Priorities, 1985.

Snepp, Frank. *Decent Interval*. New York: Random House, 1977.

Spanier, John. *Truman, MacArthur and the Korean War*. New York: W. W. Norton, 1965.

Spector, Ronald H. *The U.S. Army in Vietnam, The Early Years*. Washington, D.C.: U.S. Center of Military History, 1983.

Stanton, Shelby. *Anatomy of a Division*. San Francisco: Presidio, 1987.

———. *The Rise and Fall of an American Army*. San Francisco: Presidio, 1985.

———. *Vietnam Order of Battle*. Washington, D.C.: U.S. News Books, 1981.

Stubbing, Richard A., with Richard A. Mendel. *The Defense Game*. New York: Harper & Row, 1986.

Szulc, Tad. *The Illusion of Peace*. New York: Viking, 1978.

Talbott, Strobe. *Deadly Gambits*. New York: Knopf, 1984.

Taylor, Maxwell D. *Swords and Plowshares*. New York: W. W. Norton, 1972.

———. *The Uncertain Trumpet*. New York: Harper & Row, 1959.

Taylor, Robert L., and William E. Rosenback, eds. *Military Leadership*. Boulder: Westview Press, 1984.

Trask, Roger R. *The Secretaries of Defense: A Brief History, 1947–1985*. Washington, D.C.: Office of the Secretary of Defense, 1985.

Turner, Stansfield. *Secrecy and Democracy*. Boston: Houghton Mifflin, 1985.

Twining, Nathan F. *Neither Liberty nor Safety: A Hard Look at U.S. Military Policy and Strategy*. New York: Holt, Rinehart, and Winston, 1966.

Tyler, Patrick. *Running Critical*. New York: Harper & Row, 1986.

Tyroler, Charles, Jr., ed. *Alerting America: The Papers of the Committee on the Present Danger*. Washington, D.C.: Pergamon-Brassey's, 1984.

United States Military Academy. *Register of Graduates*. West Point, N.Y.: Association of Graduates, 1983.

Weigley, Russell F. *Eisenhower's Lieutenants*. Bloomington, Ind.: Indiana University Press, 1981.

———. *History of the U.S. Army*. New York: Macmillan, 1967.

Westmoreland, William C. *A Soldier Reports*. New York: Doubleday, 1976.

Woodward, Bob, and Carl Bernstein. *The Final Days*. New York: Simon and Schuster, 1976.

Wyden, Peter. *Bay of Pigs: The Untold Story*. New York: Simon and Schuster, 1979.

Yarmolinsky, Adam. *The Military Establishment*. New York: Harper & Row, 1971.

Yergin, Daniel. *Shattered Peace: The Origins of the Cold War and the National Security State*. Boston: Houghton Mifflin, 1977.

York, Herbert. *Race to Oblivion: A Participant's View of the Arms Race*. New York: Simon and Schuster, 1970.

Zumwalt, Elmo R., Jr. *On Watch: A Memoir*. New York: Times Books, 1976.

———. and Elmo Zumwalt III, with John Pekkanen. *My Father, My Son*. New York: Macmillan, 1986.

ARTICLES

Adde, Nick. "Solving the Puzzle Palace." *Army Times*, October 13, 1986.

———. "Where Are They Now?" *Navy Times*, January 19, 1987.

Ahearne, John F. "Pentagon Strategy, 'WWNH.' " *Washington Post*, March 4, 1987.

Beatty, Jack. "In Harm's Way." *The Atlantic*, May 1987.

Beecher, William. "U.S. Bombing Strategy." *New York Times*, August 26, 1967.

Budahn, P. J. "Accord Reached on Major Reorganization Bill Points."
  Navy Times, September 1, 1986.
———. "Bill Would Unite Special Forces in Single Agency." *Navy
  Times*, July 21, 1986.
———. "DoD Overhaul Falls Short of Critics' Desires." *Army Times*,
  December 8, 1986.
———. "JCS Drafts Plan for Special Ops Command." *Air Force
  Times*, July 28, 1986.
———. "Senate OKs Plan to Create Special Forces Command." *Navy
  Times*, August 18, 1986.
———. "Special Forces Becomes 11th Unified Command." *Air Force
  Times*, October 27, 1986.
Bush, Ted. "Secretary to Probe Use of Admin Discharges." *Navy
  Times*, May 4, 1987.
Cannon, Lou. "McFarlane's Appointment Tipped the Scales." *Wash-
  ington Post*, October 24, 1983.
———. "Standing Fast." *Washington Post*, October 25, 1983.
———. "Reagan's Upbeat Mood Returns After Week That Rocked
  Nation." *Washington Post*, October 30, 1983.
Center for Defense Information. *The Defense Monitor*. "America's
  Special Soldiers: The Buildup of U.S. Special Operations Forces,"
  1985.
———. "Militarism in America," 1986.
———. "The Pentagon Spending Juggernaut: Will Congress Put On
  the Brakes?" 1985.
———. "The Soviet Navy: Still Second Best," 1985.
———. "U.S.-Soviet Nuclear Arms: 1985," 1985.
———. "War Games," 1984.
———. "Waste in Military Procurement: The Prospects for Reform,"
  1986.
Claiborne, William. "Toll at 192." *Washington Post*, October 25, 1983.
Clifford, Clark. "A Vietnam Reappraisal." *Foreign Affairs*, July 1969.
Fallows, James. "M-16: A Bureaucratic Horror Story." *The Atlantic*,
  June 1981.
Fouquet, David. "Rogers to Step Down as NATO Chief in June."
  Washington Post, February 27, 1987.
Fulghum, David. "U.S. to Continue Nuclear Reliance, Hill Told." *Air
  Force Times*, December 8, 1986.
Getler, Michael. "Security Questioned at Marines' Bombed Building."
  Washington Post, October 27, 1983.
Gilpatric, Roswell L. "An Expert Looks at the Joint Chiefs." *New York
  Times Magazine*, March 29, 1964.
Gorman, Paul F. "Toward a Stronger Defense Establishment." In
  Clark et al., *The Defense Reform Debate*. Baltimore: Johns Hopkins,
  1984.

Gruetzner, James K. "DoD Reorganization." *Proceedings*, May 1987.

Hiatt, Fred. "Can Congress Quell Rivalry in the Military?" *Washington Post*, March 8, 1986.

———. "U.S. Flotilla Remains Near Grenada After Lebanon Bombings." *Washington Post*, October 25, 1983.

Heinl, Robert J. "The Collapse of the Armed Forces." *Armed Forces Journal*, June 7, 1971.

Holloway, James L., III. "The Quality of Military Advice." *AEI Foreign Policy and Defense Review*, February 1980.

Holloway Report. "The Holloway Report: Iran Rescue Mission #1." *Aviation Week and Space Technology*, September 15, 1980.

———. "The Holloway Report: Iran Rescue Mission #2." *Aviation Week and Space Technology*, September 22, 1980.

———. "The Holloway Report: Iran Rescue Mission #3." *Aviation Week and Space Technology*, September 29, 1980.

Ingersoll, Bruce. "Army May Scrap Turret to Save New M-1 Tank." *Chicago Sun-Times*, February 28, 1982.

Jones, David C. "What's Wrong with Our Defense Establishment?" *New York Times Magazine*, November 7, 1982.

———. "Why the Joint Chiefs of Staff Must Change." *Directors and Boards*, The Hays Associates Magazine, February 1982.

Kaufmann, William. "The Requirements of Deterrence." Memorandum #7, Princeton Center of International Studies, Princeton, N.J., 1954.

Kester, John G. "The Future of the Joint Chiefs of Staff." *AEI Foreign Policy and Defense Review*, February 1980.

Leepson, Marc. "An Interview with Clark Clifford." *The Veteran*, October 1986.

Longo, James. "House Panel Fails to Stop 'Joint Duty' Rejection." *Air Force Times*, July 21, 1986.

Luttwak, Edward. "Ollie North Was Right About Bureaucrats at the CIA and Pentagon." *Washington Post*, March 8, 1987.

Mandlebaum, Michael, and Strobe Talbott. "Reykjavik and Beyond." *Foreign Affairs*, Winter 1986/87, pp. 215–35.

Matthews, William. "Koch: Pentagon Indifference May Have Encouraged Beirut Bombing." *Defense News*, September 29, 1986.

Meyer, Edward C. "The JCS — How Much Reform Is Needed?" *Armed Forces Journal International* (119), April 1982.

Mintz, Morton. "Depth Charge: Cost Overruns on New Trident Sub Leave a Muddied Wake." *Washington Post*, October 4, 1981.

Mohr, Charles. "Drop in U.S. Arms Spurs Debate on Military Policy." *New York Times*, October 24, 1982.

Oberdorfer, Don. "At Reykjavik, Soviets Were Prepared and U.S. Improvised." *Washington Post*, February 16, 1987.

———. "U.S. Resources Worldwide Face Further Strain." *Washington Post*, October 24, 1983.

Perry, Mark. "Defense Reform." *American Politics*, August 1987.

———. "The I.S.A. Behind the NSC." *The Nation*, January 17, 1987.

———. "John Paul Vann." *The Veteran*, July 1988.

———. "Just for the Record, Gen. Bruce Palmer Doesn't Buy the Conventional Wisdom." *The Veteran*, December 1985.

———. "The Fire Last Time." *The Veteran*, August 1987.

———. "The Messiah of Ap Bac." *The Veteran*, August 1988.

———. "Unsung Hero." *The Veteran*, October 1986.

Peterzell, Jay. "Reagan's Covert Act Policy (I)." *First Principles*, Center for National Security Studies, January 1982.

———. "Reagan's Covert Act Policy (II)." *First Principles*, Center for National Security Studies, February 1982.

———. "Reagan's Covert Act Policy (III)." *First Principles*, Center for National Security Studies, March 1982.

———. "Reagan's Covert Act Policy (IV)." *First Principles*, Center for National Security Studies, September/October 1982.

Pincus, Walter, and R. Jeffrey Smith. "U.S., Heeding NATO, Limits Geneva Arms Cut Proposals." *Washington Post*, October 15, 1986.

Reid, T. R., and Helen Dewar. "Reappraisal." *Washington Post*, October 25, 1983.

Schram, Martin. "Battle of Defense Cuts, Cabinet Loses Oneness." *Washington Post*, September 14, 1981.

Smith, Hedrick. "McNamara Doubts Bombing in North Can End the War." *New York Times*, August 26, 1967.

Triplett, William C. "Chaos in the Ia Drang." *The Veteran*, October 1986.

Tyler, Patrick, E., and David Hoffman. "U.S. Invades Grenada, Fights Cubans." *Washington Post*, October 26, 1983.

Weinberger, Caspar W. "U.S. Defense Strategy." *Foreign Affairs*, Spring 1986, pp. 675–97.

White, Thomas D. "Strategy and the Defense Intellectuals." *Saturday Evening Post*, May 4, 1963.

Wilson, George. "The Chiefs Take a Dive." *Washington Post*, June 22, 1986.

———. "Goldwater Is Right, Colleagues Say." *Washington Post*, May 8, 1986.

———. "Pentagon Reform Bill Sweeps Through Senate." *Washington Post*, May 8, 1986.

———. "Rift Seen Between Reagan, Joint Chiefs." *Washington Post*, November 25, 1986.

———. "600-Ship Navy Is Sailing Toward Rough Fiscal Seas." *Washington Post*, March 16, 1987.

DOCUMENTS

Center for Strategic and International Studies. "Toward a More Effective Defense." Washington, D.C.: Georgetown University, February 1985.

Condit, Kenneth W. "The History of the Joint Chiefs of Staff." The Joint Chiefs of Staff and National Policy, vol. II, 1947–1949, Historical Division, Joint Secretariat, Joint Chiefs of Staff, December 1978.

Conference Report. "U.S. Senate and House of Representatives Report on Military Reorganization." In Congressional Record (121). Washington, D.C.: Government Printing Office, September 16, 1986.

Congressional Research Service. "The U.S. Government and the Vietnam War," Washington, D.C.: U.S. Government Printing Office, December 1984.

Cuba Study Group (Taylor Report). Operation Zapata: The "Ultrasensitive" Report and Testimony of the Board of Inquiry on the Bay of Pigs. Reprint of "Narrative of the Anti-Castro Cuban Operation Zapata." Frederick, Md.: University Publications of America, 1981.

Defense 86 Almanac (September/October). U.S. Department of Defense. Washington, D.C.: U.S. Government Printing Office, September 1986.

Department of the Navy. "Sea Plan 2000: Naval Force Planning Study" (unclassified executive study). Washington, D.C.: U.S. Department of the Navy, 1978.

Department of State. Foreign Relations of the United States, 1950, vol. I. Washington, D.C.: U.S. Government Printing Office.

Holloway Report (classified). "Report on the Mission to Rescue American Hostages Held in Iran." Department of Defense (internal JCS study), 1980.

Joint Chiefs of Staff. "A Concise History of the Organization of the Joint Chiefs of Staffs, 1942–1979." Joint Chiefs of Staff Special Historical Study, Historical Division, Joint Secretariat, Joint Chiefs of Staff, July 1980.

———. "Construction of 6A Carrier." Modern Military Records Division, National Archives and Records Service, CCS 561, May 26, 1948.

———. "The Evolving Role of the Joint Chiefs of Staff in the National Security Structure." Joint Chiefs of Staff Special Historical Study, Historical Division, Joint Secretariat, Joint Chiefs of Staff, July 7, 1977.

———. "Function of the Armed Forces and the Joint Chiefs of Staff," Modern Military Records Division, National Archives and Records Service, CCS 370, sec. 7, March 8, 1948.

——— "Memorandum." Modern Military Records Division,

National Archives, Record Group 319 (Army Operations), June 2 1948.

———. "The Military Importance of Korea." Modern Military Records Division, National Archives and Records Service, CCS 383.21 (Korea), March 19, 1945.

———. "The Military Organization for Psychological and Covert Operations (JCS 1735/32). Modern Military Records Division, National Archives, Record Group 319 (Army Operations), October 28, 1949.

———. "Modern Evolution of the Armed Forces." Modern Military Records Division, National Archives and Records Service, CCS 045.8 (Naval War College), May 25, 1954.

———. "Study on Guerrilla Warfare." Modern Military Records Division, National Archives, Record Group 319 (Army Operations), March 1, 1949.

———. "Summary of Major Activities of Office of Covert and Psychological Warfare," Modern Military Records Division, National Archives, Record Group 319 (Army Operations), April 7, 1953.

Johnson, Lyndon Baines. "Peace in Vietnam and Southeast Asia." Address to the Nation, March 31, 1968, in *Public Papers of the Presidents of the United States, 1968–1969*, Washington, D.C.: U.S. Government Printing Office, 1970.

Long Commission Report. *Congressional Record.* Washington, D.C.: U.S. Government Printing Office, January 30, 1984.

Medical Readiness (classified). "Medical Readiness Planning in the U.S. European Command." Department of Defense, Medical Readiness Review Group, April 18, 1984 (in the author's possession).

Meyer, Edward C. "Remarks to World Affairs Council." Boston, September 24, 1981.

Moore, John Norton, and Robert F. Turner. "The Legal Structure of Defense Organization." President's Blue Ribbon Commission on Defense Management. Washington, D.C.: U.S. Government Printing Office, January 15, 1986.

Office of Technology Assessment. "Technologies for NATO's Follow-On Forces Attack Concept." Washington, D.C.: U.S. Government Printing Office, July 1986.

Packard, David, et al. "A Formula for Action." A Report to the President on Defense Acquisition, President's Blue Ribbon Commission on Defense Management. Washington, D.C.: U.S. Government Printing Office, April 1986.

———. "A Quest for Excellence." President's Blue Ribbon Commission on Defense Management. Washington, D.C.: U.S. Government Printing Office, June 1986.

———. "An Interim Report to the President." President's Blue Ribbon Commission on Defense Management. Washington, D.C.: U.S. Government Printing Office, February 28, 1986.

————. "National Security Planning & Budgeting." President's Blue Ribbon Commission on Defense Management. Washington, D.C.: U.S. Government Printing Office, June 1986.

"The Peers Report." *Report of the Department of the Army Review of the Preliminary Investigations in the My Lai Incident.* Washington, D.C.: Department of the Army, March 14, 1970.

Poole, Walter S. "The History of the Joint Chiefs of Staff." The Joint Chiefs of Staff and National Policy, vol. IV, 1950–1952, Historical Division, Joint Secretariat, Joint Chiefs of Staff, September 1979.

Radford, Arthur. "Modern Evolution of the Armed Forces." Records of the JCS, National Archives, 045.8 (Naval War College).

Schnabel, James F. "The History of the Joint Chiefs of Staff." The Joint Chiefs of Staff and National Policy, vol. I, 1945–1947. Historical Division, Joint Secretariat, Joint Chiefs of Staff, February 1979.

———— and Robert J. Watson, "The History of the Joint Chiefs of Staff." The Joint Chiefs of Staff and National Policy, vol. III, The Korean War. Historical Division, Joint Secretariat, Joint Chiefs of Staff, April 12, 1978, March 1979.

Tower, John, Edmund Muskie, and Brent Scowcroft. "Report of the President's Special Review Board." Washington, D.C.: U.S. Government Printing Office, March 1987.

United States. "The Paris Peace Accords." In *United States Treaties and Other International Agreements*, vol. 24, part 1, 1973. Washington, D.C.: U.S. Government Printing Office.

United States Army War College. "Study on Military Professionalism." Carlisle, Pa.: Carlisle Barracks, June 30, 1970.

U.S. Congress. "National Security Act of 1947," PL 253. 80th Congress. Washington, D.C.: U.S. Government Printing Office, 1947.

U.S. House of Representatives, Committee on Armed Services. "Background Material on Structural Reform of the Department of Defense." Washington, D.C.: U.S. Government Printing Office, March 1986.

————. "HASC Unveils 'Revolutionary' New Pentagon Reorganization Bill" (press release). Washington, D.C.: U.S. Government Printing Office, June 17, 1986.

————. "House-Senate Conference Wraps Up Defense Reorganization Bill." Washington, D.C.: U.S. Government Printing Office, September 11, 1986.

————. "Joint Chiefs of Staff Reorganization Act of 1983." Report to Accompany HR 3718, 98th Congress, 1st Session. Washington, D.C.: U.S. Government Printing Office, 1983.

————. "National Defense Program, Unification and Strategy," 81st

Congress, 1st Session. Washington, D.C.: U.S. Government Printing Office, 1949.

——. "Reorganization Proposals for the Joint Chiefs of Staff." Hearings before the Investigations Subcommittee. Washington, D.C.: U.S. Government Printing Office, April 21, 22, 28, 29, May 5, 6, 20, June 8, 16, 17, 23, July 14, 16, 21, 28, August 5, 1982.

——. "Reorganization Proposals for the Joint Chiefs of Staff — 1985." Hearings before the Investigations Subcommittee. Washington, D.C.: U.S. Government Printing Office, June 13, 19, and 26, 1985.

——. "Sundry Legislation Affecting the Naval and Military Establishments." 81st Congress, 1st Session, vols. I, II. Washington, D.C.: U.S. Government Printing Office, 1949.

U.S. Senate, Committee on Armed Services. "Department of Defense Reorganization Act of 1958." Hearings on HR 12541, 85th Congress, 2nd Session. Washington, D.C.: U.S. Government Printing Office, June–July 1958.

——. "Hearings on Military Preparedness." 96th Congress, 2nd Session. Washington, D.C.: U.S. Government Printing Office, November 1981.

——. "The Situation in Lebanon." 98th Congress, 1st Session. Washington, D.C.: U.S. Government Printing Office, October 25, 31, 1983.

——. Subcommittee on Military Preparedness. "Inquiry into Satellite and Missile Program." 85th Congress, 2nd Session. Washington, D.C.: U.S. Government Printing Office, 1958.

——. Preparedness Investigating Subcommittee. "Hearings on the Air War in Vietnam." 90th Congress, 1st Session. Washington, D.C.: U.S. Government Printing Office, 1967.

——. Select Committee to Study Governmental Operations with Respect to Intelligence Activities. "Final Report," Books 1–4. Washington, D.C.: U.S. Government Printing Office, 1976.

——. Staff Report to the Committee on Armed Services. "Defense Organization: The Need for Change." Washington, D.C.: U.S. Government Printing Office, October 16, 1985.

U.S. Senate, Committee on Military Affairs. "Hearings on S. 84 and S. 1482: Department of the Armed Forces; Department of Military Security." 79th Congress, 1st Session. Washington, D.C.: U.S. Government Printing Office, 1958.

U.S. Senate, Committees on Foreign Relations and Armed Services. "Military Situation in the Far East." 82nd Congress. Washington, D.C.: U.S. Government Printing Office, 1951.

Westmoreland, William C. "Report on the War in Vietnam" (Section II: Report on Operations in South Vietnam, January 1964–June 1968). Washington, D.C.: U.S. Government Printing Office, 1968.

ORAL HISTORIES

United States Army, Military History Institute, Carlisle Barracks,
Pennsylvania

General Omar N. Bradley
General Mark W. Clark
General J. Lawton Collins
General George H. Decker
Lieutenant General Ira C. Eaker
General Anderew J. Goodpaster
General Paul D. Harkins
General Hamilton H. Howze
General Harold K. Johnson
Lieutenant General Harry W. O. Kinnard
General Lyman L. Lemnitzer
General Bruce Palmer, Jr.
General Matthew B. Ridgway
General William B. Rosson
General Maxwell D. Taylor
General William C. Westmoreland

United States Air Force, History Division, Bolling Air Force Base,
Washington, D.C.

General Curtis LeMay
General Glen Martin
General Paul M. McConnell
General John D. Ryan
General Nathan Twining
General Thomas White

United States Navy and U.S. Marine Corps, History Division,
Anacostia Naval Air Station, Washington, D.C.

Admiral Arleigh Burke
Admiral Thomas H. Moorer
Admiral U. S. Grant Sharp
Admiral Elmo Zumwalt, Jr.

RECORDS OF THE JOINTS CHIEFS OF STAFF

JCS Papers: Modern Military Branch, National Archives, Washington,
D.C. (to 1962). *Note:* All JCS papers except those dealing with current
matters of national security are declassified after twenty years.

JCS Papers: Library of Congress, Washington, D.C. Curtis LeMay Papers, Carl Spaatz Papers, Nathan Twining Papers, Hoyt Vandenberg Papers, Thomas White Papers.

JCS Papers: U.S. Department of the Army, U.S. Department of the Navy (and Marine Corps Division), and U.S. Department of the Air Force (all in Washington, D.C.) maintain biographical data on each JCS member, issuing the information to the public in the form of biographical press releases. In addition, the Office of the Joint Chiefs of Staff maintains biographical information releases on each current and former member of the JCS.

I N D E X

Haig, Alexander (*cont.*)
JCS spy ring, 234, 235, 236;
resignation of, 307, 310
Halberstam, David, 118
Halsey, William "Bull," 8, 18, 52,
210
Harkins, Paul, 124, 128–29, 136
Harriman, Averell, 130, 195–97, 198,
200
Hawkins, Jack, 107–8
Hayward, Thomas B., 272, 276, 280,
282, 305; and arms control, 295; as
CNO, 271, 346
Heinl, Robert D., 240
Helms, Richard, 182, 189, 202, 248
Herres, Robert T., 346
Holloway, James L., Jr., 254–55
Holloway, James L., III, 263, 264,
270, 276; as CNO, 254, 255,
256–57, 346; and military reform,
303; quoted, 244
Hoover, Herbert, 16
House Appropriations Committee,
260
House Armed Services Committee,
16–19, 260, 270, 272–73; on
military reform, 300–303
House Subcommittee on Military
Preparedness, 199
Howze, Hamilton H., 122
Humphrey, Hubert, 189

Iklé, Fred, 279, 292, 294, 297

Jackson, Henry, 279
Jessup, Philip, 23
Johnson, Harold K., 32, 164, 172,
301; as Army chief of staff,
135–36, 345; career of, 136, 150–51;
and DePuy, 186; replaced as
Army chief of staff, 197; on Special Forces, 276, 342–43; and
Vietnam War, 137–38, 141, 142,
148–60 *passim*, 164, 165–66,
173–78, 192, 194, 274
Johnson, Louis, 13–14, 15, 23
Johnson, Lyndon B., 71, 130–31, 199,
277, 287; and Bay of Pigs, 108; his

decision not to seek re-election,
194; Great Society of, 143;
hearings of, on Eisenhower's
defense policies, 82–83; and Paris
peace talks, 195–97, 198; his
relations with JCS, 133, 134, 140,
196; and Taylor, 137; his victory
over Goldwater, 143; and
Vietnam War, 138–48 *passim*,
152–63 *passim*, 169, 174, 177–80,
184–95 *passim*, 198, 204, 205, 223,
225; and Wheeler, 201, 203
Joint Analysis Directorate, 37
Joint Army-Navy Committee, 1, 2
*Joint Chiefs of Staff and the War in
Vietnam, The*, 242–43
Joint Emergency War Plans, 16, 20
Joint Secretariat, 37
Joint Special Operations Agency,
37
Jones, David C., 264, 269, 271, 277,
287; as Air Force chief of staff,
252–53, 346; and arms control, 293,
295–98; his chairmanship of JCS,
270, 272, 280, 289, 345; characterized, 253; criticism of, 253–54;
and military reform, 293,
298–304, 328, 333; on nuclear war,
292; quoted, 278; and Reagan's
military strategy, 290; and rescue
operation in Iran, 274, 275, 276,
305; retirement of, 304; successor
to, 305; and Weinberger, 280,
281–83, 284

Karnow, Stanley, 128
Kaufmann, William W., 70–71
Kelley, Paul X., 323, 327, 330; career
of, 324; characterized, 324; as
Marine Corps commandant, 313,
347; and Marines in Beirut, 313,
314, 316, 324–26; quoted, 312
Kennedy, John F., 70, 71, 132, 195,
287; assassination of, 130, 132, 136,
143; and Bay of Pigs, 94, 97, 101–11
passim, 114–17; budgets of, 289;
and Cuban missile crisis, 124–26;
and Green Berets, 150; his